GREAT BRITAIN & IR

TOURIST and MOTORING ATLAS / ATLAS ROUTIER et TOURISTIQUE / STRASSEN- und REISEATLAS
TOERISTISCHE WEGENATLAS / ATLANTE STRADALE e TURISTICO / ATLAS DE CARRETERAS y TURÍSTICO

Contents
Sommaire / Inhaltsübersicht / Inhoud / Sommario / Sumario

Inside front cover: key to map pages
Intérieur de couverture : tableau d'assemblage / Umschlaginnenseite: Übersicht / Binnenzijde van het omslag: overzichtskaart
-Copertina interna: quadro d'insieme / Portada interior: mapa índice

II - III

Channel Tunnel - Tunnel sous la Manche
Folkestone Terminal - Terminal de Calais (F)
Shipping Services
Liaisons maritimes / Schiffsverbindungen / Scheepvaartverbindingen / Collegamenti marittimi / Líneas marítimas

IV - XXI

Main road map
Grands axes routiers / Durchgangsstraßen / Grote verbindingswegen / Grandi arterie stradali / Carreteras principales
1 inch = 15.8 miles - 1:1 000 000 - 1 cm = 10 km

1 - 119

Key   **1**
Légende / Zeichenerklärung / Verklaring van de tekens / Legenda / Signos convencionales

Great Britain & Ireland   **2 - 119**
Grande-Bretagne & Irlande / Großbritannien & Irland / Groot-Brittannië & Ierland
Gran Bretagna & Irlanda / Gran Bretaña & Irlanda
1 inch = 4.75 miles - 1: 300 000 - 1 cm = 3 km

120 - 147

Index Great Britain   **120 - 138**
Index Grande-Bretagne / Register Großbritannien / Register Groot-Brittannië / Indice Gran Bretagna / Índice Gran Bretaña

Index Ireland   **139 - 147**
Index Irlande / Register Irland / Register Ierland / Indice Irlanda / Índice Irlanda

148 - 192

Key   **148**
Légende / Zeichenerklärung / Verklaring van de tekens / Legenda / Signos convencionales

Town plans Great Britain   **149 - 185**
Plans de ville Grande-Bretagne / Stadtpläne Großbritannien / Stadsplattegronden Groot-Brittannië
Piante di città Gran Bretagna / Planos de ciudades Gran Bretaña

Town plans Ireland   **186 - 191**
Plans de ville Irlande / Stadtpläne Irland / Stadsplattegronden Ierland / Piante di città Irlanda / Planos de ciudades Irlanda

Eochair / Allwedd / Comnarthai ar phleanna bailte / Symbolau ar gynlluniau'r trefi   **192**

Back of the guide: distances
En fin de volume : distances / Am Ende des Buches: Entfernungen / Achter in het boek: afstanden
Alla fine del volume: distanze / Al final del volumen: distancias

Channel Tunnel
Tunnel sous la Manche

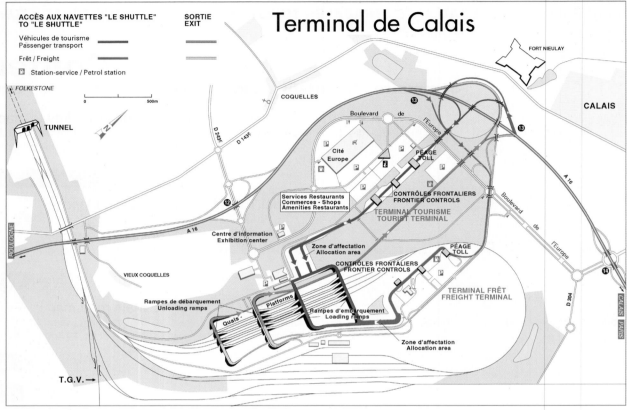

Terminal de Calais

ACCÈS AUX NAVETTES "LE SHUTTLE"
TO "LE SHUTTLE"

SORTIE
EXIT

Véhicules de tourisme
Passenger transport

Frêt / Freight

Station-service / Petrol station

FOLKESTONE

TUNNEL

0   500m

N

COQUELLES

D 243E

D 143E

A 16

FOLKESTONE

BOULOGNE

Boulevard   de   l'Europe

FORT NIEULAY

CALAIS

Cité
Europe

PÉAGE
TOLL

CONTRÔLES FRONTALIERS
FRONTIER CONTROLS

TERMINAL TOURISME
TOURIST TERMINAL

Services Restaurants
Commerces - Shops
Amenities Restaurants

Centre d'information
Exhibition center

Zone d'affectation
Allocation area

CONTRÔLES FRONTALIERS
FRONTIER CONTROLS

PÉAGE
TOLL

Boulevard   de   l'Europe

A 16

VIEUX COQUELLES

Rampes de débarquement
Unloading ramps

Platforms

Quais

Rampes d'embarquement
Loading ramps

TERMINAL FRÊT
FREIGHT TERMINAL

Zone d'affectation
Allocation area

D 304

CALAIS PARIS

T.G.V. →

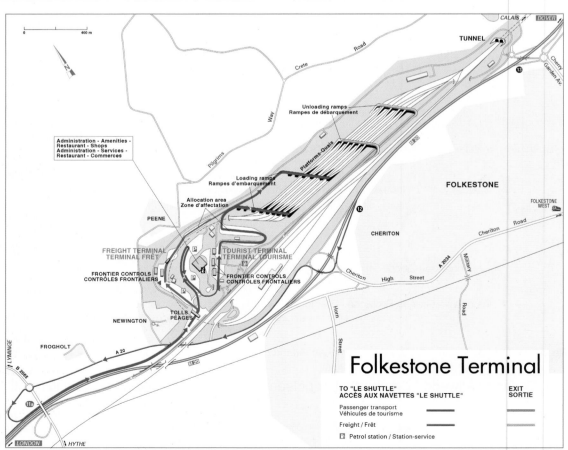

CALAIS   DOVER

TUNNEL

0   400 m

N

Crete   Road

Way

Pilgrims

Administration - Amenities -
Restaurant - Shops
Administration - Services -
Restaurant - Commerces

Unloading ramps
Rampes de débarquement

Platforms-Quais

M 20

Cherry Garden Av.

FOLKESTONE

FOLKESTONE
WEST

Loading ramps
Rampes d'embarquement

Allocation area
Zone d'affectation

PEENE

FREIGHT TERMINAL
TERMINAL FRÊT

TOURIST TERMINAL
TERMINAL TOURISME

CHERITON

Cheriton   Road

A 2034

Military   Road

Horn   Road

FRONTIER CONTROLS
CONTRÔLES FRONTALIERS

FRONTIER CONTROLS
CONTRÔLES FRONTALIERS

Cheriton   High   Street

NEWINGTON

TOLLS
PÉAGES

Street

FROGHOLT

A 20

M 20

LYMINGE

B 2065

LONDON   HYTHE

Folkestone Terminal

TO "LE SHUTTLE"
ACCÈS AUX NAVETTES "LE SHUTTLE"

EXIT
SORTIE

Passenger transport
Véhicules de tourisme

Freight / Frêt

Petrol station / Station-service

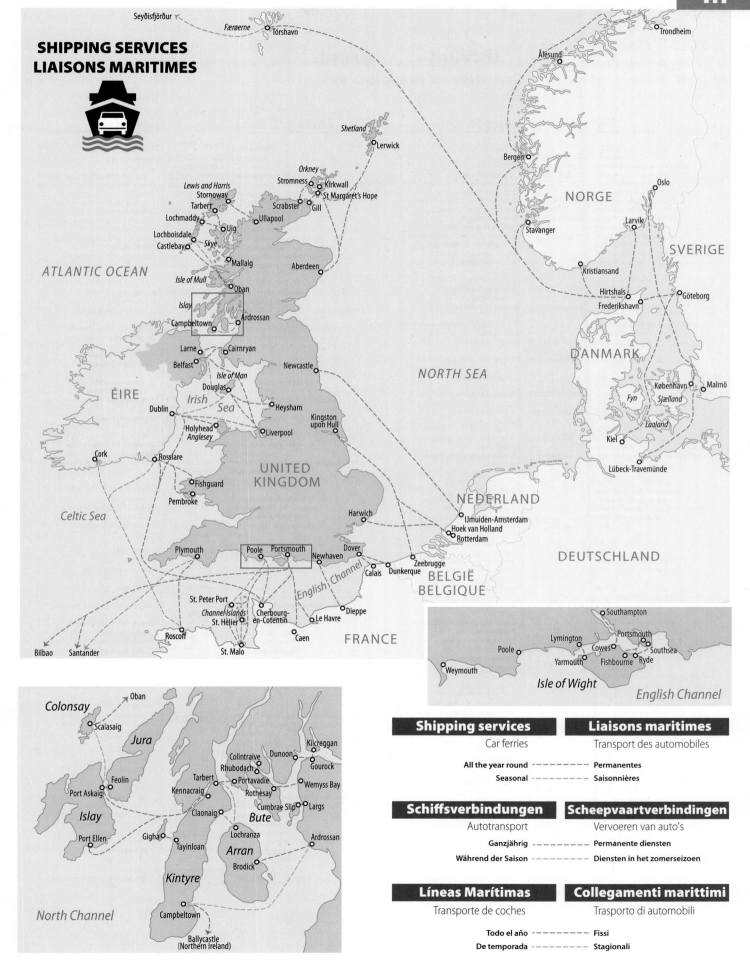

SHIPPING SERVICES
LIAISONS MARITIMES

Seyðisfjörður
Færøerne
Tórshavn
Trondheim
Ålesund
Shetland
Lerwick
Bergen
Oslo
NORGE
Orkney
Stromness Kirkwall
St Margaret's Hope
Gill
Scrabster
Stavanger
Larvik
Lewis and Harris
Stornoway
Tarbert
Ullapool
SVERIGE
Lochmaddy
Uig
Kristiansand
Lochboisdale
Skye
Castlebay
Mallaig
Aberdeen
Hirtshals
Göteborg
ATLANTIC OCEAN
Isle of Mull
Oban
Frederikshavn
Islay
Ardrossan
DANMARK
Campbeltown
København
Malmö
Larne Cairnryan
Fyn
Sjælland
Belfast
Newcastle
NORTH SEA
Kiel
Laaland
Isle of Man
Douglas
Lübeck-Travemünde
ÉIRE
Irish
Sea
Dublin
Heysham
Holyhead
Anglesey
Liverpool
Kingston upon Hull
Cork
Rosslare
UNITED
KINGDOM
NEDERLAND
Fishguard
IJmuiden-Amsterdam
Hoek van Holland
Pembroke
Rotterdam
Celtic Sea
Harwich
DEUTSCHLAND
Plymouth
Poole Portsmouth
Dover
Newhaven
Zeebrugge
Calais Dunkerque
BELGIË
BELGIQUE
English Channel
St. Peter Port
Dieppe
Channel Islands
St. Hélier
Cherbourg-en-Cotentin
Le Havre
Roscoff
Caen
FRANCE
Bilbao Santander
St. Malo

Southampton
Lymington
Portsmouth
Poole
Cowes
Southsea
Weymouth
Yarmouth
Fishbourne Ryde
Isle of Wight
English Channel

Colonsay
Oban
Scalasaig
Jura
Kilcreggan
Colintraive Dunoon
Rhubodach
Gourock
Feolin
Tarbert Portavadie
Port Askaig
Kennacraig
Rothesay
Wemyss Bay
Islay
Claonaig
Cumbrae Slip
Largs
Bute
Port Ellen
Gigha
Lochranza
Ardrossan
Tayinloan
Arran
Kintyre
Brodick
North Channel
Campbeltown
Ballycastle
(Northern Ireland)

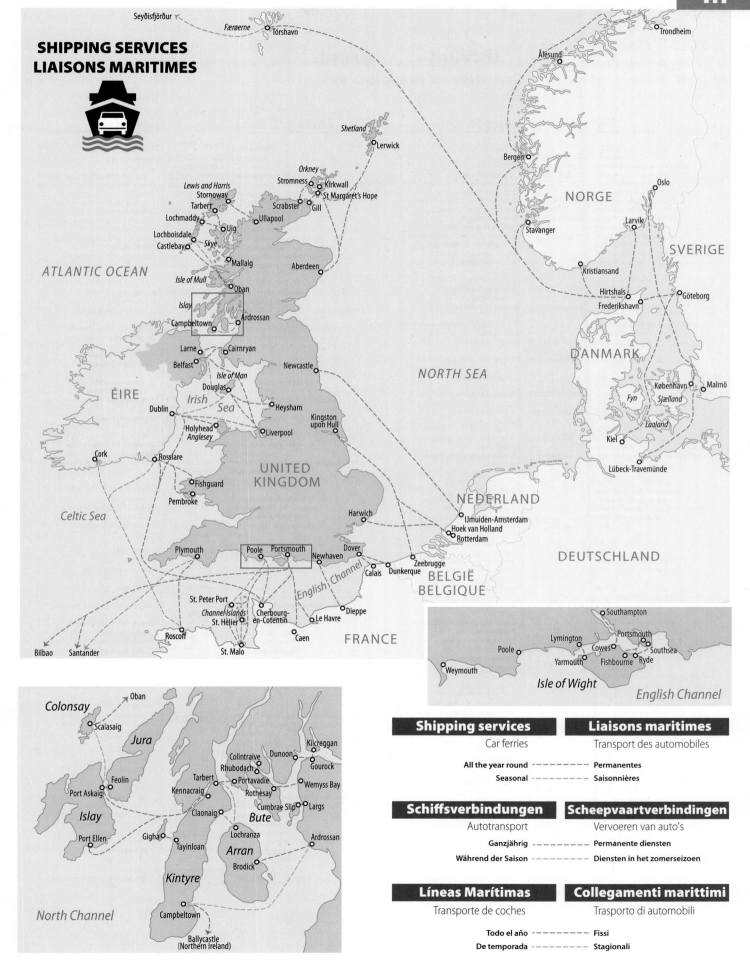

Shipping services
Car ferries

All the year round	---- Permanentes
Seasonal	---- Saisonnières

Liaisons maritimes
Transport des automobiles

Schiffsverbindungen
Autotransport

Ganzjährig	---- Permanente diensten
Während der Saison	---- Diensten in het zomerseizoen

Scheepvaartverbindingen
Vervoeren van auto's

Líneas Marítimas
Transporte de coches

Todo el año	---- Fissi
De temporada	---- Stagionali

Collegamenti maríttimi
Trasporto di automobili

Main road map
Grands axes routiers / Durchgangsstraßen / Grote verbindingswegen
Grandi arterie stradali / Carreteras principales

Key	Légende	Zeichenerklärung	Legenda
Roads	**Routes**	**Straßen**	**Strade**
Motorway	Autoroute	Autobahn	Autostrada
Motorway: single carriageway	Route-auto	Autostraße	Strada-auto
Motorway (unclassified)	Route et assimilée	Autobahn oder Schnellstraße	Autostrada, strada di tipo autostradale
Dual carriageway with motorway characteristics	Double chaussée de type autoroutier	Schnellstraße mit getrennten Fahrbahnen	Doppia carreggiata di tipo autostradale
Interchanges:	Échangeurs :	Anschlussstellen:	Svincoli:
complete, limited, not specified	complet, partiels, sans précision	Voll- bzw. Teilanschluss, ohne Angabe	completo, parziale, imprecisato
Interchange numbers	Numéros d'échangeurs	Anschlussstellennummern	Svincoli numerati
Recommended MICHELIN main itinerary	Itinéraire principal recommandé par MICHELIN	Von MICHELIN empfohlene Hauptverkehrsstraße	Itinerario principale raccomandato da MICHELIN
Recommended MICHELIN regional itinerary	Itinéraire régional ou de dégagement recommandé par MICHELIN	Von MICHELIN empfohlene Regionalstraße	Itinerario regionale raccomandato da MICHELIN
Road surfaced - unsurfaced	Route revêtue - non revêtue	Straße mit Belag - ohne Belag	Strada rivestita - non rivestita
Motorway/Road under construction	Autoroute - Route en construction	Autobahn/Straße im Bau	Autostrada - Strada in costruzione
Road widths	**Largeur des routes**	**Straßenbreiten**	**Larghezza delle strade**
Dual carriageway	Chaussées séparées	Getrennte Fahrbahnen	Carreggiate separate
2 wide lanes	2 voies larges	2 breite Fahrspuren	2 corsie larghe
2 lanes - 2 narrow lanes	2 voies - 2 voies étroites	2 Fahrspuren - 2 schmale Fahrspuren	2 corsie - 2 corsie strette
Distances (total and intermediate)	**Distances** (totalisées et partielles)	**Straßenentfernungen** (Gesamt- und Teilentfernungen)	**Distanze** (totali e parziali)
On motorway in kilometers	Sur autoroute en kilomètres	Auf der Autobahn in Kilometern	Su autostrada in chilometri
Toll roads - Toll-free section	Section à péage - Section libre	Mautstrecke - Mautfreie Strecke	Tratto a pedaggio - Tratto esente da pedaggio
On road in kilometers	Sur route en kilomètres	Auf der Straße in Kilometern	Su strada in chilometri
On motorway (GB) in miles - in kilometers	Sur autoroute (GB) en miles - en kilomètres	Auf der Autobahn (GB) in Meilen - in Kilometern	Su autostrada (GB) in miglia - in chilometri
Toll roads - Toll-free section	Section à péage - Section libre	Mautstrecke - Mautfreie Strecke	Tratto a pedaggio - Tratto esente da pedaggio
On road in miles	Sur route en miles	Auf der Straße in Meilen	Su strada in miglia
Numbering - Signs	**Numérotation - Signalisation**	**Nummerierung - Wegweisung**	**Numerazione - Segnaletica**
European route - Motorway	Route européenne - Autoroute	Europastraße - Autobahn	Strada europea - Autostrada
Other roads	Autres routes	Sonstige Straßen	Altre strade
Destination on primary route network	Localités jalonnant les itinéraires principaux	Richtungshinweis auf der empfohlenen Fernverkehrsstraße	Località delimitante gli itinerari principali
Safety Warnings	**Alertes Sécurité**	**Sicherheitsalerts**	**Segnalazioni stradali**
Snowbound, impassable road during the period shown	Enneigement : période probable de fermeture	Eingeschneite Straße: voraussichtl. Wintersperre	Innevamento: probabile periodo di chiusura
Pass and its height above sea level	Col et sa cote d'altitude	Pass mit Höhenangabe	Passo ed altitudine
Steep hill - Toll barrier	Forte déclivité - Barrière de péage	Starke Steigung - Mautstelle	Forte pendenza - Casello
Ford	Gué	Furt	Guado
Transportation	**Transports**	**Verkehrsmittel**	**Trasporti**
Airport	Aéroport	Flughafen	Aeroporto
Transportation of vehicles: year-round - seasonal	Transport des autos : permanent - saisonnier	Autotransport: ganzjährig - saisonbedingte Verbindung	Trasporto auto: tutto l'anno - stagionale
by boat	par bateau	per Schiff	su traghetto
by ferry	par bac	per Fähre	su chiatta
Ferry (passengers and cycles only)	Bac pour piétons et cycles	Fähre für Personen und Fahrräder	Traghetto per pedoni e biciclette
Motorail	Auto/Train	Autoreisezug	Auto/treno
Administration	**Administration**	**Verwaltung**	**Amministrazione**
Administrative district seat	Capitale de division administrative	Verwaltungshauptstadt	Capoluogo amministrativo
Parador / Pousada	Parador / Pousada	Parador / Pousada	Parador / Pousada
Administrative boundaries	Limites administratives	Verwaltungsgrenzen	Confini amministrativi
National boundary	Frontière	Staatsgrenze	Frontiera
Principal customs post	Douane principale	Hauptzollamt	Dogana principale
Secondary customs post	Douane avec restriction	Zollstation mit Einschränkung	Dogana con limitazioni
Restricted area for foreigners / Military property	Zone interdite aux étrangers / Zone militaire	Sperrgebiet für Ausländer / Militärgebiet	Zona vietata agli stranieri / Zona militare
Sights	**Lieux touristiques**	**Sehenswürdigkeiten**	**Mete e luoghi d'interesse**
2- and 3-star	Sites classés 2 et 3 étoiles	Sehenswürdigkeiten mit 2 und 3 Sternen	Siti segnalati con 2 e 3 stelle
MICHELIN Green Guide sites	par le Guide Vert MICHELIN	im Grünen Reiseführer MICHELIN	dalla Guida Verde MICHELIN
Religious building	Édifice religieux	Sakral-Bau	Edificio religioso
Historic house, castle	Château	Schloss, Burg	Castello
Monastery	Monastère	Kloster	Monastero
Stave church	Église en bois debout	Stabkirche	Chiesa in legno di testa
Wooden church	Église en bois	Holzkirche	Chiesa in legno
Open air museum	Musée de plein air	Freilichtmuseum	Museo all'aperto
Antiquities	Site antique	Antike Fundstätte	Sito antico
Rock carving - Prehistoric monument	Gravure rupestre - Monument mégalithique	Felsbilder - Vorgeschichtliches Steindenkmal	Incisione rupestre - Monumento megalitico
Rune stone - Ruins	Pierre runique - Ruines	Runenstein - Ruine	Pietra runica - Rovine
Cave - Windmill	Grotte - Moulin à vent	Höhle - Windmühle	Grotta - Mulino a vento
Other places of interest	Autres curiosités	Sonstige Sehenswürdigkeit	Altri luoghi d'interesse
Scenic route	Parcours pittoresque	Landschaftlich schöne Strecke	Percorso pittoresco
Other signs	**Signes divers**	**Sonstige Zeichen**	**Simboli vari**
Recreation ground	Parc de loisirs	Erholungspark	Parco divertimenti
Dam - Waterfall	Barrage - Cascade	Staudamm - Wasserfall	Diga - Cascata
National park / Nature park	Parc national / Parc naturel	Nationalpark / Naturpark	Parco nazionale / Parco naturale

Signos Convencionales

Carreteras
Autopista
Carretera
Autopista, Autovía
Autovía
Accesos:
completo, parcial, sin precisar
Números de los accesos
Itinerario principal recomendado
por MICHELIN
Itinerario regional recomendado
por MICHELIN
Carretera asfaltada - sin asfaltar
Autopista - Carretera en construcción

Ancho de las carreteras
Calzadas separadas
Dos carriles anchos
Dos carriles - Dos carriles estrechos

Distancias (totales y parciales)
En autopista en kilómetros
Tramo de peaje - Tramo libre

En carretera en kilómetros

En autopista (GB)
en millas - en kilómetros
Tramo de peaje - Tramo libre

En carretera en millas

Numeración - Señalización
Carretera europea - Autopista
Otras carreteras
Localidades situadas en los principales
itinerarios

Alertas Seguridad
Nevada:
Período probable de cierre
Puerto y su altitud
Pendiente Pronunciada - Barrera de peaje
Vado

Transportes
Aeropuerto
Transporte de coches:
todo el año - de temporada
por barco
por barcaza
Barcaza para el paso de peatones y vehículos dos ruedas
Auto-tren

Administración
Capital de división administrativa
Parador / Pousada
Limites administrativos
Frontera
Aduana principal
Aduana con restricciones
Zona prohibida a los extranjeros / Propiedad militar

Curiosidades
Lugares clasificados con 2 y 3 estrellas
por la Guía Verde MICHELIN
Edificio religioso
Castillo
Monasterio
Iglesia de madera
Iglesia de madera
Museo al aire libre
Zona de vestigios antiguos
Grabado rupestre - Monumento megalítico
Piedra rúnica - Ruinas
Cueva - Molino de viento
Otras curiosidades
Recorrido pintoresco

Signos diversos
Zona recreativa
Presa - Cascada

Parque nacional / Parque natural

Verklaring van de tekens

Wegen
Autosnelweg
Autoweg
Autosnelweg of gelijksoortige weg
Gescheiden rijbanen van het type autosnelweg
Aansluitingen: volledig, gedeeltelijk,
zonder aanduiding
Afritnummers
Hoofdweg

Regionale weg

Verharde weg - onverharde weg
Autosnelweg - Weg in aanleg

Breedte van de wegen
Gescheiden rijbanen
2 brede rijstroken
2 rijstroken - 2 smalle rijstroken

Afstanden (totaal en gedeeltelijk)
Op autosnelwegen in kilometers
Gedeelte met tol - Tolvrij gedeelte

Op andere wegen in kilometers

Op autosnelwegen (GB)
in mijlen - in kilometers
Gedeelte met tol - Tolvrij gedeelte

Op andere wegen in mijlen

Wegnummers - Bewegwijzering
Europaweg - Autosnelweg
Andere wegen
Plaatsen langs een hoofdweg met
bewegwijzering

Veiligheidswaarschuwingen
Sneeuw:
vermoedelijke sluitingsperiode
Bergpas en hoogte boven de zeespiegel
Steile helling - Tol
Wad

Vervoer
Luchthaven
Vervoer van auto's:
het hele jaar - tijdens het seizoen
per boot
per veerpont
Veerpont voor voetgangers en fietsers
Autotrein

Administratie
Hoofdplaats van administratief gebied
Parador / Pousada
Administratieve grenzen
Staatsgrens
Hoofddouanekantoor
Douanekantoor met beperkte bevoegdheden
Terrein verboden voor buitenlanders / Militair gebied

Bezienswaardigheden
Locaties met 2 en 3 sterren volgens de
Groene Gids van MICHELIN
Kerkelijk gebouw
Kasteel
Klooster
Stavkirke (houten kerk)
Houten kerk
Openluchtmuseum
Overblijfsel uit de Oudheid
Rotstekening - Megaliet
Runensteen - Ruïne
Grot - Molen
Andere bezienswaardigheden
Schilderachtig traject

Diverse tekens
Recreatiepark
Stuwdam - Waterval

Nationaal park / Natuurpark

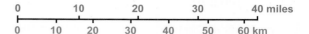

0 10 20 30 40 miles
0 10 20 30 40 50 60 km

**Republic of Ireland: All distances
and speed limits are signed in kilometres.**

**République d'Irlande: Les distances
et les limitations de vitesse sont exprimées en
kilomètres.**

**Irland: Alle Entfernungsangaben und
Geschwindigkeitsbegrenzungen in km.**

**Ierland: Alle afstanden en
maximumsnelheden zijn uitsluitend
in kilometers aangegeven.**

**Repubblica d'Irlanda: Distanze e limiti
di velocità sono espressi soltanto in chilometri.**

**República de Irlanda: Distancias y límites de
velocidad están expresados sólo en kilómetros.**

Key to 1:1 000 000 map pages
Légende des cartes au 1/1 000 000
Zeichenerklärung der Karten 1:1 000 000
Verklaring van de tekens voor kaarten met schaal 1:1 000 000
Legenda carte scala 1:1 000 000
Signos convencionales de los mapas a escala 1:1 000 000

ENGLAND

UNITARY AUTHORITIES

1	Bath and North East Somerset
	Bedford
	Blackburn with Darwen
	Blackpool
	Bracknell Forest
	Brighton and Hove
7	Buckinghamshire
8	Cambridgeshire
9	Central Bedfordshire
10	Cheshire East
11	Cheshire West and Chester
	City of Bristol
13	Cornwall
14	Cumbria
	Derby
16	Derbyshire
17	Devon
18	Dorset
19	Durham
20	East Riding of Yorkshire
21	East Sussex
22	Essex
23	Gloucestershire
	Greater London
	Greater Manchester
26	Halton
27	Hampshire
	Hartlepool
29	Herefordshire
30	Hertfordshire
31	Kent
	Kingston-upon-Hull
33	Lancashire
	Leicester
35	Leicestershire
36	Lincolnshire
	Luton
38	Medway
39	Merseyside
	Middlesbrough
41	Milton Keynes
42	Norfolk

43	North East Lincolnshire
44	North Lincolnshire
45	North Somerset
46	North Yorkshire
47	Northamptonshire
48	Northumberland
49	Nottinghamshire
	Nottingham
51	Oxfordshire
	Peterborough
	Plymouth
	Portsmouth
	Reading
56	Redcar and Cleveland
57	Rutland
58	Shropshire
59	Somerset
60	South Gloucestershire
61	South Yorkshire
	Southend-on-Sea
63	Staffordshire
	Stockton-on-Tees
	Stoke-on-Trent
66	Suffolk
67	Surrey
	Swindon
69	Telford and Wrekin
70	Thurrock
	Torbay
72	Tyne and Wear
	Warrington
74	Warwickshire
75	West Berkshire
76	West Midlands
77	West Sussex
78	West Yorkshire
79	Wiltshire
	Windsor and Maidenhead
	Wokingham
82	Worcestershire
	York

 = **UNITARY AUTHORITIES**

32

SCOTLAND

UNITARY AUTHORITIES

1	1	Aberdeen City
2	2	Aberdeenshire
3	3	Angus
4	4	Argyll and Bute
5	5	Clackmannanshire
6		City of Edinburgh
7		City of Glasgow
8	8	Dumfries and Galloway
9	9	Dundee City
10	10	East Ayrshire
11	11	East Dunbartonshire
12	12	East Lothian
13	13	East Renfrewshire
14	14	Falkirk
15	15	Fife
16	16	Highland

17	17	Inverclyde
18	18	Midlothian
19	19	Moray
20	20	North Ayrshire
21	21	North Lanarkshire
22	22	Orkney Islands
23	23	Perth and Kinross
24	24	Renfrewshire
25	25	Scottish Borders
26	26	Shetland Islands
27	27	South Ayrshire
28	28	South Lanarkshire
29	29	Stirling
30	30	West Dunbartonshire
31	31	West Lothian
32	32	Na H-Eileanan Siar (Western Isles)

NORTHERN IRELAND

DISTRICT COUNCILS

1	1	Antrim and Newtownabbey
2	2	Ards and North Down
3	3	Armagh, Banbridge and Craigavon
4	4	Belfast
5	5	Causeway Coast and Glens
6	6	Derry and Strabane

7	7	Fermanagh and Omagh
8	8	Lisburn and Castlereagh
9	9	Mid and East Antrim
10	10	Mid Ulster
11	11	Newry, Mourne and Down

WALES

UNITARY AUTHORITIES

1	1	Anglesey/Sir Fôn
2	2	Blaenau Gwent
3	3	Bridgend/Pen-y-bont ar Ogwr
4	4	Caerphilly/Caerffili
5	5	Cardiff/Caerdydd
6	6	Carmarthenshire/Sir Gaerfyrddin
7	7	Ceredigion
8	8	Conwy
9	9	Denbighshire/Sir Ddinbych
10	10	Flintshire/Sir y Fflint
11	11	Gwynedd

12	12	Merthyr Tydfil/Merthyr Tudful
13	13	Monmouthshire/Sir Fynwy
14	14	Neath Port Talbot/Castell-nedd Phort Talbot
15	15	Newport/Casnewydd
16	16	Pembrokeshire/Sir Benfro
17	17	Powys
18	18	Rhondda Cynon Taff/Rhondda Cynon Taf
19	19	Swansea/Abertawe
20	20	Torfaen/Tor-faen
21	21	Vale of Glamorgan/Bro Morgannwg
22	22	Wrexham/Wrecsam

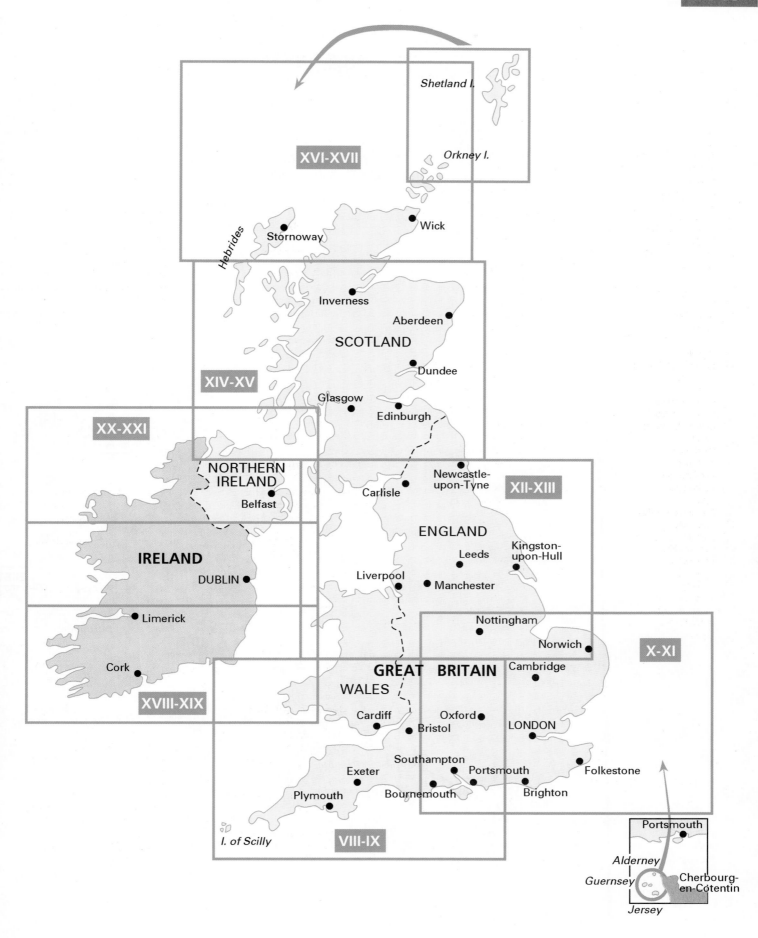

XVI-XVII

Shetland I.

Orkney I.

Hebrides

Stornoway

Wick

Inverness

Aberdeen

SCOTLAND

XIV-XV

Dundee

Glasgow

Edinburgh

XX-XXI

NORTHERN
IRELAND

Belfast

Newcastle-
upon-Tyne

XII-XIII

Carlisle

ENGLAND

IRELAND

Leeds

Kingston-
upon-Hull

Liverpool

DUBLIN

Manchester

Limerick

Nottingham

Norwich

X-XI

Cork

Cambridge

GREAT BRITAIN

WALES

XVIII-XIX

Cardiff

Oxford

Bristol

LONDON

Southampton

Portsmouth

Folkestone

Exeter

Plymouth

Bournemouth

Brighton

I. of Scilly

VIII-IX

Portsmouth

Alderney

Guernsey

Cherbourg-
en-Cotentin

Jersey

ST. GEORGE'S CHANNEL

Saltee Islands
e Harbour/ Ros Láir
Point

Stumble Head
Pembrokeshire Coast National Park
Newport
Fishguard/ Abergwaun
St. David's Head
St. David's
St. Bride's Bay
Haverfordwest/Hwlffordd
Pembrokeshire Coast National Park
Milford Haven/ Aberdaugleddau
Neyland
Pembroke Dock
Pembroke
St. Govan's Head
Narberth
Whitland
Saundersfoot
Pendine
Tenby/ Dinbych-y-pysgod
Carmarthen Bay
Worms Head
Rhossili
Port Eynon
The Mumbles

Aberaeron
New Quay
Aberporth
Synod Inn
Cardigan
Newcastle Emlyn
Crymmych
Llandysul
Lampeter
Tregaron
Elan Valley

Carmarthen/ Caerfyrddin
St. Clears
Kidwelly
Burry Port
Llanelli
SWANSEA/ ABERTAWE
Port Talbot
Porthcawl
Bridgend/ Pen-y-bont

Llandovery
Llandeilo
Llangadog
Black Mountain
Brecon National
Sennybridge
Ammanford
Cross Hands
Pontardawe
Pontarddulais
Neath/ Castell-Nedd
Merthyr
Hirwaun
Aberdare
Maesteg

BRISTOL CHANNEL

Lundy
Combe Martin
Lynton
Lynmouth
Porlock
Ilfracombe
Exmoor National
Simonsbath
Tarr steps
Croyde
Braunton
Barnstaple
Northam
South Molton
Hartland Point
Clovelly
Bideford
Great Torrington
Tiverton
Cliffs of Morwenstow
Kilkhampton
Stratton
Holsworthy
Hatherleigh
Winkleigh
Bude
Crediton
EXETER
Okehampton
Moretonhampstead
Tintagel
High Willhays
Dartmoor National Park
Camelford
Launceston
Lydford Gorge
Bovey Tracey
Padstow
Tavistock
Princetown
Ashburton
Newton Abbot
Wadebridge
Callington
Buckfastleigh
Bodmin
Liskeard
Buckland Abbey
Plympton
Newquay
Lostwithiel
Saltash
Plymstock
Totnes
Fraddon
West Looe
Torpoint
Plymouth
Modbury
Dartmouth
St. Austell
Fowey
Polperro
PLYMOUTH
Newton Ferrers
Kingsbridge
Truro
Trewithen
Tregony
Mevagissey
Salcombe
Camborne
Trelissick Garden
Start Po
St. Ives
Hayle
Redruth
Penryn
St. Mawes
St. Just
Penzance
Falmouth
Land's End
St. Michael's Mount
Helston
Glendurgan Garden
Sennen
Mount's Bay
St. Keverne
Lizard
Lizard Point

Subtropical Gardens
Tresco
St. Martin's
Isles of Scilly
St. Mary's

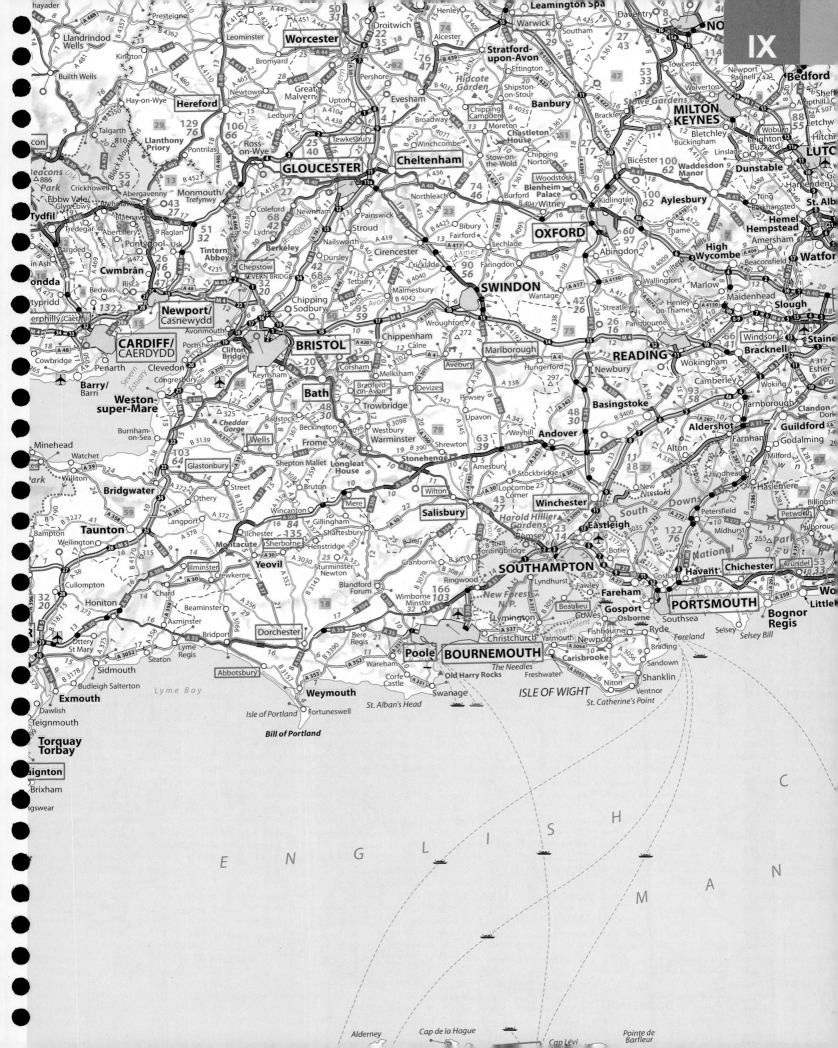

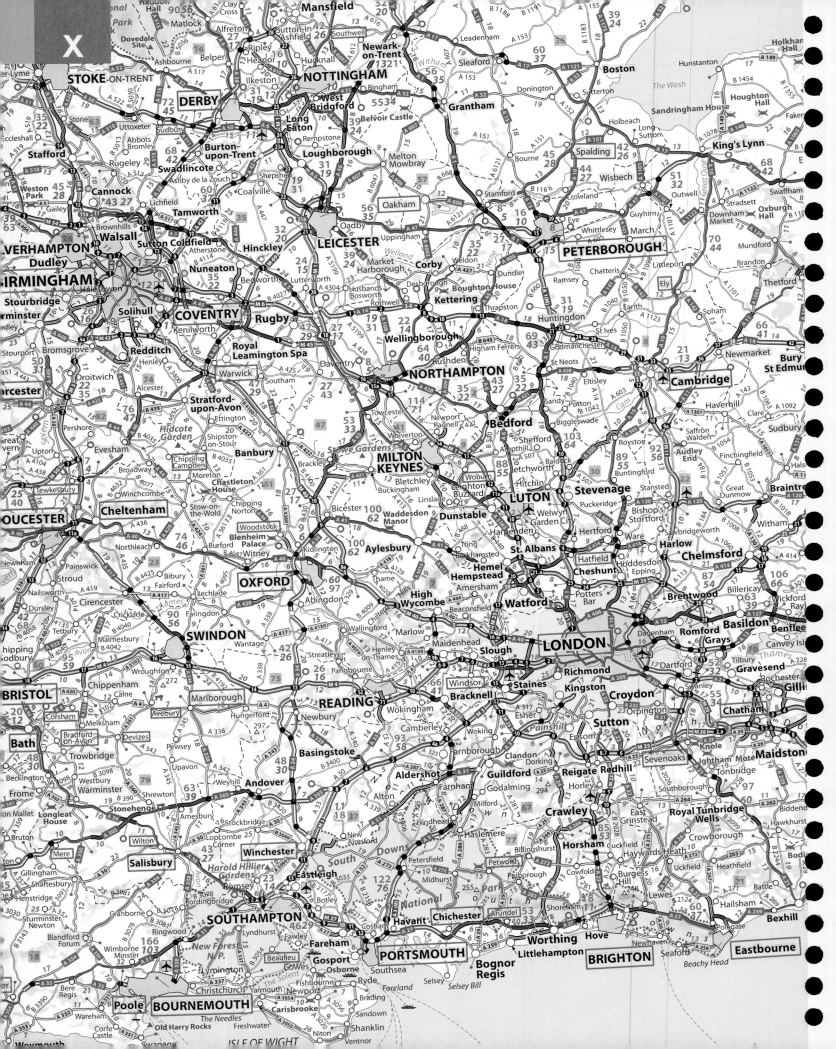

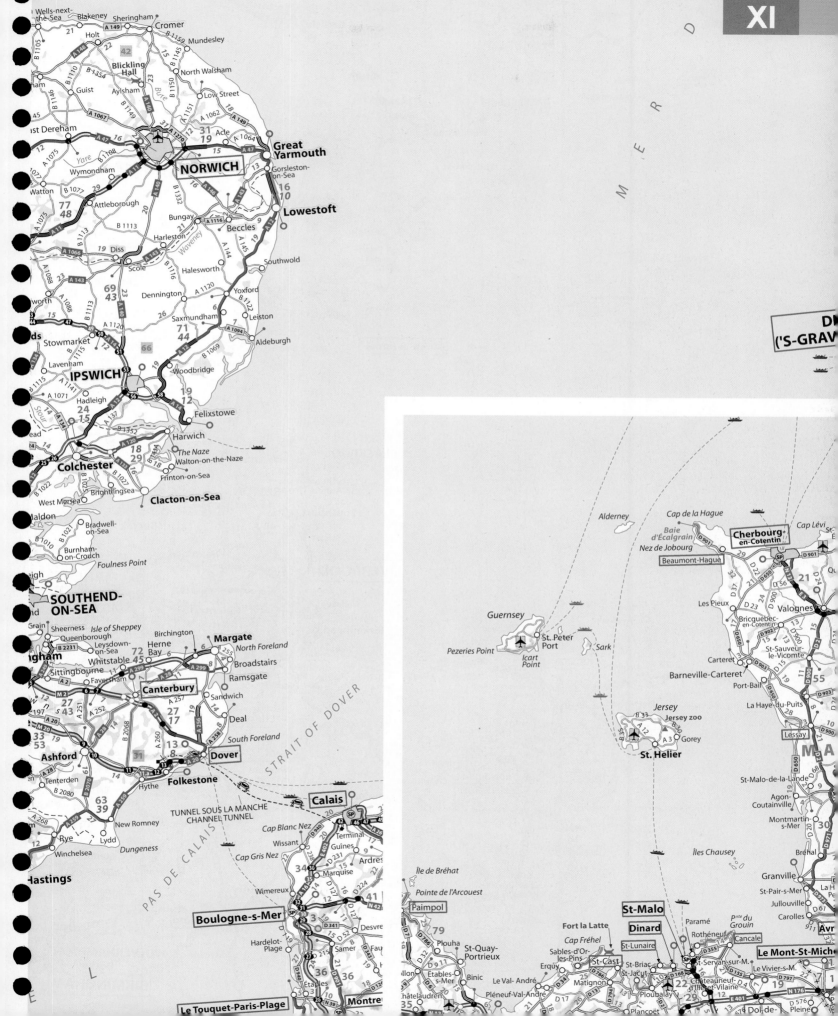

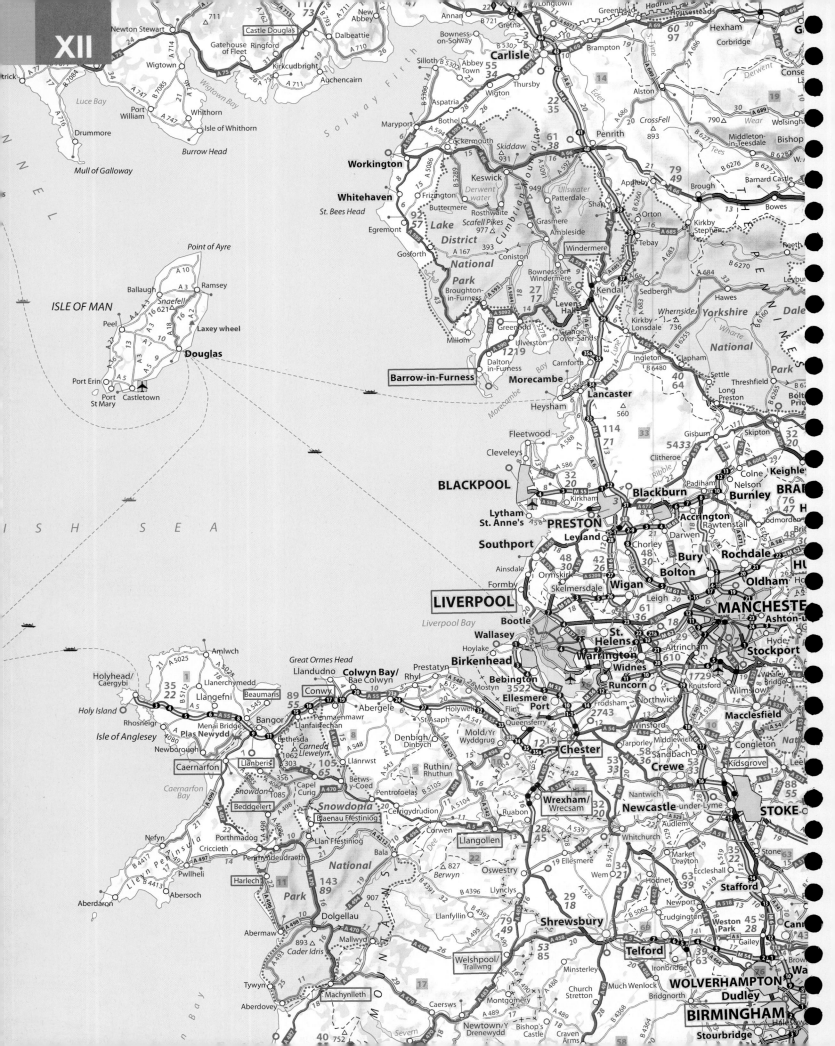

South Shields
SUNDERLAND
Washington
Houghton-le-Spring
Seaham
Durham
Hartlepool
Peterlee
Sedgefield
Stockton-on-Tees
Billingham
Redcar
Marske-by-the-Sea
Saltburn-by-the-Sea
Brotton
Loftus
Whitby
Darlington
MIDDLESBROUGH
Guisborough
Eaglescliffe
Northallerton
Cleveland Hills
North York Moors National Park
Richmond
Scarborough
Scalby
Bedale
Thirsk
Rievaulx Abbey
Helmsley
Pickering
Filey
Ripon
Easingwold
Malton
Norton
Flamborough Head
Boroughbridge
Bridlington
Knaresborough
YORK
Wetwang
Driffield
Beeford
Harrogate
Wetherby
Tadcaster
Market Weighton
Leven
Hornsea
Otley
Bingley
Harewood
LEEDS
Selby
Barlby
Beverley
KINGSTON UPON HULL
Halifax
Garforth
Castleford
Howden
Goole
Hedon
Withernsea
Snaith
River Humber
Barton-upon-Humber
Patrington
Kilnsea
Dewsbury
Wakefield
Pontefract
Thorne
Crowle
Scunthorpe
Immingham Dock
Immingham
Spurn Head
HUDDERSFIELD
Barnsley
Doncaster
Grimsby
Cleethorpes
under-Lyne
Conisbrough
Bentley
Brigg
Caistor
Stocksbridge
Rotherham
Bawtry
Epworth
Market Rasen
SHEFFIELD
Maltby
Gainsborough
Louth
Mablethorpe
Sutton-on-Sea
High Peak
Castleton
Worksop
Retford
Wragby
Chapel-en-le-Frith
Dronfield
Staveley
Tuxford
Alford
District
Chesterfield
Ollerton
Lincoln
Horncastle
Partney
Spilsby
Skegness
Bakewell
Chatsworth House
Hardwick Hall
Mansfield
Woodhall Spa
Haddon Hall
Clay Cross
Southwell
Matlock
Alfreton
Sutton-in-Ashfield
Leadenham
Holkham
Wells-next-the-Sea
Blakeney
Sheringham
Dovedale
Ashbourne
Ripley
Belper
Heanor
Hucknall
Newark-on-Trent
Sleaford
Boston
Hunstanton
Holt
Ilkeston
NOTTINGHAM
Bingham
Grantham
Donington
Sutterton
Sandringham House
Houghton Hall
Blickling Hall
DERBY
West Bridgford
Belvoir Castle
Holbeach
Long Sutton
King's Lynn
East Dereham
Fakenham
Guist
Aylsham
Uttoxeter
Sudbury
Long Eaton
Rempstone
Bourne
Spalding
Wisbech
Burton-upon-Trent
Loughborough
Melton Mowbray
Crowland
Outwell
Downham Market
Oxburgh Hall
Swaffham
Wymondham
Watton
Swadlincote
Shepshed
Stamford
Ashby de la Zouch
Coalville
Oakham
Guyhirn
Eye
March
Attleborough
Lichfield
Tamworth
Oadby
LEICESTER
Uppingham
Whittlesey
PETERBOROUGH
Mundford
Brandon
Sutton Coldfield
Hinckley
Atherstone
Market Harborough
Corby
Weldon
Oundle
Chatteris
Littleport
Ely
Thetford
Diss
Nuneaton
Bedworth
Lutterworth
Husbands Bosworth
Rothwell
Kettering
Boughton House
Ramsey

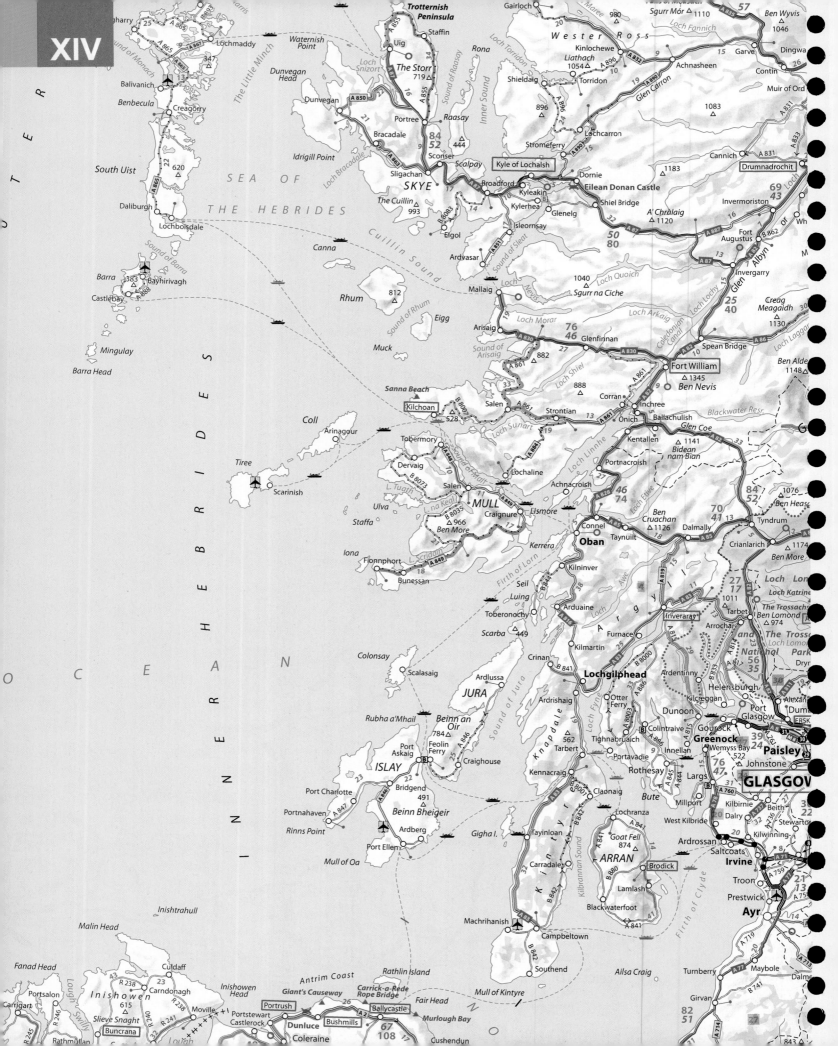

Alness, Invergordon, Cromarty, Black Isle, Fortrose, Nairn, Forres, Elgin, Lossiemouth, Buckie, Cullen, Banff, Macduff, Fraserburgh, Loch of Strathbeg, Rattray Head

Tore, Fochabers, Keith, Turriff, New Deer, Mintlaw, Peterhead, Buchan Ness

Inverness, Findhorn, Rothes, Craigellachie, Huntly, Rhynie, Oldmeldrum, Ellon, Cruden Bay, Newburgh

Glen More, Dava, Grantown-on-Spey, Dufftown, Mossat, Alford, Inverurie, Kintore, Pitmedden Garden

Carrbridge, Dulnain Bridge, Tomintoul, Colnabaichin, Craigievar Castle, Crathes Castle, **ABERDEEN**

Aviemore, Glenmore Forest Park, Cairn Gorm, Crathie Castle

Kingussie, Cairngorm Mountains, Ben Macdui, Balmoral Castle, Braemar, Ballater, Aboyne, Banchory, Dee, Stonehaven

Newtonmore, **Cairngorms National Park**, Laurencekirk, Inverbervie

Laggan, Dalwhinnie, Pass of Drumochter, Devil's Elbow, Glas Maol, The Pleasance, Marykirk, Brechin, Montrose

Blair Castle, Blair Atholl, Kinloch Rannoch, S Esk, N Esk, Kirriemuir, Forfar, Glamis Castle, Arbroath

Pitlochry, Schiehallion, Aberfeldy, Dunkeld, Blairgowrie, Rattray, Alyth, Meigle, Coupar Angus, Glamis, **DUNDEE**, Carnoustie, Monifieth

Ben Lawers, Loch Tay, BenChonzie, Crieff, **Perth**, Newburgh, Tayport, Newport-on-Tay, Buddon Ness, Leuchars

Killin, Lochearnhead, Callander, Auchterarder, Ochil Hills, Auchtermuchty, Cupar, **St. Andrews**, Fife Ness

Ben Vorlich, Crail, Falkland, Anstruther, Pittenweem, Saint Monans

Doune, Dunblane, Dollar, Kinross, Glenrothes, Leven, Elie, Methil, Buckhaven

Stirling, Bridge of Allan, Alva, **Alloa**, **Dunfermline**, Lochgelly, **Kirkcaldy**, Firth of Forth

Kincardine, Culross, Cowdenbeath, Burntisland

Denny, Grangemouth, Bo'ness, Inverkeithing, North Berwick, Dunbar

Kilsyth, **Falkirk**, Linlithgow, Hopetoun House, Queensferry, Leith, Prestonpans, Aberlady, East Linton, Cockburnspath, St Abb's Head National Nature Reserve

Kirkintilloch, **Cumbernauld**, Bathgate, **Livingston**, Musselburgh, Tranent, Haddington, Eyemouth

Clydebank, Airdrie, Armadale, Whitburn, **EDINBURGH**, Dalkeith, Loanhead, Lammermuir Hills

Coatbridge, Motherwell, Penicuik, RosslynChapel, Duns, **Berwick-upon-Tweed**

Barrhead, Hamilton, Wishaw, Carluke, West Linton, Carnwath, Lauder, Greenlaw, Holy Island

East Kilbride, Strathaven, Lanark, Biggar, Peebles, Galashiels, Mellerstain, Coldstream, Belford, Bamburgh Castle

Kilmarnock, Galston, Douglas, Innerleithen, Melrose, Abbey Dryburgh, Kelso, Newtown St Boswells, Wooler, The Cheviot

Mauchline, Muirkirk, Abington, Broad Law, Selkirk, Jedburgh, Alnwick

Cumnock, Elvanfoot, Hawick, Carter Bar, Northumberland National Park, Warkworth, Amble

New Cumnock, Sanquhar, Moffat, Otterburn, Rothbury, Felton

Drumlanrig castle, Thornhill, Beattock, Kielder Resr., Ashington, Newbiggin-by-the-Sea, Morpeth, Blyth

Lochmaben, Lockerbie, Langholm

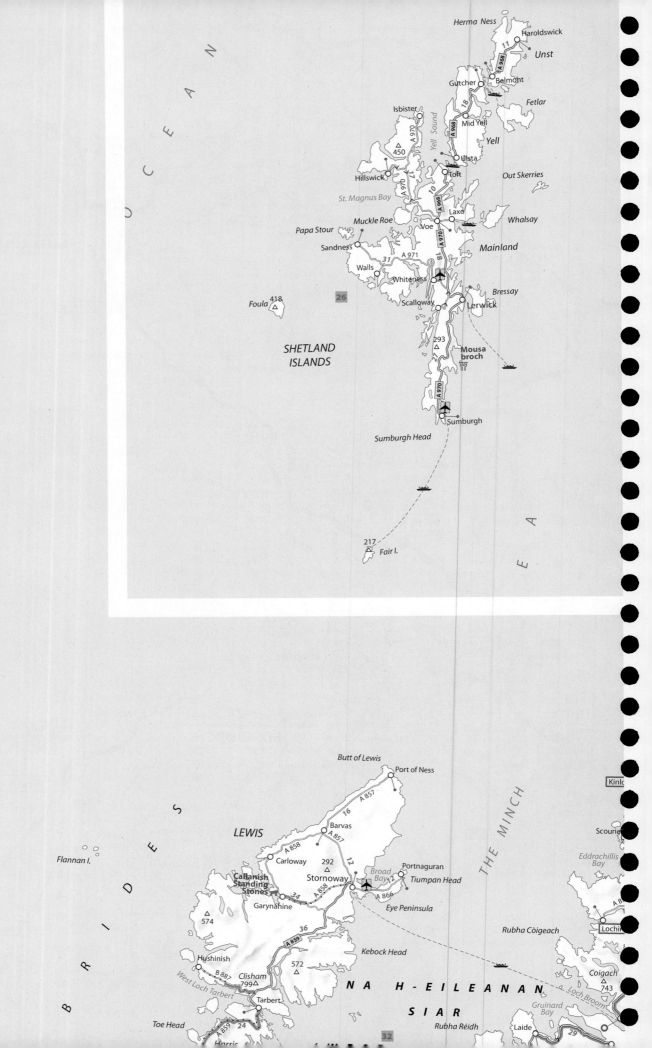

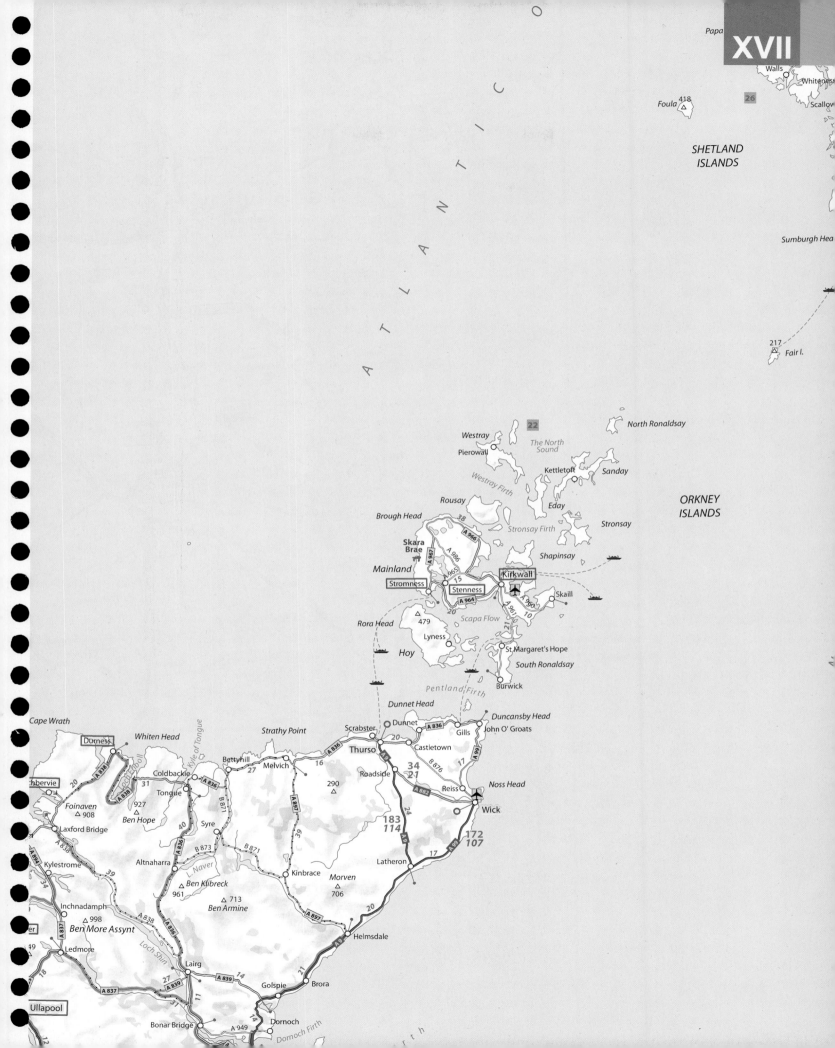

Papa

Walls

Whiteness

Foula 418 △

26

Scallow

SHETLAND
ISLANDS

Sumburgh Hea

A T L A N T I C

217 △ Fair I.

22

North Ronaldsay

Westray

Pierowall

The North
Sound

Kettletoft

Sanday

ORKNEY
ISLANDS

Westray Firth

Rousay

Brough Head

Eday

Stronsay

Stronsay Firth

38

A 966

Skara
Brae

A 967

A 966

Shapinsay

Mainland

A 965

15

Stromness

Stenness

Kirkwall

A 990

Skaill

A 964

A 961

10

20

Scapa Flow

479 △

21

Rora Head

Lyness

Hoy

St Margaret's Hope

South Ronaldsay

Burwick

Pentland Firth

Dunnet Head

Duncansby Head

Cape Wrath

Whiten Head

Kyle of Tongue

Strathy Point

Scrabster

Dunnet

A 836

Gills

John O' Groats

Durness

20

Thurso

Castletown

A 99

Bettyhill

Melvich

16

Roadside

34
21

B 876

17

Noss Head

Loch Eriboll

A 838

Coldbackie

A 836

27

A 882

Reiss

chbervie

20

31

Tongue

290 △

A 882

Wick

Foinaven
△ 908

927 △

B 871

Syre

24

927

Ben Hope

40

39

183
114

172
107

Laxford Bridge

A 836

B 873

B 871

A 897

Latheron

17

Kylestrome

Altnaharra

L. Naver

Kinbrace

A 99

39

Ben Klibreck

Morven
706

Inchnadamph

961

713 △

20

A 838

Ben Armine

A 897

△ 998

A 838

A 836

Ben More Assynt

Loch Shin

Helmsdale

Ledmore

Lairg

A 839

49

A 837

27

14

Golspie

Brora

A 839

21

Ullapool

18

A 837

Bonar Bridge

A 949

Dornoch

Dornoch Firth

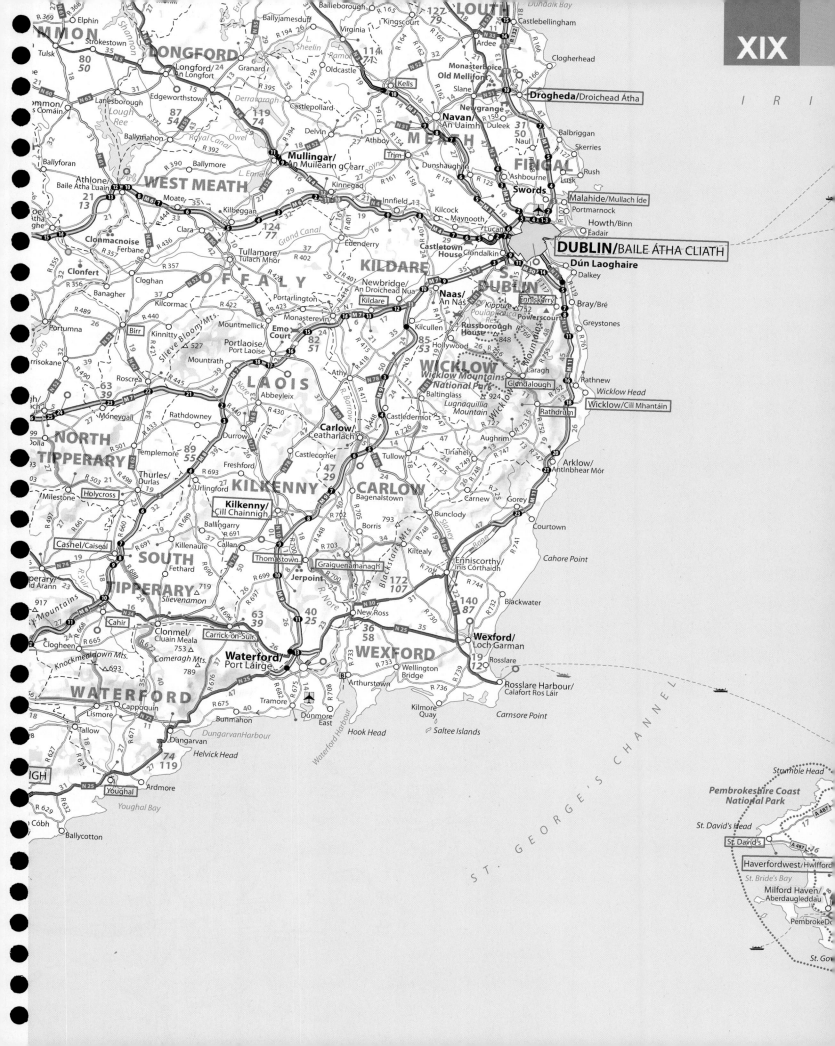

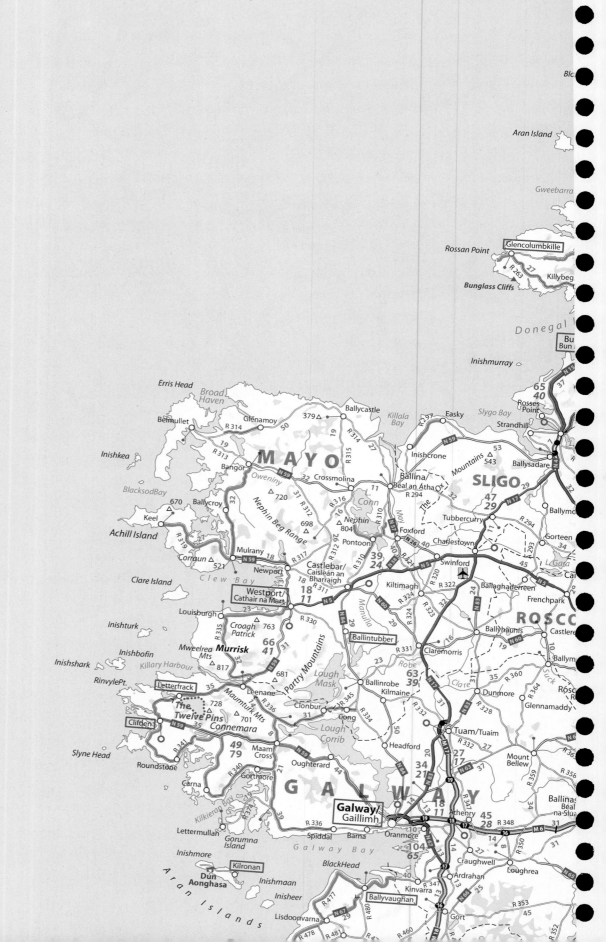

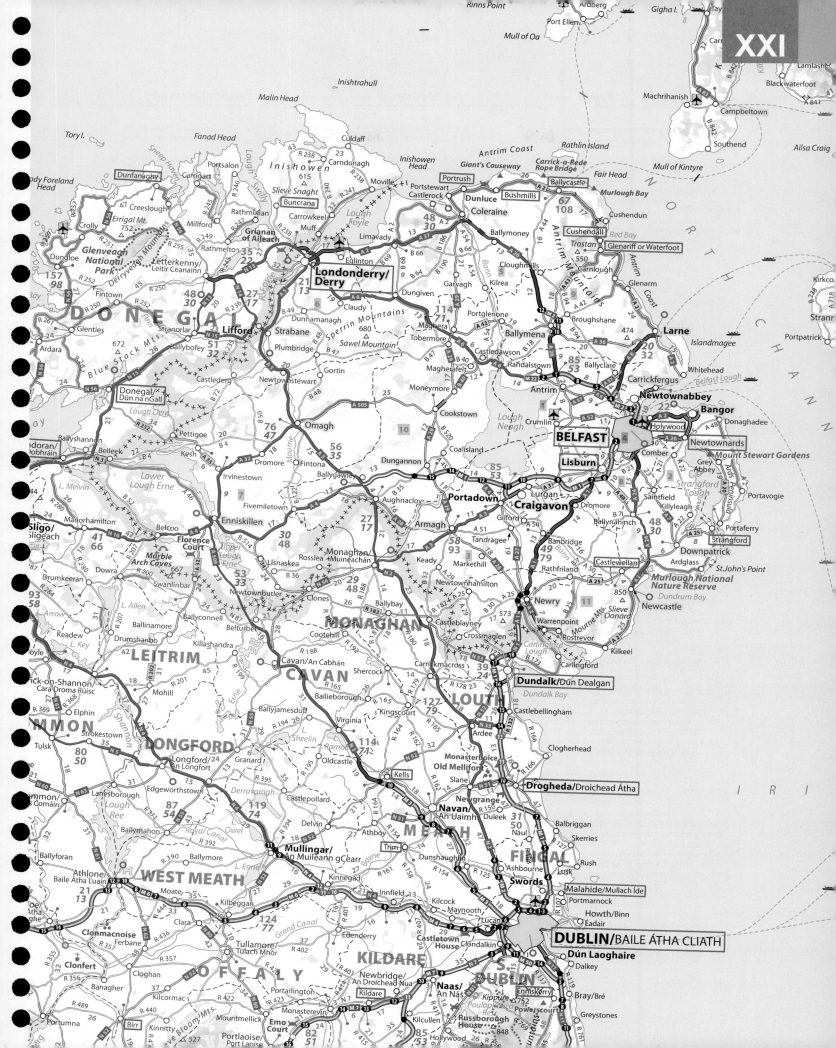

Key	Légende	Zeichenerklärung

Roads / Routes / Straßen

Motorway - Service areas	Autoroute - Aires de service	Autobahn - Tankstelle mit Raststätte
Dual carriageway with motorway characteristics	Double chaussée de type autoroutier	Schnellstraße mit getrennten Fahrbahnen
Interchanges: complete, limited	Échangeurs : complet, partiels	Anschlussstellen: Voll - bzw. Teilanschlussstellen
Interchange numbers	Numéros d'échangeurs	Anschlussstellennummern
International and national road network	Route de liaison internationale ou nationale	Internationale bzw.nationale Hauptverkehrsstraße
Interregional and less congested road	Route de liaison interrégionale ou de dégagement	Überregionale Verbindungsstraße oder Umleitungsstrecke
Road surfaced - unsurfaced	Route revêtue - non revêtue	Straße mit Belag - ohne Belag
Footpath - Waymarked footpath / Bridle path	Sentier - Sentier balisé/Allée cavalière	Pfad - Ausgeschilderter Weg / Reitpfad
Motorway / Road under construction	Autoroute - Route en construction	Autobahn - Straße im Bau
(when available: with scheduled opening date)	(le cas échéant : date de mise en service prévue)	(ggf. voraussichtliches Datum der Verkehrsfreigabe)

Road widths / Largeur des routes / Straßenbreiten

Dual carriageway	Chaussées séparées	Getrennte Fahrbahnen
4 lanes - 2 wide lanes	4 voies - 2 voies larges	4 Fahrspuren - 2 breite Fahrspuren
2 lanes - 2 narrow lanes	2 voies - 2 voies étroites	2 Fahrspuren - 1 Fahrspur

Distances (total and intermediate) / Distances (totalisées et partielles) / Entfernungen (Gesamt- und Teilentfernungen)

Toll roads on motorway	Section à péage sur autoroute	Mautstrecke auf der Autobahn
Toll-free section on motorway	Section libre sur autoroute	Mautfreie Strecke auf der Autobahn
in miles - en kilometers	en miles - en kilomètres	in Meilen - in Kilometern
on road	sur route	Auf der Straße

Numbering - Signs / Numérotation - Signalisation / Nummerierung - Wegweisung

Motorway - GB: Primary route	Autoroute - GB : itinéraire principal (Primary route)	Autobahn - GB: Empfohlene Fernverkehrsstraße (Primary route)
IRL : National primary and secondary route	IRL : itinéraire principal (National primary et secondary route)	IRL: Empfohlene Fernverkehrsstraße (National primary und secondary route)
Other roads	Autres routes	Sonstige Straßen
Destination on primary route network	Localités jalonnant les itinéraires principaux	Richtungshinweis auf der empfohlenen Fernverkehrsstraße

M 5 A 38
N 20 N 31
A 190 B 629 R 561
YORK

Obstacles / Obstacles / Verkehrshindernisse

Roundabout - Pass and its height above sea level (meters)	Rond-point - Col et sa cote d'altitude (en mètres)	Verkehrsinsel - Pass mit Höhenangabe (in Meter)
Steep hill (ascent in direction of the arrow)	Forte déclivité (flèches dans le sens de la montée)	Starke Steigung (Steigung in Pfeilrichtung)
IRL: Difficult or dangerous section of road	IRL : Parcours difficile ou dangereux	IRL: Schwierige oder gefährliche Strecke
In Scotland: narrow road with passing places	En Écosse : route très étroite avec emplacements pour croisement	In Schottland: sehr schmale Straße mit Ausweichstellen (passing places)
Level crossing: railway passing, under road, over road	Passages de la route : à niveau, supérieur, inférieur	Bahnübergänge: schienengleich, Unterführung, Überführung
Prohibited road - Road subject to restrictions	Route interdite - Route réglementée	Gesperrte Straße - Straße mit Verkehrsbeschränkungen
Toll barrier - One way road (on major and regional roads)	Barrière de péage - Route à sens unique	Mautstelle - Einbahnstraße
Height limit under 15'6'' IRL, 16'6'' GB	Hauteur limitée au dessous de 15'6'' IRL, 16'6''GB	Beschränkung der Durchfahrtshöhe bis 15'6'' IRL, 16'6' GB
Load limit (under 16 t.)	Limites de charge (au-dessous de 16 t.)	Höchstbelastung (angegeben, wenn unter 16 t)

Transportation / Transports / Verkehrsmittel

Railway - Passenger station	Voie ferrée - Gare	Bahnlinie - Bahnhof
Airport - Airfield	Aéroport - Aérodrome	Flughafen - Flugplatz
Transportation of vehicles: (seasonal services in red)	Transport des autos: (liaison saisonnière en rouge)	Autotransport: (rotes Zeichen: saisonbedingte Verbindung)
by boat	par bateau	per Schiff
by ferry (load limit in tons)	par bac (charge maximum en tonnes)	per Fähre (Höchstbelastung in t)
Ferry (passengers and cycles only)	Bac pour piétons et cycles	Fähre für Personen und Fahrräder

Accommodation - Administration / Hébergement - Administration / Unterkunft - Verwaltung

Administrative boundaries	Limites administratives	Verwaltungshauptstadt
Scottish and Welsh borders	Limite de l'Écosse et du Pays de Galles	Grenze von Schottland und Wales
National boundary - Customs post	Frontière - Douane	Staatsgrenze - Zoll

Sport & Recreation Facilities / Sports - Loisirs / Sport - Freizeit

Golf course - Horse racetrack	Golf - Hippodrome	Golfplatz - Pferderennbahn
Racing circuit - Pleasure boat harbour	Circuit automobile - Port de plaisance	Rennstrecke - Yachthafen
Caravan and camping sites	Camping, caravaning	Campingplatz
Waymarked footpath - Country park	Sentier balisé - Base ou parc de loisirs	Ausgeschilderter Weg - Freizeitanlage
Safari park, zoo - Bird sanctuary, refuge	Parc animalier, zoo - Réserve d'oiseaux	Tierpark, Zoo - Vogelschutzgebiet
IRL: Fishing - Greyhound track	IRL : Pêche - Cynodrome	IRL: Angeln - Windhundrennen
Tourist train	Train touristique	Museumseisenbahn
Funicular, cable car, chairlift	Funiculaire, téléphérique, télésiège	Standseilbahn, Seilbahn, Sessellift

Sights / Curiosités / Sehenswürdigkeiten

Principal sights:	Principales curiosités :	Hauptsehenswürdigkeiten:
see THE GREEN GUIDE	voir LE GUIDE VERT	siehe GRÜNER REISEFÜHRER
Towns or places of interest, Places to stay	Localités ou sites intéressants, lieux de séjour	Sehenswerte Orte, Ferienorte
Religious building - Historic house, castle	Édifice religieux - Château	Sakral-Bau - Schloss, Burg
Ruins - Prehistoric monument - Cave	Ruines - Monument mégalithique - Grotte	Ruine - Vorgeschichtliches Steindenkmal - Höhle
Garden, park - Other places of interest	Jardin, parc - Autres curiosités	Garten, Park - Sonstige Sehenswürdigkeit
IRL: Fort - Celtic cross - Round Tower	IRL : Fort - Croix celte - Tour ronde	IRL: Fort, Festung - Keltisches Kreuz - Rundturm
Panoramic view - Viewpoint - Scenic route	Panorama - Point de vue - Parcours pittoresque	Rundblick - Aussichtspunkt - Landschaftlich schöne Strecke

Rye (▲)
Ergol

Other signs / Signes divers / Sonstige Zeichen

Industrial cable way	Transporteur industriel aérien	Industrieschwebebahn
Telecommunications tower or mast - Lighthouse	Tour ou pylône de télécommunications - Phare	Funk-, Sendeturm - Leuchtturm
Power station - Quarry	Centrale électrique - Carrière	Kraftwerk - Steinbruch
Mine - Industrial activity	Mine - Industries	Bergwerk - Industrieanlagen
Refinery - Cliff	Raffinerie - Falaise	Raffinerie - Klippen
National forest park - National park	Parc forestier national - Parc national	Waldschutzgebiet - Nationalpark

Verklaring van de tekens | ## Legenda | ## Signos convencionales

Wegen
Autosnelweg - Serviceplaatsen
Gescheiden rijbanen van het type autosnelweg

Aansluitingen: volledig, gedeeltelijk
Afritnummers
Internationale of nationale verbindingsweg
Interregionale verbindingsweg
Verharde weg - Onverharde weg
Pad - Bewegwijzerd wandelpad / Ruiterpad
Autosnelweg in aanleg - weg in aanleg
(indien bekend: datum openstelling)

Breedte van de wegen
Gescheiden rijbanen
4 rijstroken - 2 brede rijstroken
2 rijstroken - 2 smalle rijstroken

Afstanden (totaal en gedeeltelijk)
Gedeelte met tol op autosnelwegen
Tolvrij gedeelte op autosnelwegen
in mijlen - in kilometers
op andere wegen

Wegnummers - Bewegwijzering
Autosnelweg - GB: Hoofdweg (Primary route)
IRL: Hoofdweg (National primary en secondary route)
Andere wegen
Plaatsen langs een autosnelweg of Primary route met bewegwijzering

Hindernissen
Rotonde - Bergpas en hoogte boven de zeespiegel (in meters)
Steile helling (pijlen in de richting van de helling)
IRL: Moeilijk of gevaarlijk traject
In Schotland: smalle weg met uitwijkplaatsen
Wegovergangen: gelijkvloers, overheen, onderdoor
Verboden weg - Beperkt opengestelde weg
Tol - Weg met eenrichtingsverkeer
Vrije hoogte indien lager dan 15' 6'' IRL, 16'6'' GB

Maximum draagvermogen (indien minder dan 16 t)

Vervoer
Spoorweg - Reizigersstation
Luchthaven - Vliegveld
Vervoer van auto's: (tijdens het seizoen: rood teken)
per boot
per veerpont (maximum draagvermogen in t.)
Veerpont voor voetgangers en fietsers

Verblijf - Administratie
Administratieve grenzen
Grens van Schotland en Wales

Staatsgrens - Douanekantoor

Sport - Recreatie
Golfterrein - Renbaan
Autocircuit - Jachthaven
Kampeerterrein (tent, caravan)
Sentiero segnalato - Recreatiepark
Safaripark, dierentuin - Vogelreservaat
IRL: Vissen - Hondenrenbaan
Toeristentreintje
Kabelspoor, kabelbaan, stoeltjeslift

Bezienswaardigheden
Belangrijkste bezienswaardigheden:
zie DE GROENE GIDS
Interessante steden of plaatsen, vakantieoorden
Kerkelijk gebouw - Kasteel
Ruïne - Megaliet - Grot
Tuin, park - Andere bezienswaardigheden
IRL: Fort - Keltisch kruis - Ronde toren
Panorama - Uitzichtpunt - Schilderachtig traject

Diverse tekens
Kabelvrachtvervoer
Telecommunicatietoren of -mast - Vuurtoren
Elektriciteitscentrale - Steengroeve
Mijn - Industrie
Raffinaderij - Klif
Staatsbos - Nationaal park

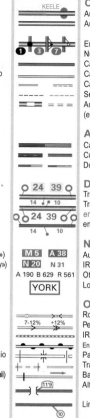

Strade
Autostrada - Aree di servizio
Doppia carreggiata di tipo autostradale

Svincoli: completo, parziale
Svincoli numerati
Strada di collegamento internazionale o nazionale
Strada di collegamento interregionale o di disimpegno
Strada rivestita - non rivestita
Sentiero - Sentiero segnalato / Pista per cavalli
Autostrada, strada in costruzione
(data di apertura prevista)

Larghezza delle strade
Carreggiate separate
4 corsie - 2 corsie larghe
2 corsie - 2 corsie strette

Distanze (totali e parziali)
Tratto a pedaggio su autostrada
Tratto esente da pedaggio su autostrada
in miglia - in chilometri
su strada

Numerazione - Segnaletica
Autostrada - GB: itinerario principale (Strada «Primary»)
IRL: itinerario principale (Strada «National primary» e «Secondary»)
Altre Strade
Località delimitante gli itinerari principali

Ostacoli
Rotonda - Passo ed altitudine (in metri)
Forte pendenza (salita nel senso della freccia)
IRL: Percorso difficile o pericoloso
In Scozia: Strada molto stretta con incrocio
Passaggi della strada: a livello, cavalcavia, sottopassaggio
Strada vietata - Strada a circolazione regolamentata
Casello - Strada a senso unico (su collegamenti principali e regionali)
Limite di altezza inferiore a 15'6'' IRL, 16'6''GB

Limite di portata (inferiore a 16 t.)

Trasporti
Ferrovia - Stazione viaggiatori
Aeroporto - Aerodromo
Trasporto auto: (stagionale in rosso)
su traghetto
su chiatta (carico massimo in t.)
Traghetto per pedoni e biciclette

Risorse alberghiere - Amministrazione
Confini amministrativi
Confine di Scozia e Galles

Frontiera - Dogana

Sport - Divertimento
Golf - Ippodromo
Circuito Automobilistico - Porto turistico
Campeggi, caravaning
Sentiero segnalato - Area o parco per attività ricreative
Parco con animali, zoo - Riserva ornitologica
IRL: Pesca - Cinodromo
Trenino turistico
Funicolare, funivia, seggiovia

Mete e luoghi d'interesse
Principali luoghi d'interesse,
vedere LA GUIDA VERDE
Località o siti interessanti, luoghi di soggiorno
Edificio religioso - Castello
Rovine - Monumento megalitico - Grotta
Giardino, parco - Altri luoghi d'interesse
IRL: Forte - Croce celtica - Torre rotonda
Panorama - Vista - Percorso pittoresco

Simboli vari
Teleferica industriale
Torre o pilone per telecomunicazioni - Faro
Centrale elettrica - Cava
Miniera - Industrie
Raffineria - Falesia
Parco forestale nazionale - Parco nazionale

Carreteras
Autopista - Áreas de servicio
Autovía

Enlaces: completo, parciales
Números de los accesos
Carretera de comunicación internacional o nacional
Carretera de comunicación interregional o alternativo
Carretera asfaltada - sin asfaltar
Sendero - Sendero señalado / Camino de caballos
Autopista, carretera en construcción
(en su caso: fecha prevista de entrada en servicio)

Ancho de las carreteras
Calzadas separadas
Cuatro carriles - Dos carriles anchos
Dos carriles - Dos carriles estrechos

Distancias (totales y parciales)
Tramo de peaje en autopista
Tramo libre en autopista
en millas - en kilómetros
en carretera

Numeración - Señalización
Autopista - GB: Vía principal (Primary route)
IRL: Vía principal (National primary et secondary route)
Otras carreteras
Localidad en itinerario principal

Obstáculos
Rotonda - Puerto y su altitud (en métros)
Pendiente Pronunciada (las flechas indican el sentido del ascenso)
IRL: Recorrido difícil o peligroso
En escocia: carretera muy estrecha con ensanchamientos para poder cruzarse
Pasos de la carretera: a nivel, superior, inferior
Tramo prohibido - Carretera restringida
Barrera de peaje - Carretera de sentido único
Altura limitada (15'6'' IRL, 16'6''GB)

Limite de carga (inferior a 16 t)

Transportes
Línea férrea - Estación de viajeros
Aeropuerto - Aeródromo
Transporte de coches: (Enlace de temporada: signo rojo)
por barco
por barcaza (carga máxima en toneladas)
Barcaza para el paso de peatones y vehículos dos ruedas

Alojamiento - Administración
Límites administrativos
Límites de Escocia y del País de Gales

Frontera - Puesto de aduanas

Deportes - Ocio
Golf - Hipódromo
Circuito de velocidad - Puerto deportivo
Camping, caravaning
Sendero señalado - Parque de ocio
Reserva de animales, zoo - Reserva de pájaros
IRL: Pêche - Cynodrome
Tren turístico
Funicular, Teleférico, telesilla

Curiosidades
Principales curiosidades:
ver LA GUÍA VERDE
Localidad o lugar interesante, lugar para quedarse
Edificio religioso - Castillo
Ruinas - Monumento megalítico - Cueva
Jardín, parque - Curiosidades diversas
IRL: Fortaleza - Cruz celta - Torre redonda
Vista panorámica - Vista parcial - Recorrido pintoresco

Signos diversos
Transportador industrial aéreo
Emisor de Radiodifusión - Faro
Central eléctrica - Cantera
Mina - Industrias
Refinería - Acantilado
Parque forestal nacional - Parque nacional

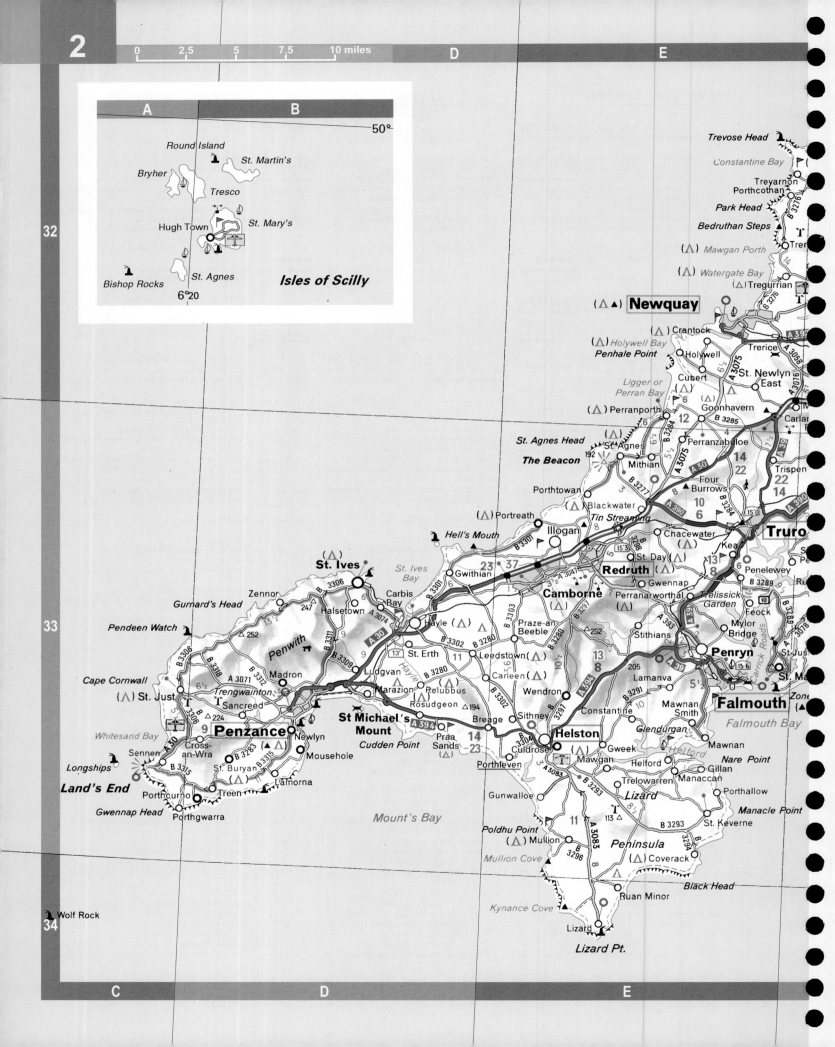

0   2.5   5   7.5   10 miles

D   E

A   B
50°

Round Island
St. Martin's
Bryher
Tresco
Hugh Town   St. Mary's
St. Agnes
Bishop Rocks
6°20

32

Isles of Scilly

Trevose Head
Constantine Bay
Treyarnon
Porthcothan
Park Head
Bedruthan Steps
(∧) *Mawgan Porth*   Tre
(∧) *Watergate Bay*
(∧) Tregurrian

(∧ ▲) **Newquay**
(∧) Crantock
(∧) *Holywell Bay*   Holywell   St. Newlyn
Penhale Point   Cubert   East
Ligger or   Goonhavern
Perran Bay   12
(∧) Perranporth   6   Perranzabuloe
St. Agnes Head   St Agnes   14
The Beacon   192   Mithian   22
Porthtowan   Four   10   Trispen
Blackwater   Burrows   6   22
(∧) Portreath   *Tin Streaming*   14
Hell's Mouth   Illogan   Chacewater   **Truro**
23 37   St. Day   13   Penelewey
Gwithian   **Redruth**   8
St. Ives   Gwennap
St. Ives   **Camborne**   Perranarworthal   Trelissick
(∧) **St. Ives**   Carbis   Garden
Zennor   Bay   Feock
Gurnard's Head   247   Halsetown   Hayle (∧)   Stithians   Mylor
Pendeen Watch   252   St. Erth   11   Penryn
Penwith   Ludgvan   Leedstown(∧)   13   Lamanva   **Penryn**
Madron   Carleen (∧)   8   205   **Falmouth**
(∧) St. Just   Marazion   Wendron   Mawnan
Cape Cornwall   Trengwainton   Relubbus   Constantine   Smith   *Falmouth Bay*
Sancreed   Rosudgeon   Glendurgan
Whitesand Bay   9   Breage   14   Helston   Mawnan
Penzance   Sithney   23   Helford   *Nare Point*
Cross-an-Wra   Newlyn   Praa   Culdrose   Gweek   Helford   Gillan
Sennen   Mousehole   Sands   Porthleven   Mawgan   Trelowarren   Manaccan
St Michael's   (∧)   *Lizard*   Porthallow
Longships   St. Buryan   Mount   *Cudden Point*   Gunwalloe   11   St. Keverne
Land's End   (∧)   Lamorna   *Mount's Bay*   *Poldhu Point*   113   *Manacle Point*
Porthcurno   Treen   (∧) Mullion   *Peninsula*   *Black Head*
Gwennap Head   Porthgwarra   *Mullion Cove*   (∧) Coverack
Ruan Minor
Wolf Rock   *Kynance Cove*   Lizard
Lizard Pt.

33

34

C   D   E

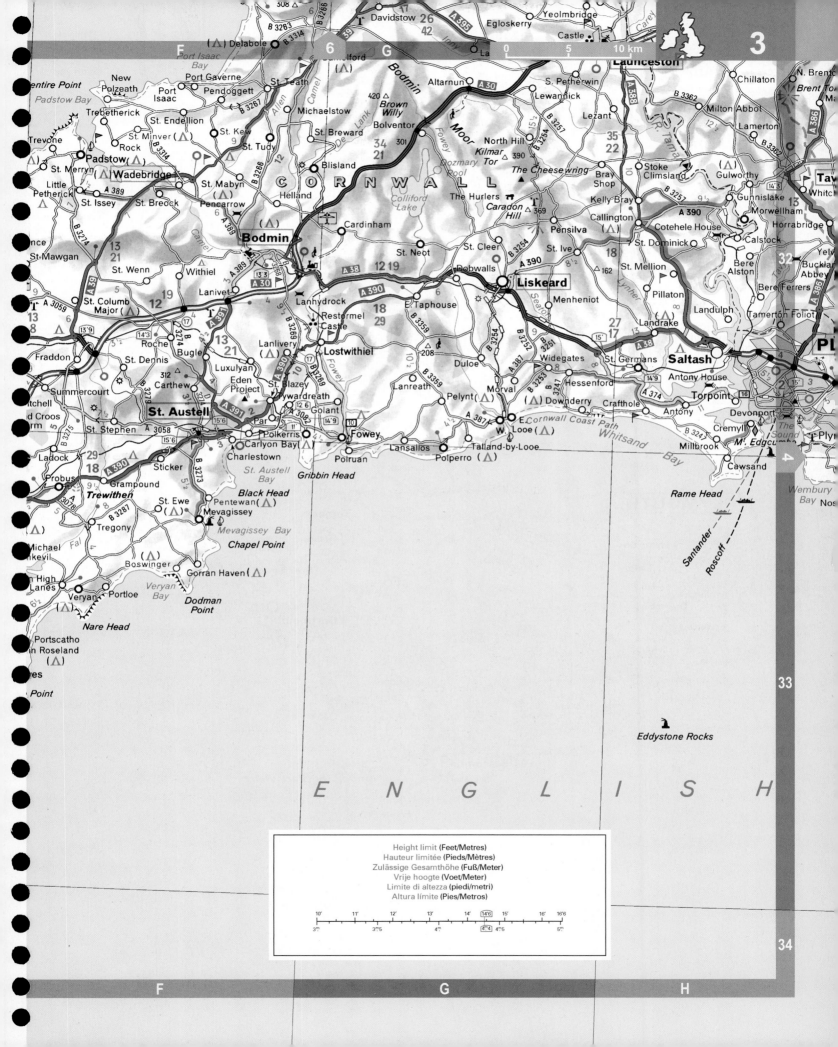

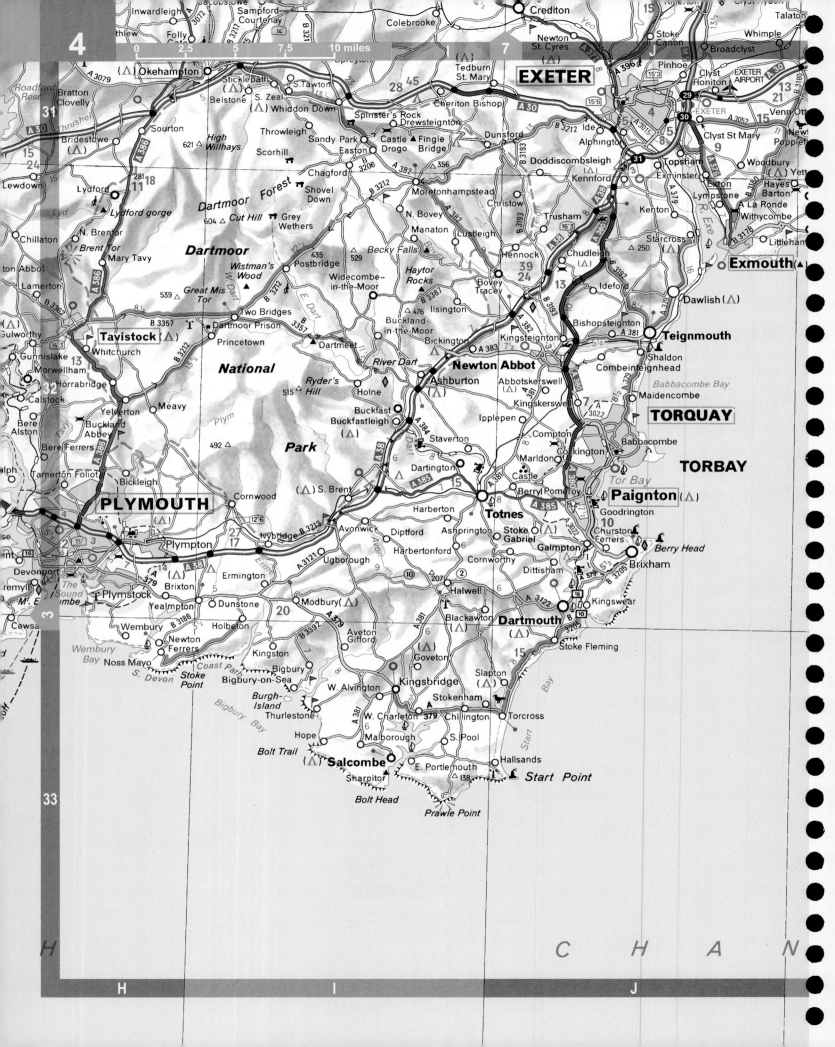

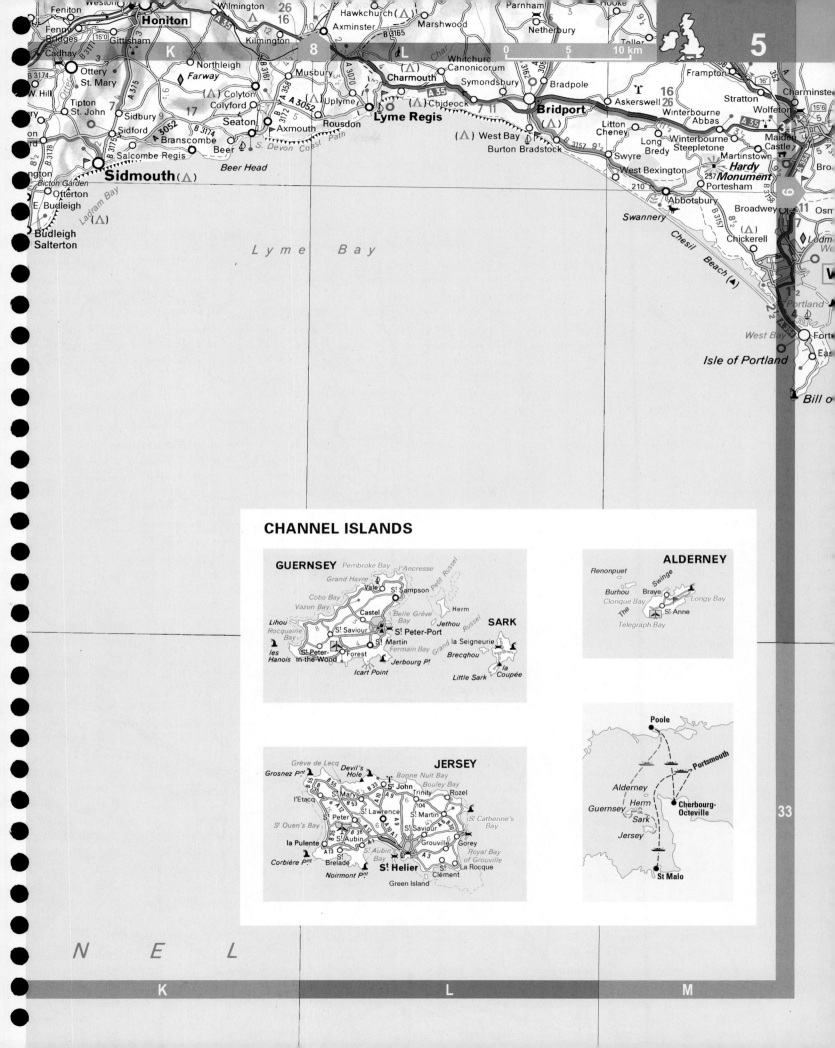

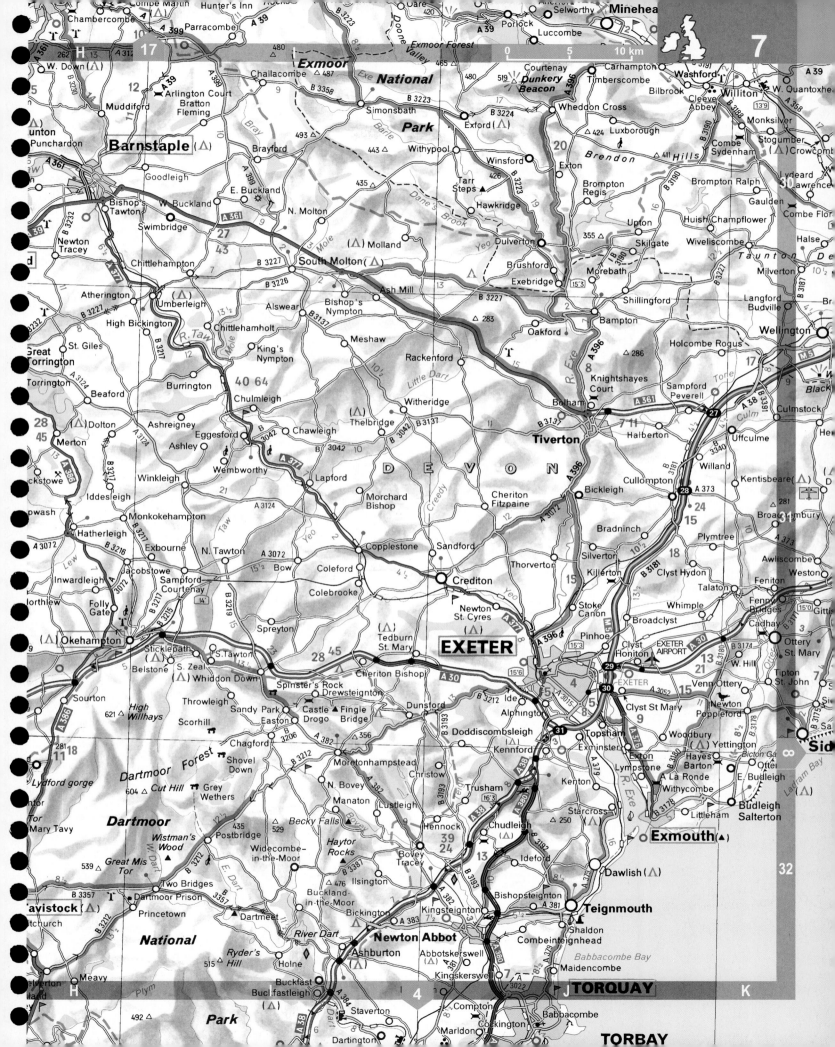

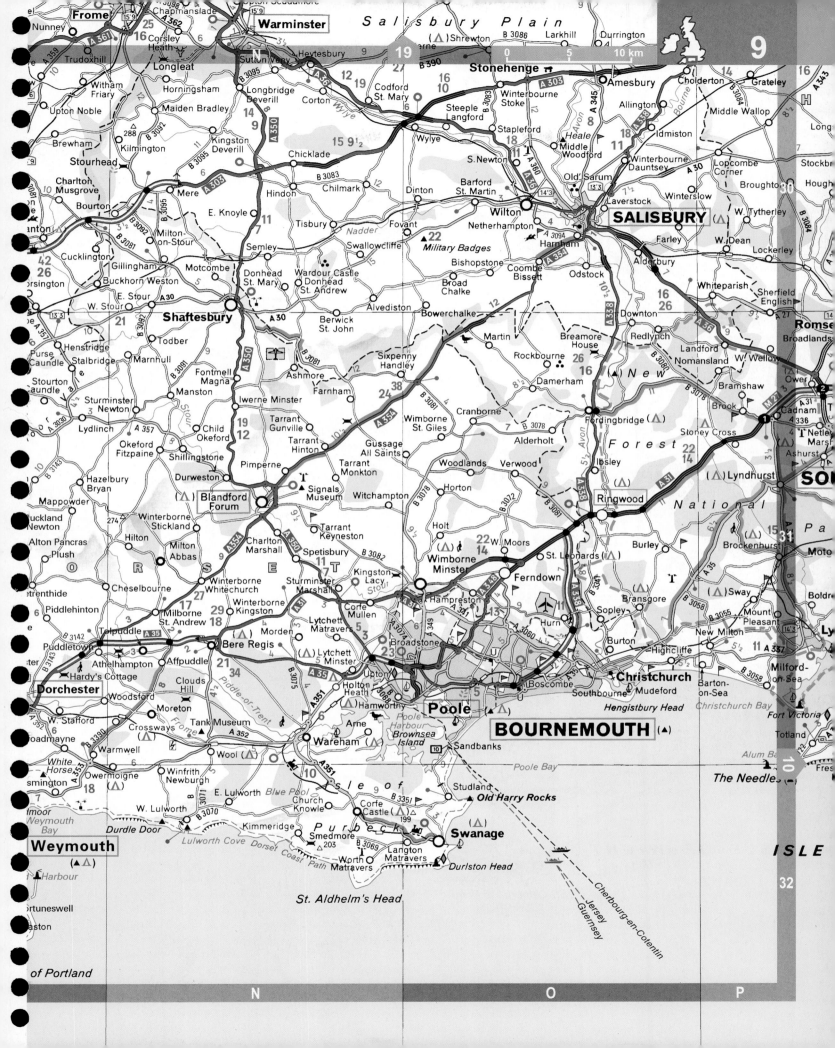

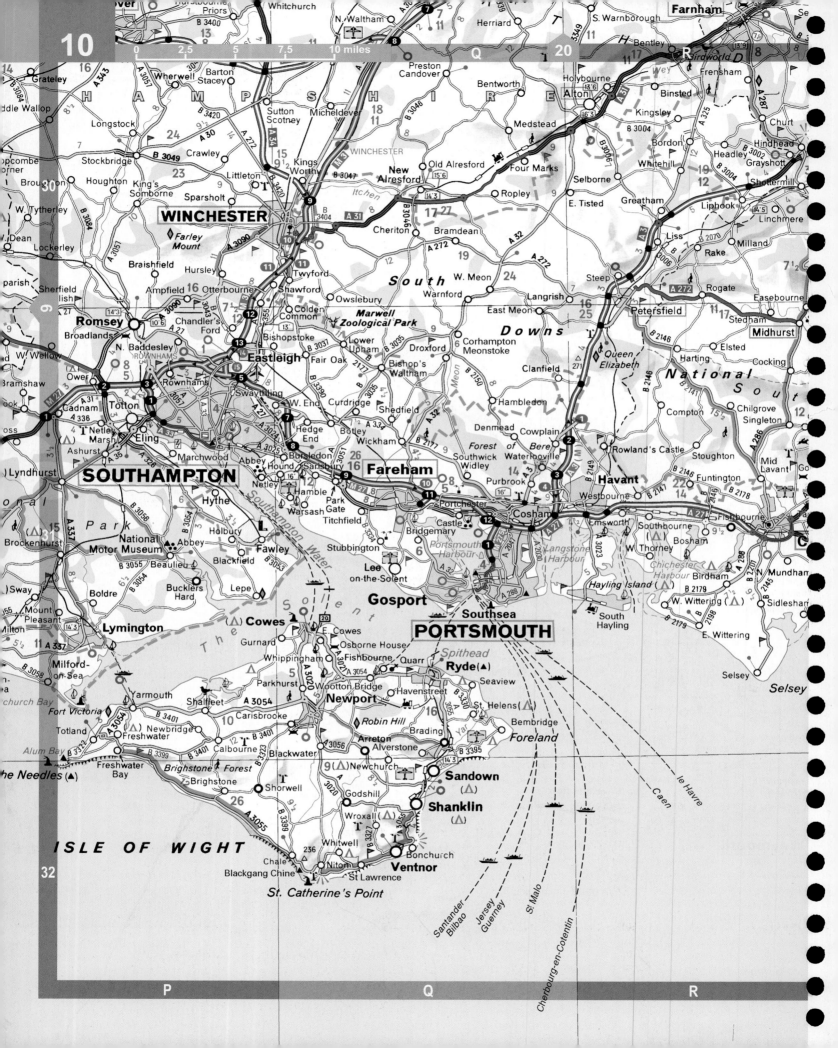

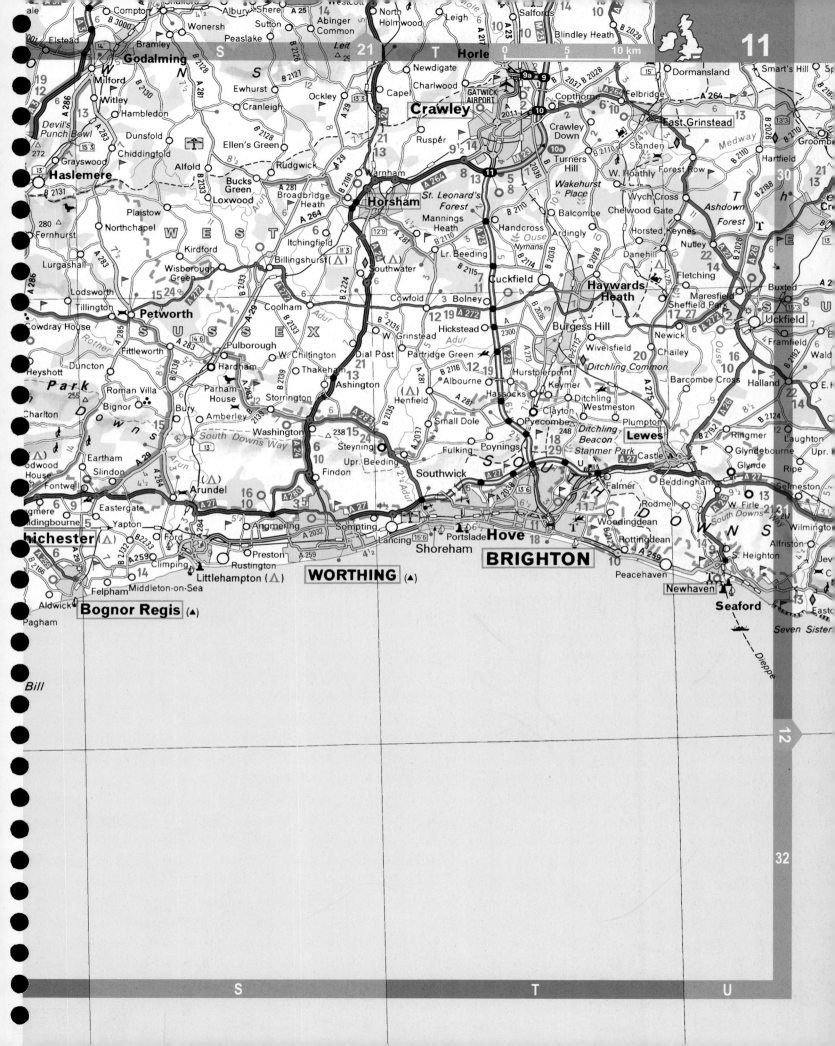

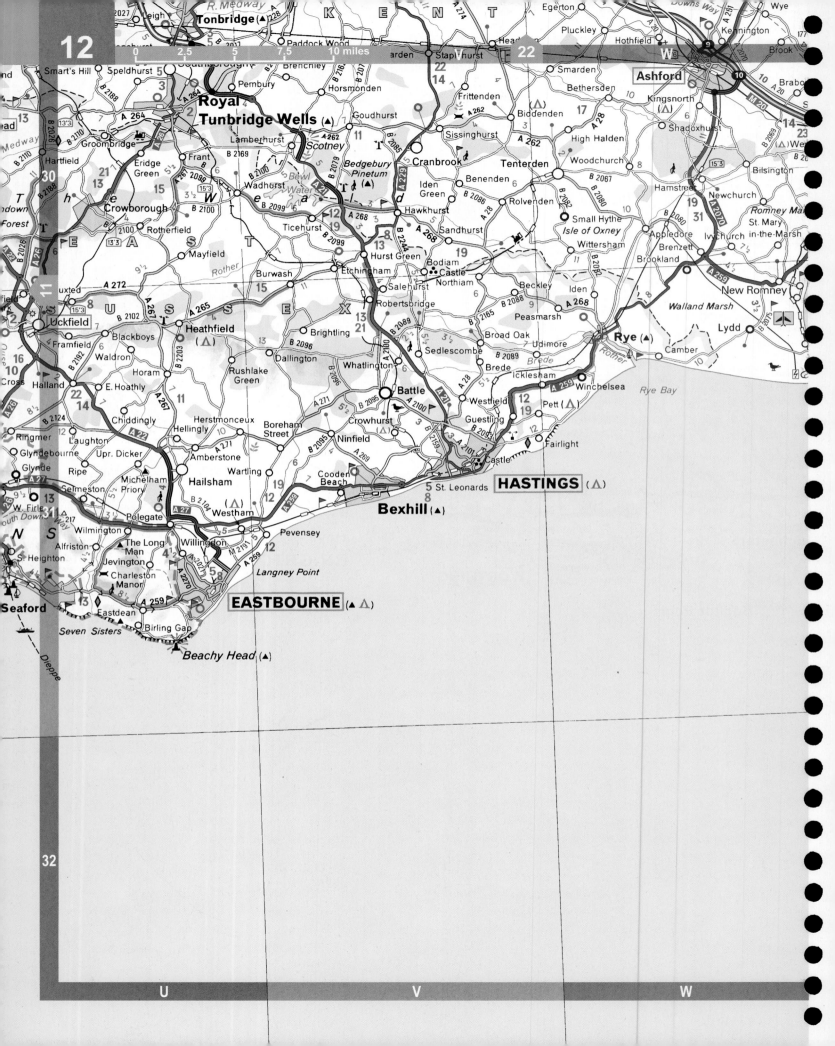

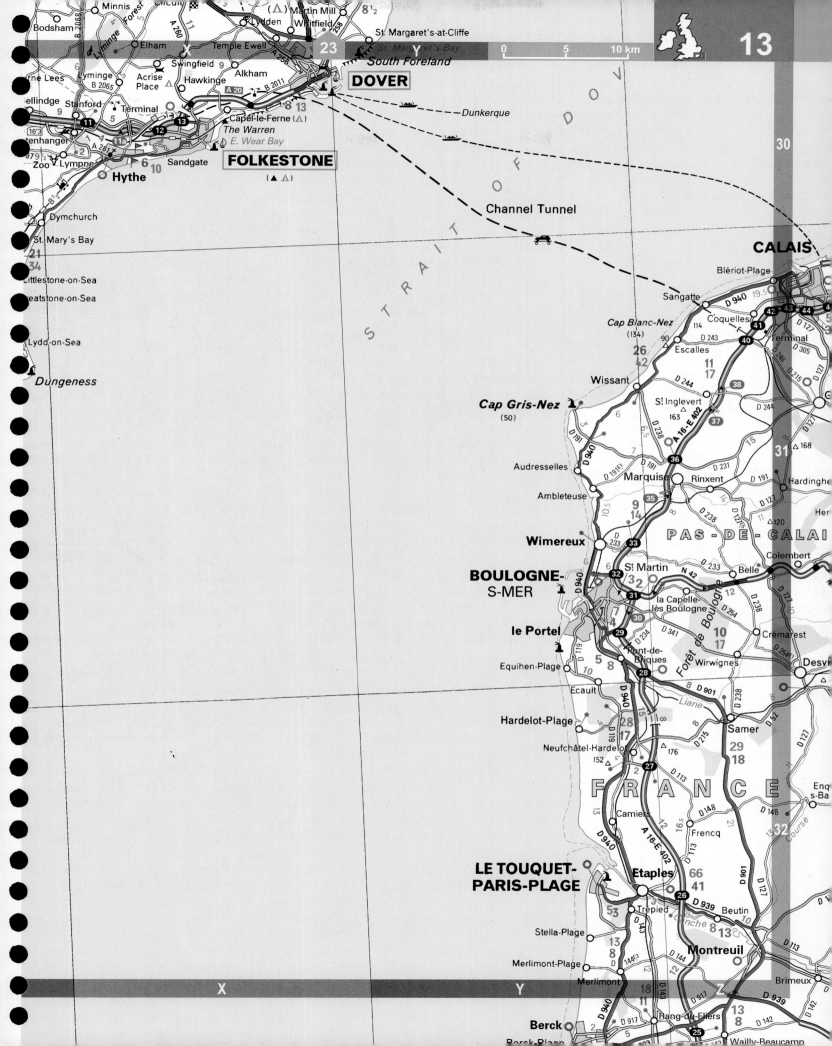

Bodsham

Minnis

Martin Mill
Lydden
Whitfield

St. Margaret's-at-Cliffe

Lyminge Forest
Elham
Temple Ewell

A 260

Swingfield
Hawkinge
Alkham

St. Margaret's Bay

South Foreland

DOVER

0   5   10 km

ne Lees
Acrise Place
B 2065

Stanford
Terminal

A 20
B 2011

Dunkerque

11

5

13

Capel-le-Ferne

8   13

The Warren

E. Wear Bay

12

enhanger

A 261

11a

Zoo   Lympne

Sandgate

FOLKESTONE

Hythe

6   10

Dymchurch

St. Mary's Bay

Channel Tunnel

21
34

Littlestone-on-Sea

eatstone-on-Sea

STRAIT OF DOV

30

CALAIS

Blériot-Plage

Lydd-on-Sea

Sangatte

D 940   19.5

42   43   44

Dungeness

Cap Blanc-Nez
(134)

Coquelles

41

114

D 243

40   Terminal

26
42

90

Escalles

D 246

D 305

Wissant

11
17

D 244

38

D 215   D 127

D 191

S! Inglevert

D 244

163

37

31

Cap Gris-Nez
(50)

A 16·E 402

168

36

D 231

D 191

Audresselles

D 191E1   D 191

Marquise

Rinxent

Hardinghe

Ambleteuse

35

D 238

D 127

120

9
14

D 238

PAS-DE-GALAI

Her

D 233   33

Wimereux

Colembert

6

St Martin

N 42   D 233

Belle

D 121

BOULOGNE-
S-MER

32

32

la Capelle-
lès Boulogne

12

D 238

31

D 254

10
17

Crémarest

le Portel

29

D 234

D 341

Wirwignes

D 254E

Desv

Pont-de-
Briques

28

5
8

Equihen-Plage

10

Ecault

D 940

D 901

Liane

Hardelot-Plage

28
17

Samer

D 52

Neufchâtel-Hardelo

176

D 215

29
18

152

27

D 113

FRANCE

Enq
s-Ba

Camiers

D 148

D 148

16.5

A 16·E 402

D 113

Frencq

21

32
Course

LE TOUQUET-
PARIS-PLAGE

Etaples

66
41

D 901

D 127

26

D 939

Beutin

53

Trépied

D 143

8   13

Stella-Plage

13
8

D 143

Montreuil

Merlimont-Plage

144E3

D 144

D 113

Merlimont

18
11

D 143

D 917

D 939

Brimeux

D 142

X   Y

Berck

Rang-du-Fliers

13
8

D 142

25

Wailly-Beaucamp

0 2.5 5 7.5 10 miles

27

28

29

D

E

C

F

Rosslare

Pembrokeshire Coast

Western Cleddau

St. *G E O R G E' S* Channel

Strumble Head (▲)

3½

213

Goodwick

St. Nicholas

Ynysdeullyn Abercastle

Penclegyr Mathry

Trevine 17

Portgain

Abereiddy Croes-goch

St. David's Head (▲)

181 △ *Carn Llidi* B 4330

2½

Whitesand Bay 6 *Solva*

Bishop's A 487 Llandeloy Hayscastle

Palace **P E M B R O K E S**

Ramsey Island **St. David's** 100 Solva

Tyddewi (△)

Bishops and Clerks *Pembrokeshire Coast Path* Newgale

Ramsey Sound

Camrose

St. Bride's Bay Nolton 16

5

Broad Haven B 4341 B 4327

(△)

Lit. Haven

8½

The Smalls *Grassholme I.*

Skomer Island *Martin's Haven* St. Brides B 4327 Johnston

(▲) St.= 13 Steynton

Broad Sound Marloes Herbrandston

6 St.

Ishmael's **Milford Haven**

Skokholm Island (▲) Dale *Aberdaugleddau* Neyland

71 *Milford Haven* **Pembroke Dock**

Thorn I. Angle Doc Penfro

St. Ann's Head (▲) Rhoscrowther **Pembroke**

Rosslare Penfro

Freshwater West

Castlemartin 12

National Park

Linney Head

Stackpole

Bosherston

Stack Rocks Stackpole H

St. Govan's Head (▲)

P e m b r o k e s h i r e

Trwyn

Dinas Head *Newp*

Newp Bay

Fishguard Bay Bryn-

3½ Henllan

Dinas A 487

Llanychaer

Fishguard / Abe

Pem

Trecwn

334

A 487 Letterston Puncheston

A 4331 347

164 Welsh Hook

Wolf's Castle 12

15 Spittal Wal

24 Scolton Man

51 Clar

Rudbaxton Roa

B 4329 Wiston

B 4330

A 40 Picto

Haverfordwest National Park

14'9 Hwlffordd

B A 4076

A 471 10 Llangwm Mi

Rosemarket Lawrenny

Cre

16 Cas

4½ 27 10

15' A 4

4075 Bisho

A 4 Pa

14'6 Lamphey Ja

B 4320 Hundleton B 415

B 4319 *Freshwater East*

Freshwater East

Dinas Head

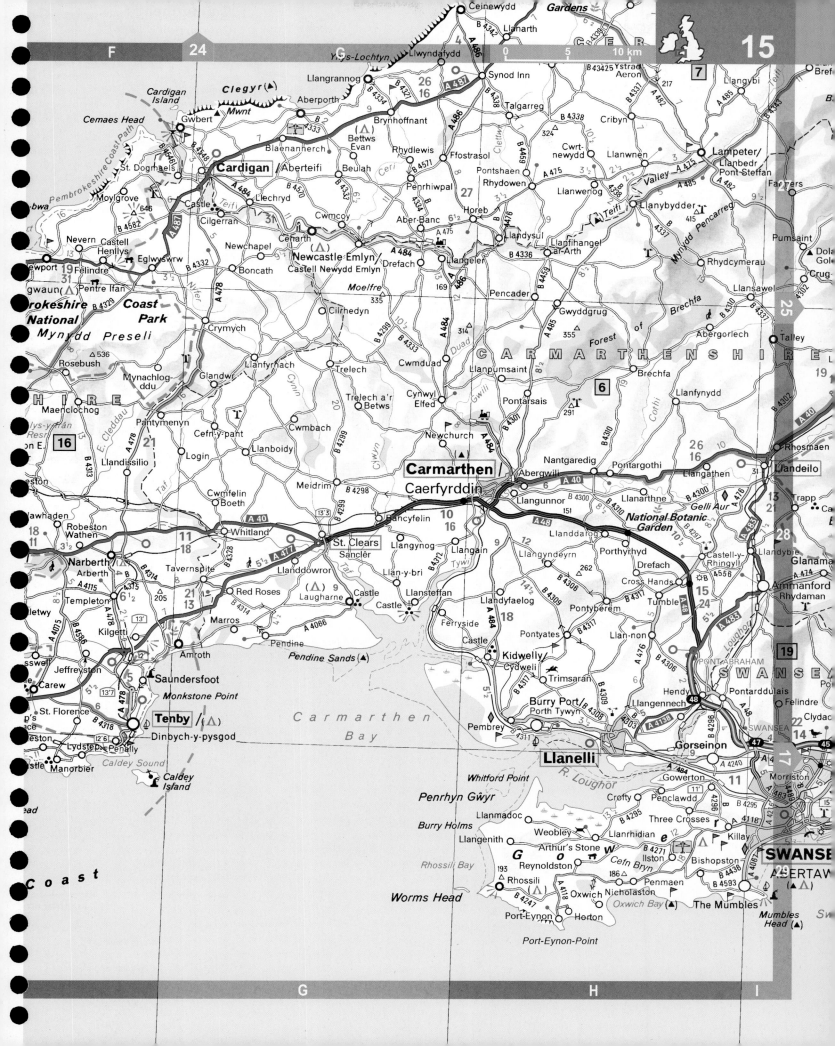

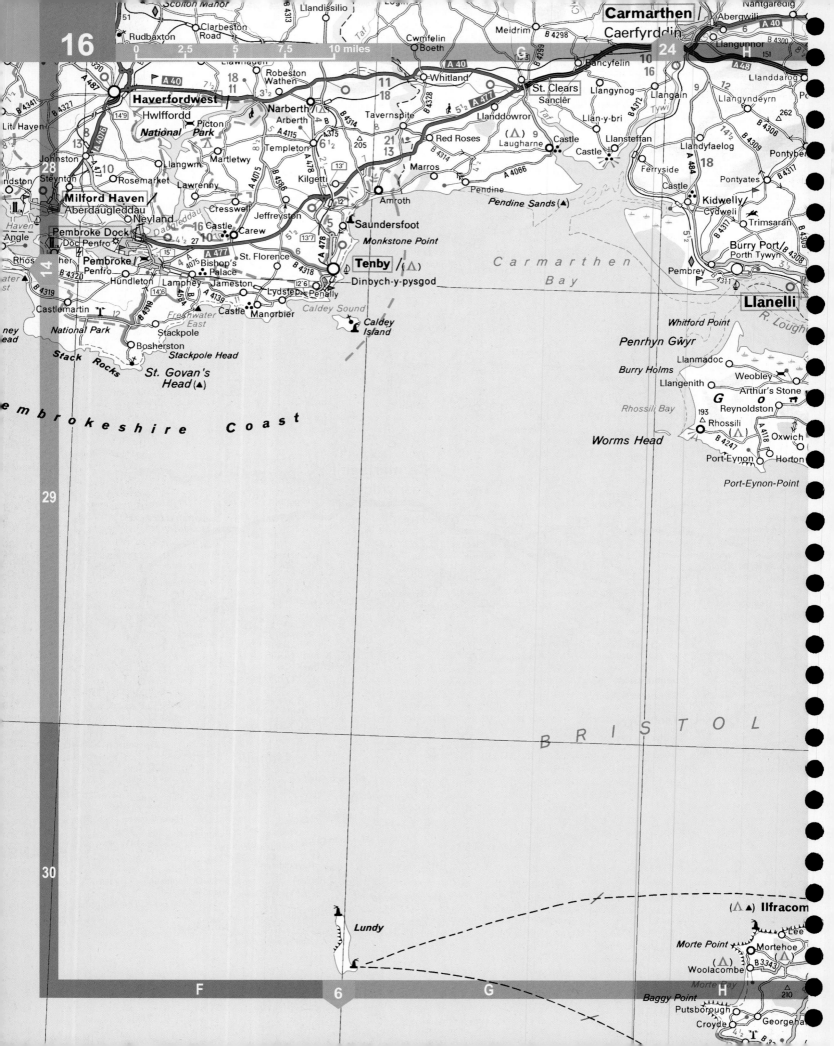

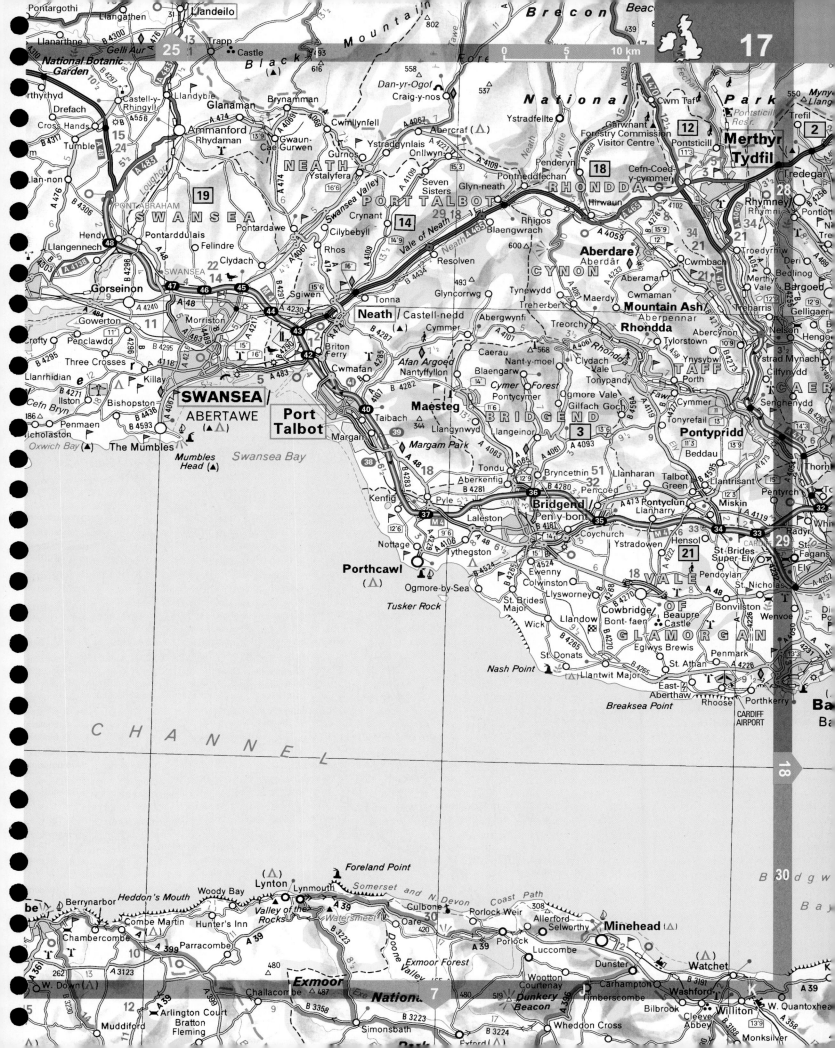

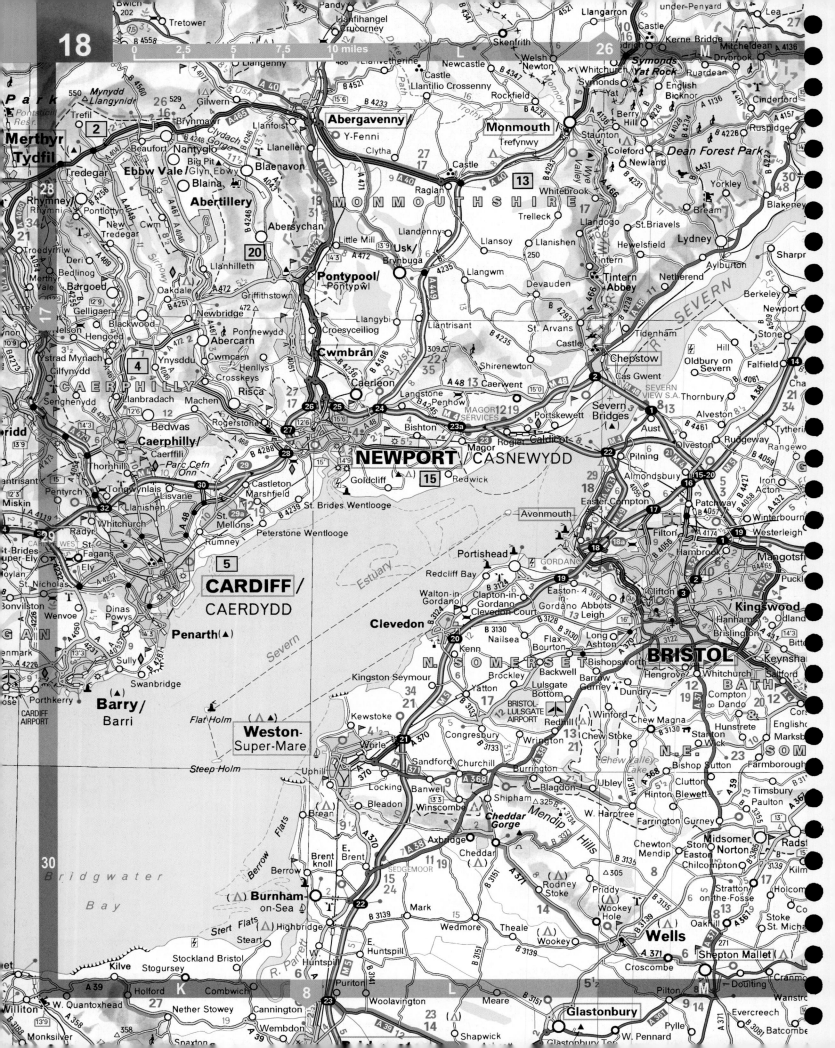

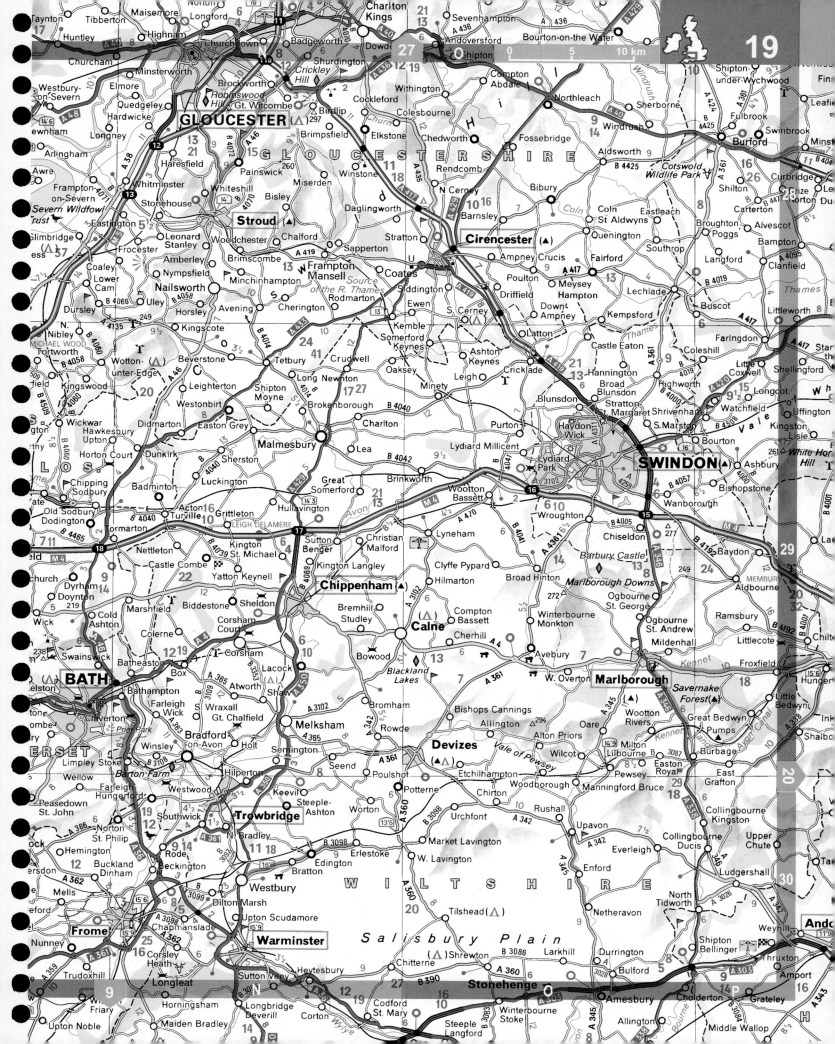

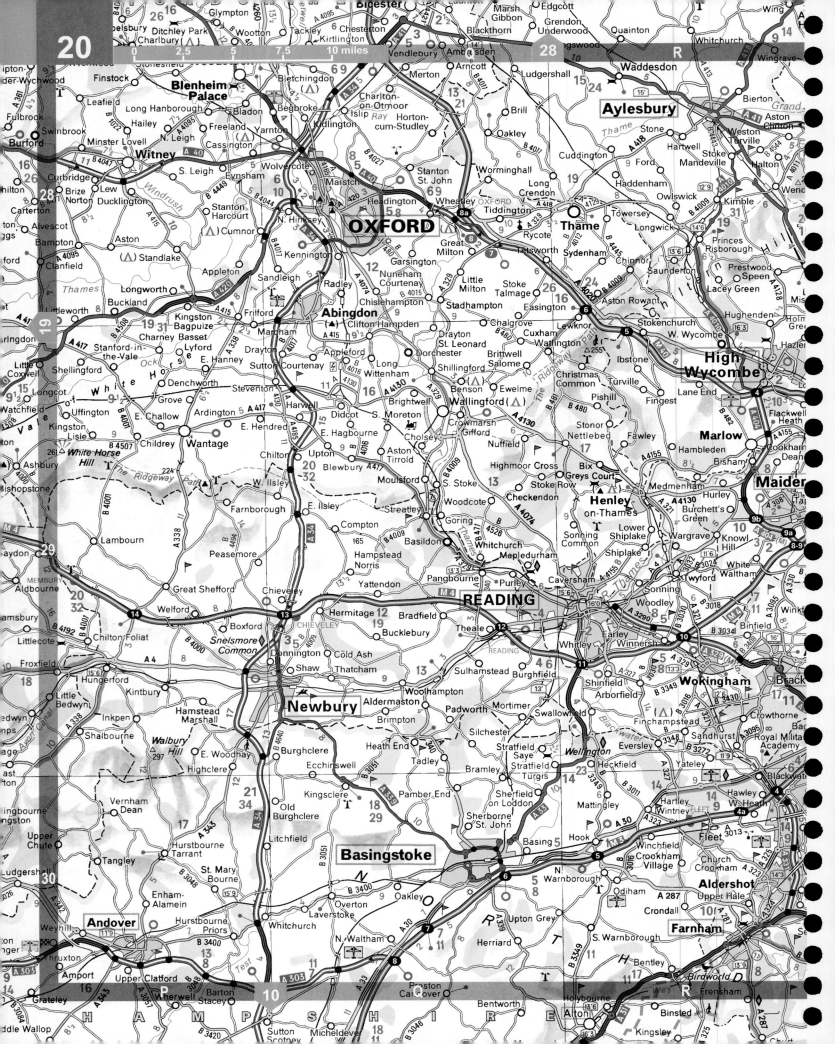

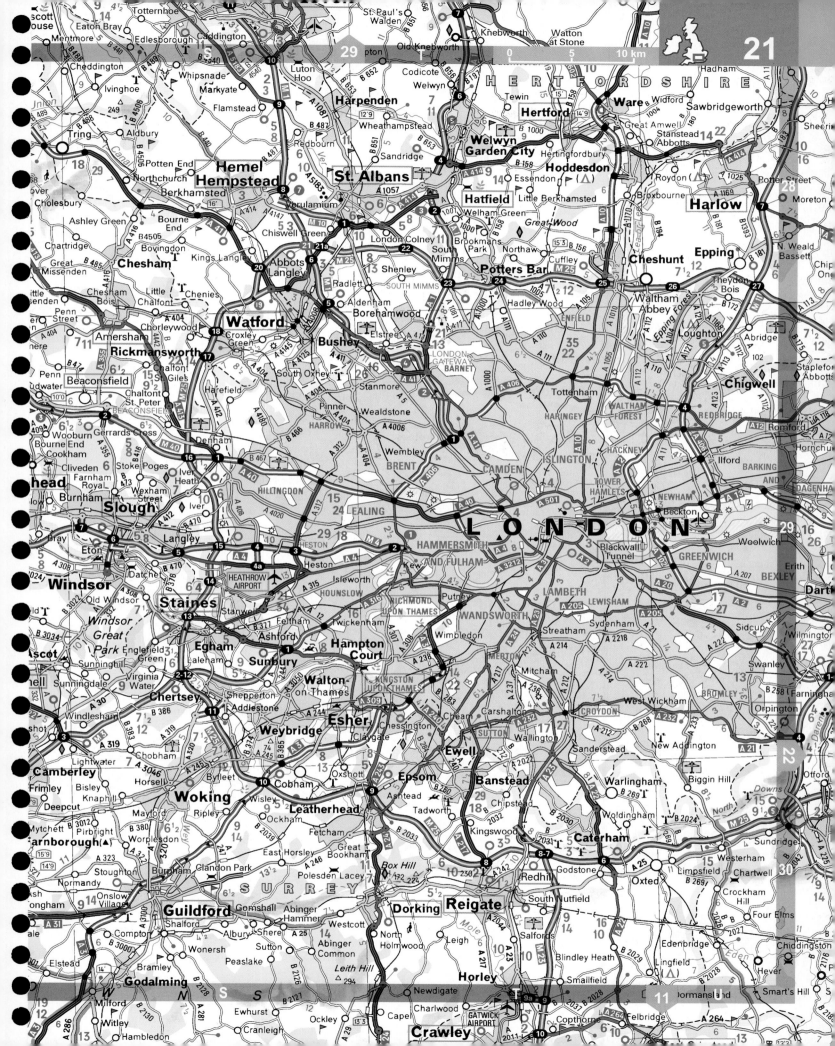

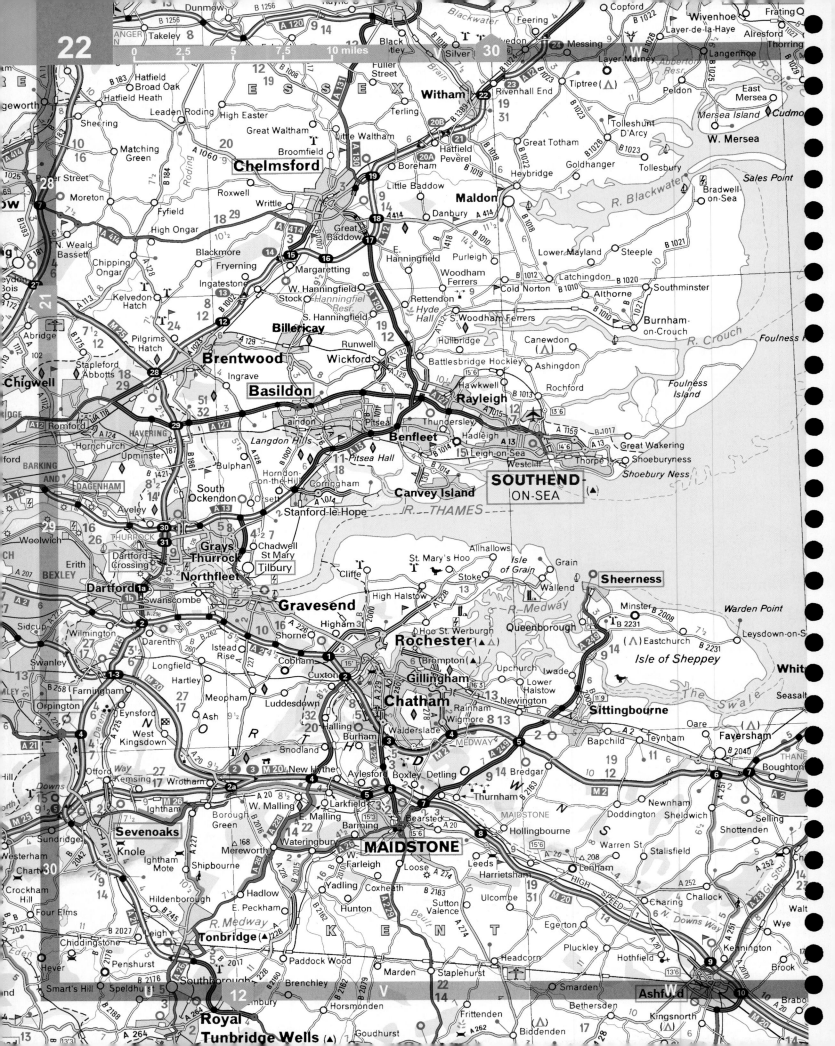

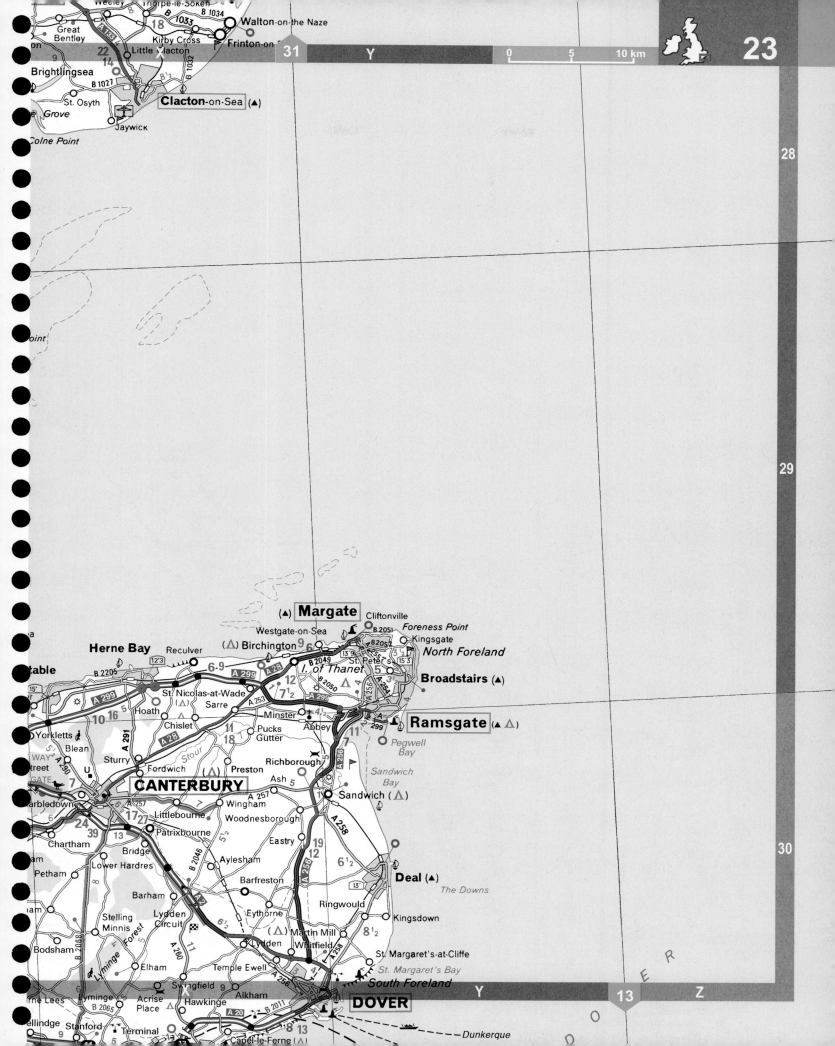

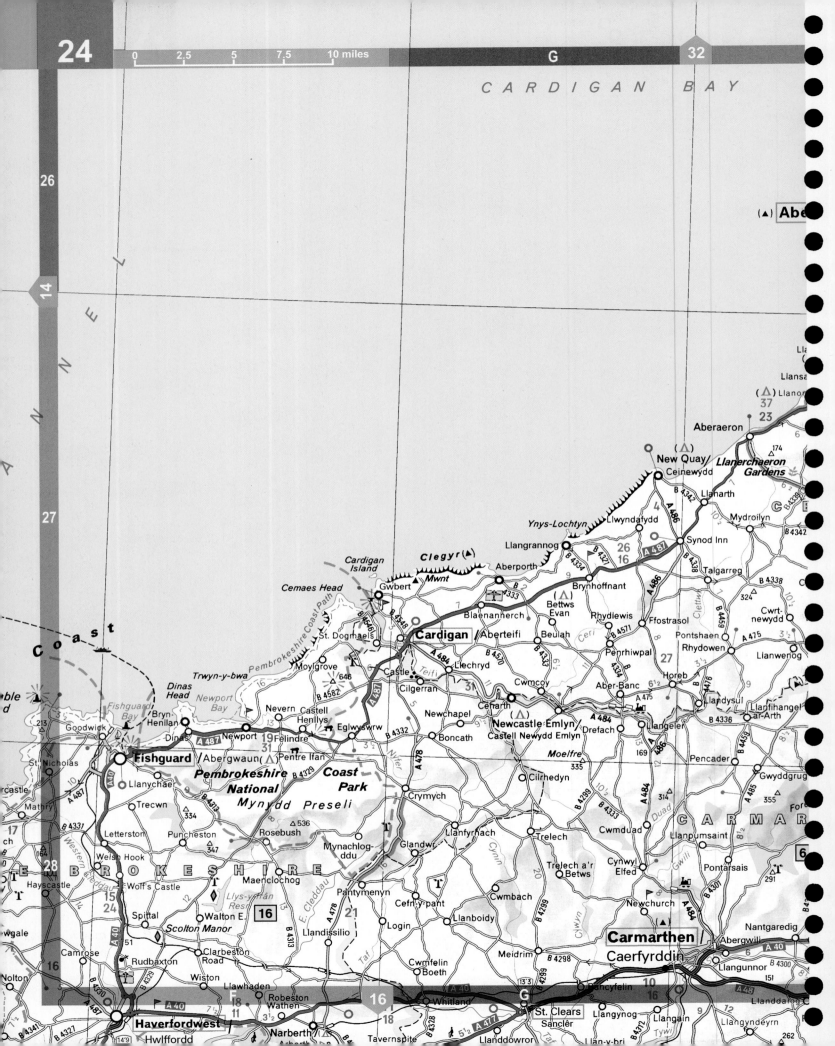

CARDIGAN BAY

(▲) **Abe**

0 2.5 5 7.5 10 miles

Llan

Llansa

(△) Llanor
37

Aberaeron 23

(△) 174 6

New Quay/ *Llanerchaeron*
Ceinewydd *Gardens* G

Llanarth B 4342

Ynys-Lochtyn Llwyndafydd Mydroilyn B 4342

Clegyr(▲) Llangrannog 26 A 487 Synod Inn Talgarreg 324

Aberporth 16 B 4321 B 4338 Cwrt-
newydd

*Cardigan
Island* Gwbert ▲ *Mwnt* Bettws Brynhoffnant Rhydlewis Ffostrasol B 4459

A 4333 Evan (△) Pontshaen Rhydowen Llanwenog

Cemaes Head **Cardigan** / Aberteifi Blaenannerch Beulah Penrhiwpal 27

St. Dogmaels Llechryd B 4520 B 4333 Aber-Banc Horeb Llandysul

Trwyn-y-bwa Moylgrove 646 Castle *Teifi* Cwmcoy A 475 Llanfihangel
ar-Arth

*Dinas
Head* *Newport
Bay* B 4582 Cilgerran 31 Newchapel Newcastle Emlyn Llangeler B 4336

Nevern Castell (△) Castell Newydd Emlyn Drefach

Goodwick Bryn- Henllys Eglwyswrw Boncath *Moelfre* Pencader

213 Henllan Dinas A 487 Newport 19 Felindre B 4332 169 A 486 Gwyddgrug

St. Nicholas 31 Pentre Ifan *Nifer* A 478 335 Llanpumsaint 355

Fishguard / Abergwaun (△) Cilrhedyn CARMAR

Mathry Llanychaer **Pembrokeshire** *Coast* Crymych Llanfyrnach Trelech Cwmduad 314

Trecwn **National** *Park* 536 Mynachlog- 291

Letterston 334 *Mynydd Preseli* ddu Glandwr Trelech a'r Cynwyl Pontarsais

Welsh Hook 347 Rosebush Mynachlog- Betws Elfed

28 Hayscastle Maenclochog Pantymenyn Cefn-y-pant Cwmbach Newchurch

15 Wolf's Castle B 4313 A 478 21 Login Llanboidy Nantgaredig

24 *Llys-y-frân
Res.* 16 **Carmarthen** / **Caerfyrddin** Abergwili

Spittal Walton E. Meidrim A 40

Scolton Manor 51 Llandissilio Cwmfelin Llangunnor B 4300

Camrose Clarbeston Boeth 151

Rudbaxton Road *Taf* 16 G

Nolton Wiston Llawhaden Robeston **St. Clears** Llangynog Llangain Llangyndeyrn

Haverfordwest / Hwlffordd 18 Wathen 16 Whitland Sanclêr *Tywi* 262

Narberth / 18 Tavernspite Llanddowror A 48 Llanddarog

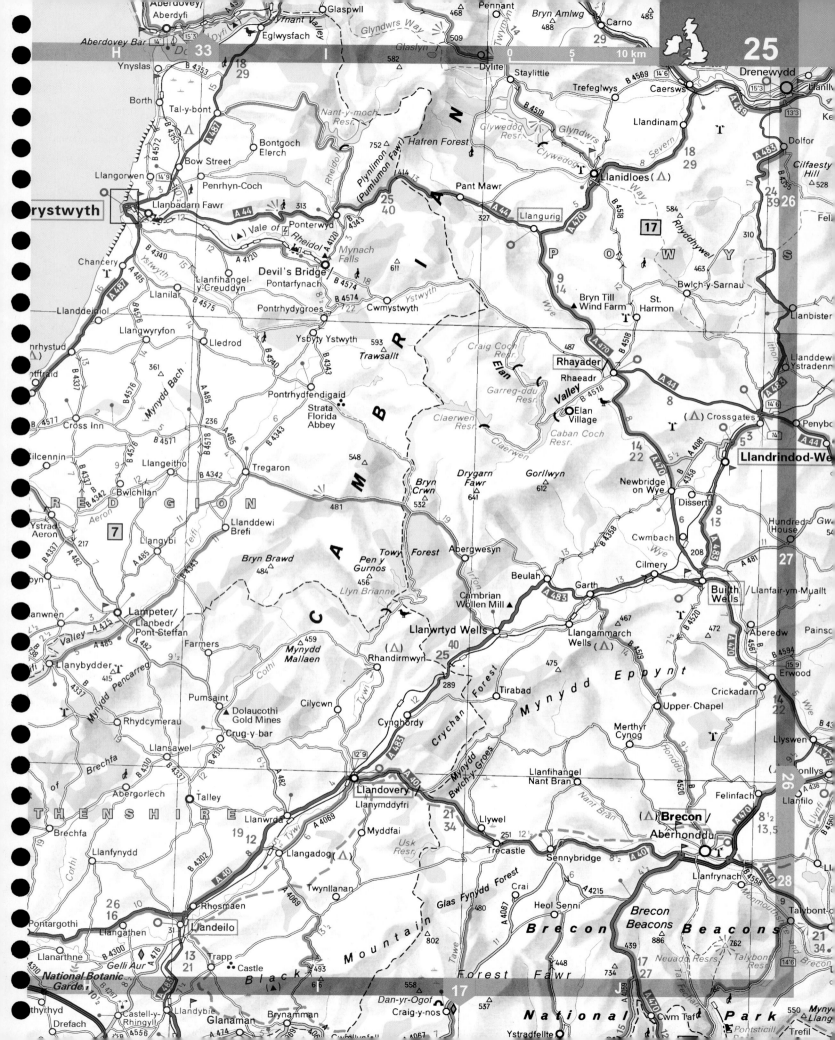

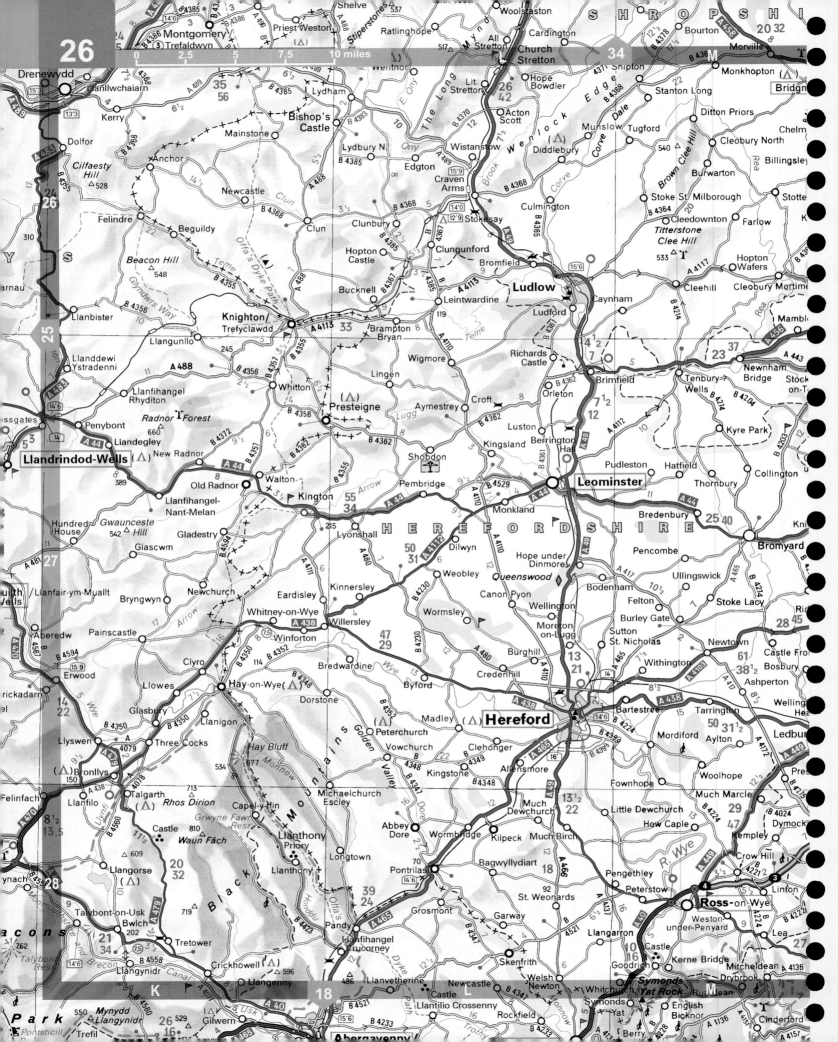

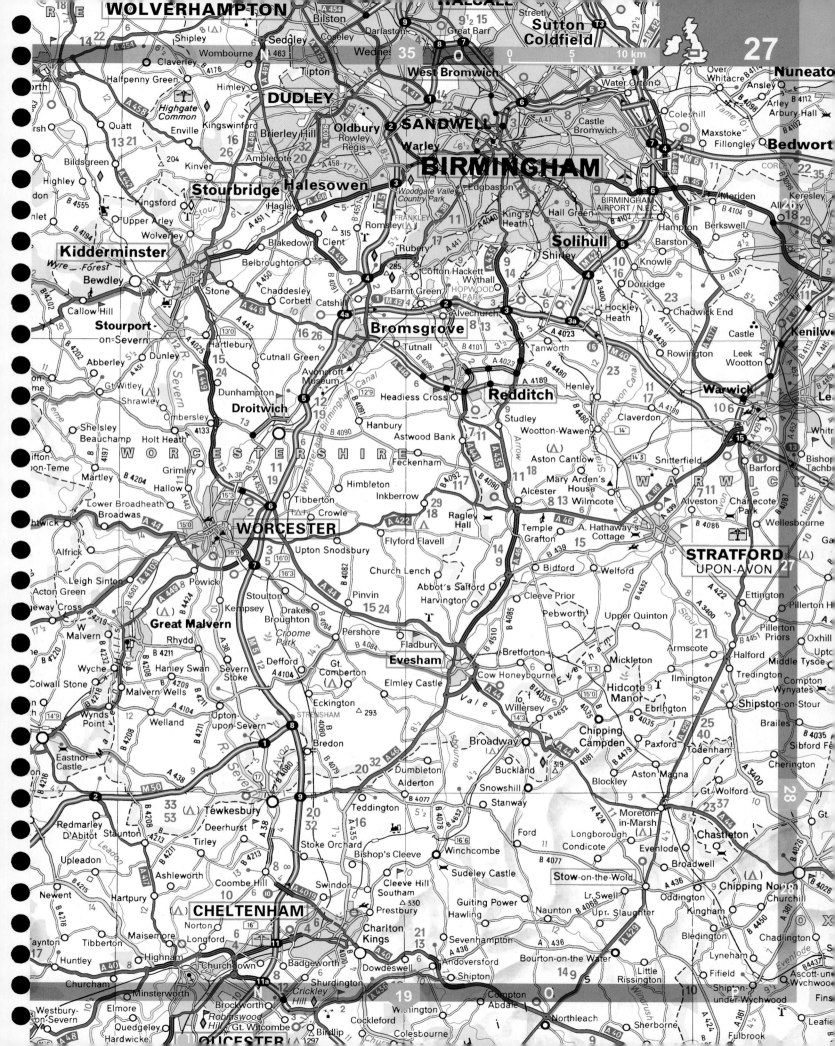

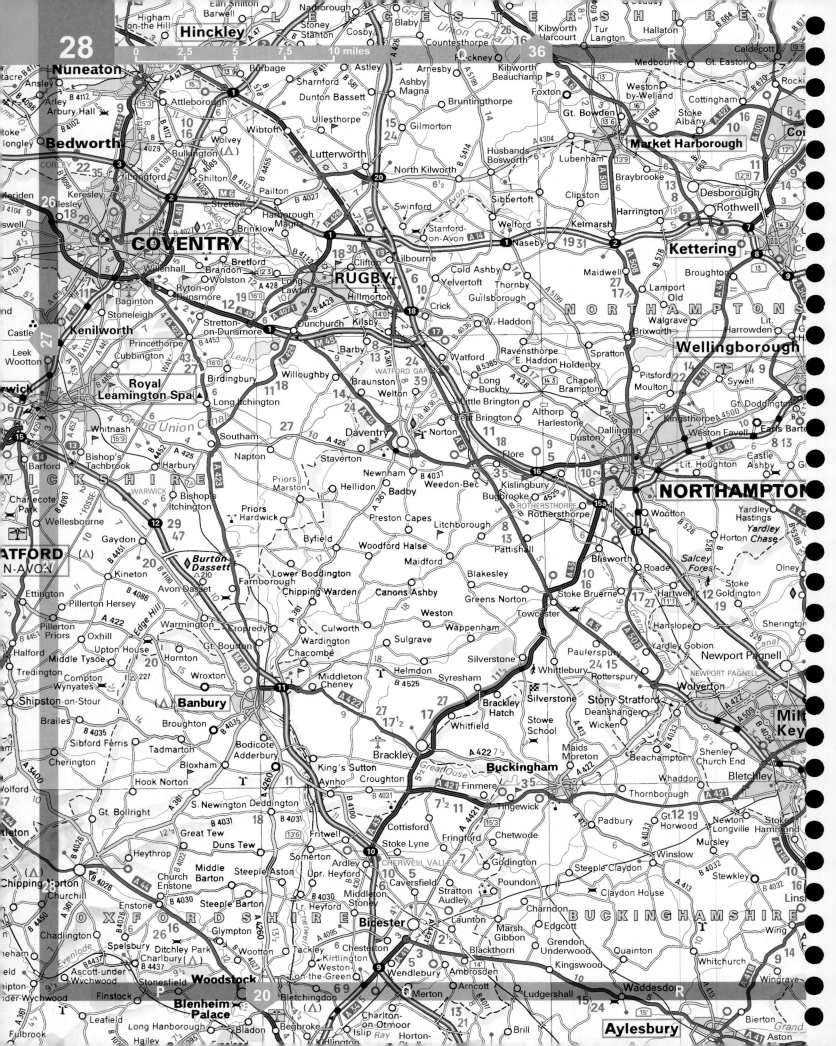

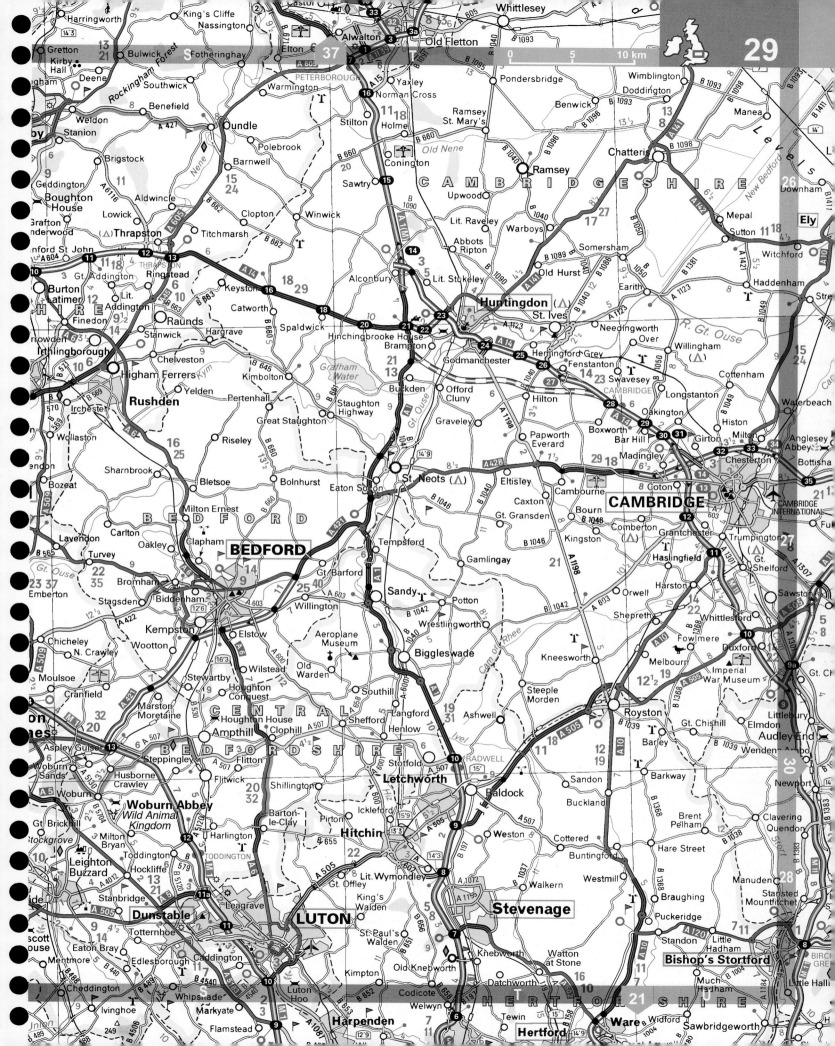

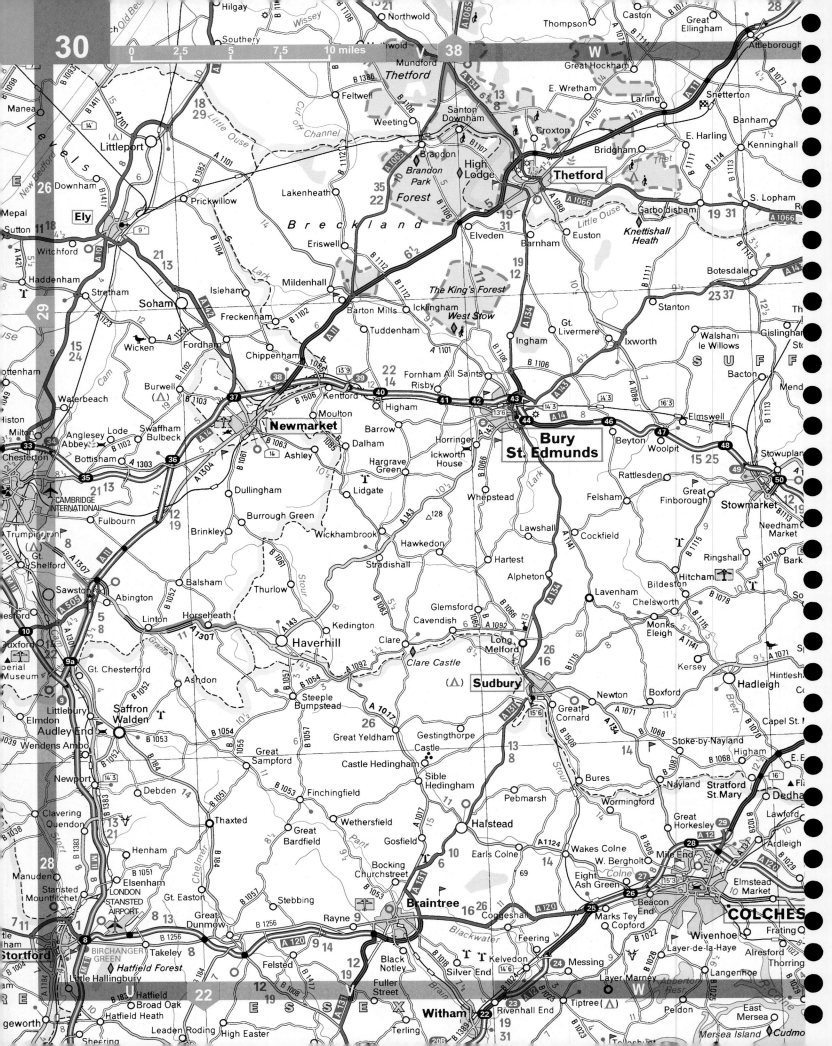

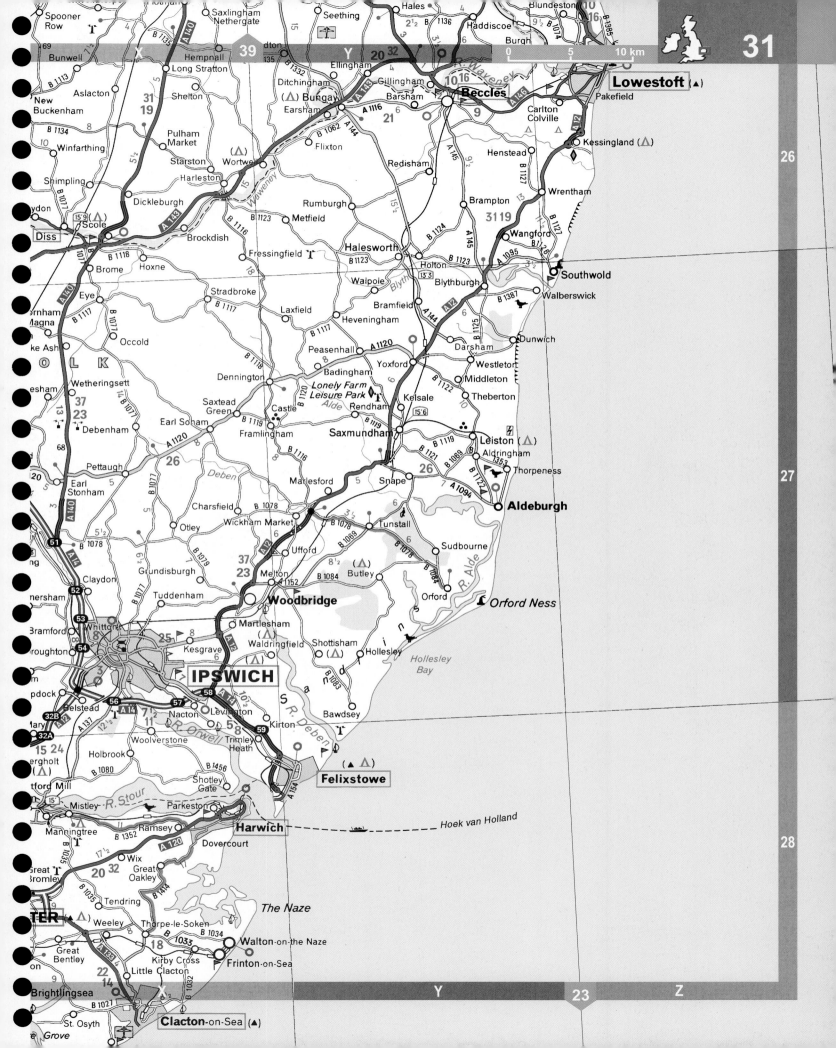

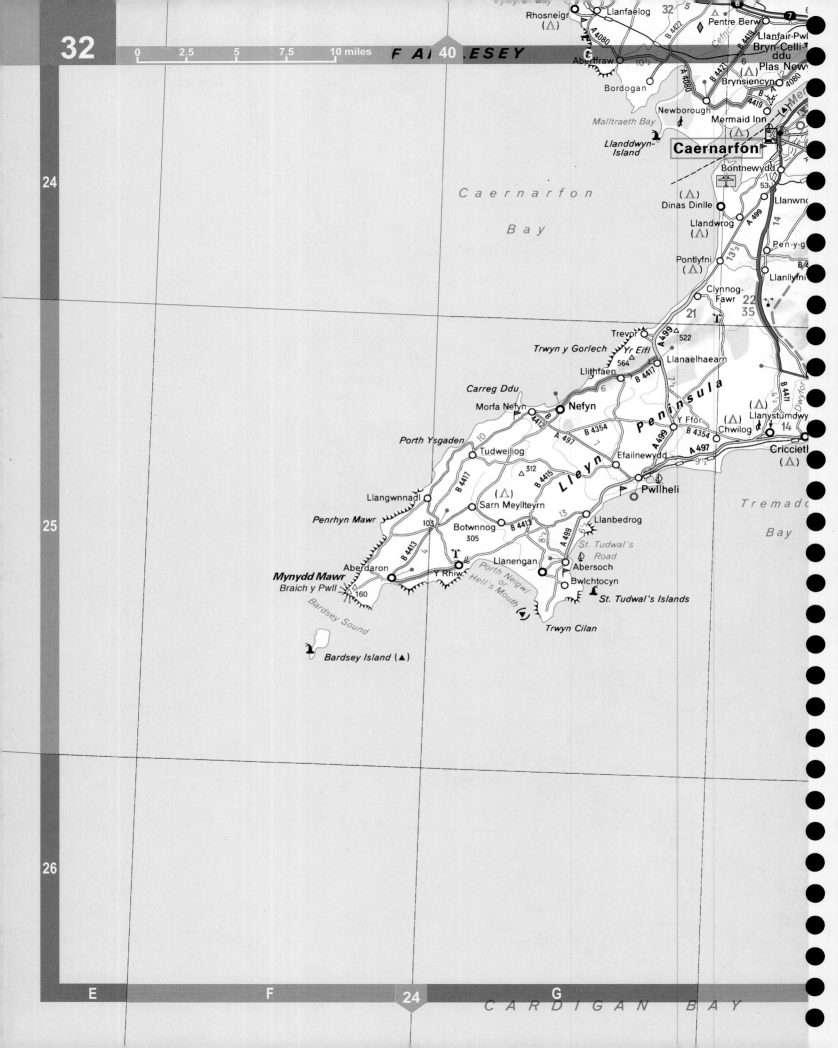

0   2.5   5   7.5   10 miles

F A 40 **ESEY**

Rhosneig
(△)

Llanfaelog 32 5

Pentre Berw

Llanfair-Pwl
Bryn-Celli-
ddu

Aberffraw 10½ Plas New

Bordogan Brynsiencyn

Newborough Mermaid Inn

Malltraeth Bay Llanddwyn-
Island

Caernarfon

Bontnewydd

C a e r n a r f o n

B a y

Dinas Dinlle (△) Llanwn

Llandwrog
(△)

Pen-y-g

Pontlyfni
(△) 13½ 14

Llanllyfni

Clynnog-
Fawr 22
35

21

Trevor A 499 522

Trwyn y Gorlech Yr Eifl Llanaelhaearn

Carreg Ddu 564 Llithfaen 6 B 4417

Morfa Nefyn Nefyn

Porth Ysgaden B 4354 Y Ffor (△) Llanystumdwy

Tudweiliog 10 A 497 7 Chwilog 14

Lleyn Efailnewydd A 497 Criccieth
(△)

△ 312 B 4415

Llangwnnadl (△) Pwllheli *Tremad*

Sarn Meyllteyrn 13 *Bay*

Penrhyn Mawr 103 Botwnnog 305 Llanbedrog

B 4413 Llanengan St. Tudwal's *Road*

Aberdaron Abersoch

Mynydd Mawr Y Rhiw Bwlchtocyn

Braich y Pwll △ 160 *Porth Neigwl* St. Tudwal's Islands

Bardsey Sound *Hell's Mouth*

Trwyn Cilan

Bardsey Island (▲)

24

25

26

E   F   24   G

C A R D I G A N   B A Y

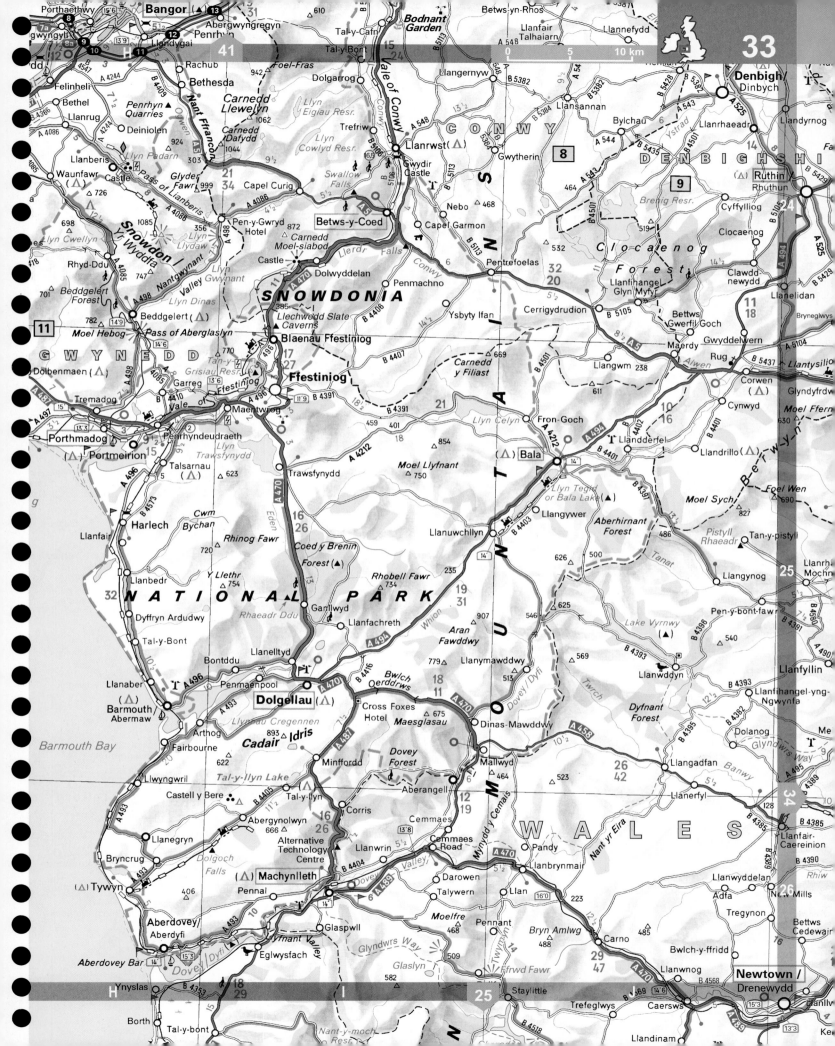

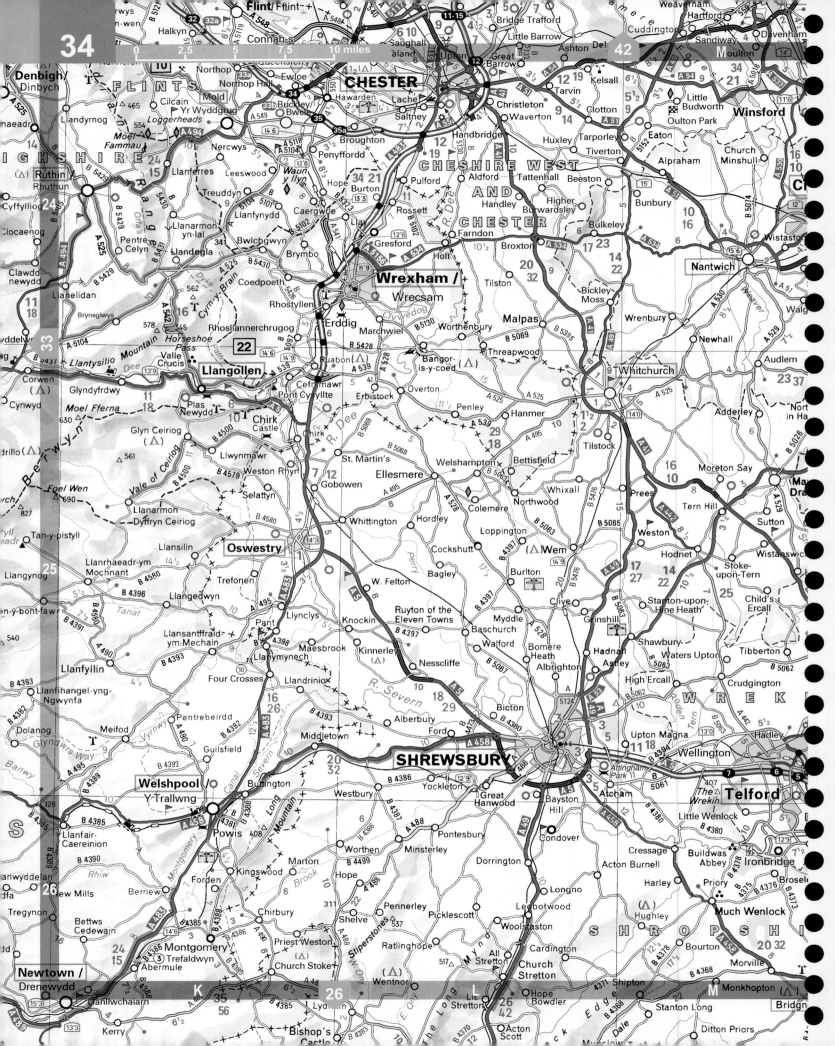

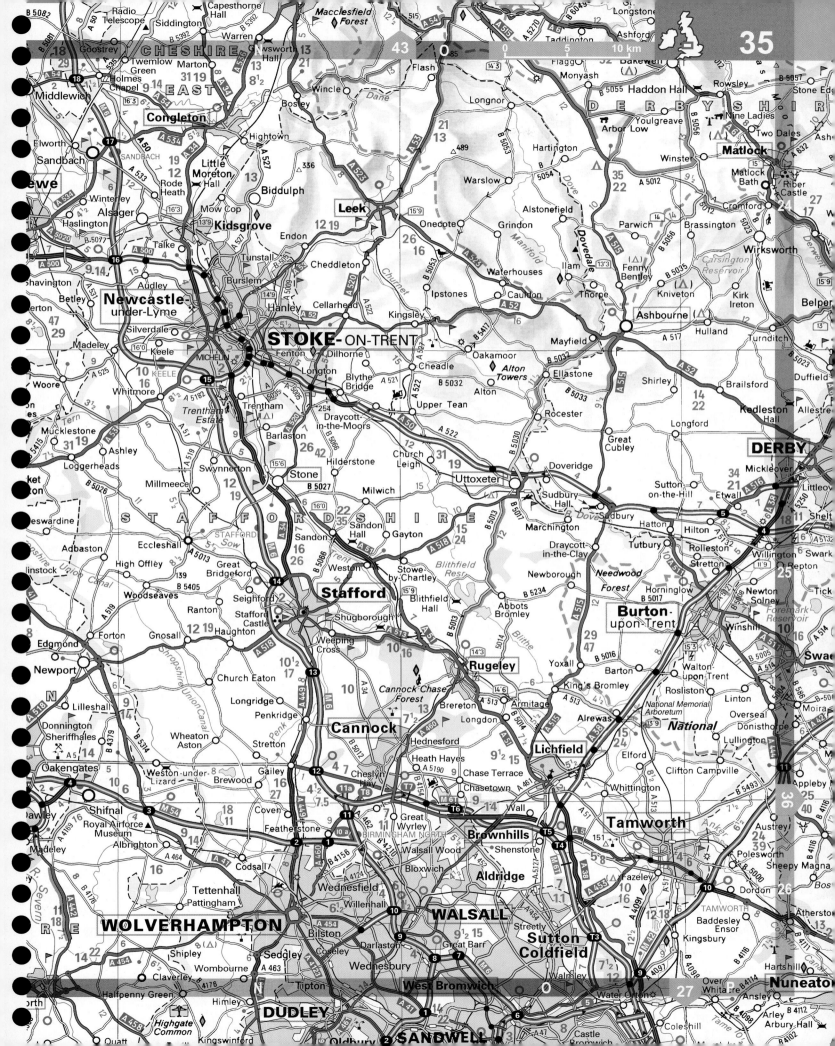

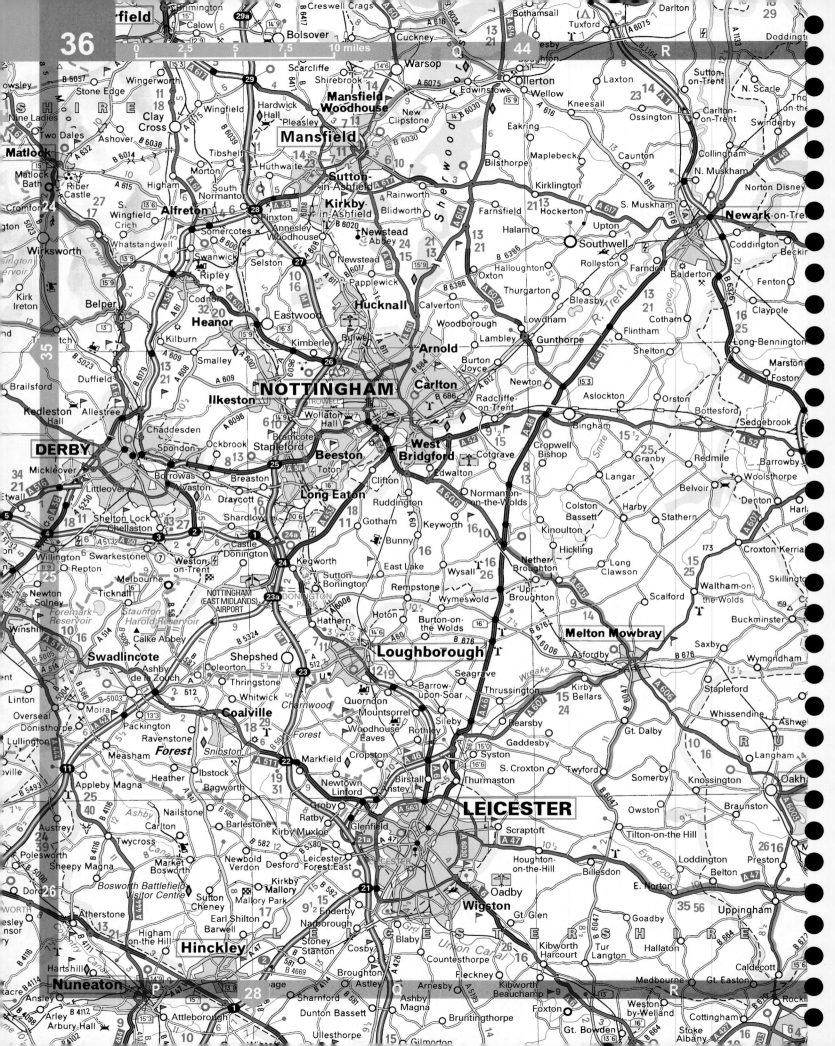

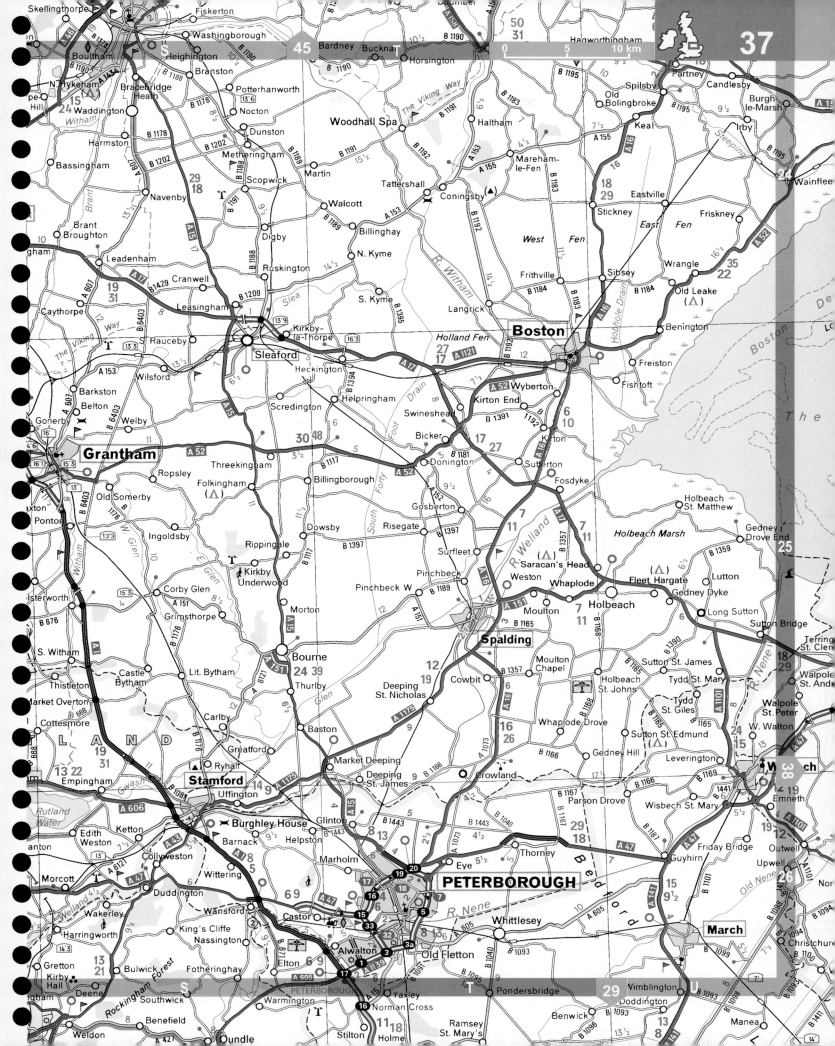

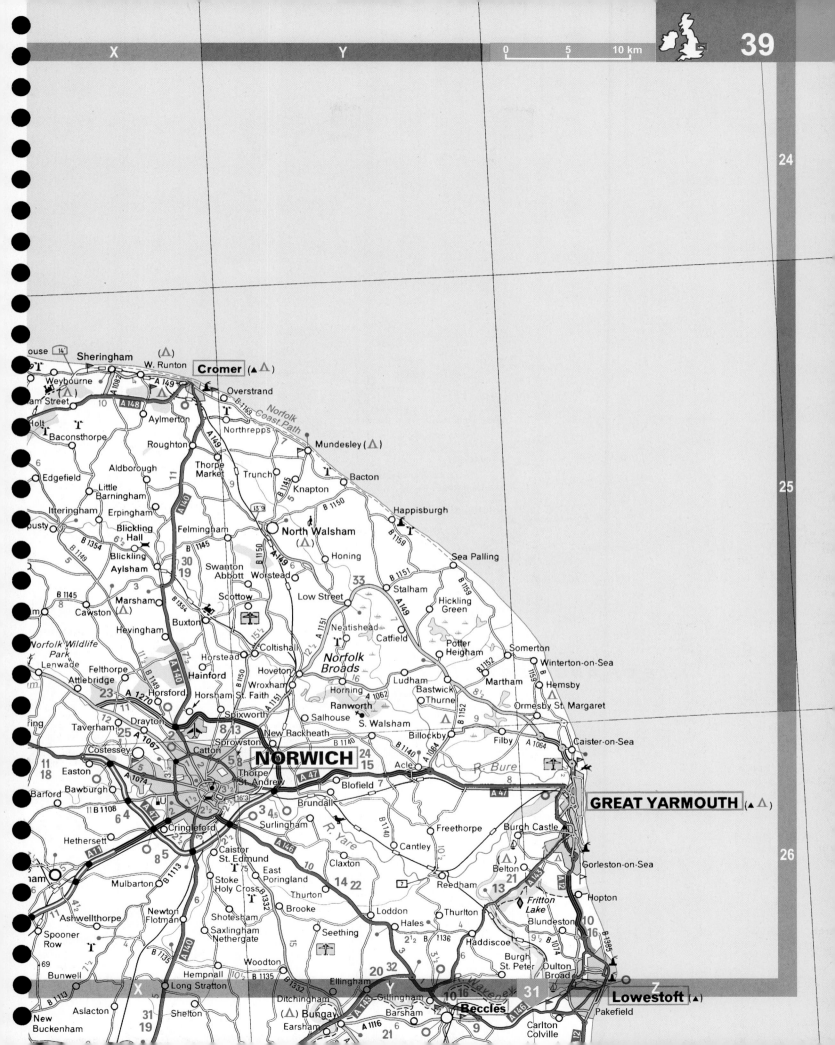

X   Y   0   5   10 km

24

25

26

ouse 14' Sheringham (△)
Weybourne W. Runton **Cromer** (▲△)
(△) A 149 Overstrand
am Street A 148 Norfolk Coast Path
Holt Aylmerton Northrepps 7
Baconsthorpe Roughton A 149 Mundesley (△)
Edgefield Aldborough Thorpe Market Trunch Bacton
6 Little Barningham 11 9 Knapton B 1145
Itteringham Erpingham Felmingham 13'9 B 1150 Happisburgh
busty Blickling Hall B 1354 6½ North Walsham B 1159
B 1149 Blickling B 1145 (△) Sea Palling
5 Aylsham 30 19 Swanton Abbott Worstead Honing B 1151
B 1145 Marsham 3 Scottow 33 Stalham B 1159
8 Cawston (△) B 1354 Low Street A 149 Hickling Green
Hevingham 15'2 Buxton Neatishead Catfield Potter Heigham Somerton
Norfolk Wildlife Park Horstead Coltishall A 1151 Norfolk Broads Ludham B 1152 Winterton-on-Sea
Lenwade Felthorpe Hainford Hoveton 16 Bastwick Martham Hemsby
Attlebridge 11½ B 1149 A 140 Wroxham A 1062 Thurne 8½ Ormesby St Margaret
23 A 1270 Horsford Horsham St. Faith Horning Ranworth B 1152
ring Taverham 12 Drayton Spixworth Salhouse S. Walsham Billockby Filby A 1064 Caister-on-Sea
25 A 1067 2 8 13 New Rackheath B 1140 Acle R. Bure
Costessey Catton Sprowston B 1140 A 1064 8
11 18 Easton 5 8 **NORWICH** 24 15 **GREAT YARMOUTH** (▲△)
Barford Bawburgh A 1074 Thorpe St. Andrew A 47 Blofield 7
11 B 1108 6 4 U 16'3 Brundall B 1140 Freethorpe Burgh Castle
Hethersett A 47 Cringleford 3 4 5 Surlingham R. Yare Cantley 10½ (△)
A 11 8 5 Caister St. Edmund 2½ Claxton Reedham Belton Gorleston-on-Sea
ham Mulbarton B 1113 7'5 East Poringland 10 14 22 7 13 A 143 A 12 Hopton
Newton Flotman B 1332 Thurton Brooke Loddon Thurlton Fritton Lake Blundeston 10
Ashwellthorpe 11 Shotesham Hales 2½ B 1136 Haddiscoe 9½ A 1074 16
Spooner Row Saxlingham Nethergate 15 Seething 3 3½ Burgh St. Peter Oulton Broad
69 Bunwell 7½ Woodton B 1135 20 32 R. Waveney 31 **Lowestoft** (▲)
New Buckenham B 1113 Long Stratton B 1332 Hempnall 10½ Ellingham Gillingham 10 16 Pakefield
Aslacton 31 19 Shelton Ditchingham (△) Bungay **Beccles** A 146 Carlton Colville
Barsham Earsham A 1116 21 9

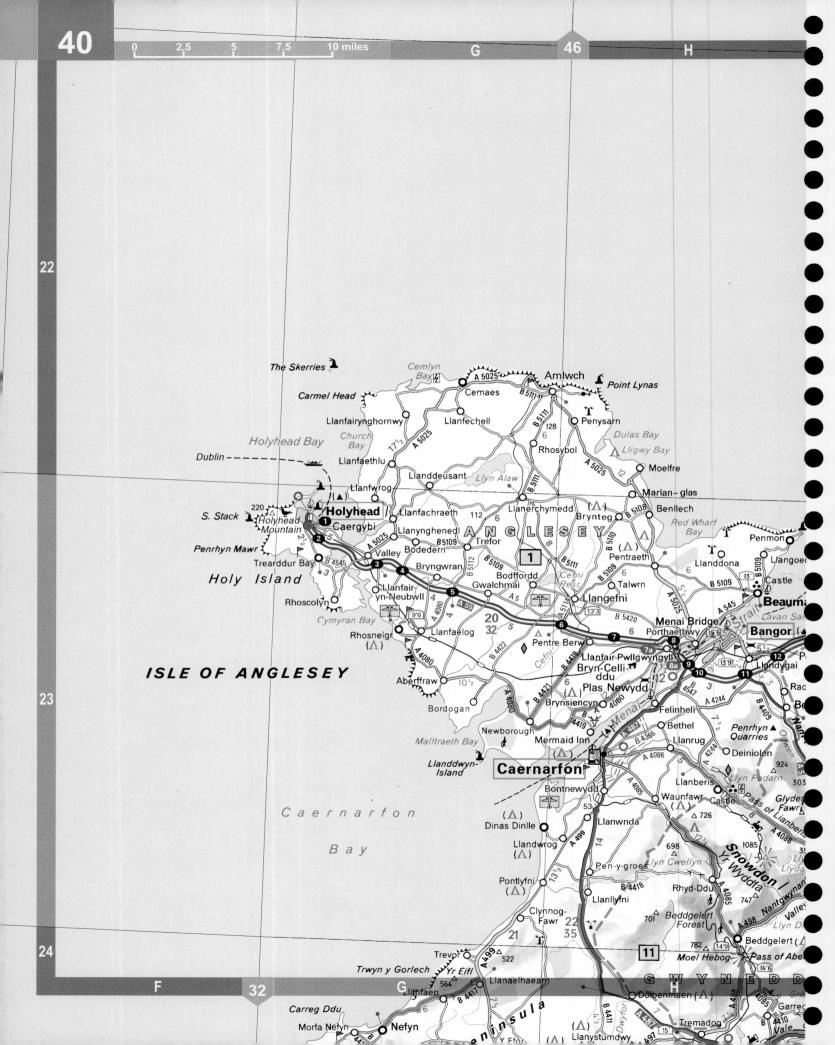

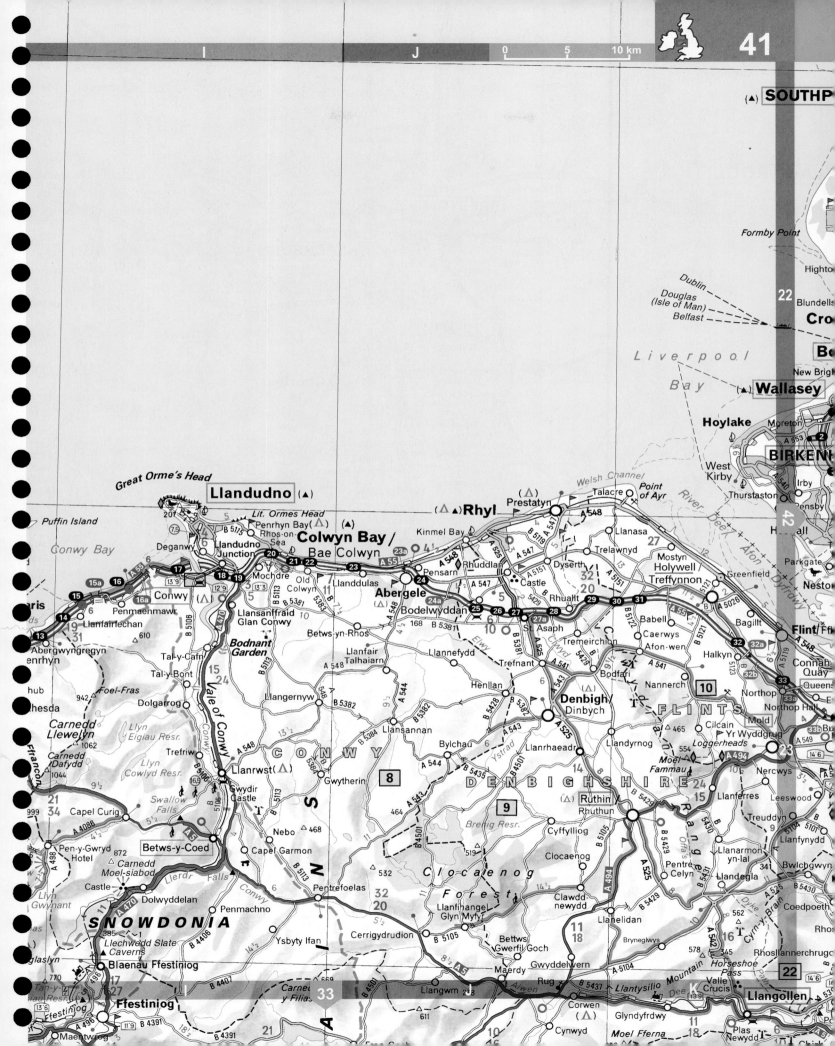

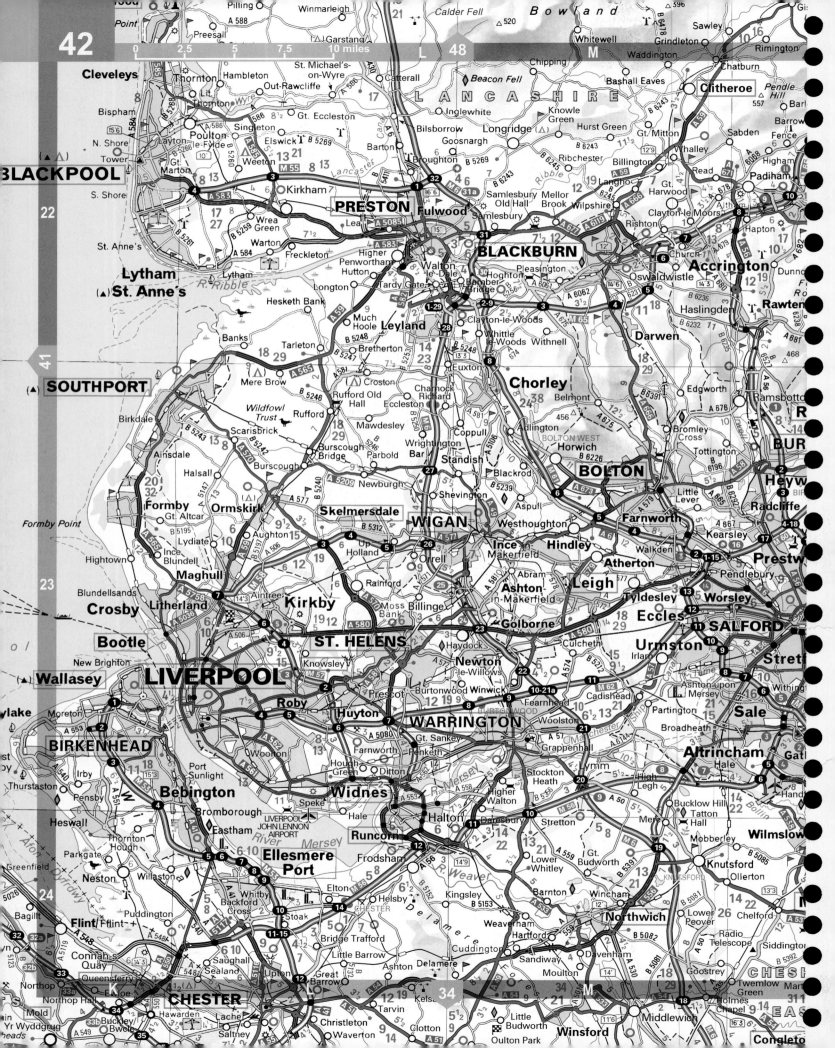

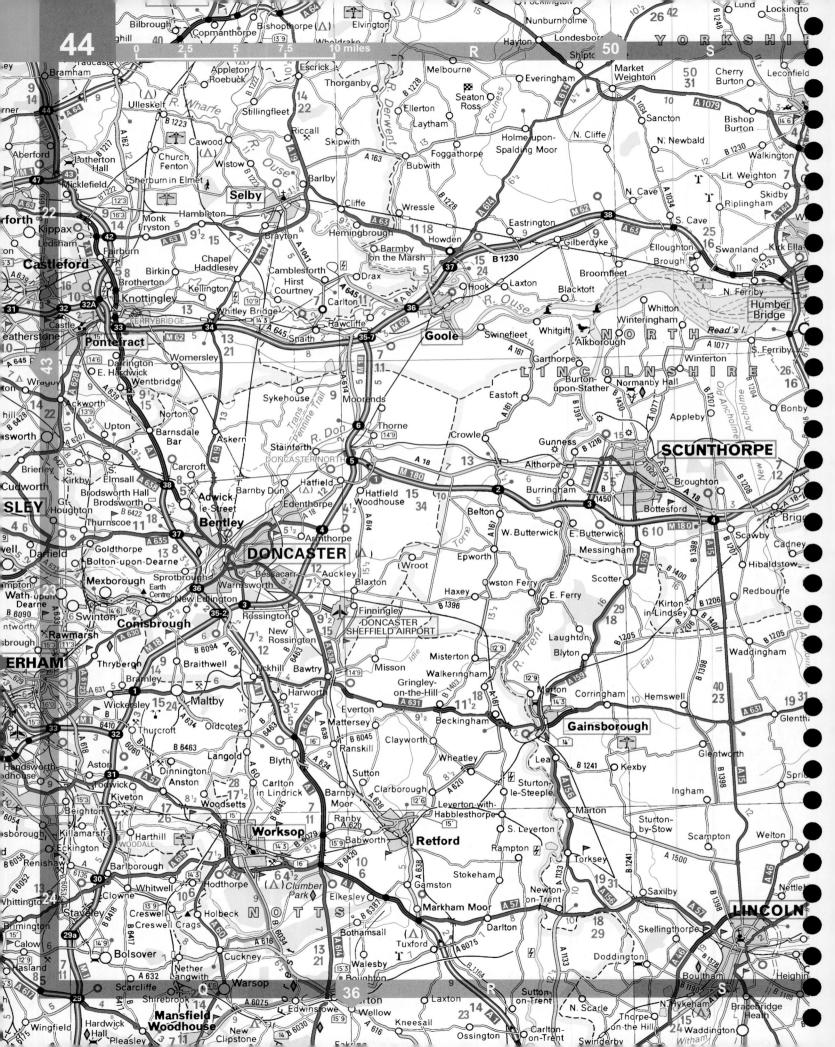

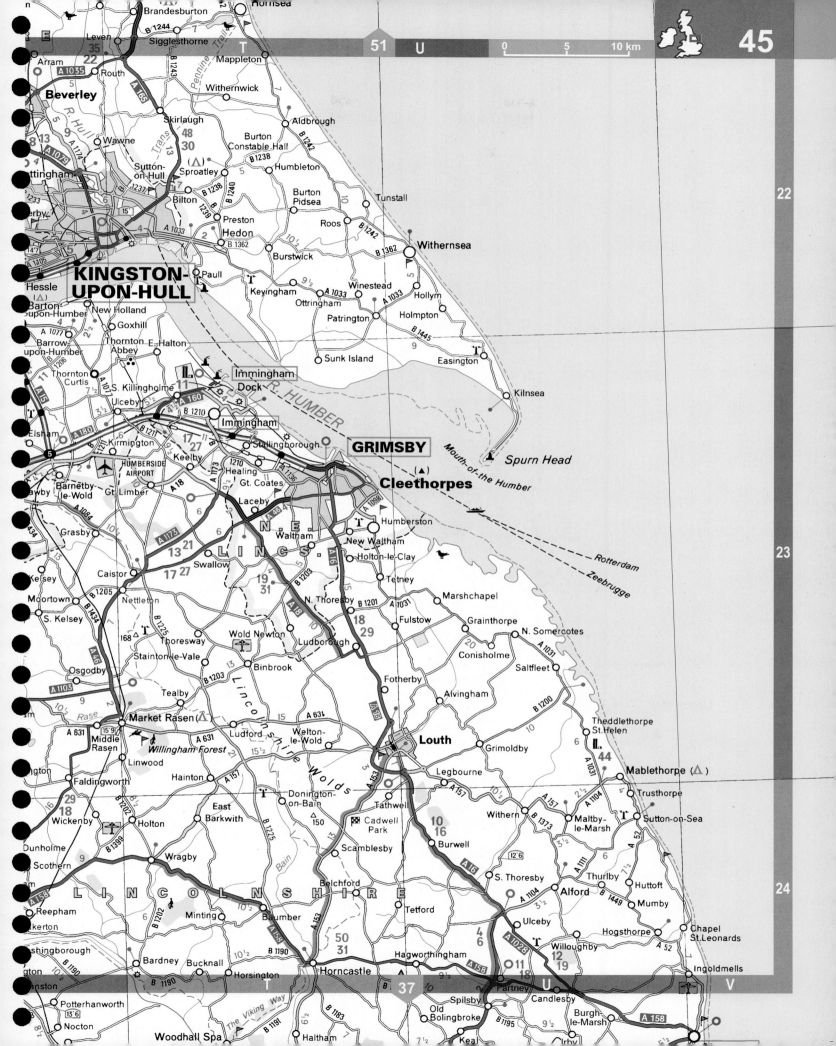

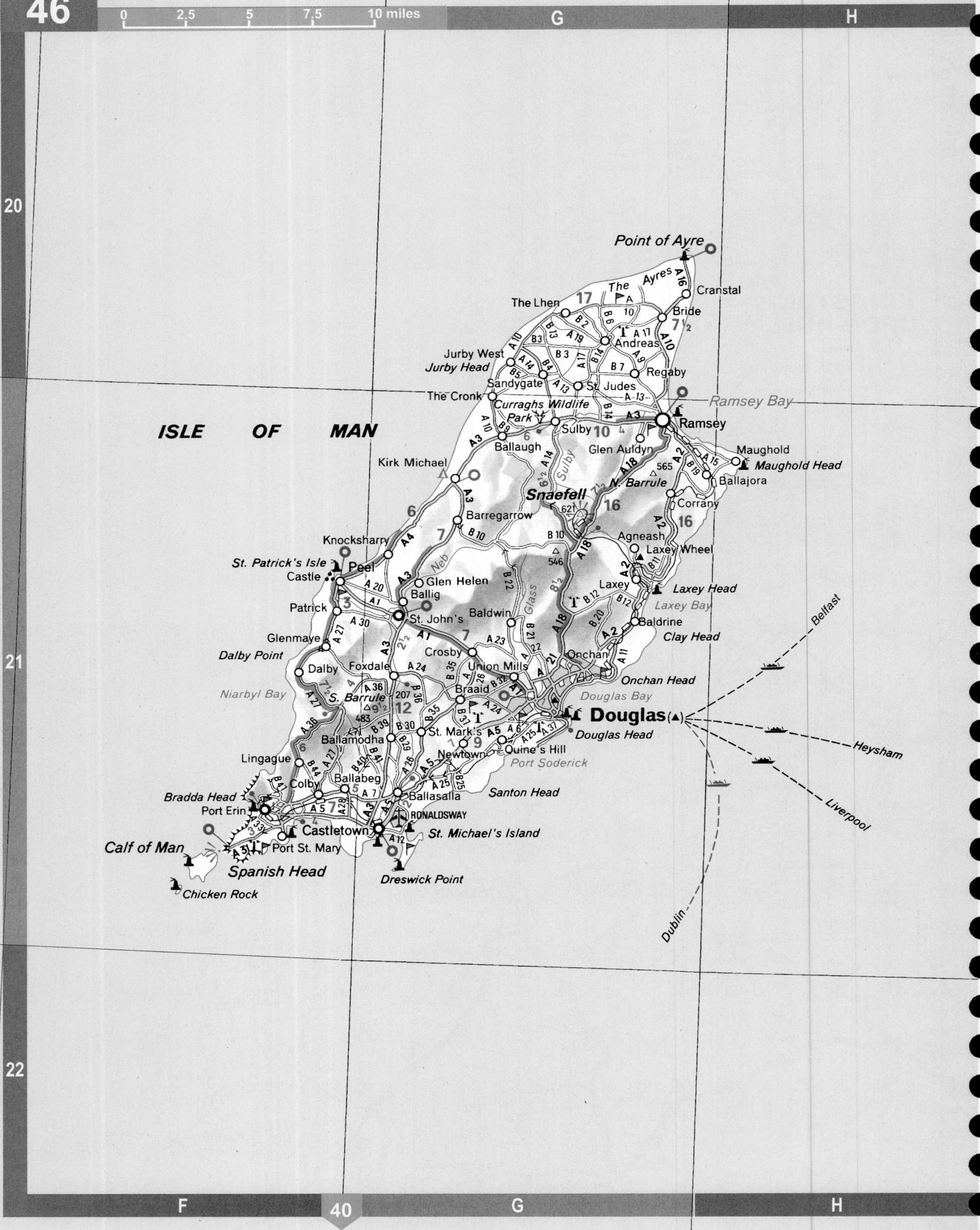

0   2.5   5   7.5   10 miles

20

Point of Ayre

The Ayres A16

Cranstal

The Lhen 17   A
B 2   B 6   10
A 17
B 3   B 13   A 19   Bride 7½
Andreas   A 10   A 9

Jurby West   A 10   A 14   B 3   A 17   B 4
Jurby Head   B 5   B 4   A 13   B 7   Regaby
Sandygate   St. Judes   A-13
The Cronk   Curraghs Wildlife   B 14   A 3
Park   Sulby   10   A 3   Ramsey

ISLE   OF   MAN   A 10   B 8   Ballaugh   A 14   4   Maughold
Kirk Michael   A 3   *Sulby*   Glen Auldyn   A 2   B 15   *Maughold Head*
A 18   565   B 19   Ballajora
N. Barrule   Corrany
Snaefell   16   A 2   16
6   Barregarrow   621
B 10   B 10   Agneash
Knocksharry   7   A 4   546   Laxey Wheel
St. Patrick's Isle   B 22   A 18
Castle   Peel   A 3   Glen Helen   B 12   Laxey
Ballig   B 21   *Laxey Head*
Patrick   3   A 20   St. John's   7   *Laxey Bay*
A 1   Baldwin   A 23   A 2   Baldrine
Glenmaye   A 27   A 30   Crosby   B 20   *Clay Head*
Dalby Point   A 1   Union Mills   Onchan   A 11
Dalby   Foxdale   A 24   B 35   A
Niarbyl Bay   7½   *S. Barrule*   207   B 36   Braaid   *Onchan Head*
A 27   483   9½   12   B 36   *Douglas Bay*
A 36   B 39   B 30   St. Mark's   A 5   A 6   **Douglas** (▲)
Lingague   6   Ballamodha   B 29   1   9   Quine's Hill   *Douglas Head*
A 5   B 44   A 41   Newtown   *Port Soderick*
Colby   Ballabeg   A 25
Bradda Head   A 7   Ballasalla   *Santon Head*
Port Erin   A 5   RONALDSWAY
Castletown   A 12   *St. Michael's Island*
Calf of Man   Port St. Mary   *Dreswick Point*
Spanish Head

Chicken Rock

Belfast
Heysham
Liverpool
Dublin

21

22

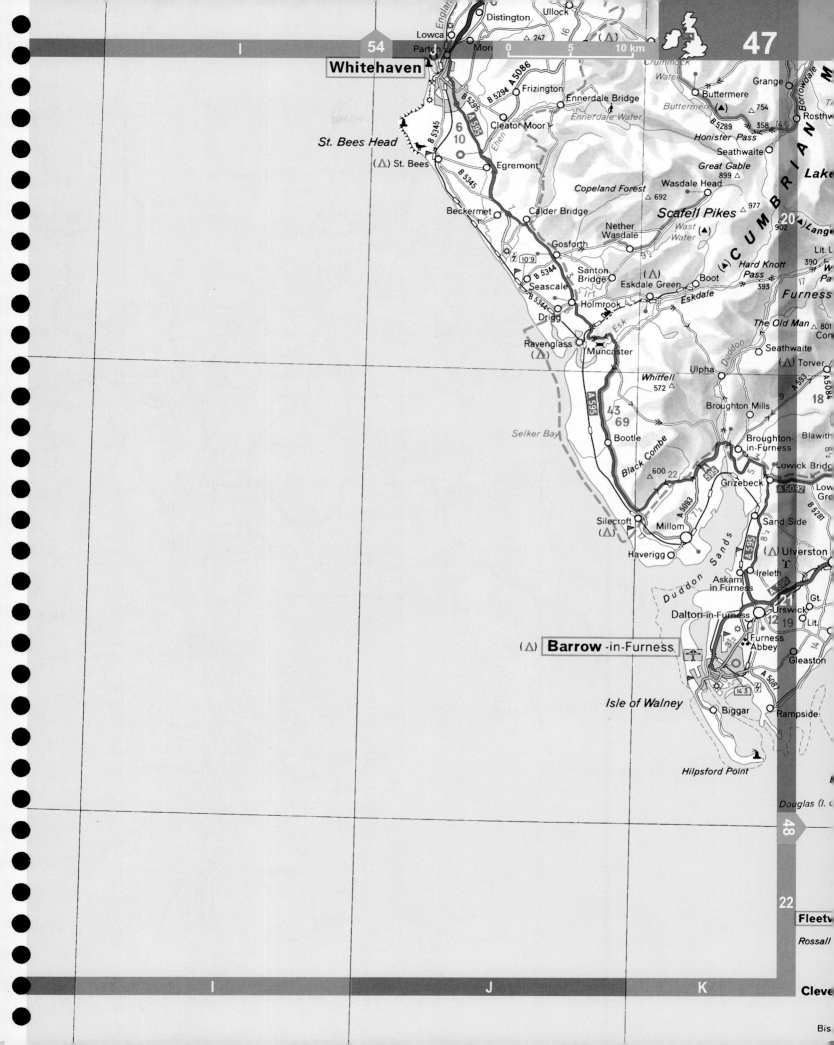

Distington
Ullock
Lowca
Morc
△ 247
16

Partch
0   5   10 km

Whitehaven

Crummock Water
Grange
B 5294 A 5086
Frizington
Buttermere ▲
△ 754
Borrowdale
Rosthw

B 5295
Ennerdale Bridge
Buttermere
B 5289
358 14⅛

A 595
Cleator Moor
Ennerdale Water
Honister Pass
B 5345
Seathwaite

St. Bees Head
6
10
Etten
Great Gable
899 △
CUMBRIAN M

(△) St. Bees
Egremont
Wasdale Head
Lake

B 5345
Copeland Forest
△ 692
Scafell Pikes 977 △
20
902
Lang

Beckermet
Calder Bridge
Nether Wasdale
Wast Water
(▲)
Lit. L
W

B 5344
Gosforth
Hard Knott Pass
390
Pa
17

10'9
Santon Bridge
(△)
Boot
393
Furness

Seascale
Irt
Eskdale Green
Eskdale
B 5344
Holmrook
The Old Man △ 801
Con

Drigg
Esk
Seathwaite

Ravenglass
Muncaster
Ulpha
(△) Torver
18

(△)
Duddon
Whitfell
572 △
A 5084
A 593

A 595
43
69
Broughton Mills

Selker Bay
Bootle
Broughton-in-Furness
Blawith

Black Combe
△ 600 22
A 595
Lowick Bridge

Grizebeck
A 5092
Low
Gre

Silecroft
A 5083 7½
Sand Side
B 5281

(△)
Millom
8⅖
(△) Ulverston

Haverigg
Duddon Sands
A 595
Ireleth

Askam in Furness
A 590
21
Gt.

Dalton-in-Furness
Urswick
12 19 Lit.

(△) **Barrow** -in-Furness
Furness Abbey

14 3
A 5087
Gleaston

Isle of Walney
Biggar
Rampside

Hilpsford Point

Douglas (I. d

22

Fleetw

Rossall

I   J   K   **Cleve**
Bis

Braithwaite | Castlerigg | Pooley Bridge | Gt. Strickland | Morland
Brackenthwaite | Stair | Watermillock | Helton | King's Meauburn
Derwent- | Thirlspot | Sandwick | Martindale | Sleagill
0 2.5 5 7.5 10 miles | K 54 55 L | Ulswater | Crosby Raven
Frizington | Grange | Thirlspot | Glenridding | Dale Head | Rosgill | Shap
Ennerdale Bridge | Buttermere | Borrowdale | Glenridding | Patterdale | Shap Summit
Cleator Moor | Rosthwaite | Helvellyn | High Street | Haweswater Resr. | Orton
Egremont | Honister Pass | Great Gable | Lake District National Park | Harter Fell | Shap Fells
Calder Bridge | Seathwaite | Wasdale Head | Grasmere | Dove Cottage | Sadgill | Tebay
Nether Wasdale | Copeland Forest | Scafell Pikes | Rydal | Kentmere
Gosforth | Wast Water | Langdale Valley | Chapel Stile | Ambleside | Troutbeck | Tebay
Santon Bridge | Hard Knott Pass | Lit. Langdale | Skelwith Bridge | Waterhead | Staveley | Watchgate
Seascale | Eskdale Green | Boot | Wrynose Pass | Furness Fells | The Tarn | Windermere | Ings | Burneside | Grayrigg
Holmrook | Eskdale | Windermere | Hawkshead | Bowness | Meal Bank
Drigg | The Old Man | Coniston | Brantwood | Hill Top | Winster | Crook | Kendal
Ravenglass | Seathwaite | Sawrey | Underbarrow | Old Hutton
Muncaster | Ulpha | Torver | Grizedale | Crosthwaite | Levens
Whitfell | Broughton Mills | Coniston Water | Forest | Satterthwaite | Cartmel Fell | Endmoor | Crooklands
Bootle | Blawith | Rusland | Levens Hall | Heversham
Broughton-in-Furness | Lowick Bridge | Oxen Park | Newby Bridge | Witherslack | Lupton
Grizebeck | Lowick Green | Ayside | Haverthwaite | Lindale | Milnthorpe | Beetham | Holme
Silecroft | Sand Side | Greenodd | High Newton | Arnside | Kirkby Lonsdale
Millom | Ulverston | Cark | Cartmel | Grange-Over-Sands | Burton West | Burton | Whittington
Haverigg | Ireleth | Cartmel Sands | Flookburgh | Kents Bank | Silverdale | Yealand Conyers | Warton
Askam in Furness | Gt. Urswick | Bardsea | Carnforth | Nether Kellet | Over Kellet | Wennington
Dalton-in-Furness | Lit. | Baycliff | Morecambe Bay | Bolton-le-Sands | Aughton | Wray
Barrow -in-Furness | Furness Abbey | Gleaston | Hest Bank | Slyne | Halton | Claughton
Isle of Walney | Biggar | Rampside | Morecambe | Caton | Salter
Hilpsford Point | Heysham | Lancaster | Crossgill
Belfast | Overton | Ward's Stone
Douglas (I. of Man) | Glasson | Galga
Fleetwood | Cockerham | Dolphinholme | Marshaw
Rossall Point | Pilling | Winmarleigh | Garstang | Calder Fell
Preesall | Stalmine
Cleveleys | Thornton | Hambleton | St. Michael's-on-Wyre | Catterall | Beacon Fell
Bispham | Lit. Thornton | Out-Rawcliffe | Inglewhite
Singleton | Gt. Eccleston | Bilsborrow

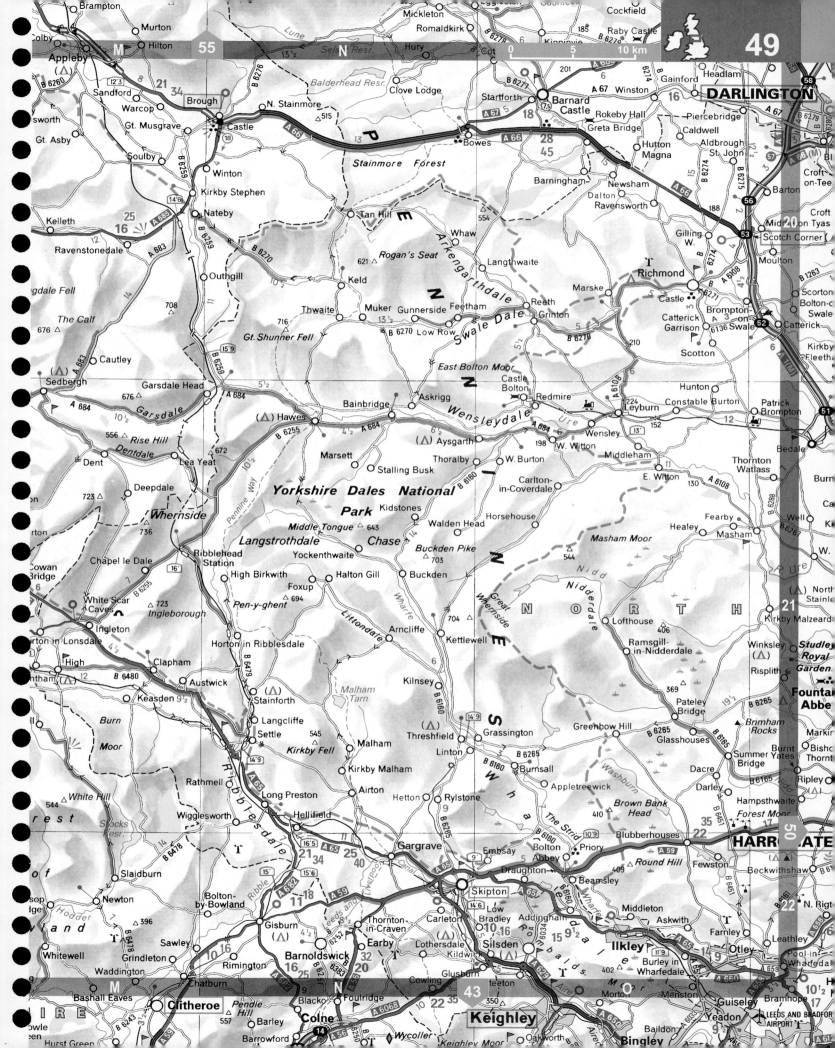

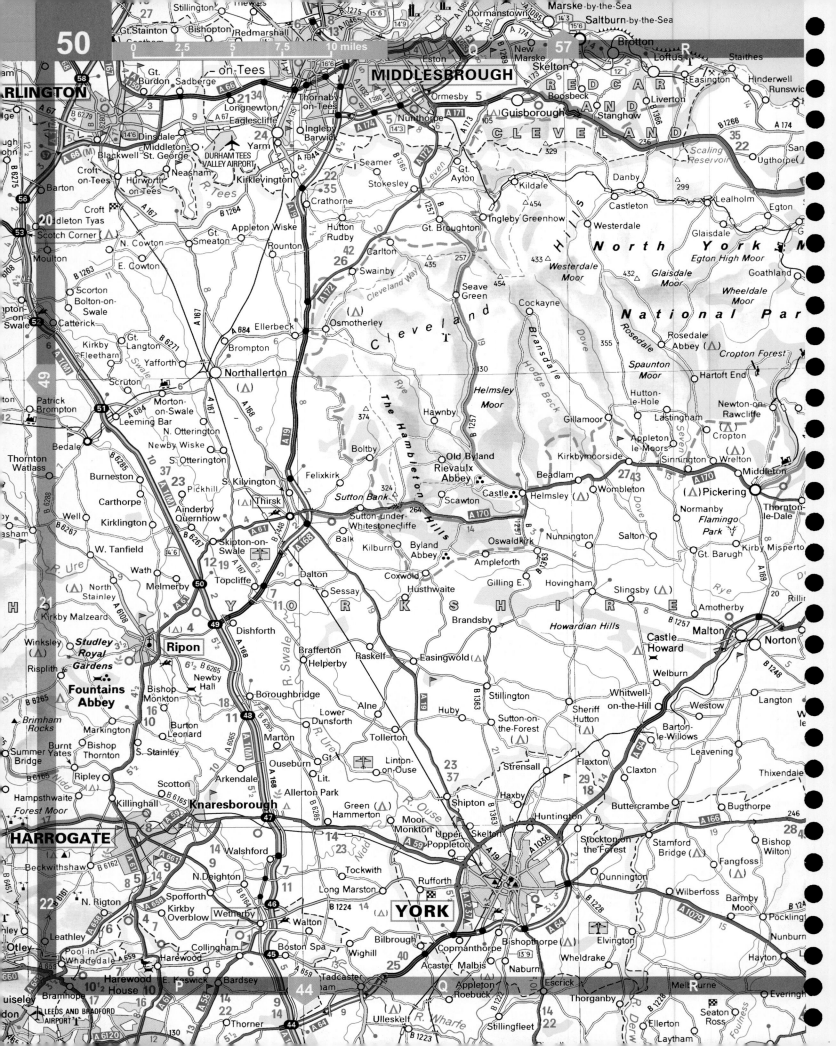

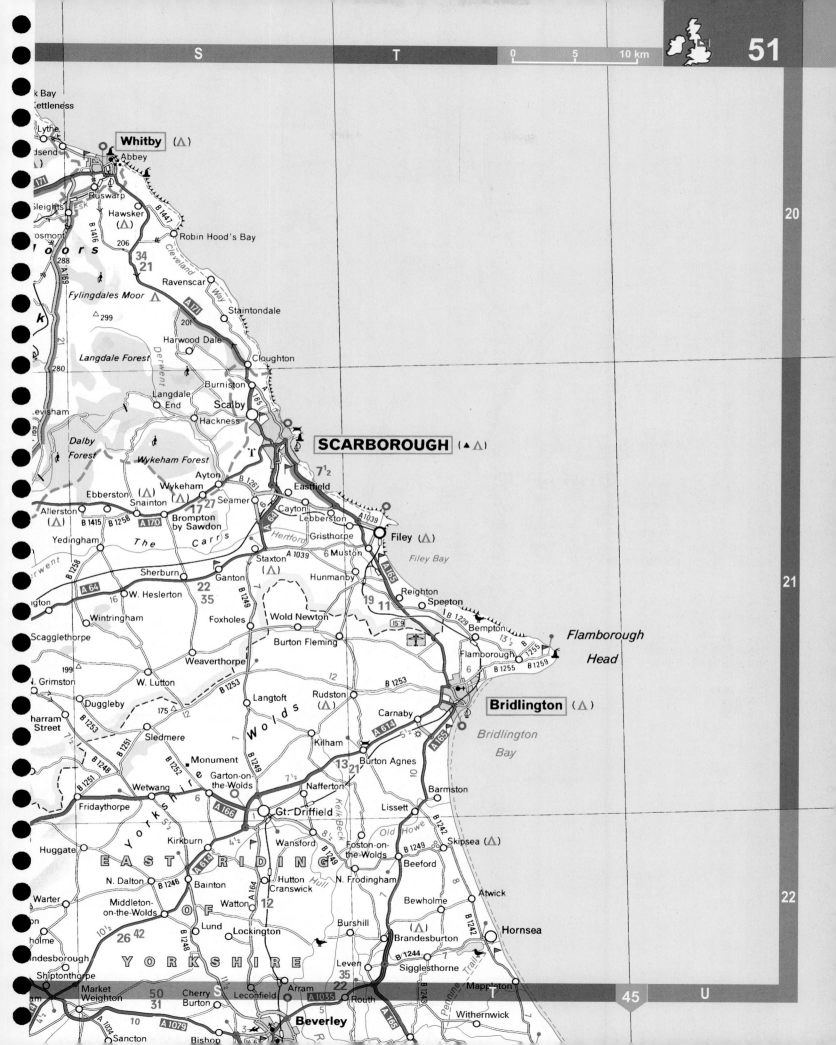

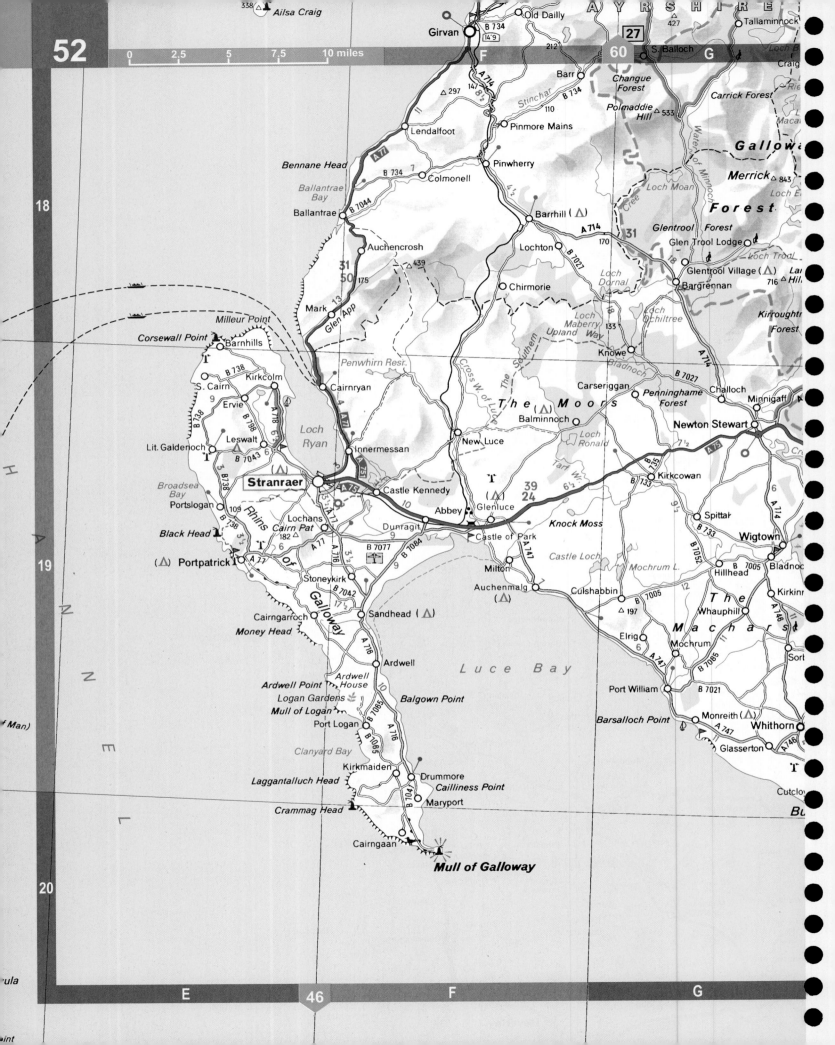

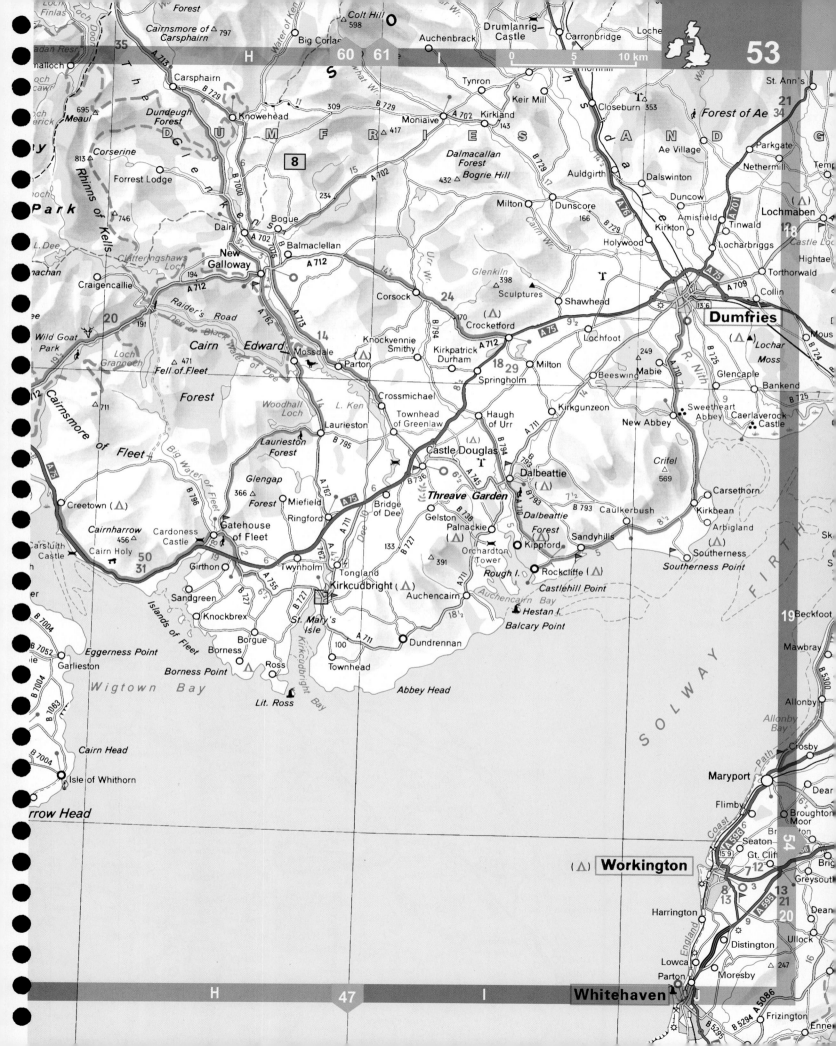

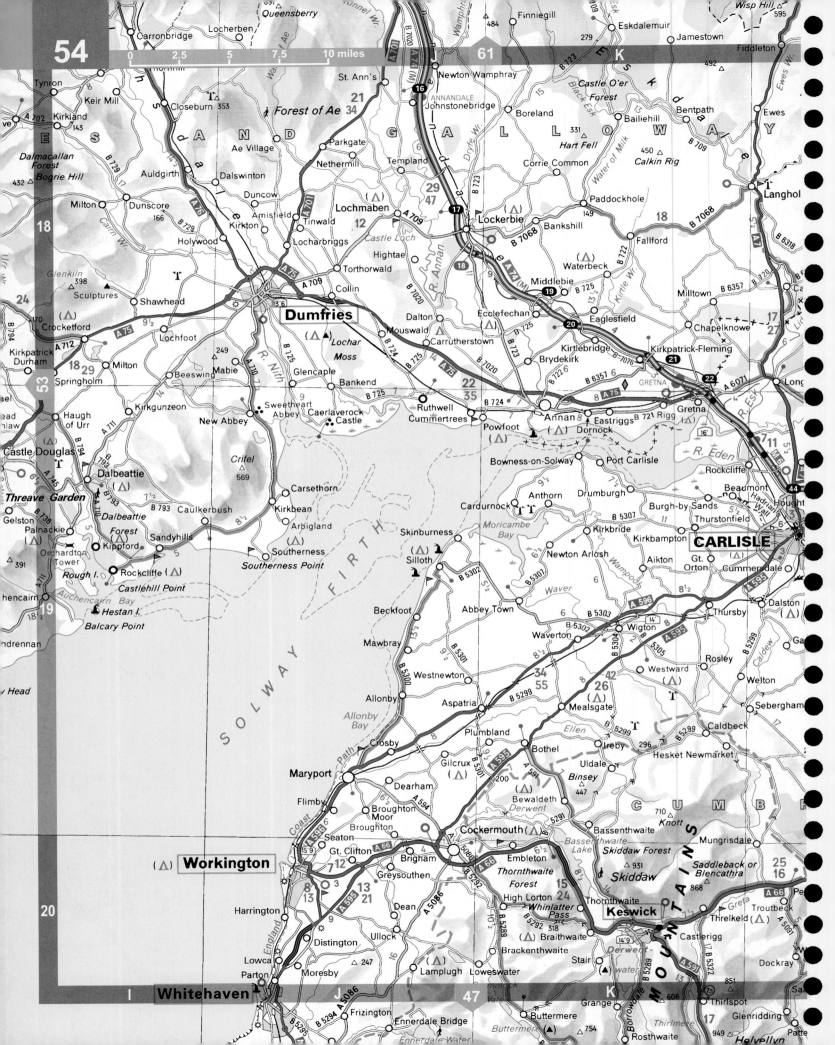

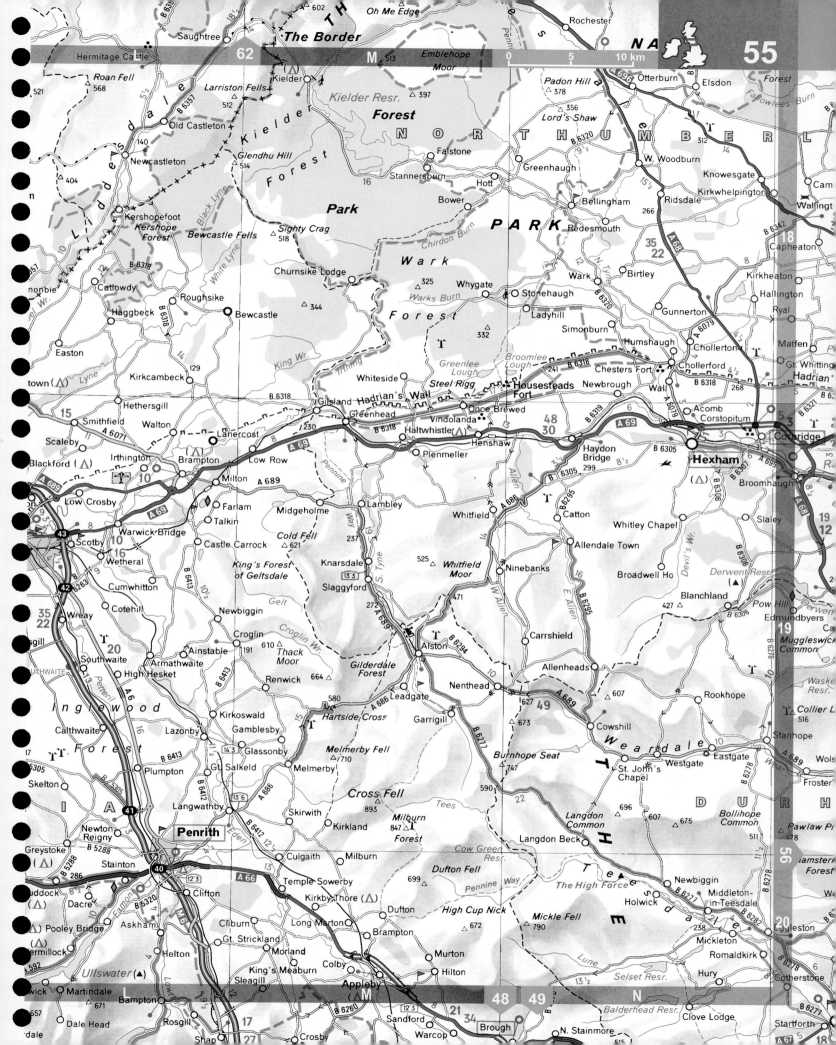

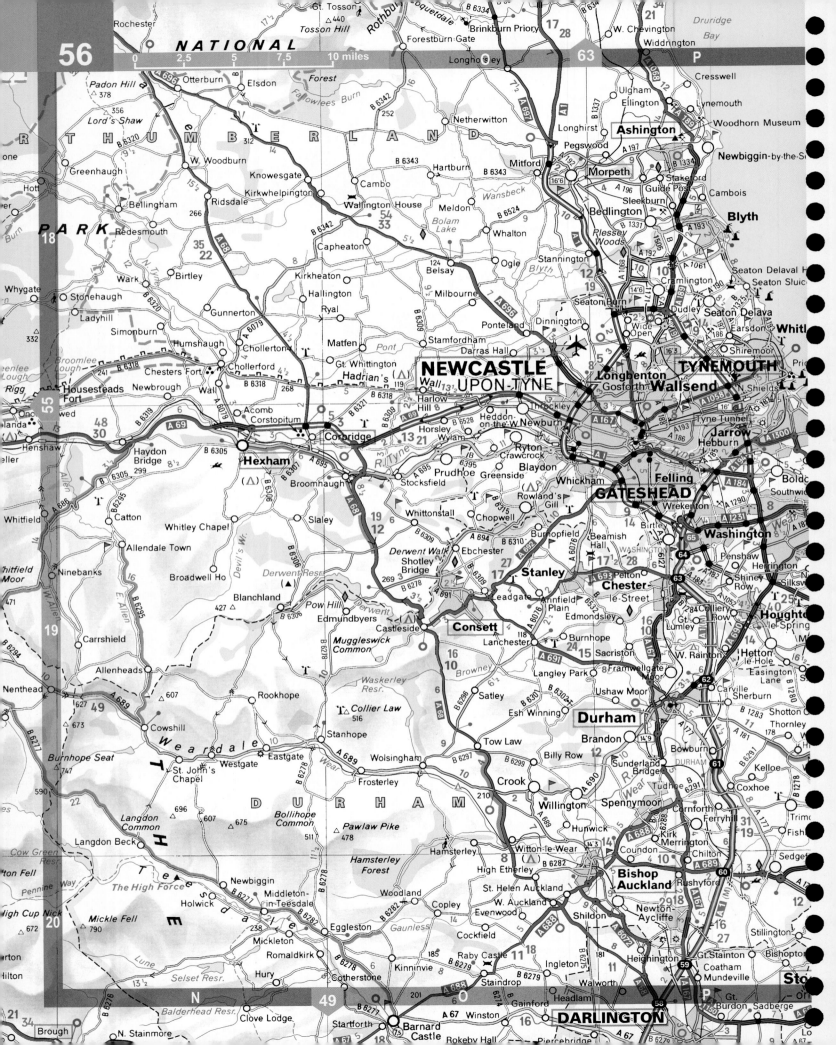

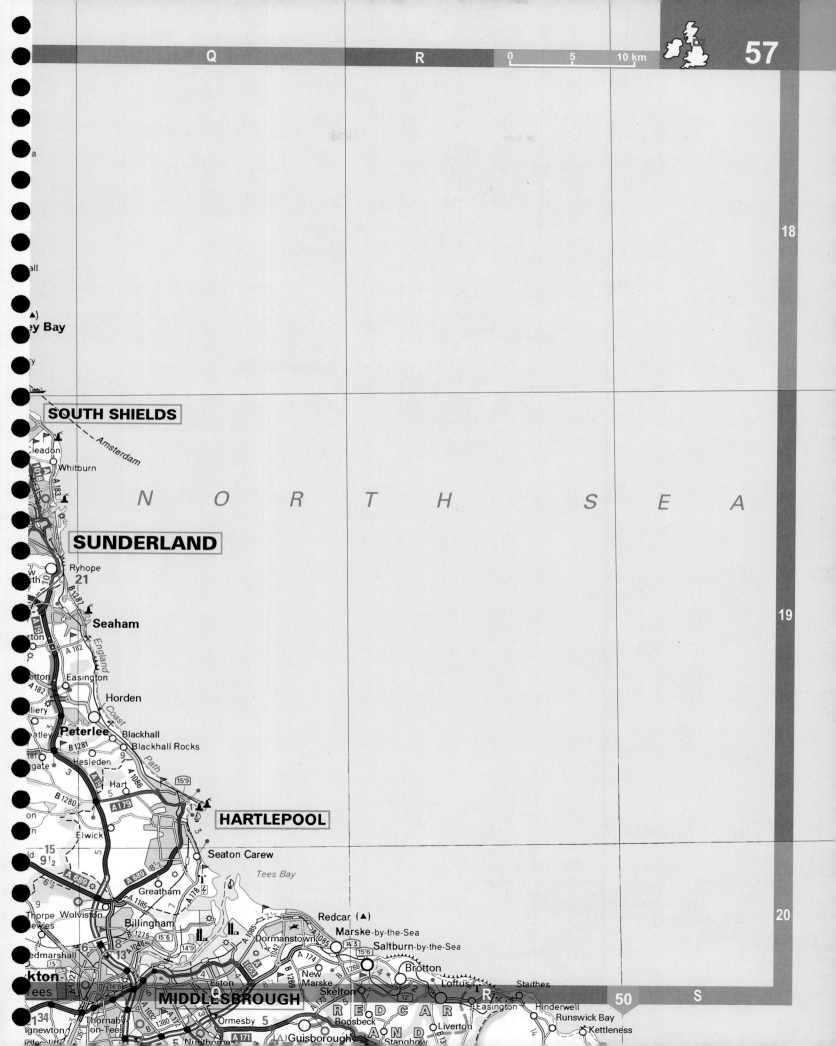

18

SOUTH SHIELDS

Amsterdam

Cleadon Whitburn

N O R T H S E A

SUNDERLAND

Ryhope
21

Seaham

19

Easington

Horden

Peterlee Blackhall
Blackhall Rocks

Hesleden

Hart

15'9

HARTLEPOOL

Elwick

15
9½

Seaton Carew

Tees Bay

Greatham

Thorpe Wolviston
Bewles Redcar (▲)

Billingham Marske-by-the-Sea
Saltburn-by-the-Sea

20

edmarshall Dormanstown

kton **6 13** Brotton

Tees New Marske Loftus Staithes

MIDDLESBROUGH Skelton Easington Hinderwell

50 S

Thornaby Ormesby **5** Boosbeck Liverton Runswick Bay
on-Tees Guisborough Kettleness

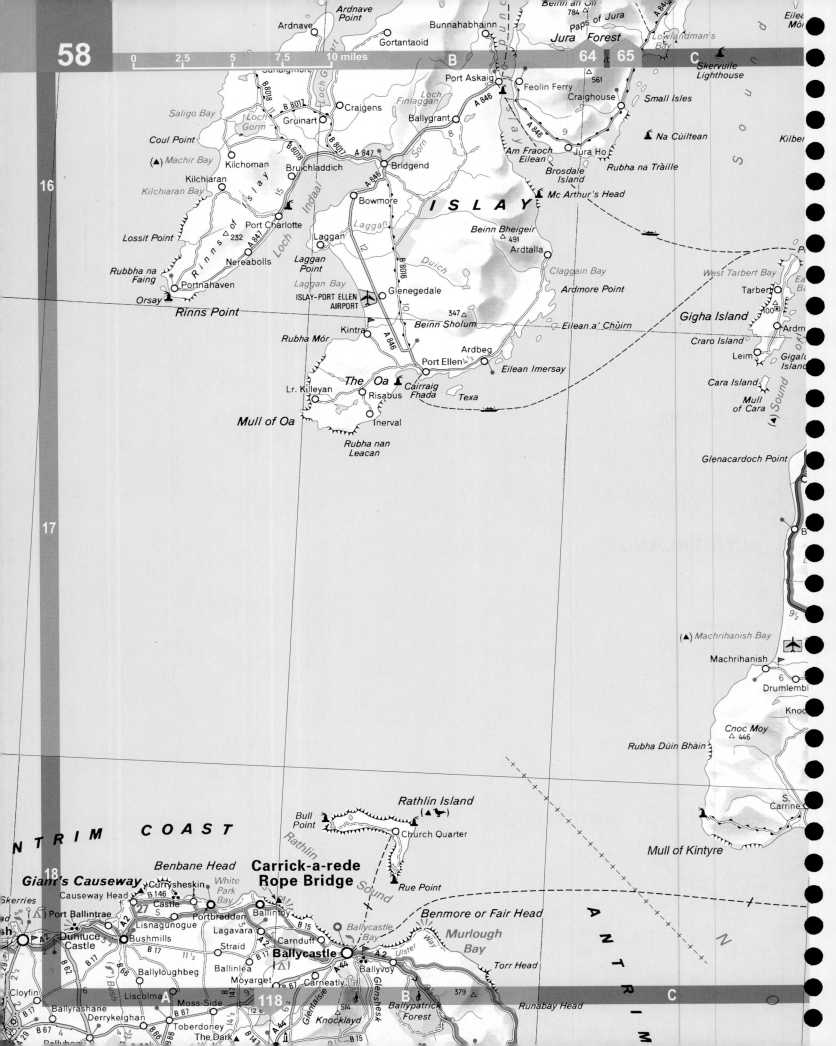

Ardnave
Point
Ardnave
Bunnahabhainn
Beinn an Oir
784 △
Paps of Jura
Lowlandman's
Bay
Jura Forest
Gortantaoid
Skervuile
Lighthouse
0   2.5   5   7.5   10 miles
B
C
Port Askaig
Feolin Ferry
561
Craighouse
Small Isles
Sanaigmore
Saligo Bay
B 8018
B 8017
Craigens
Loch
Finlaggan
A 846
A 846
9
Na Cùiltean
Loch Gr...
Gruinart
Ballygrant
Loch
Gorm
Bruichladdich
Bridgend
Am Fraoch
Eilean
Jura Ho
Brosdale
Island
Rubha na Tràille
Coul Point
B 8017
Sorn
Kilber
(▲) Machir Bay
Kilchoman
A 847
Bowmore
I S L A Y
Mc Arthur's Head
16
Kilchiaran
A 846
15
Port Charlotte
Laggan
Beinn Bheigeir
△ 491
Kilchiaran Bay
Lossit Point
Rinns of Islay
△ 232
A 847
Laggan
Laggan
Ardtalla
Duich
Claggain Bay
West Tarbert Bay
Nereabolls
B 8016
Ardmore Point
Rubbha na
Faing
Laggan
Point
12
Glenegedale
Tarbert
100
Portnahaven
Laggan Bay
Eilean a' Chùirn
Gigha Island
Orsay
ISLAY-PORT ELLEN
AIRPORT
10
Beinn Sholum
Craro Island
Ardm...
Rinns Point
Kintra
347 △
Leim
Gigal...
Island
Rubha Mór
A 846
Ardbeg
Cara Island
Ardbeg
42
The Oa
Port Ellen
Eilean Imersay
Mull
of Cara
Lr. Killeyan
Risabus
Cairraig
Fhada
Texa
(▲)
Mull of Oa
Inerval
Rubha nan
Leacan
Glenacardoch Point
17
B...
9½
(▲) Machrihanish Bay
Machrihanish
6
Drumlembl
Knoc
Cnoc Moy
△ 446
Rubha Dùin Bhàin
S.
Carrine
N T R I M   C O A S T
Rathlin Island
Mull of Kintyre
Bull
Point
Church Quarter
Rathlin
18
Benbane Head
**Carrick-a-rede
Rope Bridge**
Rue Point
Sound
Giant's Causeway
Currysheskin
White
Park
Bay
Benmore or Fair Head
Skerries
Causeway Head
B 146
Castle
Ballintoy
B 15
Murlough
Bay
Port Ballintrae
A 2
27
5
Portbradden
Ballycastle
Bay
A N
Dunluce
Castle
Lisnagunogue
Lagavara
Carnduff
Ballycastle
Ulster
Torr Head
Bushmills
B 17
Straid
A 2
Ballyvoy
Way
Cloyfin
B 62
Ballyloughbeg
Ballinlea
Moyarget
Carneatly
A 44
T
Liscolman
Moss-Side
A
118
B
514
379
Runabay Head
R
Ballyrashane
Derrykeighan
B 67
Toberdoney
The Dark
Knocklayd
Ballypatrick
Forest
I
M

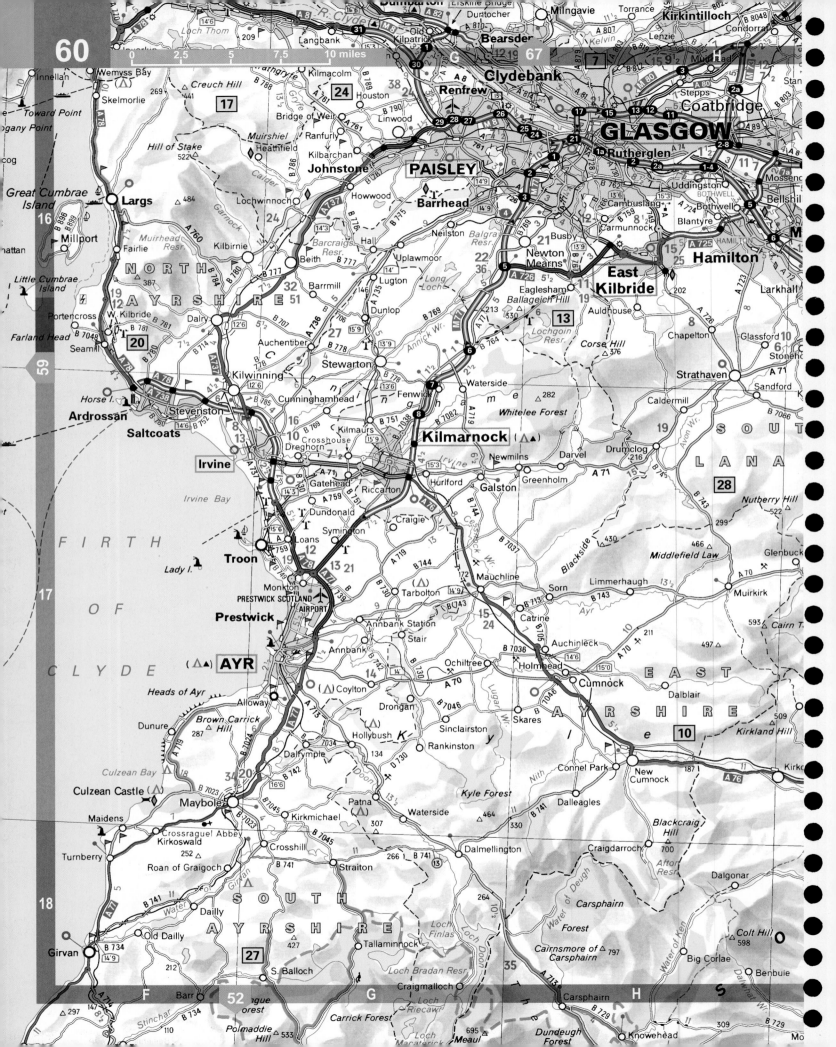

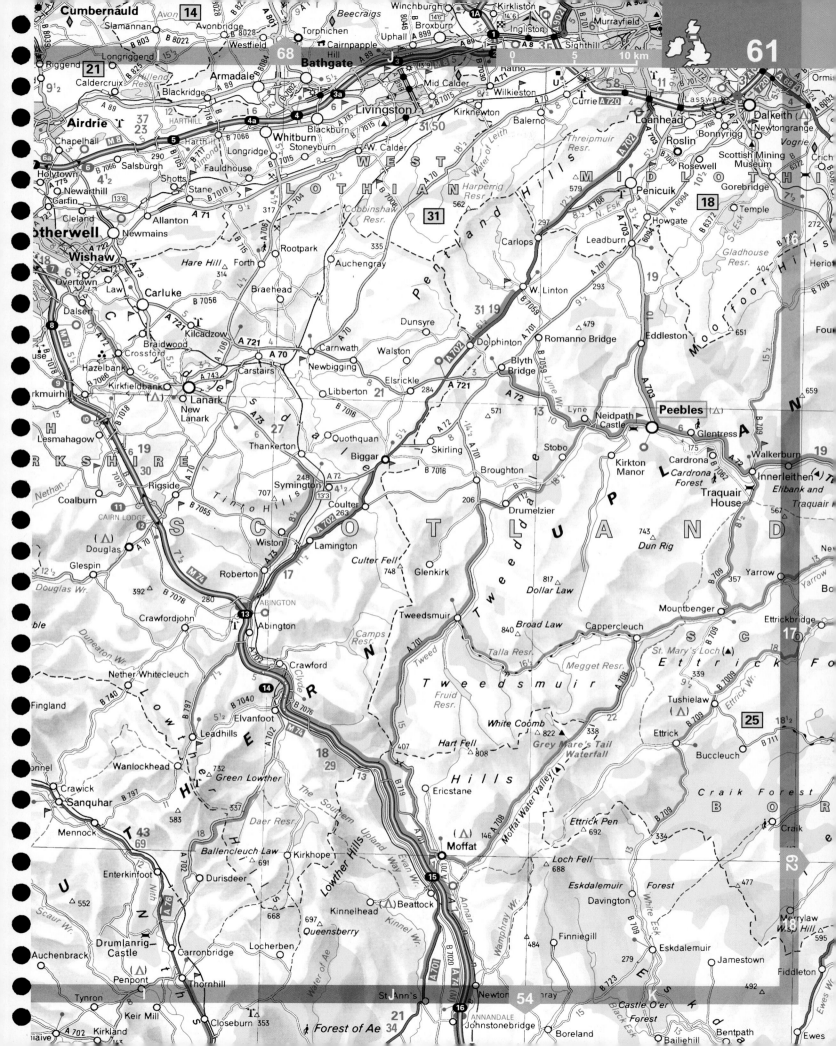

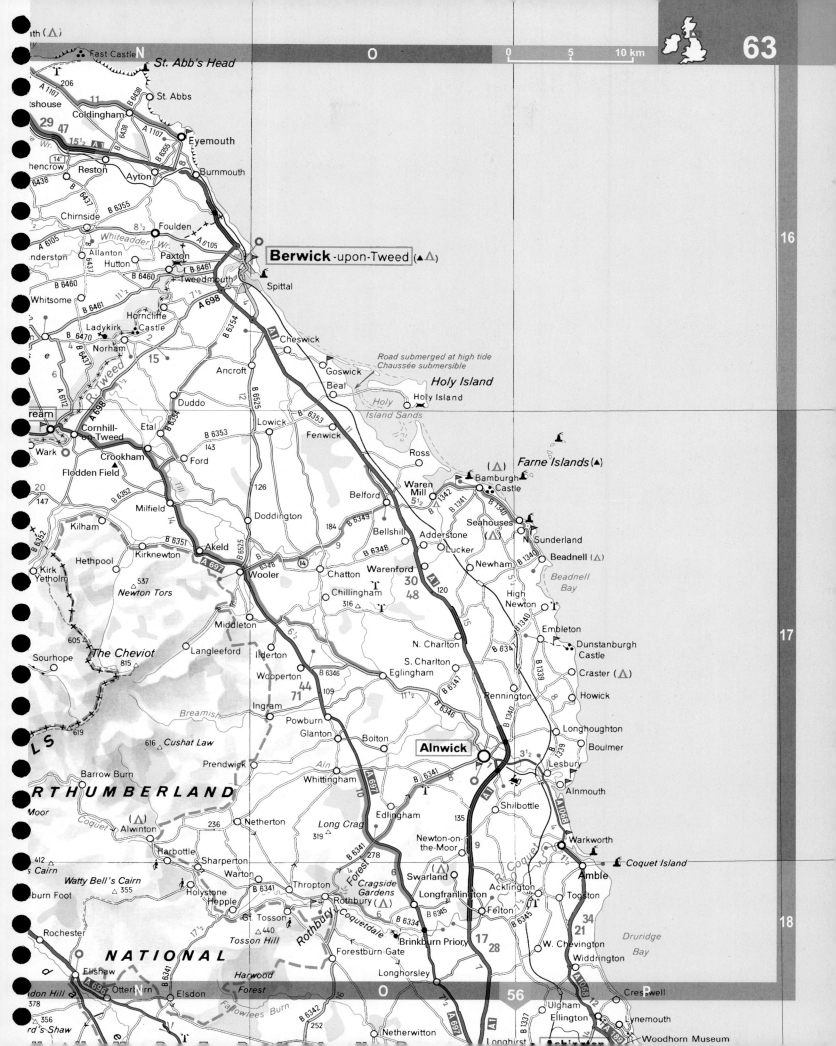

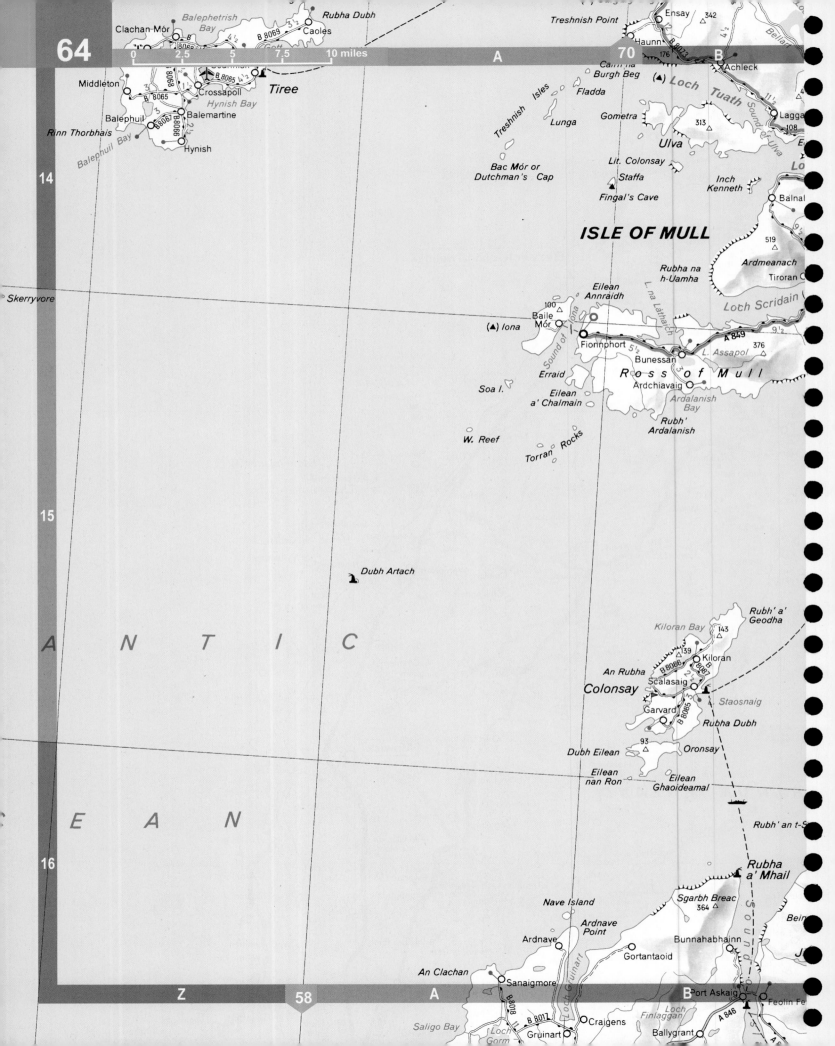

Clachan-Mór
Balephetrish Bay
Rubha Dubh

0   2.5   5   7.5   10 miles

Treshnish Point
Ensay   342
Haunn   176
B 8073
Achleck   B

Middleton
Crossapoll
B 8065
Balephuil
B8067 B8066
Balemartine
Hynish Bay
Hynish
Rinn Thorbhais
Balephuil Bay
Tiree
B 8065
B 8069
Caoles
Gott
Carn na
Burgh Beg
Fladda
Treshnish Isles
Lunga
Gometra
313
Ulva
108
Lagga
Bac Mór or
Dutchman's Cap
Lit. Colonsay
Staffa
Fingal's Cave
Inch
Kenneth
Balnal

(▲) *Loch Tuath*

ISLE OF MULL

14

Skerryvore

Eilean
Annraidh
Baile
Mór
100
(▲) Iona
Fionnphort   5½
A 849
L. Assapol
Bunessan
Erraid
Soa I.
Eilean
a' Chalmain
Ardchiavaig
Rubha na
h-Uamha
Ross of Mull
376
Loch Scridain
Ardmeanach
Tiroran
519

Rubh'
Ardalanish
*Ardalanish
Bay*

W. Reef
Torran Rocks

15

Dubh Artach

A   N   T   I   C

Kiloran Bay   143
Rubh' a'
Geodha
139
An Rubha
B 8086
Kiloran
Scalasaig
B 8087
Colonsay
Garvard
B 8065
Staosnaig
Rubha Dubh
Dubh Eilean   93
Oronsay
Eilean
nan Ron
Eilean
Ghaoideamal

E   A   N

16

Rubh' an t-S

Rubha
a' Mhail
Nave Island
Sgarbh Breac
364
Ardnave
Point
Ardnave
Bunnahabhainn
An Clachan
Sanaigmore
Gortantaoid

Port Askaig
Feolin Fe
A 846
Saligo Bay
B 8017
Craigens
Gruinart
Loch
Finlaggan
Ballygrant
Loch Gruinart
Loch
Gorm

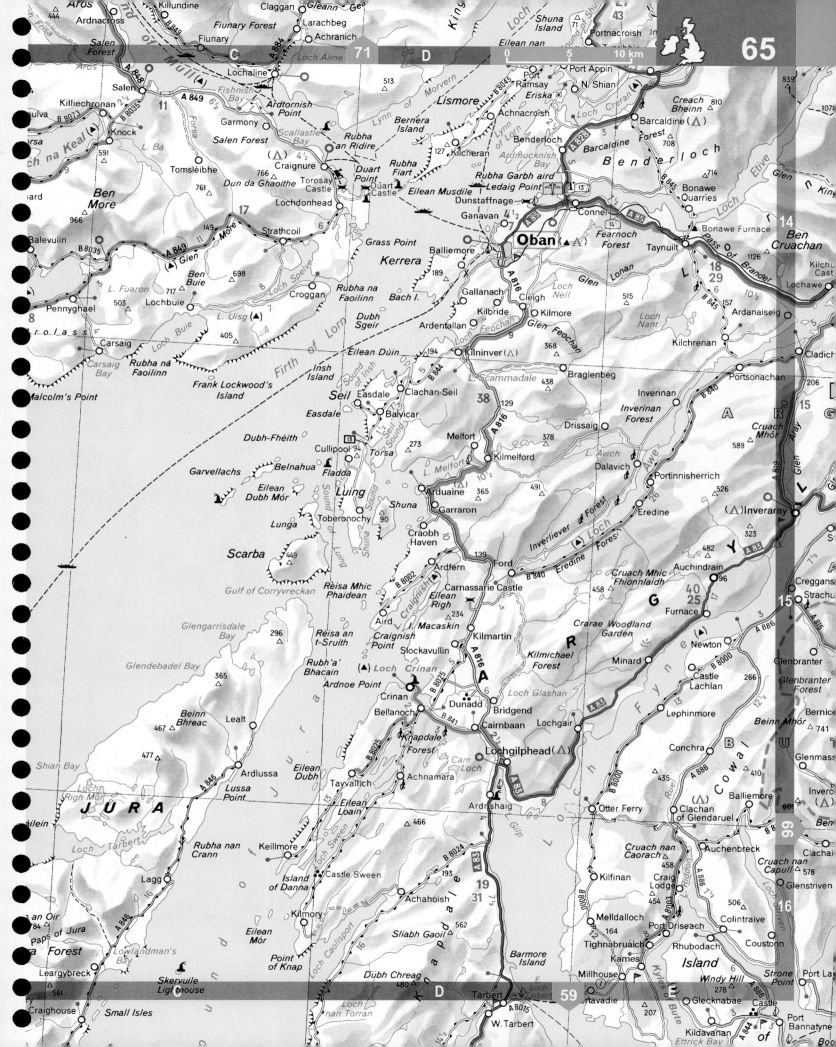

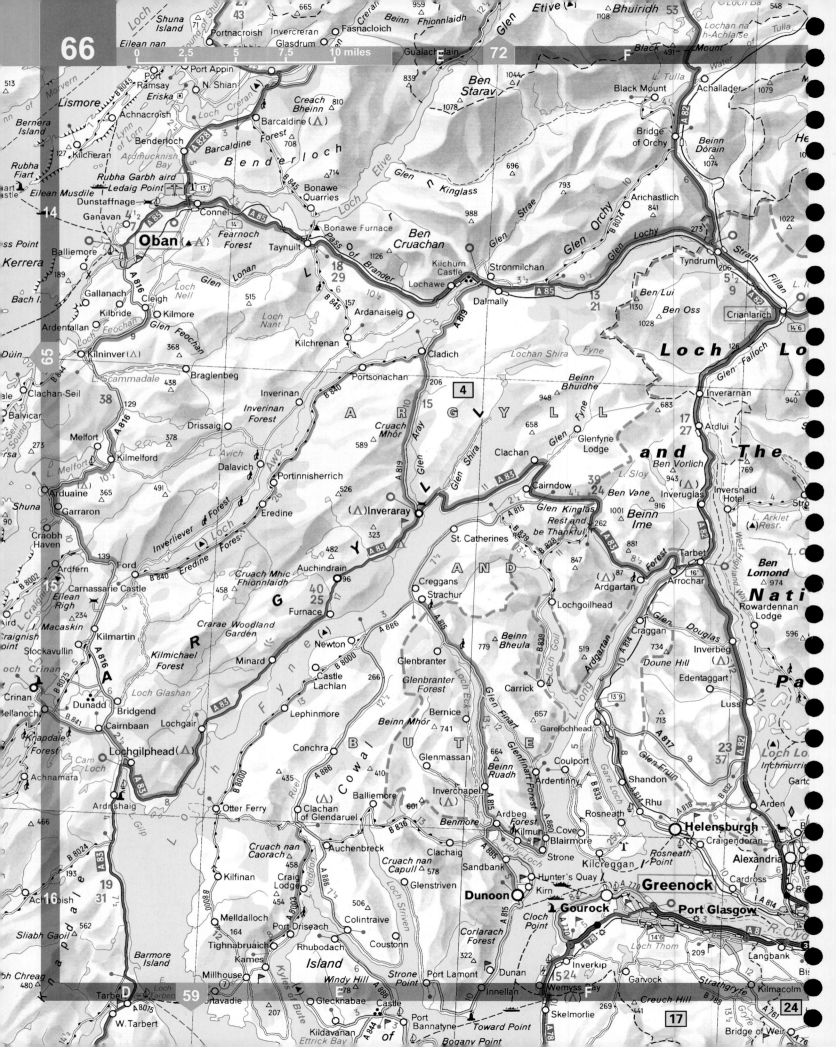

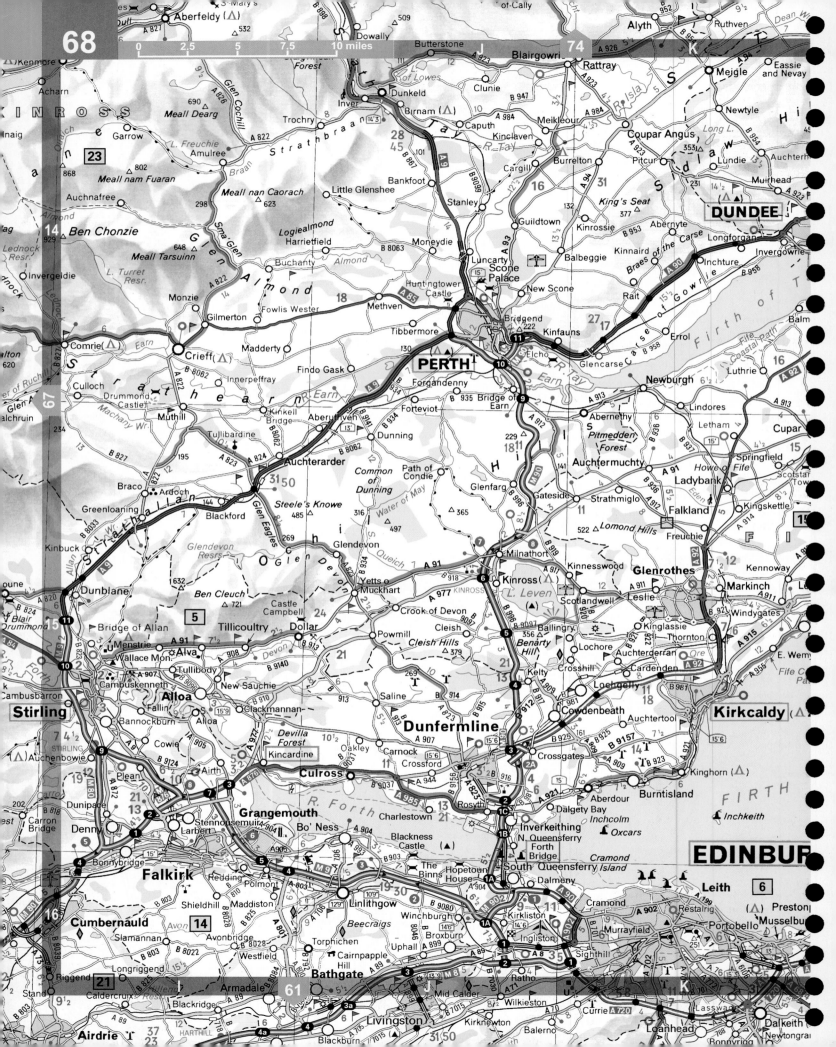

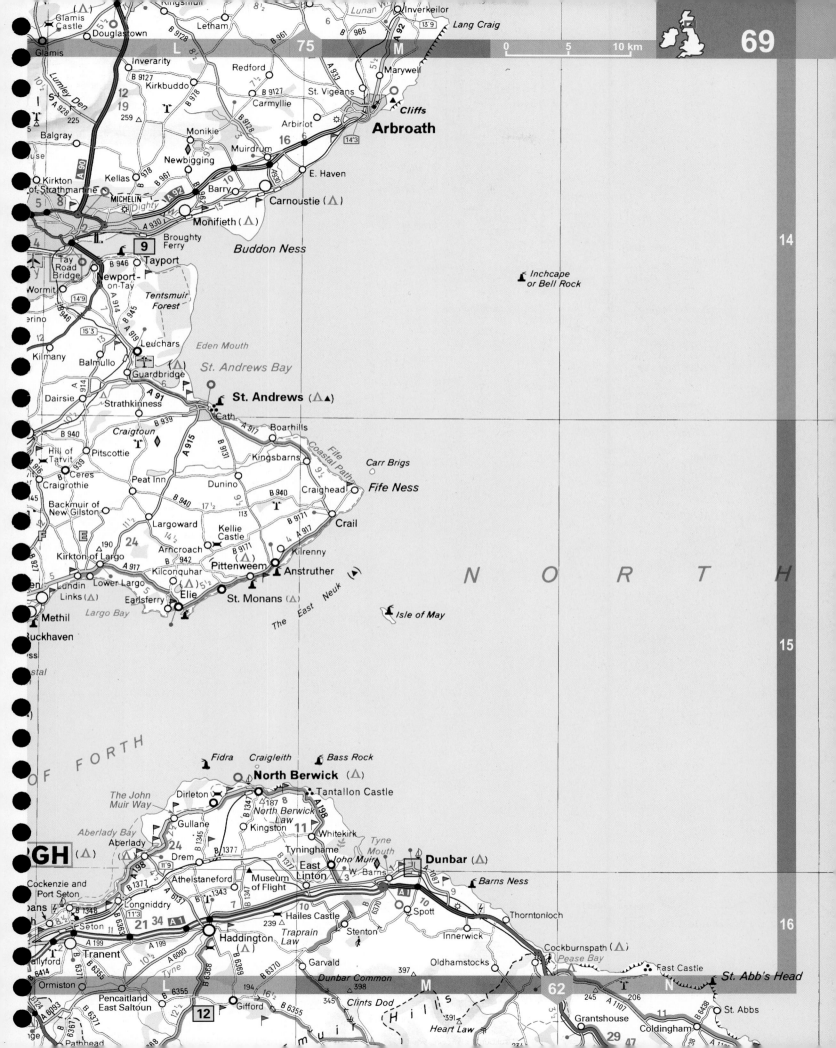

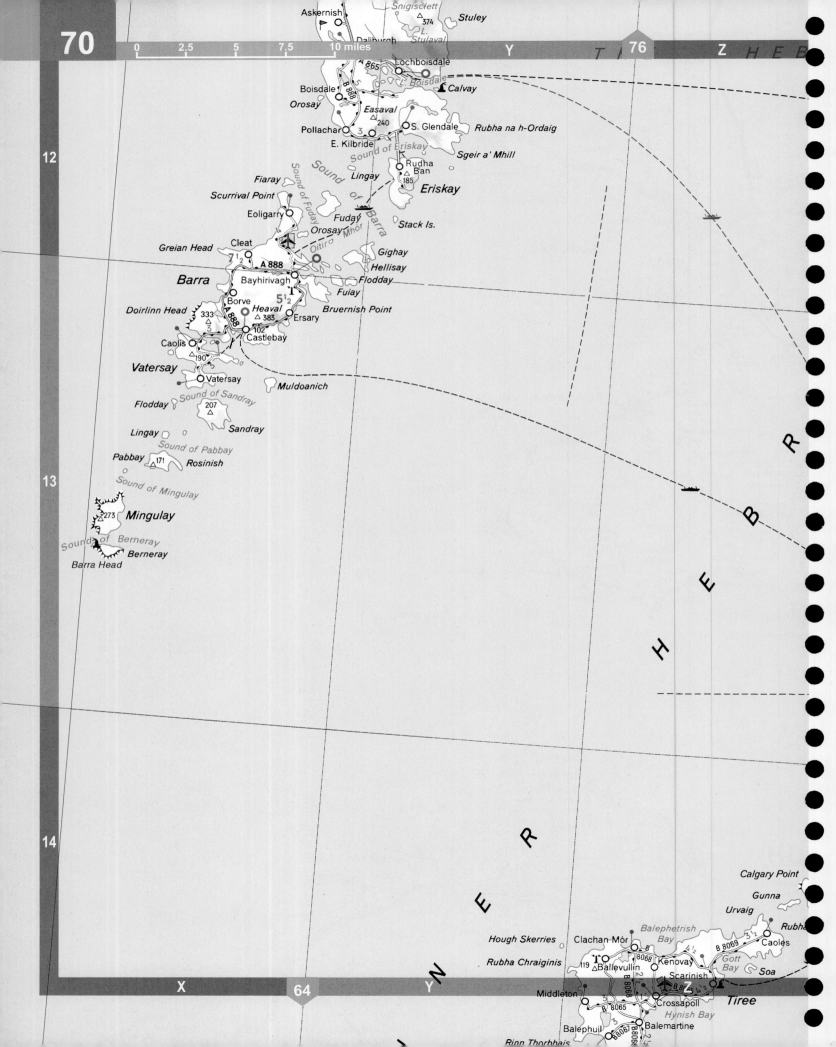

Askernish

Snigisclett

374

Stuley

Daliburgh

L. Stulaval

Y   T I   Z   H E B

Lochboisdale

A 865

Boisdale

B 888

L. Boisdale

Calvay

Orosay

Easaval

240

Pollachar   3   S. Glendale   *Rubha na h-Ordaig*

E. Kilbride

Sgeir a' Mhill

Rudha

Sound of Eriskay

Lingay   Ban

185

12

Fiaray   *Sound of Fuday*

Eriskay

Scurrival Point

Sound of Barra

Eoligarry   Fuday   *Stack Is.*

Orosay Mhór

Cleat   *Oitir*

Greian Head   *Gighay*

7 ½   *Hellisay*

A 888   *Flodday*

Barra   Bayhirivagh   *Fuiay*

5 ½   1

Borve   *Bruernish Point*

Doirlinn Head   *Heaval*   383   Ersary

333   A 888

102 Castlebay

Caolis   190

Vatersay   Vatersay

Flodday   *Sound of Sandray*

207

Lingay   Sandray

Sound of Pabbay

Pabbay   171   *Rosinish*

Sound of Mingulay

13

273   *Mingulay*

Sound of Berneray

Berneray

Barra Head

Muldoanich

R

E   B

H   E

14   *Calgary Point*

N   *Gunna*

E   *Urvaig*

Rubha

R   *Balephetrish*

Bay

Hough Skerries   Clachan-Mòr   Caoles

B   B 8069

Rubha Chraiginis   119   B 8068   *Gott*   Soa

Ballevullin   Kenovay   *Bay*

X   Y   Z   B

64   Middleton   Crossapoll   *Tiree*

B 8065   *Hynish Bay*

Balephuil   Balemartine

Rinn Thorbhais

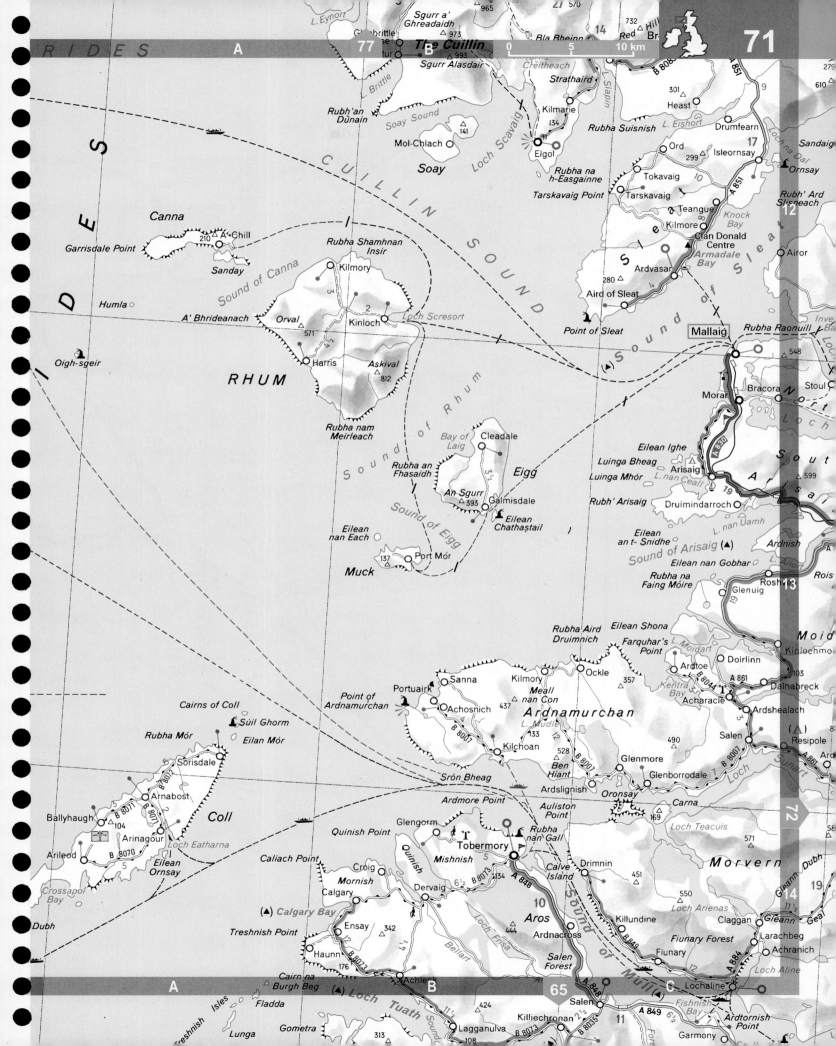

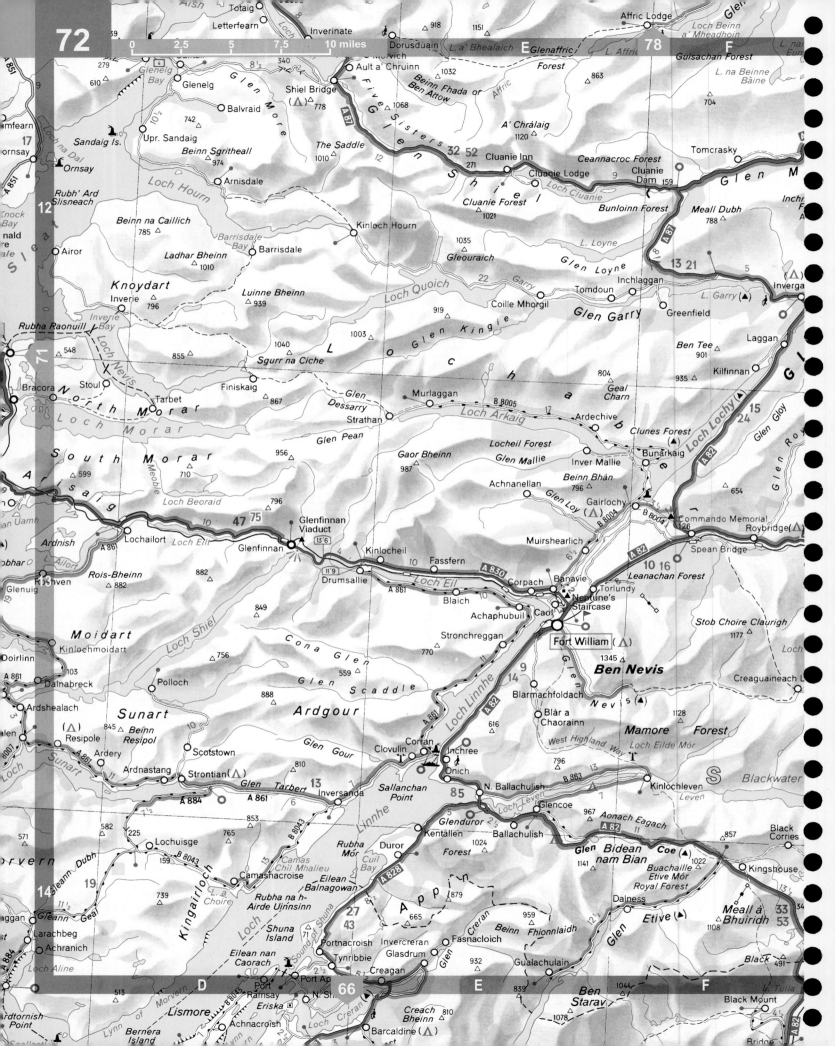

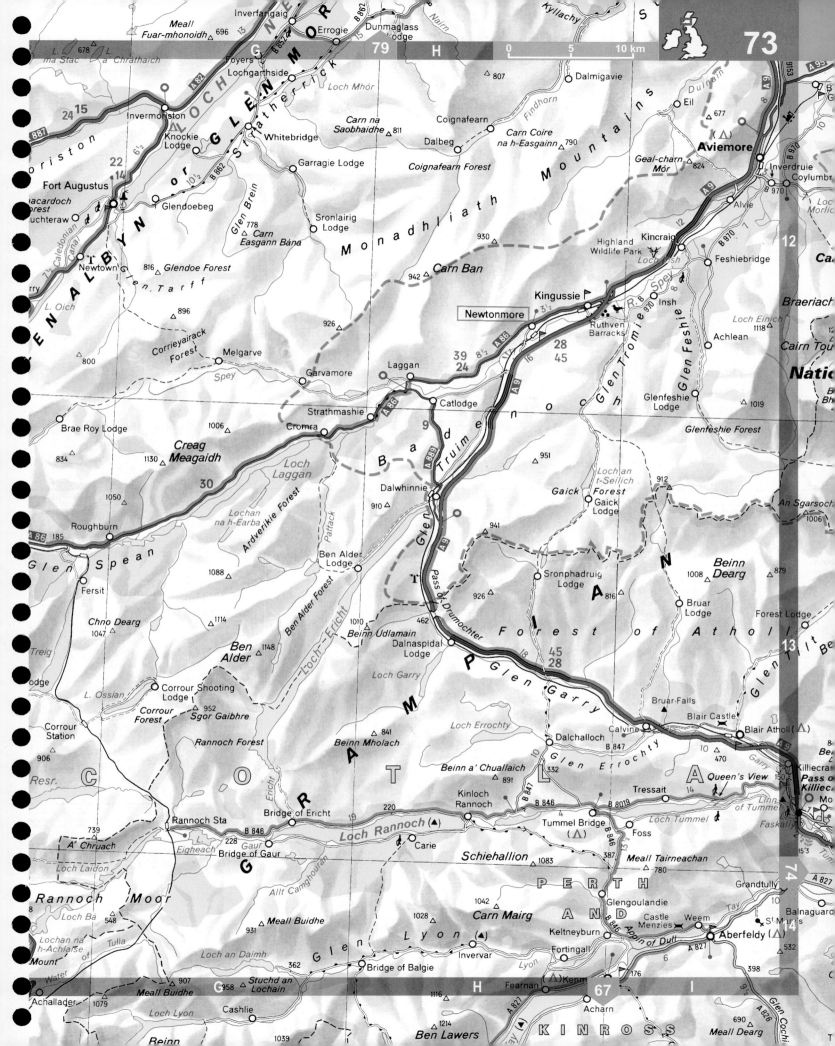

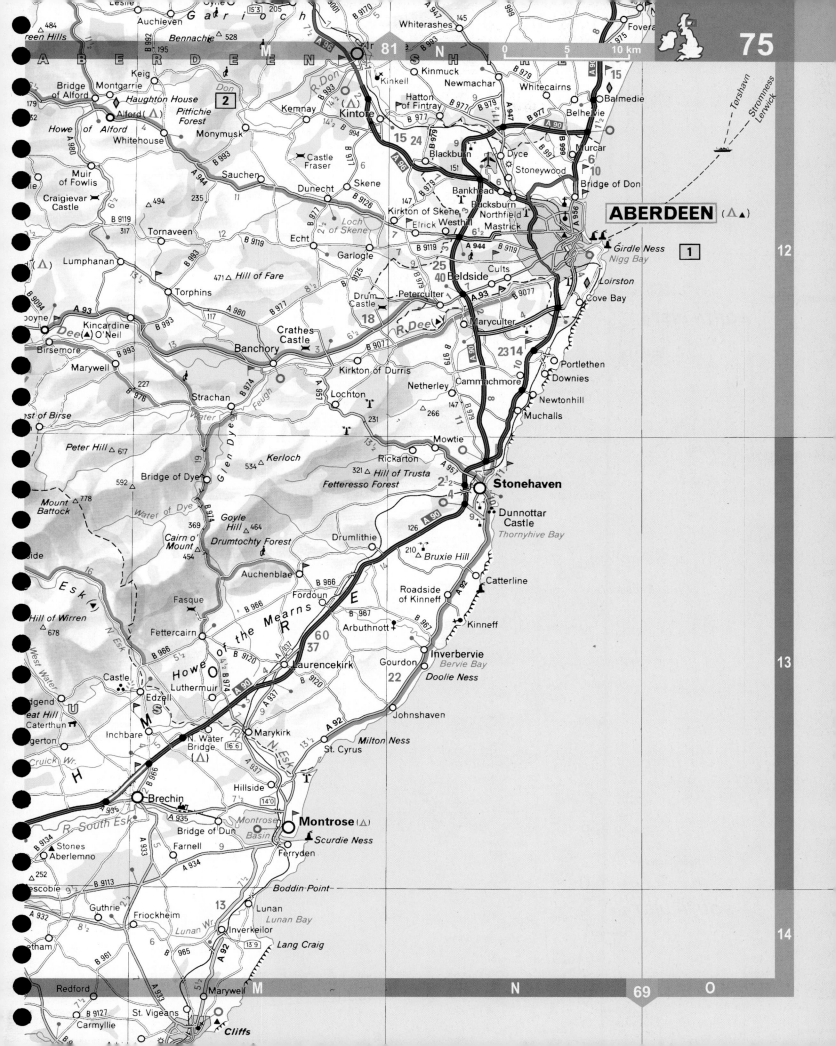

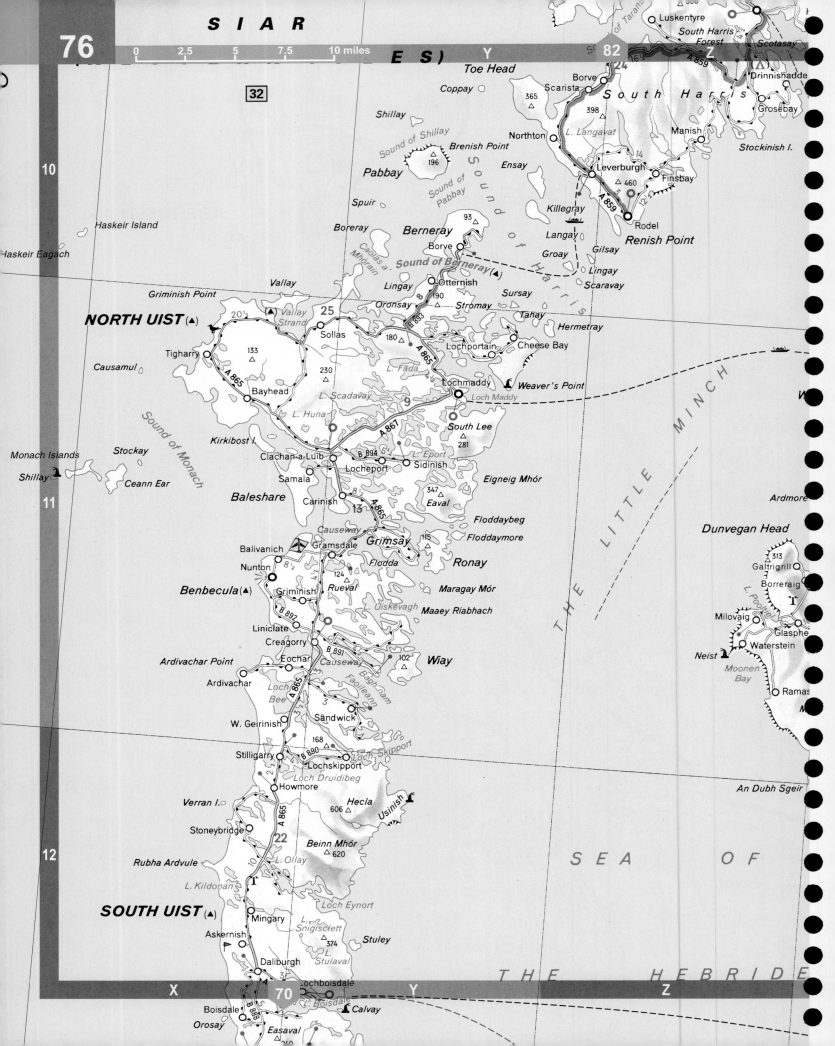

0   2.5   5   7.5   10 miles

32

Luskentyre
South Harris Forest
Scotasay

Toe Head
Drinnishadde
Coppay
Borve
Scarista
365
398
South Harris
Grosebay
Shillay
Northton
L. Langavat
Manish
Pabbay
Leverburgh
Finsbay
Stockinish I.
Sound of Shillay
Brenish Point
460
Spuir
Ensay
A 859
Killegray
Rodel
Boreray
Berneray
93
Langay
Gilsay
Renish Point
Borve
Groay
Lingay
Scaravay
Sound of Berneray
Vallay
Lingay
Otternish
Sursay
Griminish Point
Oronsay
Stromay
Tahay
NORTH UIST
Valley Strand
25
180
Hermetray
Sollas
Tigharry
133
L. Fada
Lochportain
Cheese Bay
Causamul
230
9
Lochmaddy
Bayhead
L. Scadavay
Loch Maddy
Weaver's Point
L. Huna
Kirkibost I.
A 867
South Lee
Monach Islands
Stockay
Clachan-a-Luib
B 894
L. Eport
281
Eigneig Mhór
Shillay
Ceann Ear
Samala
Locheport
Sidinish
Baleshare
Carinish
347
Eaval
Floddaybeg
13
Eaval
Floddaymore
Causeway
115
THE LITTLE MINCH
Balivanich
Gramsdale
Grimsay
Ronay
Dunvegan Head
Nunton
Flodda
313
Benbecula
124
Galtrigrill
Griminish
Rueval
Maragay Mór
Borreraig
B 892
L. Uiskevagh
Maaey Riabhach
Milovaig
Liniclate
Glasphe
Creagorry
B 891
Waterstein
Ardvachar Point
Eochar
Causeway
102
Wiay
Neist
Ardvachar
Loch Bee
Moonen Bay
W. Geirinish
Sandwick
Ramas
168
Loch Skipport
Stilligarry
B 880
An Dubh Sgeir
Lochskipport
Howmore
Loch Druidibeg
SEA   OF
Verran I.
Hecla
Usinish
Stoneybridge
606
22
Rubha Ardvule
Beinn Mhór
L. Ollay
620
L. Kildonan
Loch Eynort
SOUTH UIST
Mingary
L. Snigisclett
Stuley
Askernish
374
L. Stulaval
Daliburgh
THE   HEBRIDE
70
Lochboisdale
X   Y   Z
Boisdale
Calvay
Orosay
Easaval

10

11

12

Haskeir Island
Haskeir Eagach
Sound of Monach

A 865
A 865
A 865
A 865
A 865
A 867
B 893

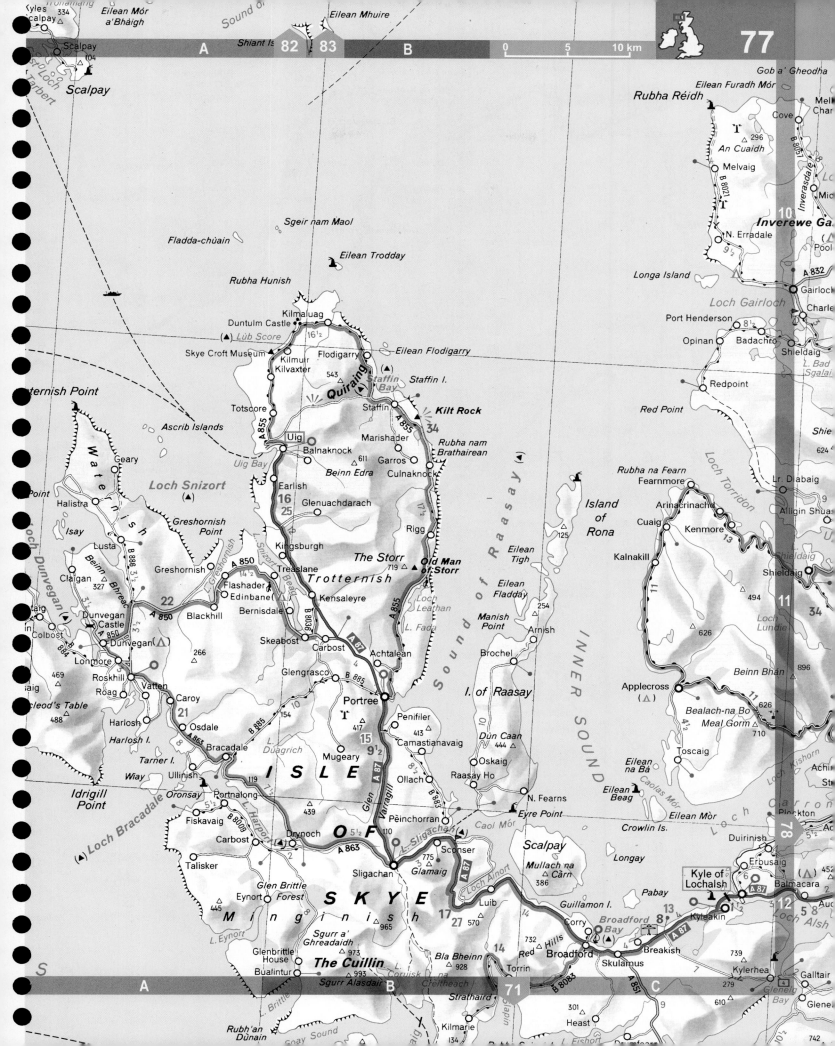

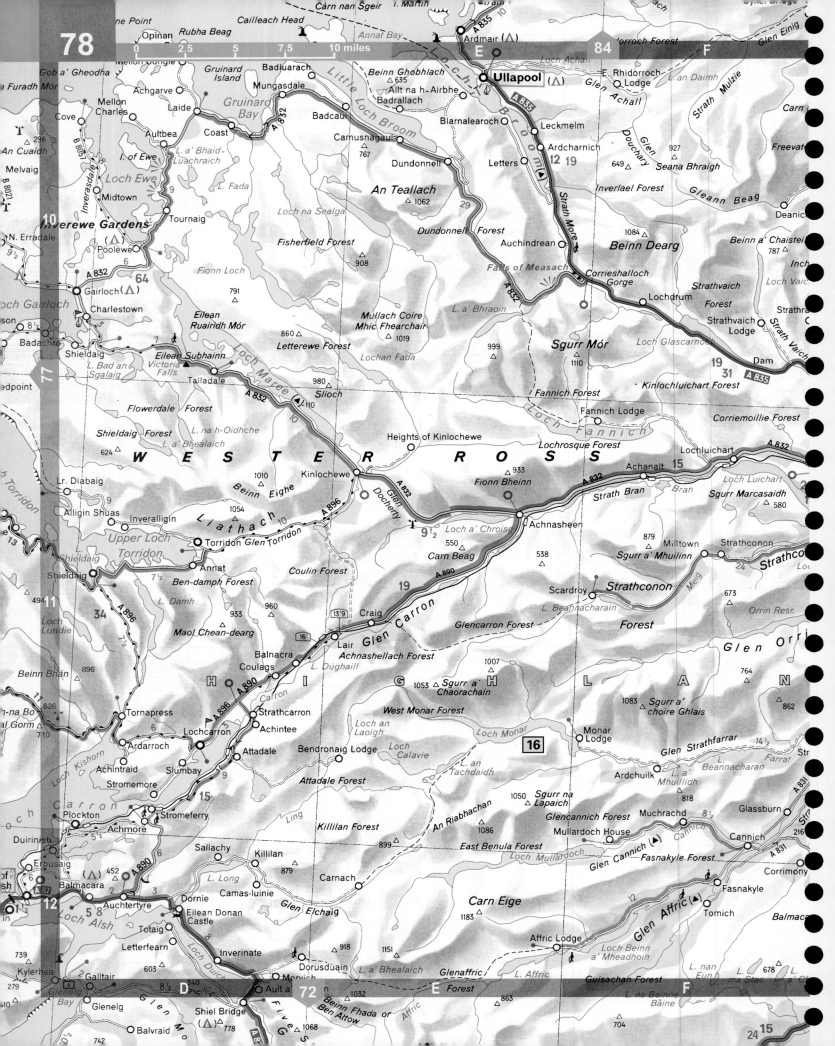

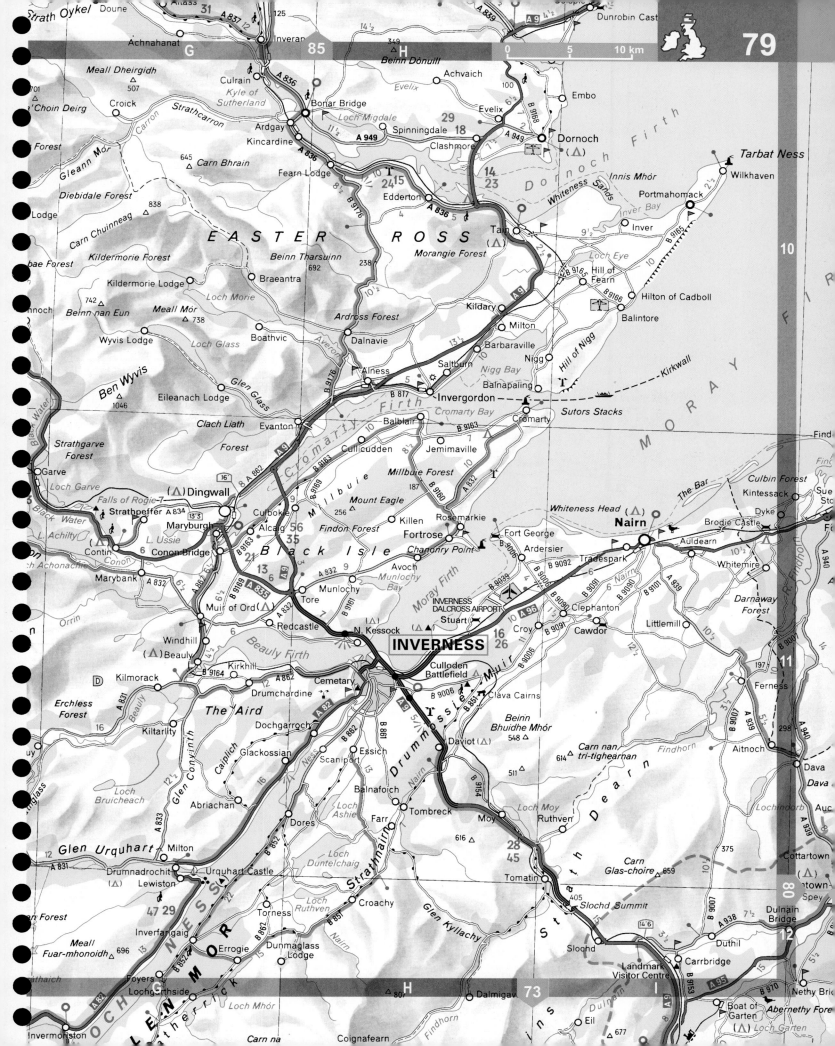

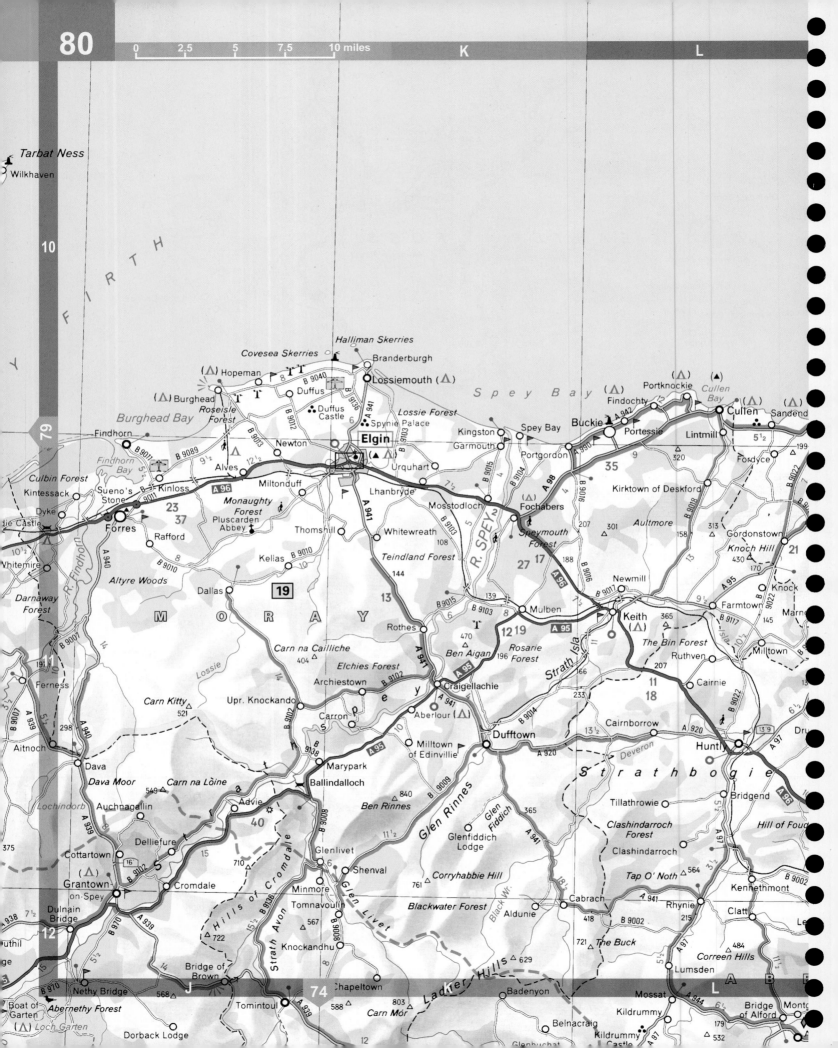

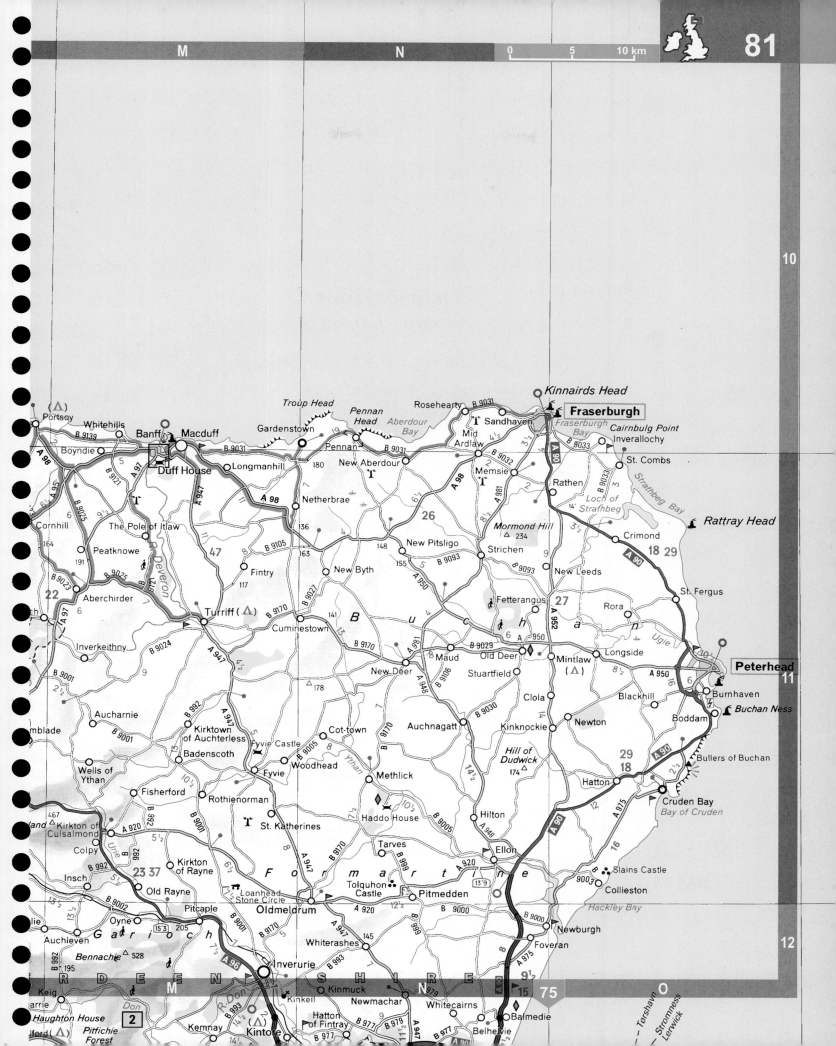

0   2.5   5   7.5   10 miles

Z   A

8

HEBRIDES

ISLE OF LEWIS
AND HARRIS

Galson

A8...

Borve

Shader   150

16

Barvas

Arnol   Co

Bragar   12   *L. Urrahag*   28

50   Shawbost   12

Loch Breivat

Garenin   261   110

Carloway   A 858   12   A 857

Little Bernera   Dun Carloway Broch

Gallan Head   *West Loch Roag*   Tobson   Beinn Mholach   Tong

Aird Uig   Pabay Mór   Tolsta Chaolais   △ 292

Valtos   Breaclete   *L. Laxavat Ard*   Newmarket

205   Miavaig   **Great**   Breasclete

Vuia Mór   **Bernera**   *Eilean*   Callanish   **Stornoway**

Timsgarry   Floday   *Kearstay*   Garynahine

Uig   **Standing Stones**   Crulivig   13½   A 859   B 897

Mangersta   *L.*   *Suainaval*   Enaclete   13   Garynahine   A 858   7

9   *Camas Uig*   B 8011   **LEWIS**   Achmore   112   Leurbost   B 897

Islivig   574   B 8059   *L. nam*   8   L. Grasay

Aird Brenish   △   *L.*   20   *Falcag*   Crossbost   Ranish

Brenish   *Grunavat*   Loch Airigh   *L. Trealaval*   *Barkin Isles*

Mealasta I.   na h-Airde   281   Laxay   Keose   *Eilean Chaluim Chill*

Caolas an Eilein   △   Balallan   *L. Erisort*   Cromore

Kearstay   *L. Tamanavay*   *Morsgail Forest*   *Loch Langavat*   Kershader   *Eilean T*

Braigh Mór   Arivruaich   B 8060   Marvig

Scarp   308   303   *Loch Resort*   *Ulladale*   492   *L. Sgibacleit*   Glenside   14

△   △   36   A 859   Seaforth   Gravir   *L. Odhairn*

Gasker   Hushinish   **Tirga Mór**   Stulaval   217   Head   401   **Park**   B 8060   *Kebo*

Hushinish Point   B 887   △ 679   579   △   17½   **or**   Eishken   Lemreway

Forest of Harris   Ardvourlie   *Seaforth*   572   **Pairc**   *Loch Shell or Loch Seaig*

Amhuinnsuidhe   13   *Island*   *Beinn Mhór*   *Eilean Iubhard*

HARRIS   *Meavaig*   Meavaig   **Clisham**   Maaruig   *Crionaig*   371   *Sound of Shiant*

Taransay Glorigs   *Soay Mór*   **North Harris**   △ 799   467   △

10   *Taransay*   Ardhasaig   *West Loch Tarbert*   Rhenigidale   *Eilean Mór*   *Eilear*

ANAN   267   *Isay*   3   Tarbert   *Lo ch*   *a'Bháigh*   *Shiant Islands*

506   Luskentyre   Kyles   334   △   *East L*

SLES)   *South Harris*   *Scotasay*   Scalpay   104   **Scalpay**

Toe Head   *Forest*   Scalpay

Y   76   Z   Drinnishadder   A

Coppay   Scarista   365   398   S o u t h   H a r r i s   Grosebay

Shillay

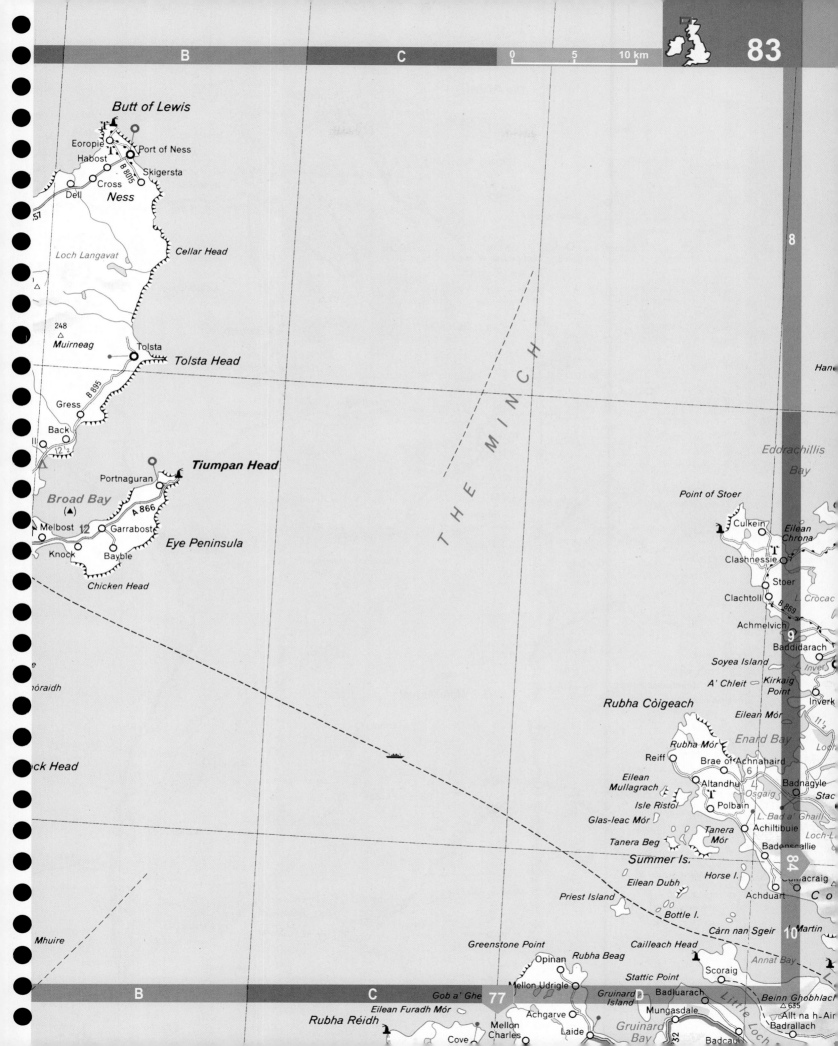

8

Butt of Lewis

Eoropie
Habost
Port of Ness
Cross
Skigersta
Dell
Ness

Loch Langavat

Cellar Head

248
Muirneag
Tolsta
Tolsta Head

B 895

Gress

Back

Tiumpan Head

Portnaguran

Broad Bay
(▲)

Melbost
Garrabost
12
A 866

Knock
Bayble
Eye Peninsula

Chicken Head

THE MINCH

Eddrachillis
Bay

Point of Stoer

Culkein
Eilean
Chrona

Clashnessie
Stoer

Clachtoll
B 869
L. Crocac

Achmelvich
9
Baddidarach

Soyea Island

A' Chleit
Kirkaig
Point
Inverk
Rubha Còigeach

Eilean Mór
Enard Bay
Rubha Mór

Reiff
Brae of Achnahaird
6
Eilean
Mullagrach
Altandhu
L.
Osgaig
Badnagyle
Isle Ristol
Polbain
Stac
Glas-leac Mór
L. Bad a' Ghaill
Achiltibuie
Loch L
Tanera
Mór
Badenscallie
Tanera Beg
Summer Is.

Horse I.
84
Eilean Dubh
Cumacraig
Priest Island
Achduart
Co
Bottle I.

Càrn nan Sgeir
10
Martin

Greenstone Point
Cailleach Head
Annat Bay

Opinan
Rubha Beag
Scoraig

Mellon Udrigle
Stattic Point
Badluarach
Beinn Ghobhlach

Gob a' Ghe
77
Gruinard
Island
Mungasdale
Badrallach
635

Eilean Furadh Mór
Achgarve
Laide
Allt na h-Ain
Rubha Réidh
Mellon
Charles
Gruinard
Bay
32
Badcaul
Cove

Mhuire
Mhoraidh
ck Head

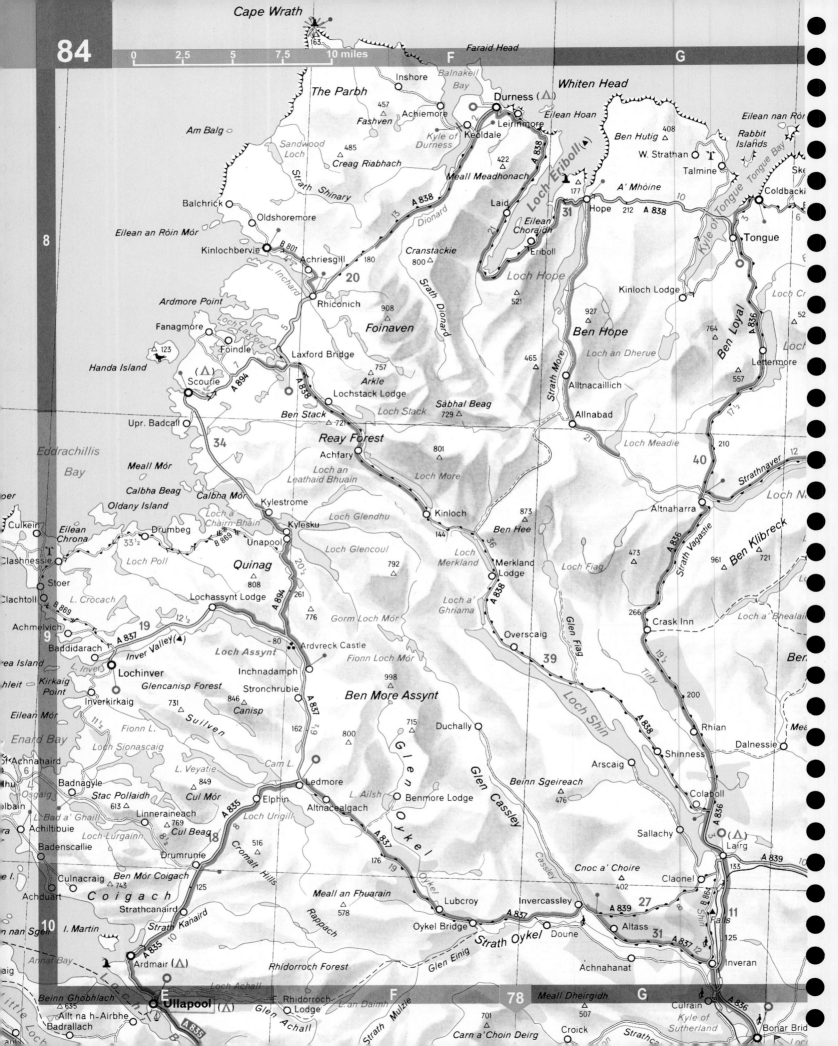

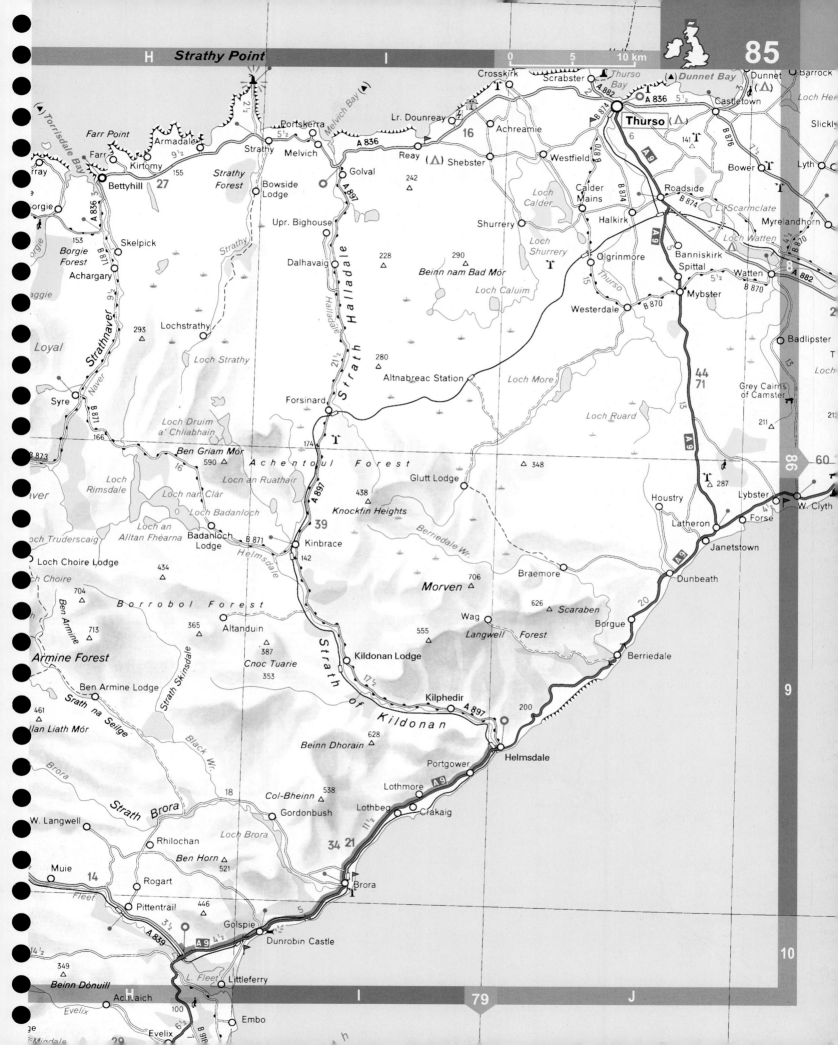

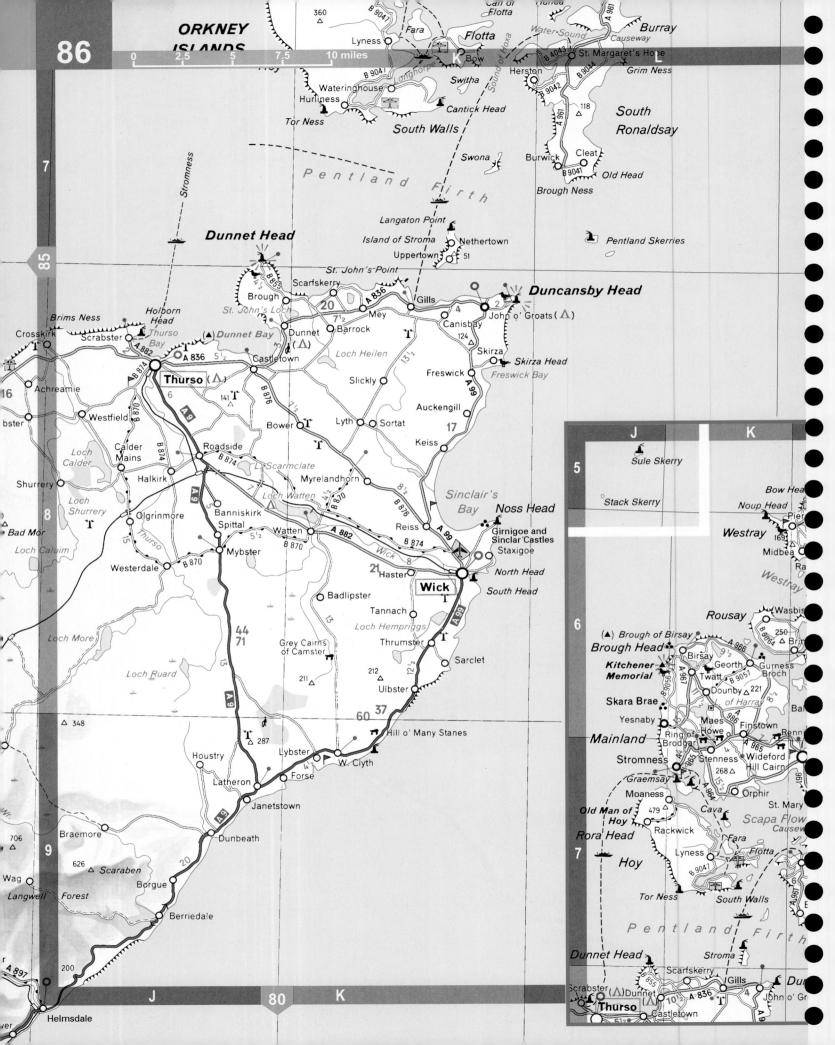

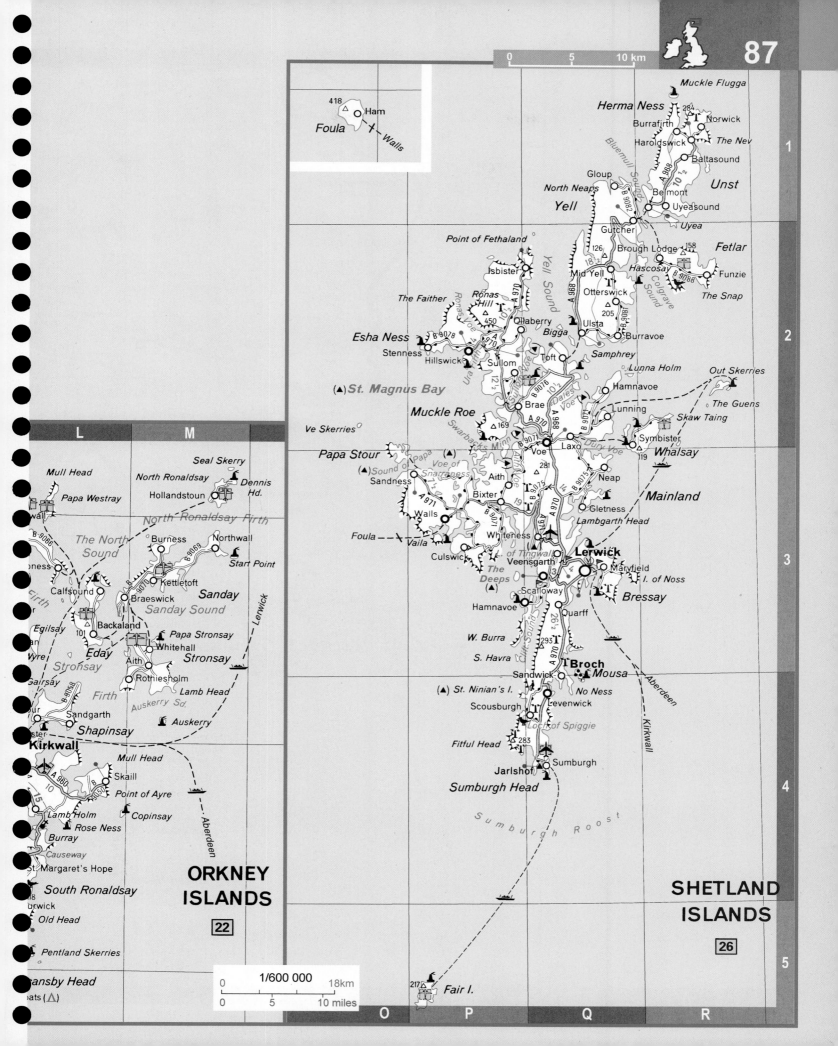

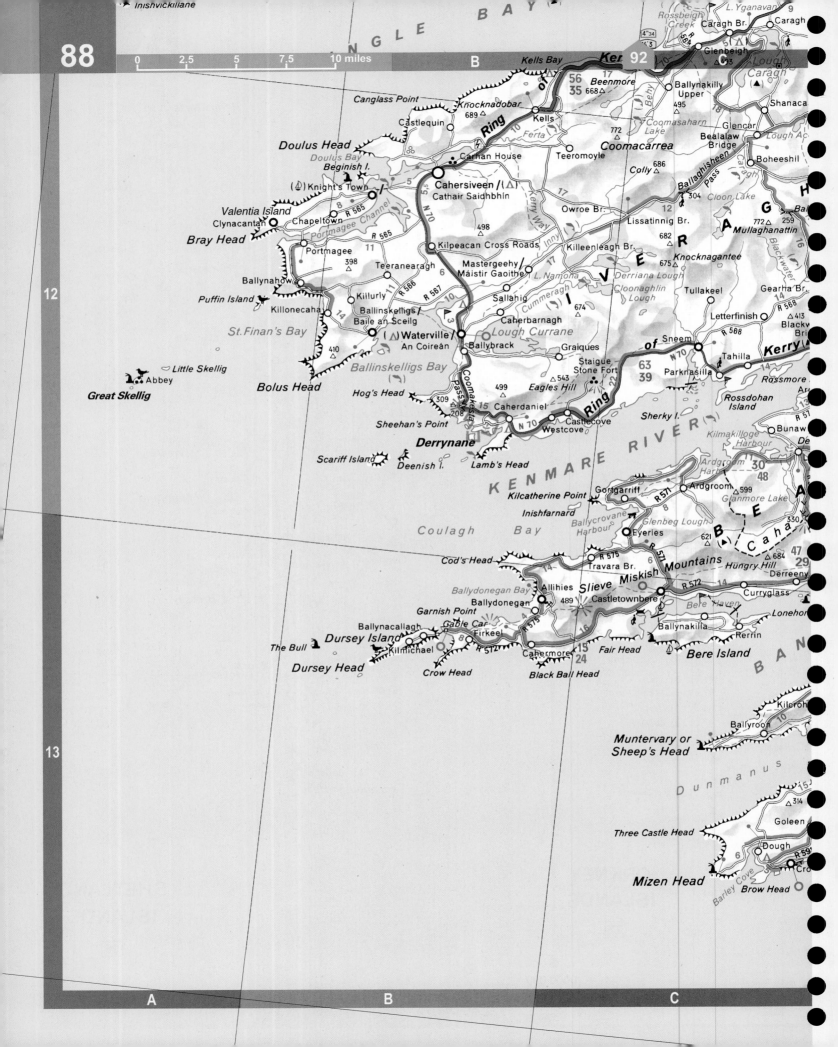

INGLE BAY

Inishvickillane

Kells Bay

Rossbeigh Creek
Caragh Br.   Caragh
L. Yganavan   9
Glenbeigh   564
Caragh (Lough)
Shanaca

0   2.5   5   7.5   10 miles

Canglass Point

Knocknadobar
689

56
35   668   Beenmore
Ballynakilly Upper
495   Ballynakilla Lower
772   Coomasaharn Lake
18
Glencar
Lough Ac
Boheeshil

Castlequin
Carhan House
Teeromoyle
686   Colly
Coomacarrea
Bealalaw Bridge

Doulus Head
Doulus Bay
Beginish I.
Knight's Town
Valentia Island
Clynacantan
Bray Head
Chapeltown
R 565
Portmagee Channel
Cahersiveen
Cathair Saidhbhín
498
Owroe Br.
Lissatinnig Br.
682
304
Cloon Lake
Kerry Way
Ferta
17
12
KE
VERAG
772   259
Mullaghanattin
Blackwater

12

Portmagee
398
Teeranearagh
R 565
R 566
R 567
11
6
Killurly
Ballinskelligs / Baile an Sceilg
Kilpeacan Cross Roads
Inny
Mastergeehy / Máistir Gaoithe
Killeenleagh Br.
675   Knocknagantee
Tullakeel
17
Letterfinish
R 568
413
Blackw
Bri

Ballynahow
Puffin Island
Killonecaha
14
L. Namona
Sallahig
Caherbarnagh
674   Derriana Lough
Cloonaghlin Lough
Cummeragh
IVERAG

St.Finan's Bay
Waterville / An Coireán
Lough Currane
Ballybrack
Graigues
Sneem
R 568
Kerry
N 70
Tahilla
Rossmore
Ar

Little Skellig
Abbey
Great Skellig
Bolus Head
Hog's Head
309
208
15
Caherdaniel
Caherdaniel
Staigue Stone Fort
499   543   Eagles Hill
63
39
Parknasilla
Ring of
Rossdohan Island
R 57

Sheehan's Point
Coomakesta Pass
N 70
Castlecove
Westcove
Sherky I.
Kilmakilloge Harbour
Bunaw
De

Derrynane
Scariff Island
Deenish I.
Lamb's Head
KENMARE RIVER
Kilcatherine Point
Gortgarriff
R 571
Ardgroom Harb.
Ardgroom
599
Glanmore Lake
30
48

Inishfarnard
Ballycrovane Harbour
Coulagh   Bay
Eyeries
621
684
47
29
BE
B
Caha
330

Cod's Head
Travara Br.
R 575
6   571
Slieve Miskish Mountains
Hungry Hill
R 572
14
Derreeny

13

Ballydonegan Bay
Allihies
489
Castletownbere
Bere Haven
Curryglass
Lonehor

Garnish Point
Gable Car
Ballynacallagh
Ballydonegan
R 575
R 572
16
Ballynakilla
Rerrin
Bere Island

The Bull
Dursey Island
Firkeel
R 572
Cahermore
15
24
Fair Head
BAN

Kilmichael
Dursey Head
Crow Head
Black Ball Head

Kilcroh
Ballyroon
10

Muntervary or Sheep's Head

Dunmanus

314
15
Goleen

Three Castle Head
6
Dough
589

Mizen Head
Barley Cove
Brow Head
Cro

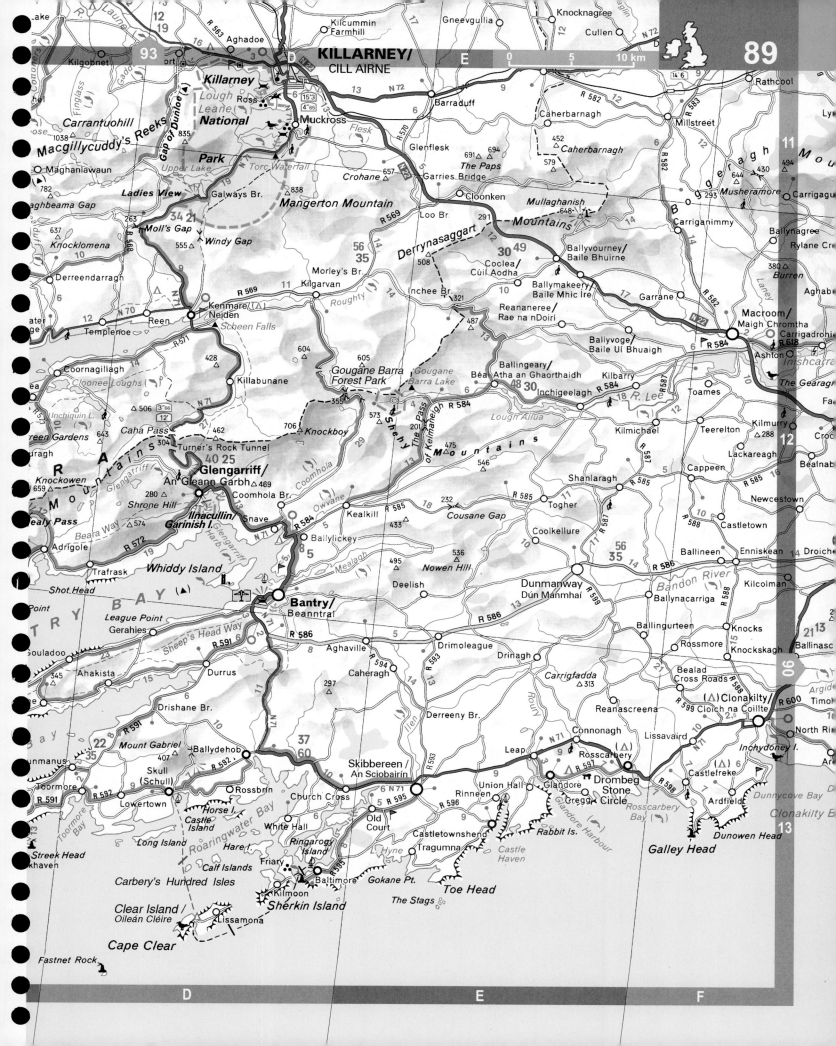

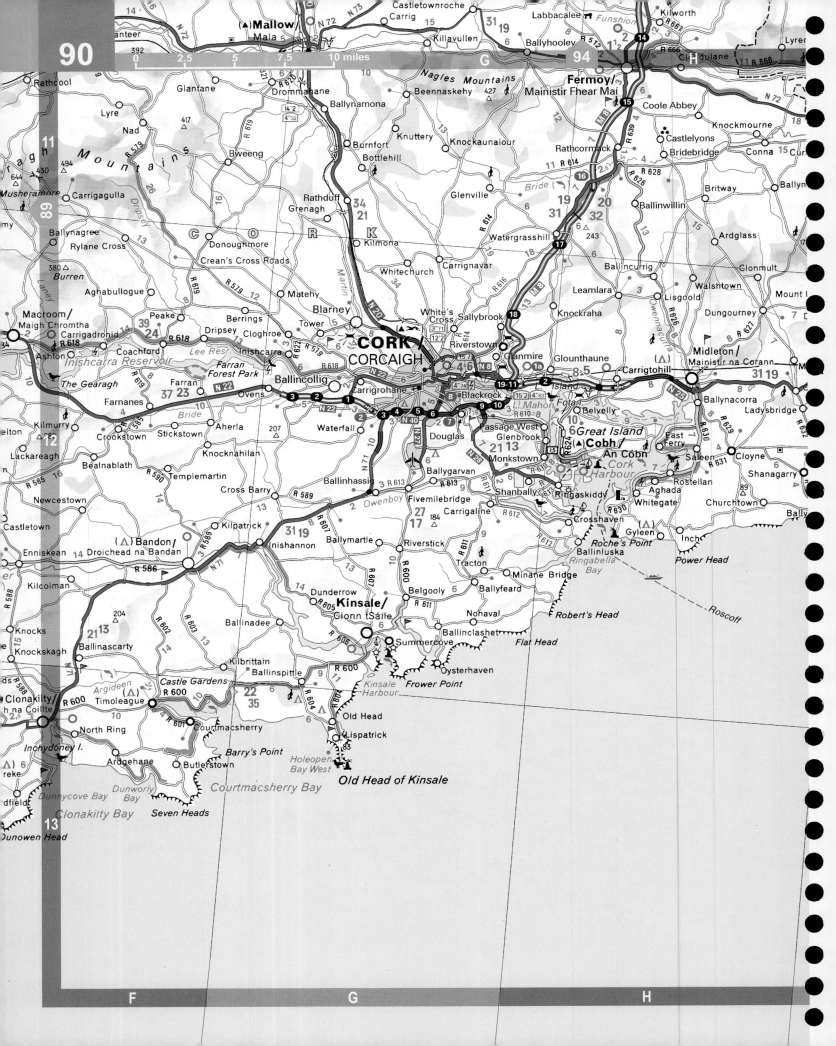

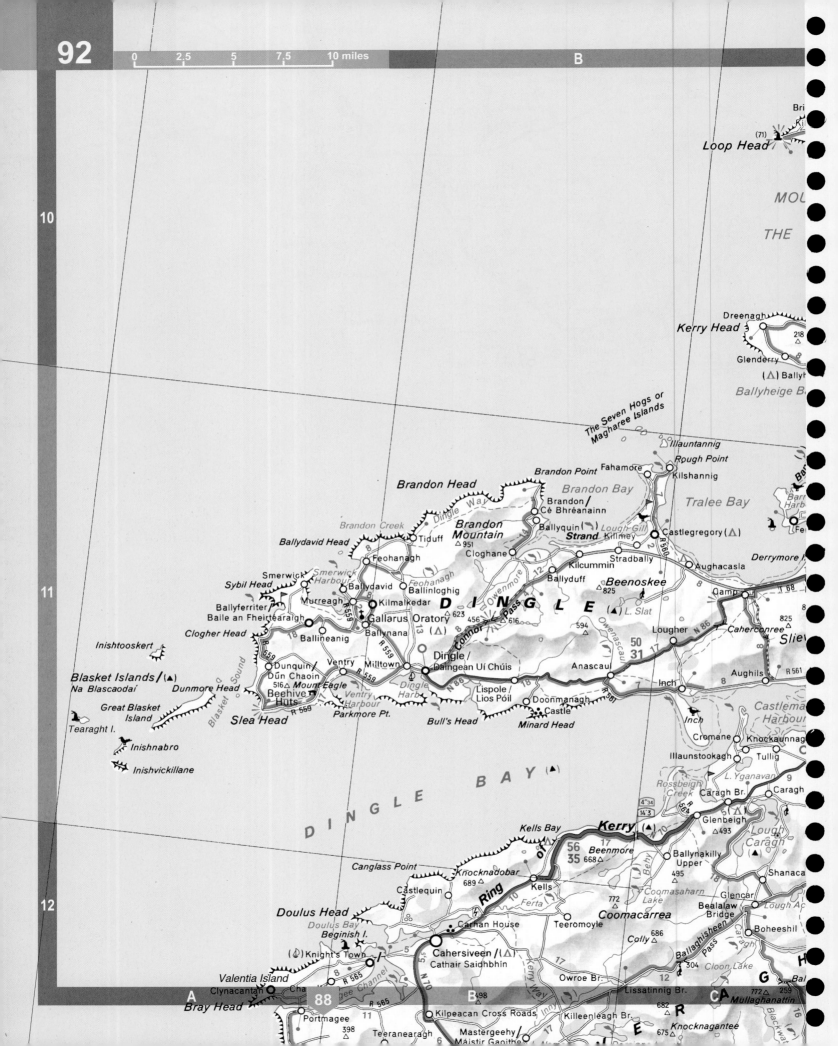

0   2.5   5   7.5   10 miles

B

Loop Head (71)

Bri

MO

THE

Dreenagh

Kerry Head

218

Glenderry

(△) Bally

Ballyheige B.

The Seven Hogs or Magharee Islands

Illauntannig

Brandon Head

Brandon Point   Fahamore

Rough Point

Kilshannig

Barr

Brandon Bay

Tralee Bay

Barr Harb

Dingle Way

Brandon / Cé Bhréanainn

Ballyquin ( ) *Lough Gill*

Castlegregory (△)

Fe

Brandon Creek

Brandon Mountain

△ 951

Ballyquin ( )   **Strand** Killmey

R 560

Ballydavid Head

Tiduff

Cloghane

Killmey

2

△

Stradbally

Derrymore I.

Feohanagh

Kilcummin

Aughacasla

8

Smerwick

Smerwick Harbour

Ballydavid

Feohanagh

Ballyduff

Beenoskee

△ 825

Camp

T 68

Sybil Head

Ballinloghig

D I N G L E

(▲) *L. Slat*

Ballyferriter

Murreagh

Kilmalkedar

△ 623

456 △

616

594

Lougher   N 86

Caherconree

825

Baile an Fheirtearaigh

Gallarus Oratory (△)

13

8

Connor Pass

50

31 17

△

Slie

Clogher Head

Ballineanig

Ballynana

R 559

Dingle / Daingean Uí Chúis

Owenascaul

Aughils   R 561

18

R 559

Inishtooskert

Ventry

Milltown   R 559

Anascaul

7

Inch

8

Blasket Islands / (▲)

Na Blascaodaí

Dunquin / Dún Chaoin

516 △ *Mount Eagle*

Beehive Huts

R 559

Ventry Harbour

Lispole / Lios Póil

18

Dunmore Head

Inch

Castlemai Harbour

Great Blasket Island

Blasket Sound

Doonmanagh

Castle

Tearaght I.

Slea Head

Parkmore Pt.

Bull's Head

Minard Head

Cromane

Knockaunnag

Inishnabro

Illaunstookagh

Tullig

C

Inishvickillane

D I N G L E   B A Y (▲)

Rossbeigh Creek

L. Yganavan

9

Caragh Br.

Caragh

4°34

14·3

Kerry (▲)

Glenbeigh

△ 493

Lough Caragh

Kells Bay

56

35   **Beenmore**

668 △

17

Ballynakilly Upper

495

Shanaca

Canglass Point

Knocknadobar

689 △

Kells

10

Coomasaharn Lake

772

Glencar

Lough Ac

Doulus Head

Ferta

Coomacarrea

Bealalaw Bridge

18

Doulus Bay

Carhan House

Teeromoyle

△

Beginish I.

Colly

686

Ballaghisheen Pass

Boheeshil

( ) Knight's Town

5

Cahersiveen / (△)

Cathair Saidhbhín

Kerry Way

304

Cloon Lake

G

5·5

H

Valentia Island

R 565

Channel

Owroe Br.

12

Lissatinnig Br.

772   259

Clynacantan

Cha

B 498

CA

Mullaghanattin

Bray Head

R 565

N 710

Inny

682

Blackwa

Portmagee

11

Kilpeacan Cross Roads

Killeenleagh Br.

Knocknagantee

398

Mastergeehy /

675 △

Máistir Gaoithe

Teeranearagh

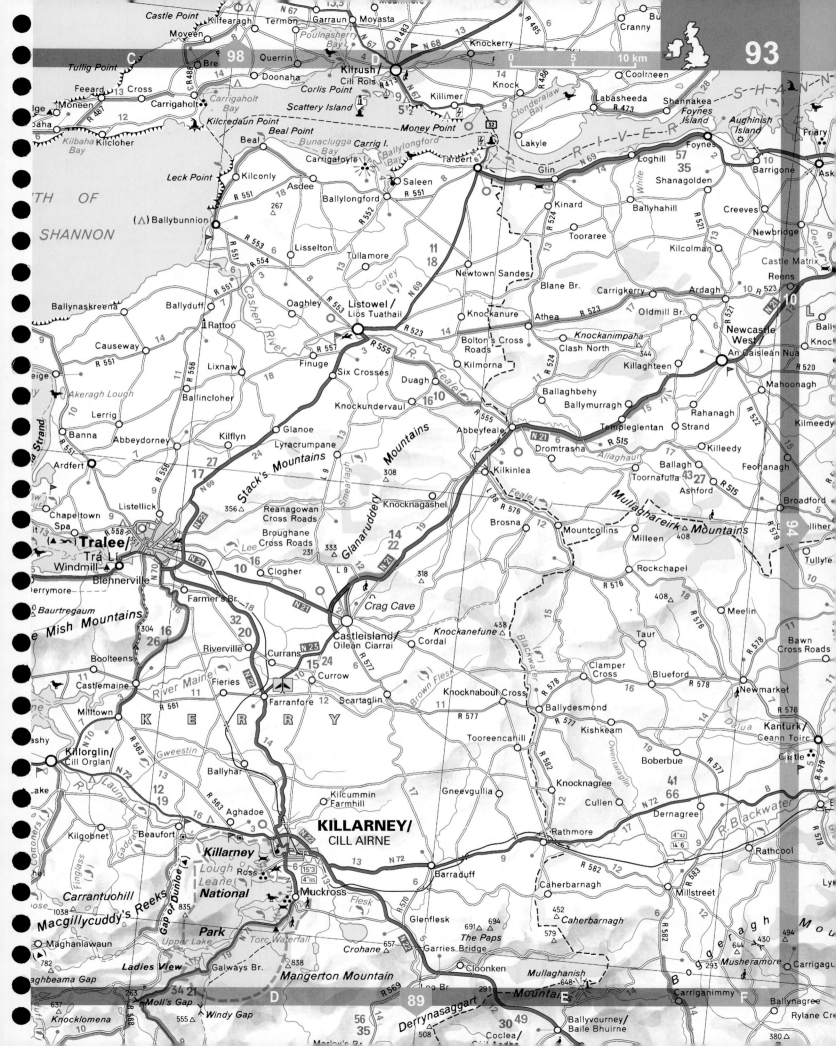

SHANNON AIRPORT
Folk Park
Cratloe Woodcock Hill
Shannon
Rineanna Point
Bunratty
LIMERICK/ LUIMN 100 H
G
Cloonlara
Castleconnell
Newport
Toor
Slie

S H A N N O N
Shannakea Foynes Island
Aughinish Island
Ballysteen
Creggaun
Coonagh
Parteen
Lisnagry
Clare Glens
Slievefelim Mountains
Murroe
Clonteen
Cappamore

Foynes
Pallaskenry
Bleach Lake
Dromore Lake
Mungret
Friary
Kilcornan
New Kildimo
Clarina
Bohereen
Barringtonsbridge
Abington
Brittas

Shanagolden
Barrigone
Askeaton
Old Kildimo
Ferry Bridge
Ballyneety
Caherconlish
Kilmurry

Creeves
Cappagh
Ballinagarrane
Adare
Patrickswell
Crecora
Fedamore
Ballybrood
Dromkeen
Pallas Green
Cloonlusk

Newbridge
Castle Matrix
Croagh
Croom
Monaster
Monasteranenagh Abbey
Interpretive Centre
Pallasgreen
Oola

Kilcolman
Reens
Rathkeale/ Ráth Caola
Kilfinny
L I M E R I C K
Meanus
Holycross
Lough Gur
Herbertstown
Kilteely
Cullen
Monard

Newcastle West/ An Caislean Nua
Ballyallinan
Knockaderry
Ballingarry
Morenane
Bruff
Knockainy
Knockaunavoher
Emly
Lattin
Tipp Tiob

Mahoonagh
Cloncagh
Corronoher
Ballinleeny
Athlacca
Newtown
R 515
Hospital

Rahanagh
Strand
Kilmeedy
Castletown
Killacolla
Rockhill
Dromin
Bulgaden
Elton
Knocklong
Kilross

Killeedy
Ballagh
Feohanagh
Ballyagran
Garryfine
Bruree
Kilmallock/ Cill Mocheallóg
Garryspillane
Galbally
Lisvarrinane
New

Ashford
Feenagh
Martinstown
Glenbrohane
Ballylanders
Barna

Mountains
Broadford
Newtownshandrum
Charleville/ An Ráth
Blackpool
Kilfinnane
Cullane
Anglesborough

Dromcolliher
Milford
R 515
Ardpatrick
784

Tullylease
Dromina
Ballyhaght
Ballyorgan
Kilbeheny

Meelin
Freemount
Newtown
B a l l y h o u r a   M o u n t a i n s
Knockanevin
Killaclug
Mitchelstown/ Baile Mhistéala

Liscarroll
Castle
Churchtown
Farahy
Kildorrery
Kilworth
Moun

Bawn Cross Roads
Buttevant
Friary
Rockmills
Glanworth

Blueford
Newmarket
Kilbrin
Doneraile
Shanballymore
Castletownroche
Kilworth

Boberbue
Kanturk/ Ceann Toirc
Castlecor
Old Twopothouse
New Twopothouse Village
Carrig
Labbacallee
Kilworth

Castle
Ballyclogh
Cecilstown
Annes Grove Gardens
Glanworth
Clondulan

Dernagree
Banteer
R. Blackwater
Mallow/ Mala
N 72
Castletownroche
Killavullen
Ballyhooley
Kilavullen

Rathcool
Lombardstown
Glantane
Drommahane
Nagles Mountains
Fermoy/ Mainistir Fhear Mai

Lyre
Nad
Ballynamona
Beennaskehy
Coole Abbey
Castlelyons
Bridebridge

Millstreet
Boggeragh Mountains
Musheramore
Carrigagulla
Bweeng
Burnfort
Bottlehill
Knuttery
Knockaunalour
Rathcormack
Glenville
Bride

Carriganimmy
Ballynagree
F   C O R K   G
Rylane Cross
Donoughmore
Creans Cross Roads
Rathduff
Grenagh
Watergrasshill
Whitechurch
Carrignavar
Ballincurrig
Britv

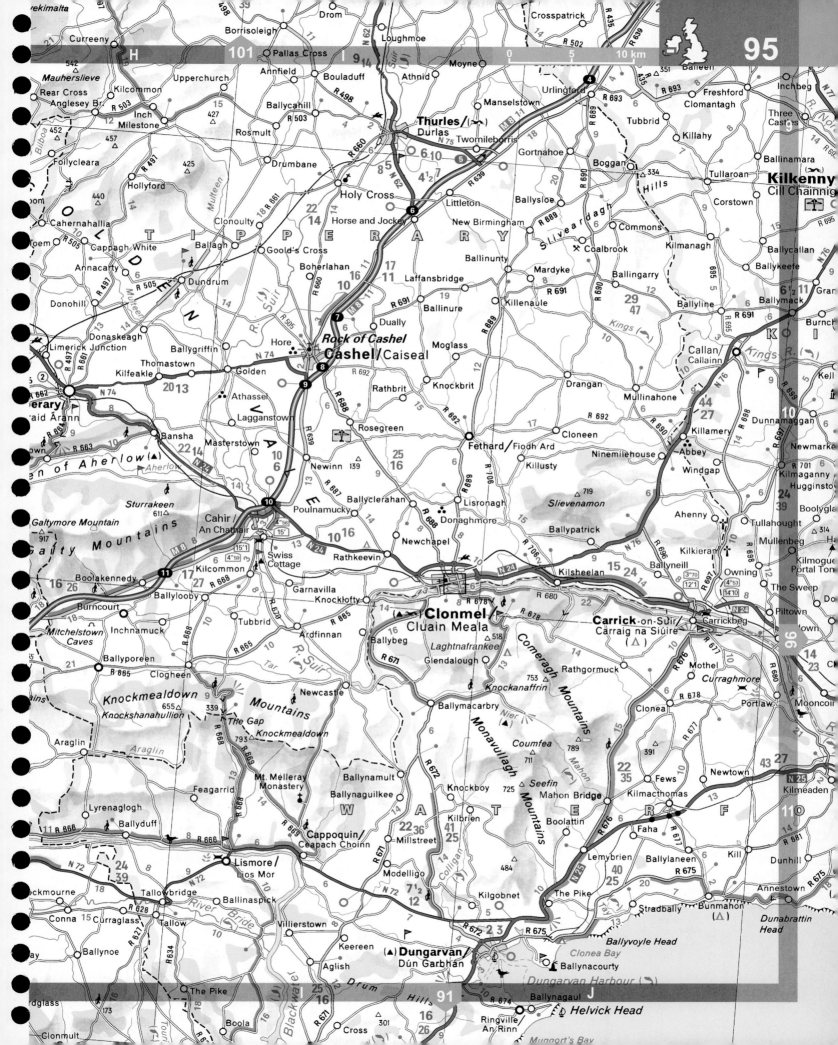

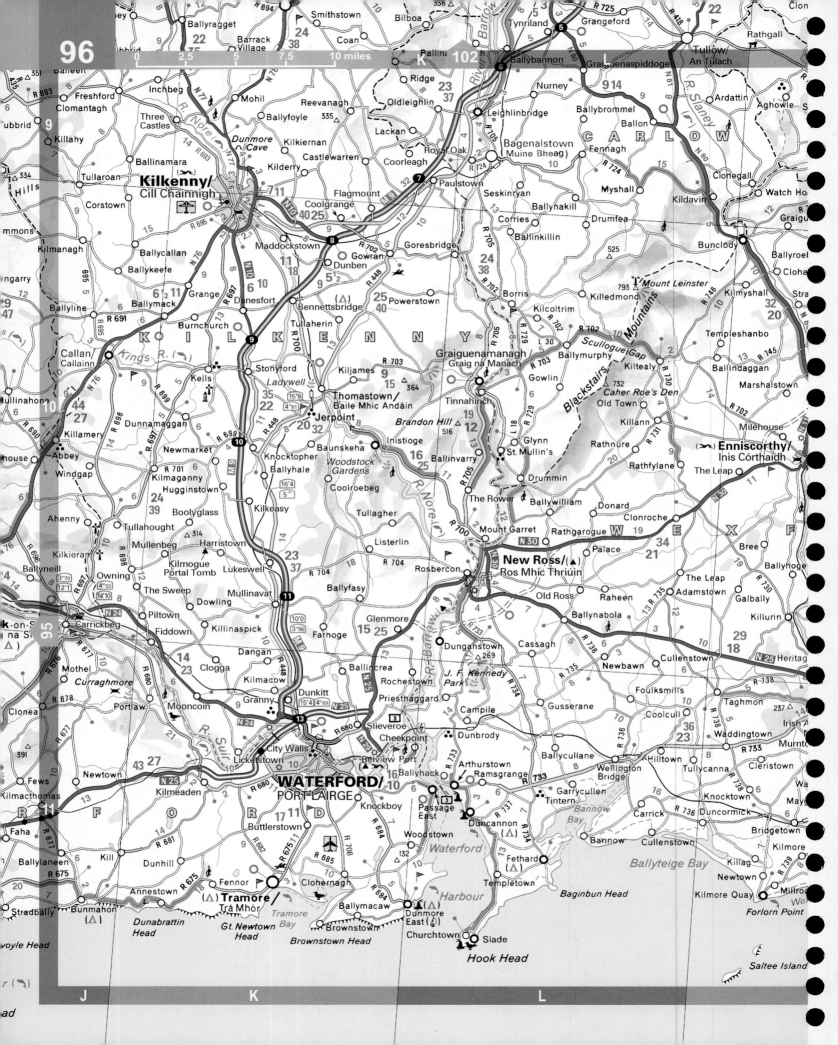

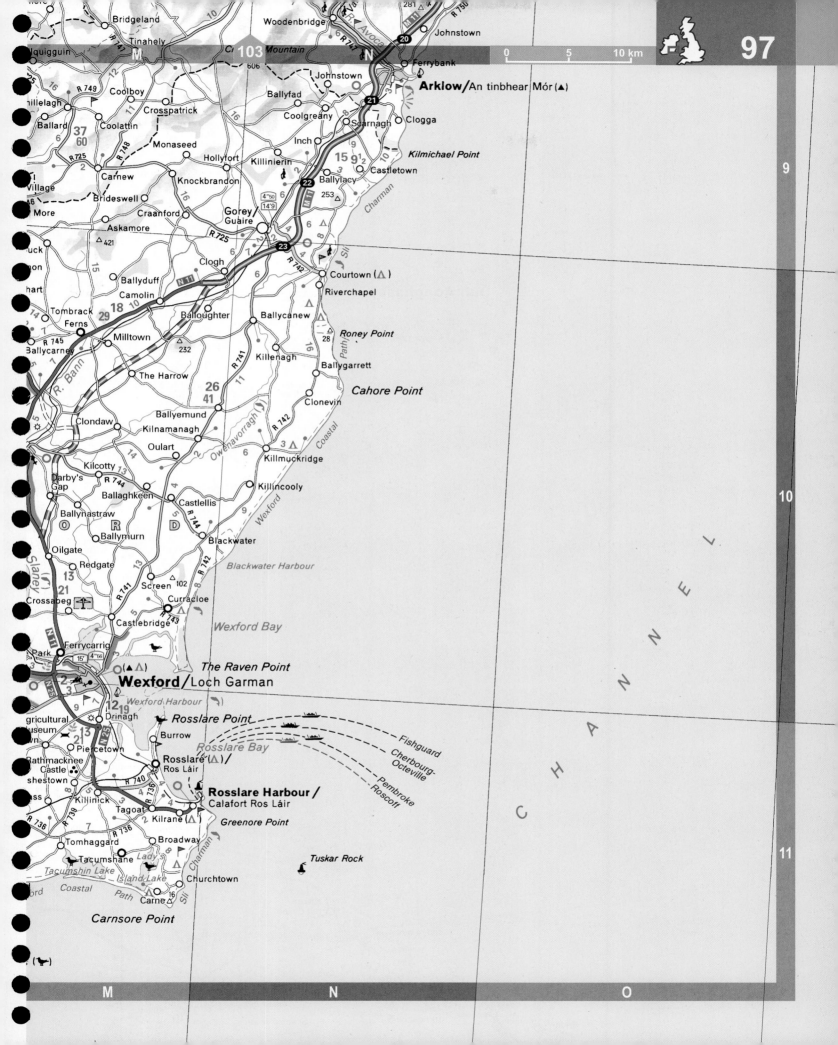

Bridgeland
Woodenbridge
Johnstown
Tinahely
R 750
M 11
20
Crı 103 Mountain
Ferrybank
0   5   10 km
lquigguin
R 747
606
Johnstown
Arklow/An tinbhear Mór (▲)
25
Coolboy
R 749
Ballyfad
21
9
Ballard
Crosspatrick
Coolgreany
Scarnagh
Clogga
Coolattin
16
Inch
Kilmichael Point
37
60
Monaseed
Hollyfort
Killinierin
15 9
Castletown
Village
Carnew
R 725
Knockbrandon
22
Ballylacy
46
Brideswell
R 748
4 50
253
Charman
More
Craanford
14 9
Gorey/
Guaire
253
R 741
9
Askamore
R 725
△ 421
6
23
Clogh
R 742
Courtown (△)
Ballyduff
N 11
6
Riverchapel
Camolin
Balloughter
Ballycanew
14
Tombrack
18 10
Roney Point
Ferns
29
△ 232
28
Milltown
Killenagh
Ballygarrett
Ballycarney
R 745
The Harrow
26
41
Cahore Point
R. Bann
Ballyemund
Owenavorragh
Clonevin
Clondaw
Kilnamanagh
542
Oulart
6
3
Kilcotty
14
Killmuckridge
Darby's
Gap
R 744
Killincooly
Ballaghkeen
Castlellis
Ballynastraw
R 744
9
Wexford
O R D
Ballymurn
Blackwater
Oilgate
Blackwater Harbour
Redgate
13
Slaney
13
R 741
Screen
102
Curracloe
21
R 743
Crossabeg
Castlebridge
N 11
Wexford Bay
Ferrycarrig
15 4 56
Park
The Raven Point
(▲△)
2
Wexford/Loch Garman
3
N 25
9
Wexford Harbour
agricultural
museum
12 19
Drinagh
Rosslare Point
own
Burrow
Fishguard
Piercetown
Rosslare Bay
Cherbourg-
Octeville
Rathmacknee
Castle
Rosslare (△)/
Ros Láir
shestown
R 740
Pembroke
ass
Rosslare Harbour/
Killinick
R 736
Calafort Ros Láir
Roscoff
R 739
Tagoat
4
Greenore Point
R 736
7
Kilrane (△)
Tomhaggard
Broadway
Tuskar Rock
Tacumshane
Lady
△
Tacumshin Lake
Island Lake
Churchtown
ord *Coastal Path*
Carne
Charman
Sil
Carnsore Point

C H A N N E L

9

10

11

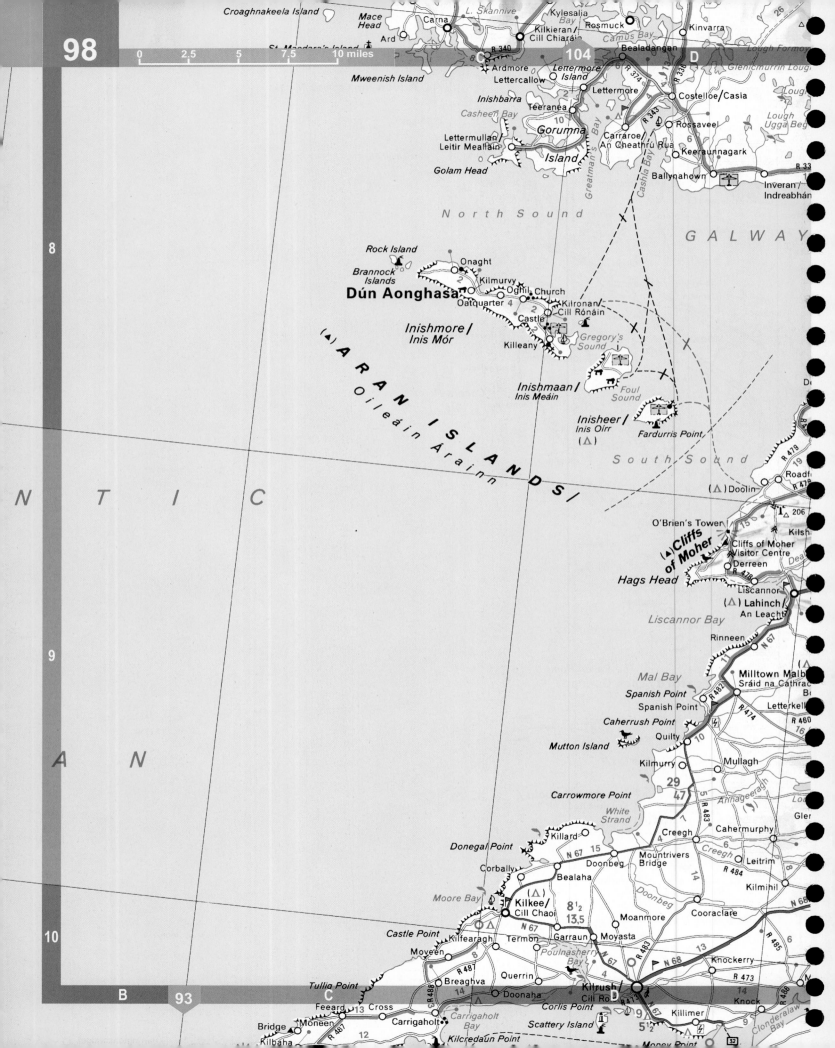

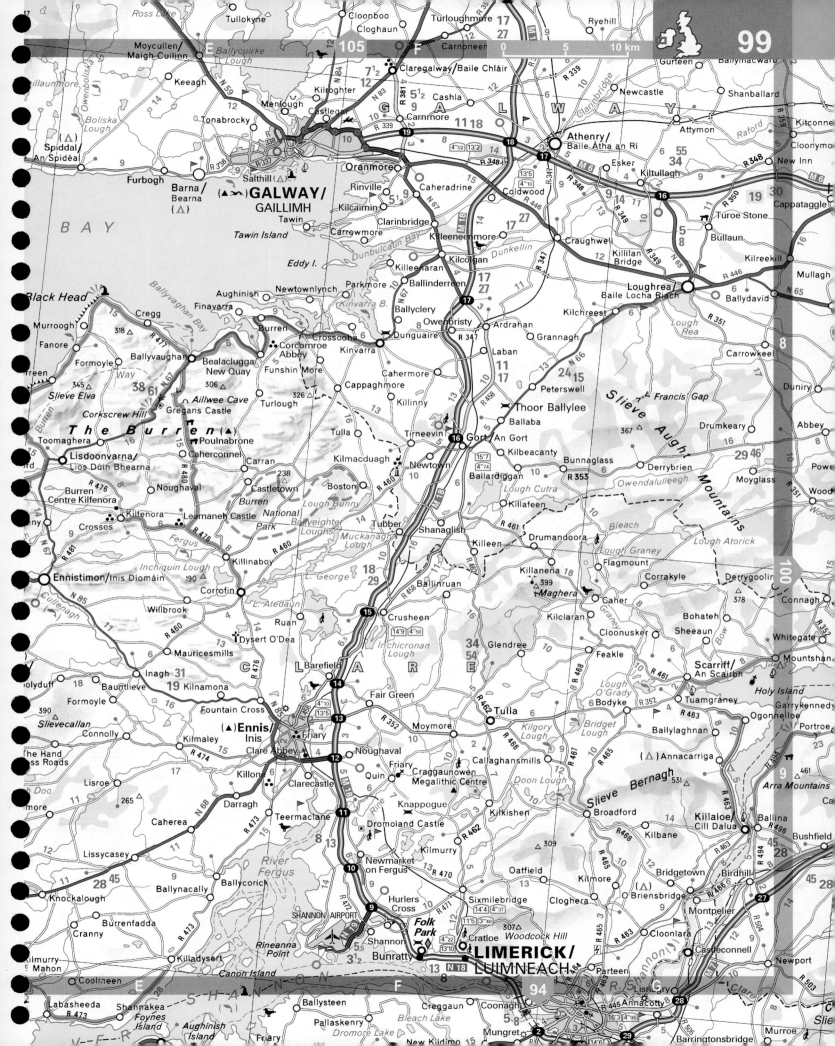

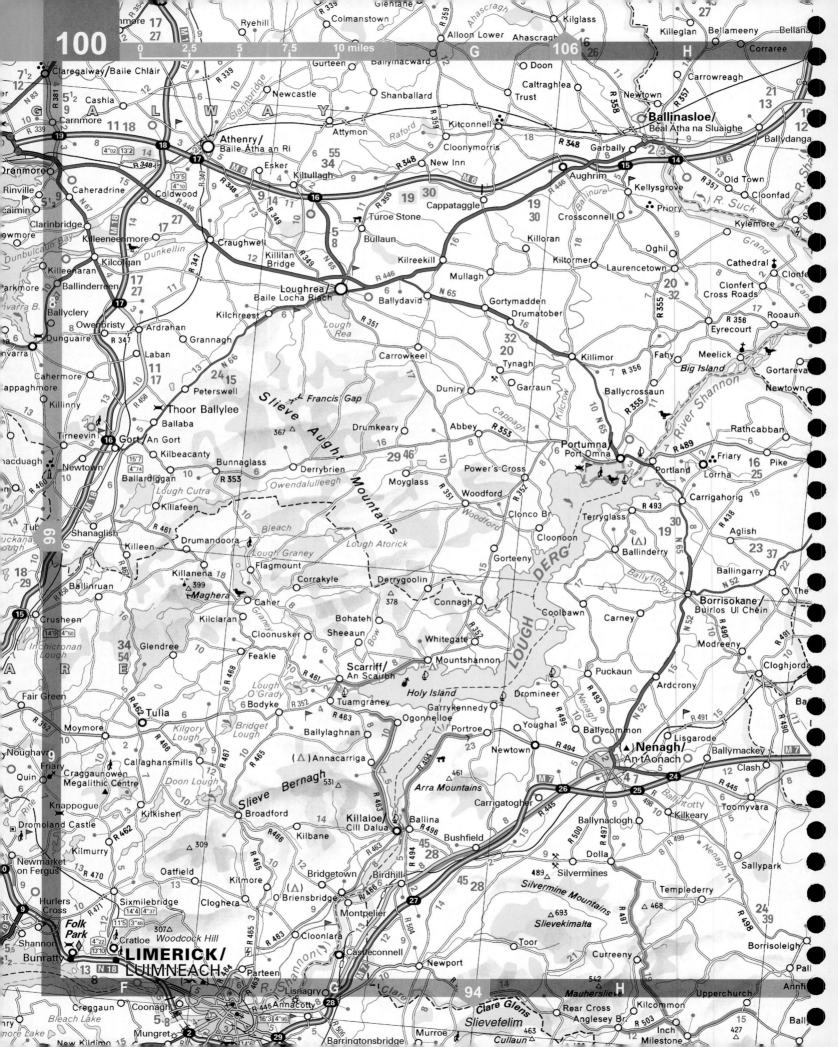

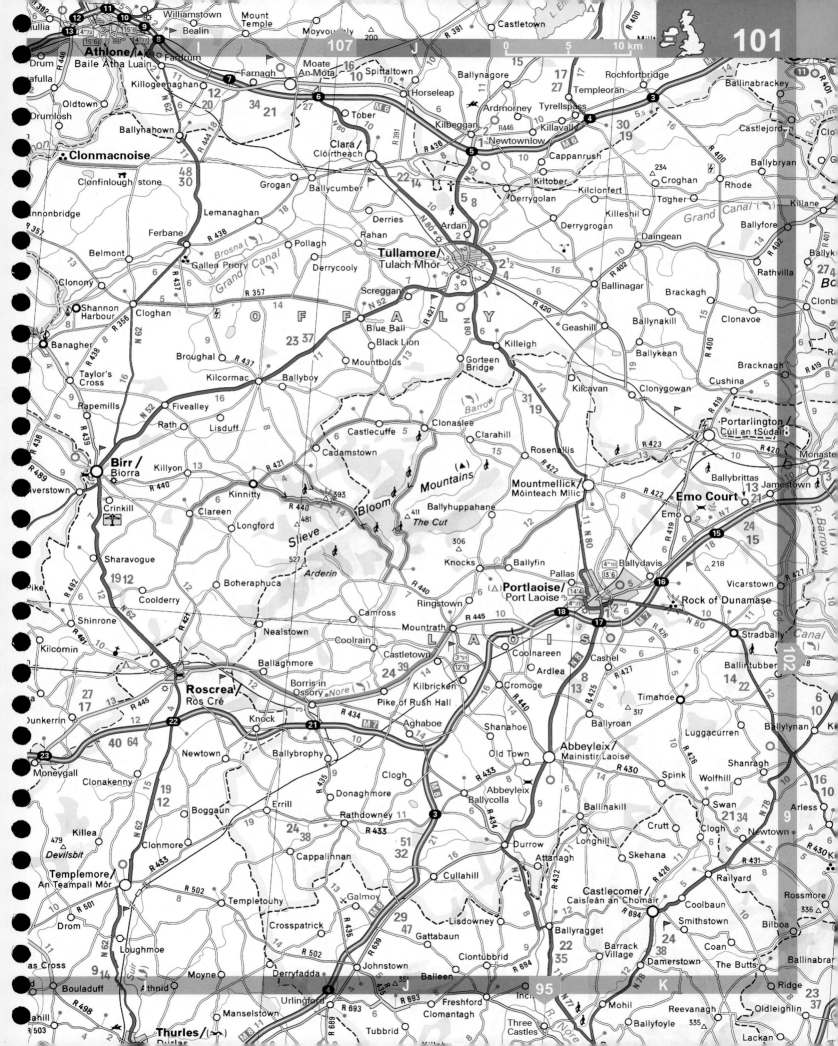

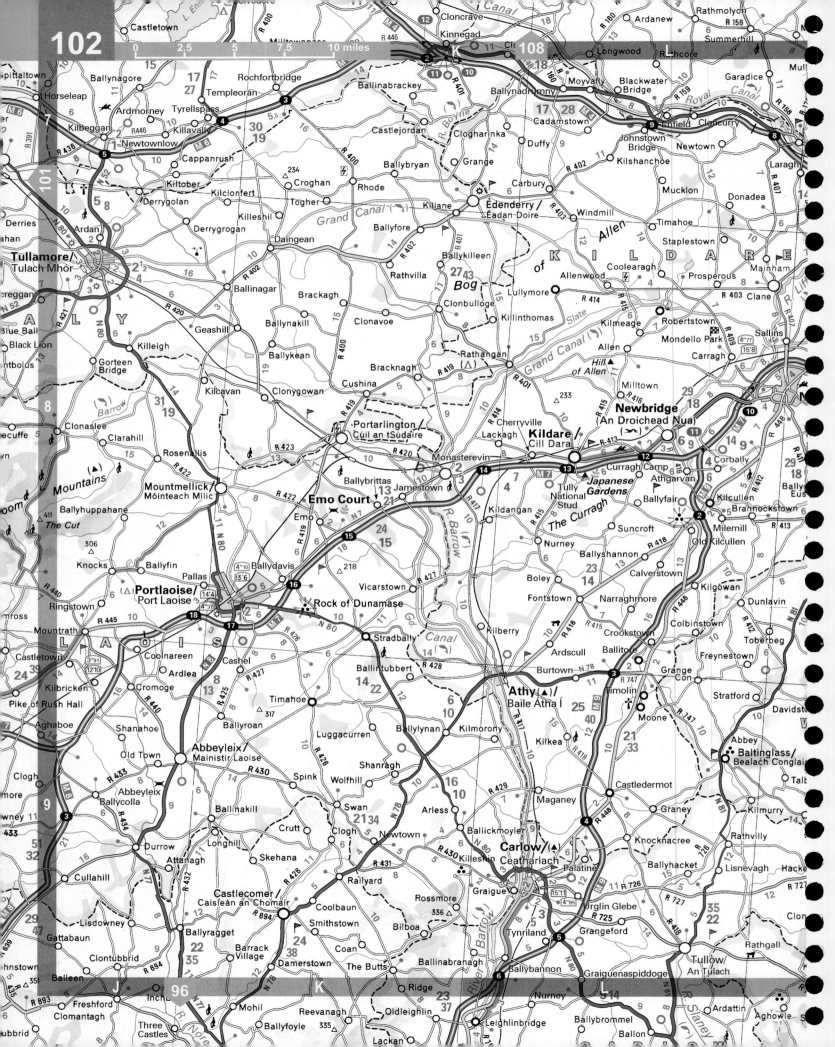

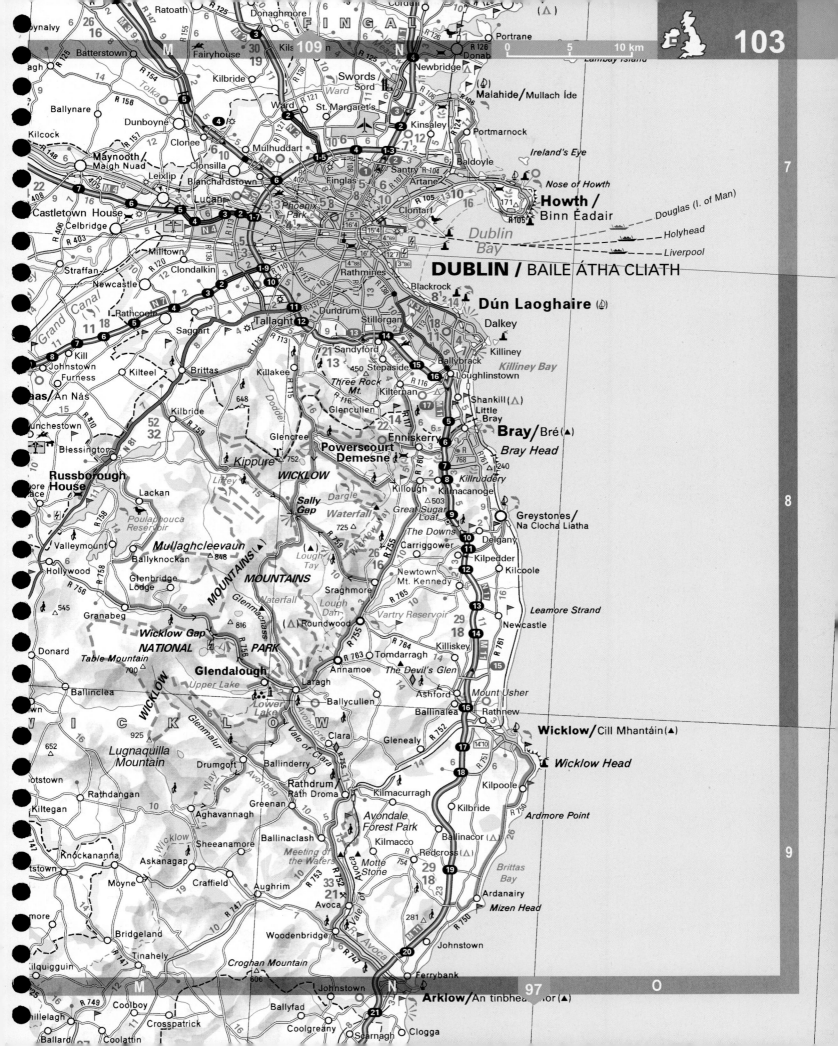

Achill Head
Croaghaun
△ 667 Dooagh
Keel
Keel Lough
River
Inishbiggle
Castlehill
Bellag
R 319
Ryteoge Head
Keem Strand
B
110
Bunacurry
Aghagh
Island
C
Claggan
63
39

0   2.5   5   7.5   10 miles

Cathedral Rocks ▲
Cashel
Salia

(▲) ACHILL ISLAND
Dooega Head
△ 464
Knockmore
Achill
Achill Sound / Gob an Choire
R 319

Dooega / Dumha Éige
△ 340
Belfarsad
36
△ 382
Mul
An Mha

Ashleam Bay
Derreen
Corraun

Bills Rocks
△ Corraun Hill
58

Cloghmore
An Chloich Mhóir
521 Glassillaun
Peninsula

Achillbeg Island
Dooghbeg

Bolinglanna

6

Clare Island
Ballytoohy
CLEW   BA
Isla

△
461

Old Head
Kilsallag
△

Roonagh Quay
Louisburgh
13

Emlagh Point
7

Formoyle
Mullagh

Roonah Lough
R 335

Inishturk
Caher Island
Killadoon
Cregganbaun

Bridge
Silver Strand
(▲) MURRI

Kinnadoohy
Doo Lough
Pass
Sh

Inishbofin
Tonakeera Point
817 △
Doo
Lough
△
761

Crump Island
Mweelrea Mountains
Delphi

Inishshark
Bofin
Rinvyle Point
Rinvyle Castle
Ardnagreevagh
700 △ Ben

Rinvyle (△)
R 335

Cashleen
356
Gowlaun
Salrock
10

High Island
Ballynakill Harbour
19
Tully Cross
600 △ Lough
Fee
Leenane

Aughrus More
4
8
Dawros
Garraun
Kylemore Abbey
624 △

Claddaghduff
14
N 59
10
Letterfrack
Kylemore
Lough
667 △
Ki

7

Omey Island
Cleggan /
An Cloigeann
Moyard
Connemara
National Park
R 344
16
Maumturk Moun

Kingstown
(△) Sky Road
Streamstown
294
(▲) J

Talbot Island
Clifden /
An Clochán
728 △ Benbaun
710 △ Lough
Inagh
Finnisglin

Errislannan
Cascade
Derrylea
The Twelve Pins
Benbreen
692
701

Owenglin
Bencorr

Mannin
Bay
9
Ballinaboy
Ballynahinch
Lake
CONNEMAR
Derryclare Lough
Derryn

Doonloughan
R 341
Toombeola
Ballinafad
Recess /
Sraith Salach
1

Ballyconneely
6
R 342
Cashel / An Caiseal
R 340

Callow
Maumeen Lough
R 341
6

Slyne Head
Errisbeg
300 △
Bunnahown
10
Lou

Ballyconneely
Bay
12 Roundstone
Gowla

Inishnee
Bertraghboy Bay
Derryrush

Glinsk / Glinsce
354

Lough
Bola
Kilkieran
Bay

Moyrus
12
L. Skannive
Kylesalia
Rosm

Croaghnakeela Island
Mace
Head
Carna
Kilkieran /
Cill Chiaráin

Ard
St. Macdara's Island
R 340
Lett

Mweenish Island
Ardmore
Lettercallow
Lettermore
Island

8

Inishbarra
Teeranea

Casheen Bay
Gorumna

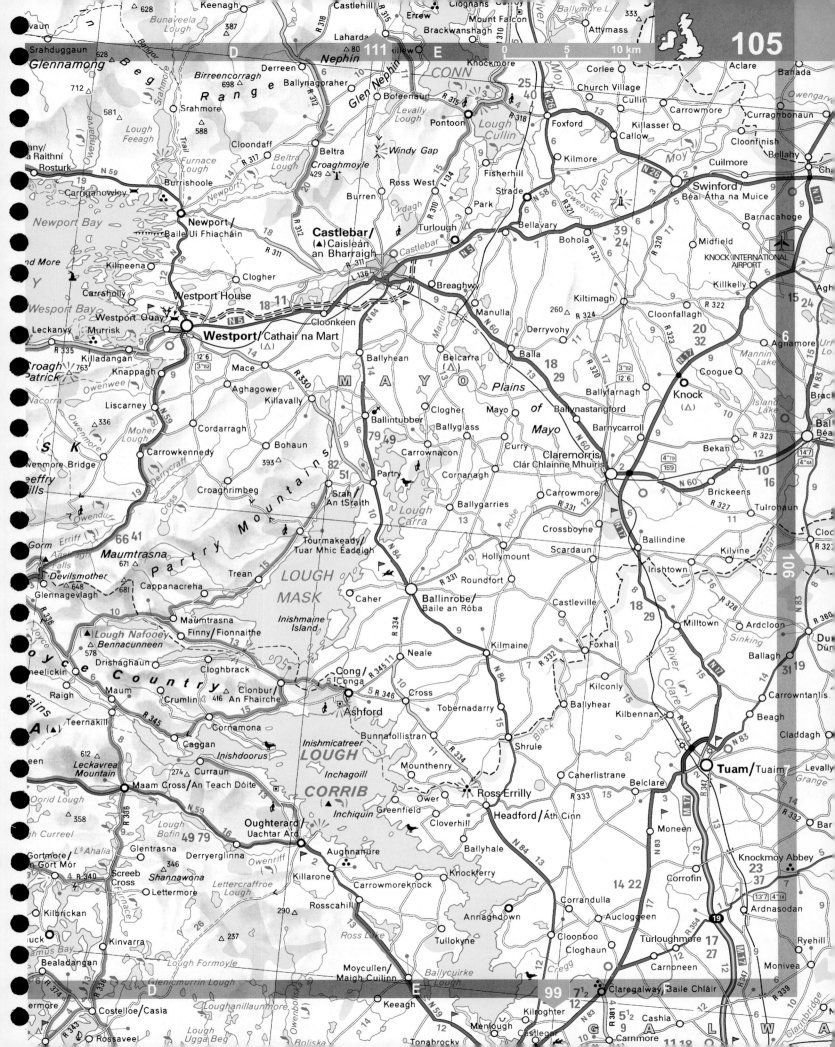

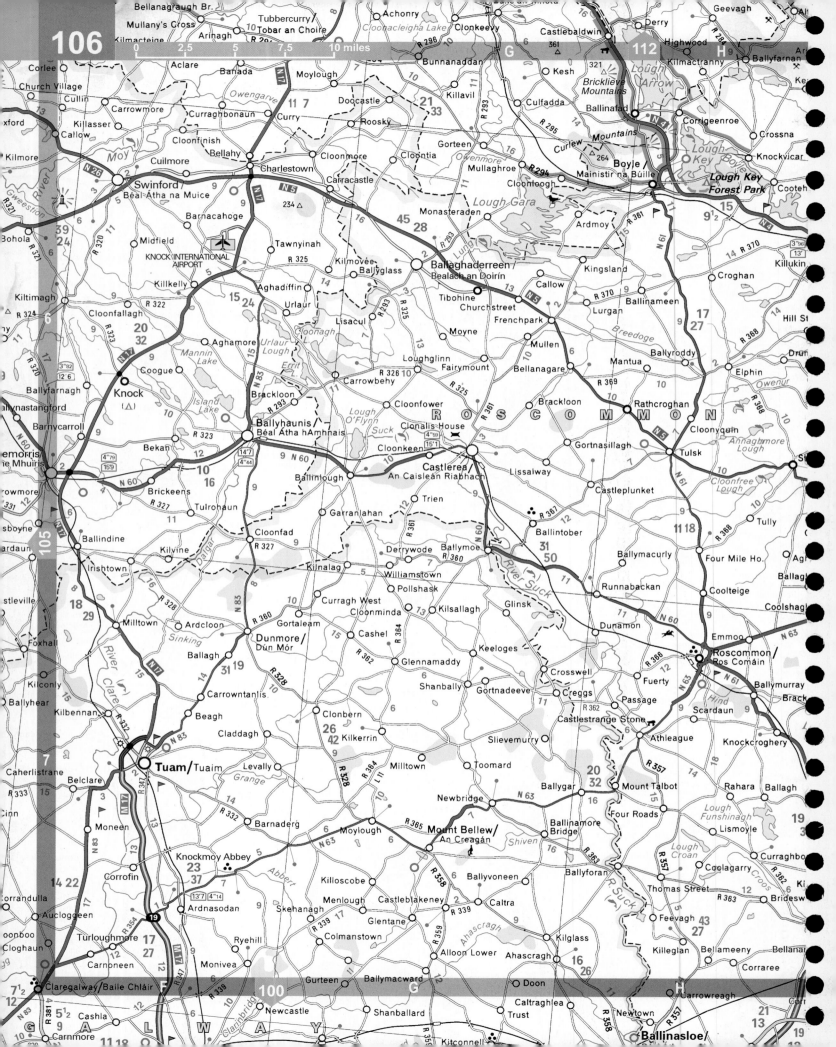

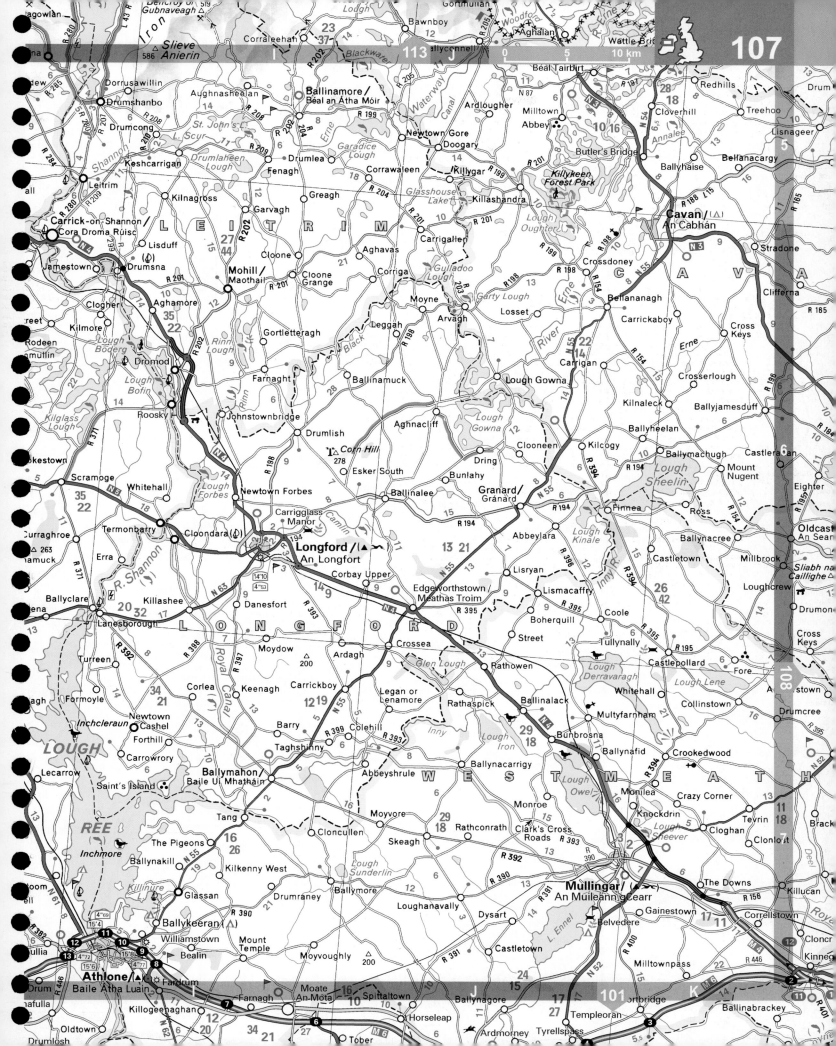

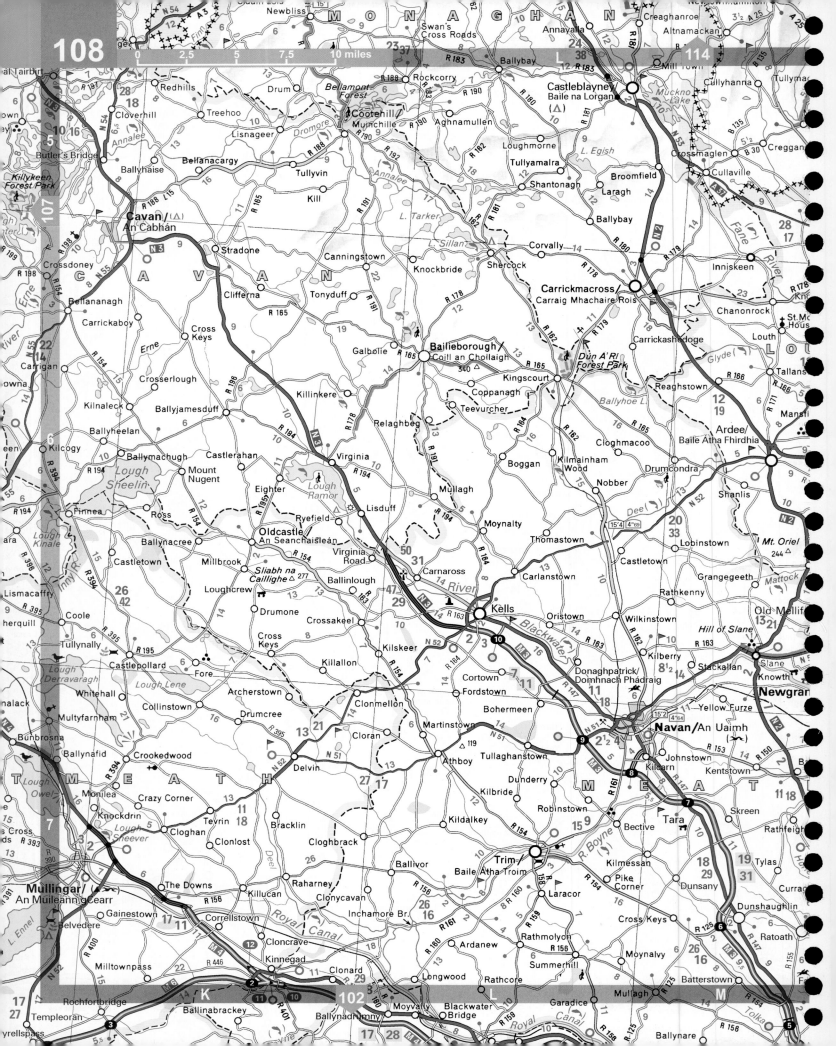

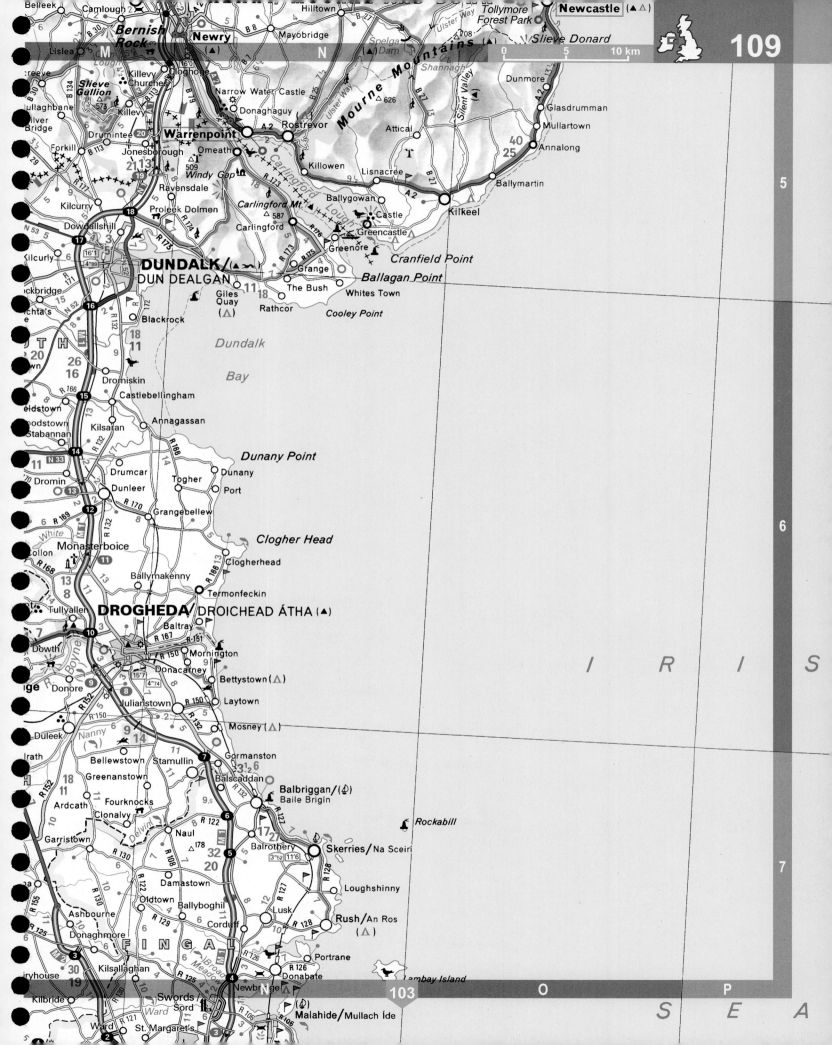

0   2.5   5   7.5   10 miles

A T L A N T

4

B

5

6

A   104   B   C

Benwee Hea
Kid Island
Erris Head
Broad Haven
Rinroe Point
Eagle Island
Aghadoon
Annagh Head   Corclogh   6   138   Knocknalina   11   266
Inver
10
Belmullet /
Inishglora   Béal an Mhuirthead
R 313
Corraun Point   An Geata Mór   R 313   11   Barnati
Bar na
Drumreagh   Trawmore   R 314   Bunnahowen /
Mullet Peninsula   Bay   Bun na hAbhna
11   240
Elly Bay   12
10   12
Inishkea North   Doolough Point   19
R 313   Srahmore
Inishkea South   Tristia   11
Aghleam   Dooyork
105
Fallmore   10   Blacksod   Dooagh   Geesala /
Point   10   6   Gaoth Saile
Black Rock   Duvillaun More   Duvillaun Beg   Blacksod
Bay   Tullaghan
Bay
Doohooma   Shranamani
Owenduff (r)
Saddle Head   Ridge Point   Fahy Lough   Doona   N 59
Slievemore   671   Valley   Ballycroy
Doogort
Achill Head   Croaghaun   Keel Lough   Inishbiggle   Castlehill   Bellaga
667   Dooagh   Keel   River   Annagh   Claggan
R 319   2   2   Island   63
Moyteoge Head   Keem Strand   Bunacurry   39
Cathedral Rocks
(▲) ACHILL ISLAND   Cashel   Salia
Dooega Head   464
Knockmore   340   Achill
Dooega / Dumha Éige   R 319

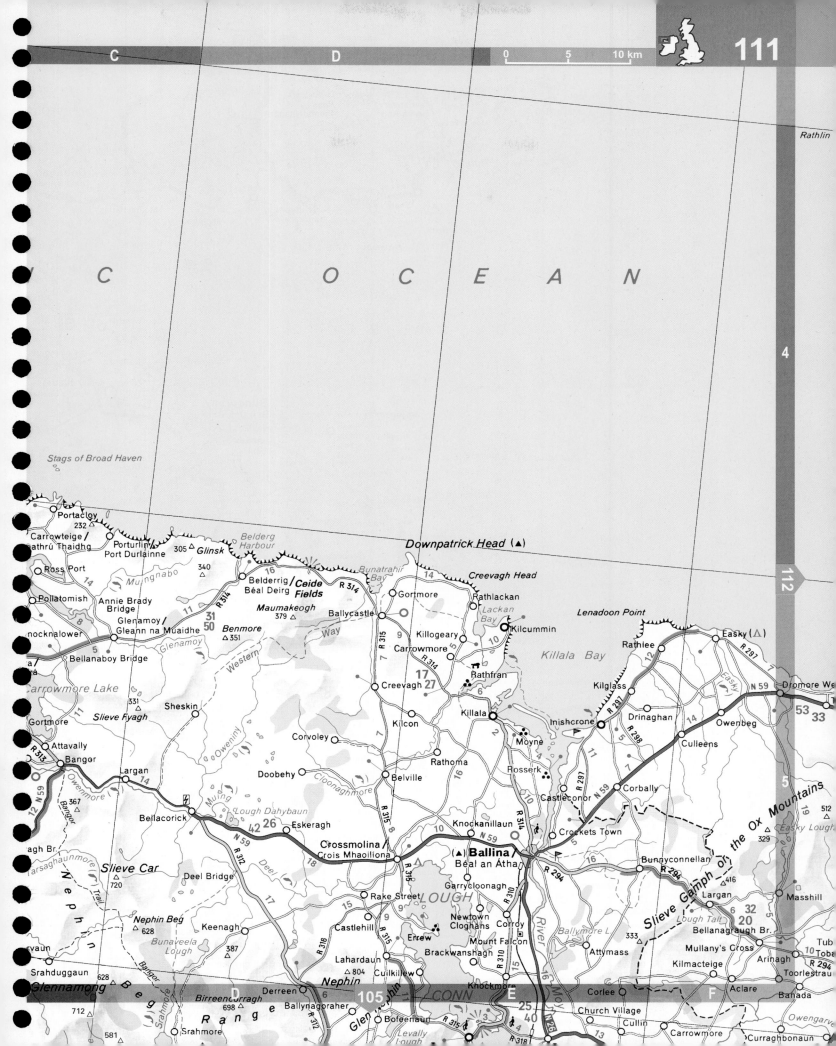

C   D   0   5   10 km

4

112

A T L A N T I C   O C E A N

Rathlin

Stags of Broad Haven

Portacloy 232

Carrowteige / Cathrú Thaidhg
Porturlin Port Durlainne   305   Glinsk

Belderg Harbour

Downpatrick Head (▲)

Ross Port   14   Muingnabo   340

16   Belderrig / Béal Deirg   Ceide Fields   R 314   Bunatrahir Bay   14   Creevagh Head

Pollatomish   11   Annie Brady Bridge   Maumakeogh 379   Ballycastle   Gortmore   Rathlackan

Knocknalower   8   Glenamoy / Gleann na Muaidhe   31 50   Benmore 351   Way   Killogeary   Lackan Bay

Lenadoon Point   Easky (△)

5   Bellanaboy Bridge   Glenamoy   9   Carrowmore   R 314   5   Kilcummin   10   Rathlee   12   R 297   7

Carrowmore Lake   11   331   Sheskin   Slieve Fyagh   Western   7 R 315   17   Rathfran   Killala Bay   Kilglass   Easky   N 59   Dromore We

Gortmore   Creevagh   27   6   Inishcrone   Drinaghan   14   Owenbeg   53 33

Attavally   R 313   Bangor   Owenny   Kilcon   Killala   2   Moyne   5 R 298   Culleens   7   5

Largan   14   Corvoley   Rathoma   Rosserk   R 297   11   Corbally

N 59   Owenmore   367   Doobehy   Cloonaghmore   Belville   16   Castleconor   N 59   19   512

12   Bangor   Bellacorick   Muing   Lough Dahybaun   42 26   Eskeragh   R 315   10   Knockanillaun   Crockets Town   Slieve Gamph or the Ox Mountains   Easky Lough   329

N 59   R 312   Crossmolina / Crois Mhaoilíona   18   N 59   Bunnyconnellan   R 294   Lough Talt   416

Slieve Car 720   Deel Bridge   Deel   17   (▲) Ballina / Béal an Átha   R 294   16   Largan   6   32 20   Masshill

Nephin Beg 628   Keenagh   387   15   Rake Street   9   LOUGH   Garrycloonagh   Bellanagraugh Br.   333   Mullany's Cross   10 Tobe

Bunaveela Lough   Castlehill   R 315   Newtown Cloghans   Corroy   Ballymore L   Kilmacteige   Arinagh   R 294

Srahduggaun   628   Lahardaun   804   Cuilkillew   Mount Falcon   Brackwanshagh   R 310   Attymass   Toorlestraun

Glennamong   712   Derreen   Nephin   Glen Nephin   CONN   Knockmore   Corlee   Aclare   Banada

581   Srahmore   Birreencorragh 698   Ballynagoraher   Bofeenaun   R 315   3   40   Church Village   Cullin   Carrowmore   Curraghbonaun

Bangor Beg Range   Levally Lough   R 318   River Moy   R 26   13   Owengara

D   105   E   25   F

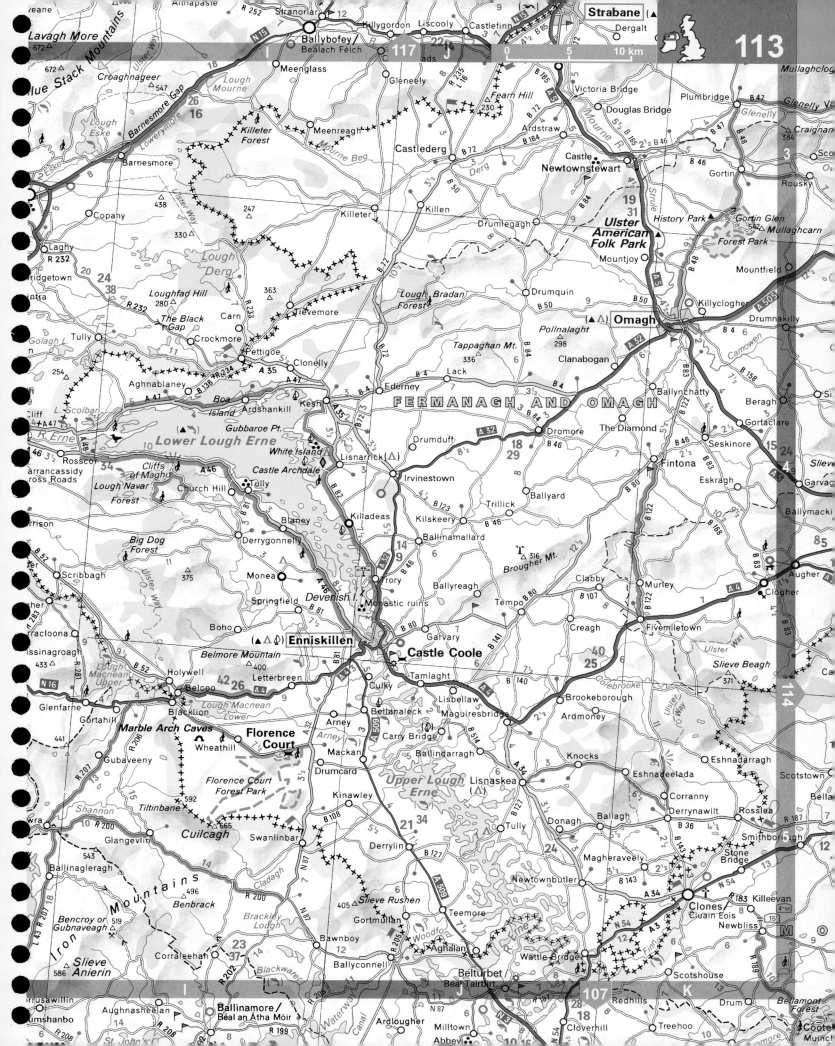

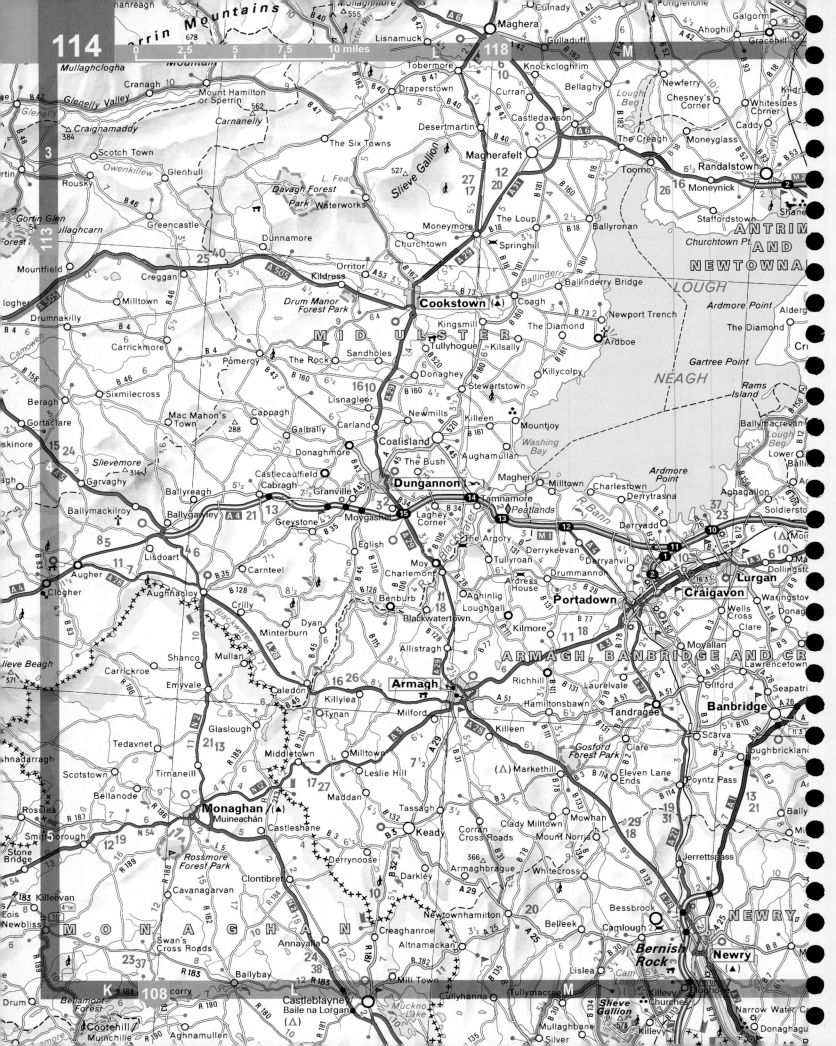

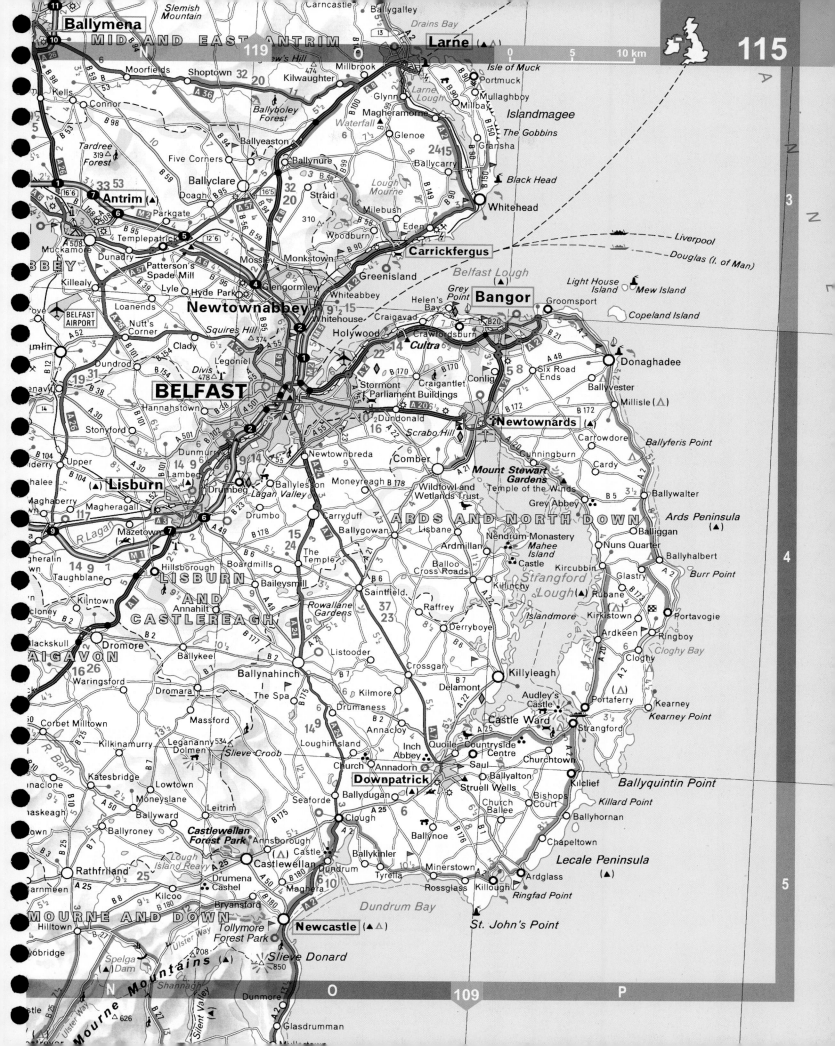

0 2.5 5 7.5 10 miles

2

West Town
East Town

Tory

Bloody Foreland Head

R 257

316△ Meenaclady

Brinlack
Bun na Leaca

13

Gweedore

Go
Gort

Gola Island /
Gabhla

Derrybeg

Tievea
△431

Owey Island /
Llaighe

Bunbeg /
An Bun Beag

Middletown

R 258

Gweedore /
Gaoth Dobha

Cruit
Island

Inishfree
Bay

R 257

Dore

Clady

Torneady Point

Rosses
Bay

DONEGAL
AIRPORT

6

5

Kincasslagh

R 259

Crolly /
Croithlí

L.
Na

Aran or
Aranmore Island /
Árainn Mhór

228△ Leabgarrow

Annagary

Loughanure

Ballintra

Burtonport /
Ailt an Chorráin

L.
Anure

519

Meencorwick

Rosses
(▲)

Rutland
Island

R 259

Teela

Owenator

Inishfree Upper

Dungloe /
An Clochán Liath

(△)

Lough
Croangar

396△

Com

Crohy Head

Maghery

Meenatotan

R 252

R 254

Owen

Derrydruel

Gweebarra
Bay

Roaninish

Dooey Point

Meenacross

Trawenagh
Bay

Doocharry /
An Dúchoraidh

Gweebarra

R 252

17
27

9

384△

Dunmore Head

Derrylough

Ballynacarrick

Baile

Dawros Head

(△)Portnoo

2

Clooney

Lettermacaward /
Leitir Mhic an Bhaird

5

Narin

5

Gweebarra
Bridge

14

Aghla M

Rossbeg

Maas

335△

596△

5

Kilclooney

R 261

N 56

R 250

D

Graff

Loughros More
Bay

△

Glenties

Stracashel

Loughros Point

R 253

L.
Machugh

14

Tanga

Glendorragha

Crannogeboy

Owenea

9

Kilrean

Slievetooey
443△

Maghera

Laconnell

Ardara

Carnawee

60

Port

521

Glen Head

Olencolmcille
Folk Village

374△

Stravally

Lough
Nalughraman

50
31

Neck of the Ballagh

Meenybraddan

Glen Bay

3

Rossan Point
Malin More

Glencolumbkille /
Gleann Cholm Cille

Crove

Glengesh
Pass

Malin
Bay

Malin Beg /
Málainn Bhig

9

Meenaneary /
Mín na Aoire

R 263

6

Meentullynagarn

Tullynaha

Meenavean

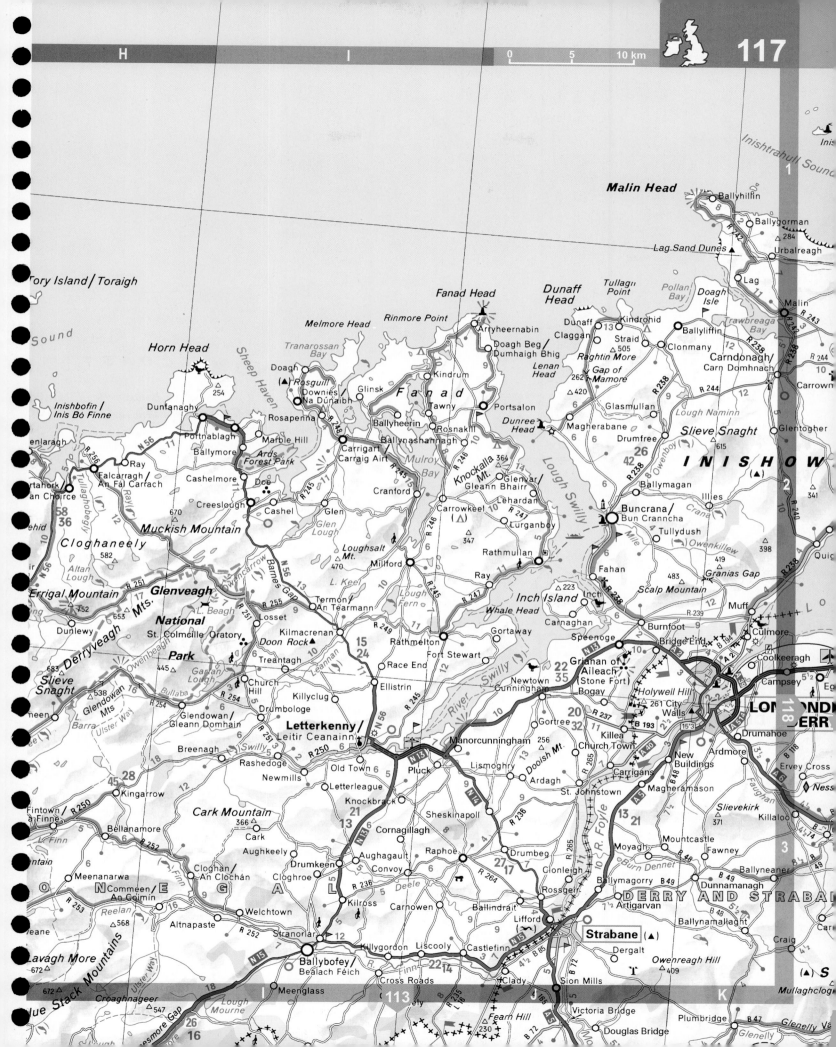

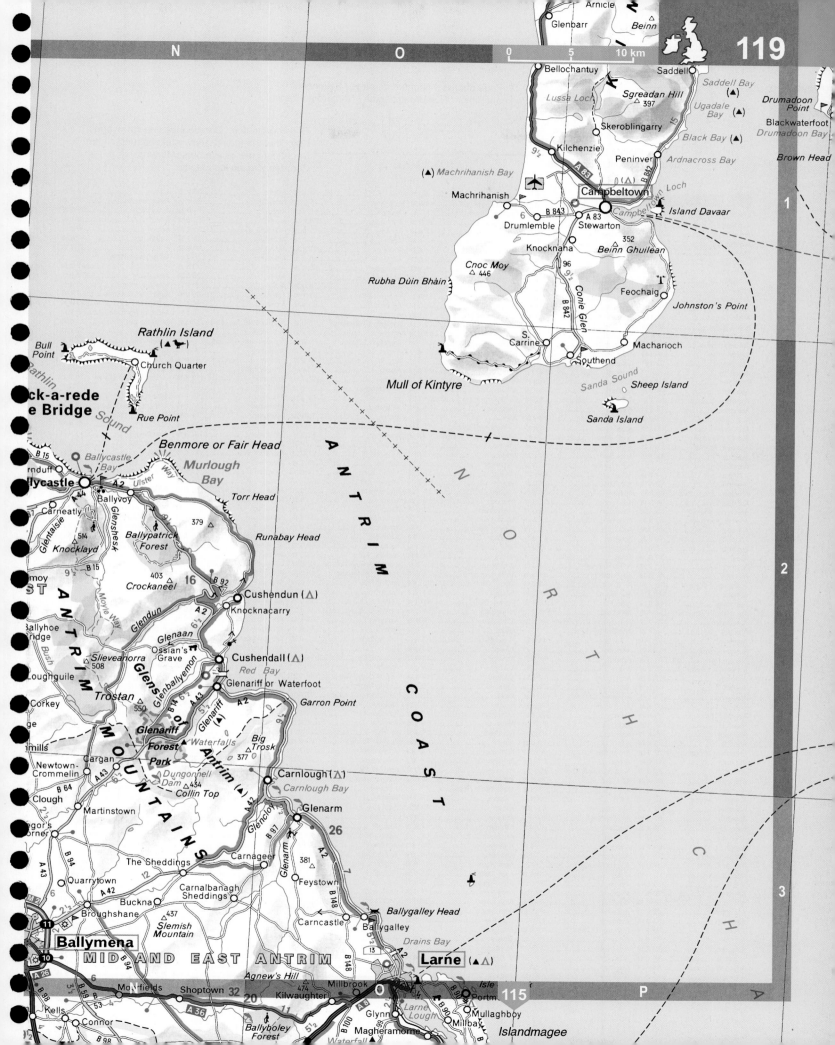

0   5   10 km

Arnicle
Glenbarr   Beinn

Bellochantuy   Saddell
Lussa Loch   Saddell Bay
Sgreadan Hill (▲)
397   Ugadale (▲)
Bay   Drumadoon
Point
Skeroblingarry   Black Bay (▲)   Blackwaterfoot
Drumadoon Bay
Kilchenzie   15   Peninver   Ardnacross Bay   Brown Head
9½   A 83   B 842

(▲) Machrihanish Bay

Machrihanish   (▲) (△)
Campbeltown   Campbeltown Loch   Island Davaar
6   B 843   Stewarton
Drumlemble   B 843   A 83
Knocknaha   Beinn Ghuilean   352
397
Cnoc Moy   96
△ 446   9½   Conie Glen   Feochaig
Rubha Dùin Bhàin   B 842   Johnston's Point

S.
Carrine   Macharioch
Southend
Mull of Kintyre   Sanda Sound   Sheep Island

Sanda Island

Rathlin Island
(▲)
Bull   (▲)
Point   Church Quarter
Rue Point

ck-a-rede
e Bridge   Benmore or Fair Head
Sound
B 15   Ballycastle   Murlough
rnduff   Bay   Bay
llycastle   A 2   Ulster Way
A 44   Ballyvoy
1   Carneatly   Torr Head   A N T R I M
Glentaisie   379 △
514 ▲
Knocklayd   Ballypatrick   Runabay Head
moy   Forest
9½   B 15   403 △   16   B 92   N
Crockaneel
Cushendun (△)   O
Knocknacarry
A 2   R
Ballyhoe   Glendun   6½
ridge   Glenaan   T
Bush   Ossian's   H
Grave   Cushendall (△)
Slieveanorra   Glenballyemon   Red Bay   C
508 ▲   Glenariff or Waterfoot   O
Loughguile   B 14   A 2   Garron Point   A
Trostan   Glenariff   S
Corkey   550 ▲   (▲)   T
ge   Glenariff   Waterfalls   Big
Forest   Trosk
mills   Park   377
Newtown-   Cargan   Dungonnell   434
Crommelin   A 43   Dam △   Carnlough (△)
Collin Top   Carnlough Bay
Clough   Martinstown   A 42   Glenarm
gor's   B 64   Glenclo   26
rner   A 2   B 97   Glenarm
The Sheddings   Carnagee   A 2
B 94   381
Quarrytown   12   Feystown   7
A 42   Carnalbanagh   B 148
Buckna   Sheddings
Broughshane   437   Ballygalley Head
11   Slemish   Carncastle   Ballygalley
10   Mountain   B 148   Drains Bay
Ballymena   13   A 2
A 26   M I D A N D E A S T A N T R I M   Larne (▲ △)   P
A 26   Agnew's Hill   A
B 98   Moorfields   Shoptown 32   Millbrook   Isle
Kilwaughter   474   Portm   115
Kells   A 36   A 8   Larne
Connor   Glynn   Mullaghboy
Ballyboley   B 100   Milbay
Forest   Magheramorne   Islandmagee
Waterfall

A B C D E F G H I J K L M N O P Q R S T U V W X Y Z

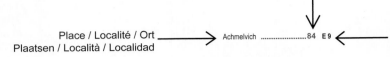

Page number / Numéro de page / Seitenzahl
Paginanummer / Numero di pagina / Numéro de Página

Place / Localité / Ort
Plaatsen / Località / Localidad

Achmelvich ....84 E 9

Grid coordinates / Coordonnées de carroyage
Koordinatenangabe / Verwijstekens ruitsysteem
Coordinate riferite alla quadrettatura
Coordenadas en los mapas

A

A Chill 71 A 12
A La Ronde 4 J 32
Abbas Combe 9 M 30
Abberley 27 M 27
Abbey 23 X 30
Abbey Dore 26 L 28
Abbey Town 54 K 19
Abbeydale 43 P 23
Abbeystead 48 L 22
Abbots Bromley 35 O 25
Abbots Langley 21 S 28
Abbots Leigh 18 M 29
Abbots Ripton 29 T 26
Abbotsbury 5 M 32
Abbotsford House 62 L 17
Abbotskerswell 4 J 32
Aber Banc 15 G 27
Aberaeron 24 H 27
Aberaman 17 J 28
Aberangell 33 I 25
Abercarn 18 K 29
Abercastle 14 E 28
Aberchirder 81 M 11
Abercynon 17 J 29
Aberdâr / Aberdare 17 J 28
Aberdare / Aberdâr 17 J 28
Aberdaron 32 F 25
Aberdaugleddau / Milford Haven 14 E 28
Aberdeen 75 N 12
Aberdour 68 K 15
Aberdour Bay 81 N 10
Aberdovey / Aberdyfi 33 H 26
Aberdyfi / Aberdovey 33 H 26
Aberedw 25 J 27
Abereiddy 14 E 28
Aberfeldy 73 I 14
Aberffraw 32 G 24
Aberford 43 P 22
Aberfoyle 67 G 15
Abergavenny / Y-Fenni 18 K 28
Abergele 41 J 23
Abergolech 15 H 28
Abergwaun / Fishguard 24 F 28
Abergwesyn 25 I 27
Abergwili 15 H 28
Abergwynfi 17 J 29
Abergwyngregyn 41 H 23
Abergynolwyn 33 I 26
Aberhonddu / Brecon 25 J 28
Aberkenfig 17 J 29
Aberlady 69 L 15
Aberlemno 75 L 13
Aberlour 80 K 11
Abermaw / Barmouth 33 H 25
Abermule 34 K 26
Abernethy 68 K 15
Abernyte 68 K 14
Aberpennar / Mountain Ash 17 J 28
Aberporth 15 G 27
Abersoch 32 G 25
Abersychan 18 K 28
Abertawe / Swansea 17 I 29
Aberteifi / Cardigan 15 G 27
Abertillery 18 K 28
Aberuthven 67 J 15
Aberystwyth 25 H 26
Abingdon 20 Q 28
Abinger Common 21 S 30
Abinger Hammer 21 S 30
Abingto *Cambs.* 30 U 27
Abington *South Lanarkshire* 61 I 17
Aboyne 75 L 12
Abriachan 79 G 11
Abridge 21 U 29
Accrington 42 M 22
Achahoish 65 D 16
Achallader 66 F 14
Achanalt 78 F 11
Achaphubuil 72 E 13
Acharacle 71 C 13
Achargary 85 H 8
Acharn 67 H 14
Achduart 83 E 10
Achgarve 78 D 10
Achiemore 84 F 8
Achiltibuie 83 D 9
Achintee 78 D 11
Achintraid 78 D 11
Achlean 73 I 12
Achleck 64 B 14
Achmelvich 84 E 9
Achmore 78 D 11
Achnahanat 84 G 10
Achnamara 65 D 15
Achnanellan 72 E 13
Achnasheen 78 E 11
Achnashellach Forest 78 E 11
Achosnich 71 B 13
Achranich 71 C 14
Achray (Loch) 67 G 15
Achreamie 85 I 8
Achriesgill 84 F 8
Achtalean 77 B 11
Achvaich 79 H 10
Acklington 63 P 18
Ackworth 44 P 23
Acle 39 Y 26
Acomb 55 N 19
Acrise Place 13 X 30
Acton Burnell 34 L 26
Acton Scott 26 L 26
Acton Turville 19 N 29
Adbaston 35 M 25
Adderbury 28 Q 27
Adderley 34 M 25
Adderstone 63 O 17
Addingham 49 O 22
Addlestone 21 S 29
Adfa 33 J 26
Adlington 42 M 23
Adlington Hall 43 N 24
Advie 80 J 11
Adwick-le-Street 44 Q 23
Ae (Forest of) 53 J 18
Ae Village 53 J 18
Afan Argoed 17 J 29
Affric (Glen) 78 F 12
Affric Lodge 78 E 12
Afon Dyfrdwy / Dee (River) 34 K 24
Afon Dyfrdwy (River) / Dee *Wales* 41 K 23
Afon-wen 41 K 23
Agneash 46 G 21
Aikton 54 K 19
Ailort (Loch) 72 C 13
Ailsa Craig 59 E 18
Ainderby Quernhow 50 P 21
Ainort (Loch) 77 B 12
Ainsdale 42 K 23
Air Uig 82 Y 9
Aird 65 D 15
Aird (The) 79 G 11
Aird of Sleat 71 C 12
Airdrie 61 I 16
Airigh na h-Airde (Loch) 82 Z 9
Airor 72 C 12
Airth 67 I 15
Airton 49 N 21
Aith *Orkney Is.* 87 M 6
Aith *Shetland Is.* 87 P 3
Aitnoch 80 I 11
Akeld 63 N 17
Albourne 11 T 31
Albrighton 35 N 26
Albyn or Mor (Glen) 73 F 12
Alcaig 79 G 11
Alcester 27 O 27
Alconbury 29 T 26
Aldborough 39 X 25
Aldbourne 19 P 29
Aldbrough 45 T 22
Aldbrough St. John 49 O 20
Aldbury 21 S 28
Alde (River) 31 Y 27
Aldeburgh 31 Y 27
Aldenham 21 S 28
Alderbury 9 O 30
Alderholt 9 O 31
Alderley Edge 43 N 24
Alderney *Channel I.* 5
Aldershot 20 R 30
Alderton 27 N 28
Aldford 34 L 24
Aldingbourne 11 R 31
Aldridge 35 O 26
Aldringham 31 Y 27
Aldsworth 19 O 28
Aldunie 80 K 12
Aldwick 11 R 31
Alexandria 66 G 16
Alfold Crossways 11 S 30
Alford *Aberdeenshire* 75 L 12
Alford *Lincs.* 45 U 24
Alfreton 36 P 24
Alfrick 27 M 27
Alfriston 12 U 31
Aline (Loch) 65 C 14
Alkborough 44 S 22
Alkham 13 X 30
All Stretton 34 L 26
Allanaquoich 74 J 12
Allanton *North Lanarkshire* 61 I 16
Allanton *Scottish Borders* 63 N 16
Allendale Town 55 N 19
Allenheads 55 N 19
Allensmore 26 L 27
Allerford 17 J 30
Allerston 51 S 21
Allestree 36 P 25
Allhallows 22 V 29
Alligin Shuas 78 D 11
Allington *Kennet* 19 O 29
Allington *Salisbury* 9 O 30
Allnabad 84 G 8
Alloa 67 I 15
Allonby 54 J 19
Alloway 60 G 17
Allt na h-Airbhe 78 E 10
Alltan Fhèarna (Loch an) 85 H 9
Alltnacaillich 84 G 8
Almond (Glen) 67 I 14
Almondbank 68 J 14
Almondsbury 18 M 29
Alness 79 H 10
Alnmouth 63 P 17
Alnwick 63 O 17
Alpheton 30 W 27
Alphington 4 J 31
Alpraham 34 M 24
Alresford 30 X 28
Alrewas 35 O 25
Alsager 35 N 24
Alsh (Loch) 78 D 12
Alston 55 M 19
Alstonefield 35 O 24
Alswear 7 I 31
Altadnduin 85 H 9
Altandhu 83 D 9
Altarnun 3 G 32
Altass 84 G 10
Alternative Technology Centre 33 I 26
Altham 42 M 22
Althorne 22 W 29
Althorpe 44 R 23
Altnabreac Station 85 I 8
Altnacealgach 84 F 9
Altnaharra 84 G 9
Alton *Hants.* 10 R 30
Alton *Staffs.* 35 O 25
Alton Pancras 9 M 31
Alton Priors 19 O 29
Alton Towers 35 O 25
Altrincham 42 M 23
Alum Bay 10 P 31
Alva 67 I 15
Alvaston 36 P 25
Alvechurch 27 O 26
Alvediston 9 N 30
Alves 80 J 11
Alvescot 19 P 28
Alvie 73 I 12
Alvingham 45 U 23
Alwinton 63 N 17
Alyth 74 K 14
Amberley 11 S 31
Amble 63 P 18
Amblecote 27 N 26
Ambleside 48 L 20
Ambrosden 28 Q 28
Amersham 21 S 29
Amesbury 9 O 30
Amhuinnsuidhe 82 Y 10
Amisfield 53 J 18
Amlwch 40 G 22
Ammanford / Rhydaman 15 I 28
Amotherby 50 R 21
Ampleforth 50 Q 21
Amport 20 P 30
Ampthill 29 S 27
Amroth 15 G 28
Amulree 67 I 14
An Riabhachan 78 E 11
An Socach 74 J 13
An Teallach 78 E 10
Anchor 26 K 26
Ancroft 63 O 16
Ancrum 62 M 17
Andover 20 P 30
Andoversford 27 O 28
Andreas 46 G 20
Angle 14 E 28
Anglesey (Isle of) 40
Anglesey Abbey 30 U 27
Angmering 11 S 31
Annan 54 K 19
Annan (River) 61 J 18
Annat 78 D 11
Annat Bay 83 E 10
Annbank 60 G 17
Annbank Station 60 G 17
Anne Hathaway's Cottage 27 O 27
Annesley-Woodhouse 36 Q 24
Annfield Plain 56 O 19
Ansley 28 P 26
Anstey 36 Q 25
Anston 44 Q 23
Anstruther 69 L 15
Anthorn 54 K 19
Antony House 3 H 32
Appin 72 E 14
Appleby *Eden* 55 M 20
Appleby *North Lincolnshire* 44 S 23
Appleby Magna 36 P 25
Applecross 77 C 11
Appledore *Devon* 6 H 30
Appledore *Kent* 12 W 30
Appleford 20 Q 29
Appleton 20 P 28
Appleton Roebuck 44 Q 22
Appleton Wiske 50 P 20
Appletreewick 49 O 21
Aran Fawddwy 33 I 25
Arberth / Narberth 15 F 28
Arbigland 53 J 19
Arbirlot 69 M 14
Arbor Low 35 O 24
Arborfield 20 R 29
Arbroath 69 M 14
Arbury Hall 28 P 26
Arbuthnott 75 N 13
Archiestown 80 K 11
Ard (Loch) 67 G 15
Ardanaiseig 66 E 14
Ardarroch 78 D 11
Ardcharnich 78 E 10
Ardchiavaig 64 B 15
Ardchuilk 78 F 11
Ardchyle 67 G 14
Ardechive 72 E 13
Arden 66 G 15
Ardentallan 65 D 14
Ardeonaig 67 H 14
Ardersier 79 H 11
Ardery 72 C 13
Ardfern 65 D 15
Ardgartan 66 F 15
Ardgay 79 G 10
Ardgour 72 D 13
Ardhasaig 82 Z 10
Ardingly 11 T 30
Ardington 20 P 29
Ardivachar 76 X 11
Ardleigh 30 W 28
Ardley 28 Q 28
Ardlui 66 F 15
Ardlussa 65 C 15
Ardmair 84 E 10
Ardminish 58 C 16
Ardmore Point *Isle of Skye* 77 A 11
Ardnacross 71 C 14
Ardnamurchan 71 B 13
Ardnastang 72 D 13
Ardnave 64 A 16
Ardnave Point 64 B 16
Ardpatrick 59 D 16
Ardrishaig 65 D 15
Ardrossan 59 F 17
Ardshealach 71 C 13
Ardslignish 71 C 13
Ardtalla 58 B 16
Ardtalnaig 67 H 14
Ardtoe 71 C 13
Ardvasar 71 C 12
Ardverikie Forest 73 G 13
Ardvorlich 67 H 14
Ardwell 52 F 19
Argyll 65 D 15
Argyll Forest Park 66 F 15
Arichastlich 66 F 14
Arienas (Loch) 71 C 14
Arileod 71 A 14
Arinacrinachd 77 C 11
Arinagour 71 A 14
Arisaig 71 C 13
Arivruaich 82 Z 9
Arkaig (Loch) 72 E 13
Arkendale 50 P 21
Arkengarthdale 49 O 20
Arkholme 48 M 21
Arklet (Loch) 66 G 15
Arley 27 P 26
Arlingham 19 M 28
Arlington Court 7 I 30
Armadale *Highland* 85 H 8
Armadale *West Lothian* 61 I 16
Armadale Bay 71 C 12
Armitage 35 O 25
Armthorpe 44 Q 23
Arnabost 71 A 14
Arncliffe 49 N 21
Arncott 20 Q 28
Arncroach 69 L 15
Arne 9 N 31
Arnesby 28 Q 26
Arnicle 59 D 17
Arnisdale 72 D 12
Arnish 77 B 11
Arnol 82 A 8
Arnold 36 Q 25
Arnprior 67 H 15
Arnside 48 L 21
Aros 65 B 14
Arram 45 S 22
Arran (Isle of) 59 E 17
Arreton 10 Q 31
Arrochar 66 F 15
Arscaig 84 G 9
Arundel 11 S 31
Ascog 59 E 16
Ascot 21 R 29
Ascott House 29 R 28
Ascott-under-Wychwood 28 P 28
Ascrib Islands 77 A 11
Asfordby 36 R 25
Ash *Kent* 23 X 30
Ash *Surrey* 20 R 30
Ash Mill 7 I 31
Ashbourne 35 O 24
Ashburton 4 I 32
Ashbury 19 P 29
Ashby de la Zouch 36 P 25
Ashby Magna 28 Q 26
Ashcott 8 L 30
Ashdon 30 U 27
Ashford *Kent* 12 W 30
Ashford *Surrey* 21 S 29
Ashford-in-the-Water *Derbs.* 43 O 24
Ashie (Loch) 79 H 11
Ashill *Breckland* 38 W 26
Ashill *South Somerset* 8 L 31
Ashingdon 22 W 29
Ashington *Northumb* 56 P 18
Ashington *West Sussex* 11 S 31
Ashkirk 62 L 17
Ashleworth 27 N 28
Ashley *East Cambridgeshire* 30 V 27
Ashley *Newcastle-under-Lyme* 35 M 25
Ashley *Torridge* 7 I 31
Ashley Green 21 S 28
Ashmore 9 N 31
Ashover 36 P 24
Ashperton 26 M 27
Ashreigney 7 I 31
Ashtead 21 T 30
Ashton 34 L 24
Ashton-in-Makerfield 42 M 23
Ashton Keynes 19 O 29
Ashton-under-Lyne 43 N 23
Ashton-upon-Mersey 42 M 23
Ashurst 10 P 31
Ashwell *North Hertfordshire* 29 T 27
Ashwell *Rutland* 36 R 25
Ashwellthorpe 39 X 26
Askam in Furness 47 K 21
Askern 44 Q 23
Askernish 76 X 12
Askerswell 5 L 31
Askham 55 L 20
Askrigg 49 N 21
Askwith 49 O 22
Aslacton 31 X 26
Aslockton 36 R 25
Aspatria 54 K 19
Aspley Guise 29 S 27
Assynt (Loch) 84 E 9
Astley 34 L 25
Aston *Vale Royal* 44 Q 23
Aston *West Oxfordshire* 20 P 28
Aston Clinton 20 R 28
Aston Magna 27 O 27
Aston Rowant 20 R 28
Aston Tirrold 20 Q 29
Astwood Bank 27 O 27
Atcham 34 L 25
Athelhampton Hall 9 N 31
Athelney 8 L 30
Athelstaneford 69 L 16
Atherington 7 H 31
Athersley 43 P 23
Atherstone 36 P 26
Atherton 42 M 23
Atholl (Forest of) 73 H 13
Attadale 78 D 11
Attleborough *Breckland* 38 X 26
Attleborough *Nuneaton and Bedworth* 28 P 26
Attlebridge 39 X 25
Atwick 51 T 22
Atworth 19 N 29
Aucharnie 81 M 11
Auchavan 74 K 13
Auchenblae 75 M 13
Auchenbowie 67 I 15
Auchenbrack 61 I 18
Auchenbreck 65 E 16
Auchencairn 53 I 19
Auchencrosh 52 F 18
Auchencrow 63 N 16
Auchengray 61 J 16
Auchenmalg 52 F 19
Auchentiber 60 G 16

Auchindrean ...78 E 10
Auchinleck ...60 H 17
Auchleven ...81 M 12
Auchlyne ...67 G 14
Auchnafree ...67 I 14
Auchnagallin ...80 J 11
Auchnagatt ...81 N 11
Aucholzie ...74 K 12
Auchronie ...74 L 13
Auchterarder ...67 I 15
Auchteraw ...73 F 12
Auchterderran ...68 K 15
Auchterhouse ...68 K 14
Auchtermuchty ...68 K 15
Auchtertyre ...78 D 12
Auckengill ...86 K 8
Auckley ...44 Q 23
Audenshaw ...43 N 23
Audlem ...34 M 25
Audley ...35 N 24
Audley End ...30 U 27
Aughton near Lancaster ...48 L 21
Aughton near Ormskirk ...42 L 23
Auldearn ...79 I 11
Auldgirth ...53 I 18
Auldhouse ...60 H 16
Ault a' Chruinn ...72 D 12
Aultbea ...78 D 10
Aust ...18 M 29
Austrey ...35 P 26
Austwick ...49 M 21
Avebury ...19 O 29
Aveley ...22 U 29
Avening ...19 N 28
Aveton Gifford ...4 I 33
Aviemore ...73 I 12
Avoch ...79 H 11
Avon (Glen) ...74 J 12
Avon (River) R. Severn ...28 Q 26
Avon (River) Wilts. ...9 O 31
Avonbridge ...67 I 16
Avonmouth ...18 L 29
Avonwick ...4 I 32
Awe (Loch) ...65 E 15
Awliscombe ...8 K 31
Awre ...19 M 28
Axbridge ...18 L 30
Axminster ...8 L 31
Axmouth ...5 K 31
Aylburton ...18 M 28
Aylesbury ...20 R 28
Aylesford ...22 V 30
Aylesham ...23 X 30
Aylsham ...39 X 25
Aylton ...26 M 27
Aymestrey ...26 L 27
Aynho ...28 Q 28
Ayr ...60 G 17
Aysgarth ...49 O 21
Ayside ...48 L 21
Ayton Scarborough ...51 S 21
Ayton Scottish Borders ...63 N 16

B

Bà (Loch) ...65 C 14
Babbacombe Bay ...4 J 32
Babcary ...8 M 30
Babell ...41 K 23
Babworth ...44 R 24
Back ...83 B 9
Backaland ...87 L 6
Backmuir of New Gilston ...69 L 15
Backwater Reservoir ...74 K 13
Backwell West Town ...18 L 29
Baconsthorpe ...39 X 25
Bacton Mid Suffolk ...30 X 27
Bacton North Norfolk ...39 Y 25
Bacup ...43 N 22
Bad a' Ghaill (Loch) ...84 E 9
Bad an Sgalaig (Loch) ...78 D 10
Badachro ...77 C 10
Badanloch (Loch) ...85 H 9
Badanloch Lodge ...85 H 9
Badcaul ...78 D 10
Baddesley Ensor ...35 P 26
Baddidarach ...84 E 9
Badenoch ...73 H 13
Badenscallie ...83 E 9
Badenyon ...74 K 12
Badlipster ...86 K 8
Badluarach ...78 D 10
Badminton ...19 N 29
Badrallach ...78 E 10
Bae Colwyn / Colwyn Bay ...41 I 23
Bagh nam Faoileann ...76 Y 11
Bagillt ...41 K 23
Bagley ...34 L 25

Bagshot ...21 R 29
Bagworth ...36 P 25
Bagwyllydiart ...26 L 28
Baile Mór ...64 A 15
Bailiehill ...54 K 18
Bainbridge ...49 N 21
Bainton ...51 S 22
Bakewell ...35 O 24
Bala ...33 J 25
Balallan ...82 A 9
Balbeggie ...68 J 14
Balblair ...79 H 10
Balcary Point ...53 I 19
Balcombe ...11 T 30
Balderton ...36 R 24
Baldrine ...46 G 21
Baldwin ...46 G 21
Balemartine ...64 Z 14
Balephetrish Bay ...70 Z 14
Balephuil ...64 Z 14
Balephuil Bay ...64 Z 14
Balerno ...61 J 16
Baleshare ...76 X 11
Balevulin ...65 B 14
Balfour ...87 L 6
Balfron ...67 H 15
Balgray ...69 L 14
Balintore Angus ...74 K 13
Balintore Highland ...79 I 10
Balivanich ...76 X 11
Balk ...50 Q 21
Ballabeg ...46 F 21
Ballachulish ...72 E 13
Ballajora ...46 G 21
Ballamodha ...46 G 21
Ballantrae ...52 E 18
Ballasalla ...46 G 21
Ballater ...74 K 12
Ballaugh ...46 G 21
Ballevullin ...70 Z 14
Balliemore near Dunoon ...65 E 15
Balliemore near Oban ...65 D 14
Ballig ...46 G 21
Ballingry ...68 K 15
Ballinluig ...74 J 14
Ballochan ...75 L 12
Ballochroy ...59 D 16
Ballyhaugh ...71 A 14
Balmacara ...53 H 18
Balmaclellan ...53 H 18
Balmaha ...67 G 15
Balmedie ...75 N 12
Balminnoch ...52 F 19
Balmoral Castle ...74 K 12
Balmullo ...69 L 14
Balnacra ...78 D 11
Balnafoich ...79 H 11
Balnaguard ...74 I 14
Balnahard ...64 B 14
Balnakeil Bay ...84 F 8
Balnaknock ...77 B 11
Balnapaling ...79 H 10
Baltonsborough ...8 M 30
Balvicar ...65 D 15
Balvraid ...72 D 12
Bamburgh Castle ...63 O 17
Bamford ...43 O 23
Bampton Cumbria ...48 L 20
Bampton Devon ...7 J 31
Bampton Oxon. ...20 P 28
Banavie ...72 E 13
Banbury ...28 P 27
Banchory ...75 M 12
Bancyfelin ...15 G 28
Bandenscoth ...81 M 11
Banff ...81 M 10
Bangor ...40 H 23
Bankend ...53 J 18
Bankfoot ...68 J 14
Bankhead ...75 N 12
Banks ...42 L 22
Bankshill ...54 K 18
Banniskirk ...85 J 8
Bannockburn ...67 I 15
Banstead ...21 T 30
Banwell ...18 L 30
Bapchild ...22 W 30
Bar Hill ...29 U 27
Barbaraville ...79 H 10
Barbon ...48 M 21
Barcaldine ...65 E 14
Barcombe Cross ...11 U 31
Bardney ...45 T 24
Bardsea ...48 K 21
Bardsey ...43 P 22
Bardsey Island ...32 F 25

Barford ...39 X 26
Barford-St. Martin ...9 O 30
Barfreston ...23 X 30
Bargoed ...18 K 28
Bargrennan ...52 G 18
Barham ...23 X 30
Barking ...30 X 27
Barking and Dagenham
  London Borough ...21 U 29
Barkston ...37 S 25
Barkway ...29 U 28
Barlaston ...35 N 25
Barlborough ...44 Q 24
Barlestone ...36 P 26
Barley North Hertfordshire ...29 U 27
Barley Pendle ...42 N 22
Barlow ...43 P 24
Barmby on the Marsh ...44 R 22
Barming ...22 V 30
Barmouth / Abermaw ...33 H 25
Barmouth Bay ...33 H 25
Barmston ...51 T 21
Barnack ...37 S 26
Barnard Castle ...49 O 20
Barnby Dun ...44 Q 23
Barnby Moor
  East Riding of Yorks. ...50 R 22
Barnby Moor Notts. ...44 Q 23
Barnet London Borough ...21 T 29
Barnetby-le-Wold ...45 S 23
Barney ...38 W 25
Barnham ...30 W 26
Barnham Broom ...38 X 26
Barnhill ...80 J 11
Barnhills ...52 E 18
Barningham ...49 O 20
Barnoldswick ...49 N 22
Barnsley ...43 P 23
Barnstaple ...7 H 30
Barnston ...42 M 24
Barnwell ...29 S 26
Barr ...52 F 18
Barra ...70 X 13
Barra (Sound of) ...70 X 12
Barra Head ...70 X 13
Barregarrow ...46 G 21
Barrhead ...60 G 16
Barrhill ...52 F 18
Barri / Barry ...18 K 29
Barrington ...8 L 31
Barrisdale ...72 D 12
Barrisdale Bay ...72 D 12
Barrmill ...60 G 16
Barrock ...86 K 8
Barrow ...30 V 27
Barrow Burn ...63 N 17
Barrow Gurney ...18 L 29
Barrow-in-Furness ...47 K 21
Barrow-upon-Humber ...45 S 22
Barrow-upon-Soar ...36 Q 25
Barrowby ...36 R 25
Barrowford ...43 N 22
Barry Angus ...69 L 14
Barry / Barri
  Vale of Glamorgan ...18 K 29
Barsham ...31 Y 26
Barston ...27 O 26
Bartestree ...26 M 27
Barton Eden ...49 P 20
Barton Lancs. ...42 L 22
Barton-le-Clay ...29 S 28
Barton le Willows ...50 R 21
Barton Mills ...30 V 26
Barton-on-Sea ...9 P 31
Barton-under-Needwood ...35 O 25
Barton-upon-Humber ...44 S 22
Barvas ...82 A 8
Barwell ...36 P 26
Barwick-in-Elmet ...43 P 22
Baschurch ...34 L 25
Bashall Eaves ...42 M 22
Basildon Berks. ...20 Q 29
Basildon Essex ...22 V 29
Basing ...20 Q 30
Basingstoke ...20 Q 30
Baslow ...43 P 24
Bass Rock ...69 M 15
Bassenthwaite ...54 K 19
Bassingham ...37 S 24
Baston ...37 S 25
Bastwick ...39 Y 25
Batcombe ...8 M 31
Bath ...19 M 29
Bathampton ...19 N 29
Batheaston ...19 N 29
Bathgate ...61 J 16
Batley ...43 P 22

Battle ...12 V 31
Baumber ...45 T 24
Bawburgh ...39 X 26
Bawdeswell ...38 X 25
Bawdsey ...31 Y 27
Bawtry ...44 Q 23
Bayble ...83 B 9
Baycliff ...48 K 21
Baydon ...19 P 29
Bayhead ...76 X 11
Bayston Hill ...34 L 25
Beachampton ...28 R 27
Beachy Head ...12 U 31
Beacon (The) ...2 E 33
Beacon End ...30 W 28
Beaconsfield ...21 S 29
Beadlam ...50 R 21
Beadnell Bay ...63 P 17
Beaford ...7 H 31
Beal ...63 O 16
Beaminster ...8 L 31
Beamish Hall ...56 P 19
Beamsley ...49 O 22
Bearsden ...67 G 16
Bearsted ...22 V 30
Beattock ...61 J 18
Beauchief ...43 P 24
Beaufort ...18 K 28
Beaulieu ...10 P 31
Beauly ...79 G 11
Beauly Firth ...79 G 11
Beaumaris ...40 H 23
Beaumont ...54 K 19
Beaupré Castle ...17 J 29
Bebington ...42 L 23
Beccles ...31 Y 26
Beckfoot ...54 J 19
Beckingham ...44 R 23
Beckington ...19 N 30
Beckley ...12 V 31
Beckton ...21 U 29
Bedale ...50 P 21
Beddau ...17 J 29
Beddgelert ...33 H 24
Beddingham ...11 U 31
Bedford ...29 S 27
Bedgebury Pinetum ...12 V 30
Bedlington ...56 P 18
Bedlinog ...17 K 28
Bedrule ...62 M 17
Bedwas ...18 K 29
Bedworth ...28 P 26
Bee (Loch) ...76 X 11
Beer ...5 K 31
Beeston ...36 Q 25
Beeswing ...53 I 18
Begdbroke ...20 Q 28
Beguildy ...26 K 26
Beighton ...44 P 23
Beinn a' Ghlò ...74 I 13
Beinn a' Mheadhoin (Loch) ...78 F 12
Beinn Dearg Highland ...78 F 10
Beinn Dearg
  Perthshire and Kinross ...73 I 13
Beinn Heasgarnich ...67 G 14
Beinn Ime ...66 F 15
Beith ...60 G 16
Belbroughton ...27 N 26
Belchford ...45 T 24
Belford ...63 O 17
Belhelvie ...75 N 12
Bellabeg ...74 K 12
Bellanoch ...65 D 15
Bellingham ...55 N 18
Bellshill
  Berwick-upon-Tweed ...63 O 17
Bellshill North Lanarkshire ...60 H 16
Belmont ...87 R 1
Belnacraig ...74 K 12
Belper ...36 P 24
Belsay ...56 O 18
Belstead ...31 X 27
Belton Lincs. ...37 S 25
Belton Norfolk ...39 Y 26
Belton North Lincs. ...44 R 23
Belton Rutland ...36 R 26
Belvoir ...36 R 25
Bembridge ...10 Q 31
Bempton ...51 T 21
Ben Alder ...73 G 13
Ben Alder Lodge ...73 G 13
Ben Armine Forest ...85 H 9
Ben Armine Lodge ...85 H 9
Ben Chonzie ...67 I 14
Ben Cruachan ...65 E 14
Ben-damph Forest ...78 D 11

Ben Hope ...84 G 8
Ben Klibreck ...84 G 9
Ben Lawers ...67 H 14
Ben Ledi ...67 H 15
Ben Lomond ...66 G 15
Ben Loyal ...84 G 8
Ben Macdui ...74 I 12
Ben More Argyll and Bute ...65 B 14
Ben More Stirling ...67 G 14
Ben More Assynt ...84 F 9
Ben Nevis ...72 E 13
Ben Starav ...66 E 14
Ben Vorlich ...67 H 14
Ben Wyvis ...79 G 10
Benbecula ...76 X 11
Benbuie ...60 H 18
Benderloch Argyll and Bute ...65 D 14
Benderloch Mountain ...65 E 14
Benenden ...12 V 30
Benfleet ...22 V 29
Benington ...37 U 25
Benllech ...40 H 23
Benmore ...67 G 14
Benmore Lodge ...84 F 9
Benson ...20 Q 29
Bentley Doncaster ...44 Q 23
Bentley East Hampshire ...20 R 30
Bentpath ...54 K 18
Bentworth ...10 Q 30
Benwick ...29 T 26
Beoraid (Loch) ...72 D 13
Bere Alston ...3 H 32
Bere Ferrers ...3 H 32
Bere Regis ...9 N 31
Berkeley ...18 M 28
Berkhamsted ...21 S 28
Berneray near Barra ...70 X 13
Berneray near North Uist ...76 Y 10
Bernice ...66 E 15
Bernisdale ...77 B 11
Berriew ...34 K 26
Berrington Hall ...26 L 27
Berrow ...18 K 30
Berry Head ...4 J 32
Berry Hill ...18 M 28
Berry Pomeroy ...4 J 32
Berrynarbor ...17 H 30
Bervie Bay ...75 N 13
Berwick-St. John ...9 N 31
Berwick-upon-Tweed ...63 O 16
Berwyn ...33 J 25
Bessacarr ...44 Q 23
Bethel ...33 H 24
Bethersden ...12 W 30
Bethesda ...33 H 24
Betley ...35 M 24
Bettisfield ...34 L 25
Bettws Cedewain ...34 K 26
Bettws Evan ...15 G 27
Bettws Gwerfil Goch ...33 J 24
Bettyhill ...85 H 8
Betws-y-Coed ...33 I 24
Betws yn Rhos ...41 I 23
Beulah near Cardigan ...15 G 27
Beulah
  near Llandrindod-Wells ...25 J 27
Beverley ...45 S 22
Beverstone ...19 N 29
Bewaldeth ...54 K 19
Bewcastle ...55 L 18
Bewdley ...27 N 26
Bewholme ...51 T 22
Bexhill ...12 V 31
Bexley London Borough ...21 U 29
Beyton ...30 W 27
Bhaid-Luachraich (Loch) ...78 D 10
Bhealaich (Loch a') ...84 G 9
Bhraoin (Loch a') ...78 E 10
Bhrollum (Loch) ...82 A 10
Bibury ...19 O 28
Bicester ...28 Q 28
Bicker ...37 T 25
Bickington ...4 I 32
Bickleigh Mid Devon ...7 J 31
Bickleigh South Hams ...4 H 32
Bicton ...34 L 25
Bicton gardens ...5 K 31
Biddenden ...12 V 30
Biddenham ...29 S 27
Biddestone ...19 N 29
Biddulph ...35 N 24
Bidean nam Bian ...72 E 14
Bideford ...6 H 30
Bidford ...27 O 27
Bielside ...75 N 12
Bierton ...20 R 28

Big Corlae ...60 H 18
Bigbury ...4 I 33
Bigbury-on-Sea ...4 I 33
Biggar Barrow-in-Furness ...47 K 21
Biggar South Lanarkshire ...61 J 17
Biggin Hill ...21 U 30
Biggleswade ...29 T 27
Bignor ...11 S 31
Bildeston ...30 W 27
Bildsgreen ...27 M 26
Bill of Portland ...8 M 32
Billericay ...22 V 29
Billesdon ...36 R 26
Billingborough ...37 S 25
Billinge ...42 L 23
Billingham ...57 Q 20
Billinghay ...37 T 24
Billingshurst ...11 S 30
Billingsley ...27 M 26
Billington ...42 M 22
Billockby ...39 Y 26
Billy Row ...56 O 19
Bilsington ...12 W 30
Bilsthorpe ...36 Q 24
Bilston ...35 N 26
Bilton ...45 T 22
Binbrook ...45 T 23
Binfield ...20 R 29
Bingham ...36 R 25
Bingley ...43 O 22
Binham ...38 W 25
Binns (The) ...68 J 16
Binsted ...10 R 30
Birchington ...23 X 29
Birdham ...10 R 31
Birdingbury ...28 P 27
Birdwell ...43 P 23
Birdworld ...10 R 30
Birgham ...62 N 17
Birkdale ...42 K 23
Birkenhead ...42 K 23
Birkin ...44 Q 22
Birling Gap ...12 U 31
Birmingham ...27 O 26
Birsay ...86 K 6
Birsemore ...75 L 12
Birstall ...36 Q 25
Birtley Gateshead ...56 P 19
Birtley Tynedale ...55 N 18
Birtsmorton Court ...27 N 27
Bisham ...20 R 29
Bishop Auckland ...56 P 20
Bishop Burton ...44 S 22
Bishop Monkton ...50 P 21
Bishop Sutton ...18 M 29
Bishop Thornton ...50 P 21
Bishop Wilton ...50 R 22
Bishops Cannings ...19 O 29
Bishop's Castle ...26 L 26
Bishop's Caundle ...9 M 31
Bishop's Cleeve ...27 N 28
Bishop's Itchington ...28 P 27
Bishops Lydeard ...8 K 30
Bishop's Nympton ...7 I 31
Bishop's Palace
  near St. David's ...14 E 28
Bishop's Palace near Tenby 16 F 28
Bishop's Stortford ...30 U 28
Bishop's Tachbrook ...28 P 27
Bishop's Tawton ...7 H 30
Bishop's Waltham ...10 Q 31
Bishopsteignton ...4 J 32
Bishopstocke ...10 Q 31
Bishopston ...15 H 29
Bishopstone Salisbury ...9 O 30
Bishopstone Swindon ...19 P 29
Bishopthorpe ...50 Q 22
Bishopton Darlington ...56 P 20
Bishopton Renfrewshire ...67 G 16
Bishton ...18 L 29
Bisley ...19 N 28
Bispham ...42 K 22
Bix ...20 R 29
Bixter ...87 P 3
Blaby ...36 Q 26
Black Bay ...59 D 17
Black Corries ...72 F 13
Black Down Hills ...8 K 31
Black Isle ...79 G 11
Black Mount ...66 F 14
Black Mountain ...25 I 28
Black Mountains ...26 K 28
Black Notley ...30 V 28
Black Torrington ...6 H 31
Black Water Valley ...78 F 11
Blackawton ...4 I 32

A
B
C
D
E
F
G
H
I
J
K
L
M
N
O
P
Q
R
S
T
U
V
W
X
Y
Z

A B C D E F G H I J K L M N O P Q R S T U V W X Y Z

Blackburn *Aberdeenshire* ...75 N 12
Blackburn *Lancs.* ...42 M 22
Blackburn *West Lothian* ...61 J 16
Blackfield ...10 P 31
Blackford *Cumbria* ...54 L 19
Blackford *Perthshire and Kinross* ...67 I 15
Blackhall ...57 Q 19
Blackhall Rocks ...57 Q 19
Blackhill *Aberdeenshire* ...81 O 11
Blackhill *Highland* ...77 A 11
Blacklunans ...74 J 13
Blackmoor Gate ...17 I 30
Blackmore ...22 U 28
Blackness Castle ...68 J 15
Blacko ...43 N 22
Blackpool ...42 K 22
Blackridge ...61 I 16
Blackthorn ...28 Q 28
Blacktoft ...44 R 22
Blackwater *Hart* ...20 R 30
Blackwater *Isle of Wight* ...10 Q 31
Blackwater (River) ...22 W 28
Blackwater Reservoir ...72 F 13
Blackwaterfoot ...59 D 17
Blackwell ...50 P 20
Blackwood ...18 K 29
Bladnoch ...52 G 19
Bladon ...20 P 28
Blaenannherch ...15 G 27
Blaenau Ffestiniog ...33 I 25
Blaenavon ...18 K 28
Blaengarw ...17 J 29
Blaengrwrach ...17 J 28
Blagdon ...18 L 30
Blaich ...72 E 13
Blaina ...18 K 28
Blair Atholl ...73 I 13
Blair Castle ...73 I 13
Blairgowrie ...68 J 14
Blairmore ...66 F 16
Blakeney *Glos.* ...18 M 28
Blakeney *Norfolk* ...38 X 25
Blakesley ...28 Q 27
Blamerino ...68 K 14
Blandford Forum ...9 N 31
Blanefield ...67 H 16
Blàr a Chaorainn ...72 E 13
Blarmachfoldach ...72 E 13
Blarnalearoch ...78 E 10
Blawith ...48 K 21
Blaxton ...44 R 23
Blaydon ...56 O 19
Bleadon ...18 L 30
Bleaklow Hill ...43 O 23
Blean ...23 X 30
Bleasby ...36 R 24
Blenheim Palace ...20 P 28
Bletchingdon ...20 Q 28
Bletchley ...28 R 27
Bletsoe ...29 S 27
Blewbury ...20 Q 29
Blickling ...39 X 25
Blickling Hall ...39 X 25
Blidworth ...36 Q 24
Blindley Heath ...21 T 30
Blisland ...3 F 32
Blisworth ...28 R 27
Blithe ...35 O 25
Blithfield Hall ...35 O 25
Blithfield Reservoir ...35 O 25
Blockley ...27 O 27
Blofield ...39 Y 26
Bloxham ...28 P 27
Blubberhouses ...49 O 22
Blue John Cavern ...43 O 23
Bluemull Sound ...87 Q 1
Blundellsands ...42 K 23
Blundeston ...39 Z 26
Blyth *Northumb.* ...56 P 18
Blyth *Notts.* ...44 Q 23
Blythburgh ...31 Y 27
Blythe Bridge ...35 N 25
Blyton ...44 R 23
Bo' Ness ...68 J 15
Boarhills ...69 L 15
Boat of Garten ...74 I 12
Boathvic ...79 G 10
Bocking Churchstreet ...30 V 28
Boddam ...81 O 11
Bodedern ...40 G 23
Bodelwyddan ...41 J 23
Bodenham ...26 L 27
Bodfari ...41 J 23
Bodfordd ...40 G 23
Bodham Street ...39 X 25
Bodiam Castle ...12 V 30

Bodicote ...28 Q 27
Bodmin ...3 F 32
Bodmin Moor ...3 G 32
Bodnant Garden ...41 I 23
Bognor Regis ...11 R 31
Bogue ...53 H 18
Boisdale ...70 X 12
Boisdale (Loch) ...70 Y 12
Boldon ...56 P 19
Bolham ...7 J 31
Bollin (River) ...42 N 23
Bollington ...43 N 24
Bolney ...11 T 31
Bolnhurst ...29 S 27
Bolsover ...44 Q 24
Boltby ...50 Q 21
Bolton *Alnwick* ...63 O 17
Bolton *Bolton* ...42 M 23
Bolton Abbey ...49 O 22
Bolton-by-Bowland ...49 N 22
Bolton-le-Sands ...48 L 21
Bolton on Swale ...50 P 20
Bolton-upon-Dearne ...44 Q 23
Bomere Heath ...34 L 25
Bonar Bridge ...79 G 10
Bonawe Quarries ...65 E 14
Bonby ...44 S 23
Boncath ...15 G 27
Bonchester Bridge ...62 M 17
Bonhill ...66 G 16
Bonnybridge ...67 I 16
Bont-faen / Cowbridge ...17 J 29
Bontgoch Elerch ...25 I 26
Bontnewydd ...32 H 24
Boosbeck ...50 R 20
Boot ...47 K 20
Bootle *Cumbria* ...47 J 21
Bootle *Merseyside* ...42 K 23
Border Forest Park (The) ...55 M 18
Bordogan ...32 G 24
Boreham ...22 V 28
Boreham Street ...12 V 31
Borehamwood ...21 T 29
Boreland ...54 K 18
Borgue *Dumfries and Galloway* ...53 H 19
Borgue *Highland* ...85 J 9
Borness ...53 H 19
Borough Green ...22 U 30
Boroughbridge ...50 P 21
Borreraig ...77 Z 11
Borrobol Forest ...85 H 9
Borrowash ...36 P 25
Borth ...25 H 26
Borve *Barra Isle* ...70 X 13
Borve *Eilean Siar* ...70 X 13
Borve *Isle of Lewis* ...82 A 8
Borve *South Harris* ...76 Y 10
Borwick ...48 L 21
Bosbury ...26 M 27
Boscastle ...6 F 31
Boscombe ...9 O 31
Bosham ...10 R 31
Bosherston ...16 F 29
Bosley ...35 N 24
Boston ...37 T 25
Boston Spa ...50 P 22
Boswinger ...3 F 33
Botesdale ...30 W 26
Bothamsall ...44 R 24
Bothel ...54 K 19
Bothwell ...60 H 16
Botley ...10 Q 31
Bottesfor *Melton* ...36 R 25
Bottesford *North Lincolnshire* ...44 S 23
Bottisham ...30 U 27
Botwnnog ...32 G 25
Boughton ...36 Q 24
Boughton House ...29 R 26
Boughton Street ...22 W 30
Boulmer ...63 P 17
Boultham ...44 S 24
Bourn ...29 T 27
Bourne ...37 S 25
Bournemouth ...9 O 31
Bourton *North Dorset* ...9 N 30
Bourton *Vale of White Horse* ...19 P 29
Bourton-on-the-Water ...27 O 28
Bovey Tracey ...4 I 32
Bovingdon ...21 S 28
Bow ...7 I 31
Bow Street ...25 H 26
Bowden ...62 L 17
Bower *Highland* ...85 K 8

Bower *Tynedale* ...55 M 18
Bowerchalke ...9 O 30
Bowes ...49 N 20
Bowhill ...62 L 17
Bowland ...62 L 17
Bowland (Forest of) ...49 M 22
Bowmore ...58 B 16
Bowness ...48 L 20
Bowness-on-Solway ...54 K 19
Bowood House ...19 N 29
Box ...19 N 29
Box Hill ...21 T 30
Boxford *Babergh* ...30 W 27
Boxford *West Berkshire* ...20 P 29
Boxley ...22 V 30
Boxworth ...29 T 27
Boyton ...6 G 31
Bozeat ...29 R 27
Braaid ...46 G 21
Brabourne Lees ...12 W 30
Bracadale (Loch) ...77 A 12
Bracebridge Heath ...37 S 24
Brackley ...28 Q 27
Brackley Hatch ...28 Q 27
Bracknell ...20 R 29
Braco ...67 I 15
Bracora ...72 C 13
Bradan Resr (Loch) ...60 G 18
Bradfield *Sheffield* ...43 P 23
Bradfield *West Berkshire* ...20 Q 29
Bradford *Bradford* ...43 O 22
Bradford *Taunton Deane* ...8 K 31
Bradford Abbas ...8 M 31
Bradford-on-Avon ...19 N 29
Brading ...10 Q 31
Bradninch ...7 J 31
Bradpole ...5 L 31
Bradwell ...43 O 24
Bradwell-on-Sea ...22 W 28
Bradworthy ...6 G 31
Brae ...87 P 2
Brae of Achnahaird ...83 D 9
Braeantra ...79 G 10
Braemar ...74 J 12
Braemore ...85 J 9
Braeriach ...74 I 12
Braeswick ...87 L 6
Brafferton Helperby ...50 Q 21
Bragar ...82 A 8
Braglenbeg ...65 D 15
Braich y Pwll ...32 F 25
Braidwood ...61 I 16
Bràigh Mòr ...82 Y 9
Brailes ...28 P 27
Brailsford ...35 P 25
Braintree ...30 V 28
Braishfield ...10 P 30
Braithwaite ...54 K 20
Braithwell ...44 Q 23
Bramcote ...36 Q 25
Bramfield ...31 Y 27
Bramford ...31 X 27
Bramhall ...43 N 23
Bramham ...43 P 22
Bramhope ...43 P 22
Bramley *Basingstoke and Deane* ...20 Q 30
Bramley *South Yorks.* ...44 Q 23
Bramley *Surrey* ...21 S 30
Brampton *Cambs.* ...29 T 27
Brampton *Cumbria* ...55 L 19
Brampton *Eden* ...55 M 20
Brampton *Rotherham.* ...43 P 23
Brampton *Suffolk* ...31 Y 26
Brampton Bryan ...26 L 26
Brancaster ...38 V 25
Branderburgh ...80 K 10
Brandesburton ...51 T 22
Brandon *Durham* ...56 P 19
Brandon *Suffolk* ...30 V 26
Brandsby ...50 Q 21
Branscombe ...5 K 31
Bransgore ...9 O 31
Branston ...37 S 24
Brant Broughton ...37 S 24
Brassington ...35 P 24
Bratton ...19 N 30
Bratton Clovelly ...6 H 31
Bratton Fleming ...7 I 30
Braughing ...29 U 28
Braunston *Daventry* ...28 Q 27
Braunston *Rutland* ...36 R 26
Braunton ...6 H 30
Bray-on-Thames ...21 R 29

Bray Shop ...3 G 32
Braybrooke ...28 R 26
Brayford ...7 I 30
Brayton ...44 Q 22
Breaclete ...82 Z 9
Breadalbane ...67 G 14
Breage ...2 D 33
Bream ...18 M 28
Breamore House ...9 O 31
Brean ...18 K 30
Breasclete ...82 Z 9
Breaston ...36 Q 25
Brechin ...75 M 13
Breckland ...30 V 26
Brecon / Aberhonddu ...25 J 28
Brecon Beacons National Park ...25 J 28
Bredbury ...43 N 23
Bredenbury ...26 M 27
Bredgar ...22 W 30
Bredon ...27 N 27
Bredwardine ...26 L 27
Bremhill ...19 N 29
Brenchley ...12 V 30
Brendon Hills ...7 J 30
Brenig Reservoir ...33 J 24
Brenish ...82 Y 9
Brent *London Borough* ...21 T 29
Brent Knoll ...18 L 30
Brent Pelham ...29 U 28
Brentwood ...22 U 29
Brenzett ...12 W 30
Brereton ...35 O 25
Bressay ...87 Q 3
Bretford ...28 P 26
Bretherton ...42 L 22
Brewham ...9 M 30
Brewlands Bridge ...74 K 13
Brewood ...35 N 25
Bride ...46 G 20
Bridestowe ...4 H 31
Bridge ...23 X 30
Bridge of Alford ...75 L 12
Bridge of Allan ...67 I 15
Bridge of Avon ...80 J 11
Bridge of Balgie ...73 H 14
Bridge of Brown ...74 J 12
Bridge of Buchat ...74 L 12
Bridge of Craigisla ...74 K 13
Bridge of Dee ...53 I 19
Bridge of Don ...75 N 12
Bridge of Dun ...75 M 13
Bridge of Dye ...75 M 13
Bridge of Earn ...68 J 14
Bridge of Ericht ...73 G 13
Bridge of Gairn ...74 K 12
Bridge of Gaur ...73 G 13
Bridge of Orchy ...66 F 14
Bridge of Weir ...60 G 16
Bridge Trafford ...42 L 24
Bridgemary ...10 Q 31
Bridgend *Aberdeenshire* ...80 L 11
Bridgend *Angus* ...75 L 13
Bridgend *Argyll and Bute* ...65 D 15
Bridgend *Islay* ...58 B 16
Bridgend *Perthshire and Kinross* ...68 J 14
Bridgend / Pen-y-bont ...17 J 29
Bridgend of Lintrathen ...74 K 13
Bridgerule ...6 G 31
Bridgham ...30 W 26
Bridgnorth ...27 M 26
Bridgwater ...8 L 30
Bridlington ...51 T 21
Bridport ...5 L 31
Brierfield ...43 N 22
Brierley ...43 P 23
Brierley Hill ...27 N 26
Brigg ...44 S 23
Brigham ...54 J 20
Brighouse ...43 O 22
Brighstone ...10 P 32
Brighstone Forest ...10 P 32
Brightling ...12 V 31
Brightlingsea ...22 X 28
Brighton ...11 T 31
Brightwell ...20 Q 29
Brigstock ...29 S 26
Brill ...20 Q 28
Brimfield ...26 L 27
Brimham Rocks ...49 O 21
Brimington ...43 P 24
Brimpsfield ...19 N 28
Brimpton ...20 Q 29
Brinkburn Priory ...63 O 18
Brinkley ...30 V 27

Brinklow ...28 P 26
Brinkworth ...19 O 29
Brinyan ...86 L 6
Brisley ...38 W 25
Brislington ...18 M 29
Bristol ...18 M 29
Briston ...38 X 25
Briton Ferry ...17 I 29
Brittle (Loch) ...71 B 12
Brittwell Salome ...20 Q 29
Brixham ...4 J 32
Brixton ...4 I 32
Brixworth ...28 R 27
Brize Norton ...20 P 28
Broad Bay ...83 B 9
Broad Blunsdon ...19 O 29
Broad Chalke ...9 O 30
Broad Haven ...14 E 28
Broad Hinton ...19 O 29
Broad Law ...61 J 17
Broad Oak ...12 V 31
Broadbridge Heath ...11 S 30
Broadclyst ...7 J 31
Broadlands ...10 P 31
Broadmayne ...9 M 31
Broadstairs ...23 Y 29
Broadstone ...9 O 31
Broadwas ...27 M 27
Broadway ...27 O 27
Broadwell Ho ...55 N 19
Broadwey ...8 M 32
Broadwindsor ...8 L 31
Broadwoodwidger ...6 H 31
Brochel ...77 B 11
Brockdish ...31 X 26
Brockenhurst ...10 P 31
Brockley ...18 L 29
Brockworth ...19 N 28
Brodick ...59 E 17
Brodick Bay ...59 E 17
Brodick Castle ...59 E 17
Brodie Castle ...79 I 11
Brodsworth ...44 Q 23
Brodsworth Hall ...44 Q 23
Brokenborough ...19 N 29
Brolass ...65 B 14
Bromborough ...42 L 24
Brome ...31 X 26
Bromfield ...26 L 26
Bromham *Bedford* ...29 S 27
Bromham *Kennet* ...19 N 29
Bromley *London Borough* ...21 U 29
Brompton *Kent* ...22 V 29
Brompton *near Northallerton* ...50 P 20
Brompton-by-Sawdon ...51 S 21
Brompton on Swale ...49 O 20
Brompton Ralph ...7 K 30
Brompton Regis ...7 J 30
Bromsgrove ...27 N 26
Bromyard ...26 M 27
Bronllys ...26 K 27
Brook ...22 W 30
Brooke ...39 Y 26
Brookmans Park ...21 T 28
Broom (Loch) ...78 E 10
Broomfield *Chelmsford* ...22 V 28
Broomfield *Sedgemoor* ...8 K 30
Broomfleet ...44 S 22
Broomhaugh ...56 O 19
Brora ...85 I 9
Broseley ...34 M 26
Brotherton ...44 Q 22
Brotton ...57 R 20
Brough *East Riding of Yorkshire* ...44 S 22
Brough *Eden* ...49 N 20
Brough *Highland* ...86 J 8
Brough Head ...86 J 6
Brough Lodge ...87 R 2
Brough of Birsay ...86 J 6
Broughton *Cumbria* ...54 J 19
Broughton *Flintshire / Sir y Fflint* ...34 L 24
Broughton *Hants.* ...10 P 30
Broughton *Lancs.* ...42 L 22
Broughton *North Lincs.* ...44 S 23
Broughton *Northants.* ...28 R 26
Broughton *Oxon.* ...28 P 27
Broughton *Scottish Borders* ...61 J 17
Broughton-in-Furness ...47 K 21
Broughton Mills ...47 K 21
Broughton Moor ...54 J 19
Broughton Poggs ...19 P 28
Broughty Ferry ...69 L 14
Brownhills ...35 O 26
Brownsea Island ...9 O 31

Broxbourne ...21 T 28
Broxburn ...68 J 16
Bruar Lodge ...73 I 13
Bruichladdich ...58 A 16
Brundall ...39 Y 26
Brushford ...7 J 30
Bruton ...8 M 30
Brydekirk ...54 K 18
Brymbo ...34 K 24
Bryn-Henllan ...24 F 27
Brynamman ...17 I 28
Brynbuga / Usk ...18 L 28
Bryncethin ...17 J 29
Bryneglwys ...34 K 24
Bryngwran ...40 G 23
Bryngwyn ...26 K 27
Brynhoffnant ...15 G 27
Brynmawr ...18 K 28
Brynsiencyn ...32 H 24
Brynteg ...40 H 23
Bualintur ...71 B 12
Bubwith ...44 R 22
Buccleuch ...61 K 17
Buchanty ...67 I 14
Buchlyvie ...67 H 15
Buckden *Cambs.* ...29 T 27
Buckden *North Yorks.* ...49 N 21
Buckfast ...4 I 32
Buckfast Abbey ...4 I 32
Buckfastleigh ...4 I 32
Buckhaven ...68 K 15
Buckhorn Weston ...9 M 30
Buckie ...80 L 10
Buckingham ...28 R 27
Buckland *Herts.* ...29 T 28
Buckland *Oxon.* ...20 P 28
Buckland Abbey ...4 H 32
Buckland Brewer ...6 H 31
Buckland Dinham ...19 M 30
Buckland in-the-Moor ...4 I 32
Buckland Newton ...8 M 31
Buckland St. Mary ...8 K 31
Bucklebury ...20 Q 29
Bucklers Hard ...10 P 31
Buckley / Bwcle ...34 K 24
Buckminster ...36 R 25
Bucknall ...37 T 24
Bucknell ...26 L 26
Bucksburn ...75 N 12
Bucks green ...11 S 30
Bude ...6 G 31
Budleigh Salterton ...5 K 32
Bugbrooke ...28 Q 27
Bugle ...3 F 32
Bugthorpe ...50 R 21
Buildwas Abbey ...34 M 26
Builth Wells / Llanfair-ym-Muallt ...25 J 27
Bulford ...19 O 30
Bulkeley ...34 L 24
Bulkington ...28 P 26
Bulwark ...36 Q 24
Bulwick ...37 S 26
Bunarkaig ...72 F 13
Bunessan ...64 B 15
Bungay ...31 Y 26
Bunnahabhainn ...64 B 16
Bunny ...36 Q 25
Buntingford ...29 T 28
Burbage *Leics.* ...28 P 26
Burbage *Wilts.* ...19 O 29
Burchett's Green ...20 R 29
Bures ...30 W 28
Burford ...19 P 28
Burgess Hill ...11 T 31
Burgh-by-Sands ...54 K 19
Burgh Castle ...39 Y 26
Burgh-le-Marsh ...38 U 24
Burgh-St. Peter ...39 Y 26
Burghead ...80 J 10
Burghfield ...20 Q 29
Burghill ...26 L 27
Burghley House ...37 S 26
Burham ...22 V 30
Burley ...9 O 31
Burley-in-Wharfedale ...49 O 22
Burlton ...34 L 25
Burneside ...48 L 20
Burneston ...50 P 21
Burnfoot ...62 L 17
Burnham ...21 S 29
Burnham Market ...38 W 25
Burnham Mills ...44 S 22
Burnham-on-Crouch ...22 W 29
Burnham-on-Sea ...18 L 30
Burnhaven ...81 O 11
Burnhope ...56 O 19
Burniston ...51 S 21

Burnley .... 43 N 22
Burntisland .... 68 K 15
Burrafirth .... 87 R 1
Burravoe .... 87 Q 2
Burray .... 87 L 7
Burrelton .... 68 K 14
Burringham .... 44 R 23
Burrington North Devon ...... 7 I 31
Burrington North Somerset ..18 L 30
Burrough Green .... 30 V 27
Burrow Head .... 53 G 19
Burry Port /Porth Tywyn ...15 H 28
Burscough .... 42 L 23
Burscough Bridge .... 42 L 23
Burshill .... 51 S 22
Bursledon .... 10 Q 31
Burslem .... 35 N 24
Burstwick .... 45 T 22
Burton Christchurch ....9 O 31
Burton Ellesmere
    Port and Neston .... 48 L 21
Burton South Lakeland .... 48 L 21
Burton Wrecsam / Wrexham 34 L 24
Burton Agnes .... 51 T 21
Burton Bradstock .... 5 L 31
Burton Constable Hall .... 45 T 22
Burton Fleming .... 51 S 21
Burton in Lonsdale .... 49 M 21
Burton Joyce .... 36 Q 25
Burton Latimer .... 29 R 26
Burton Leonard .... 50 P 21
Burton Pidsea .... 45 T 22
Burton-upon-Stather .... 44 R 23
Burton-upon-Trent .... 35 O 25
Burwarton .... 26 M 26
Burwash .... 12 V 31
Burwell Cambs. .... 30 U 27
Burwell Lincs. .... 45 U 24
Bury Bury .... 42 N 23
Bury Chichester .... 11 S 31
Bury St. Edmunds .... 30 W 27
Busby .... 60 H 16
Buscot .... 19 P 28
Bushey .... 21 S 29
Bute (Island of) .... 59 E 16
Bute (Kyles of) .... 59 E 16
Bute (Sound of) .... 59 E 16
Butleigh .... 8 L 30
Butley .... 31 Y 27
Butt of Lewis .... 83 B 8
Buttercrambe .... 50 R 21
Buttermere .... 47 K 20
Butterstone .... 68 J 14
Buttington .... 34 K 25
Buxted .... 12 U 31
Buxton Derbs. .... 43 O 24
Buxton Norfolk .... 39 X 25
Bwcle / Buckley .... 34 K 24
Bwlch .... 26 K 28
Bwlch Oerddrws .... 33 I 25
Bwlch y Ffridd .... 33 J 26
Bwlch-y-Groes .... 25 I 28
Bwlch-y-Sarnau .... 25 J 26
Bwlchgwyn .... 34 K 24
Bwlchllan .... 25 H 27
Byfield .... 28 Q 27
Byfleet .... 21 S 30
Byland Abbey .... 50 Q 21
Byrness .... 62 M 18

C

Cabrach .... 80 K 12
Cadair Idris .... 33 I 25
Caddington .... 29 S 28
Caddonfoot .... 62 L 17
Cadhay .... 5 K 31
Cadishead .... 42 M 23
Cadnam .... 10 P 31
Cadney .... 44 S 23
Cadwell Park .... 45 T 24
Caerau .... 17 J 29
Caerdydd / Cardiff .... 18 K 29
Caerffili / Caerphilly .... 18 K 29
Caerfyrddin / Carmarthen ...15 H 28
Caergwrle .... 34 K 24
Caergybi / Holyhead .... 40 G 23
Caerlaverock Castle .... 53 J 19
Caerleon .... 18 L 29
Caernarfon .... 32 H 24
Caernarfon Bay .... 32 G 24
Caerphilly / Caerffili .... 18 K 29
Caersws .... 25 J 26
Caerwent .... 18 L 29
Caerwys .... 41 K 23
Cailliness Point .... 52 F 19
Cairn Edward Forest .... 53 H 18
Cairn Gorm .... 74 J 12

Cairn Table .... 60 H 17
Cairn Toul .... 74 I 12
Cairnborrow .... 80 L 11
Cairndow .... 66 F 15
Cairngaan .... 52 F 20
Cairngarroch .... 52 E 19
Cairnie .... 80 L 11
Cairnpapple Hill .... 67 J 16
Cairnryan .... 52 E 19
Cairnsmore of Carsphairn ..60 H 18
Cairnsmore of Fleet .... 53 G 19
Cairraig Fhada .... 58 B 17
Caister-on-Sea .... 39 Z 26
Caistor .... 45 T 23
Calbourne .... 10 P 31
Caldback .... 54 K 19
Caldecott .... 36 R 26
Calder (Loch) .... 85 J 8
Calder Bridge .... 47 J 20
Calder Mains .... 85 J 8
Caldercruix .... 61 I 16
Calderdale .... 43 N 22
Caldermill .... 60 H 17
Caldey Island .... 15 F 29
Caldicot .... 18 L 29
Caldwell .... 49 O 20
Calf of Man .... 46 F 21
Calfsound .... 87 L 6
Calgary .... 71 B 14
Calgary Bay .... 71 B 14
Caliach Point .... 71 B 14
Calke Abbey .... 36 P 25
Callander .... 67 H 15
Callander (Glen) .... 74 J 13
Callington .... 3 H 32
Calne .... 19 N 29
Calow .... 43 P 24
Calstock .... 3 H 32
Calthwaite .... 55 L 19
Calvay .... 70 Y 12
Calver .... 43 P 24
Calverton .... 36 Q 24
Calvine .... 73 I 13
Cam .... 29 U 27
Cam Loch .... 84 E 9
Camas Chil Mhalieu .... 72 D 14
Camas-luinie .... 78 D 12
Camasnacroise .... 72 D 14
Camastianavaig .... 77 B 11
Camber .... 12 W 31
Camberley .... 20 R 30
Camblesforth .... 44 Q 22
Cambo .... 56 O 18
Cambois .... 56 P 18
Camborne .... 2 E 33
Cambrian Mountains .... 25 I 27
Cambridge .... 29 U 27
Cambusbarron .... 67 I 15
Cambuskenneth .... 67 I 15
Camden London Borough ...21 T 29
Camelford .... 6 F 32
Cammachmore .... 75 N 12
Campbeltown .... 59 D 17
Campsie Fells .... 67 H 15
Campton .... 62 M 17
Campville .... 35 P 25
Camrose .... 24 E 28
Camusnagaul .... 78 E 10
Candlesby .... 37 U 24
Canewdon .... 22 W 29
Canisbay .... 86 K 8
Canna .... 71 A 12
Cannich .... 78 F 11
Cannich (Glen) .... 78 F 11
Cannington .... 8 K 30
Cannock .... 35 N 25
Canonbie .... 54 L 18
Canons Ashby .... 28 Q 27
Canterbury .... 23 X 30
Cantley .... 39 Y 26
Canvey Island .... 22 V 29
Caol .... 72 E 13
Caolas a' Mhòrain .... 76 Y 10
Caoles .... 70 Z 14
Caolis .... 70 X 13
Caolisport (Loch) .... 65 D 16
Cape Cornwall .... 2 C 33
Cape Wrath .... 84 E 8
Capel .... 11 T 30
Capel Curig .... 33 I 24
Capel Garmon .... 33 I 24
Capel Le Ferne .... 13 X 30
Capel St. Mary .... 31 X 27
Capel-y-Ffin .... 26 K 28
Capesthorne Hall .... 43 N 24
Capheaton .... 56 O 18
Cappercleuch .... 61 K 17

Caputh .... 68 J 14
Cara Island .... 58 C 17
Carbis Bay .... 2 D 33
Carbost Minginish .... 77 A 12
Carbost Trotternish .... 77 B 11
Cardenden .... 68 K 15
Cardiff / Caerdydd .... 18 K 29
Cardigan / Aberteifi .... 15 G 27
Cardigan Bay .... 24 G 26
Cardington .... 34 L 26
Cardinham .... 3 G 32
Cardrona .... 61 K 17
Cardross .... 66 G 16
Cardurnock .... 54 K 19
Carew .... 15 F 28
Carfraemill .... 62 L 16
Cargill .... 68 J 14
Carhampton .... 7 J 30
Carie .... 73 H 13
Carinish .... 76 Y 11
Carisbrooke .... 10 Q 31
Cark .... 48 L 21
Carlbt .... 37 S 25
Carleen .... 2 D 33
Carleton .... 49 N 22
Carlisle .... 55 L 19
Carlops .... 61 J 16
Carloway .... 82 Z 9
Carlton Bedford .... 29 S 27
Carlton Hambleton .... 50 Q 20
Carlton
    Hinckley and Bosworth ...36 P 26
Carlton North Yorks. .... 44 Q 22
Carlton Notts. .... 36 Q 25
Carlton Colville .... 31 Z 26
Carlton in Lindrick .... 44 Q 23
Carlton-on-Trent .... 36 R 24
Carluke .... 61 I 16
Carmarthen / Caerfyrddin ...15 H 28
Carmel Head .... 40 G 22
Carmunnock .... 60 H 16
Carmyllie .... 69 L 14
Carn Ban .... 73 H 12
Carn Coire na h-Easgainn ..73 H 12
Carn Eige .... 78 E 12
Carn Glas-choire .... 79 I 11
Carn Mairg .... 73 H 14
Carnaby .... 51 T 21
Carnach .... 78 E 12
Carnassarie Castle .... 65 D 15
Carnedd Llewelyn .... 33 I 24
Carnforth .... 48 L 21
Carno .... 33 J 26
Carnock .... 68 J 15
Carnoustie .... 69 L 14
Carnwath .... 61 J 16
Carradale .... 59 D 17
Carradale Bay .... 59 D 17
Carrbridge .... 79 I 12
Carrick .... 66 F 15
Carrick Roads .... 2 E 33
Carron .... 80 K 11
Carron (Loch) .... 77 C 11
Carron Bridge .... 67 H 15
Carrshield .... 55 N 19
Carrutherstown .... 54 J 18
Carsaig .... 65 C 15
Carse of Gowrie .... 68 K 14
Carseriggan .... 52 G 19
Carsethorn .... 53 J 19
Carsluith .... 53 G 19
Carsphairn .... 53 H 18
Carstairs .... 61 I 16
Carterton .... 19 P 28
Carterway Heads .... 56 O 19
Carthew .... 3 F 32
Carthorpe .... 50 P 21
Cartmel .... 48 L 21
Carville .... 56 P 19
Cas-Gwent / Chepstow ...... 18 M 29
Cashlie .... 67 G 14
Casnewydd / Newport .... 18 L 29
Castell-Nedd / Neath .... 17 I 29
Castell Newydd Emlyn /
    Newcastle Emlyn .... 15 G 27
Castell-y-Rhingyll .... 15 H 28
Castle Acre .... 38 W 25
Castle Ashby .... 28 R 27
Castle Bolton .... 49 O 21
Castle Bytham .... 37 S 25
Castle Campbell .... 67 I 15
Castle Cary .... 8 M 30
Castle Combe .... 19 N 29
Castle Donington .... 36 P 25
Castle Douglas .... 53 I 19

Castle Drogo .... 4 I 31
Castle Eaton .... 19 O 29
Castle Fraser .... 75 M 12
Castle frome .... 26 M 27
Castle Hedingham .... 30 V 28
Castle Howard .... 50 R 21
Castle Kennedy .... 52 F 19
Castle Lachlan .... 65 E 15
Castle Loch .... 53 J 19
Castle Rising .... 38 V 25
Castlebay .... 70 X 13
Castleford .... 43 P 22
Castlemartin .... 16 E 29
Castlerigg .... 54 K 20
Castleton
    Casnewydd / Newport ...18 K 29
Castleton Derbs. .... 43 O 23
Castleton North Yorks. .... 50 R 20
Castletown Highland .... 85 J 8
Castletown Isle of Man ...... 46 G 21
Catacol .... 59 E 16
Catacol Bay .... 59 D 16
Caterham .... 21 T 30
Catfield .... 39 Y 25
Catlodge .... 73 H 12
Caton .... 48 L 21
Catrine .... 60 H 17
Catterall .... 42 L 22
Catterick .... 50 P 20
Catterick Garrison .... 49 O 20
Catterline .... 75 N 13
Cattistock .... 8 M 31
Catton Broadland .... 39 X 26
Catton Tynedale .... 55 N 19
Catworth .... 29 S 26
Cauldcleuch Head .... 62 L 18
Cauldon .... 35 O 24
Caulkerbush .... 53 I 19
Cautley .... 49 M 20
Cava .... 86 K 7
Cavendish .... 30 V 27
Caversfield .... 28 Q 28
Caversham .... 20 R 29
Cawdor .... 79 I 11
Cawood .... 44 Q 22
Caxton .... 29 T 27
Caynham .... 26 M 26
Caythorpe .... 37 S 24
Cayton .... 51 S 21
Ceall (Loch nan) .... 71 C 13
Cefn Bryn .... 15 H 29
Cefn-Coed-y-cymmer .... 17 J 28
Cefn-mawr .... 34 K 25
Cefn-y-Pant .... 15 G 28
Ceinewydd / New Quay ...... 24 G 27
Ceiriog (Vale of) .... 34 K 25
Cemaes .... 40 G 22
Cemaes Head .... 15 F 27
Cemmaes .... 33 I 26
Cemmaes road .... 33 I 26
Cenarth .... 15 G 27
Ceres .... 69 L 15
Cerne Abbas .... 8 M 31
Cerrigydrudion .... 33 J 24
Chacewater .... 2 E 33
Chacombe .... 28 Q 27
Chadderton .... 43 N 23
Chaddesden .... 36 P 25
Chadlington .... 28 P 28
Chadwell St. Mary .... 22 V 29
Chagford .... 4 I 31
Chailey .... 11 T 31
Chàirn Bhain (Loch a') ...... 84 E 9
Chalfont St. Giles .... 21 S 29
Chalfont St. Peter .... 21 S 29
Chalford .... 19 N 28
Chalgrove .... 20 Q 29
Challacombe .... 7 I 30
Challoch .... 52 G 19
Challock .... 22 W 30
Chalkerell .... 5 M 32
Chamber combe Manor .... 17 H 30
Chandler's Ford .... 10 P 31
Channel Islands 5
Chapel Brampton .... 28 R 27
Chapel-en-le-Frith .... 43 O 24
Chapel Haddlesey .... 44 Q 22
Chapel le Dale .... 49 M 21
Chapel St. Leonards .... 45 V 24
Chapel Stile .... 48 K 20
Chapelhall .... 61 I 16
Chapelknowe .... 54 K 18
Chapelton .... 60 H 16
Chapeltown Moray .... 74 K 12
Chapeltown Sheffield .... 43 P 23
Chapmanslade .... 19 N 30
Chard .... 8 L 31

Chardstock .... 8 L 31
Charfield .... 19 M 29
Charing .... 22 W 30
Charlbury .... 28 P 28
Charlecote Park .... 27 P 27
Charleston Manor .... 12 U 31
Charlestown Highland .... 78 C 10
Charlestown Restormel .... 3 F 33
Charlton .... 19 N 29
Charlton Horethorne .... 8 M 30
Charlton Kings .... 27 N 28
Charlton Marshall .... 9 N 31
Charlton Musgrove .... 9 M 30
Charlton on Otmoor .... 20 Q 28
Charlwood .... 11 T 30
Charminster .... 8 M 31
Charmouth .... 5 L 31
Charney Basset .... 20 P 29
Charsfield .... 31 X 27
Chartham .... 23 X 30
Chartridge .... 21 S 28
Chartwell .... 21 U 30
Chastleton .... 27 P 28
Chatburn .... 42 M 22
Chatham .... 22 V 29
Chatsworth House .... 43 P 24
Chatteris .... 29 U 26
Chatton .... 63 O 17
Chawleigh .... 7 I 31
Cheadle Gtr. Mches. .... 43 N 23
Cheadle Staffs. .... 35 O 25
Checkendon .... 20 Q 29
Cheddar .... 18 L 30
Cheddar Gorge .... 18 L 30
Cheddington .... 21 S 28
Cheddleton .... 35 N 24
Chedington .... 8 L 31
Chedworth .... 19 O 28
Cheese Bay .... 76 Y 11
Chelford .... 42 N 24
Chellaston .... 36 P 25
Chelmarsh .... 27 M 26
Chelmsford .... 22 V 28
Cheltenham .... 27 N 28
Chelveston .... 29 S 27
Chelwood Gate .... 11 U 30
Chepstow / Cas-Gwent ...... 18 L 29
Cherhill .... 19 O 29
Cherington Cotswold .... 19 N 28
Cherington
    Stratford-on-Avon .... 27 P 27
Cheriton .... 10 Q 30
Cheriton Bishop .... 4 I 31
Cheriton Fitzpaine .... 7 J 31
Cherry Burton .... 44 S 22
Chertsey .... 21 S 29
Cherwell (River) .... 28 Q 28
Cheselbourne .... 9 M 31
Chesham .... 21 S 28
Chesham Bois .... 21 S 28
Cheshunt .... 21 T 28
Chesil Beach .... 8 M 32
Cheslyn Hay .... 35 N 26
Chester .... 34 L 24
Chester-le-Street .... 56 P 19
Chesterfield .... 43 P 24
Chesters Fort .... 55 N 18
Chesterton Cambridge .... 29 U 27
Chesterton Cherwell .... 28 Q 28
Cheswardine .... 35 M 25
Cheswick .... 63 O 16
Cheviot (The) .... 63 N 17
Cheviot Hills (The) .... 62 M 17
Chew Magna .... 18 M 29
Chew Stoke .... 18 M 29
Chewton Mendip .... 18 M 30
Chicheley .... 29 R 27
Chichester .... 10 R 31
Chickerell .... 5 M 32
Chicklade .... 9 N 30
Chiddingfold .... 11 S 30
Chiddingstone .... 22 U 30
Chideock .... 5 L 31
Chidham .... 10 R 31
Chigwell .... 21 U 29
Chilcompton .... 18 M 30
Child Okeford .... 9 N 31
Childrey .... 20 P 29
Child's Ercall .... 34 M 25
Chilham .... 22 W 30
Chillingham .... 63 O 17
Chilmark .... 9 N 30
Chiltern Hills .... 20 R 29
Chilton Sedgefield .... 56 P 20

Chilton
    Vale of White Horse ...... 20 Q 29
Chilton Folia .... 20 P 29
Chippenham
    East Cambridgeshire ..... 30 V 27
Chippenham
    North Wiltshire .... 19 N 29
Chipping .... 42 M 22
Chipping Campden .... 27 O 27
Chipping Norton .... 28 P 28
Chipping Ongar .... 22 U 28
Chipping Sodbury .... 19 M 29
Chipping Warden .... 28 Q 27
Chirbury .... 34 K 26
Chirk .... 34 K 25
Chirk Castle .... 34 K 25
Chirmorie .... 52 F 18
Chirnside .... 63 N 16
Chirton .... 19 O 30
Chiseldon .... 19 O 29
Chislet .... 23 X 30
Chiswell Green .... 21 S 28
Chitterne .... 19 N 30
Chittlehamholt .... 7 I 31
Chittlehampton .... 7 I 30
Chobham .... 21 S 29
Cholderton .... 9 O 30
Cholesbury .... 21 S 28
Chollerton .... 55 N 18
Cholsey .... 20 Q 29
Chon (Loch) .... 67 G 15
Chopwell .... 56 O 19
Chorley .... 42 M 23
Chorleywood .... 21 S 29
Christchurch Christchurch ...9 O 31
Christchurch Fenland .... 38 U 26
Christian Malford .... 19 N 29
Christleton .... 34 L 24
Christmas Common .... 20 R 29
Christow .... 4 J 32
Chroisg (Loch a') .... 78 E 11
Chudleigh .... 4 J 32
Chulmleigh .... 7 I 31
Church .... 42 M 22
Church Crookham .... 20 R 30
Church Eaton .... 35 N 25
Church Enstone .... 28 P 28
Church Fenton .... 44 Q 22
Church Knowle .... 9 N 32
Church Leigh .... 35 O 25
Church Lench .... 27 O 27
Church Minshull .... 34 M 24
Church Stoke .... 34 K 26
Church Stretton .... 34 L 26
Churcham .... 19 M 28
Churchdown .... 27 N 28
Churchill North Somerset ... 18 L 29
Churchill Oxon. .... 27 P 28
Churchingford .... 8 K 31
Churnet .... 35 N 24
Churnsike Lodge .... 55 M 18
Churston Ferrers .... 4 J 32
Churt .... 10 R 30
Chwilog .... 32 H 25
Cifynydd .... 17 K 29
Cilcain .... 34 K 24
Cilcennin .... 25 H 27
Cilgerran .... 15 G 27
Cilmery .... 25 J 27
Cilrhedyn .... 15 G 28
Cilybebyll .... 17 I 28
Cilycwm .... 25 I 27
Cinderford .... 18 M 28
Cirencester .... 19 O 28
City of London
    London Borough .... 21 T 29
Clachaig .... 66 E 16
Clachan Argyl .... 66 F 15
Clachan Kintyre .... 59 D 16
Clachan Mòr .... 70 Z 14
Clachan of Campsie .... 67 H 16
Clachan of Glendaruel .... 65 E 15
Clachtoll .... 83 E 9
Clackavoid .... 74 J 13
Clackmannan .... 67 I 15
Clacton-on-Sea .... 23 X 28
Claggain Bay .... 58 B 16
Claggan .... 71 C 14
Claidh (Loch) .... 82 A 10
Claigan .... 77 A 11
Clandon Park .... 21 S 30
Clanfield .... 10 Q 31
Claonel .... 84 G 9
Clapham Beds. .... 29 S 27
Clapham North Yorks. .... 49 M 21
Clapton-in-Gordano .... 18 L 29

A B C D E F G H I J K L M N O P Q R S T U V W X Y Z

Clàr (Loch nan) .... 85 H 9
Clarbeston Road .... 24 F 28
Clare .... 30 V 27
Clashindarroch .... 80 L 11
Clashmore .... 79 H 10
Clashnessie .... 84 E 9
Clatt .... 80 L 12
Clatteringshaws (Loch) .... 53 H 18
Clauchlands Point .... 59 E 17
Clavering .... 29 U 28
Claverley .... 27 N 26
Claverton Manor .... 19 N 29
Clawdd-newydd .... 33 J 24
Clawton .... 6 G 31
Claxton Ryedale .... 50 R 21
Claxton South Norfolk .... 39 Y 26
Clay Cross .... 36 P 24
Claydon .... 31 X 27
Claydon House .... 28 R 28
Claypole .... 36 R 24
Clayton .... 11 T 31
Clayton-le-Moors .... 42 M 22
Clayton West .... 43 P 23
Cleadale .... 71 B 13
Cleadon .... 57 P 19
Cleat .... 70 X 12
Cleator Moor .... 47 J 20
Cleckheaton .... 43 O 22
Cleedownton .... 26 M 26
Cleehill .... 26 M 26
Cleethorpes .... 45 T 23
Cleeve Abbey .... 7 J 30
Cleeve Prior .... 27 O 27
Clehonger .... 26 L 27
Cleigh .... 65 D 14
Clenchwarton .... 38 V 25
Clent .... 27 N 26
Cleobury Mortimer .... 26 M 26
Cleobury North .... 26 M 26
Clephanton .... 79 I 11
Clevedon .... 18 L 29
Clevedon-Court .... 18 L 29
Cleveland Hills .... 50 Q 20
Cleveleys .... 42 K 22
Cley Next the Sea .... 38 X 25
Cliburn .... 55 M 20
Cliffe Edway .... 22 V 29
Cliffe Selby .... 44 R 22
Clifton
　City of Nottingham .... 36 Q 25
Clifton Eden .... 55 L 20
Clifton Rugby .... 28 Q 26
Clifton Hampden .... 20 Q 29
Clifton-upon-Teme .... 27 M 27
Clipston .... 28 R 26
Clisham .... 82 Z 10
Clitheroe .... 42 M 22
Clive .... 34 L 25
Cliveden House .... 21 R 29
Clocaenog .... 33 J 24
Clocaenog Forest .... 33 J 24
Clola .... 81 O 11
Clophill .... 29 S 27
Clopton .... 29 S 26
Closeburn .... 53 I 18
Clotton .... 34 L 24
Clouds Hill .... 9 N 31
Cloughton .... 51 S 20
Clova .... 74 K 13
Clova (Glen) .... 74 K 13
Clove Lodge .... 49 N 20
Clovelly .... 6 G 31
Clovenfords .... 62 L 17
Clovulin .... 72 E 13
Clowne .... 44 Q 24
Cluanie Loch .... 72 E 12
Cluanie Lodge .... 72 E 12
Clumber Park .... 44 Q 24
Clun .... 26 K 26
Clunbury .... 26 L 26
Clunes Forest .... 72 F 13
Clungunford .... 26 L 26
Clunie .... 68 J 14
Clutton .... 18 M 30
Clwydian Range .... 34 K 24
Clydach .... 17 I 28
Clyde (Firth of) .... 59 F 17
Clyde (River) .... 61 J 17
Clydebank .... 60 G 16
Clydesdale .... 61 I 16
Clyffe Pypard .... 19 O 29
Clynnog-Fawr .... 32 G 24
Clyro .... 26 K 27
Clyst Honiton .... 4 J 31
Clyst Hydon .... 7 J 31
Clytha .... 18 L 28
Clywedog Resr. .... 25 J 26

Coalburn .... 61 I 17
Coaley .... 19 N 28
Coalville .... 36 P 25
Coast .... 78 D 10
Coatbridge .... 60 H 16
Coates .... 19 N 28
Cobham .... 21 S 30
Cockayne .... 50 Q 20
Cockburnspath .... 69 M 16
Cockenzie and Port Seton .... 69 L 16
Cockerham .... 48 L 22
Cockermouth .... 54 J 20
Cockfield Babergh .... 30 W 27
Cockfield Teesdale .... 56 O 20
Cocking .... 10 R 31
Cockleford .... 19 N 28
Cockshutt .... 34 L 25
Coddington .... 36 R 24
Codford St. Mary .... 9 N 30
Codicote .... 21 T 28
Codnor .... 36 P 24
Codsall .... 35 N 26
Coe (Glen) .... 72 F 14
Coed y Brenin Forest .... 33 I 25
Coedpoeth .... 34 K 24
Coggeshall .... 30 W 28
Coigach .... 84 E 10
Coignafearn .... 73 H 12
Coignafearn Forest .... 73 H 12
Coille Mhorgil .... 72 E 12
Colaboll .... 84 G 9
Colbost .... 77 A 11
Colby Eden .... 55 M 20
Colby Isle of Man .... 46 F 21
Colchester .... 30 W 28
Cold Ash .... 20 Q 29
Cold Ashby .... 28 Q 26
Cold Ashton .... 19 M 29
Cold Fell .... 55 M 19
Cold Norton .... 22 W 28
Coldbackie .... 84 G 8
Colden Common .... 10 Q 31
Coldingham .... 63 N 16
Coldstream .... 63 N 17
Colebrooke .... 7 I 31
Coleford Glos. .... 18 M 28
Coleford Somerset .... 18 M 30
Colemere .... 34 L 25
Coleorton .... 36 P 25
Coleshill
　North Warwickshire .... 27 O 26
Coleshill
　Vale of White Horse .... 19 P 29
Colgrave Sound .... 87 R 2
Colkirk .... 38 W 25
Coll Argyll and Bute .... 71 A 14
Coll Eilean Siar .... 83 B 9
Colliery Row .... 56 P 19
Collieston .... 81 O 11
Collin .... 53 J 18
Collingbourne Ducis .... 19 P 30
Collingbourne Kingston .... 19 P 30
Collingham Notts. .... 36 R 24
Collingham West Yorks. .... 50 P 22
Collington .... 26 M 27
Collyweston .... 37 S 26
Colmonell .... 52 F 18
Coln (River) .... 19 O 28
Colnabaichin .... 74 K 12
Colne .... 43 N 22
Colne (River) .... 22 X 28
Colonsay .... 64 B 15
Colpy .... 81 M 11
Colsterworth .... 37 S 25
Coltishall .... 39 Y 25
Colwall Stone .... 27 M 27
Colwinston .... 17 J 29
Colwyn Bay / Bae Colwyn .... 41 I 23
Colyton .... 5 K 31
Combe Florey .... 8 K 30
Combe Martin .... 17 H 30
Combe-St. Nicholas .... 8 L 31
Combeinteignhead .... 4 J 32
Comberton .... 29 U 27
Combwich .... 8 K 30
Come-to-Good .... 2 E 33
Compton Berks. .... 20 Q 29
Compton Guildford .... 21 S 30
Compton West Sussex .... 10 R 31
Compton Abdale .... 19 O 28
Compton Basset .... 19 O 29
Compton Castle .... 4 J 32
Compton Dando .... 18 M 29
Compton Wynyates .... 28 P 27
Comrie .... 67 I 14
Cona Glen .... 72 D 13

Conchra .... 65 E 15
Condicote .... 27 O 28
Condover .... 34 L 26
Congleton .... 35 N 24
Congresbury .... 18 L 29
Coningsby .... 37 T 24
Conington .... 29 T 26
Connah's Quay .... 42 K 24
Connel .... 65 D 14
Connel Park .... 60 H 17
Conon Bridge .... 79 G 11
Consett .... 56 O 19
Constantine Bay .... 2 E 32
Contin .... 79 G 11
Convinth (Glen) .... 79 G 11
Conway Falls .... 33 I 24
Conwy .... 41 I 23
Conwy (River) .... 33 I 24
Conwy (Vale of) .... 33 I 24
Cooden Beach .... 12 V 31
Cookham .... 21 R 29
Coolham .... 11 S 31
Coombe Bissett .... 9 O 30
Copdock .... 31 X 27
Copford .... 30 W 28
Copley .... 56 O 20
Copmanthorpe .... 50 Q 22
Copplestone .... 7 I 31
Coppull .... 42 M 23
Copthorne .... 11 T 30
Coquet (River) .... 63 N 17
Corbridge .... 55 N 19
Corby .... 28 R 26
Corby Glen .... 37 S 25
Corfe Castle .... 9 N 32
Corfe Mullen .... 9 N 31
Corgarff Castle .... 74 K 12
Corhampton .... 10 Q 31
Cornforth .... 56 P 19
Cornhill .... 81 L 11
Cornhill-on-Tweed .... 63 N 17
Cornwood .... 4 I 32
Cornworthy .... 4 J 32
Corpach .... 72 E 13
Corpusty .... 39 X 25
Corran .... 72 E 13
Corrany .... 46 G 21
Corrie .... 59 E 17
Corrie Common .... 54 K 18
Corrimony .... 78 F 11
Corringham Thurrock .... 22 V 29
Corringham West Lindsey .... 44 R 23
Corris .... 33 I 26
Corry .... 77 C 12
Corryvreckan (Gulf of) .... 65 C 15
Corscombe .... 8 L 31
Corsham .... 19 N 29
Corsham Court .... 19 N 29
Corsley Heath .... 19 N 30
Corsock .... 53 I 18
Corstopitum .... 55 N 19
Corton .... 9 N 30
Corwen .... 33 J 25
Cosby .... 36 Q 26
Cosham .... 10 Q 31
Costessey .... 39 X 26
Cot-town .... 81 N 11
Cotehill .... 55 L 19
Cotgrave .... 36 Q 25
Cotham .... 36 R 24
Cotherstone .... 49 O 20
Cothi River .... 25 H 28
Coton .... 29 U 27
Cottenham .... 29 U 27
Cottered .... 29 T 28
Cottesmore .... 37 S 25
Cottingham
　East Riding of Yorks. .... 45 S 22
Cottingham Northants. .... 28 R 26
Cottisford .... 28 Q 28
Cottonshopeburn Foot .... 62 M 18
Coulags .... 78 D 11
Coulport .... 66 F 15
Coulter .... 61 J 17
Coundon .... 56 P 20
Countesthorpe .... 36 Q 26
Coupar Angus .... 68 K 14
Coustonn .... 66 E 16
Cove Argyll and Bute .... 66 F 15
Cove Highland .... 78 C 10
Cove Bay .... 75 N 12
Coventry .... 28 P 26
Coverack .... 2 E 33
Cow Honeybourne .... 27 O 27

Cowal .... 65 E 15
Cowan Bridge .... 48 M 21
Cowbit .... 37 T 25
Cowbridge / Bont-faen .... 17 J 29
Cowdenbeath .... 68 J 15
Cowdray House .... 10 R 31
Cowes Isle of Wight .... 10 Q 31
Cowfold .... 11 T 31
Cowie .... 67 I 15
Cowling .... 43 N 22
Cowplain .... 10 Q 31
Coxheath .... 22 V 30
Coxhoe .... 56 P 19
Coxwold .... 50 Q 21
Coylton .... 60 G 17
Coylumbridge .... 74 I 12
Crackington Haven .... 6 G 31
Crafthole .... 3 H 32
Craggan .... 68 F 15
Cragside Gardens .... 63 O 18
Crai .... 25 J 28
Craig .... 78 E 11
Craig Lodge .... 65 E 16
Craig-y-nos .... 17 I 28
Craigdarroch .... 60 H 18
Craigellachie .... 80 K 11
Craigencallie .... 53 G 18
Craigendoran .... 66 F 16
Craigens .... 58 B 16
Craighead .... 69 M 15
Craighouse .... 58 C 16
Craigie .... 60 G 17
Craigievar Castle .... 75 L 12
Craigmalloch .... 53 G 18
Craignish (Loch) .... 65 D 15
Craignure .... 65 C 14
Craigrothie .... 69 L 15
Craigton .... 74 K 14
Craik .... 62 K 17
Crail .... 69 M 15
Crailing .... 62 M 17
Crailinghall .... 62 M 17
Crakaig .... 85 I 9
Cramlington .... 56 P 18
Cramond .... 68 K 16
Cranborne .... 9 O 31
Cranbrook .... 12 V 30
Crane Moor .... 43 P 23
Cranford St. John .... 29 S 26
Cranleigh .... 11 S 30
Cranmore .... 18 M 30
Cranshaws .... 62 M 16
Cranstal .... 46 G 20
Cranwell .... 37 S 24
Cranworth .... 38 W 26
Crask Inn .... 84 G 9
Craster .... 63 P 17
Crathes Castle .... 75 M 12
Crathie .... 74 K 12
Crathorne .... 50 Q 20
Craven Arms .... 26 L 26
Crawcrook .... 56 O 19
Crawford .... 61 J 17
Crawfordjohn .... 61 I 17
Crawick .... 61 I 17
Crawley Hants. .... 10 P 30
Crawley West Sussex .... 11 T 30
Crawley Down .... 11 T 30
Creag Meagaidh .... 73 G 13
Creagan .... 65 E 14
Creagorry .... 76 Y 11
Creake South .... 38 W 25
Credenhill .... 26 L 27
Crediton .... 7 J 31
Creech St. Michael .... 8 K 30
Creetown .... 53 G 19
Creggans .... 66 E 15
Creran (Loch) .... 65 D 14
Cressage .... 34 M 26
Cresswell Castle Morpeth .... 56 P 18
Cresswell Pembrokeshire /
　Sir Benfro .... 15 F 28
Cresswell .... 44 Q 24
Cruden Bay .... 81 O 11
Crewe .... 35 M 24
Crewkerne .... 8 L 31
Crianlarich .... 66 G 14
Crug-y-bar .... 25 I 27
Cribyn .... 15 H 27
Criccieth .... 33 H 25
Crich .... 36 P 24
Crichton .... 62 L 16
Crick .... 28 Q 26
Crickadarn .... 25 K 27
Cricket St. Thomas .... 8 L 31
Crickhowell .... 26 K 28
Cricklade .... 19 O 29
Crickley Hill .... 19 N 28
Crieff .... 67 I 14

Crimond .... 81 O 11
Crimplesham .... 38 V 26
Crinan .... 65 D 15
Crinan (Loch) .... 65 D 15
Cringleford .... 39 X 26
Croachy .... 79 H 12
Crocketford .... 53 I 18
Crockham Hill .... 21 U 30
Croes-goch .... 14 E 28
Croesyceiliog .... 18 L 29
Croft Herefordshire .... 26 L 27
Croft Richmondshire .... 50 P 20
Croft-on-Tees .... 50 P 20
Crofty .... 15 H 29
Croggan .... 65 C 14
Croglin .... 55 M 19
Croick .... 79 G 10
Cromalt Hills .... 84 E 9
Cromar .... 74 L 12
Cromarty .... 79 H 10
Cromarty Bay .... 79 H 10
Cromarty Firth .... 79 H 11
Cromdale .... 80 J 11
Cromdale (Hills of) .... 80 J 12
Cromer .... 39 X 25
Cromford .... 35 P 24
Cromra .... 73 G 13
Crondall .... 20 R 30
Cronk (The) .... 46 G 21
Crook South Lakeland .... 48 L 20
Crook Wear Valley .... 56 O 19
Crook of Devon .... 68 J 15
Crookham .... 63 N 17
Crookham Village .... 20 R 30
Crooklands .... 48 L 21
Cropredy .... 28 Q 27
Cropston .... 36 Q 25
Cropwell Bishop .... 36 R 25
Crosby Allerdale .... 54 J 19
Crosby Isle of Man .... 46 G 21
Crosby Sefton .... 42 K 23
Crosby Ravensworth .... 48 M 20
Croscombe .... 18 M 30
Cross .... 83 B 8
Cross Fell .... 55 M 19
Cross Hands .... 15 H 28
Cross Inn .... 25 H 27
Crossaig .... 59 D 16
Crossapoll .... 64 Z 14
Crossbost .... 82 A 9
Crossford .... 61 I 16
Crossgates .... 68 J 15
Crossgill .... 48 L 21
Crosshill Fife .... 68 K 15
Crosshill South Ayrshire .... 60 G 18
Crosshouse .... 60 G 17
Crosskeys .... 18 K 29
Crosskirk .... 85 J 8
Crossmichael .... 53 I 19
Crossraguel Abbey .... 60 F 18
Crossways .... 9 N 31
Croston .... 42 L 23
Crouch (River) .... 22 W 29
Croughton .... 28 Q 28
Crovie .... 81 N 11
Crow Hill .... 26 M 28
Crowborough .... 12 U 30
Crowcombe .... 8 K 30
Crowhurst .... 12 V 31
Crowland .... 37 T 25
Crowle Doncaster .... 44 R 23
Crowle Wychavon .... 27 N 27
Crowlin Island .... 77 C 11
Crowmarsh Gifford .... 20 Q 29
Crowthorne .... 20 R 29
Croxley Green .... 21 S 29
Croxton Kerrial .... 36 R 25
Croy .... 79 H 11
Croyde .... 6 H 30
Croydon London Borough .... 21 T 29
Cruckton .... 34 L 26
Crudgington .... 34 M 25
Crudwell .... 19 N 29
Crulivig .... 82 Z 9
Crymmych .... 15 G 28
Crynant .... 17 I 28
Cuaig .... 77 C 11
Cubbington .... 28 P 27
Cubert .... 2 E 32
Cuckfield .... 11 T 30
Cucklington .... 9 M 30
Cuckney .... 44 Q 24
Cuddington Aylesbury .... 20 R 28
Cuddington Vale Royal .... 42 M 24

Cudworth .... 43 P 23
Cuffley .... 21 T 28
Cuxham .... 20 Q 29
Cuilcudden .... 79 H 11
Cuillin Sound .... 71 B 12
Cuillin (The) .... 77 B 12
Culbokie .... 79 G 11
Culdrose .... 2 E 33
Culgaith .... 55 M 20
Culkein .... 83 D 9
Cullen .... 80 L 10
Cullen Bay .... 80 L 10
Cullingworth .... 43 O 22
Cullipool .... 65 D 15
Culloch .... 67 I 14
Cullompton .... 7 J 31
Culmington .... 26 L 26
Culmstock .... 8 K 31
Culnacraig .... 84 E 10
Culrain .... 79 G 10
Culross .... 68 J 15
Culshabbin .... 52 G 19
Culswic .... 87 P 3
Culter Fell .... 61 J 17
Cults .... 75 N 12
Culzean Castle .... 59 F 17
Cumbernauld .... 67 I 16
Cumbrian Moutains .... 48 K 20
Cuminestown .... 81 N 11
Cummersdale .... 54 L 19
Cummertrees .... 54 J 19
Cumnock .... 60 H 17
Cumnor .... 20 P 28
Cumwhitton .... 55 L 19
Cunninghamhead .... 60 G 17
Cupar .... 69 K 15
Curbridge .... 20 P 28
Curdridge .... 10 Q 31
Currie .... 61 K 16
Curry Rivel .... 8 L 30
Cutcloy .... 53 G 19
Cutnall green .... 27 N 27
Cuxton .... 22 V 29
Cwm .... 18 K 28
Cwm Bychan .... 33 H 25
Cwm Taf .... 17 J 28
Cwmafan .... 17 I 29
Cwmaman .... 17 J 28
Cwmbach Carmarthenshire /
　Sir Gaerfyrddin .... 15 G 28
Cwmbach Powys / Powys .... 25 J 27
Cwmbach Rhondda, Cynon, Taf /
　Rhondda, Cynon, Taff .... 17 J 28
Cwmbrân .... 18 L 29
Cwmcarn .... 18 K 29
Cwmcoy .... 15 G 27
Cwmllynfell .... 17 I 28
Cwmystwyth .... 25 I 26
Cwnduad .... 15 G 28
Cwnfelin Boeth .... 15 G 28
Cwrt-Newydd .... 15 H 27
Cydweli / Kidwelly .... 15 H 28
Cyffylliog .... 33 J 24
Cymmer .... 17 J 29
Cymyran Bay .... 40 G 23
Cynwyl Elfed .... 15 G 28

D

Dacre Eden .... 55 L 20
Dacre Harrogate .... 49 O 21
Daglingworth .... 19 N 28
Dailly .... 60 F 18
Daimh (Loch an) .... 73 G 14
Dairsie or Osnaburgh .... 69 L 14
Dalavich .... 65 E 15
Dalbeattie .... 53 I 19
Dalbeg .... 73 H 12
Dalblair .... 60 H 17
Dalby .... 46 F 21
Dalchalloch .... 73 H 13
Dalchruin .... 67 H 15
Dale .... 14 E 28
Dale Head .... 48 L 20
Dalgonar .... 60 H 18
Dalham .... 30 V 27
Dalhavaig .... 85 I 8
Daliburgh .... 76 X 12
Dalkeith .... 61 K 16
Dallas .... 80 J 11
Dalleagles .... 60 H 17
Dallington Northampton .... 28 R 27
Dallington Rother .... 12 V 31
Dalmally .... 66 F 14
Dalmellington .... 60 G 18
Dalmeny .... 68 J 16
Dalmigavie .... 73 H 12
Dalnabreck .... 71 C 13

Dalnaspidal Lodge ...73 H 13
Dalnavaid ...74 J 13
Dalnavie ...79 H 10
Dalness ...72 F 14
Dalry
  Dumfries and Galloway ...53 H 18
Dalry North Ayrshire ...60 F 16
Dalrymple ...60 G 17
Dalston ...54 L 19
Dalswinton ...53 I 18
Dalton
  Dumfries and Galloway ...54 J 18
Dalton North Yorks. ...50 P 21
Dalton in Furness ...47 K 21
Damerham ...9 O 31
Damh (Loch) ...78 D 11
Dan-yr-Ogof ...17 I 28
Danbury ...22 V 28
Danby ...50 R 20
Dane ...35 N 24
Danehill ...11 U 30
Darenth ...22 U 29
Darfield ...43 P 23
Darlington ...50 P 20
Darowen ...33 I 26
Darras Hall ...56 O 18
Darrington ...44 Q 22
Darsham ...31 Y 27
Dartford ...22 U 29
Dartford Tunnel ...22 U 29
Dartington ...4 I 32
Dartmeet ...4 I 32
Dartmoor National Park ...4 I 32
Dartmouth ...4 J 32
Darton ...43 P 23
Darvel ...60 H 17
Darwen ...42 M 22
Datchet ...21 S 29
Datchworth ...29 T 28
Dava ...80 J 11
Daventry ...28 Q 27
Davidstow ...6 G 32
Davington ...61 K 18
Daviot ...79 H 11
Dawley ...34 M 26
Dawlish ...4 J 32
Deal ...23 Y 30
Dean ...54 J 20
Dean Forest Park ...18 M 28
Deanich Lodge ...78 F 10
Deanston ...67 H 15
Dearham ...54 J 19
Debden ...30 U 28
Deben (River) ...31 X 27
Debenham ...31 X 27
Deddington ...28 Q 28
Dedham ...30 W 28
Dee / Afon Dyfrdwy (River)
  Wales ...41 K 23
Dee (River) Scotland ...75 N 12
Dee (River) / Afon Dyfrdwy ...34 K 24
Deene ...29 S 26
Deepcut ...21 R 30
Deepdale ...49 M 21
Deeping-St. James ...37 T 25
Deeping St. Nicholas ...37 T 25
Deeps (The) ...87 P 3
Defford ...27 N 27
Deiniolen ...33 H 24
Delabole ...6 F 32
Delamere ...34 M 24
Delamere Forest ...42 L 24
Dell ...83 B 8
Dellifure ...80 J 11
Delnadamph Lodge ...74 K 12
Delph ...43 N 23
Denbigh / Dinbych ...33 J 24
Denby Dale ...43 P 23
Denchworth ...20 P 29
Denham ...21 S 29
Denholm ...62 L 17
Denmead ...10 Q 31
Dennington ...31 Y 27
Denny ...67 I 15
Dent ...49 M 21
Denton South Kesteven ...36 R 25
Denton Stockport ...43 N 23
Denver ...38 V 26
Derby ...36 P 25
Deri ...18 K 28
Dersingham ...38 V 25
Dervaig ...71 B 14
Derwent (River) R. Ouse ...44 R 22
Derwent (River) R. Trent ...36 P 24
Derwent (River) R. Tyne ...56 O 19
Derwent Dale ...43 O 23
Derwent Reservoir Derbs. ...43 O 23

Derwent Reservoir
  Northumb. ...56 N 19
Derwent Water ...54 K 20
Desborough ...28 R 26
Desford ...36 Q 26
Detling ...22 V 30
Devauden ...18 L 28
Deveron (River) ...81 M 11
Devil's Beef Tub ...61 J 17
Devil's Bridge / Pontarfynach 25 I 26
Devil's Elbow ...74 J 13
Devil's Punch Bowl ...10 R 30
Devizes ...19 O 29
Dewsbury ...43 P 22
Dherue (Loch an) ...84 G 8
Dial Post ...11 S 31
Dickleburgh ...31 X 26
Didcot ...20 Q 29
Diddlebury ...26 L 26
Digby ...37 S 24
Dilhorne ...35 N 25
Dilton Marsh ...19 N 30
Dilwyn ...26 L 27
Dinas ...24 F 27
Dinas Dinlle ...32 G 24
Dinas Head ...24 F 27
Dinas-Mawddwy ...33 I 25
Dinas Powys ...18 K 29
Dinbych / Denbigh ...33 J 24
Dinbych-y-pysgod / Tenby ...15 F 28
Dingwall ...79 G 11
Dinnet ...74 L 12
Dinnington
  Newcastle upon Tyne ...56 O 18
Dinnington Rotherham ...44 Q 23
Dinsdale ...50 P 20
Dinton ...9 O 30
Diptford ...4 I 32
Dirleton ...69 L 15
Dishforth ...50 P 21
Diss ...31 X 26
Disserth ...25 J 27
Distington ...53 J 20
Ditcheat ...8 M 30
Ditchingham ...31 Y 26
Ditchley Park ...28 P 28
Ditchling ...11 T 31
Ditton Priors ...26 M 26
Doc Penfro /
  Pembroke Dock ...16 F 28
Docherty (Glen) ...78 E 11
Docking ...38 V 25
Dockray ...54 L 20
Dodburn ...62 L 17
Doddington Cambs. ...29 U 26
Doddington Kent ...22 W 30
Doddington Lincs. ...44 S 24
Doddington Northumb. ...63 O 17
Dodington ...19 M 29
Dodman Point ...3 F 33
Dodworth ...43 P 23
Doirlinn ...71 C 13
Dolanog ...33 J 25
Dolbenmaen ...33 H 25
Dolfor ...26 K 26
Dolgarrog ...33 I 24
Dolgellau ...33 I 25
Dolgoch Falls ...33 I 26
Dollar ...67 I 15
Dolphinholme ...48 L 22
Dolton ...7 H 31
Don (River) R. Ouse ...44 Q 23
Don (River) R. Spey ...74 K 12
Doncaster ...44 Q 23
Donhead-St. Andrew ...9 N 30
Donhead-St. Mary ...9 N 30
Donington ...37 T 25
Donington-on-Bain ...45 T 24
Donington Park Circuit ...36 P 25
Donisthorpe ...36 P 25
Donnington Berks. ...20 Q 29
Donnington Salop ...35 M 25
Donyatt ...8 L 31
Doon (Loch) ...60 G 18
Dorback Lodge ...74 J 12
Dorchester Dorset ...8 M 31
Dorchester Oxon. ...20 Q 29
Dordon ...35 P 26
Dore ...43 P 24
Dores ...79 H 11
Dorking ...21 T 30
Dormansland ...11 U 30
Dormanstown ...57 Q 20
Dornie ...78 D 12
Dornoch ...79 H 10

Dornoch Firth ...79 H 10
Dornock ...54 K 19
Dorrington ...34 L 26
Dorstone ...26 K 27
Dorusduan ...78 D 12
Douchary (Glen) ...78 F 10
Dougarie ...59 D 17
Douglas Isle of Man ...46 G 21
Douglas
  South Lanarkshire ...61 I 17
Douglastown ...74 L 14
Dounby ...86 K 6
Doune Highland ...84 G 10
Doune Stirling ...67 H 15
Dove (River) ...35 O 24
Dove Cottage ...48 K 20
Dove Holes ...43 O 24
Dovedale ...35 O 24
Dover ...13 X 30
Dovercourt ...31 X 28
Doveridge ...35 O 25
Dovey / Dyfi (River) ...33 I 26
Dowally ...74 J 14
Dowdeswell ...27 N 28
Dowlish Wake ...8 L 31
Down Ampney ...19 O 28
Downham ...30 U 26
Downham Market ...38 V 26
Downies ...75 N 12
Downton ...9 O 31
Dowsby ...37 S 25
Doynton ...19 M 29
Drakes Broughton ...27 N 27
Draughton ...49 O 22
Drax ...44 R 22
Draycott ...36 P 25
Draycott-in-the-Clay ...35 O 25
Draycott-in-the-Moors ...35 N 25
Drayton Norfolk ...39 X 26
Drayton Oxon. ...20 Q 29
Drayton-St. Leonard ...20 Q 29
Drefach near Carmarthen ...15 H 28
Drefach
  near Newcastle-Emlyn ...15 G 27
Dreghorn ...60 G 17
Drem ...69 L 15
Drenewydd / Newtown ...26 K 26
Dreswick Point ...46 G 21
Driffield ...19 O 28
Drigg ...47 J 20
Drighlington ...43 P 22
Drimnin ...71 C 14
Drinnishadder ...76 Z 10
Drissaig ...65 E 15
Droitwich ...27 N 27
Dronfield ...43 P 24
Drongan ...60 G 17
Droxford ...10 Q 31
Druidibeg (Loch) ...76 Y 12
Druim a' Chliabhain (Loch) .85 H 8
Druimdarroch ...71 C 13
Druimindarroch ...71 C 13
Drum Castle ...75 M 12
Drumbeg ...84 E 9
Drumblade ...81 L 11
Drumburgh ...54 K 19
Drumchardine ...79 G 11
Drumclog ...60 H 17
Drumelzier ...61 J 17
Drumfearn ...71 C 12
Drumlanrig Castle ...61 I 18
Drumlemble ...58 C 17
Drumlithie ...75 M 13
Drummond Castle ...67 I 14
Drummore ...52 F 19
Drummossie Muir ...79 H 11
Drumnadrochit ...79 G 11
Drumrunie ...84 E 9
Drumsallie ...72 D 13
Drumtochty Forest ...75 M 13
Druridge Bay ...63 P 18
Drybrook ...18 M 28
Dryburgh Abbey ...62 M 17
Drygarn Fawr ...25 J 27
Drymen ...67 G 15
Drynoch ...77 B 12
Duchally ...84 F 9
Ducklington ...20 P 28
Duddington ...37 S 26
Duddo ...63 N 16
Dudley Dudley ...27 N 26
Dudley North Tyneside ...56 P 18
Duff House ...81 M 11
Duffield ...36 P 25
Dufftown ...80 K 11
Duffus ...80 J 10
Dufton ...55 M 20

Duggleby ...51 S 21
Duich (Loch) ...78 D 12
Duirinish ...77 C 12
Duke's Pass ...67 G 15
Dukinfield ...43 N 23
Dullingham ...30 V 27
Dulnain Bridge ...80 J 12
Duloe ...3 G 32
Dulverton ...7 J 30
Dumbarton ...67 G 16
Dumbleton ...27 O 27
Dumfries ...53 J 18
Dun Carloway Broch ...82 Z 9
Dunan ...66 F 16
Dunbar ...69 M 15
Dunbeath ...85 J 9
Dunblane ...67 I 15
Duncansby Head ...86 K 8
Dunchurch ...28 Q 26
Duncow ...53 J 18
Dundee ...69 K 14
Dundonald ...60 G 17
Dundrennan ...53 I 19
Dundry ...18 M 29
Dunecht ...75 M 12
Dunfermline ...68 J 15
Dungeness ...13 W 31
Dunholme ...44 S 24
Dunino ...69 L 15
Dunipace ...67 I 15
Dunkeld ...68 J 14
Dunkery Beacon ...7 J 30
Dunkeswell ...8 K 31
Dunkirk ...19 N 29
Dunley ...27 N 27
Dunlop ...60 G 16
Dunmaglass Lodge ...79 H 12
Dunnet ...85 J 8
Dunnet Bay ...85 J 8
Dunnet Head ...86 J 7
Dunning ...68 J 15
Dunnington ...50 R 22
Dunnockshaw ...42 N 22
Dunnottar Castle ...75 N 13
Dunoon ...66 F 16
Dunragit ...52 F 19
Dunrobin Castle ...85 I 10
Duns ...62 M 16
Duns Tew ...28 P 28
Dunscore ...53 I 18
Dunsfold ...11 S 30
Dunsford ...4 I 31
Dunsop Bridge ...49 M 22
Dunstable ...29 S 28
Dunstaffnage Castel ...65 D 14
Dunstanburgh Castle ...63 P 17
Dunster ...17 J 30
Dunston ...37 S 24
Dunstone ...4 I 32
Dunsyre ...61 J 16
Duntelchaig (Loch) ...79 H 11
Dunton bassett ...28 Q 26
Dunure ...59 F 17
Dunvegan ...77 A 11
Dunvegan (Loch) ...77 A 11
Dunvegan Castle ...77 A 11
Dunvegan Head ...76 Z 11
Dunwich ...31 Y 27
Durdle Door ...9 N 32
Durham ...56 P 19
Durisdeer ...61 I 18
Durlston Head ...9 O 32
Durness ...84 F 8
Durrington ...19 O 30
Dursley ...19 M 28
Dury Voe ...87 Q 2
Duston ...28 R 27
Duthil ...79 I 12
Duxford ...29 U 27
Dyce ...75 N 12
Dyfi / Dovey (River) ...33 I 26
Dyke ...80 I 11
Dykehead ...74 K 13
Dykends ...74 K 13
Dymchurch ...13 W 30
Dymock ...27 M 28
Dyrham ...19 M 29
Dyserth ...41 J 23

E

Eaglescliffe ...50 P 20
Eaglesfield ...54 K 18
Eaglesham ...60 H 16
Eakring ...36 R 24
Ealing London Borough ...21 T 29
Earba (Lochan na h-) ...73 G 13

Earby ...49 N 22
Eardisley ...26 K 27
Earl Shilton ...36 Q 26
Earl Soham ...31 X 27
Earl Stonham ...31 X 27
Earley Winnersh ...20 R 29
Earlish ...77 A 11
Earls Barton ...28 R 27
Earls Colne ...30 W 28
Earlsferry ...69 L 15
Earlston ...62 L 17
Earn (Loch) ...67 H 14
Earn (River) ...67 J 14
Earsdon ...56 P 18
Earsham ...31 Y 26
Eartham ...11 S 31
Easdale ...65 D 15
Easebourne ...10 R 31
Easington Easington ...57 P 19
Easington
  East Riding of Yorkshire ...45 U 23
Easington
  Redcar and Cleveland ...50 R 20
Easington
  South Oxfordshire ...20 Q 28
Easingwold ...50 Q 21
Easington Lane ...56 P 19
Eassie and Nevay ...68 K 14
East Aberthaw ...17 J 29
East Barkwith ...45 T 24
East Bergholt ...30 X 28
East Brent ...18 L 30
East Budleigh ...5 K 32
East Butterwick ...44 R 23
East Chinnock ...8 L 31
East-Challow ...20 P 29
East-Coker ...8 M 31
East Cowes ...10 Q 31
East Cowton ...50 P 20
East Dereham ...38 W 25
East Ferry ...44 R 23
East Glen (River) ...37 S 25
East Grafton ...19 P 29
East Grinstead ...11 T 30
East Hagbourne ...20 Q 29
East-Halton ...45 T 23
East Hanney ...20 P 29
East Hardwick ...44 Q 23
East Harling ...30 W 26
East Haven ...69 L 14
East Hendred ...20 P 29
East Hoathly ...12 U 31
East Horsley ...21 S 30
East Huntspill ...18 L 30
East Ilsley ...20 Q 29
East Keswick ...50 P 22
East Kilbride Eilean Siar ...70 X 12
East Kilbride
  South Lanarkshire ...60 H 16
East-Knoyle ...9 N 30
East Knoyle ...9 N 30
East Lambrook ...8 L 31
East Leake ...36 Q 25
East Linton ...69 M 16
East Loch Roag ...82 Z 9
East Loch Tarbet ...77 Z 10
East Looe ...3 G 32
East Lulworth ...9 N 32
East-Malling ...22 V 30
East Markham ...44 R 24
East Meon ...10 Q 31
East Mersea ...22 W 28
East Midlands Airport ...36 Q 25
East Moor ...35 P 24
East Norton ...36 R 26
East-Poringland ...39 Y 26
East Portlemouth ...4 I 33
East Rhidorroch Lodge ...78 F 10
East-Rudham ...38 W 25
East-Saltoun ...62 L 16
East Tisted ...10 R 30
East Wemyss ...68 K 15
East-Winch ...38 V 25
East Wittering ...10 R 31
East Witton ...49 O 21
East-Woodhay ...20 P 29
East-Wretham ...30 W 26
Eastbourne ...12 U 31
Eastchurch ...22 W 29
Eastdean ...12 U 31
Easter-Compton ...18 M 29
Easter Ross ...79 G 10
Eastergate ...11 S 31
Eastfield ...51 S 21
Eastgate ...55 N 19
Eastham ...42 L 24
Eastington ...19 N 28

Eastleach ...19 O 28
Eastleigh ...10 P 31
Eastoft ...44 R 23
Easton Carlisle ...55 L 18
Easton Dorset ...8 M 32
Easton Norfolk ...39 X 26
Easton-Grey ...19 N 29
Easton-in-Gordano ...18 L 29
Easton-Royal ...19 O 29
Eastriggs ...54 K 19
Eastrington ...44 R 22
Eastry ...23 X 30
Eastville ...37 U 24
Eastwood ...36 Q 24
Eaton ...34 M 24
Eaton Bray ...29 S 28
Eaton Socon ...29 T 27
Ebbw Vale / Glyn Ebwy ...18 K 28
Ebchester ...56 O 19
Ebrington ...27 O 27
Eccles ...62 M 17
Ecchinswell ...20 Q 29
Ecclefechan ...54 K 18
Eccles ...42 M 23
Eccleshall ...35 N 25
Echt ...75 M 12
Eckford ...62 M 17
Eckington Derbs. ...43 P 24
Eckington Worc. ...27 N 27
Edale ...43 O 23
Eday ...87 L 6
Eddelston ...61 K 16
Edderton ...79 H 10
Eddrachillis Bay ...84 E 9
Eden (River) ...55 M 19
Eden Project ...3 F 32
Edenbridge ...21 U 30
Edentaggart ...66 F 15
Edenthorpe ...44 Q 23
Edgefield ...39 X 25
Edgmond ...35 M 25
Edgton ...26 L 26
Edinbane ...77 A 11
Edinburgh ...68 K 16
Edington ...19 N 30
Edith Weston ...37 S 26
Edlesborough ...29 S 28
Edlingham ...63 O 17
Edmondsley ...56 P 19
Edmundbyers ...56 O 19
Edwalton ...36 Q 25
Edwinstowe ...36 Q 24
Edzell ...75 M 13
Efailnewydd ...32 G 25
Egerton ...22 W 30
Eggerness Point ...53 G 19
Eggleston ...56 N 20
Egham ...21 S 29
Egilsay ...87 L 6
Eglingham ...63 O 17
Egloskerry ...6 G 32
Eglwys Brewis ...17 J 29
Eglwyswsrw ...15 F 27
Egremont ...47 J 20
Egton ...50 R 20
Eigg ...71 B 13
Eigheach (Loch) ...73 G 13
Eight Ash Green ...30 W 28
Eil ...73 I 12
Eil (Loch) ...72 E 13
Eilde Mór (Loch) ...72 F 13
Eilean a' Chalmain ...64 A 15
Eilean Beag ...77 C 11
Eilean Chathastail ...71 B 13
Eilean Donan Castle ...78 D 12
Eilean Flodigarry ...77 B 10
Eilean Mhuire ...82 A 10
Eilean Mòr ...77 C 11
Eilean Mullagrach ...83 D 9
Eilean na Bà ...77 C 11
Eilean nan Each ...71 B 13
Eilean Trodday ...77 B 10
Eileanach Lodge ...79 G 10
Eilt (Loch) ...72 D 13
Eishken ...82 A 9
Eishort (Loch) ...71 C 12
Elan Valley ...25 J 27
Elan Village ...25 J 27
Elcho ...68 J 14
Elgin ...80 K 11
Elgol ...71 B 12
Elham ...23 X 30
Elie ...69 L 15
Eling ...10 P 31
Elkesley ...44 R 24
Elkstone ...19 N 28

A
B
C
D
E
F
G
H
I
J
K
L
M
N
O
P
Q
R
S
T
U
V
W
X
Y
Z

A
B
C
D
E
F
G
H
I
J
K
L
M
N
O
P
Q
R
S
T
U
V
W
X
Y
Z

Elland ....43 O 22
Ellastone ....35 O 25
Ellen's Green ....11 S 30
Ellerbeck ....50 P 20
Ellerton ....44 R 22
Ellesmere ....34 L 25
Ellesmere Port ....42 L 24
Ellingham ....31 Y 26
Ellington ....56 P 18
Ellon ....81 N 11
Elloughton ....44 S 22
Elmdon ....29 U 27
Elmley Castle ....27 N 27
Elmore ....19 N 28
Elmstead Market ....30 W 28
Elmswell ....30 W 27
Elphin ....84 E 9
Elrick ....75 N 12
Elrig ....52 G 19
Elsdon ....55 N 18
Elsenham ....30 U 28
Elsham ....45 S 23
Elsrickle ....61 J 16
Elstead ....21 R 30
Elstree ....21 T 29
Elswick ....42 L 22
Eltisley ....29 T 27
Elton ....37 S 26
Elveden ....30 W 26
Elvington ....50 R 22
Elwick ....57 Q 19
Elworth ....35 M 24
Ely ....30 U 26
Emberton ....28 R 27
Embleton Allerdale ....54 K 20
Embleton Alnwick ....63 P 17
Embo ....79 I 10
Embsay ....49 O 22
Emneth ....37 U 26
Empingham ....37 S 25
Emsworth ....10 R 31
Enaclete ....82 Z 9
Enard Bay ....83 D 9
Enderby ....36 Q 26
Endmoor ....48 L 21
Endon ....35 N 24
Enfield London Borough ....21 T 29
Enford ....19 O 30
Englefield Green ....21 S 29
English Bicknor ....18 M 28
Englishcombe ....19 M 29
Enham Alamein ....20 P 30
Enmore ....8 K 30
Ensay ....71 B 14
Enstone ....28 P 28
Enterkinfoot ....61 I 18
Enville ....27 N 26
Eochar ....76 X 11
Eoligarry ....70 X 12
Eoropie ....83 B 8
Eport (Loch) ....76 Y 11
Epping ....21 U 28
Epping Forest ....21 U 29
Epsom ....21 T 30
Epworth ....44 R 23
Erddig ....34 K 24
Eredine ....65 E 15
Eredine Forest ....65 D 15
Eriboll ....84 F 8
Eriboll (Loch) ....84 F 8
Ericht (Loch) ....73 G 13
Ericstane ....61 J 17
Eridge Green ....12 U 30
Eriska ....65 D 14
Eriskay ....70 Y 12
Erisort (Loch) ....82 A 9
Eriswell ....30 V 26
Erlestoke ....19 N 30
Ermington ....4 I 32
Erpingham ....39 X 25
Erraid ....64 A 15
Errochty (Loch) ....73 H 13
Errogie ....79 G 12
Errol ....68 K 14
Ersary ....70 X 13
Erskine Bridge ....67 G 16
Ervie ....52 E 19
Erwood ....25 K 27
Esh Winning ....56 O 19
Esha Ness ....87 P 2
Esher ....21 S 29
Esk (Glen) ....75 L 13
Esk (River) ....54 K 19
Eskdale ....54 K 18
Eskdalemuir ....61 K 18
Essendon ....21 T 28

Essich ....79 H 11
Eston ....57 Q 20
Etal ....63 N 17
Etchilhampton ....19 O 29
Etchingham ....12 V 30
Etherow (River) ....43 N 23
Etherow Park ....43 N 23
Eton ....21 S 29
Ettington ....27 P 27
Ettrick ....61 K 17
Ettrick Forest ....62 K 17
Ettrick Pen ....61 K 17
Etwall ....35 P 25
Euston ....30 W 26
Euxton ....42 L 22
Evanton ....79 G 11
Evelix ....79 H 10
Evenlode ....27 O 28
Evenwood ....56 O 20
Evercreech ....8 M 30
Everingham ....44 R 22
Everleigh ....19 O 30
Evershot ....8 M 31
Eversley ....20 R 29
Everton ....44 R 23
Evesham ....27 O 27
Evesham (Vale of) ....27 O 27
Ewe (Isle of) ....78 D 10
Ewell ....21 T 29
Ewelme ....20 Q 29
Ewenny ....17 J 29
Ewes ....54 L 18
Ewhurst ....11 S 30
Exbourne ....7 I 31
Exe (River) ....7 J 31
Exebridge ....7 J 30
Exeter ....4 J 31
Exford ....7 J 30
Exminster ....4 J 31
Exmoor National Park ....7 I 30
Exmouth ....4 J 32
Exton ....7 J 30
Eyam ....43 O 24
Eye Cambs. ....37 T 26
Eye Suffolk ....31 X 27
Eye Peninsula ....83 B 9
Eyemouth ....63 N 16
Eynort ....77 A 12
Eynort (Loch) Highland ....77 A 12
Eynort (Loch) Western Isles ....76 Y 12
Eynsford ....22 U 29
Eynsham ....20 P 28
Eyre Point ....77 B 12
Eythorne ....23 X 30

F

Fada (Loch) ....76 Y 11
Failsworth ....43 N 23
Fair Isle ....87 P 5
Fair Oak ....10 Q 31
Fairbourne ....33 H 25
Fairford ....19 O 28
Fairlie ....59 F 16
Fairlight ....12 V 31
Fakenham ....38 W 25
Fala ....62 L 16
Faldingworth ....45 S 23
Falfield ....18 M 29
Falkirk ....67 I 16
Falkland ....68 K 15
Fallin ....67 I 15
Falmer ....11 T 31
Falmouth ....2 E 33
Falstone ....55 M 18
Fanagmore ....84 E 8
Fangfoss ....50 R 22
Fannich (Loch) ....78 E 11
Fannich Lodge ....78 F 11
Fara ....86 K 7
Fareham ....10 Q 31
Faringdon ....19 P 29
Farley ....9 O 30
Farley Mount ....10 P 30
Farlow ....26 M 26
Farmborough ....18 M 29
Farmers ....25 I 27
Farmtown ....80 L 11
Farnborough Hants. ....20 R 30
Farnborough Warw. ....28 P 27
Farnborough
    West Berkshire ....20 P 29

Farndon Chester ....34 L 24
Farndon
    Newark and Sherwood ......36 R 24
Farne Islands ....63 P 17
Farnell ....75 M 13
Farnham Dorset ....9 N 31
Farnham Surrey ....20 R 30
Farnham Royal ....21 S 29
Farningham ....22 U 29
Farnley ....49 O 22
Farnsfield ....36 Q 24
Farnworth ....42 M 23
Farr ....85 H 8
Farrington Gurney ....18 M 30
Farway ....5 K 31
Fasnakyle ....78 F 12
Fasnakyle Forest ....78 F 11
Fasque ....75 M 13
Fassfern ....72 E 13
Fauldhouse ....61 I 16
Faversham ....22 W 30
Fawley ....10 P 31
Fazeley ....35 O 26
Fearby ....49 O 21
Fearn Lodge ....79 H 10
Fearnan ....67 H 14
Fearnmore ....77 C 11
Featherstone Staffs. ....35 N 26
Featherstone West Yorks. ......43 P 22
Feckenham ....27 N 27
Feering ....30 W 28
Feetham ....49 N 20
Felbridge ....11 T 30
Felindre Carmarthenshire /
    Sir Gaerfyrddin ....25 I 28
Felindre Powys ....26 K 26
Felinfach ....25 K 28
Felinheli ....33 H 24
Felixkirk ....50 Q 21
Felixstowe ....31 Y 28
Felling ....56 P 19
Felmingham ....39 Y 25
Felpham ....11 S 31
Felsham ....30 W 27
Felsted ....30 V 28
Feltham ....21 S 29
Felthorpe ....39 X 25
Felton ....63 O 18
Feltwell ....30 V 26
Fence ....42 N 22
Feniton ....8 K 31
Fenny Bentley ....35 O 24
Fenstanton ....29 T 27
Fenton Stoke-on-Trent ....35 N 25
Fenton West Lindsey ....44 R 24
Fenwick
    Berwick-upon-Tweed ....63 O 17
Fenwick East Ayrshire ....60 G 17
Feochaig ....59 D 17
Feochan (Loch) ....65 D 14
Feock ....2 E 33
Feolin Ferry ....58 B 16
Fern ....74 L 13
Ferndown ....9 O 31
Ferness ....79 I 11
Fernhurst ....11 R 30
Ferryden ....75 M 13
Ferryhill ....56 P 19
Ferryside ....15 G 28
Fersit ....73 F 13
Feshie (Glen) ....73 I 12
Feshiebridge ....73 I 12
Fetcham ....21 S 30
Fetlar ....87 R 2
Fetterangus ....81 N 11
Fettercairn ....75 M 13
Fewston ....49 O 22
Ffestiniog ....33 I 25
Ffestiniog (Vale of) ....33 H 25
Fflint / Flint ....42 K 24
Fforest Fawr ....17 J 28
Ffostrasol ....15 G 27
Fiaray ....70 X 12
Fiddleton ....62 L 18
Fifield ....27 P 28
Filby ....39 Y 26
Filey ....51 T 21
Fillongley ....27 P 26
Filton ....18 M 29
Finchampstead ....20 R 29
Finchingfield ....30 V 28
Findhorn ....80 J 11
Findhorn (River) ....73 H 12
Findhorn Bay ....80 J 11
Findo Gask ....68 J 14
Findochty ....80 L 10
Findon ....11 S 31

Finedon ....29 S 26
Fingest ....20 R 29
Fingland ....60 I 17
Finiskaig ....72 D 13
Finmere ....28 Q 28
Finnart ....66 F 15
Finniegill ....61 K 18
Finningley ....44 R 23
Finsbay ....76 Z 10
Finstock ....20 P 28
Finstown ....86 K 6
Fintry Aberdeenshire ....81 M 11
Fintry Stirling ....67 H 15
Fionn Loch ....78 D 10
Fionn Loch Mór ....84 F 9
Fionnphort ....64 A 15
Fishbourne Chichester ....10 R 31
Fishbourne Isle of Wight ......10 Q 31
Fishburn ....56 P 19
Fisherfield Forest ....78 D 10
Fisherford ....81 M 11
Fishguard / Abergwaun ....24 F 28
Fishnish Bay ....65 B 14
Fishtoft ....37 U 25
Fiskavaig ....77 A 12
Fiskerton ....45 S 24
Fittleworth ....11 S 31
Fiunary ....71 C 14
Fivehead ....8 L 30
Flackwell Heath ....21 R 29
Fladbury ....27 N 27
Fladda-Chùain ....77 A 10
Flagg ....35 O 24
Flamborough ....51 T 21
Flamborough Head ....51 T 21
Flamingo Park ....50 R 21
Flamstead ....21 S 28
Flash ....35 O 24
Flashader ....77 A 11
Flatford Mill ....30 X 28
Flax Bourton ....18 L 29
Flaxton ....50 R 21
Fleckney ....36 Q 26
Fleet ....20 R 30
Fleet (Islands of) ....53 H 19
Fleet (Loch) ....79 H 10
Fleet Hargate ....37 U 25
Fleetwood ....48 K 22
Flimby ....53 J 19
Flint / Fflint ....42 K 24
Flintham ....36 R 24
Flitton ....29 S 27
Flitwick ....29 S 27
Flodday near Hellisay ....70 X 13
Flodday near Sandray ....70 X 13
Flodden Field ....63 N 17
Flodigarry ....77 B 11
Flookburgh ....48 L 21
Floors Castle ....62 M 17
Flotta ....86 K 7
Flowerdale Forest ....78 D 11
Flyford Flavell ....27 N 27
Fochabers ....80 K 11
Foggathorpe ....44 R 22
Foinaven ....84 F 8
Foindle ....84 E 8
Folkestone ....13 X 30
Folkingham ....37 S 25
Folly Gate ....7 H 31
Fontmell Magna ....9 N 31
Ford Argyll and Bute ....65 D 15
Ford Arun ....11 S 31
Ford
    Berwick-upon-Tweed ....63 N 17
Ford
    Buckinghamshire ....20 R 28
Ford Cotswold ....27 O 28
Ford
    Shrewsbury and Atcham ..34 L 25
Forde Abbey ....8 L 31
Forden ....34 K 26
Fordham ....30 V 27
Fordingbridge ....9 O 31
Fordoun ....75 M 13
Fordwich ....23 X 30
Fordyce ....80 L 11
Foreland ....10 Q 31
Foreland Point ....17 I 30
Foremark Reservoir ....36 P 25
Forest Lodge ....74 I 13
Forest Row ....11 U 30
Forestburn Gate ....63 O 18
Forfar ....74 L 14
Forgandenny ....68 J 14
Forgie ....80 L 11
Formby ....42 K 23
Formby Point ....42 K 23
Fornham All Saints ....30 W 27

Forres ....80 J 11
Forrest Lodge ....53 H 18
Forse ....85 K 9
Forsinard ....85 I 8
Fort Augustus ....73 F 12
Fort George ....79 H 11
Fort Victoria ....10 P 31
Fort William ....72 E 13
Forteviot ....68 J 14
Forth ....61 I 16
Forth (Firth of) ....68 K 15
Forth (River) ....67 G 15
Forth Bridges ....68 J 15
Fortingall ....73 H 14
Forton ....35 M 25
Fortrose ....79 H 11
Forter ....74 K 13
Fortuneswell ....8 M 32
Fosdyke ....37 T 25
Foss ....73 I 13
Foston ....36 R 25
Foston on the Wolds ....51 T 22
Fotherby ....45 T 23
Fotheringhay ....29 S 26
Foulden ....63 N 16
Foulness Point ....22 W 29
Foulridge ....43 N 22
Foulsham ....38 X 25
Fountainhall ....62 L 16
Fountains Abbey ....50 P 21
Four Crosses ....34 K 25
Four Elms ....21 U 30
Four Marks ....10 Q 30
Fovant ....9 O 30
Foveran ....81 N 12
Fowey ....3 G 32
Fowlmere ....29 U 27
Fownhope ....26 M 27
Foxdale ....46 G 21
Foxholes ....51 S 21
Foxton ....28 R 26
Foxup ....49 N 21
Foyers ....73 G 12
Fraddon ....3 F 32
Framfield ....12 U 31
Framlingham ....31 Y 27
Frampton-on-Severn ....19 M 28
Framwellgate Moor ....56 P 19
Frant ....12 U 30
Fraserburgh ....81 O 10
Fraserburgh Bay ....81 O 10
Freckenham ....30 V 27
Freckleton ....42 L 22
Freeland ....20 P 28
Freethorpe ....39 Y 26
Freevater Forest ....79 F 10
Freiston ....37 U 25
Fremington ....7 H 30
Frensham ....10 R 30
Freshwater ....10 P 31
Freshwater Bay ....10 P 31
Freshwater East ....16 F 29
Freshwater West ....14 E 29
Fressingfield ....31 X 26
Freswick ....86 K 8
Freuchie ....68 K 15
Freuchie (Loch) ....67 I 14
Friday Bridge ....37 U 26
Fridaythorpe ....51 S 21
Frimley ....21 R 30
Fringford ....28 Q 28
Frinton-on-Sea ....31 X 28
Friockheim ....75 M 14
Frisa (Loch) ....71 B 14
Friskney ....37 U 24
Frithville ....37 T 24
Frittenden ....12 V 30
Fritwell ....28 Q 28
Frizington ....47 J 20
Frocester ....19 N 28
Frodsham ....42 L 24
Froggatt ....43 P 24
Frome ....19 N 30
Frosterley ....56 O 19
Froxfield ....20 P 29
Froyde ....80 L 11
Fuday ....70 X 12
Fuiay ....70 X 13
Fulbourn ....30 U 27
Fulking ....11 T 31
Fuller Street ....22 V 28
Fulwood ....42 M 22
Funtington ....10 R 31
Funzie ....87 R 2
Furness Abbey ....47 K 21
Furness Fells ....48 K 20
Fyfield ....22 U 28
Fyvie ....81 M 11

G

Gaddesby ....36 R 25
Gaick Lodge ....73 H 13
Gainford ....49 O 20
Gainsborough ....44 R 23
Gairloch ....78 C 10
Gairlochy ....72 F 13
Gairsay ....87 L 6
Gaitsgill ....54 L 19
Galashiels ....62 L 17
Galgate ....48 L 22
Gallan Head ....82 Y 9
Gallanach ....65 D 14
Galloway Forest Park ....52 G 18
Galltair ....72 D 12
Galmisdale ....71 B 13
Galmpton ....4 J 32
Galson ....82 A 8
Galston ....60 G 17
Galtrigill ....76 Z 11
Gamblesby ....55 M 19
Gamlingay ....29 T 27
Gamston ....44 R 24
Ganavan ....65 D 14
Ganton ....51 S 21
Garboldisham ....30 W 26
Gardenstown ....81 N 10
Garelochhead ....66 F 15
Garenin ....82 Z 9
Garforth ....43 P 22
Gargrave ....49 N 22
Gargunnock ....67 H 15
Garioch ....81 M 12
Garlieston ....53 G 19
Garlogie ....75 M 12
Garmony ....65 C 14
Garmouth ....80 K 11
Garrabost ....83 B 9
Garragie Lodge ....73 G 12
Garraron ....65 D 15
Garreg ....33 H 25
Garrigill ....55 M 19
Garrisdale Point ....71 A 12
Garros ....77 B 11
Garrow ....67 I 14
Garry (Glen) Highland ....72 E 12
Garry (Glen)
    Perthshire and Kinross ....73 H 13
Garry (Loch) ....72 F 12
Garsington ....20 Q 28
Garten (Loch) ....74 I 12
Garth ....25 J 27
Garthorpe ....44 R 23
Gartmore ....67 G 15
Gartocharn ....67 G 15
Garton-on-The-Wolds ....51 S 21
Garvald ....69 M 16
Garvamore ....73 G 12
Garve ....79 F 11
Garvellachs ....65 C 15
Garvestone ....38 W 26
Garvock ....66 F 16
Garway ....26 L 28
Garynahine ....82 Z 9
Gatehouse of Fleet ....53 H 19
Gateshead ....56 P 19
Gateside ....68 K 15
Gatley ....42 N 23
Gatwick Airport ....11 T 30
Gaulden Manor ....8 K 30
Gavard ....64 B 15
Gaydon ....28 P 27
Gayton King's Lynn
    and West Norfolk ....38 V 25
Gayton Stafford ....35 N 25
Gaywood ....38 V 25
Geary ....77 A 11
Geddington ....29 R 26
Gedney Drove End ....37 U 25
Gedney Hill ....37 T 25
Gelligaer ....18 K 29
Gelston ....53 I 19
Georgeham ....6 H 30
Georth ....86 K 6
Gerrards Cross ....21 S 29
Gestingthorpe ....30 V 27
Gifford ....62 L 16
Gigha (Sound of) ....58 C 17
Gigha Island ....58 C 16
Gighay ....70 Y 12
Gilberdyke ....44 R 22
Gilcrux ....54 J 19
Gildersome ....43 P 22
Gilfach Goch ....17 J 29
Gillamoor ....50 R 21
Gilling East ....50 Q 21

Gilling West ....49 O 20
Gillingham Dorset ....9 N 30
Gillingham Kent ....22 V 29
Gillingham South Norfolk ...31 Y 26
Gills ....86 K 8
Gilmerton ....67 I 14
Gilmorton ....28 Q 26
Gilston ....62 L 16
Gilwern ....18 K 28
Girthon ....53 H 19
Girton ....29 U 27
Girvan ....59 F 18
Gisburn ....49 N 22
Gisland ....55 M 19
Gittisham ....8 K 31
Gladestry ....26 K 27
Glaisdale ....50 R 20
Glamis ....74 K 14
Glamis Castle ....74 L 14
Glanaman ....17 I 28
Glandwr ....15 G 28
Glanton ....63 O 17
Glas-allt-Shiel ....74 K 13
Glas-leac Mór ....83 D 9
Glas Maol ....74 J 13
Glasbury ....26 K 27
Glascarnoch (Loch) ....78 F 10
Glascwm ....26 K 27
Glasdrum ....72 E 14
Glasgow ....60 H 16
Glasphein ....76 Z 11
Glaspwll ....33 I 26
Glass (Loch) ....79 G 10
Glassburn ....78 F 11
Glasserton ....52 G 19
Glassford ....60 H 16
Glasshouses ....49 O 21
Glasson ....48 L 22
Glassonby ....55 M 19
Glastonbury ....8 L 30
Gleadless ....43 P 23
Gleann Beag ....78 F 10
Gleann Mór ....79 G 10
Gleaston ....48 K 21
Glecknabae ....59 E 16
Glemsford ....30 V 27
Glen auldyn ....46 G 21
Glen Brittle Forest ....77 B 12
Glen Finglas Reservoir ....67 G 15
Glen More Forest Park ....74 I 12
Glen Shee ....74 J 13
Glen Trool Lodge ....52 G 18
Glenbarr ....59 C 17
Glenborrodale ....71 C 13
Glenbranter ....66 E 15
Glenbrittle House ....77 B 12
Glenbuchat Castle ....74 K 12
Glenbuck ....60 I 17
Glencaple ....53 J 18
Glencarse ....68 K 14
Glencoe ....72 E 13
Glencoul (Loch) ....84 F 9
Glendoebeg ....73 G 12
Glendurgan Garden ....2 E 33
Glenegedale ....58 B 16
Glenelg ....72 D 12
Glenelg Bay ....72 D 12
Glenfarg ....68 J 15
Glenfeshie Lodge ....73 I 12
Glenfiddich Lodge ....80 K 11
Glenfield ....36 Q 26
Glenfinnan ....72 D 13
Glenforsa Airport ....65 C 14
Glenfyne Lodge ....66 F 15
Glengorm ....71 B 14
Glengoulandie ....73 H 14
Glengrasco ....77 B 11
Glenkens (The) ....53 H 18
Glenkin die ....74 L 12
Glenkirk ....61 J 17
Glenlivet ....80 J 11
Glenluce ....52 F 19
Glenmassan ....66 E 15
Glenmaye ....46 F 21
Glenmore ....71 C 13
Glenprosen Village ....74 K 13
Glenridding ....48 L 20
Glenrothes ....68 K 15
Glenside ....82 A 9
Glenstriven ....66 E 16
Glentham ....44 S 23
Glentress ....61 K 17
Glentrool Village ....52 G 18
Glentworth ....44 S 23
Glenuachdarach ....77 B 11
Glenuig ....71 C 13
Glespin ....61 I 17

Gletness ....87 Q 3
Glinton ....37 T 26
Glossop ....43 O 23
Gloucester ....27 N 28
Gloup ....87 Q 1
Glusburn ....49 O 22
Glyn Ceiriog ....34 K 25
Glyn-Ebwy / Ebbw Vale ....18 K 28
Glyn-neath ....17 J 28
Glyncorrwg ....17 J 28
Glynde ....11 U 31
Glyndebourne ....11 U 31
Glyndyfrdwy ....34 K 25
Gnosall ....35 N 25
Goadby ....36 R 26
Goat Fell ....59 E 17
Goathland ....50 R 20
Gobowen ....34 K 25
Godalming ....21 S 30
Godmanchester ....29 T 27
Godmanstone ....8 M 31
Godshill ....10 Q 32
Godstone ....21 T 30
Goil (Loch) ....66 F 15
Golborne ....42 M 23
Goldcliff ....18 L 29
Goldhanger ....22 W 28
Goldthorpe ....44 Q 23
Golspie ....85 I 10
Gomersal ....43 O 22
Gometra ....64 B 14
Gomshall ....21 S 30
Goodleigh ....7 I 30
Goodrich ....26 M 28
Goodrington ....4 J 32
Goodwick ....24 F 27
Goodwood House ....10 R 31
Goole ....44 R 22
Goonhavern ....2 E 32
Goostrey ....42 M 24
Gordon ....62 M 16
Gordonbush ....85 I 9
Gordonstown ....80 L 11
Gorebridge ....61 K 16
Goring ....20 Q 29
Gorm Loch Mór ....84 F 9
Gorran Haven ....3 F 33
Gorseinon ....15 H 29
Gorsleston-on-Sea ....39 Z 26
Gortantaoid ....64 B 16
Gosberton ....37 T 25
Gosfield ....30 V 28
Gosforth Cumbria ....47 J 20
Gosforth
    Newcastle upon Tyne ....56 P 18
Gosport ....10 Q 31
Goswick ....63 O 16
Gotham ....36 Q 25
Gott Bay ....70 Z 14
Goudhurst ....12 V 30
Gourdon ....75 N 13
Gourock ....66 F 16
Gowerton ....15 H 29
Goxhill ....45 T 22
Graemsay ....86 K 7
Grafton Underwood ....29 S 26
Grain ....22 W 29
Grainthorpe ....45 U 23
Granby ....36 R 25
Grandtully ....74 I 14
Grange-over-Sands ....48 L 21
Grangemouth ....67 I 15
Grantchester ....29 U 27
Grantham ....37 S 25
Grantown-on-Spey ....80 J 12
Grantshouse ....62 N 16
Grasby ....45 S 23
Grasmere ....48 K 20
Grassington ....49 O 21
Grateley ....9 P 30
Graveley ....29 T 27
Gravesend ....22 V 29
Gravir ....82 A 9
Grayrigg ....48 M 20
Grays Thurrock ....22 V 29
Grayshott ....10 R 30
Grayswood ....11 R 30
Greasbrough ....43 P 23
Great Addington ....29 S 26
Greenfield
    Flintshire / Sir y Fflint .....41 K 23
Greenfield Highland .....72 F 12
Greenhaugh ....55 N 18
Greenhead ....55 M 19
Great Altcar ....42 K 23
Great Amwell ....21 T 28
Great Ayton ....50 Q 20
Great Baddow ....22 V 28

Great Bardfield ....30 V 28
Great Barford ....29 S 27
Great Barr ....35 O 26
Great Barrow ....34 L 24
Great Barugh ....50 R 21
Great Bedwyn ....19 P 29
Great Bentley ....31 X 28
Great Bernera ....82 Z 9
Great Bircham ....38 V 25
Great-Bollright ....28 P 28
Great Bookham ....21 S 30
Great Bourton ....28 Q 27
Great Bowden ....28 R 26
Great Brickhill ....29 R 28
Great Bridgeford ....35 N 25
Great Bromley ....30 X 28
Great Broughton ....50 Q 20
Great-Budworth ....42 M 24
Great Burdon ....50 P 20
Great Chalfield ....19 N 29
Great Chesterford ....30 U 27
Great Chishill ....29 U 27
Great Clifton ....53 J 20
Great Coates ....45 T 23
Great-Comberton ....27 N 27
Great Cornard ....30 W 27
Great Cubley ....35 O 25
Great Cumbrae Island ....59 F 16
Great-Dalby ....36 R 25
Great Doddington ....28 R 27
Great Driffield ....51 S 21
Great-Dunham ....38 W 25
Great Dunmow ....30 V 28
Great Easton Essex ....30 U 28
Great Easton Leics. ....28 R 26
Great Eccleston ....42 L 22
Great Ellingham ....38 W 26
Great Finborough ....30 W 27
Great Glen ....36 Q 26
Great Gonerby ....37 S 25
Great Gransden ....29 T 27
Great Harrowden ....28 R 27
Great Harwood ....42 M 22
Great Hockham ....30 W 26
Great Horkesley ....30 W 28
Great Horwood ....28 R 28
Great Houghton ....43 P 23
Great Langton ....50 P 20
Great-Limber ....45 T 23
Great Livermere ....30 W 27
Great Lumley ....56 P 19
Great Malvern ....27 N 27
Great Marton ....42 K 22
Great Massingham ....38 W 25
Great Milton ....20 Q 28
Great Missenden ....21 R 28
Great Mitton ....42 M 22
Great Musgrave ....49 M 20
Great Oakley ....31 X 28
Great Ormes Head ....41 I 22
Great Orton ....54 K 19
Great Ouse (River) ....38 V 25
Great Ouseburn ....50 Q 21
Great Ponton ....37 S 25
Great Ryburgh ....38 W 25
Great Salkeld ....55 L 19
Great Sampford ....30 V 28
Great Shefford ....20 P 29
Great Shelford ....29 U 27
Great Smeaton ....50 P 20
Great Somerford ....19 N 29
Great Stainton ....56 P 20
Great Strickland ....55 L 20
Great Torrington ....6 H 31
Great Tosson ....63 O 18
Great Totham ....22 W 28
Great Urswick ....48 K 21
Great Wakering ....22 W 29
Great Waltham ....22 V 28
Great Whernside ....49 O 21
Great Whittington ....56 O 18
Great Witley ....27 M 27
Great Wolford ....27 P 27
Great Wyrley ....35 N 26
Great Yarmouth ....39 Z 26
Great Yeldham ....30 V 27
Greatford ....37 S 25
Greatham Cleveland ....57 Q 20
Greatham Hants. ....10 R 30
Greatstone-on-Sea ....12 W 31
Greenfield

Greenhow Hill ....49 O 21
Greenlaw ....62 M 16
Greenloaning ....67 I 15
Greenock ....66 F 16
Greenodd ....48 K 21
Greens Norton ....28 Q 27
Greenside ....56 O 19
Greenwich
    London Borough ....21 U 29
Grendon ....28 R 27
Grendon Underwood ....28 Q 28
Gresford ....34 L 24
Greshornish ....77 A 11
Greshornish (Loch) ....77 A 11
Gress ....83 B 9
Gretna ....54 K 19
Gretton ....37 R 26
Greys Court ....20 R 29
Greysouthen ....54 J 20
Greystoke ....55 L 19
Griffithstown ....18 K 28
Griminish ....76 X 11
Grimley ....27 N 27
Grimoldby ....45 U 23
Grimsay ....76 Y 11
Grimsby ....45 T 23
Gringley on the Hill ....44 R 23
Grinshill ....34 L 25
Grinton ....49 O 20
Gristhorpe ....51 T 21
Grittleton ....19 N 29
Groby ....36 Q 26
Grogport ....59 D 17
Groombridge ....12 U 30
Grosebay ....76 Z 10
Grosmont Monmouthshire /
    Sir Fynwy ....26 L 28
Grosmont Scarborough ....50 R 20
Grove ....20 P 29
Gruinard Bay ....78 D 10
Gruinard Island ....78 D 10
Gruinart ....58 B 16
Gruinart (Loch) ....64 B 16
Grunavat (Loch) ....82 Z 9
Grundisburgh ....31 X 27
Gualachulain ....66 E 14
Guardbridge ....69 L 14
Guernsey Channel I. 5
Guesting ....12 V 31
Guildford ....21 S 30
Guildtown ....68 J 14
Guilsborough ....28 Q 26
Guisborough ....50 Q 20
Guiseley ....43 O 22
Guist ....38 W 25
Gullane ....69 L 15
Gunna ....70 Z 14
Gunnerside ....49 N 20
Gunnerton ....55 N 18
Gunness ....44 R 23
Gunnislake ....3 H 32
Gunthorpe ....36 R 25
Gurnard ....10 Q 31
Gurness Broch ....86 K 6
Gurnos ....17 I 28
Gussage All Saints ....9 O 31
Gutcher ....87 Q 1
Guthrie ....75 L 14
Guyhirn ....37 U 26
Gwalchmai ....40 G 23
Gwaun-Cae-Gurwen ....17 I 28
Gwbert-on-Sea ....15 F 27
Gweek ....2 E 33
Gwennap ....2 E 33
Gwithian ....2 D 33
Gwyddelwern ....33 J 24
Gwyddgrug ....15 H 28
Gwydir Castle ....33 I 24
Gwytherin ....33 I 24

H

Habost ....83 B 8
Hackney London Borough ..21 T 29
Haddenham Bucks. ....20 R 28
Haddenham Cambs. ....29 U 26
Haddington ....69 L 16
Haddiscoe ....39 Y 26
Haddo House ....81 N 11
Haddon Hall ....35 P 24
Hadfield ....43 O 23
Hadleigh Essex ....22 V 29
Hadleigh Suffolk ....30 W 27
Hadley ....34 M 25
Hadlow ....22 V 30
Hadnall ....34 L 25
Hadrian's Wall ....55 M 18
Haggbeck ....55 L 18

Hagley ....27 N 26
Hagworthingham ....45 U 24
Hailsham ....12 U 31
Hainford ....39 X 25
Hainton ....45 T 23
Halam ....36 R 24
Halberton ....7 J 31
Halcro ....42 M 23
Hales ....39 Y 26
Halesowen ....27 N 26
Halesworth ....31 Y 26
Halford ....27 P 27
Halifax ....43 O 22
Halistra ....77 A 11
Halkirk ....85 J 8
Hall ....60 G 16
Halland ....12 U 31
Hallaton ....36 R 26
Hallington ....55 N 18
Halloughton ....36 R 24
Hallow ....27 N 27
Hallsands ....4 J 33
Halsall ....42 L 23
Halse ....8 K 30
Halsetown ....2 D 33
Halstead ....30 V 28
Halstock ....8 M 31
Haltham ....37 T 24
Halton Aylesbury Vale ....20 R 28
Halton Lancaster ....48 L 21
Halton Gill ....49 N 21
Haltwhistle ....55 M 19
Halwell ....4 I 32
Halwill Junction ....6 H 31
Hambledon ....20 R 29
Hambleton Hants. ....10 Q 31
Hambleton Surrey ....11 S 30
Hambleton Lancs. ....42 L 22
Hambleton North Yorks. ....44 Q 22
Hambleton Hills (The) ....50 Q 21
Hambridge ....8 L 31
Hamersley ....56 O 19
Hamhaugh ....21 T 29
Hamnavoe near Brae ....87 Q 2
Hamnavoe near Scallway ...87 P 3
Hampreston ....9 O 31
Hampstead Norris ....20 Q 29
Hampsthwaite ....50 P 21
Hampton Court ....21 S 29
Hampton in Arden ....27 O 26
Hamstead Marshall ....20 P 29
Hamsterley ....56 O 19
Hamstreet ....12 W 30
Hamworthy ....9 N 31
Handa Island ....84 E 8
Handbridge ....34 L 24
Handcross ....11 T 30
Handforth ....43 N 23
Handley ....34 L 24
Handsworth ....43 P 23
Hanley ....35 N 24
Hanley Swan ....27 N 27
Hanningfield ....22 V 28
Hannington ....19 O 29
Hanslope ....28 R 27
Happisburgh ....39 Y 25
Hapton ....42 N 22
Harberton ....4 I 32
Harbertonford ....4 I 32
Harbledown ....23 X 30
Harborough Magna ....28 Q 26
Harbottle ....63 N 17
Harbury ....28 P 27
Harby ....36 R 25
Hardham ....11 S 31
Hardwick ....44 Q 24
Hardwick Hall ....36 Q 24
Hardwicke ....19 N 28
Hardy Monument ....5 M 31
Hardy's Cottage ....9 M 31
Hare Street ....29 U 28
Haresfield ....19 N 28
Harewood House ....50 P 22
Hargrave Green ....30 V 27
Haringey London Borough ..21 T 29
Harlaxton ....36 R 25
Harlech ....33 H 25
Harleston ....31 X 26
Harlestone ....28 R 27
Harley ....34 M 26
Harlington ....29 S 28

Harlosh ....77 A 11
Harlow ....21 U 28
Harlow Hill ....56 O 18
Harmston ....37 S 24
Haroldswick ....87 R 1
Harpenden ....21 S 28
Harpley ....38 V 25
Harport (Loch) ....77 A 12
Harray (Loch of) ....86 K 6
Harrietfield ....67 J 14
Harrington Allerdale ....53 J 20
Harrington Kettering ....28 R 26
Harringworth ....37 S 26
Harris Highland ....71 A 13
Harris Western Isles ....82 Y 10
Harris (Sound of) ....76 Y 10
Harrogate ....50 P 22
Harrow London Borough ...21 S 29
Harston ....29 U 27
Hartburn ....56 O 18
Hartest ....30 W 27
Hartfield ....11 U 30
Harthill North Lanarkshire ...61 I 16
Harthill Rotherham ....44 Q 24
Harting ....10 R 31
Hartington ....35 O 24
Hartland ....6 G 31
Hartland Quay ....6 G 31
Hartlebury ....27 N 26
Hartlepool ....57 Q 19
Hartley ....22 U 29
Hartley Wintney ....20 R 30
Hartpury ....27 N 28
Hartshill ....36 P 26
Hartwell ....20 R 28
Hartwell ....28 R 27
Harvington ....27 O 27
Harwell ....20 Q 29
Harwich ....31 X 28
Harwood Dale ....51 S 20
Harworth ....44 Q 23
Hascosay ....87 R 2
Haselbury Plucknett ....8 L 31
Hasland ....43 P 24
Haslemere ....11 R 30
Haslingden ....42 N 22
Haslingfield ....29 U 27
Haslington ....35 M 24
Hassocks ....11 T 31
Haster ....86 K 8
Hastings ....12 V 31
Hatch Court ....8 L 31
Hatfield
    County of Herefordshire ..26 M 27
Hatfield Herts. ....21 T 28
Hatfield South Yorks. ....44 Q 23
Hatfield Broad Oak ....22 U 28
Hatfield Heath ....22 U 28
Hatfield Peverel ....22 V 28
Hatfield Woodhouse ....44 R 23
Hatherleigh ....7 H 31
Hathern ....36 Q 25
Hathersage ....43 P 24
Hatton Aberdeenshire ....81 O 11
Hatton Derbs. ....35 O 25
Hatton of Fintray ....75 N 12
Haugh of Urr ....53 I 19
Haughton ....35 N 25
Haunn ....71 B 14
Havant ....10 R 31
Havenstreet ....10 Q 31
Haverfordwest / Hwlffordd ..16 F 28
Haverhill ....30 V 27
Haverigg ....47 K 21
Havering London Borough ..22 U 29
Haverthwaite ....48 K 21
Hawarden ....34 K 24
Hawes ....49 N 21
Hawick ....62 L 17
Hawkchurch ....8 L 31
Hawkedon ....30 V 27
Hawkesbury Upton ....19 M 29
Hawkhurst ....12 V 30
Hawkridge ....7 J 30
Hawkshead ....48 L 20
Hawkwell ....22 V 29
Hawley ....20 R 30
Hawling ....27 O 28
Haworth ....43 O 22
Hawsker ....51 S 20
Haxby ....50 Q 21
Haxey ....44 R 23
Hay-on-Wye ....26 K 27
Haydock ....42 M 23
Haydon Bridge ....55 N 19
Haydon Wick ....19 O 29
Hayfield ....43 O 23

A B C D E F G H I J K L M N O P Q R S T U V W X Y Z

A B C D E F G H I J K L M N O P Q R S T U V W X Y Z

Hayle .... 2 D 33
Hayling Island .... 10 R 31
Hayscastle .... 14 E 28
Hayton .... 50 R 22
Haywards Heath .... 11 T 31
Hazel Grove .... 43 N 23
Hazelbank .... 61 I 16
Hazelbury Bryan .... 9 M 31
Hazlemere .... 21 R 29
Heacham .... 38 V 25
Headcorn .... 22 V 30
Headington .... 20 Q 28
Headless Cross .... 27 O 27
Headley .... 10 R 30
Heads of Ayr .... 60 F 17
Healey .... 49 O 21
Healing .... 45 T 23
Heanor .... 36 P 24
Heast .... 71 C 12
Heath End .... 20 Q 29
Heath Hayes .... 35 O 25
Heather .... 36 P 25
Heathfield Renfrewshire ...... 60 F 16
Heathfield Wealden .... 12 U 31
Heathrow Airport .... 21 S 29
Hebburn .... 56 P 19
Hebden Bridge .... 43 N 22
Hebrides (Sea of the) .....76 Z 12
Heckfield .... 20 R 29
Heckington .... 37 T 25
Heddon on the Wall .... 56 O 19
Hedge End .... 10 Q 31
Hednesford .... 35 O 25
Hedon .... 45 T 22
Heighington Durham ...... 56 P 20
Heighington Lincs. .... 44 S 24
Heights of Kinlochewe ...78 E 11
Helensburgh .... 66 F 15
Helford .... 2 E 33
Hellifield .... 49 N 22
Hellingly .... 12 U 31
Hellisay .... 70 X 12
Hell's Mouth
    or Porth Neigwl .... 32 G 25
Helmdon .... 28 Q 27
Helmsdale .... 85 J 9
Helmsley .... 50 Q 21
Helpringham .... 37 T 25
Helpston .... 37 S 26
Helsby .... 42 L 24
Helston .... 2 E 33
Helton .... 55 L 20
Helvellyn .... 48 K 20
Hemel Hempstead .... 21 S 28
Hemingbrough .... 44 R 22
Hemingford Grey .... 29 T 27
Hemington .... 19 M 30
Hempnall .... 39 X 26
Hempton .... 38 W 25
Hemsby .... 39 Z 25
Hemswell .... 44 S 23
Hemsworth .... 43 P 23
Hemyock .... 8 K 31
Hendy .... 15 H 28
Henfield .... 11 T 31
Hengoed .... 18 K 29
Henham .... 30 U 28
Henley .... 27 O 27
Henley-on-Thames .... 20 R 29
Henllan .... 33 J 24
Henllys .... 18 K 29
Henlow .... 29 T 27
Hennock .... 4 J 32
Henshaw .... 55 M 19
Henstead .... 31 Y 26
Henstridge .... 9 M 31
Heol Senni .... 25 J 28
Hepple .... 63 N 18
Heptonstall .... 43 N 22
Herbrandston .... 14 E 28
Hereford .... 26 L 27
Heriot .... 62 L 16
Herm Channel I. 5
Herma Ness .... 87 R 1
Hermitage .... 20 Q 29
Hermitage Castle .... 62 L 18
Herne Bay .... 23 X 29
Herriard .... 20 Q 30
Herringfleet .... 39 Y 26 .... [uncertain]
Herrington .... 56 P 19
Herstmonceux .... 12 U 31
Hertford .... 21 T 28
Hesket Newmarket .... 54 K 19
Hesketh Bank .... 42 L 22
Hesleden .... 57 Q 19
Hessenford .... 3 G 32
Hessle .... 45 S 22
Hest Bank .... 48 L 21

Heswall .... 42 K 24
Hethersgill .... 55 L 19
Hethpool .... 63 N 17
Hetton-le-Hole .... 56 P 19
Heveningham .... 31 Y 27
Hever .... 21 U 30
Heversham .... 48 L 21
Hevingham .... 39 X 25
Hewelsfield .... 18 M 28
Hexham .... 55 N 19
Heybridge .... 22 W 28
Heysham .... 48 L 21
Heyshott .... 11 R 31
Heytesbury .... 9 N 30
Heythrop .... 28 P 28
Heywood .... 43 N 23
Hibaldstow .... 44 S 23
Hickling .... 36 R 25
Hickling Green .... 39 Y 25
Hidcote Manor Garden ...27 O 27
High Bentham .... 49 M 21
High Bickington .... 7 I 31
High Birkwith .... 49 N 21
High Easter .... 22 V 28
High Ercall .... 34 M 25
High Etherley .... 56 O 20
High Force (The) .... 55 N 20
High Halden .... 12 W 30
High Halstow .... 22 V 29
High Ham .... 8 L 30
High Hesket .... 55 L 19
High Newton Alnwick .....63 P 17
High Newton
    South Lakeland .... 48 L 21
High Offley .... 35 N 25
High Ongar .... 22 U 28
High Peak .... 43 O 23
High Willhays .... 4 I 31
High Wycombe .... 20 R 29
Higham Kent .... 22 V 29
Higham Lancs. .... 42 N 22
Higham
    North East Derbyshire ...36 P 24
Higham Suffolk .... 30 V 27
Higham Ferrers .... 29 S 27
Higham on the Hill .... 36 P 26
Highbridge .... 18 L 30
Highclere .... 20 P 29
Highcliffe .... 9 O 31
Higher Penwortham .... 42 L 22
Highland Wildlife Park ...73 I 12
Highley .... 27 M 26
Highmoor Cross .... 20 R 29
Highnam .... 27 N 28
Hightae .... 54 J 18
Hightown Congleton ...... 35 N 24
Hightown Sefton .... 42 K 23
Highworth .... 19 O 29
Hilborough .... 38 W 26
Hildenborough .... 22 U 30
Hilderstone .... 35 N 25
Hilgay .... 38 V 26
Hill .... 18 M 29
Hill of Fearn .... 79 I 10
Hill of Tarvit .... 69 L 15
Hillhead .... 52 G 19
Hillingdon
    London Borough .... 21 S 29
Hillington .... 38 V 25
Hillside .... 75 M 13
Hillswick .... 87 P 2
Hilmarton .... 19 O 29
Hilperton .... 19 N 30
Hilpsford Point .... 47 K 21
Hilton Aberdeenshire .... 81 N 11
Hilton Eden .... 55 M 20
Hilton Huntingdonshire ...29 T 27
Hilton North Dorset .... 9 N 31
Hilton South Derbyshire ...35 P 25
Hilton of Cadboll .... 79 I 10
Himbleton .... 27 N 27
Hinchingbrooke House ...29 T 27
Hinckley .... 36 P 26
Hinderwell .... 50 R 20
Hindhead .... 10 R 30
Hindley .... 42 M 23
Hindolveston .... 38 X 25
Hindon .... 9 N 30
Hingham .... 38 W 26
Hinstock .... 34 M 25
Hintlesham .... 31 X 27
Hinton-Blewett .... 18 M 30
Hirst Courtney .... 44 Q 22
Hirwaun .... 17 J 28
Histon .... 29 U 27
Hitcham .... 30 W 27
Hitchin .... 29 T 28

Hockering .... 38 X 25
Hockerton .... 36 R 24
Hockley .... 22 V 29
Hockley Heath .... 27 O 26
Hockliffe .... 29 S 28
Hoddesdon .... 21 T 28
Hodnet .... 34 M 25
Hodthorpe .... 44 Q 24
Hogsthorpe .... 45 U 24
Holbeach .... 37 U 25
Holbeach-St. Johns ...... 37 T 25
Holbeach-St. Matthew ...37 U 25
Holbeck .... 44 Q 24
Holbrook .... 31 X 28
Holbury .... 10 P 31
Holcombe .... 18 M 30
Holcombe Rogus .... 7 J 31
Holdenby .... 28 R 27
Holford .... 8 K 30
Holkam Hall .... 38 W 25
Hollandstoun .... 87 M 5
Hollesley .... 31 Y 27
Hollesley Bay .... 31 Y 27
Hollingbourne .... 22 V 30
Hollingworth .... 43 O 23
Hollybush .... 60 G 17
Hollym .... 45 U 22
Holmbridge .... 43 O 23
Holme Huntingdonshire ...29 T 26
Holme South Lakeland ...48 L 21
Holme-next-the-Sea ..... 38 V 25
Holme
    upon Spalding-Moor ...44 R 22
Holmer Green .... 21 R 29
Holmes Chapel .... 35 M 24
Holmesfield .... 43 P 24
Holmfirth .... 43 O 23
Holmhead .... 60 H 17
Holmpton .... 45 U 22
Holnest .... 8 M 31
Holt Dorset .... 9 O 31
Holt Norfolk .... 38 X 25
Holt Wilts. .... 19 N 29
Holt Wrexham .... 34 L 24
Holt Heath .... 27 N 27
Holton Lincs. .... 45 T 24
Holton Norfolk .... 31 Y 26
Holton South Somerset ...8 M 30
Holton Heath .... 9 N 31
Holton-le-Clay .... 45 T 23
Holwick .... 55 N 20
Holy Island Anglesey .....40 F 23
Holy Island North Ayrshire ...59 E 17
Holy Island Northumb. ...63 O 16
Holybourne .... 10 R 30
Holyhead / Caergybi ..... 40 G 23
Holystone .... 63 N 18
Holywell .... 2 E 32
Holywell / Treffynnon .... 41 K 23
Holywell Bay .... 2 E 32
Holywood .... 53 J 18
Honing .... 39 Y 25
Honington .... 36 S 25 .... [uncertain]
Honiton .... 8 K 31
Hoo St. Werburgh .... 22 V 29
Hook
    Basingstoke and Deane ...20 R 30
Hook
    East Riding of Yorkshire ...44 R 22
Hook Norton .... 28 P 28
Hooke .... 8 M 31
Hope Derbs. .... 43 O 23
Hope Flintshire .... 34 K 24
Hope Highland .... 84 G 8
Hope South Shropshire ...34 L 26
Hope (Loch) .... 84 G 8
Hope Bowdler .... 26 L 26
Hope under Dinmore ..... 26 L 27
Hopeman .... 80 J 10
Hopetoun House .... 68 J 16
Hopton .... 39 Z 26
Horam .... 12 U 31
Horbury .... 43 P 23
Horden .... 57 Q 19
Hordley .... 34 L 25
Horeb .... 15 G 27
Horley .... 21 T 30
Hornby .... 48 M 21
Horncastle .... 45 T 24
Hornchurch .... 22 U 29
Horncliffe .... 63 N 16
Horning .... 39 Y 25
Horninglow .... 35 P 25
Horn's Cross .... 6 H 31
Hornsea .... 51 T 22
Hornton .... 28 P 27
Horrabridge .... 4 H 32

Horseheath .... 30 V 27
Horsehouse .... 49 O 21
Horsell .... 21 S 30
Horsford .... 39 X 25
Horsforth .... 43 P 22
Horsham .... 11 T 30
Horsham St. Faith .... 39 X 25
Horsington East Lindsey ...37 T 24
Horsington
    South Somerset .... 9 M 30
Horsley Stroud .... 19 N 28
Horsley Tynedale .... 56 O 19
Horsmonden .... 12 V 30
Horstead .... 39 Y 25
Horsted Keynes .... 11 T 30
Horton Abertawe /
    Swansea .... 15 H 29
Horton East Dorset .... 9 O 31
Horton South Somerset ...8 L 31
Horton Court .... 19 M 29
Horton-in-Ribblesdale ...49 N 21
Horwich .... 42 M 23
Hoton .... 36 Q 25
Hott .... 55 M 18
Houghton .... 10 P 30
Houghton Hall .... 38 V 25
Houghton House .... 29 S 27
Houghton-le-Spring ...... 56 P 19
Houghton-on-the-Hill ... 36 R 26
Hounslow
    London Borough .... 21 S 29
Hourn (Loch) .... 72 D 12
Housesteads Fort .... 55 N 18
Houston .... 60 G 16
Houstry .... 85 J 9
Hove .... 11 T 31
Hoveton .... 39 Y 25
Hovingham .... 50 R 21
Howick .... 63 P 17
Howmore .... 76 X 12
Hownam .... 62 M 17
Howwood .... 60 G 16
Hoxa (Sound of) .... 86 K 7
Hoxne .... 31 X 26
Hoy .... 86 J 7
Hoylake .... 41 K 22
Hoyland Nether .... 43 P 23
Huby .... 50 Q 21
Hucknall .... 36 Q 24
Huddersfield .... 43 O 23
Huggate .... 51 S 22
Hugh Town I. of Scilly 2
Hughenden .... 20 R 29
Hughley .... 34 M 26
Huish Champflower .... 7 J 30
Huish Episcopi .... 8 L 30
Hull (River) .... 45 S 22
Hulland .... 35 P 24
Hullavington .... 19 N 29
Hullbridge .... 22 V 29
Humber (River) .... 45 T 23
Humber Bridge .... 44 S 22
Humberston .... 45 T 23
Humbleton .... 45 T 22
Hume Castle .... 62 M 17
Humshaugh .... 55 N 18
Hundleton .... 16 F 28
Hundred House .... 26 K 27
Hungerford .... 20 P 29
Hunmanby .... 51 T 21
Hunstanton .... 38 V 25
Hunter's Inn .... 17 I 30
Hunter's Quay .... 66 F 16
Huntingdon .... 29 T 26
Huntingtower Castle ..... 68 J 14
Huntly .... 80 L 11
Hunton .... 12 V 30
Huntspill .... 18 L 30
Hunwick .... 56 O 19
Hurlford .... 60 G 17
Hurn .... 9 O 31
Hursley .... 10 P 30
Hurst Green .... 12 V 30
Hurstbourne Priors .... 20 P 30
Hurstbourne Tarrant ..... 20 P 30
Hurstpierpoint .... 11 T 31
Hurworth-on-Tees .... 50 P 20
Husbands Bosworth ...... 28 Q 26
Huthwaite .... 36 Q 24
Huttoft .... 45 U 24
Hutton Scottish Borders ...63 N 16

Hutton South Ribble ..... 42 L 22
Hutton Cranswick .... 51 S 22
Hutton Rudby .... 50 Q 20
Huxley .... 34 L 24
Huyton .... 42 L 23
Hwlffordd / Haverfordwest ...16 F 28
Hyde .... 43 N 23
Hynish .... 64 Z 14
Hynish Bay .... 64 Z 14
Hythe Hants. .... 10 P 31
Hythe Kent .... 13 X 30

I

Ibsley .... 9 O 31
Ibstock .... 36 P 25
Ickleford .... 29 T 28
Icklingham .... 30 V 27
Ickworth House .... 30 V 27
Iddesleigh .... 7 H 31
Ideford .... 4 J 32
Iden .... 12 W 31
Iden Green .... 12 V 30
Idmiston .... 9 O 30
Idrigill Point .... 77 A 12
Ightham .... 22 U 30
Ightham Mote .... 22 U 30
Ilchester .... 8 L 30
Ilderton .... 63 O 17
Ilfracombe .... 17 H 30
Ilkeston .... 36 Q 25
Ilkley .... 49 O 22
Illogan .... 2 E 33
Ilmington .... 27 O 27
Ilminster .... 8 L 31
Ilsington .... 4 I 32
Ilton .... 8 L 31
Immingham .... 45 T 23
Immingham Dock .... 45 T 23
Ince Blundell .... 42 K 23
Ince-in-Makerfield .... 42 M 23
Inch Kenneth .... 64 B 14
Inchard (Loch) .... 84 E 8
Inchbare .... 75 M 13
Inchgrundle .... 74 L 13
Inchkeith .... 68 K 15
Inchlaggan .... 72 E 12
Inchmarnock .... 59 E 16
Inchnadamph .... 84 F 9
Inchture .... 68 K 14
Indaal (Loch) .... 58 A 16
Inerval .... 58 B 17
Ingatestone .... 22 V 28
Ingbirchworth .... 43 P 23
Ingham .... 30 W 27
Ingleby Barwick .... 50 Q 20
Ingleton Durham .... 56 O 20
Ingleton North Yorks. ....49 M 21
Inglewhite .... 42 L 22
Inglewood Forest .... 55 L 19
Ingliston .... 68 J 16
Ingoldmells .... 38 V 24
Ingoldsby .... 37 S 25
Ingram .... 63 O 17
Ings .... 48 L 20
Inkpen .... 20 P 29
Innellan .... 59 F 16
Inner Hebrides .... 70 Y 14
Inner Sound .... 77 C 11
Innerleithen .... 61 K 17
Innerleven .... 69 M 16 .... [uncertain]
Innerpeffray .... 67 I 14
Innerwick .... 69 M 16
Insch .... 81 M 11
Insh .... 73 I 12
Inshore .... 84 F 8
Instow .... 6 H 30
Inver Highland .... 79 I 10
Inver Perth and Kinross ...68 J 14
Inver (Loch) .... 84 E 9
Inver Bay .... 79 I 10
Inver Mallie .... 72 E 13
Inver Valley .... 84 E 9
Inverallligin .... 78 D 11
Inverallochy .... 81 O 10
Inveran .... 84 G 10
Inveraray .... 66 E 15
Inverarity .... 69 L 14
Inverarnan .... 66 F 15
Inverbeg .... 66 G 15
Inverbervie .... 75 N 13
Invercassley .... 84 G 10
Invercauld House .... 74 J 12
Inverchapel .... 66 F 15
Invercreran .... 72 E 14
Inverdruie .... 73 I 12
Inverewe Gardens .... 78 C 10
Inverey .... 74 J 13
Inverfarigaig .... 79 G 12

Invergarry .... 72 F 12
Invergeldie .... 67 H 14
Invergordon .... 79 H 10
Invergowrie .... 68 K 14
Inverie .... 72 C 13
Inverinan .... 65 E 15
Inverinate .... 78 D 12
Inverkeithing .... 68 J 15
Inverkeithny .... 81 M 11
Inverkip .... 66 F 16
Inverkirkaig .... 84 E 9
Inverliever Forest .... 65 D 15
Inverlochlarig .... 67 G 15
Invermoriston .... 73 G 12
Inverness .... 79 H 11
Inversanda .... 72 D 13
Inversnaid Hotel .... 66 F 15
Inveruglas .... 66 F 15
Inverurie .... 81 M 12
Invervar .... 73 H 14
Inwardleigh .... 7 H 31
Iona .... 64 A 15
Ipplepen .... 4 J 32
Ipstones .... 35 O 24
Ipswich .... 31 X 27
Irby East Lindsey .... 37 U 24
Irby Wirral .... 42 K 23
Irchester .... 29 S 27
Ireby .... 54 K 19
Ireleth .... 47 K 21
Irlam .... 42 M 23
Iron Acton .... 18 M 29
Ironbridge .... 34 M 26
Irthington .... 55 L 19
Irthlingborough .... 29 S 27
Irvine .... 60 F 17
Irwell (River) .... 42 N 23
Isbyty Ystwyth .... 25 I 27
Isla (Glen) .... 74 K 13
Islay (Sound of) .... 64 B 16
Isle of Whithorn .... 53 G 19
Isleham .... 30 V 26
Isleornsay .... 71 C 12
Isleworth .... 21 S 29
Islington London Borough ...21 T 29
Islip .... 20 Q 28
Islivig .... 82 Y 9
Itchingfield .... 11 S 30
Ithon (River) .... 25 K 27
Itteringham .... 39 X 25
Iver .... 21 S 29
Iver Heath .... 21 S 29
Ivinghoe .... 21 S 28
Ivybridge .... 4 I 32
Ivychurch .... 12 W 30
Iwade .... 22 W 29
Iwerne Minster .... 9 N 31
Ixworth .... 30 W 27

J

Jacobstow .... 6 G 31
Jacobstowe .... 7 H 31
Jameston .... 15 F 29
Jamestown
    Dumfries and Galloway ...61 K 18
Jamestown
    West Dunbartonshire ...66 G 16
Janetstown .... 85 J 9
Jarrow .... 56 P 19
Jaywick .... 23 X 28
Jedburgh .... 62 M 17
Jedburgh Abbey .... 62 M 17
Jeffreyston .... 15 F 28
Jemimaville .... 79 H 11
Jersey Channel I. 5
Jevington .... 12 U 31
John Muir .... 69 M 15
John o' Groats .... 86 K 8
Johnshaven .... 75 N 13
Johnston .... 16 F 28
Johnstone .... 60 G 16
Johnstonebridge .... 54 J 18
Jura (Isle of) .... 58 B 16
Jura (Sound of) .... 65 C 16
Jura Forest .... 65 C 16
Jura Ho .... 58 B 16
Jurby West .... 46 G 20

K

Kainakill .... 77 C 11
Kames .... 65 E 16
Katrine (Loch) .... 67 G 15
Kea .... 2 E 33
Keal .... 37 U 24
Keal (Loch na) .... 65 B 14
Kearsley .... 42 M 23
Keasden .... 49 M 21

Kebock Head .... 82 A 9
Kedington .... 30 V 27
Kedleston Hall .... 36 P 25
Keelby .... 45 T 23
Keevil .... 19 N 30
Kegworth .... 36 Q 25
Keig .... 75 M 12
Keighley .... 43 O 22
Keillmore .... 65 C 16
Keinton Mandeville .... 8 M 30
Keir Mill .... 53 I 18
Keiss .... 86 K 8
Keith .... 80 L 11
Keld .... 49 N 20
Kellas *Angus* .... 69 L 14
Kellas *Moray* .... 80 J 11
Kelleth .... 49 M 20
Kellie Castle .... 69 L 15
Kellington .... 44 Q 22
Kelloe .... 56 P 19
Kelly Bray .... 3 H 32
Kelmarsh .... 28 R 26
Kelsall .... 34 L 24
Kelso .... 62 M 17
Kelston .... 19 M 29
Keltneyburn .... 73 H 14
Kelty .... 68 J 15
Kelvedon .... 30 W 28
Kelvedon Hatch .... 22 U 29
Kemble .... 19 N 28
Kemnay .... 75 M 12
Kempley .... 26 M 28
Kempsey .... 27 N 27
Kempsford .... 19 O 28
Kempston .... 29 S 27
Kemsing .... 22 U 30
Kendal .... 48 L 21
Kenfig .... 17 I 29
Kenilworth .... 27 P 26
Kenknock .... 67 G 14
Kenmore *Highland* .... 77 C 11
Kenmore
  Perthshire and Kinross .... 67 I 14
Kenn .... 18 L 29
Kennet (River) .... 19 O 29
Kennethmont .... 80 L 11
Kenninghall .... 30 X 26
Kennington *Kent* .... 22 W 30
Kennington *Oxon.* .... 20 Q 28
Kennoway .... 68 K 15
Kenovay .... 70 Z 14
Kensaleyre .... 77 B 11
Kentallen .... 72 E 13
Kentford .... 30 V 27
Kentisbeare .... 7 K 31
Kentmere .... 48 L 20
Kenton .... 4 J 32
Kents Bank .... 48 L 21
Keoldale .... 84 F 8
Keresley .... 28 P 26
Kerrera .... 65 D 14
Kerry .... 26 K 26
Kersey .... 30 W 27
Kershader .... 82 A 9
Kershopefoot .... 55 L 18
Kesgrave .... 31 X 27
Kessingland .... 31 Z 26
Keswick .... 54 K 20
Kettering .... 28 R 26
Kettleness .... 50 R 20
Kettleshulme .... 43 N 24
Kettletoft .... 87 M 6
Kettlewell .... 49 N 21
Ketton .... 37 S 26
Kew .... 21 T 29
Kewstoke .... 18 L 29
Kexbrough .... 43 P 23
Kexby .... 44 R 23
Keyingham .... 45 T 22
Keymer .... 11 T 31
Keynsham .... 18 M 29
Keyworth .... 36 Q 25
Kibworth Harcourt .... 36 R 26
Kidderminster .... 27 N 26
Kidermorie Lodge .... 79 G 10
Kidlington .... 20 Q 28
Kidsgrove .... 35 N 24
Kidstones .... 49 N 21
Kidwelly / Cydweli .... 15 H 28
Kielder .... 55 M 18
Kielder Forest .... 55 M 18
Kielder Reservoir .... 55 M 18
Kiiphedir .... 85 I 9
Kilamarsh .... 44 Q 24
Kilbarchan .... 60 G 16
Kilbirnie .... 60 F 16
Kilbrannan Sound .... 59 D 17

Kilbride .... 65 D 14
Kilburn *Amber Valley* .... 36 P 24
Kilburn *Hambleton* .... 50 Q 21
Kilchattan .... 59 E 16
Kilchenzie .... 59 C 17
Kilcheran .... 65 D 14
Kilchiaran .... 58 A 16
Kilchoan .... 71 B 13
Kilchoman .... 58 A 16
Kilchrenan .... 65 E 14
Kilconquhar .... 69 L 15
Kilcreggan .... 66 F 16
Kildale .... 50 Q 20
Kildary .... 79 H 10
Kildavanan .... 59 E 16
Kildonan .... 59 E 17
Kildonan Lodge .... 85 I 9
Kildrummy .... 74 L 12
Kildrummy Castle .... 74 L 12
Kilfinnan .... 72 F 12
Kilgetti .... 15 F 28
Kilham
  Berwick-upon-Tweed .... 63 N 17
Kilham
  East Riding of Yorkshire .... 51 S 21
Kilkhampton .... 6 G 31
Killay .... 15 H 29
Killean .... 59 D 17
Killearn .... 67 G 15
Killen .... 79 H 11
Killerton .... 7 J 31
Killiechronan .... 65 C 14
Killilan .... 78 D 12
Killin .... 67 H 14
Killinghall .... 50 P 21
Killundine .... 71 C 14
Kilmacolm .... 60 G 16
Kilmaluag .... 77 B 10
Kilmany .... 69 L 14
Kilmarie .... 71 B 12
Kilmarnock .... 60 G 17
Kilmartin .... 65 D 15
Kilmaurs .... 60 G 17
Kilmelford .... 65 D 15
Kilmersdon .... 19 M 30
Kilmington *East Devon* .... 8 K 31
Kilmington *Salisbury* .... 9 N 30
Kilmorack .... 79 G 11
Kilmore *Ardnamurchan* .... 71 B 13
Kilmore *Argyll and Bute* .... 65 C 16
Kilmory *I. Rhum* .... 71 A 12
Kilmory *North Ayrshire* .... 59 E 17
Kilmuir .... 77 A 11
Kilmun .... 66 F 16
Kilncadzow .... 61 I 16
Kilninver .... 65 D 14
Kilnsey .... 49 N 21
Kiloran .... 64 B 15
Kilpeck .... 26 L 28
Kilrenny .... 69 L 15
Kilsby .... 28 Q 26
Kilsyth .... 67 H 16
Kiltarlity .... 79 G 11
Kilvaxter .... 77 A 11
Kilwinning .... 60 F 17
Kimberley *Broxtowe* .... 36 Q 25
Kimberley *South Norfolk* .... 38 X 26
Kimble .... 20 R 28
Kimbolton .... 29 S 27
Kimmeridge .... 9 N 32
Kimpton .... 21 T 28
Kinbrace .... 85 I 9
Kinbuck .... 67 I 15
Kincardine *Fife* .... 67 I 15
Kincardine *Highland* .... 79 G 10
Kincardine *O'Neil* .... 75 L 12
Kinclaven .... 68 J 14
Kincraig .... 73 I 12
Kineton .... 28 P 27
Kinfauns .... 68 J 14
Kingairloch .... 72 D 14
Kingarth .... 59 E 16
Kinghorn .... 68 K 15
King's Bromley .... 35 O 25
King's Cliffe .... 37 S 26
Kings Langley .... 21 S 28
King's Lynn .... 38 V 25
King's Meaburn .... 55 M 20
King's Somborne .... 10 P 30
King's Sutton .... 28 Q 27
King's Walden .... 29 T 28
Kings Worthy .... 10 Q 30
Kingsbarns .... 69 M 15
Kingsbridge .... 4 I 33
Kingsburgh .... 77 A 11

Kingsbury Episcopi .... 8 L 31
Kingsclere .... 20 Q 30
Kingscote .... 19 N 29
Kingsdon .... 8 L 30
Kingsdown .... 23 Y 30
Kingsgate .... 23 Y 29
Kingshouse *Highland* .... 72 F 14
Kingshouse *Stirling* .... 67 H 14
Kingskerswell .... 4 J 32
Kingskettle .... 68 K 15
Kingsland .... 26 L 27
Kingsley *East Hampshire* .... 10 R 30
Kingsley
  Staffordshire Moorlands .... 35 O 24
Kingsmuir .... 74 L 14
Kingsnorth .... 12 W 30
Kingsteignton .... 4 J 32
Kingsthorpe .... 28 R 27
Kingston *Devon* .... 4 I 33
Kingston *East Hampshire* .... 69 L 15
Kingston *Moray* .... 80 K 10
Kingston
  South Cambridgeshire .... 29 T 27
Kingston Bagpuize .... 20 P 28
Kingston Deverill .... 9 N 30
Kingston Lacy .... 9 N 31
Kingston Lisle .... 20 P 29
Kingston Seymour .... 18 L 29
Kingston-St. Mary .... 8 K 30
Kingston-upon-Hull .... 45 S 22
Kingston-upon-Thames
  London Borough .... 21 T 29
Kingstone .... 26 L 27
Kingswear .... 4 J 32
Kingswinford .... 27 N 26
Kingswood .... 19 M 29
Kingswood *Powys* .... 34 K 26
Kingswood *South Glos.* .... 18 M 29
Kington .... 26 K 27
Kington Langley .... 19 N 29
Kington-St. Michael .... 19 N 29
Kingussie .... 73 H 12
Kinkell .... 75 M 12
Kinkell Bridge .... 67 I 15
Kinknockie .... 81 O 11
Kinlet .... 27 M 26
Kinloch .... 71 B 12
Kinloch Hourn .... 72 D 12
Kinloch Lodge .... 84 G 8
Kinloch Rannoch .... 73 H 13
Kinlochard .... 67 G 15
Kinlochbervie .... 84 E 8
Kinlocheil .... 72 E 13
Kinlochewe .... 78 E 11
Kinlochleven .... 72 F 13
Kinlochmoidart .... 71 C 13
Kinloss .... 80 J 11
Kinmuck .... 75 N 12
Kinnaird .... 68 K 14
Kinneff .... 75 N 13
Kinnelhead .... 61 J 18
Kinnerley .... 34 L 25
Kinnersley .... 26 L 27
Kinnesswood .... 68 K 15
Kinninvie .... 56 O 20
Kinoulton .... 36 R 25
Kinross .... 68 J 15
Kinrossie .... 68 K 14
Kintbury .... 20 P 29
Kintessack .... 80 I 11
Kintore .... 75 M 12
Kintra .... 58 B 17
Kintyre (Peninsula) .... 59 D 17
Kinver .... 27 N 26
Kippax .... 43 P 22
Kippen .... 67 H 15
Kippford .... 53 I 19
Kirby Bellars .... 36 R 25
Kirby Cross .... 31 X 28
Kirby Hall .... 29 S 26
Kirby Misperton .... 50 R 21
Kirby Muxloe .... 36 Q 26
Kirby Underwood .... 37 S 25
Kirdford .... 11 S 30
Kirk Ella .... 45 S 22
Kirk Ireton .... 35 P 24
Kirk Merrington .... 56 P 19
Kirk Michael .... 46 G 21
Kirk Yetholm .... 63 N 17
Kirkbampton .... 54 K 19
Kirkbean .... 53 J 19
Kirkbride .... 54 K 19
Kirkbuddo .... 69 L 14
Kirkburn .... 51 S 22
Kirkburton .... 43 O 23
Kirkby .... 42 L 23
Kirkby Fleetham .... 50 P 20

Kirkby-in-Ashfield .... 36 Q 24
Kirkby-la-Thorpe .... 37 S 25
Kirkby Lonsdale .... 48 M 21
Kirkby Malham .... 49 N 21
Kirkby Mallory .... 36 Q 26
Kirkby Malzeard .... 49 P 21
Kirkby Overblow .... 50 P 22
Kirkby Stephen .... 49 M 20
Kirkby Thore .... 55 M 20
Kirkbymoorside .... 50 R 21
Kirkcaldy .... 68 K 15
Kirkcolm .... 52 E 19
Kirkconnel .... 60 I 17
Kirkcowan .... 52 G 19
Kirkcudbright .... 53 H 19
Kirkcudbright Bay .... 53 H 19
Kirkfieldbank .... 61 I 16
Kirkgunzeon .... 53 I 19
Kirkham .... 42 L 22
Kirkheaton .... 56 O 18
Kirkhill .... 79 G 11
Kirkhope .... 61 J 18
Kirkinner .... 52 G 19
Kirkintilloch .... 67 H 16
Kirkland
  Dumfries and Galloway .... 53 I 18
Kirkland *Eden* .... 55 M 19
Kirklees .... 43 O 23
Kirklevington .... 50 P 20
Kirkliston .... 68 J 16
Kirkmaiden .... 52 F 19
Kirkmichael
  Perthshire and Kinross .... 74 J 13
Kirkmichael
  South Ayrshire .... 60 G 17
Kirkmuirhill .... 61 I 17
Kirknewton
  Berwick-upon-Tweed .... 63 N 17
Kirknewton
  West Lothian .... 61 J 16
Kirkoswald .... 59 F 18
Kirkpatrick Durham .... 53 I 18
Kirkpatrick-Fleming .... 54 K 18
Kirkstone Pass .... 48 L 20
Kirkton
  Dumfries and Galloway .... 53 J 18
Kirkton *Scottish Borders* .... 62 L 17
Kirkton Manor .... 61 K 17
Kirkton of Culsalmond .... 81 M 11
Kirkton of Durris .... 75 M 12
Kirkton of Glenisla .... 74 K 13
Kirkton of Kingoldrum .... 74 K 13
Kirkton of Largo .... 69 L 15
Kirkton of Skene .... 75 N 12
Kirkton of Strathmartine .... 69 K 14
Kirktown of Auchterless .... 81 M 11
Kirktown of Deskford .... 80 L 11
Kirkwall .... 86 L 7
Kirkwhelpington .... 56 N 18
Kirmington .... 45 T 23
Kirn .... 66 F 16
Kirriemuir .... 74 K 13
Kirtlebridge .... 54 K 18
Kirtlington .... 28 Q 28
Kirtomy .... 85 H 8
Kirton *Boston* .... 37 T 25
Kirton *Suffolk Coastal* .... 31 X 27
Kirton End .... 37 T 25
Kirton-in-Lindsey .... 44 S 23
Kishorn (Loch) .... 78 D 11
Kislingbury .... 28 R 27
Kitchener Memorial .... 86 J 6
Kiveton .... 44 Q 23
Knaresborough .... 50 P 21
Knarsdale .... 55 M 19
Knebworth .... 29 T 28
Kneesall .... 36 R 24
Kneesworth .... 29 T 27
Knighton / Trefyclawdd .... 26 K 26
Knightshayes Court .... 7 J 31
Kniveton .... 35 O 24
Knock *Argyll and Bute* .... 65 C 14
Knock *Moray* .... 80 L 11
Knock *Western Isles* .... 83 B 9
Knockandhu .... 80 K 12
Knockbrex .... 53 H 19
Knockie Lodge .... 73 G 12
Knockin .... 34 L 25
Knocknaha .... 59 D 17
Knocksharry .... 46 G 21
Knockvennie Smithy .... 53 I 18
Knole .... 22 U 30
Knossington .... 36 R 25

Knottingley .... 44 Q 22
Knowe .... 52 G 18
Knowehead .... 53 H 18
Knowesgate .... 55 N 18
Knowle .... 27 O 26
Knowsley .... 42 L 23
Knoydart .... 72 D 12
Knutsford .... 42 M 24
Kyle Forest .... 60 G 17
Kyle of Durness .... 84 F 8
Kyle of Lochalsh .... 77 C 12
Kyle of Sutherland .... 79 G 10
Kyle of Tongue .... 84 G 8
Kyleakin .... 77 C 12
Kylerhea .... 72 C 12
Kyles Scalpay .... 82 Z 10
Kylestrome .... 84 E 9
Kynance Cove .... 2 E 34
Kyre park .... 26 M 27

L

La Rocque *Jersey I.* 5
Laceby .... 45 T 23
Lacey Green .... 20 R 28
Lache .... 34 L 24
Lacock .... 19 N 29
Ladder Hills .... 74 K 12
Ladock .... 3 F 33
Ladybank .... 68 K 15
Ladybower Reservoir .... 43 O 23
Ladyhill .... 55 N 18
Lagg .... 65 C 16
Lagg *Argyll and Bute* .... 58 B 16
Laggan *near Invergarry* .... 72 F 12
Laggan
  near Newtonmore .... 73 H 12
Laggan (Loch) .... 73 G 13
Laggan Point .... 58 B 16
Lagganulva .... 64 B 14
Laide .... 78 D 10
Lair .... 78 E 11
Lairg .... 84 G 9
Lake District National Park .48 K 20
Lakenheath .... 30 V 26
Lamanva .... 2 E 33
Lamberhurst .... 12 V 30
Lambeth *London Borough* .21 T 29
Lambley *Gedling* .... 36 Q 24
Lambley *Tynedale* .... 55 M 19
Lambourn .... 20 P 29
Lamerton .... 3 H 32
Lamington .... 61 J 17
Lamlash .... 59 E 17
Lamlash Bay .... 59 E 17
Lammermuir Hills .... 62 L 16
Lampeter /
  Llanbedr Pont Steffan .... 15 H 27
Lamplugh .... 54 J 20
Lamport .... 28 R 26
Lanark .... 61 I 16
Lancaster .... 48 L 21
Lanchester .... 56 O 19
Lancing .... 11 T 31
Landmark Visitor Centre .... 79 I 12
Landrake .... 3 H 32
Land's End .... 2 C 33
Landulph .... 3 H 32
Lane End .... 20 R 29
Laneast .... 6 G 32
Lanercost .... 55 L 19
Langar .... 36 R 25
Langavat (Loch) *Lewis* .... 82 Z 9
Langavat (Loch)
  South Harris .... 76 Z 10
Langbank .... 66 G 16
Langcliffe .... 49 N 21
Langdale End .... 51 S 21
Langdale Valley .... 48 K 20
Langdon Beck .... 55 N 19
Langenhoe .... 30 W 28
Langford
  Mid Bedfordshire .... 29 T 27
Langford
  West Oxfordshire .... 19 P 28
Langford Budville .... 8 K 31
Langham .... 36 R 25
Langholm .... 54 L 18
Langleeford .... 63 N 17
Langley .... 21 S 29
Langley Park .... 56 O 19
Langold .... 44 Q 23
Langport .... 8 L 30
Langrick .... 37 T 24
Langrish .... 10 Q 30
Langsett .... 43 O 23
Langshaw .... 62 L 17
Langstrothdale Chase .... 49 N 21

Langthwaite .... 49 O 20
Langtoft .... 51 S 21
Langton .... 50 R 21
Langton Matravers .... 9 O 32
Langwathby .... 55 L 19
Lanhydrock .... 3 F 32
Lanivet .... 3 F 32
Lanlivery .... 3 F 32
Lanreath .... 3 G 32
Lansallos .... 3 G 32
Lanton .... 62 M 17
Lapford .... 7 I 31
Larachbeg .... 71 C 14
Larbert .... 67 I 15
Largs .... 59 F 16
Larkhall .... 61 I 16
Larkhill .... 19 O 30
Larling .... 30 W 26
Lasswade .... 61 K 16
Lastingham .... 50 R 21
Latchingdon .... 22 W 28
Latton .... 19 O 29
Lauder .... 62 L 16
Lauderdale .... 62 L 16
Laugharne .... 15 G 28
Laughton *Wealden* .... 12 U 31
Laughton *West Lindsey* .... 44 R 23
Launcells .... 6 G 31
Launceston .... 6 G 32
Laurencekirk .... 75 M 13
Laurieston .... 53 H 19
Lauriston Castle .... 68 K 16
Lavendon .... 29 S 27
Lavenham .... 30 W 27
Laverstock .... 9 O 30
Laverstoke .... 20 Q 30
Lawford .... 30 X 28
Lawrenny .... 16 F 28
Lawshall .... 30 W 27
Laxay .... 82 A 9
Laxey .... 46 G 21
Laxey Bay .... 46 G 21
Laxfield .... 31 Y 27
Laxford (Loch) .... 84 E 8
Laxford Bridge .... 84 E 8
Laxo .... 87 Q 2
Laxton
  East Riding of Yorkshire ... 44 R 22
Laxton
  Newark and Sherwood .... 36 R 24
Layer-de-la-Haye .... 30 W 28
Layer Marney .... 22 W 28
Laytham .... 44 R 22
Layton .... 42 K 22
Lazonby .... 55 L 19
Lea *Herefordshire* .... 26 M 28
Lea *North Wiltshire* .... 19 N 29
Lea *West Lindsey* .... 44 R 23
Leaden Roding .... 22 U 28
Leadenham .... 37 S 24
Leadgate *Derwentside* .... 56 O 19
Leadgate *Eden* .... 55 M 19
Leadhills .... 61 I 17
Leafield .... 20 P 28
Leagrave .... 29 S 28
Lealholm .... 50 R 20
Lealt .... 65 C 15
Leargybreck .... 65 C 16
Leasingham .... 37 S 24
Leathaid Bhuain (Loch an) .84 F 9
Leatherhead .... 21 T 30
Leathley .... 49 P 22
Leavening .... 50 R 21
Lebberston .... 51 S 21
Lechlade .... 19 O 28
Lecht Road .... 74 K 12
Leckmelm .... 78 E 10
Leconfield .... 44 S 22
Ledbury .... 27 M 27
Ledmore .... 84 F 9
Ledsham .... 44 Q 22
Ledston .... 44 Q 22
Lee .... 16 H 30
Lee-on-the-Solent .... 10 Q 31
Leebotwood .... 34 L 26
Leeds *Kent* .... 22 V 30
Leeds *West Yorks.* .... 43 P 22
Leedstown .... 2 D 33
Leek .... 35 N 24
Leek Wootton .... 27 P 27
Leeming Bar .... 50 P 21
Leeswood .... 34 K 24
Legbourne .... 45 U 23
Legerwood .... 62 M 16
Leicester .... 36 Q 26
Leicester Forest East .... 36 Q 26
Leigh .... 42 M 23

A B C D E F G H I J K L M N O P Q R S T U V W X Y Z

Leigh *Mole Valley* ....21 T 30
Leigh *North Wiltshire* ....19 O 29
Leigh *Sevenoaks* ....22 U 30
Leigh *West Dorset* ....8 M 31
Leigh-on-Sea ....22 V 29
Leigh Sinton ....27 N 27
Leighterton ....19 N 29
Leighton Buzzard ....29 S 28
Leim ....58 C 17
Leintwardine ....26 L 26
Leirinmore ....84 F 8
Leiston ....31 Y 27
Leith ....68 K 16
Leitholm ....62 M 16
Lemreway ....82 A 9
Lendalfoot ....52 F 18
Lenham ....22 W 30
Lennoxtown ....67 H 16
Leominster ....26 L 27
Leonard Stanley ....19 N 28
Lepe ....10 P 31
Lephinmore ....65 E 15
Lerwick ....87 Q 3
Lesbury ....63 P 17
Leslie *Aberdeenshire* ....81 L 12
Leslie *Fife* ....68 K 15
Lesmahagow ....61 I 17
Leswalt ....52 E 19
Letchworth ....29 T 28
Letham *Angus* ....75 L 14
Letham *Fife* ....68 K 15
Letheringsett ....38 X 25
Letterewe Forest ....78 D 10
Letterfearn ....78 D 12
Lettermore ....84 G 8
Letters ....78 E 10
Letterston ....24 F 28
Leuchars ....69 L 14
Leurbost ....82 A 9
Leven
  East Riding of Yorks. ....51 T 22
Leven *Fife* ....69 K 15
Leven (Loch) ....72 E 13
Leven (River) ....72 F 13
Levens ....48 L 21
Levens Hall ....48 L 21
Levenwick ....87 Q 4
Leverington ....37 U 25
Leverton
  with Habblesthorpe ....44 R 24
Levington ....31 X 27
Levisham ....50 R 21
Lewannick ....3 G 32
Lewdown ....6 H 32
Lewes ....11 U 31
Lewis (Isle of) ....82 Z 9
Lewis and Harris (Isle of) ...82 Z 8
Lewisham
  London Borough ....21 T 29
Lewknor ....20 R 28
Leyburn ....49 O 21
Leyland ....42 L 22
Leysdown-on-Sea ....22 W 29
Lezant ....3 G 32
Lhanbryde ....80 K 11
Lhen (The) ....46 G 20
Liathach ....78 D 11
Libberton ....61 J 16
Lichfield ....35 O 25
Liddesdale ....55 L 18
Lidgate ....30 V 27
Lifton ....6 H 32
Ligger or Perran Bay ....2 E 32
Lilbourne ....28 Q 26
Lilleshall ....35 M 25
Lilliesleaf ....62 L 17
Limmerhaugh ....60 H 17
Limpsfield ....21 U 30
Linchmere ....10 R 30
Lincoln ....44 S 24
Lincolnshire Wolds ....45 T 23
Lindfield ....11 T 30
Lindores ....68 K 14
Lingague ....46 F 21
Lingay *near Eriskay* ....70 X 12
Lingay *near Pabbay* ....70 X 13
Lingen ....26 L 27
Lingfield ....21 T 30
Liniclate ....76 X 11
Linlithgow ....67 J 16
Linn of Dee ....74 J 13
Linn of Tummel ....74 I 13
Linneraineach ....84 E 9
Linney Head ....14 E 29
Linnhe (Loch) ....72 D 14
Linslade ....29 R 28
Lintmill ....80 L 10

Linton *Craven* ....49 N 21
Linton *Herefordshire* ....26 M 28
Linton *Scottish Borders* ....62 M 17
Linton
  South Cambridgeshire ....30 U 27
Linton *South Derbyshire* ....35 P 25
Linton-on-Ouse ....50 Q 21
Lintrathen (Loch of) ....74 K 13
Linwood *Renfrewshire* ....60 G 16
Linwood *West Lindsey* ....45 T 23
Liphook ....10 R 30
Liskeard ....3 G 32
Lismore ....65 D 14
Liss ....10 R 30
Lisset ....51 T 21
Lisvane ....18 K 29
Litcham ....38 W 25
Litchborough ....28 Q 27
Litchfield ....20 P 30
Litherland ....42 L 23
Little-Baddow ....22 V 28
Little-Barningham ....39 X 25
Little Berkhamsted ....21 T 28
Little Brington ....28 Q 27
Little Budworth ....34 M 24
Little Bytham ....37 S 25
Little Chalfont ....21 S 28
Little Clacton ....31 X 28
Little Colonsay ....64 B 14
Little-Coxwell ....19 P 29
Little Cumbrae Island ....59 F 16
Little Dewchurch ....26 L 28
Little Galdenoch ....52 E 19
Little Glenshee ....67 J 14
Little Hadham ....29 U 28
Little Hallingbury ....22 U 28
Little Harrowden ....28 R 27
Little Houghton ....28 R 27
Little Loch Broom ....78 D 10
Little Loch Roag ....82 Z 9
Little Mill ....18 L 28
Little-Milton ....20 Q 28
Little Minch (The) ....76 Z 11
Little Moreton Hall ....35 N 24
Little Ouse (River) ....30 V 26
Little Ouseburn ....50 Q 21
Little-Raveley ....29 T 26
Little Snoring ....38 W 25
Little-Stretton ....26 L 26
Little-Stukeley ....29 T 26
Little Torrington ....6 H 31
Little Urswick ....48 K 21
Little Walsingham ....38 W 25
Little Waltham ....22 V 28
Little Wenlock ....34 M 26
Littleborough ....43 N 23
Littlebourne ....23 X 30
Littlebury ....30 U 27
Littlecote House ....20 P 29
Littleferry ....79 H 10
Littleham ....4 J 32
Littlehampton ....11 S 31
Littlemill ....79 I 11
Littleport ....30 U 26
Littlestone-on-Sea ....12 W 31
Littleton ....10 P 30
Littleworth ....20 P 28
Litton Cheney ....5 M 31
Liverpool ....42 L 23
Liverton ....50 R 20
Livet (Glen) ....80 K 12
Livingston ....61 J 16
Lizard ....2 E 34
Lizard Peninsula ....2 E 33
Llaim ....35 O 24
Llan ....33 J 26
Llan-non ....15 H 28
Llan-y-Bri ....15 G 28
Llanarmon-yn-Ial ....34 K 24
Llanarthne ....24 H 28
Llanarthney ....15 H 28
Llanasa ....41 J 23
Llanbadarn Fawr ....25 H 26
Llanbedr ....33 H 25
Llanbedr Pont Steffan /
  Lampeter ....15 H 27
Llanbedrog ....32 G 25
Llanberis ....33 H 24
Llanberis (Pass of) ....33 H 24
Llanbister ....26 K 26
Llanboidy ....15 G 28
Llanbradach ....18 K 29
Llanbrynmair ....33 J 26
Llanddarog ....15 H 28
Llanddeiniol ....25 H 27
Llandderfel ....33 J 25
Llanddeusant ....40 G 22

Llanddewi Brefi ....25 I 27
Llanddewi Ystradenni ....26 K 27
Llanddona ....40 H 23
Llanddowror ....15 G 28
Llanddulas ....41 J 23
Llandegla ....34 K 24
Llandeilo ....15 H 28
Llandenny ....18 L 28
Llandinam ....25 J 26
Llandissilio ....15 G 28
Llandogo ....18 L 28
Llandovery / Llanymddyfri ...25 I 28
Llandrindod Wells ....25 J 27
Llandrinio ....34 K 25
Llandudno ....41 I 23
Llandudno Junction ....41 I 23
Llandwrog ....32 H 24
Llandybie ....15 H 28
Llandyfaelog ....15 H 28
Llandygai ....40 H 23
Llandysul ....15 H 27
Llanegryn ....33 H 26
Llanelidan ....34 K 24
Llanellen ....18 K 28
Llanelli ....15 H 28
Llanelltyd ....33 I 25
Llanengan ....32 G 25
Llanerchymedd ....40 G 23
Llanerfyl ....33 J 25
Llanfachraeth ....40 G 23
Llanfaethlu ....40 G 22
Llanfair ....33 H 25
Llanfair-Caereinion ....34 K 26
Llanfair-Pwllgwyngyll ....40 H 23
Llanfair-ym-Muallt /
  Builth Wells ....25 J 27
Llanfair-yn-Neubwll ....40 G 23
Llanfairfechan ....41 I 23
Llanfairynghornwy ....40 G 22
Llanfechell ....40 G 22
Llanferres ....34 K 24
Llanfihangel-ar-arth ....15 H 27
Llanfihangel Glyn Myfyr ...33 J 24
Llanfihangel Nant Bran ....25 J 28
Llanfihangel Rhyditon ....26 K 27
Llanfihangel-y-Creuddyn ..25 I 26
Llanfilo ....26 K 28
Llanfoist ....18 K 28
Llanfrynach ....25 J 28
Llanfwrog ....40 G 23
Llanfyllin ....34 K 25
Llanfynydd *Carmarthenshire /
  Sir Gaerfyrddin* ....15 H 28
Llanfynydd *Flintshire /
  Sir y Fflint* ....34 K 24
Llanfyrnach ....15 G 28
Llangadfan ....33 J 25
Llangadog ....25 I 28
Llangain ....15 G 28
Llangammarch Wells ....25 J 27
Llangarron ....26 L 28
Llangathen ....15 H 28
Llangedwyn ....34 K 25
Llangefni ....40 H 23
Llangeinor ....17 J 29
Llangeitho ....25 H 27
Llangeler ....15 G 27
Llangelynin ....15 H 29
Llangennech ....15 H 28
Llangernyw ....33 I 24
Llangoed ....40 H 23
Llangollen ....34 K 25
Llangorse ....26 K 28
Llangorwen ....25 H 26
Llangrannog ....15 G 27
Llangunllo ....26 K 27
Llangunnor ....15 H 28
Llangurig ....25 J 26
Llangwm *Monmouthshire /
  Sir Fynwy* ....18 L 28
Llangwm *Pembrokeshire /
  Sir Benfro* ....16 F 28
Llangwnnadl ....32 F 25
Llangwyryfon ....25 H 27
Llangybi ....15 H 27
Llangyndeyrn ....15 H 28
Llangynidr ....26 K 28
Llangynog *Carmarthenshire /
  Sir Gaerfyrddin* ....15 G 28
Llangynog *Powys* ....33 J 25
Llangynwyd ....17 J 29
Llangywer ....33 J 25
Llanharan ....17 J 29
Llanharry ....17 J 29
Llanhilleth ....18 K 28
Llanidloes ....25 J 26

Llanilar ....25 H 26
Llanishen ....18 L 28
Llanllwchaiarn ....26 K 26
Llanllyfni ....32 H 24
Llanmadoc ....15 H 29
Llannefydd ....41 J 23
Llanon ....25 H 27
Llanpumsaint ....15 H 28
Llanrhaeadr ....33 J 24
Llanrhaeadr-ym-
  Mochnant ....34 K 25
Llanrhidian ....15 H 29
Llanrhystud ....25 H 27
Llanrug ....33 H 24
Llanrwst ....33 I 24
Llansanffraid Glan Conwy ...41 I 23
Llansannan ....33 J 24
Llansantffraid ....25 H 27
Llansantffraid-ym-Mechain ...34 K 25
Llansawel ....15 H 27
Llansilin ....34 K 25
Llansoy ....18 L 28
Llansteffan ....15 G 28
Llanthony ....26 K 28
Llanthony Priory ....26 K 28
Llantilio Crossenny ....18 L 28
Llantwit Major ....17 J 29
Llanuwchllyn ....33 I 25
Llanvetherine ....18 L 28
Llanwddyn ....33 J 25
Llanwenog ....15 H 27
Llanwnda ....32 H 24
Llanwnen ....15 H 27
Llanwnog ....25 J 26
Llanwrda ....15 I 28
Llanwrin ....33 I 26
Llanwrtyd Wells ....25 J 27
Llanwyddelan ....33 J 26
Llanybydder ....15 H 27
Llanychaer ....24 F 28
Llanymawddwy ....33 J 25
Llanymddyfri / Llandovery ...25 I 28
Llanymynech ....34 K 25
Llanynghenedl ....40 G 23
Llanystumdwy ....32 H 25
Llawhaden ....15 F 28
Llechryd ....15 G 27
Lledrod ....25 I 27
Lleyn Peninsula ....32 G 25
Llithfaen ....32 G 25
Llowes ....26 K 27
Llston ....15 H 29
Llwydafydd ....24 G 27
Llwyngwril ....33 H 25
Llwynmawr ....34 K 25
Llyfnant Valley ....33 I 26
Llyn Brianne ....25 I 27
Llyn Celyn ....33 I 25
Llyn Tegid or Bala Lake ...33 J 25
Llyswen ....26 K 27
Llysworney ....17 J 29
Llywel ....25 J 28
Loanhead ....61 K 16
Lochailort ....72 D 13
Lochaline ....65 C 14
Lochans ....52 E 19
Locharbriggs ....53 J 18
Lochassynt Lodge ....84 E 9
Lochawe ....66 E 14
Lochay (Glen) ....67 G 14
Lochboisdale ....70 Y 12
Lochbuie ....65 C 14
Lochcarron ....78 D 11
Lochdonhead ....65 C 14
Lochdrum ....78 F 10
Lochearnhead ....67 H 14
Locheport ....76 Y 11
Locherben ....61 J 18
Lochfoot ....53 I 18
Lochgair ....65 D 15
Lochgarthside ....73 G 12
Lochgelly ....68 K 15
Lochgilphead ....65 D 15
Lochgoilhead ....66 F 15
Lochinver ....84 E 9
Lochluichart ....78 F 11
Lochmaben ....54 J 18
Lochmaddy ....76 Y 11
Lochore ....68 K 15
Lochportain ....76 Y 11
Lochranza ....59 E 16
Lochsie (Glen) ....74 J 13
Lochstack ....84 F 8
Lochton *Aberdeenshire* ...75 M 12
Lochton *South Ayrshire* ...52 F 18
Lochtyn / Ynys ....15 G 27

Lochuisge ....72 D 14
Lochwinnoch ....60 G 16
Lochy (Loch) ....72 F 13
Lockerbie ....54 J 18
Lockerley ....9 P 30
Locking ....18 L 30
Loddington ....28 R 26
Loddon ....39 Y 26
Lode ....30 U 27
Lodsworth ....11 R 31
Lofthouse ....49 O 21
Loftus ....50 R 20
Logan Gardens ....52 F 19
Loggerheads ....35 M 25
Logie Coldstone ....74 L 12
Logiealmond ....67 I 14
Login ....15 F 28
Lomond (Loch) ....66 G 15
Londesborough ....51 R 22
London ....21 T 29
London Colney ....21 T 28
Long (Loch) *Angus* ...68 K 14
Long (Loch)
  Argyll and Bute ...66 F 15
Long Ashton ....18 M 29
Long Bennington ....36 R 25
Long Bredy ....5 M 31
Long Buckby ....28 Q 27
Long Clawson ....36 R 25
Long Crendon ....20 R 28
Long Eaton ....36 Q 25
Long Hanborough ....20 P 28
Long Itchington ....28 P 27
Long Lawford ....28 Q 26
Long Man (The) ....12 U 31
Long Marston ....50 Q 22
Long Marton ....55 M 20
Long Melford ....30 W 27
Long Mountain ....34 K 26
Long Mynd (The) ....26 L 26
Long Preston ....49 N 21
Long Stratton ....31 X 26
Long Sutton *Lincs.* ....37 U 25
Long Sutton *Somerset* ...8 L 30
Long Wittenham ....20 Q 29
Longay ....77 C 12
Longbenton ....56 P 18
Longborough ....27 O 28
Longbridge Deverill ....9 N 30
Longburton ....8 M 31
Longcot ....19 P 29
Longdon ....35 O 25
Longfield ....22 U 29
Longford
  Derbyshire Dales ...35 O 25
Longford *Tewkesbury* ...27 N 28
Longforgan ....68 K 14
Longformacus ....62 M 16
Longham ....38 W 25
Longhirst ....56 P 18
Longhorsley ....56 O 18
Longhoughton ....63 P 17
Longleat House ....19 N 30
Longmanhil ....81 M 11
Longnewton ....50 P 20
Longney ....19 M 28
Longniddry ....69 L 16
Longnor ....35 O 24
Longparish ....20 P 30
Longridge *Ribble Valley* ...42 M 22
Longridge
  South Staffordshire ...35 N 25
Longridge *West Lothian* ...61 I 16
Longside ....81 O 11
Longstanton ....29 U 27
Longton *South Ribble* ...42 L 22
Longton *Stoke-on-Trent* ...35 N 25
Longtown *Carlisle* ...54 L 18
Longtown *Herefordshire* ...26 L 28
Longwick ....20 R 28
Longworth ....20 P 28
Lonmore ....77 A 11
Looe ....3 G 32
Loose ....22 V 30
Loppington ....34 L 25
Lorn ....65 E 14
Lorn (Firth of) ....65 D 14
Lossiemouth ....80 K 10
Lostwithiel ....3 G 32
Lothersdale ....49 N 22
Lothmore ....85 I 9
Loudwater ....21 R 29
Loughborough ....36 Q 25
Loughor (River) ....17 H 29
Loughton ....21 U 29
Louth ....45 U 23
Lovington ....8 M 30

Low Bradley ....49 O 22
Low Crosby ....55 L 19
Low Row *Carlisle* ...55 M 19
Low Row *Richmondshire* ...49 N 20
Low Street ....39 Y 25
Lowca ....53 J 20
Lowdham ....36 Q 24
Lower Beeding ....11 T 30
Lower Bentham ....49 M 21
Lower Boddington ....28 Q 27
Lower Broadheath ....27 N 27
Lower Cam ....19 M 28
Lower Diabaig ....78 C 11
Lower Dounreay ....85 I 8
Lower Dunsforth ....50 Q 21
Lower Halstow ....22 W 29
Lower Hardres ....23 X 30
Lower Heyford ....28 Q 28
Lower Killeyan ....58 B 17
Lower Largo ....69 L 15
Lower Mayland ....22 W 28
Lower Peover ....42 M 24
Lower Upham ....10 Q 31
Lower-Whitley ....42 M 24
Lowestoft ....31 Z 26
Lowgill ....49 M 21
Lowick
  Berwick-upon-Tweed ...63 O 17
Lowick
  East Northamptonshire ...29 S 26
Lowick Bridge ....48 K 21
Lowther ....55 L 20
Lowther Hills ....61 J 18
Loxwood ....11 S 30
Loyal (Loch) ....84 G 8
Loyne (Loch) ....72 E 12
Lùb Score ....77 A 10
Lubcroy ....84 F 10
Lubenham ....28 R 26
Lubnaig (Loch) ....67 H 15
Luccombe ....17 J 30
Luce Bay ....52 F 19
Lucker ....63 O 17
Luddesdown ....22 V 29
Ludford *East Lindsey* ...45 T 23
Ludford *South Shropshire* ...26 L 26
Ludgershall *Bucks* ...20 Q 28
Ludgershall *Wilts.* ...19 P 30
Ludgvan ....2 D 33
Ludham ....39 Y 25
Ludlow ....26 L 26
Lugton ....60 G 16
Luib *Highland* ...77 B 12
Luib *Stirling* ...67 G 14
Luichart (Loch) ....78 F 11
Luing ....65 D 15
Lullington ....35 P 25
Lulsgate Bottom ....18 L 29
Lulworth Cove ....9 N 32
Lumphanan ....75 L 12
Lumsden ....80 L 12
Lunan ....75 M 14
Lunanhead ....74 L 14
Luncarty ....68 J 14
Lund ....51 S 22
Lundie ....68 K 14
Lundie (Loch) ....78 C 11
Lundin Links ....69 L 15
Lundy ....16 G 30
Lunning ....87 Q 2
Lurgainn (Loch) ....84 E 9
Lurgashall ....11 S 30
Luskentyre ....82 Z 10
Luss ....66 G 15
Lusta ....77 A 11
Lustleigh ....4 I 32
Luston ....26 L 27
Luthermuir ....75 M 13
Luthrie ....68 K 14
Luton ....29 S 28
Luton Hoo ....21 S 28
Lutterworth ....28 Q 26
Lutton ....37 U 25
Luxborough ....7 J 30
Lybster ....86 K 9
Lydbury North ....26 L 26
Lydd ....12 W 31
Lydd-on-Sea ....12 W 31
Lydden ....23 X 30
Lydeard-St. Lawrence ...8 K 30
Lydford *Mendip* ...8 M 30
Lydford *West Devon* ...4 H 32
Lydham ....26 L 26
Lydiard Millicent ....19 O 29
Lydiard Park ....19 O 29
Lydiate ....42 L 23
Lydlinch ....9 M 31

Lydney .... 18 M 28
Lydstep .... 15 F 29
Lyme Bay .... 5 L 32
Lyme Park .... 43 N 23
Lyme Regis .... 5 L 31
Lyminge .... 13 X 30
Lymington .... 10 P 31
Lymm .... 42 M 23
Lympne .... 13 X 30
Lympstone .... 4 J 32
Lyndhurst .... 10 P 31
Lyne .... 61 K 17
Lyneham *North Wiltshire* .. 19 O 29
Lyneham
   West Oxfordshire ..... 27 P 28
Lynemouth .... 56 P 18
Lyness .... 86 K 7
Lynmouth .... 17 I 30
Lynton .... 17 I 30
Lyon (Glen) .... 73 H 14
Lyonshall .... 26 L 27
Lytchett Matravers ...... 9 N 31
Lytchett Minster .... 9 N 31
Lytes Cary .... 8 L 30
Lyth .... 86 K 8
Lytham .... 42 L 22
Lytham St. Anne's ...... 42 K 22
Lythe .... 51 R 20

M

Maaruig .... 82 Z 10
Mabie .... 53 J 18
Mablethorpe .... 45 U 23
Macaskin (Island) ...... 65 D 15
Macclesfield .... 43 N 24
Macduff .... 81 M 10
Machars (The) .... 52 G 19
Machen .... 18 K 29
Machir Bay .... 58 A 16
Machrihanish .... 58 C 17
Machrihanish Bay .... 58 C 17
Machynlleth .... 33 I 26
Madderty .... 67 I 14
Maddiston .... 67 I 16
Maddy (Loch) .... 76 Y 11
Madeley *Staffs* .... 35 M 24
Madeley
   Telford and Wrekin ... 35 M 26
Madingley .... 29 U 27
Madron .... 2 D 33
Maenclochog .... 15 F 28
Maentwrog .... 33 I 25
Maerdy *Conwy* .... 33 J 25
Maerdy
   Rhondda, Cynon, Taf .. 17 J 28
Maes Howe .... 86 K 7
Maesbrook .... 34 K 25
Maesteg .... 17 J 29
Maghull .... 42 L 23
Magor .... 18 L 29
Maiden Bradley .... 9 N 30
Maiden Castle .... 8 M 31
Maiden Newton .... 8 M 31
Maidenhead .... 20 R 29
Maidens .... 59 F 17
Maidford .... 28 Q 27
Maids Morelon .... 28 Q 27
Maidstone .... 22 V 30
Maidwell .... 28 R 26
Mainland *Orkney Islands* .. 86 J 6
Mainland *Shetland Islands* .87 R 3
Mainstone .... 26 K 26
Maisemore .... 27 N 28
Malborough .... 4 I 33
Maldon .... 22 W 28
Malham .... 49 N 21
Mallaig .... 71 C 12
Mallory Park Circuit .... 36 P 26
Mallwyd .... 33 I 25
Malmesbury .... 19 N 29
Malpas .... 34 L 24
Maltby .... 44 Q 23
Maltby-le-Marsh .... 45 U 24
Malton .... 50 R 21
Malvern Wells .... 27 N 27
Mamble .... 26 M 26
Mamore Forest .... 72 F 13
Man (Isle of) .... 46 G 21
Manaccan .... 2 E 33
Manaton .... 4 I 32
Manchester .... 43 N 23
Manderston .... 62 N 16
Manea .... 29 U 26
Mangersta .... 82 Y 9
Manish .... 76 Z 10
Manningford Bruce ...... 19 O 30

Mannings Heath .... 11 T 30
Manningtree .... 31 X 28
Manorbier .... 15 F 29
Mansfield .... 36 Q 24
Mansfield Woodhouse ... 36 Q 24
Manston .... 9 N 31
Manton .... 36 R 26
Manuden .... 30 U 28
Maplebeck .... 36 R 24
Mapledurham .... 20 Q 29
Mappleton .... 45 T 22
Mappowder .... 9 M 31
Mar (Forest of) .... 74 J 12
Marazion .... 2 D 33
March .... 37 U 26
Marcham .... 20 P 29
Marchington .... 35 O 25
Marchwood .... 10 P 31
Marden .... 22 V 30
Maree (Loch) .... 78 D 10
Mareham-le-Fen .... 37 T 24
Maresfield .... 11 U 31
Margam .... 17 I 29
Margaretting .... 22 V 28
Margate .... 23 Y 29
Margnaheglish .... 59 E 17
Marham .... 38 V 26
Marhamchurch .... 6 G 31
Marholm .... 37 T 26
Marian-Glas .... 40 H 22
Marishader .... 77 B 11
Mark *Sedgemoor* ...... 18 L 30
Mark *South Ayrshire* .. 52 E 18
Market Bosworth .... 36 P 26
Market Deeping .... 37 T 25
Market Drayton .... 34 M 25
Market Harborough ..... 28 R 26
Market Lavington ...... 19 O 30
Market Overton .... 36 R 25
Market Rasen .... 45 T 23
Market Weighton .... 44 S 22
Markfield .... 36 Q 25
Markinch .... 68 K 15
Marks Tey .... 30 W 28
Marksbury .... 18 M 29
Markyate .... 21 S 28
Marlborough .... 19 O 29
Marldon .... 4 J 32
Marlesford .... 31 Y 27
Marloes .... 14 E 28
Marlow .... 20 R 29
Marnhull .... 9 N 31
Marple .... 43 N 23
Marros .... 15 G 28
Marsden .... 43 O 23
Marsett .... 49 N 21
Marsh Gibbon .... 28 Q 28
Marsham .... 39 X 25
Marshaw .... 48 M 22
Marshchapel .... 45 U 23
Marshfield
   Casnewydd / Newport .. 18 K 29
Marshfield
   South Gloucestershire .. 19 N 29
Marshwood .... 8 L 31
Marske .... 49 O 20
Marske-by-the-Sea ..... 57 Q 20
Marston .... 20 Q 28
Marston .... 37 R 25
Marston Magna .... 8 M 31
Marston Moretaine ..... 29 S 27
Martham .... 39 Y 25
Martin *New Forest* ..... 9 O 31
Martin *North Kesteven* .. 37 T 24
Martin (Isle) .... 84 E 10
Martin Mill .... 23 Y 30
Martindale .... 48 L 20
Martinstown .... 5 M 31
Martlesham .... 31 X 27
Martletwy .... 15 F 28
Martley .... 27 M 27
Martock .... 8 L 31
Marton *Harrogate* ..... 50 P 21
Marton *Macclesfield* .. 35 N 24
Marvig .... 82 A 9
Marwell Zoological Park .. 10 Q 31
Mary Arden's House .... 27 O 27
Mary Tavy .... 4 H 32
Marybank .... 79 G 11
Maryburgh .... 79 G 11
Maryculter .... 75 N 12
Maryfield .... 87 Q 3
Marykirk .... 75 M 13
Marypark .... 80 J 11
Maryport *Allerdale* ... 53 J 19
Maryport
   Dumfries and Galloway .. 52 F 19

Marywell *Aberdeenshire* .. 75 L 12
Marywell *Angus* ...... 69 M 14
Masham .... 49 P 21
Matching Green .... 22 U 28
Mathry .... 14 E 28
Matlock .... 36 P 24
Matlock Bath .... 35 P 24
Mattersey .... 44 R 23
Mattingley .... 20 R 30
Mattishall .... 38 X 26
Mauchline .... 60 G 17
Maud .... 81 N 11
Maughold .... 46 H 21
Maughold Head .... 46 H 21
Mawbray .... 54 J 19
Mawnan .... 2 E 33
Maxstoke .... 27 P 26
Maxton .... 62 M 17
Maybole .... 60 F 17
Mayfield *East Sussex* .. 12 U 30
Mayfield *Staffs* ..... 35 O 24
Mc Arthur's Head ...... 58 B 16
Meadie (Loch) .... 84 G 9
Meal Bank .... 48 L 20
Mealsgate .... 54 K 19
Meare .... 8 L 30
Measach (Falls of) .... 78 E 10
Measham .... 36 P 25
Meavaig .... 82 Z 10
Meavy .... 4 H 32
Medbourne .... 28 R 26
Medmenham .... 20 R 29
Medstead .... 10 Q 30
Medway (River) .... 22 W 29
Meidrim .... 15 G 28
Meifod .... 34 K 25
Meigle .... 68 K 14
Meikleour .... 68 J 14
Meikleour .... 68 J 14
Meikleour .... 68 J 14
Meikleour .... 68 J 14
Meikleour .... 68 J 14
Melbost .... 83 B 9
Melbourn .... 29 U 27
Melbourne
   East Riding of Yorkshire .44 R 22
Melbourne
   South Derbyshire .... 36 P 25
Melbury Osmond .... 8 M 31
Meldon .... 56 O 18
Melfort .... 65 D 15
Melgarve .... 73 G 12
Melksham .... 19 N 29
Melldalloch .... 65 E 16
Mellerstain .... 62 M 17
Melling .... 48 M 21
Mellon Charles .... 78 D 10
Mellon Udrigle .... 78 D 10
Mells .... 19 M 30
Melmerby *Eden* .... 55 M 19
Melmerby *Harrogate* .. 50 P 21
Melrose .... 62 L 17
Meltham .... 43 O 23
Melton .... 31 X 27
Melton Mowbray .... 36 R 25
Melvaig .... 77 C 10
Melvich .... 85 I 8
Memsie .... 81 N 11
Menai Bridge /
   Porthaethwy .... 40 H 23
Menai Strait .... 33 H 24
Mendip Hills .... 18 L 30
Mendlesham .... 31 X 27
Menheniot .... 3 G 32
Mennock .... 61 I 17
Menston .... 43 O 22
Menstrie .... 67 I 15
Menteith Hills .... 67 H 15
Mentmore .... 29 R 28
Meonstoke .... 10 Q 31
Meopham .... 22 V 29
Mepal .... 29 U 26
Mere *Cheshire* .... 42 M 24
Mere *Wilts* .... 9 N 30
Mereworth .... 22 V 30
Meriden .... 27 P 26
Merkland Lodge .... 84 F 9
Mermaid Inn .... 32 H 24
Merrick .... 52 G 18
Merriott .... 8 L 31
Merrylaw .... 62 K 18
Mersey (River) .... 42 M 23
Merthyr Cynog .... 25 J 27
Merthyr Tydfil .... 17 J 28
Merton *Cherwell* ..... 20 Q 28
Merton *Devon* .... 7 H 31
Merton *London Borough* .. 21 T 29
Meshaw .... 7 I 31
Messing .... 30 W 28
Messingham .... 44 S 23
Metfield .... 31 Y 26

Metheringham .... 37 S 24
Methil .... 69 K 15
Methlick .... 81 N 11
Methven .... 68 J 14
Methwold .... 38 V 26
Mevagissey .... 3 F 33
Mexborough .... 44 Q 23
Mhór (Loch) .... 73 G 12
Miavaig .... 82 Z 9
Michaelchurch Escley .. 26 L 27
Michaelstow .... 3 F 32
Micheldever .... 10 Q 30
Michelham Priory ...... 12 U 31
Micklefield .... 44 Q 22
Mickleover .... 36 P 25
Mickleton *Cotswold* .. 27 O 27
Mickleton *Teesdale* .. 55 N 20
Mid Ardlaw .... 81 N 10
Mid Calder .... 61 J 16
Mid Lavant .... 10 R 31
Mid Sannox .... 59 E 17
Mid Yell .... 87 Q 2
Midbea .... 86 L 6
Middle Barton .... 28 P 28
Middle Rasen .... 45 S 23
Middle Tysoe .... 28 P 27
Middle Wallop .... 9 P 30
Middle Woodford .... 9 O 30
Middlebie .... 54 K 18
Middleham .... 49 O 21
Middlesbrough .... 57 Q 20
Middlestown .... 43 P 23
Middleton *Argyll and Bute* .. 64 Z 14
Middleton
   Berwick-upon-Tweed .. 63 O 17
Middleton *Bradford* .. 49 O 22
Middleton *Gtr. Mches.* .. 43 N 23
Middleton Cheney ...... 28 Q 27
Middleton-in-Teesdale .. 55 N 20
Middleton on the Wolds .. 51 S 22
Middleton St. George .. 50 P 20
Middleton Tyas .... 49 P 20
Middletown *Powys* .... 34 K 25
Middlewich .... 35 M 24
Midgeholme .... 55 M 19
Midhurst .... 10 R 31
Midlem .... 62 L 17
Midsomer Norton ...... 18 M 30
Midtown .... 78 C 10
Miefield .... 53 H 19
Migdale (Loch) .... 79 H 10
Milborne Port .... 8 M 31
Milborne St. Andrew .... 9 N 31
Milbourne .... 56 O 18
Milburn .... 55 M 19
Mildenhall *Forest Heath* .30 V 26
Mildenhall *Kennet* ... 19 O 29
Mile End .... 30 W 28
Milfield .... 63 N 17
Milford .... 11 S 30
Milford Haven /
   Aberdaugleddau ..... 14 E 28
Milford-on-Sea .... 9 P 31
Milland .... 10 R 30
Millbrook .... 3 H 32
Millhouse .... 59 E 16
Millmeece .... 35 N 25
Millom .... 47 K 21
Millport .... 59 F 16
Milltown
   Dumfries and Galloway .. 54 K 18
Milltown *Highland* .... 78 F 11
Milltown *Moray* ...... 80 L 11
Milnathort .... 68 J 15
Milngavie .... 67 H 16
Milnrow .... 43 N 23
Milnthorpe .... 48 L 21
Milovaig .... 76 Z 11
Milton .... 79 H 10
Milton *Cambs* .... 29 U 27
Milton *Carlisle* ..... 55 L 19
Milton *Dumfries* ..... 53 I 18
Milton *Highland* ..... 79 G 11
Milton *Stranraer* .... 52 F 19
Milton Abbas .... 9 N 31
Milton Abbot .... 3 H 32
Milton Bryan .... 29 S 28
Milton Ernest .... 29 S 27
Milton Keynes .... 28 R 27
Milton Libourne ...... 19 O 29
Milton of Campsie .... 67 H 16
Milton of Cushnie .... 75 L 12
Milton-on-Stour .... 9 N 30
Miltonduff .... 80 J 11
Miltown of Edinvillie .. 80 K 11
Milverton .... 8 K 30

Milwich .... 35 N 25
Minard .... 65 E 15
Minch (The) .... 83 C 9
Minehead .... 17 J 30
Minety .... 19 O 29
Mingary .... 76 X 12
Minginish .... 77 B 12
Mingulay .... 70 X 13
Minigaff .... 52 G 19
Minnigaff .... 52 G 19
Minster *near Sheerness* .. 22 W 29
Minster *near Ramsgate* .. 23 X 29
Minsterley .... 34 L 26
Minsterworth .... 19 N 28
Minterne Magna .... 8 M 31
Minting .... 45 T 24
Mintlaw .... 81 O 11
Minto .... 62 L 17
Mirfield .... 43 O 22
Miserden .... 19 N 28
Misson .... 44 R 23
Misterton *Notts* ..... 44 R 23
Misterton *Somerset* ... 8 L 31
Mistley .... 31 X 28
Mitcham .... 21 T 29
Mitcheldean .... 26 M 28
Mitchell .... 2 E 32
Mitford .... 56 O 18
Mithian .... 2 E 33
Moaness .... 86 K 7
Mochdre .... 41 I 23
Mochrum .... 52 G 19
Modbury .... 4 I 32
Moelfre .... 40 H 22
Moffat .... 61 J 17
Moidart .... 72 C 13
Moira .... 36 P 25
Mol-Chlach .... 71 B 12
Mold / Yr Wyddgrug .... 34 K 24
Molland .... 7 I 30
Monach Islands .... 76 W 11
Monadhliath Mountains .. 73 H 12
Monar (Loch) .... 78 E 11
Monar Lodge .... 78 F 11
Monaughty Forest ...... 80 J 11
Moneydie .... 68 J 14
Moniaive .... 53 I 18
Monifieth .... 69 L 14
Monikie .... 69 L 14
Monk Fryston .... 44 Q 22
Monkland .... 26 L 27
Monkokehampton .... 7 H 31
Monks Eleigh .... 30 W 27
Monksilver .... 7 K 30
Monkton .... 60 G 17
Monmouth / Trefynwy .. 18 L 28
Monreith .... 52 G 19
Montacute .... 8 L 31
Montgarrie .... 75 L 12
Montgomery / Trefaldwyn .. 34 K 26
Montrose .... 75 M 13
Monyash .... 35 O 24
Monymusk .... 75 M 12
Monzie .... 67 I 14
Moonen Bay .... 76 Z 11
Moor Monkton .... 50 Q 21
Moorends .... 44 R 23
Moorfoot Hills .... 61 K 16
Moors (The) .... 52 F 19
Moortown .... 45 S 23
Morar .... 71 C 13
Moray Firth .... 79 H 11
Morchard Bishop .... 7 I 31
Morcott .... 37 S 26
Morden .... 9 N 31
Mordiford .... 26 M 27
More (Glen) *near Kinloch* .. 84 F 9
More (Loch)
   near Westerdale .... 85 J 8
Morebath .... 7 J 30
Morebattle .... 62 M 17
Morecambe .... 48 L 21
Morecambe Bay .... 48 L 21
Moresby .... 53 J 20
Moreton *Epping Forest* .. 22 U 28
Moreton *Purbeck* ...... 9 N 31
Moreton-in-Marsh ...... 27 O 28
Moreton-on-lugg ...... 26 L 27
Moreton Say .... 34 M 25
Moretonhampstead ...... 4 I 32
Morfa Nefyn .... 32 G 25
Morie (Loch) .... 79 G 10
Moriston (Glen) ...... 72 F 12
Morland .... 55 M 20
Morley .... 43 P 22
Morlich (Loch) .... 74 I 12

Morpeth .... 56 O 18
Morriston .... 17 I 29
Morte Bay .... 6 H 30
Mortehoe .... 16 H 30
Mortimer .... 20 Q 29
Morton *near Bourne* .. 37 S 25
Morton
   North East Derbyshire .. 36 P 24
Morton
   near Gainsborough ... 44 R 23
Morton on Swale ...... 50 P 21
Morval .... 3 G 32
Morvah .... 85 I 9
Morven .... 71 C 14
Morvich .... 72 D 12
Morville .... 34 M 26
Morwelham .... 3 H 32
Morwenstow .... 6 G 31
Mosborough .... 43 P 24
Moss Bank .... 42 L 23
Mossdale .... 53 H 18
Mossend .... 60 H 16
Mossley .... 43 N 23
Mosstodloch .... 80 K 11
Mostyn .... 41 K 23
Motherwell .... 61 I 16
Moulin .... 74 I 13
Moulton *Forest Heath* .. 30 V 27
Moulton *Lincs* .... 37 T 25
Moulton *Northants* ... 28 R 27
Moulton Chapel .... 37 T 25
Mount Pleasant .... 9 P 31
Mountain Ash /
   Aberpennar .... 17 J 28
Mount's Bay .... 2 D 33
Mountsorrel .... 36 Q 25
Mousa .... 87 Q 4
Mousehole .... 2 D 33
Mouswald .... 54 J 18
Mow Cop .... 35 N 24
Mowtie .... 75 N 13
Moy .... 79 H 11
Muasdale .... 59 C 17
Much Dewchurch .... 26 L 28
Much Hadham .... 29 U 28
Much Hoole .... 42 L 22
Much Marcle .... 26 M 28
Much Wenlock .... 34 M 26
Muchalls .... 75 N 12
Muchelney .... 8 L 30
Muchrachd .... 78 F 11
Muck .... 71 B 13
Muckle Roe .... 87 P 2
Mucklestone .... 35 M 25
Muddiford .... 7 H 30
Mudford .... 8 M 31
Mugeary .... 77 B 11
Muick (Loch) .... 74 K 13
Muie .... 85 H 9
Muir of Fowlis .... 75 L 12
Muir of Ord .... 79 G 11
Muirdrum .... 69 L 14
Muirhead .... 60 H 16
Muirkirk .... 60 H 17
Muirshearlich .... 72 E 13
Muker .... 49 N 20
Mulbarton .... 39 X 26
Mulben .... 80 K 11
Muldoanich .... 70 X 13
Mull (Isle of) .... 64 B 14
Mull (Sound of) ...... 71 C 14
Mull of Galloway ..... 52 F 20
Mull of Oa .... 58 A 17
Mullardoch (Loch) .... 78 E 12
Mullardoch House ..... 78 F 11
Mullion .... 2 E 33
Mumbles (The) .... 15 H 29
Mumby .... 45 U 24
Mundesley .... 39 Y 25
Mundford .... 30 V 26
Mundham .... 10 R 31
Munlochy .... 79 H 11
Munlochy Bay .... 79 H 11
Munslow .... 26 L 26
Murlaggan .... 72 E 13
Murrayfield .... 68 K 16
Mursley .... 28 R 28
Murton *Easington* ... 57 P 19
Murton *Eden* .... 55 M 20
Musbury .... 5 K 31
Musselburgh .... 68 K 16
Muston .... 51 T 21
Muthill .... 67 I 15
Mwnt .... 15 G 27
Mybster .... 85 J 8
Myddfai .... 25 I 28
Myddle .... 34 L 25

A B C D E F G H I J K L M N O P Q R S T U V W X Y Z

132 Great Britain

Mydroilyn 15 H 27
Mynach Falls 25 I 26
Mynachlog-ddu 15 F 28
Mynydd Eppynt 25 J 27
Mynydd Mawr 32 F 25
Mynydd Preseli 15 F 28
Myrelandhorn 86 K 8
Mytchett 21 R 30
Mytholmroyd 43 O 22

N

Na Cùiltean 58 C 16
Naburn 50 Q 22
Nacton 31 X 27
Nafferton 51 S 21
Nailsea 18 L 29
Nailstone 36 P 26
Nailsworth 19 N 28
Nairn 79 I 11
Nant (Loch) 65 E 14
Nant-y-Moch Reservoir 25 I 26
Nant-y-moel 17 J 29
Nantgwynant Valley 33 H 24
Nantwich 34 M 24
Nantyglo 18 K 28
Napton 28 Q 27
Narberth / Arberth 15 F 28
Narborough *Blaby* 36 Q 26
Narborough *Breckland* 38 V 25
Naseby 28 R 26
Nash Point 17 J 29
Nassington 37 S 26
Nateby 49 M 20
National Exhibition Centre 27 O 26
National Motor Museum 10 P 31
Naunton 27 O 28
Navenby 37 S 24
Naver (Loch) 84 G 9
Nayland 30 W 28
Naze (The) 31 X 28
Neap 87 Q 3
Neath / Castell-nedd 17 I 29
Neath (River) 17 I 28
Nebo 33 I 24
Necton 38 W 26
Needham Market 31 X 27
Needingworth 29 T 27
Needles (The) 10 P 32
Nefyn 32 G 25
Neidpath Castle 61 K 17
Neilston 60 G 16
Neist Point 76 Z 11
Nelson
Caerffili / Caerphilly 18 K 29
Nelson *Pendle* 43 N 22
Nene (River) 37 T 26
Nenthead 55 M 19
Nercwys 34 K 24
Nereabolls 58 A 16
Ness 83 B 8
Ness (Loch) 73 G 12
Nesscliffe 34 L 25
Nestley Marsh 10 P 31
Neston 42 K 24
Nether Broughton 36 R 25
Nether Kellet 48 L 21
Nether Langwith 44 Q 24
Nether Stowey 8 K 30
Nether Wasdale 47 J 20
Nether Whitecleuch 61 I 17
Netheravon 19 O 30
Netherbrae 81 M 11
Netherbury 2 L 31
Netherend 18 M 28
Netherhampton 9 O 30
Nethermill 54 J 18
Netherthong 43 O 23
Netherton 63 N 17
Nethertown 86 K 7
Netherwitton 56 O 18
Nethy Bridge 74 J 12
Netley 10 P 31
Nettlebed 20 R 29
Nettleham 44 S 24
Nettleton 45 T 23
Nevern 15 F 27
Nevis (Glen) 72 E 13
Nevis (Loch) 72 C 12
New Abbey 53 J 19
New Aberdour 81 N 11
New Alresford 10 Q 30
New Buckenham 31 X 26
New Byth 81 N 11
New Clipstone 36 Q 24
New Cumnock 60 H 17
New Deer 81 N 11
New Edlington 44 Q 23
New Forest National Park 9 P 31
New Galloway 53 H 18
New Holland 45 S 22
New Hythe 22 V 30
New Leeds 81 N 11
New Luce 52 F 19
New Marske 57 Q 20
New Mills 43 O 23
New Mills *Powys* 33 K 26
New Milton 9 P 31
New Pitsligo 81 N 11
New Quay / Ceinewydd 24 G 27
New Rackheat 39 Y 26
New Radnor 26 K 27
New Romney 12 W 31
New Rossington 44 Q 23
New Sauchie 67 I 15
New Scone 68 J 14
New Silksworth 57 P 19
New Tredegar 18 K 28
New Waltham 45 T 23
Newark-on-Trent 36 R 24
Newbiggin *Eden* 55 L 19
Newbiggin *Teesdale* 55 N 20
Newbiggin-by-the-Sea 56 P 18
Newbigging *Angus* 69 L 14
Newbigging
South Lanarkshire 61 J 16
Newbold Verdon 36 P 26
Newborough
East Staffordshire 35 O 25
Newborough
Isle of Anglesey 32 G 24
Newbridge *Caerffili /*
Caerphilly 18 K 29
Newbridge *Isle of Wight* 10 P 31
Newbridge-on-Wye 25 J 27
Newbrough 55 N 18
Newburgh *Aberdeenshire* 81 N 12
Newburgh *Fife* 68 K 14
Newburgh *Lancashire* 42 L 23
Newburn 56 O 19
Newbury 20 Q 29
Newby Bridge 48 L 21
Newby Hall 50 P 21
Newcastle *Monmouthshire /*
Sir Fynwy 18 L 28
Newcastle
South Shropshire 26 K 26
Newcastle Emlyn /
Castell Newydd Emlyn 15 G 27
Newcastle-under-Lyme 35 N 24
Newcastle-upon-Tyne 56 P 19
Newcastle-upon-Tyne
Airport 56 O 18
Newcastleton 55 L 18
Newchapel 15 G 27
Newchurch *Carmarthenshire /*
Sir Gaerfyrddin 15 G 28
Newchurch *Isle of Wight* 10 Q 32
Newchurch *Powys* 26 K 27
Newchurch *Shepway* 12 W 30
Newdigate 11 T 30
Newent 27 M 28
Newgale 14 E 28
Newhall 34 M 24
Newham *Isle of Wight* 63 O 17
Newham *London Borough* 21 U 29
Newhaven 11 U 31
Newick 11 U 31
Newington 22 V 29
Newland 18 M 28
Newlyn 2 D 33
Newmachar 75 N 12
Newmains 61 I 16
Newmarket *Isle of Lewis* 82 A 9
Newmarket *Suffolk* 30 V 27
Newmill *Moray* 80 L 11
Newmill *Scottish Borders* 62 L 17
Newmilns 60 G 17
Newnham *Daventry* 28 Q 27
Newnham *Glos.* 18 M 28
Newnham *Kent* 22 W 30
Newnham *Bridge* 26 M 27
Newport *Essex* 30 U 28
Newport *I.O.W.* 10 Q 31
Newport *Pembrokes* 15 F 27
Newport *Stroud* 19 M 28
Newport
Telford and Wrekin 35 M 25
Newport /
Casnewydd *Newport* 18 L 29
Newport-on-Tay 69 L 14
Newport Pagnell 28 R 27
Newquay 2 E 32
Newsham 49 O 20
Newstead 36 Q 24
Newstead Abbey 36 Q 24
Newton *Aberdeenshire* 81 O 11
Newton *Argyll and Bute* 65 E 15
Newton *Babergh* 30 W 27
Newton *Moray* 80 J 11
Newton *Ribble Valley* 49 M 22
Newton *Rushcliffe* 36 R 25
Newton Abbot 4 J 32
Newton Arlosh 54 K 19
Newton-Aycliffe 56 P 20
Newton Ferrers 4 H 33
Newton Flotman 39 X 26
Newton-le-Willows 42 M 23
Newton Longville 28 R 28
Newton Mearns 60 H 16
Newton-on-Rawcliffe 50 R 21
Newton-on-Trent 44 R 24
Newton Poppleford 5 K 31
Newton Reigny 55 L 19
Newton St. Cyres 7 J 31
Newton Stewart 52 G 19
Newton Tracey 7 H 30
Newton Wamphray 54 J 18
Newtongrange 61 K 16
Newtonhill 75 N 12
Newtonmore 73 H 12
Newtown *Cheshire* 43 N 23
Newtown *Heref.* 26 M 27
Newtown *Highland* 73 F 12
Newtown *Isle of Man* 46 G 21
Newtown /
Drenewydd *Powys* 26 K 26
Newtown Linford 36 Q 25
Newtown St. Boswells 62 L 17
Newtyle 68 K 14
Neyland 16 F 28
Nicholaston 15 H 29
Nigg 79 H 10
Nigg Bay 79 H 10
Nine Ladies 35 P 24
Ninebanks 55 M 19
Ninfield 12 V 31
Nisbet 62 M 17
Nith (River) 53 J 19
Niths 61 I 18
Niton 10 Q 32
Nocton 37 S 24
Nolton 14 E 28
Nordelph 38 U 26
Norfolk Broads 39 Y 25
Norham 63 N 16
Normanby 50 R 21
Normandy 21 S 30
Normanton 43 P 22
Normanton-on-the-Wolds 36 Q 25
North Baddesley 10 P 31
North Ballachulish 72 E 13
North Berwick 69 L 15
North Bovey 4 I 32
North Bradley 19 N 30
North Brentor 4 H 32
North Cadbury 8 M 30
North Cave 44 S 22
North-Cerney 19 O 28
North-Charlton 63 O 17
North Cliffe 44 R 22
North Cowton 50 P 20
North Crawley 29 S 27
North Creake 38 W 25
North Curry 8 L 30
North Dalton 51 S 22
North Deighton 50 P 22
North Erradale 77 C 10
North Esk (Riv.) 75 L 13
North Fearns 77 B 11
North Foreland 23 Y 29
North Frodingham 51 T 22
North Grimston 51 R 21
North Harris 82 Z 10
North Hill 3 G 32
North Hinksey 20 Q 28
North Holmwood 21 T 30
North Hykeham 37 S 24
North Kelsey 45 S 23
North Kessock 79 H 11
North Kyme 37 T 24
North Leigh 20 P 28
North-Molton 7 I 30
North Morar 72 C 13
North Newbald 44 S 22
North Nibley 19 M 29
North Otterington 50 P 21
North Petherton 8 K 30
North Petherwin 6 G 31
North Rigton 50 P 22
North Ronaldsay 87 M 5
North-Scarle 36 R 24
North-Shian 65 D 14
North Shields 56 P 18
North Shore 42 K 22
North Somercotes 45 U 23
North Sound (The) 87 L 6
North Stainley 50 P 21
North Stainmore 49 N 20
North Sunderland 63 P 17
North Tamerton 6 G 31
North-Tawton 7 I 31
North Thoresby 45 T 23
North Tidworth 19 P 30
North Uist 76 X 11
North Walsham 39 Y 25
North Warnborough 20 R 30
North Water Bridge 75 M 13
North Weald Bassett 22 U 28
North Wootton 38 V 25
North York Moors
National Park 50 R 20
Northallerton 50 P 20
Northam 6 H 30
Northampton 28 R 27
Northaw 21 T 28
Northchapel 11 S 30
Northchurch 21 S 28
Northfleet 22 V 29
Northiam 12 V 31
Northleach 19 O 28
Northleigh 5 K 31
Northlew 7 H 31
Northop 34 K 24
Northrepps 39 Y 25
Northton 76 Y 10
Northumberland
National Park 63 N 18
Northwich 42 M 24
Northwold 38 V 26
Northwood 34 L 25
Norton *Daventry* 28 Q 27
Norton *Doncaster* 44 Q 23
Norton *Ryedale* 50 R 21
Norton *Tewkesbury* 27 N 28
Norton Disney 36 R 24
Norton Fitzwarren 8 K 30
Norton in Hales 35 M 25
Norton St. Philip 19 N 30
Norwich 39 X 26
Norwick 87 R 1
Noss (Isle of) 87 Q 3
Noss Head 86 K 8
Nottingham 36 Q 25
Nuffield 20 Q 29
Nunburnholme 51 R 22
Nuneaton 28 P 26
Nuneham Courtenay 20 Q 28
Nunney 19 M 30
Nunthorpe 50 Q 20
Nunton 76 X 11
Nutley 11 U 30
Nympsfield 19 N 28

O

Oa (The) 58 B 17
Oadby 36 Q 26
Oakamoor 35 O 24
Oakdale 18 K 28
Oakengates 35 M 25
Oakford 7 J 31
Oakham 36 R 25
Oakhill 18 M 30
Oakington 29 U 27
Oakley *Aylesbury Vale* 20 Q 28
Oakley *Bedfordshire* 29 S 27
Oakley *Fife* 68 J 15
Oaksey 19 N 29
Oakworth 43 O 22
Oare *Kennet* 19 O 29
Oare *Swale* 22 W 30
Oare *West Somerset* 17 I 30
Oathlaw 74 L 13
Oban 65 D 14
Occold 31 X 27
Ochil Hills 68 I 15
Ochiltree 60 G 17
Ockbrook 36 P 25
Ockle 71 C 13
Ockley 11 S 30
Odiham 20 R 30
Odland 18 M 29
Odstock 9 O 30
Offa's Dyke Path 26 K 26
Offord Cluny 29 T 27
Ogbourne St. Andrew 19 O 29
Ogbourne St. George 19 O 29
Ogil 74 L 13
Ogle 56 O 18
Ogmore-by-Sea 17 J 29
Ogmore Vale 17 J 29
Oich (Loch) 73 F 12
Oidhche (Loch na h-) 78 D 11
Oigh-Sgeir 71 Z 13
Okeford Fitzpaine 9 N 31
Okehampton 4 H 31
Old Alresford 10 Q 30
Old Bolingbroke 37 U 24
Old Burghclere 20 Q 30
Old Castleton 55 L 18
Old Colwyn 41 I 23
Old Dailly 59 F 18
Old Deer 81 N 11
Old Fletton 37 T 26
Old Harry Rocks 9 O 32
Old Head 87 L 7
Old Hurst 29 T 26
Old Hutton 48 L 21
Old Kilpatrick 67 G 16
Old Knebworth 29 T 28
Old Leake 37 U 24
Old Man of Hoy 86 J 7
Old Man of Storr 77 B 11
Old Radnor 26 K 27
Old Rayne 81 M 11
Old' Sarum 9 O 30
Old Sodbury 19 M 29
Old Somerby 37 S 25
Old Warden 29 S 27
Old Windsor 21 S 29
Oldany Island 84 E 9
Oldbury 27 N 26
Oldbury on Severn 18 M 29
Oldcotes 44 Q 23
Oldham 43 N 23
Oldhamstocks 69 M 16
Oldmeldrum 81 N 11
Oldshoremore 84 E 8
Olgrinmore 85 J 8
Ollaberry 87 P 2
Ollach 77 B 11
Ollay (Loch) 76 X 12
Ollerton *Macclesfield* 42 M 24
Ollerton
Newark and Sherwood 36 Q 24
Olney 28 R 27
Olveston 18 M 29
Ombersley 27 N 27
Once Brewed 55 M 19
Onchan 46 G 21
Onecote 35 O 24
Onich 72 E 13
Onllwyn 17 I 28
Opinan 83 D 10
Orchy (Glen) 66 F 14
Ord 71 C 12
Ordie 74 L 12
Orford 31 Y 27
Orford Ness 31 Y 27
Orkney Islands 87
Orleton 26 L 27
Ormesby 50 Q 20
Ormesby St. Margaret 39 Z 25
Ormiston 62 L 16
Ormskirk 42 L 23
Oronsay 64 B 15
Orosay *near Fuday* 70 X 12
Orosay *near Lochboisdale* 70 X 12
Orphir 86 K 7
Orrin (Glen) 78 F 11
Orrin Reservoir 78 F 11
Orsay 58 A 16
Orsett 22 V 29
Orston 36 R 25
Orton 48 M 20
Orwell 29 T 27
Orwell (River) 31 X 28
Osborne House 10 Q 31
Osdale 77 A 11
Osgaig (Loch) 83 E 9
Osgodby 45 S 23
Oskaig 77 B 11
Osmington 9 M 32
Ossett 43 P 22
Ossington 36 R 24
Oswaldtwistle 42 M 22
Oswestry 34 K 25
Otford 22 U 30
Othery 8 L 30
Otley *Suffolk* 31 X 27
Otley *West Yorks.* 49 O 22
Otterbourne 10 P 30
Otterburn 55 N 18
Otternish 76 Y 10
Otterswick 87 Q 2
Otterton 5 K 32
Ottery St. Mary 5 K 31
Ottringham 45 T 22
Oulton Broad 39 Z 26
Oulton Park Circuit 34 M 24
Oundle 29 S 26
Ouse (River)
English Channel 11 T 30
Ouse (River) *North Sea* 50 Q 21
Out-Rawcliffe 42 L 22
Out Skerries 87 R 2
Outer Hebrides 82 Y 9
Outhgill 49 M 20
Outwell 38 U 26
Over 29 U 27
Over Compton 8 M 31
Overseal 35 P 25
Overstrand 39 Y 25
Overton *Hants.* 20 Q 30
Overton *Lancs.* 48 L 21
Overton *Wrexham* 34 L 25
Overtown 61 I 16
Ower 10 P 31
Owermoigne 9 N 32
Owlswick 20 R 28
Owslebury 10 Q 30
Owston 36 R 26
Owston Ferry 44 R 23
Oxburgh Hall 38 V 26
Oxen Park 48 K 21
Oxenhope 43 O 22
Oxford 20 Q 28
Oxnam 62 M 17
Oxted 21 T 30
Oxton
Newark and Sherwood 36 Q 24
Oxton *Scottish Borders* 62 L 16
Oxwich 15 H 29
Oxwich Bay 15 H 29
Oykel (Glen) 84 F 9
Oykel Bridge 84 F 10
Oyne 81 M 12

P

Pabay 77 C 12
Pabbay *near Harris* 76 Y 10
Pabbay *near Mingulay* 70 X 13
Pabbay (Sound of) 76 Y 10
Packington 36 P 25
Padbury 28 R 28
Paddock Wood 22 V 30
Paddockhole 54 K 18
Padiham 42 N 22
Padstow 3 F 32
Pagham 10 R 31
Paignton 4 J 32
Pailton 28 Q 26
Painscastle 26 K 27
Painswick 19 N 28
Paisley 60 G 16
Pakefield 31 Z 26
Palnackie 53 I 19
Pamber End 20 Q 30
Pandy
Monmouthshire / Sir Fynwy 26 L 28
Pandy *Powys* 33 J 26
Pangbourne 20 Q 29
Pant 34 K 25
Pantymenyn 15 F 28
Papa Stour 87 O 3
Papa Westray 87 L 5
Papplewick 36 Q 24
Paps of Jura 65 B 16
Papworth Everard 29 T 27
Parbh (The) 84 F 8
Parbold 42 L 23
Parc Cefn Onn 18 K 29
Parham House 11 S 31
Park Gate 10 Q 31
Park of Pairc 82 A 9
Parkeston 31 X 28
Parkgate 53 J 18
Parkhurst 10 Q 31
Parnham House 8 L 31
Parracombe 17 I 30
Parrett (River) 8 K 30
Parson Drove 37 U 26
Partney 37 U 24
Parton *Copeland* 54 J 20
Parton
Dumfries and Galloway 53 H 18
Partridge Green 11 T 31
Parwich 35 O 24
Patchway 18 M 29
Pateley Bridge 49 O 21
Path of Condie 68 J 15
Pathhead 62 L 16
Patna 60 G 17

A B C D E F G H I J K L M N O P Q R S T U V W X Y Z

Patrick ...46 F 21
Patrington ...45 T 22
Patrixbourne ...23 X 30
Patterdale ...48 L 20
Pattingham ...35 N 26
Pattishall ...28 Q 27
Paulerspury ...28 R 27
Paull ...45 T 22
Paulton ...18 M 30
Paxton ...63 N 16
Peacehaven ...11 T 31
Peak District
  National Park ...43 O 23
Pearsie ...74 K 13
Peasedown St. John ...19 M 30
Peasemore ...20 P 29
Peasenhall ...31 Y 27
Peaslake ...21 S 30
Peasmarsh ...12 W 31
Peat Inn ...69 L 15
Peatknowe ...81 M 11
Pebmarsh ...30 W 28
Pebworth ...27 O 27
Peebles ...61 K 17
Peel ...46 F 21
Peel Fell ...62 M 18
Pegswood ...56 P 18
Pegwell Bay ...23 Y 30
Peinchorran ...77 B 12
Peldon ...22 W 28
Pelton ...56 P 19
Pelynt ...3 G 32
Pembrey ...15 H 28
Pembridge ...26 L 27
Pembroke / Penfro ...16 F 28
Pembroke Dock /
  Doc Penfro ...16 F 28
Pembrokeshire Coast
  National Park ...15 F 29
Pembury ...12 V 30
Pen-y-bont / Bridgend ...17 J 29
Pen-y-groes ...32 H 24
Penalun ...15 F 29
Penarth ...18 K 29
Pencader ...15 H 27
Pencaitland ...62 L 16
Pencarrow ...3 F 32
Penclawdd ...15 H 29
Pencombe ...26 M 27
Penderyn ...17 J 28
Pendine ...15 G 28
Pendine Sands ...15 G 28
Pendlebury ...42 N 23
Pendoylan ...17 J 29
Penelewey ...2 E 33
Penfro / Pembroke ...16 F 28
Pengethley ...26 M 28
Penhow ...18 L 29
Penicuik ...61 K 16
Penifiler ...77 B 11
Peninver ...59 D 17
Penistone ...43 P 23
Penketh ...42 L 23
Penkridge ...35 N 25
Penley ...34 L 25
Penmaen ...15 H 29
Penmaenmawr ...41 I 23
Penmaenpool ...33 I 25
Penmark ...17 J 29
Penmon ...40 H 23
Pennal ...33 I 26
Pennant ...33 J 26
Pennerley ...34 L 26
Pennines (The) ...49 N 20
Pennyghael ...65 B 14
Penpont ...53 I 18
Penrhiwpal ...15 G 27
Penrhyn ...40 H 23
Penrhyn Bay ...41 I 23
Penrhyndeudraeth ...33 H 25
Penrith ...55 L 19
Penruddock ...55 L 20
Penryn ...2 E 33
Pensarn ...41 J 23
Penshaw ...56 P 19
Penshurst ...22 U 30
Pensilva ...3 G 32
Pentewan ...3 F 33
Pentire Point ...3 F 32
Pentland Firth ...86 K 7
Pentland Hills ...61 J 16
Pentland Skerries ...87 L 7
Pentraeth ...40 H 23
Pentre-Berw ...40 H 23
Pentre-Celyn ...34 K 24
Pentrebeirdd ...34 K 25
Penwith ...2 D 33

Penybont ...26 K 27
Penysarn ...40 H 22
Penzance ...2 D 33
Pentarddulais ...15 H 28
Pernrhyn-Coch ...25 I 26
Perranarworthal ...2 E 33
Perranporth ...2 E 32
Perranzabuloe ...2 E 33
Pershore ...27 N 27
Pertenhall ...29 S 27
Perth ...68 J 14
Peterborough ...37 T 26
Peterculter ...75 N 12
Peterhead ...81 O 11
Peterlee ...57 P 19
Petersfield ...10 R 30
Peterstone Wentlooge ...18 K 29
Peterstow ...26 M 28
Petham ...23 X 30
Petrockstowe ...7 H 31
Pett ...12 V 31
Pettaugh ...31 X 27
Petworth ...11 S 31
Pevensey Bay ...12 V 31
Pewsey ...19 O 29
Pickering ...50 R 21
Picklescott ...34 L 26
Picton Castle ...16 F 28
Piddlehinton ...9 M 31
Piddletrenthide ...9 M 31
Piercebridge ...49 O 20
Pierowall ...86 L 6
Pilgrims Hatch ...22 U 29
Pillerton Hersey ...28 P 27
Pillerton Priors ...27 P 27
Pilley ...43 P 23
Pilling ...48 L 22
Pilning ...18 M 29
Pilton ...8 M 30
Pinchbeck ...37 T 25
Pinchbeck-West ...37 T 25
Pinhoe ...4 J 31
Pinmore Mains ...52 F 18
Pinner ...21 S 29
Pinvin ...27 N 27
Pinwherry ...52 F 18
Pinxton ...36 Q 24
Pirbright ...21 S 30
Pirnmill ...59 D 17
Pirton ...29 T 28
Pishill ...20 R 29
Pitcaple ...81 M 12
Pitcombe ...8 M 30
Pitcur ...68 K 14
Pitlochry ...74 I 13
Pitmedden ...81 N 11
Pitminster ...8 K 31
Pitscottie ...69 L 15
Pitsford ...28 R 27
Pittentrail ...85 H 10
Pittenween ...69 L 15
Pladda ...59 E 17
Plaistow ...11 S 30
Plas Newydd Anglesey ...33 H 24
Plas Newydd
  Denbighshire ...34 K 25
Plean ...67 I 15
Pleasington ...42 M 22
Pleasley ...36 Q 24
Plenmeller ...55 M 19
Plockton ...78 D 11
Pluckley ...22 W 30
Plumbland ...54 K 19
Plumpton ...11 T 31
Plymouth ...4 H 32
Plympton ...4 H 32
Plymstock ...4 H 32
Plymtree ...7 J 31
Plynlimon
  (Pumlumon Fawr) ...25 I 26
Pocklington ...50 R 22
Point Lynas ...40 H 22
Point of Ayr Flintshire ...41 K 22
Point of Ayre Isle of Man ...46 G 20
Polbain ...83 D 9
Pole of Itlaw (The) ...81 M 11
Polebrook ...29 S 26
Polegate ...12 U 31
Polesden Lacey ...21 S 30
Polesworth ...35 P 26
Polkerris ...3 F 32
Polloch ...72 D 13
Pollock House ...60 H 16
Polmont ...67 I 16
Polperro ...3 G 33
Polruan ...3 G 33
Polwarth ...62 M 16
Pondersbridge ...29 T 26

Pont-ar-Gothi ...15 H 28
Pontardawe ...17 I 28
Pontarddulais ...15 H 28
Pontarfynach /
  Devil's Bridge ...25 I 26
Pontargothi ...15 H 28
Pontarsais ...15 H 28
Pontefract ...44 Q 22
Ponteland ...56 O 18
Ponterwyd ...25 I 26
Pontesbury ...34 L 26
Pontllanfraith ...18 K 28
Pontllyfni ...32 G 24
Pontneddfechan ...17 J 28
Pontrhydfendigaid ...25 I 27
Pontrhydygroes ...25 I 26
Pontrilas ...26 L 28
Pontsticill ...17 J 28
Pontyates ...15 H 28
Pontyberem ...15 H 28
Pontyclun ...17 J 29
Pontycymer ...17 J 29
Pontypool / Pontypwl ...18 K 28
Pontypridd ...17 J 29
Pontypwl / Pontypool ...18 K 28
Poole ...9 O 31
Poole Bay ...9 O 31
Poolewe ...78 D 10
Pooley Bridge ...55 L 20
Pooltiel (Loch) ...76 Z 11
Porlock ...17 J 30
Port Appin ...65 D 14
Port Askaig ...58 B 16
Port Bannatyne ...59 E 16
Port Carlisle ...54 K 19
Port Charlotte ...58 A 16
Port Driseach ...65 E 16
Port Ellen ...58 B 17
Port Erin ...46 F 21
Port-Eynon ...15 H 29
Port-Eynon Point ...15 H 29
Port Gaverne ...3 F 32
Port Glasgow ...66 F 16
Port Henderson ...77 C 10
Port Isaac ...3 F 32
Port Lamont ...59 E 16
Port Logan ...52 F 19
Port Mór ...71 B 13
Port of Menteith ...67 H 15
Port of Ness ...83 B 8
Port Ramsay ...65 D 14
Port St. Mary ...46 F 21
Port Talbot ...17 I 29
Port William ...52 G 19
Portavadie ...59 E 16
Portchester ...10 Q 31
Portencross ...59 F 16
Portesham ...5 M 31
Portgordon ...80 K 11
Portgower ...85 I 9
Porth ...17 J 29
Porth Neigwl
  or Hell's Mouth ...32 G 25
Porth Tywyn /Burry Port ...15 H 28
Porthaethwy /
  Menai Bridge ...40 H 23
Porthcawl ...17 I 29
Porthcothan ...2 E 32
Porthcurno ...2 D 33
Porthgwarra ...2 C 33
Porthkerry ...17 K 29
Porthleven ...2 E 33
Porthmadog ...33 H 25
Porthtowan ...2 E 32
Porthyrhyd ...15 H 28
Portinnisherrich ...65 E 15
Portishead ...18 L 29
Portknockie ...80 L 10
Portland (Isle of) ...8 M 32
Portlethen ...75 N 12
Portmahomack ...79 I 10
Portmeirion ...33 H 25
Portnacroish ...72 D 14
Portnaguran ...83 B 9
Portnahaven ...58 A 16
Portnalong ...77 A 12
Portobello ...68 K 16
Portreath ...2 E 33
Portree ...77 B 11
Portscatho ...3 F 33
Portskerra ...85 I 8
Portskewett ...18 L 29
Portslade ...11 T 31
Portslogan ...52 E 19
Portsmouth ...10 Q 31
Portsoy ...81 L 10
Portuairk ...71 B 13

Postbridge ...4 I 32
Potten End ...21 S 28
Potter Heigham ...39 Y 25
Potter Street ...21 U 28
Potterhanworth ...37 S 24
Potterne ...19 N 30
Potters Bar ...21 T 28
Potton ...29 T 27
Poughill ...6 G 31
Poulshot ...19 N 29
Poulton ...19 O 28
Poulton-le-Fylde ...42 L 22
Poundstock ...6 G 31
Powburn ...63 O 17
Powerstock ...8 L 31
Powick ...27 N 27
Powis ...34 K 26
Poynings ...11 T 31
Poynton ...43 N 23
Praa Sands ...2 D 33
Prawle Point ...4 I 33
Praze-an-Beeble ...2 E 33
Prees ...34 M 25
Preesall ...48 L 22
Prendwick ...63 O 17
Prescot ...42 L 23
Prestatyn ...41 J 22
Prestbury Cheltenham ...27 N 28
Prestbury Macclesfield ...43 N 24
Presteigne ...26 K 27
Preston
  East Riding of Yorks. ...45 T 22
Preston Kent ...23 X 30
Preston Lancs. ...42 L 22
Preston Rutland ...36 R 26
Preston West Sussex ...11 S 31
Preston Candover ...10 Q 30
Preston Capes ...28 Q 27
Prestonpans ...69 L 16
Prestwich ...42 N 23
Prestwick ...60 G 17
Prestwood ...20 R 28
Prickwillow ...30 V 26
Priest Island ...83 D 10
Priest Weston ...34 K 26
Princes Risborough ...20 R 28
Princethorpe ...28 P 26
Princetown ...4 I 32
Priors Marston ...28 Q 27
Probus ...3 F 33
Prosen (Glen) ...74 K 13
Prudhoe ...56 O 19
Puckeridge ...29 U 28
Pucklechurch ...19 M 29
Pucks Gutter ...23 X 30
Puddletown ...9 M 31
Pudsey ...43 P 22
Pulborough ...11 S 31
Pulford ...34 L 24
Pulham ...9 M 31
Pulham Market ...31 X 26
Puncheston ...24 F 28
Punchardon ...7 H 30
Purbeck (Isle of) ...9 N 32
Purbrook ...10 Q 31
Puriton ...8 L 30
Purleigh ...22 V 28
Purley ...20 Q 29
Purse Caundle Manor ...9 M 31
Purston Jaglin ...43 P 22
Purton ...19 O 29
Putsborough ...6 H 30
Pwllheli ...32 G 25
Pyecombe ...11 T 31
Pyle ...17 I 29
Pylle ...8 M 30

Q
Quainton ...28 R 28
Quantock Hills ...8 K 30
Quarff ...87 Q 3
Quarr ...10 Q 31
Quatt ...27 M 26
Quedgeley ...19 N 28
Queen Camel ...8 M 30
Queen Elizabeth
  Forest Park ...67 G 15
Queenborough ...22 W 29
Queensbury ...43 O 22
Queensferry ...34 K 24
Quendon ...30 U 28
Quenington ...19 O 28
Quinag ...84 E 9
Quines's Hill ...46 G 21
Quinish Point ...71 B 14
Quiraing ...77 B 11

Quoich (Loch) ...72 E 12
Quorndon ...36 Q 25
Quothquan ...61 J 17

R
Raasay (Island of) ...77 B 11
Raasay (Sound of) ...77 B 11
Raasay Ho ...77 B 11
Rachub ...33 H 24
Rackenford ...7 J 31
Rackwick ...86 J 7
Radcliffe ...42 N 23
Radcliffe-on-Trent ...36 Q 25
Radlett ...21 T 28
Radley ...20 Q 28
Radnor Forest ...26 K 27
Radstock ...18 M 30
Radyr ...18 K 29
Rafford ...80 J 11
Raglan ...18 L 28
Ragley Hall ...27 O 27
Rainford ...42 L 23
Rainham ...22 V 29
Rainworth ...36 Q 24
Rait ...68 K 14
Ramasaig ...76 Z 11
Rampisham ...8 M 31
Rampside ...47 K 21
Rampton ...44 R 24
Ramsbottom ...42 N 23
Ramsbury ...19 P 29
Ramsey Cambs. ...29 T 26
Ramsey Isle of Man ...46 G 21
Ramsey Bay ...46 G 21
Ramsey Island ...14 D 28
Ramsey St. Mary's ...29 T 26
Ramsgate ...23 Y 29
Ramsgill-in-Nidderdale ...49 O 21
Ranby ...44 Q 24
Ranfurly ...60 G 16
Rangeworthy ...18 M 29
Ranish ...82 A 9
Rankinston ...60 G 17
Rannoch (Loch) ...73 H 13
Rannoch Moor ...73 F 14
Rannoch Sta ...73 G 13
Ranskill ...44 Q 23
Ranton ...35 N 25
Ranworth ...39 Y 25
Rapness ...87 L 6
Rappach ...84 F 10
Ratby ...36 Q 26
Ratho ...68 J 16
Ratlinghope ...34 L 26
Rattlesden ...30 W 27
Rattray ...68 K 14
Rattray Head ...81 O 11
Raunds ...29 S 26
Ravenglass ...47 J 20
Ravenscar ...51 S 20
Ravensthorpe ...28 Q 27
Ravenstone ...36 P 25
Ravenstonedale ...49 M 20
Ravensworth ...49 O 20
Rawcliffe ...44 R 22
Rawmarsh ...44 P 23
Rawtenstall ...42 N 22
Rayleigh ...22 V 29
Rayne ...30 V 28
Read ...42 M 22
Reading ...20 R 29
Rearsby ...36 Q 25
Reay ...85 I 8
Reay Forest ...84 F 9
Reculver ...23 X 29
Red Wharf Bay ...40 H 23
Redbourn ...21 S 28
Redbridge
  London Borough ...21 U 29
Redcar ...57 Q 20
Redcliff Bay ...18 L 29
Reddding ...67 I 16
Redditch ...27 O 27
Redesmouth ...55 N 18
Redford ...69 L 14
Redhill North Somerset ...18 L 29
Redhill
  Reigate and Banstead ...21 T 30
Redisham ...31 Y 26
Redmarley d'Abitot ...27 M 28
Redmarshall ...57 P 20
Redmire ...49 O 21
Redpoint ...77 C 11
Redruth ...2 E 33

Redwick ...18 L 29
Reedham ...39 Y 25
Reekie Linn ...74 K 13
Reepham ...45 S 24
Reeth ...49 O 20
Regarby ...46 G 20
Reiff ...83 D 9
Reigate ...21 T 30
Reighton ...51 T 21
Reiss ...86 K 8
Relubbus ...2 D 33
Rempstone ...36 Q 25
Rendcomb ...19 O 28
Rendham ...31 Y 27
Renfrew ...60 G 16
Renishaw ...44 P 24
Rennington ...63 O 17
Renton ...66 G 16
Renwick ...55 M 19
Rescobie ...75 L 14
Resipole ...72 C 13
Resolven ...17 I 28
Resort (Loch) ...82 Z 9
Restalrig ...68 K 16
Reston ...63 N 16
Restormel Castle ...3 G 32
Retford ...44 R 24
Rettendon ...22 V 29
Reynoldston ...15 H 29
Rhaeadr / Rhayader ...25 J 27
Rhaeadr Ddu ...33 I 25
Rhandirmwyn ...25 I 27
Rhayader / Rhaeadr ...25 J 27
Rheidol (Vale of) ...25 I 26
Rhenigidale ...82 Z 10
Rhian ...84 G 9
Rhiconich ...84 F 8
Rhigos ...17 J 28
Rhilochan ...85 H 9
Rhinns of Galloway (The) ...52 E 19
Rhinns of Kells ...53 G 18
Rhondda ...17 J 29
Rhoose ...17 J 29
Rhos ...17 I 28
Rhoscolyn ...40 G 23
Rhoscrowther ...14 E 28
Rhosllanerchrugog ...34 K 24
Rhosmaen ...25 I 28
Rhosneigr ...40 G 23
Rhossili ...15 H 29
Rhostyllen ...34 K 24
Rhosybol ...40 G 23
Rhu ...66 F 15
Rhuddlan ...41 J 23
Rhum ...71 A 13
Rhuthun / Ruthin ...34 K 24
Rhyd-Ddu ...33 H 24
Rhydaman / Ammanford ...15 I 28
Rhydcymerau ...15 H 27
Rhydd ...27 N 27
Rhyddhywel ...25 J 26
Rhydowen ...15 H 27
Rhyl ...41 J 23
Rhymmi / Rhymney ...18 K 28
Rhymney / Rhymmi ...18 K 28
Rhynie ...80 L 12
Ribble (River) ...49 N 22
Ribblesdale ...49 N 21
Ribchester ...42 M 22
Riber Castle ...36 P 24
Riccall ...44 Q 22
Riccarton ...60 G 17
Richards Castle ...26 L 27
Richborough ...23 X 30
Richmond ...49 O 20
Richmond-upon-Thames
  London Borough ...21 T 29
Rickarton ...75 N 13
Rickmansworth ...21 S 29
Ridgeway Cross ...27 M 27
Ridgeway Path (The) ...20 P 29
Ridsdale ...55 N 18
Rievaulx Abbey ...50 Q 21
Rigg ...77 B 11
Rigside ...61 I 17
Rillington ...51 R 21
Rimington ...49 N 22
Rimsdale (Loch) ...85 H 9
Ringford ...53 H 19
Ringmer ...11 U 31
Ringshall ...30 W 27
Ringstead
  East Northamptonshire ...29 S 26
Ringstead King's Lynn
  and West Norfolk ...38 V 25

A B C D E F G H I J K L M N O P Q R S T U V W X Y Z

A B C D E F G H I J K L M N O P Q R S T U V W X Y Z

Ringwood ....9 O 31
Ringwould ....23 Y 30
Rinnes (Glen) ....80 K 11
Rinns of Islay ....58 A 16
Rinns Point ....58 A 16
Ripe ....12 U 31
Ripley Derbs. ....36 P 24
Ripley North Yorks. ....50 P 21
Ripley Surrey ....21 S 30
Riplingham ....44 S 22
Ripon ....50 P 21
Rippingale ....37 S 25
Ripponden ....43 O 22
Risabus ....58 B 17
Risby ....30 V 27
Risca ....18 K 29
Risegate ....37 T 25
Riseley ....29 S 27
Rishton ....42 M 22
Risplith ....50 P 21
Ristol (Isle) ....83 D 9
Roadside of Kinneff ....75 N 13
Roag ....77 A 11
Roag (Loch) ....82 Z 9
Roan of Graigoch ....60 F 18
Roberton
    Dumfries and Galloway ....61 I 17
Roberton
    Scottish Borders ....62 L 17
Robertsbridge ....12 V 31
Robin Hood's Bay ....51 S 20
Roby ....42 L 23
Rocester ....35 O 25
Rochdale ....43 N 23
Roche ....3 F 32
Rochester ....22 V 29
Rochester
    Northumberland ....63 N 18
Rochford ....22 W 29
Rock ....3 F 32
Rockcliffe Cumbria ......54 K 19
Rockcliffe
    Dumfries and Galloway ...53 I 19
Rockfield ....18 L 28
Rockingham ....28 R 26
Rode ....19 N 30
Rode Heath ....35 N 24
Rodel ....76 Z 10
Rodmel ....11 U 31
Rodney Stoke ....18 L 30
Rogart ....85 H 9
Rogerstone ....18 K 29
Rogiet ....18 L 29
Rokeby Hall ....49 O 20
Rolleston Notts. ....36 R 24
Rolleston-on-Dove Staffs. ...35 P 25
Rolvenden ....12 V 30
Romannobridge ....61 J 16
Romiley ....43 N 23
Romney Marsh ....12 W 30
Romsey ....10 P 31
Romsley ....27 N 26
Rona (Island of) ....77 C 11
Ronaldsway ....46 G 21
Ronas Voe ....87 P 2
Ronay ....76 Y 11
Rookhope ....55 N 19
Roos ....45 T 22
Rootpark ....61 I 16
Ropley ....10 Q 30
Ropsley ....37 S 25
Rora ....81 O 11
Rora Head ....86 J 7
Rosedale Abbey ....50 R 20
Rosehearty ....81 N 10
Rosemarket ....16 F 28
Rosemarkie ....79 H 11
Rosewell ....61 K 16
Rosgill ....48 L 20
Roshven ....71 C 13
Rosley ....54 K 19
Roslin ....61 K 16
Rosliston ....35 P 25
Rosneath ....66 F 15
Ross
    Berwick-upon-Tweed ...63 O 17
Ross
    Dumfries and Galloway ...53 H 19
Ross of Mull ....64 B 15
Ross-on-Wye ....26 M 28
Rossall Point ....48 K 22
Rossett ....34 L 24
Rosudgeon ....2 D 33
Rosyth ....68 J 15
Rothbury ....63 O 18
Rothbury Forest ....63 O 18
Rotherfield ....12 U 30

Rotherham ....43 P 23
Rothersthorpe ....28 R 27
Rothes ....80 K 11
Rothesay ....59 E 16
Rothienorman ....81 M 11
Rothiesholm ....87 M 6
Rothwell Leeds. ....43 P 22
Rothwell Northamp. ......28 R 26
Rotterspury ....28 R 27
Rottingdean ....11 T 31
Roughburn ....73 F 13
Roughsike ....55 L 18
Roughton ....39 X 25
Rounton ....50 P 20
Rousay ....86 K 6
Rousdon ....5 L 31
Routh ....45 S 22
Rowardennan Lodge .....66 G 15
Rowington ....27 O 27
Rowland's Castle ....10 R 31
Rowland's Gill ....56 O 19
Rownhams ....10 P 31
Rowsley ....35 P 24
Roxburgh ....62 M 17
Roxwell ....22 V 28
Roy (Glen) ....72 F 13
Royal Leamington Spa ...27 P 27
Royal Military Academy ...20 R 29
Royal Tunbridge Wells ...12 U 30
Roybridge ....72 F 13
Roydon Essex ....21 U 28
Roydon Norfolk ....31 X 26
Royston Herts. ....29 T 27
Royston South Yorks. ....43 P 23
Royton ....43 N 23
Ruabon ....34 K 25
Ruan High Lanes ....3 F 33
Ruan Minor ....2 E 34
Ruardean ....18 M 28
Rubbha na Faing ....58 A 16
Rubha a' Mhail ....64 B 16
Rubha Còigeach ....83 D 9
Rubha Dubh ....70 Z 14
Rubha Hunish ....77 A 10
Rubha na h-Easgainne ...71 B 12
Rubha Rèidh ....77 C 10
Rubha Suisnish ....71 B 12
Rubh'an Dùnain ....71 A 12
Rubhaxton ....24 F 28
Ruddington ....36 Q 25
Rudgeway ....18 M 29
Rudgwick ....11 S 30
Rudha Ban ....70 Y 12
Rudston ....51 T 21
Rufford Old Hall ....42 L 23
Rufforth ....50 Q 22
Rugby ....28 Q 26
Rugeley ....35 O 25
Rumburgh ....31 Y 26
Rumney ....18 K 29
Runcorn ....42 L 23
Runswick Bay ....50 R 20
Runtaleave ....74 K 13
Runwell ....22 V 29
Rushall ....19 O 30
Rushden ....29 S 27
Ruskington ....37 S 24
Rusland ....48 K 21
Rusper ....11 T 30
Ruspidge ....18 M 28
Rustington ....11 S 31
Ruswarp ....51 S 20
Rutherglen ....60 H 16
Ruthin / Rhuthun ....34 K 24
Ruthven Aberdeenshire ...80 L 11
Ruthven Angus ....74 K 14
Ruthven Highland ....79 I 11
Ruthven (Loch) ....79 H 12
Ruthven Barracks ....73 H 12
Ruthwell ....54 J 19
Rutland Water ....37 S 26
Ruyton
    of the Eleven Towns ...34 L 25
Ryal ....56 O 18
Ryan (Loch) ....52 E 19
Rycote ....20 Q 28
Rydal ....48 L 20
Ryde ....10 Q 31
Rye ....12 W 31
Ryhall ....37 S 25
Ryhill ....43 P 23
Ryhope ....57 P 19
Ryton ....56 O 19

S

Sabden ....42 M 22
Sacriston ....56 P 19

Sadberge ....50 P 20
Saddell ....59 D 17
Saddell Bay ....59 D 17
Sadgill ....48 L 20
Saffron Walden ....30 U 27
Saham Toney ....38 W 26
St. Abbs ....63 N 16
St. Abb's Head ....63 N 16
St. Agnes ....2 E 33
St. Albans ....21 T 28
St. Aldhelm's Head ....9 N 32
St. Andrews ....69 L 14
St. Ann's ....54 J 18
St. Ann's Head ....14 E 28
St. Arvans ....18 L 29
St. Asaph ....41 J 23
St. Athan ....17 J 29
St. Austell ....3 F 32
St. Bees ....47 J 20
St. Bees Head ....47 J 20
St. Blazey ....3 F 32
St. Boswells ....62 M 17
St. Breock ....3 F 32
St. Breward ....3 F 32
St. Briavels ....18 M 28
St. Brides ....14 E 28
St. Bride's Bay ....14 E 28
St. Brides Major ....17 J 29
St. Brides-Super-Ely ....17 K 29
St. Bridge-Wentlooge ...18 K 29
St. Buryan ....2 D 33
St. Catherine's Point ....10 Q 32
St. Clears / Sanclêr .....15 G 28
St. Cleer ....3 G 32
St. Columb Major ....3 F 32
St. Combs ....81 O 11
St. Cyrus ....75 M 13
St. David's / Tyddewi ...14 E 28
St. David's Head ....14 D 28
St. Day ....2 E 33
St. Dennis ....3 F 32
St. Dogmaels ....15 F 27
St. Dominick ....3 H 32
St. Donats ....17 J 29
St. Endellion ....3 F 32
St. Erth ....2 D 33
St. Ewe ....3 F 33
St. Fagans ....18 K 29
St. Fergus ....81 O 11
St. Fillans ....67 H 14
St. Florence ....15 F 28
St. Gennys ....6 G 31
St. Germans ....3 H 32
St. Giles ....7 H 31
St. Giles-on-the-Heath ...6 H 31
St. Govan's Head ....16 F 29
St. Harmon ....25 J 26
St. Helen Auckland ....56 O 20
St. Helens I.O.W. ....10 Q 31
St. Helens Merseyside ...42 L 23
St. Helier Jersey 5
St. Ishmael's ....14 E 28
St. Issey ....3 F 32
St. Ive ....3 G 32
St. Ives Cambs. ....29 T 27
St. Ives Cornwall ....2 D 33
St. John's ....46 G 21
St. John's Chapel ....55 N 19
St. John's Loch ....86 J 8
St. Jude ....46 G 20
St. Just ....2 C 33
St. Just in Roseland ....2 F 33
St. Keverne ....2 E 33
St. Kew ....3 F 32
St. Leonards Dorset ....9 O 31
St. Leonards East Sussex ...12 V 31
St. Mabyn ....3 F 32
St. Magnus Bay ....87 P 2
St. Margaret's at Cliffe ...23 Y 30
St. Margaret's Bay ....23 Y 30
St. Margaret's Hope ......87 L 7
St. Mark's ....46 G 21
St. Martin's ....34 K 25
St. Mary in the Marsh ...12 W 30
St. Mary's Orkney Islands ...86 L 7
St. Mary's
    Perth and Kinross ......73 I 14
St. Mary's-Bay ....13 W 30
St. Mary's-Hoo ....12 V 29
St. Mary's Loch ....61 K 17
St. Mawes ....2 E 33
St. Mawgan ....3 F 32
St. Mellion ....3 H 32
St. Mellons ....18 K 29
St. Merryn ....3 F 32
St. Michael Penkevil ....2 E 33
St. Michael's Mount ....2 D 33

St. Michaels-on-Wyre ...42 L 22
St. Minver ....3 F 32
St. Monans ....69 L 15
St. Neot ....3 G 32
St. Neots ....29 T 27
St. Nicholas Pembrokes ...14 E 28
St. Nicholas
    Vale of Glamorgan ....17 K 29
St. Nicholas-at-Wade ...23 X 29
St. Ninian's Isle ....87 P 4
St. Osyth ....23 X 28
St. Patrick's Isle ....46 F 21
St. Paul's Walden ....29 T 28
St. Peter Port Guernsey ...5
St. Peter's ....23 Y 29
St. Pool ....4 I 33
St. Stephen ....3 F 32
St. Teath ....3 F 32
St. Tudwal's Islands .....32 G 25
St. Tudy ....3 F 32
St. Vigeans ....69 M 14
St. Wenn ....3 F 32
St. Weonards ....26 L 28
Salcombe ....4 I 33
Salcombe Regis ....5 K 31
Sale ....42 N 23
Salehurst ....12 V 31
Salen Argyll and Bute ...65 C 14
Salen Highland ....71 C 13
Salford ....42 N 23
Salfords ....21 T 30
Salhouse ....39 Y 25
Saline ....68 J 15
Salisbury ....9 O 30
Salisbury Plain ....19 O 30
Sallachy ....87 Q 3
Sallachy
    Ben More Assynt ....84 G 9
Sallachy
    near Kyle of Lochalsh ...78 D 12
Saltash ....3 H 32
Saltburn ....79 H 10
Saltburn-by-the-Sea .....57 R 20
Saltcoats ....59 F 17
Salter ....48 M 21
Saltfleet ....45 U 23
Saltford ....18 M 29
Salthouse ....38 X 25
Saltney ....34 L 24
Salton ....50 R 21
Samala ....76 X 11
Samlesbury Old Hall .....42 M 22
Sampford Courtenay ....7 I 31
Sampford Peverell ....7 J 31
Sanaigmore ....58 A 16
Sancton ....44 S 22
Sancreed ....2 D 33
Sand Side ....47 K 21
Sanda Island ....59 D 18
Sanday Highland ....71 A 12
Sanday Orkney Islands ...87 M 6
Sandbach ....35 M 24
Sandbank ....66 F 16
Sandbanks ....9 O 31
Sandend ....80 L 10
Sandford Eden ....49 M 20
Sandford Mid Devon ......7 J 31
Sandford North Somerset ...18 L 30
Sandford
    South Lanarkshire .....60 H 17
Sandford Orcas ....8 M 31
Sandgate ....13 X 30
Sandgreen ....53 H 19
Sandhaven ....81 N 10
Sandhead ....52 F 19
Sandhurst Berks. ....20 R 29
Sandhurst Kent ....12 V 30
Sandleigh ....20 Q 28
Sandlins ....31 Y 27
Sandness ....87 P 3
Sandon
    North Hertfordshire ....29 T 28
Sandon Stafford ....35 N 25
Sandown ....10 Q 32
Sandray ....70 X 13
Sandridge ....21 T 28
Sandringham House ......38 V 25
Sandsend ....51 R 20
Sandside ....27 O 26
Sandwell ....27 O 26
Sandwich ....23 Y 30
Sandwick Eden ....48 L 20
Sandwick Eilean Siar ....76 Y 11
Sandwick Shetland Islands ..87 Q 4
Sandwood Loch ....84 E 8
Sandy ....29 T 27
Sandygate ....46 G 20
Sandyhills ....53 I 19

Sanna ....71 B 13
Sanquhar ....61 I 17
Santon Downham ....30 W 26
Santon Head ....46 G 21
Sapperton ....19 N 28
Saracen's Head ....37 T 25
Sarclet ....86 K 8
Sarisbury ....10 Q 31
Sark Channel I. 5
Sarn Meyllteyrn ....32 G 25
Sarre ....23 X 29
Satley ....56 O 19
Satterthwaite ....48 K 21
Sauchen ....75 M 12
Saughall ....42 L 24
Saughtree ....62 L 18
Saundersfoot ....15 F 28
Saunderton ....20 R 28
Sawbridgeworth ....21 U 28
Sawrey ....48 L 20
Sawston ....29 U 27
Sawtry ....29 T 26
Saxby ....36 R 25
Saxilby ....44 S 24
Saxlingham Nethergate ...39 X 26
Saxmundham ....31 Y 27
Saxtead Green ....31 X 27
Scadavay (Loch) ....76 Y 11
Scaddle (Glen) ....72 D 13
Scafell Pikes ....47 K 20
Scagglethorpe ....50 R 21
Scalasaig ....64 B 15
Scalby ....51 S 21
Scaleby ....55 L 19
Scalford ....36 R 25
Scalloway ....87 Q 3
Scalpay Highland ....77 C 12
Scalpay Western Isles ...77 A 10
Scamblesby ....45 T 24
Scampton ....44 S 24
Scaniport ....79 H 11
Scapa Flow ....86 K 7
Scarba ....65 C 15
Scarborough ....51 S 21
Scarcliffe ....44 Q 24
Scardroy ....78 F 11
Scarfskerry ....86 K 8
Scarisbrick ....42 L 23
Scarista ....76 Y 10
Scarp ....82 Y 9
Scavaig (Loch) ....71 B 12
Scawby ....44 S 23
Schiehallion ....73 H 13
Scilly (Isles of) ....2 B 34
Scone Palace ....68 J 14
Scopwick ....37 S 24
Scoraig ....83 D 10
Scorton ....50 P 20
Scotby ....55 L 19
Scotch-Corner ....49 P 20
Scothern ....45 S 24
Scotlandwell ....68 K 15
Scotney ....12 V 30
Scotstown ....72 D 13
Scotter ....44 S 23
Scotton Harrogate ....50 P 21
Scotton Richmondshire ...49 O 20
Scottow ....39 Y 25
Scourie ....84 E 8
Scousburgh ....87 Q 4
Scrabster ....85 J 8
Scraptoft ....36 Q 26
Scredington ....37 S 25
Scridain (Loch) ....64 B 14
Scruton ....50 P 21
Sculthorpe ....38 W 25
Scunthorpe ....44 S 23
Sea Palling ....39 Y 25
Seaford ....12 U 31
Seaforth (Loch) ....82 Z 10
Seaforth Head ....82 A 9
Seagrave ....36 Q 25
Seaham ....57 P 19
Seahouses ....63 O 17
Seal ....21 R 30
Sealga (Loch na) ....78 D 10
Seamer Hambleton ....50 Q 20
Seamer Scarborough ....51 S 21
Seamill ....59 F 16
Seasalter ....23 X 29
Seascale ....47 J 20
Seaton Allerdale ....53 J 20
Seaton East Devon ....5 K 31
Seaton Carew ....57 Q 20
Seaton Delaval ....56 P 18
Seaton Delaval Hall ......56 P 18
Seaton Ross ....44 R 22
Seaton Sluice ....56 P 18

Seave Green ....50 Q 20
Seaview ....10 Q 31
Sebergham ....54 L 19
Sedbergh ....49 M 21
Sedgebrook ....36 R 25
Sedgley ....27 N 26
Sedlescombe ....12 V 31
Seend ....19 N 29
Seething ....39 Y 26
Seighford ....35 N 25
Seil (Isle of) ....65 D 15
Seilich (Loch an t-) ....73 H 13
Selattyn ....34 K 25
Selborne ....10 R 30
Selby ....44 Q 22
Selker Bay ....47 J 21
Selkirk ....62 L 17
Sellindge ....13 W 30
Selmeston ....12 U 31
Selsey ....10 R 31
Selston ....36 Q 24
Selworthy ....17 J 30
Semley ....9 N 30
Senghenydd ....18 K 29
Sennen ....2 C 33
Sennybridge ....25 J 28
Sessay ....50 Q 21
Settle ....49 N 21
Seven Sisters
    East Sussex ....12 U 31
Seven Sisters
    Neath and Port Talbot ...17 I 28
Sevenhampton ....27 O 28
Sevenoaks ....22 U 30
Severn (River) ....27 M 27
Severn Bridge ....18 M 29
Severn Stoke ....27 N 27
Sgibacleit (Loch) ....82 A 9
Sgiwen ....17 I 29
Sgurr Mór ....78 E 10
Shader ....82 A 8
Shaftesbury ....9 N 30
Shalbourne ....20 P 29
Shaldon ....4 J 32
Shalfleet ....10 P 31
Shalford ....21 S 30
Shandon ....66 F 15
Shanklin ....10 Q 32
Shap ....48 L 20
Shapinsay ....87 L 6
Shapwick ....8 L 30
Shardlow ....36 P 25
Sharlston ....43 P 23
Sharnbrook ....29 S 27
Sharnford ....28 Q 26
Sharperton ....63 N 18
Sharpness ....18 M 28
Shavington ....34 M 24
Shaw Gtr. Mches. ....43 N 23
Shaw West Berkshire ...20 Q 29
Shaw Wilts. ....19 N 29
Shawbost ....82 Z 9
Shawbury ....34 M 25
Shawford ....10 Q 30
Shawhead ....53 I 18
Shebbear ....6 H 31
Shebster ....85 I 8
Sheepwash ....6 H 31
Sheepy Magna ....36 P 26
Sheering ....22 U 28
Sheerness ....22 W 29
Sheffield ....43 P 23
Sheffield Park ....11 T 31
Shefford ....29 S 27
Sheldon ....19 N 29
Sheldon Manor ....19 N 29
Sheldwich ....22 W 30
Shell or Sealg (Loch) ...82 A 9
Shelley ....43 O 23
Shellingford ....20 P 29
Shelsley Beauchamp ....27 M 27
Shelton Rushcliffe ....36 R 25
Shelton South Norfolk ...31 X 26
Shelton Lock ....36 P 25
Shelve ....34 L 26
Shenley Church End .....28 R 27
Shenstone ....27 O 26
Shenval ....80 K 11
Shepley ....43 O 23
Sheppey (Isle of) ....22 W 29
Shepreth ....29 U 27
Shepshed ....36 Q 25
Shepton Mallet ....18 M 30
Sherborne Cotswold .....19 O 28
Sherborne West Dorset ...8 M 31
Sherborne St. John ....20 Q 30
Sherburn Durham ....56 P 19

Sherburn *Ryedale* 51 S 21
Sherburn-in-Elmet 44 Q 22
Shere 21 S 30
Sherfield English 9 P 31
Sheriff Hutton 50 Q 21
Sheriffhales 35 M 25
Sheringham 39 X 25
Sherington 28 R 27
Shernborne 38 V 25
Sherston 19 N 29
Sherwood Forest 36 Q 24
Shetland Islands 87
Shevington 42 L 23
Shiant (Sound of) 82 A 10
Shiant Island 82 A 10
Shiel (Glen) 72 D 12
Shiel (Loch) 72 D 13
Shieldaig *Loch Gairloch* 78 C 10
Shieldaig *Loch Torridon* 78 D 11
Shieldaig (Loch) 78 C 11
Shieldhill 67 I 16
Shifnal 35 M 25
Shilbottle 63 O 17
Shildon 56 P 20
Shillay 76 W 11
Shillingford 7 J 30
Shillingstone 9 N 31
Shillington 29 S 28
Shilton *Rugby* 28 P 26
Shilton *West Oxfordshire* 19 P 28
Shimpling 31 X 26
Shin (Loch) 84 G 9
Shiney Row 56 P 19
Shinfield 20 R 29
Shipdham 38 W 26
Shiplake 20 R 29
Shipley *Salop* 35 N 26
Shipley *West Yorks.* 43 O 22
Shipston-on-Stour 27 P 27
Shipton *Bridgnorth* 26 M 26
Shipton *Cotswold* 27 O 28
Shipton *Hambleton* 50 Q 21
Shipton Moyne 19 N 29
Shipton-under-Wychwood 19 P 28
Shiptonthorpe 44 R 22
Shira (Lochan) 66 F 14
Shirebrook 36 Q 24
Shiremoor 56 P 18
Shirenewton 18 L 29
Shirley *Derbyshire* 35 O 25
Shirley *Solihull* 27 O 26
Shoadoxhurst 12 W 30
Shobdon 26 L 27
Shoeburyness 22 W 29
Shoreham 11 T 31
Shorne 22 V 29
Shotesham 39 X 26
Shotley Bridge 56 O 19
Shotley Gate 31 X 28
Shottenden 22 W 30
Shottermill 10 R 30
Shotton Colliery 57 P 19
Shotts 61 I 16
Shouldham 38 V 26
Shrewsbury 34 L 25
Shrewton 19 O 30
Shrivenham 19 P 29
Shuna Sound 65 D 15
Shurdington 27 N 28
Shurrery 85 J 8
Sibbertoft 28 Q 26
Sibford Ferris 28 P 27
Sible Hedingham 30 V 28
Sibsey 37 U 24
Sidbury 5 K 31
Siddington 19 O 28
Siddlington 43 N 24
Sidford 5 K 31
Sidinish 76 Y 11
Sidlaw Hills 68 K 14
Sidlesham 10 R 31
Sidmouth 5 K 31
Sighthill 68 K 16
Sileby 36 Q 25
Silecroft 47 K 21
Silloth 54 J 19
Silsden 49 O 22
Silver End 30 V 28
Silverdale *Lancaster* 48 L 21
Silverdale *Newcastle-under-Lyme* 35 N 24
Silverstone 28 Q 27
Silverstone Circuit 28 Q 27
Silverton 7 J 31
Simonburn 55 N 18
Simonsbath 7 I 30

Sinclair's Bay 86 K 8
Sinclairston 60 G 17
Singleton *Chichester* 10 R 31
Singleton *Fylde* 42 L 22
Sionascaig (Loch) 84 E 9
Sissinghurst 12 V 30
Sithney 2 E 33
Sittingbourne 22 W 29
Sixpenny Handley 9 N 31
Skara Brae 86 J 6
Skares 60 H 17
Skeabost 77 B 11
Skegness 38 V 24
Skellingthorpe 44 S 24
Skelmanthorpe 43 P 23
Skelmersdale 42 L 23
Skelmorlie 59 F 16
Skelpick 85 H 8
Skelton *Cleveland* 50 R 20
Skelton *Cumbria* 55 L 19
Skelwith Bridge 48 K 20
Skene 75 M 12
Skene (Loch of) 75 M 12
Skenfrith 26 L 28
Skeroblingarry 59 D 17
Skidby 44 S 22
Skiddaw 54 K 20
Skigersta 83 B 8
Skilgate 7 J 30
Skillington 37 S 25
Skinburness 54 J 19
Skipness 59 D 16
Skipport (Loch) 76 Y 12
Skipsea 51 T 22
Skipton 49 N 22
Skipton-on-Swale 50 P 21
Skipwith 44 R 22
Skirlaugh 45 T 22
Skirling 61 J 17
Skirwith 55 M 19
Skirza 86 K 8
Skokholm Island 14 E 28
Skomer Island 14 E 28
Skye (Isle of) 77 B 12
Slaggyford 55 M 19
Slaidburn 49 M 22
Slaithwaite 43 O 23
Slamannan 67 I 16
Slapin (Loch) 71 B 12
Slapton 4 J 33
Sleaford 37 S 25
Sleagill 48 M 20
Sleat (Sound of) 71 C 12
Sledmere 51 S 21
Sleekburn 56 P 18
Sleights 51 S 20
Slickly 86 K 8
Sligachan 77 B 12
Sligachan (Loch) 77 B 12
Slimbridge 19 M 28
Slindon 11 S 31
Slingsby 50 R 21
Slochd 79 I 12
Slockavullin 65 D 15
Slough 21 S 29
Sloy (Loch) 66 F 15
Slumbay 78 D 11
Slyne 48 L 21
Smailholm 62 M 17
Smailholm Tower 62 M 17
Small Dole 11 T 31
Smallfield 11 T 30
Smarden 12 W 30
Smart'Hill 12 U 30
Smedmore 9 N 32
Smithfield 55 L 19
Snaefell 46 G 21
Snainton 51 S 21
Snaith 44 Q 22
Snape 31 Y 27
Snetterton Circuit 30 W 26
Snettisham 38 V 25
Snitterfield 27 O 27
Snizort (Loch) 77 A 11
Snodland 22 V 30
Snowdon / Yr Wyddfa 33 H 24
Snowdonia National Park 33 I 24
Snowshill 27 O 27
Soa 70 Z 14
Soa Island 64 A 15
Soar (River) 36 Q 25
Soay 71 B 12
Soay Sound 71 B 12
Soham 30 V 26

Solent (The) 10 Q 31
Solihull 27 O 26
Sollas 76 X 11
Solva 14 E 28
Solway Firth 53 J 19
Somerby 36 R 25
Somercotes 36 P 24
Somerford Keynes 19 O 29
Somersham *Huntingdonshire* 29 U 26
Somersham *Mid Suffolk* 31 X 27
Somerton *Norfolk* 39 Y 25
Somerton *Oxon.* 28 Q 28
Somerton *Somerset* 8 L 30
Sompting 11 S 31
Sonning Common 20 R 29
Sopley 9 O 31
Sorbie 52 G 19
Sorisdale 71 A 13
Sorn 60 H 17
Sortat 86 K 8
Soulby 49 M 20
Sound (The) 4 H 32
Sourhope 63 N 17
South-Alloa 67 I 15
South Balloch 60 G 18
South Brent 4 I 32
South Cairn 52 E 19
South Carrine 59 C 18
South Cave 44 S 22
South Cerney 19 O 28
South Charlton 63 O 17
South Croxton 36 R 25
South Downs 11 R 31
South Elmsall 44 Q 23
South Esk (River) 75 L 13
South Ferriby 44 S 22
South Foreland 23 Y 30
South Glendale 70 Y 12
South Hanningfield 22 V 29
South Harris 76 Z 10
South Harris Forest 82 Z 10
South Hayling 10 R 31
South-Heighton 11 U 31
South Hetton 56 P 19
South Kelsey 45 S 23
South Killingholme 45 T 23
South Kirkby 44 Q 23
South Kyme 37 T 24
South Lancing 11 T 31
South Leverton 44 R 24
South Lopham 30 X 26
South-Marston 19 O 29
South Mary Bourne 20 P 30
South Mimms 21 T 28
South Molton 7 I 30
South Morar 72 C 13
South Moreton 20 Q 29
South Newington 28 P 28
South-Newton 9 O 30
South Normanton 36 P 24
South Ockendon 22 U 29
South Otterington 50 P 21
South Oxhey 21 S 29
South Petherton 8 L 31
South Petherwin 3 G 32
South Queensferry 68 J 16
South Rauceby 37 S 25
South Raynham 38 W 25
South Ronaldsay 87 L 7
South Shields 56 P 19
South Shore 42 K 22
South Stack 40 F 23
South Stainley 50 P 21
South Tawton 4 I 31
South Thoresby 45 U 24
South Uist 70 X 12
South Walls 86 K 7
South Warnborough 20 R 30
South Witham 37 S 25
South Woodham Ferrers 22 V 29
South Wootton 38 V 25
South Wraxall 19 N 29
South Zeal 4 I 31
Southam *Stratford-on-Avon* 28 P 27
Southam *Tewkesbury* 27 N 28
Southampton 10 P 31
Southborough 12 U 30
Southbourne *Dorset* 9 O 31
Southbourne *West Sussex* 10 R 31
Southend 59 D 18
Southend-on-Sea 22 W 29
Southerness 53 J 19
Southery 38 V 26
Southill 29 T 27
Southminster 22 W 29

Southport 42 K 23
Southrop 19 O 28
Southsea 10 Q 31
Southwaite 55 L 19
Southwater 11 S 30
Southwell 36 R 24
Southwick *East Northamptonshire* 29 S 26
Southwick *Sunderland* 56 P 19
Southwick *West Sussex* 11 T 31
Southwick *Widley* 10 Q 31
Southwick *Wilts.* 19 N 30
Southwold 31 Z 27
Sowerby Bridge 43 O 22
Spalding 37 T 25
Spaldwick 29 S 26
Spanish Head 46 F 21
Sparkford 8 M 30
Spaxton 8 K 30
Spean (Glen) 73 F 13
Spean Bridge 72 F 13
Speeton 51 T 21
Speldhurst 12 U 30
Spelsbury 28 P 28
Spelve (Loch) 65 C 14
Spennymoor 56 P 19
Spey (River) 73 G 12
Spey Bay 80 K 10
Speymouth Forest 80 K 11
Spilsby 37 U 24
Spinningdale 79 H 10
Spithead 10 Q 31
Spittal *Dumfries and Galloway* 52 G 19
Spittal *Highland* 85 J 8
Spittal *Northumb.* 63 O 16
Spittal *Pembrokeshire / Sir Benfro* 24 F 28
Spittal of Glenshee 74 J 13
Spixworth 39 X 25
Spofforth 50 P 22
Spondon 36 P 25
Spooner Row 39 X 26
Spott 69 M 16
Spreyton 7 I 31
Spridlington 44 S 23
Springfield 68 K 15
Springholm 53 I 18
Sproatley 45 T 22
Sprotbrough 44 Q 23
Sproughton 31 X 27
Sprouston 62 M 17
Sprowston 39 X 26
Spurn Head 45 U 23
Sronlairig Lodge 73 G 12
Sronphadruig Lodge 73 H 13
Stack (Loch) 84 F 8
Stack Island 70 Y 12
Stack Rocks 16 E 29
Staffa 64 A 14
Staffin Bay 77 B 11
Stafford 35 N 25
Stagsden 29 S 27
Staincross 43 P 23
Staindrop 56 O 20
Staines 21 S 29
Stainforth *North Yorks.* 49 N 21
Stainforth *South Yorks.* 44 Q 23
Stainton 55 L 20
Stainton-le-Vale 45 T 23
Staintondale 51 S 20
Stair *Allerdale* 54 K 20
Stair *South Ayrshire* 60 G 17
Staithes 50 R 20
Stakeford 56 P 18
Stalbridge 9 M 31
Stalham 39 Y 25
Stalisfield 22 W 30
Stalling Busk 49 N 21
Stallingborough 45 T 23
Stalmine 48 L 22
Stalybridge 43 N 23
Stamford 37 S 26
Stamford Bridge 50 R 22
Stamfordham 56 O 18
Stanbridge 29 S 28
Standford-in-the-Vale 20 P 29
Standing Stones 82 Z 9
Standish 42 M 23
Standlake 20 P 28
Standon 29 U 28
Stane 61 I 16
Stanford 13 X 30
Stanford-le-Hope 22 V 29
Stanford-on-Avon 28 Q 26
Stanghow 50 R 20
Stanhoe 38 W 25

Stanhope 55 N 19
Stanion 29 S 26
Stanley *Durham* 56 O 19
Stanley *Perthshire and Kinross* 68 J 14
Stanley *Wakefield.* 43 P 22
Stanmer Park 11 T 31
Stannington 43 P 23
Stansted Abbotts 21 U 28
Stansted Mountfitchet 30 U 28
Stanton 30 W 27
Stanton Harcourt 20 P 28
Stanton Long 26 M 26
Stanton-upon-Hine-Heath 34 M 25
Stanway 27 O 28
Stanwell 21 S 29
Stanwick 29 S 27
Staple Fitzpaine 8 K 31
Stapleford *Melton* 36 R 25
Stapleford *Notts.* 36 Q 25
Stapleford *Wilts.* 9 O 30
Staplehurst 22 V 30
Starcross 4 J 32
Start Point 4 J 33
Startforth 49 O 20
Stathern 36 R 25
Staughton Highway 29 S 27
Staunton *Forest of Dean* 27 N 28
Staunton *Monmouthshire / Sir Fynwy* 18 M 28
Staveley *Cumbria* 48 L 20
Staveley *Derbs.* 43 P 24
Staxigoe 86 K 8
Staxton 51 S 21
Staylittle 25 J 26
Staynton 16 E 28
Steart 18 K 30
Stebbing 30 V 28
Stedham 10 R 31
Steep 10 R 30
Steeple 22 W 28
Steeple Ashton 19 N 30
Steeple Aston 28 Q 28
Steeple Barton 28 P 28
Steeple Bumpstead 30 V 27
Steeple Claydon 28 R 28
Steeple Langford 9 O 30
Steeple Morden 29 T 27
Steeton 49 O 22
Stelling Minnis 23 X 30
Stenhousemuir 67 I 15
Stenness *Orkney Islands* 86 K 7
Stenness *Shetland Islands* 87 P 2
Stenton 69 M 16
Steppingley 29 S 27
Stevenage 29 T 28
Stevenston 60 F 17
Steventon 20 Q 29
Stewartby 29 S 27
Stewarton 60 G 16
Stewkley 28 R 28
Steyning 11 T 31
Steynton 16 E 28
Stichill 62 M 17
Sticker 3 F 33
Sticklepath 4 I 31
Stickney 37 U 24
Stiffkey 38 W 25
Stilligarry 76 X 12
Stillingfleet 44 Q 22
Stillington *Hambleton* 50 Q 21
Stillington *Stockton-on-Tees* 56 P 20
Stilton 29 T 26
Stirling 67 I 15
Stithians 2 E 33
Stob Choire Claurigh 72 F 13
Stobo 61 K 17
Stobs Castle 62 L 17
Stock 22 V 29
Stockbridge 10 P 30
Stocke Talmage 20 Q 28
Stockland 8 K 31
Stockland Bristol 18 K 30
Stockport 43 N 23
Stocksbridge 43 P 23
Stocksfield 56 O 19
Stockton Heath 42 M 23
Stockton-on-Tees 50 P 20
Stockton-on-Teme 27 M 27
Stockton on the Forest 50 R 22
Stoer 83 D 9
Stogumber 7 K 30
Stogursey 18 K 30
Stoke 22 V 29
Stoke Albany 28 R 26
Stoke Ash 31 X 27
Stoke-by-Nayland 30 W 28

Stoke Climsland 3 H 32
Stoke Fleming 4 J 33
Stoke Gabriel 4 J 32
Stoke Goldington 28 R 27
Stoke Hammond 28 R 28
Stoke Lacy 26 M 27
Stoke Lyne 28 Q 28
Stoke Mandeville 20 R 28
Stoke-on-Trent 35 N 24
Stoke Orchard 27 N 28
Stoke Poges 21 S 29
Stoke-St. Mary 8 K 31
Stoke-St. Michael 18 M 30
Stoke St. Milborough 26 M 26
Stoke sub Hamdon 8 L 31
Stokeham 44 R 24
Stokenchurch 20 R 29
Stokenham 4 I 33
Stokesay 26 L 26
Stokesley 50 Q 20
Stone *Bucks.* 20 R 28
Stone *Staffs.* 35 N 25
Stone Edge 36 P 24
Stonehaugh 55 N 18
Stonehaven 75 N 13
Stonehenge 9 O 30
Stonehouse *Glos.* 19 N 28
Stonehouse *South Lanarkshire* 61 I 16
Stoneleigh 28 P 26
Stonesfield 20 P 28
Stoney Cross 9 P 31
Stoney Stanton 36 Q 26
Stoneybridge 76 X 12
Stoneykirk 52 F 19
Stoneywood 75 N 12
Stony Stratford 28 R 27
Stornoway 82 A 9
Storr (The) 77 B 11
Storrington 11 S 31
Stort (River) 29 U 28
Stotfold 29 T 27
Stottesdon 26 M 26
Stoughton 10 R 31
Stoul 72 C 13
Stoulton 27 N 27
Stour (River) *English Channel* 9 N 31
Stour (River) *North Sea* 30 V 27
Stour (River) *R. Severn* 27 N 26
Stourbridge 27 N 26
Stourhead House 9 N 30
Stourport-on-Severn 27 N 26
Stourton Caundle 9 M 31
Stow 62 L 16
Stow-on-the-Wold 27 O 28
Stowbridge 38 V 26
Stowe-by-Chartley 35 O 25
Stowe School 28 Q 27
Stowmarket 30 W 27
Stowupland 30 X 27
Straad 59 E 16
Strachan 75 M 12
Strachur 66 E 15
Stradbroke 31 X 27
Stradishall 30 V 27
Stradsett 38 V 26
Straiton 60 G 18
Straloch 74 J 13
Stranraer 52 E 19
Strata Florida Abbey 25 I 27
Stratfield Saye 20 Q 29
Stratford St. Mary 30 W 28
Stratford-upon-Avon 27 O 27
Strath Brora 85 H 9
Strath Dearn 79 I 11
Strath Halladale 85 I 8
Strath Isla 80 K 11
Strath More 78 E 10
Strath Mulzie 78 F 10
Strath of Kildonan 85 I 9
Strath Oykel 84 F 10
Strath Skinsdale 85 H 9
Strath Tay 68 J 14
Strathallan 67 I 15
Strathan 72 E 13
Strathardle 74 J 13
Strathaven 60 H 16
Strathblane 67 H 16
Strathbogie 80 L 11
Strathbraan 67 I 14
Strathcanaird 84 E 10
Strathcarron 78 D 11
Strathcoil 65 C 14
Strathconon 78 F 11
Strathconon Forest 78 F 11

A
B
C
D
E
F
G
H
I
J
K
L
M
N
O
P
Q
R
S
T
U
V
W
X
Y
Z

Tullibody 67 I15
Tullymurdoch 74 K14
Tumble 15 H28
Tummel (Loch) 73 I13
Tunstall
  East Riding of Yorkshire ...45 T22
Tunstall Staffs. 35 N24
Tunstall Suffolk 31 Y27
Tur Langton 36 R26
Turnberry 59 F18
Turnditch 35 P24
Turret
  (Loch and Reservoir) 67 I14
Turriff 81 M11
Turvey 29 S27
Tusker Rock 17 I29
Tutbury 35 O25
Tuxford 44 R24
Twatt 86 K6
Tweed (River) 61 J17
Tweeddale 61 J17
Tweedmouth 63 N16
Tweedsmuir Hills 61 J17
Twemlow Green 35 N24
Twickenham 21 S29
Two Dales 35 P24
Twyford Berks. 20 R29
Twyford Hants. 10 Q30
Twyford Leics. 36 R25
Twynholm 53 H19
Twynllanan 25 I28
Tydd-St. Giles 37 U25
Tydd St. Mary 37 U25
Tyddewi / St. David's 14 E28
Tyldesley 42 M23
Tylorstown 17 J29
Tyne (River) 56 P19
Tynehead 62 L16
Tynemouth 56 P18
Tynewydd 17 J29
Tynron 53 I18
Tythegston 17 J29
Tytherington 18 M29
Tywardreath 3 F32
Tywi (River) 25 I27
Tywyn 33 H26

U
Ubiey 18 L30
Uckfield 11 U31
Uddingston 60 H16
Udimore 12 V31
Uffculme 7 K31
Uffington 37 S26
Ufford 31 Y27
Ugadale Bay 59 D17
Ugborough 4 I32
Ugbrooke House 4 J32
Ugthorpe 50 R20
Uig Highland 77 A11
Uig Western Isles 82 Y9
Uisg (Loch) 65 C14
Uiskevagh (Loch) 76 Y11
Ulbster 86 K8
Ulceby East Lindsey 45 U24
Ulceby North Lincolnshire ...45 T23
Ulcombe 22 V30
Uldale 54 K19
Uley 19 N28
Ulgham 56 P18
Ullapool 78 E10
Ulleskelf 44 Q22
Ullesthorpe 28 Q26
Ullinish 77 A11
Ullock 54 J20
Ullswater 48 L20
Ulpha 47 K21
Ulsta 87 Q2
Ulva 64 B14
Ulverston 48 K21
Unapool 84 E9
Union Mills 46 G21
Unst 87 R1
Upavon 19 O30
Upchurch 22 V29
Uphall 68 J16
Uphill 18 L30
Upleadon 27 M28
Uplyme 5 L31
Upottery 8 K31
Upper Arley 27 M26
Upper Badcall 84 E9
Upper Beeding 11 T31
Upper Bighouse 85 I8
Upper Broughton 36 R25
Upper Chapel 25 J27
Upper Chute 20 P30

Upper Dicker 12 U31
Upper Hale 20 R30
Upper Heyford 28 Q28
Upper Hindhope 62 M17
Upper Knockando 80 J11
Upper Loch Torridon ...78 D11
Upper Poppleton 50 Q22
Upper Sandaig 72 D12
Upper Tean 35 O25
Uppertown 86 K7
Uppingham 36 R26
Upton Dorset 9 N31
Upton Notts. 36 R24
Upton Vale of White Horse ..20 Q29
Upton Wakefield 44 Q23
Upton West Somerset 7 J30
Upton Grey 20 Q30
Upton House 28 P27
Upton Magna 34 M25
Upton Noble 9 M30
Upton Scudamore 19 N30
Upton-upon-Severn 27 N27
Upwell 38 U26
Upwood 29 T26
Urchfont 19 O30
Ure (River) 50 Q21
Urigill (Loch) 84 F9
Urmston 42 M23
Urquhart 80 K11
Urquhart (Glen) 79 G11
Urquhart Castle 79 G12
Urrahag (Loch) 82 A8
Ushaw Moor 56 P19
Usk / Brynbuga 18 L28
Usk (River) 18 K28
Uttoxeter 35 O25
Uyea 87 R2
Uyeasound 87 R1

V
Vallay Strand 76 X11
Valle Crucis 34 K25
Valley 40 G23
Valtos 82 Z9
Vatersay 70 X13
Vatten 77 A11
Ve Skerries 87 O2
Venachar (Loch) 67 H15
Ventnor 10 Q32
Verham Dean 20 P30
Verulamium 21 S28
Verwood 9 O31
Veryan 3 F33
Veyatie (Loch) 84 E9
Vindolanda 55 M19
Voe 87 Q2
Voil (Loch) 67 G14
Vowchurch 26 L27
Vyrnwy (Lake) 33 J25

W
Waddesdon 20 R28
Waddingham 44 S23
Waddington Lancs. 42 M22
Waddington Lincs. 37 S24
Wadebridge 3 F32
Wadhurst 12 U30
Wag 85 I9
Wainfleet All Saints 38 U24
Wainstalls 43 O22
Wakefield 43 P22
Wakerley 37 S26
Wakes Colne 30 W28
Walberswick 31 Y27
Walcott 37 T24
Walden Head 49 N21
Walderslade 22 V29
Waldringfield 31 X27
Waldron 12 U31
Walesby 44 R24
Walford 34 L25
Walgherton 34 M24
Walgrave 28 R26
Walkden 42 M23
Walkeringham 44 R23
Walkern 29 T28
Wall 35 O26
Wallace Monument 67 I15
Wallasey 42 K23
Wallend 22 W29
Wallingford 20 Q29
Wallington House 56 O18
Wallsend 56 P18
Wallyford 69 K16
Walney (Isle of) 47 K21
Walpole 31 Y27

Walpole St. Andrew 38 U25
Walpole St. Peter 38 U25
Walsall 35 O26
Walsden 43 N22
Walsham le Willows 30 W27
Walshford 50 P22
Walston 61 J16
Waltham Kent 23 X30
Waltham North East Lincs. ..45 T23
Waltham Abbey 21 U28
Waltham Forest
  London Borough 21 T29
Waltham-on-the-Wolds 36 R25
Walton Carlisle 55 L19
Walton Leeds 50 Q22
Walton Powys 26 K27
Walton-East 24 F28
Walton-in-Gordano 18 L29
Walton-le-Dale 42 M22
Walton-on-Thames 21 S29
Walton-on-the-Naze 31 X28
Walton-Upon-Trent 35 O25
Walworth 49 P20
Wanborough 19 O29
Wandsworth
  London Borough 21 T29
Wangford 31 Y26
Wanlockhead 61 I17
Wansford
  East Riding of Yorkshire ...51 S22
Wansford Peterborough ...37 S26
Wanstrow 9 M30
Wantage 20 P29
Wappenham 28 Q27
Warboys 29 T26
Warbstow 6 G31
Warcop 49 M20
Wardington 28 Q27
Wardour Castle 9 N30
Ware 21 T28
Wareham 9 N31
Wargrave 20 R29
Wark near Coldstream ...63 N17
Wark near Hexham 55 N18
Wark Forest 55 M18
Warkworth 63 P17
Warley 27 O26
Warlingham 21 T30
Warmington
  East Northamptonshire ...29 S26
Warmington
  Stratford-on-Avon ...28 P27
Warminster 19 N30
Warmsworth 44 Q23
Warmwell 9 M31
Warnborough 20 R30
Warnford 10 Q30
Warnham 11 S30
Warren 43 N24
Warren (The) 13 X30
Warrington 42 M23
Warsash 10 Q31
Warslow 35 O24
Warsop 36 Q24
Warter 51 R22
Warton Ainwick 63 O18
Warton near Morecambe ..48 L21
Warton near Preston ...42 L22
Warwick 27 P27
Warwick Bridge 55 L19
Wasbister 86 K6
Wasdale Head 47 K20
Wash (The) 38 U25
Washington
  Tyne and Wear ...56 P19
Washington West Sussex 11 S31
Wast Water 47 K20
Watchet 17 K30
Watchfield 19 P29
Watchgate 48 L20
Water Orton 27 O26
Waterbeach 30 U27
Waterbeck 54 K18
Watergate Bay 2 E32
Waterhead 74 L13
Waterhouses 35 O24
Wateringbury 22 V30
Waterlooville 10 Q31
Waternish Point 77 A11
Waters Upton 34 M25
Waterside 60 G17
Waterstein 76 Z11
Watford Daventry ...28 Q27
Watford Watford ...21 S29
Wath 50 P21
Wath-upon-Dearne 44 P23
Watlington 20 Q29

Watten 85 K8
Watton Breckland 38 W26
Watton
  East Riding of Yorkshire ...51 S22
Watton at Stone 29 T28
Waunfawr 33 H24
Waveney (River) 31 Y26
Waverton Allerdale 54 K19
Waverton Chester 34 L24
Wawne 45 S22
Wear (River) 56 O20
Weardale 55 N19
Weasenham St. Peter 38 W25
Weaver (River) 34 M24
Weaverthorpe 51 S21
Wedmore 18 L30
Wednesbury 35 N26
Wednesfield 35 N26
Weedon-Bec 28 Q27
Week St. Mary 6 G31
Weeley 31 X28
Weem 73 I14
Weeting 30 V26
Weeton 42 L22
Welburn 50 R21
Welby 37 S25
Welcombe 6 G31
Welford Daventry ...28 Q26
Welford Stratford-on-Avon ...27 O27
Welford West Berkshire ...20 P29
Welham Green 21 T28
Well 50 P21
Welland 27 N27
Welland (River) 37 T25
Wellesbourne 27 P27
Wellingborough 29 R27
Wellington
  Herefordshire ...26 L27
Wellington Salop 34 M25
Wellington Somerset 8 K31
Wellow
  Bath and North East ...19 M30
Wellow
  Newark and Sherwood ...36 R24
Wells 18 M30
Wells-next-the-Sea 38 W25
Wells of Ythan 81 M11
Welney 38 U26
Welsh Newton 26 L28
Welshampton 34 L25
Welshpool / Trallwng 34 K26
Welton Allerdale 54 K19
Welton Daventry ...28 Q27
Welton West Lindsey ...44 S24
Welton-le-Wold 45 T23
Welwyn 21 T28
Welwyn Garden City 21 T28
Wem 34 L25
Wembdon 8 K30
Wembley 21 T29
Wembury 4 H33
Wembworthy 7 I31
Wemyss Bay 59 F16
Wendens Ambo 30 U27
Wendlebury 28 Q28
Wendover 20 R28
Wendron 2 E33
Wenlock Edge 26 L26
Wennington 48 M21
Wensley 49 O21
Wensleydale 49 O21
Wentbridge 44 Q23
Wentnor 26 L26
Wentworth 43 P23
Wenvoe 18 K29
Weobley
  Hereford and Worcester ..26 L27
Wereham 38 V26
Werrington 6 G32
West Alvington 4 I33
West Auckland 56 O20
West-Barns 69 M16
West Bay 8 M32
West Bergholt 30 W28
West-Bradenham 38 W26
West Bridgford 36 Q25
West Bromwich 27 O26
West-Buckland
  North Devon ...7 I30
West-Buckland
  Taunton Deane ...8 K31
West Butterwick 44 R23
West Calder 61 J16
West Camel 8 M30
West Charleton 4 I33
West Chevington 63 P18
West Chiltington 11 S31

West-Chinnock 8 L31
West Coker 8 L31
West Dean 9 P30
West-Dereham 38 V26
West Down 7 H30
West End 10 Q31
West Farleigh 22 V30
West-Felton 34 L25
West-Firle 11 U31
West Geirinish 76 X11
West-Grinstead 11 T31
West Hanningfield 22 V28
West Harptree 18 M30
West Heath 20 R30
West Heslerton 51 S21
West-Hill 5 K31
West Hoathly 11 T30
West-Huntspill 18 L30
West Kilbride 59 F16
West Kingsdown 22 U29
West Kirby 41 K22
West Langwell 85 H9
West Lavington 19 O30
West Linton 61 J16
West Loch Roag 82 Z9
West Loch Tarbert
  Argyll and Bute ...59 D16
West Loch Tarbert
  Western Isles ...82 Z10
West Looe 3 G32
West Lulworth 9 N32
West Lutton 51 S21
West Malling 22 V30
West Malvern 27 M27
West Meon 10 Q30
West Mersea 22 W28
West Moors 9 O31
West-Overton 19 O29
West Putford 6 G31
West-Quantoxhead 8 K30
West Rainton 56 P19
West Runton 39 X25
West-Stafford 9 M31
West Strathan 84 G8
West Tanfield 50 P21
West-Tarbert 59 D16
West Thorney 10 R31
West Town 18 L29
West-Tytherley 9 P30
West Walton 37 U25
West Wellow 9 P31
West Wickham 21 T29
West Winch 38 V25
West Wittering 10 R31
West Witton 49 O21
West Woodburn 55 N18
West Wycombe 20 R29
Westbourne 10 R31
Westbury Cheshire 34 L25
Westbury Wilts. 19 N30
Westbury-on-Severn 19 M28
Westcliff 22 W29
Westcott 21 S30
Westenhanger 13 X30
Wester Ross 78 D11
Westerdale Highland 85 J8
Westerdale Scarborough ...50 R20
Westerham 21 U30
Westerleigh 19 M29
Western Cleddau 24 E28
Westfield Highland 85 J8
Westfield Rother 12 V31
Westfield West Lothian ...67 I16
Westgate-on-Sea 23 Y29
Westham 12 U31
Westhoughton 42 M23
Westleton 31 Y27
Westmeston 11 T31
Westmill 29 T28
Westnewton 54 J19
Weston
  North Hertfordshire ...29 T28
Weston South Holland ...37 T25
Weston
  South Northamptonshire ...28 Q27
Weston Staffs. 35 N25
Weston-by-Welland 28 R26
Weston Favell 28 R27
Weston-on-the-Green 28 Q28
Weston-on-Trent 36 P25
Weston Rhyn 34 K25
Weston-super-Mare 18 L29
Weston Turville 20 R28
Weston-under-Lizard 35 N25
Weston-under-Penyard 26 M28
Westonbirt 19 N29

Westonzoyland 8 L30
Westray 86 K6
Westruther 62 M16
Westward 54 K19
Westward Ho 6 H30
Westwood 19 N30
Wetheral 55 L19
Wetherby 50 P22
Wetheringsett 31 X27
Wethersfield 30 V28
Wetwang 51 S21
Wey (River) 10 R30
Weybourne 39 X25
Weybridge 21 S29
Weyhill 20 P30
Weymouth 8 M32
Whaddon 28 R28
Whaley Bridge 43 O24
Whalley 42 M22
Whalsay 87 R2
Whalton 56 O18
Whaplode 37 T25
Whaplode Drove 37 T25
Wharfe (River) 44 Q22
Wharfedale 49 O22
Whatlington 12 V31
Whatsandwell 36 P24
Whauphill 52 G19
Whaw 49 N20
Wheathampstead 21 T28
Wheatley Notts. 44 R23
Wheatley Oxon. 20 Q28
Wheatley Hill 56 P19
Wheaton Aston 35 N25
Wheldrake 50 R22
Whepstead 30 W27
Whernside 49 M21
Wherwell 10 P30
Whickham 56 O19
Whimple 7 J31
Whipsnade 21 S28
Whissendine 36 R25
Whissonsett 38 W25
Whitburn South Tyneside ...57 P19
Whitburn West Lothian ...61 I16
Whitby 51 S20
Whitchurch
  Basingstoke and Deane ..20 P30
Whitchurch
  Bath and N.E. Somerset ..18 M29
Whitchurch Bucks. 28 R28
Whitchurch
  Caerdydd / Cardiff ...18 K29
Whitchurch Devon 4 H32
Whitchurch
  Heref. and Worc. ...18 M28
Whitchurch Oxon. 20 Q29
Whitchurch Salop 34 L25
White Coomb 61 K17
White Horse Hill 20 P29
White Scarcaves 49 M21
White Waltham 20 R29
Whitebridge 73 G12
Whitecairns 75 N12
Whitchurch Canonicorum ...5 L31
Whitefield 42 N23
Whitehall 87 M6
Whitehaven 47 J20
Whitehill 10 R30
Whitehills 81 M10
Whitehouse
  Aberdeenshire ...75 M12
Whitehouse
  Argyll and Bute ...59 D16
Whitekirk 69 M15
Whiten Head 84 G8
Whiteness Sands 79 I10
Whiteparish 9 P30
Whiterashes 81 N12
Whitermire 79 I11
Whitesand Bay Cornwall ...2 C33
Whitesand Bay
  Pembrokes ...14 E28
Whiteshill 19 N28
Whiteside 55 M18
Whitewell 49 M22
Whitewreath 80 K11
Whitfield Dover 23 X30
Whitfield
  South Northamptonshire ..28 Q27
Whitfield Tynedale 55 M19
Whitgift 44 R22
Whithorn 52 G19
Whiting Bay 59 E17
Whitland 15 G28
Whitley 20 R29
Whitley Bay 56 P18

A B C D E F G H I J K L M N O P Q R S T U V W X Y Z

A B C D E F G H I J K L M N O P Q R S T U V W X Y Z

Whitley Bridge .... 44 Q 22
Whitley Chapel .... 55 N 19
Whitminster .... 19 N 28
Whitmore .... 35 N 25
Whitnash .... 28 P 27
Whitsand Bay .... 3 H 32
Whitstable .... 23 X 29
Whitstone .... 6 G 31
Whittingham .... 63 O 17
Whittington Derbs. .... 43 P 24
Whittington King's Lynn
    and West Norfolk ...... 38 V 26
Whittington Lancaster .... 48 M 21
Whittington Shrops. .... 34 L 25
Whittle le Woods .... 42 M 22
Whittlebury .... 28 R 27
Whittlesey .... 37 T 26
Whittlesford .... 29 U 27
Whitton North Lincolnshire .. 44 S 22
Whitton Powys .... 26 K 27
Whitton Suffolk .... 31 X 27
Whittonstall .... 56 O 19
Whitwell Derbs. .... 44 Q 24
Whitwell I.O.W. .... 10 Q 32
Whitwell-on-the-Hill ..... 50 R 21
Whitwick .... 36 P 25
Whitworth .... 43 N 23
Whixall .... 34 L 25
Whygate .... 55 M 18
Wiay Highland .... 77 A 11
Wiay Western Isles .... 76 Y 11
Wibtoft .... 28 Q 26
Wick Bro Morgannwg /
    The Vale of Glamorgan .... 17 J 29
Wick Highland .... 86 K 8
Wick South Glos. .... 19 M 29
Wicken Cambs. .... 28 R 27
Wicken Northants. .... 30 U 27
Wickenby .... 45 S 24
Wickersley .... 44 Q 23
Wickford .... 22 V 29
Wickham .... 10 Q 31
Wickham Market .... 31 Y 27
Wickhambrook .... 30 V 27
Wickwar .... 19 M 29
Widdrington .... 63 P 18
Wide Open .... 56 P 18
Widecombe-in-the-Moor ..... 4 I 32
Wideford Hill Cairn ...... 86 K 7
Widemouth Bay .... 6 G 31
Widford .... 21 U 28
Widnes .... 42 L 23
Wigan .... 42 M 23
Wiggenhall
    St. Mary Magdalen ... 38 V 25
Wigglesworth .... 49 N 21
Wight (Isle of) .... 10 P 32
Wighton .... 38 W 25
Wigmore Herefordshire .. 26 L 27
Wigmore Medway .... 22 V 29
Wigston .... 36 Q 26
Wigton .... 54 K 19
Wigtown .... 52 G 19

Wigtown Bay .... 53 H 19
Wilberfoss .... 50 R 22
Wilcot .... 19 O 29
Wild Animal Kingdom ..... 29 S 28
Wilkhaven .... 79 I 10
Wilkieston .... 61 J 16
Willand .... 7 J 31
Willenhall Coventry ...... 28 P 26
Willenhall Walsall .... 35 N 26
Willerby .... 45 S 22
Willersey .... 27 O 27
Willingdon .... 12 U 31
Willingham .... 29 U 27
Willingham Forest .... 45 T 23
Willington Beds. .... 29 S 27
Willington Derbs. .... 35 P 25
Willington Durham .... 56 O 19
Williton .... 7 K 30
Willoughby .... 28 Q 27
Wilmcote .... 27 O 27
Wilmington East Essex .... 12 U 31
Wilmington Kent .... 22 U 29
Wilmslow .... 43 N 24
Wiloughby .... 45 U 24
Wilpshire .... 42 M 22
Wilsford .... 37 S 25
Wilstead .... 29 S 27
Wilton .... 9 O 30
Wimbledon .... 21 T 29
Wimblington .... 29 U 26
Wimborne Minster .... 9 O 31
Wimborne St. Giles .... 9 O 31
Wincanton .... 9 M 30
Wincham .... 42 M 24
Winchburgh .... 68 J 16
Winchcombe .... 27 O 28
Winchelsea .... 12 W 31
Winchester .... 10 Q 30
Winchfield .... 20 R 30
Wincle .... 35 N 24
Windermere .... 48 L 20
Windhill .... 79 G 11
Windlesham .... 21 S 29
Windrush .... 19 O 28
Windrush (River) .... 19 O 28
Windsor .... 21 S 29
Windsor Great Park ...... 21 S 29
Windygates .... 68 K 15
Winestead .... 45 T 22
Winfarthing .... 31 X 26
Winford .... 18 M 29
Winforton .... 26 K 27
Winfrith Newburgh .... 9 N 32
Wing .... 28 R 28
Wingate .... 57 P 19
Wingerworth .... 36 P 24
Wingfield near Alfreton ....36 P 24
Wingfield
    near Chesterfield ... 36 P 24
Wingham .... 23 X 30
Wingrave .... 28 R 28
Winkfield .... 21 R 29
Winkleigh .... 7 I 31

Winksley .... 50 P 21
Winmarleigh .... 48 L 22
Winnersh .... 20 R 29
Winscombe .... 18 L 30
Winsford Cheshire .... 34 M 24
Winsford Somerset .... 7 J 30
Winsham .... 8 L 31
Winshill .... 35 P 25
Winslow .... 28 R 28
Winster Derbyshire Dales ... 35 P 24
Winster South Lakeland ...... 48 L 20
Winston .... 49 O 20
Winstone .... 19 N 28
Winterborne Kingston ...... 9 N 31
Winterborne Stickland ..... 9 N 31
Winterborne Whitechurch ... 9 N 31
Winterbourne .... 18 M 29
Winterbourne Abbas .... 5 M 31
Winterbourne Dauntsey ...... 9 O 30
Winterbourne Monkton ...... 19 O 29
Winterbourne Stoke .... 9 O 30
Winteringham .... 44 S 22
Winterton .... 44 S 23
Winterton-on-Sea .... 39 Z 25
Winton .... 49 N 20
Wintringham .... 51 S 21
Winwick .... 29 S 26
Wirksworth .... 35 P 24
Wirral .... 42 K 24
Wisbech .... 37 U 25
Wisbech-St. Mary .... 37 U 26
Wisborough Green .... 11 S 30
Wishaw .... 61 I 16
Wisley .... 21 S 30
Wissey (River) .... 38 V 26
Wistanstow .... 26 L 26
Wistanswick .... 34 M 25
Wistaston .... 34 M 24
Wiston
    Dumfries and Galloway .... 61 J 17
Wiston Pembrokeshire /
    Sir Benfro .... 16 F 28
Wistow .... 44 Q 22
Witchampton .... 9 N 31
Witchford .... 30 U 26
Witham .... 22 V 28
Witham (River) .... 37 T 24
Witham Friary .... 9 M 30
Witheridge .... 7 I 31
Withern .... 45 U 24
Withernsea .... 45 U 22
Withernwick .... 45 T 22
Withington Cotswold ..... 19 O 28
Withington Herefordshire .. 26 M 27
Withnell .... 42 M 22
Withycombe .... 4 J 32
Withypool .... 7 J 30
Witley .... 11 S 30
Witney .... 20 P 28
Witsome .... 63 N 16
Wittering .... 37 S 26
Wittersham .... 12 W 30
Witton le Wear .... 56 O 19

Wiveliscombe .... 7 K 30
Wivelsfield .... 11 T 31
Wivenhoe .... 30 W 28
Wiveton .... 38 X 25
Woburn .... 29 S 28
Woburn Abbey .... 29 S 28
Woburn Sands .... 29 S 27
Woking .... 21 S 30
Wokingham .... 20 R 29
Wold Newton .... 45 T 23
Woldingham .... 21 T 30
Wollaston .... 29 S 27
Wollaton Hall .... 36 Q 25
Wolsingham .... 56 O 19
Wolston .... 28 P 26
Wolvercote .... 20 Q 28
Wolverhampton .... 35 N 26
Wolverton .... 28 R 27
Wolvey .... 28 P 26
Wolviston .... 57 Q 20
Wombleton .... 50 R 21
Wombourne .... 27 N 26
Wombwell .... 43 P 23
Womersley .... 44 Q 22
Wonersh .... 21 S 30
Wood Dalling .... 39 X 25
Woodborough .... 36 Q 24
Woodbridge .... 31 X 27
Woodbury .... 4 J 31
Woodchurch .... 12 W 30
Woodcote .... 20 Q 29
Woodford Halse .... 28 Q 27
Woodhall Spa .... 37 T 24
Woodham Ferrers .... 22 V 29
Woodhouse .... 43 P 23
Woodhouse Eaves .... 36 Q 25
Woodingdean .... 11 T 31
Woodland .... 56 O 20
Woodlands .... 9 O 31
Woodley .... 20 R 29
Woodnesborough .... 23 X 30
Woodseaves .... 35 N 25
Woodsetts .... 44 Q 23
Woodsford .... 9 M 31
Woodstock .... 20 P 28
Woodton .... 39 Y 26
Woody Bay .... 17 I 30
Wookey .... 18 L 30
Wookey Hole .... 18 L 30
Wool .... 9 N 31
Woolacombe .... 16 H 30
Wooler .... 63 N 17
Woolfardisworthy .... 6 G 31
Woolhampton .... 20 Q 29
Woolpit .... 30 W 27
Woolsthorpe .... 36 R 25
Woolverton .... 63 O 17
Woore .... 35 M 25
Wootton .... 29 R 29
Wootton Bedford .... 29 S 27
Wootton Northampton .... 28 R 27
Wootton Bassett .... 19 O 29
Wootton Brige .... 10 Q 31
Wootton Courtenay .... 17 J 30
Wootton Rivers .... 19 O 29

Wootton-Wawen .... 27 O 27
Worcester .... 27 N 27
Workington .... 53 J 20
Worksop .... 44 Q 24
Worle .... 18 L 29
Wormbridge .... 26 L 28
Wormingford .... 30 W 28
Worminghall .... 20 Q 28
Wormit .... 69 L 14
Worms Head .... 15 H 29
Wormsley .... 26 L 27
Worplesdon .... 21 S 30
Worsbrough .... 43 P 23
Worsley .... 42 M 23
Worsthorne .... 43 N 22
Worth Matravers .... 9 N 32
Worthen .... 34 L 26
Worthenbury .... 34 L 24
Worthing .... 11 S 31
Wortley .... 43 P 23
Worton .... 19 N 30
Wortwell .... 31 Y 26
Wotton-under-Edge .... 19 M 29
Wrafton .... 6 H 30
Wragby East Lindsey ..... 45 T 24
Wragby Wakefield .... 43 P 23
Wrangle .... 37 U 24
Wrawby .... 44 S 23
Wray .... 48 M 21
Wrea Green .... 42 L 22
Wreay .... 55 L 19
Wrecsam / Wrexham .... 34 L 24
Wrekenton .... 56 P 19
Wremtham .... 31 Z 26
Wrenbury .... 34 M 24
Wrestlingworth .... 29 T 27
Wrexham / Wrecsam .... 34 L 24
Wrington .... 18 L 29
Writtle .... 22 V 28
Wroot .... 44 R 23
Wrotham .... 22 U 30
Wroughton .... 19 O 29
Wroxall .... 10 Q 32
Wroxham .... 39 Y 25
Wroxton .... 28 P 27
Wyberton .... 37 T 25
Wyche .... 27 M 27
Wye .... 22 W 30
Wye (River) .... 26 M 28
Wykeham .... 51 S 21
Wylam .... 56 O 19
Wylye .... 9 O 30
Wymeswold .... 36 Q 25
Wymondham Leics. .... 36 R 25
Wymondham Norfolk ...... 39 X 26
Wyre .... 87 L 6
Wysall .... 36 Q 25
Wyvis Lodge .... 79 G 10

Y

Y-Fenni / Abergavenny ...... 18 L 28
Y Ffor .... 32 G 25
Y Llethr .... 33 I 25

Y Rhiw .... 32 G 25
Yafforth .... 50 P 20
Yalding .... 22 V 30
Yapton .... 11 S 31
Yardley Gobion .... 28 R 27
Yardley Hastings .... 28 R 27
Yare (River) .... 38 W 26
Yarm .... 50 P 20
Yarmouth .... 10 P 31
Yarnton .... 20 Q 28
Yarrow .... 62 K 17
Yate .... 19 M 29
Yateley .... 20 R 29
Yatton .... 18 L 29
Yatton Keynell .... 19 N 29
Yaxham .... 38 W 26
Yaxley .... 29 T 26
Yeadon .... 43 O 22
Yealand Conyers .... 48 L 21
Yealmpton .... 4 I 32
Yedingham .... 51 S 21
Yelden .... 29 S 27
Yell .... 87 Q 1
Yelvertoft .... 28 Q 26
Yelverton .... 4 H 32
Yeolmbridge .... 6 G 32
Yeovil .... 8 M 31
Yeovilton .... 8 M 30
Yesnaby .... 86 J 6
Yetminster .... 8 M 31
Yetts o' Muckhart .... 68 J 15
Yielden .... 29 S 27
Ynys / Lochtyn .... 15 G 27
Ynysddu .... 18 K 29
Ynyslas .... 25 H 26
Ynysybwl .... 17 J 29
Yockenthwaite .... 49 N 21
Yockleton .... 34 L 25
York .... 50 Q 22
Yorkletts .... 23 X 30
Yorkley .... 18 M 28
Yorkshire Dales
    National Park .... 49 N 21
Yorkshire Wolds .... 51 S 21
Youlgreave .... 35 O 24
Yoxall .... 35 O 25
Yoxford .... 31 Y 27
Yr Wyddfa / Snowdon ..... 33 H 24
Yr Wyddgrug / Mold .... 34 K 24
Ysbyty Ifan .... 33 I 24
Ystalyfera .... 17 I 28
Ystrad-Aeron .... 25 H 27
Ystrad Mynach .... 18 K 29
Ystradfellte .... 17 J 28
Ystradgynlais .... 17 I 28
Ystradowen .... 17 J 29
Ystwyth (River) .... 25 H 26

Z

Zennor .... 2 D 33

A

Aasleagh .... 105 D 7
Abbert .... 106 F 7
Abbey .... 100 G 8
Abbeydorney .... 93 C 10
Abbeyfeale .... 93 E 10
Abbeylara .... 107 J 6
Abbeyleix /
  Mainistir Laoise .... 101 J 9
Abbeyshrule .... 107 J 7
Abington .... 94 G 10
Achill .... 104 C 6
Achill Head .... 110 B 6
Achill Island .... 104 B 6
Achill Sound .... 104 C 6
Achillbeg Island ...... 104 C 6
Achonry .... 112 G 5
Aclare .... 112 F 5
Acoose (Lough) .... 89 C 11
Adamstown .... 96 L 10
Adare .... 94 F 10
Adrigole .... 89 C 12
Aghaboe .... 101 J 9
Aghabullogue .... 90 F 12
Aghada .... 90 H 12
Aghadiffin .... 106 F 6
Aghadoe .... 89 D 11
Aghadoon .... 110 B 5
Aghadowey .... 118 M 2
Aghagallon .... 114 N 4
Aghagower .... 105 D 6
Aghalane .... 113 J 5
Aghalee .... 114 N 4
Aghamore *Leitrim* ... 107 I 6
Aghamore *Mayo* ...... 105 F 6
Aghamuck .... 106 H 6
Aghavannagh .... 103 M 9
Aghavas .... 107 I 6
Aghaville .... 89 D 13
Aghinlig .... 114 M 4
Aghla Mountain .... 116 H 3
Aghleam .... 110 B 5
Aghnablaney .... 113 I 4
Aghnacliff .... 107 J 6
Aghnamullen .... 108 L 5
Aghowle .... 96 M 9
Agivey .... 118 M 2
Aglish *Tipperary* ..... 100 H 8
Aglish *Waterford* ..... 91 I 11
Agnew's Hill .... 115 O 3
Ahakista .... 89 D 13
Ahalia (Loughs) .... 105 D 7
Ahascragh .... 106 G 7
Ahenny .... 95 J 10
Aherla .... 90 F 12
Aherlow .... 94 H 10
Aherlow (Glen of) ..... 95 H 10
Ahoghill .... 118 M 3
Aillwee Cave .... 99 E 8
Ailt an Chorráin /
  Burtonport .... 116 G 3
Aird Mhór / Ardmore .. 91 I 12
Akeragh Lough .... 93 C 10
Aldergrove .... 115 N 4
Allaghaun .... 93 E 10
Allen .... 102 L 8
Allen (Bog of) .... 102 K 8
Allen (Lough) .... 112 H 5
Allenwood .... 102 L 8
Allihies .... 88 B 13
Allistragh .... 114 L 4
Alloon Lower .... 106 G 7
Allow .... 94 F 11
Allua (Lough) .... 89 E 12
Altagowlan .... 112 H 5
Altan Lough .... 117 H 2
Altnamackan .... 114 M 5
Altnapaste .... 117 I 3
An Blascaod Mór /
  Blasket Islands ..... 92 A 11
An Bun Beag / Bunbeg 116 H 2
An Caisleán Nua /
  Newcastle West ..... 93 E 10
An Caisleán Riabhach /
  Castlerea .... 106 G 6
An Chathair / Caher ... 95 I 10
An Cheathrú Rua /
  Carraroe .... 98 D 8
An Chloich Mhóir /
  Cloghmore .... 104 C 6
An Clochán / Clifden .. 104 B 7
An Clochán / Cloghan
  Donegal .... 117 I 3
An Clochán Liath /
  Dungloe .... 116 G 3
An Cloigeann / Cleegan 104 B 7

An Cóbh / Cobh .... 90 H 12
An Coimín / Commeen .. 117 I 3
An Coireán / Waterville .. 88 B 12
An Corrán / Currane ... 104 C 6
An Creagán /
  Mount Bellew .... 106 G 7
An Daingean / Dingle .. 92 B 11
An Dúchoraidh /
  Doocharry .... 116 H 3
An Fál Carrach /
  Falcarragh .... 117 H 2
An Fhairche / Clonbur .. 105 D 7
An Geata Mór .... 110 B 5
An Gleann Garbh /
  Glengarriff .... 89 D 12
An Gort / Gort .... 99 F 8
An Gort Mór / Gortmore .. 105 D 7
An Leacht / Lahinch .. 98 D 9
An Longfort / Longford .. 107 I 6
An Mám / Maam Cross .. 105 D 7
An Mhala Raithní /
  Mulrany .... 104 C 6
An Móta / Moate ...... 101 I 7
An Muileann gCearr /
  Mullingar .... 107 J 7
An Nás / Naas .... 102 M 8
An Ráth / Charleville .. 94 F 10
An Ros / Rush .... 109 N 7
An Sciobairín / Skibbereen .. 89 E 13
An Seanchaisleán /
  Oldcastle .... 108 K 6
An Spidéal / Spiddal .. 99 E 8
An tAonach / Nenagh .. 100 H 9
An Teampall Mór /
  Templemore .... 101 I 9
An Tearmann / Termon .. 117 I 2
An tInbhear Mór / Arklow .. 97 N 9
An Tulach / Tullow .... 102 L 9
An Uaimh / Navan ..... 108 L 7
Anascaul .... 92 B 11
Anayalla .... 114 L 5
Anglesborough .... 94 H 10
Anglesey Bridge .... 95 H 9
Annacarriga .... 99 G 9
Annacarty .... 95 H 10
Annaclone .... 115 N 5
Annacloy .... 115 O 4
Annacotty .... 94 G 9
Annaduff .... 115 O 5
Annagary .... 116 H 2
Annagassan .... 109 M 6
Annageeragh (River) .. 98 D 9
Annagh Head .... 110 B 5
Annagh Island .... 110 C 6
Annaghdown .... 105 E 7
Annaghmore Lough ... 106 H 6
Annahilt .... 115 N 4
Annalee .... 107 J 5
Annalong .... 109 O 5
Annamoe .... 103 N 8
Annes Grove Gardens .. 94 G 11
Annestown .... 91 K 11
Annfield .... 95 I 9
Annie Brady Bridge ... 111 D 4
Annsborough .... 115 O 5
Antrim .... 115 N 3
Antrim (Glens of) ..... 119 N 2
Antrim Coast .... 119 O 2
Antrim Mountains ..... 119 N 2
Anure (Lough) .... 116 H 3
Árann Mhór /
  Aran or Aranmore Island 116 G 2
Aran Islands /
  Oileáin Árainn .... 98 C 8
Archdale (Castle) ...... 113 I 4
Archerstown .... 108 K 7
Ard .... 104 C 8
Ardagh *Donegal* ...... 117 J 3
Ardagh *Limerick* ..... 93 E 10
Ardan .... 101 J 8
Ardanairy .... 103 N 9
Ardanew .... 108 L 7
Ardara .... 116 G 3
Ardattin .... 96 L 9
Ardboe .... 114 M 4
Ardcath .... 109 M 7
Ardcloon .... 105 F 7
Ardcrony .... 100 H 9
Ardea .... 89 C 12
Arderin .... 101 J 8
Ardfert .... 93 C 11
Ardfield .... 89 F 13
Ardfinnan .... 95 I 11
Ardgehane .... 90 F 13
Ardglass .... 115 P 5
Ardglass .... 90 H 11

Ardgroom .... 88 C 12
Ardgroom Harbour .... 88 C 12
Ardkeen .... 115 P 4
Ardlea .... 101 J 9
Ardlougher .... 107 J 5
Ardmillan .... 115 O 4
Ardmoney .... 113 J 5
Ardmore *Derry* .... 117 K 3
Ardmore *Galway* ..... 104 C 8
Ardmore Point *Antrim* .. 114 N 4
Ardmore Point *Craigavon* .. 114 M 4
Ardmore Point
  Dungannon East ... 103 N 9
Ardmorney .... 101 J 7
Ardmoy .... 106 G 6
Ardnagreevagh .... 104 B 7
Ardnasodan .... 105 F 7
Ardpatrick .... 94 G 10
Ardrahan .... 99 F 8
Ardreagh .... 118 M 2
Adress House .... 114 M 4
Ardscull .... 102 L 8
Ardshankill .... 113 I 4
Ardstraw .... 113 J 3
Argideen .... 89 F 13
Arigna (The) .... 114 M 4
Arigna .... 112 F 5
Arinagh .... 112 F 5
Arless .... 102 K 9
Armagh .... 114 M 4
Armaghbrague .... 114 M 5
Armoy .... 118 N 2
Arney .... 113 J 5
Arra Mountains .... 100 G 9
Arrow (Lough) .... 106 H 5
Arryheernabin .... 117 J 2
Artane .... 103 N 7
Arthurstown .... 96 L 11
Articlave .... 118 L 2
Artigarvan .... 117 J 3
Arvagh .... 107 J 6
Asdee .... 93 D 10
Ashbourne .... 109 M 7
Ashford *Glenealy* ... 103 N 8
Ashford *Limerick* ... 93 E 10
Ashford Castle .... 105 E 7
Ashleam .... 104 B 6
Ashleam Bay .... 104 B 6
Ashton .... 90 F 12
Askamore .... 97 M 9
Askanagap .... 103 M 9
Askeaton .... 94 F 10
Askill .... 112 H 4
Atedaun (Lough) ...... 99 E 9
Áth Cinn / Headford .. 105 E 7
Athassel Abbey .... 95 I 10
Athboy .... 108 L 7
Athea .... 93 E 10
Athgarvan .... 102 L 8
Athlacca .... 94 G 10
Athleague .... 106 H 7
Athnid .... 95 I 9
Athy / Baile Átha Í .. 102 L 9
Atlantic Drive (The) .. 104 C 6
Atorick (Lough) ...... 99 G 8
Attanagh .... 101 J 9
Attavally .... 111 C 5
Attical .... 109 N 5
Attymass .... 111 E 5
Attymon .... 99 G 8
Auburn .... 107 I 7
Aucloggen .... 105 F 7
Audley's Castle .... 115 P 4
Aughacasla .... 92 C 11
Aughagault .... 117 I 3
Aughamullan .... 114 M 4
Augher .... 114 K 4
Aughils .... 92 C 11
Aughinish .... 99 E 8
Aughinish Island ..... 93 E 10
Aughnacleagh .... 118 M 3
Aughnacloy .... 114 L 4
Aughnanure Castle ... 105 E 7
Aughnasheelan .... 107 I 5
Aughris .... 112 F 5
Aughris Head .... 112 F 5
Aughrus More .... 104 B 7
Avoca .... 103 N 9
Avoca (River) .... 103 N 9
Avoca (Vale of) .... 103 N 9
Avonbeg .... 103 M 9
Avondale Forest Park .. 103 N 9
Avonmore (River) ..... 103 N 9
Awbeg .... 94 G 11

B

Baginbun Head .... 96 L 11
Baile an Fheirtéaraigh /
  Ballyferriter .... 92 A 11
Baile an Mhóta /
  Ballymote .... 112 G 5
Baile an Róba /
  Ballinrobe .... 105 E 7
Baile an Sceilg /
  Ballinskelligs .... 88 B 12
Baile Átha an Rí / Athenry .. 99 F 8
Baile Átha Cliath / Dublin .. 103 N 8
Baile Átha Fhirdhia / Ardee .. 108 M 6
Baile Átha Luain / Athlone .. 107 I 7
Baile Átha Troim / Trim .. 108 L 7
Baile Brigín / Balbriggan .. 109 N 7
Baile Chláir / Claregalway .. 99 F 7
Baile Locha Riach /
  Loughrea .... 99 G 8
Baile Mhic Andáin /
  Thomastown .... 96 K 10
Baile Mhistéala /
  Mitchelstown .... 94 H 11
Baile na Finne / Fintown .. 117 H 3
Baile na Lorgan /
  Castleblayney .... 108 L 5
Baile Uí Fhiacháin /
  Newport .... 105 D 6
Baile Uí Mhatháin /
  Ballymahon .... 107 I 7
Baileysmill .... 115 O 4
Baldoyle .... 103 N 7
Baldoyle .... 103 N 7
Balla .... 105 E 6
Ballaba .... 99 F 8
Ballagan Point .... 109 N 5
Ballagh *Fermanagh* .. 113 J 5
Ballagh *Galway* ..... 106 F 7
Ballagh *Limerick* .... 95 J 9
Ballagh *near Curraghroe* .. 107 H 6
Ballagh *near Nahara* .. 106 H 7
Ballagh *Tipperary* ... 95 I 10
Ballagh (Neck of the) .. 112 G 3
Ballaghaderreen /
  Bealach an Doirín .. 106 G 6
Ballaghbeama Gap ... 89 C 12
Ballaghbehy .... 93 E 10
Ballaghisheen Pass .. 88 C 12
Ballaghkeen .... 97 M 10
Ballaghmore .... 101 I 9
Ballaghnatrillick ...... 112 G 4
Ballard .... 97 M 9
Ballardiggan .... 99 F 8
Balleen .... 101 J 9
Ballickmoyler .... 102 K 9
Balliggan .... 115 P 4
Ballin Lough .... 108 L 6
Ballina / Béal an Átha .. 111 E 5
Ballinaboy .... 104 B 7
Ballinabrackey .... 102 K 7
Ballinabranagh .... 102 L 9
Ballinaclash .... 103 N 9
Ballinacor .... 103 N 9
Ballinadee .... 90 G 12
Ballinafad *Aghanagh* .. 106 G 5
Ballinafad *Galway* .. 104 C 7
Ballinagar .... 101 J 8
Ballinagleragh .... 113 H 5
Ballinakill .... 101 K 9
Ballinalack .... 107 J 7
Ballinalea .... 103 N 8
Ballinalee .... 107 J 6
Ballinamallard .... 113 J 4
Ballinamara .... 95 J 9
Ballinameen .... 106 H 6
Ballinamore Bridge .. 106 G 7
Ballinamuck .... 107 I 6
Ballinascarty .... 90 F 12
Ballinaspick .... 91 I 11
Ballinclashet .... 90 G 12
Ballinclea .... 103 M 9
Ballincloher .... 93 C 10
Ballincollig .... 90 G 12
Ballincrea .... 96 K 11
Ballincurrig .... 90 H 12
Ballindaggan .... 96 L 10
Ballindarragh .... 113 J 5
Ballinderreen .... 99 F 8
Ballinderry *Cookstown* .. 114 M 4
Ballinderry *Terryglass* .. 100 H 8
Ballinderry *Wicklow* .. 103 N 9
Ballinderry Bridge ... 114 M 4
Ballindine .... 105 F 6
Ballindrait .... 117 J 3
Ballineanig .... 92 A 11
Ballineen .... 89 F 12
Ballingarrane .... 94 F 10

Ballingarry *Galway* .. 100 H 8
Ballingarry *Limerick* .. 94 F 10
Ballingarry *Tipperary* .. 95 J 10
Ballingeary / Béal Átha
  an Ghaorthaidh ..... 89 E 12
Ballingurteen .... 89 E 12
Ballinhassig .... 90 G 12
Ballinkillin .... 96 L 10
Ballinlea .... 118 M 2
Ballinleeny .... 94 F 10
Ballinloghig .... 92 B 11
Ballinlough *Meath* .. 108 K 6
Ballinlough *Roscommon* .. 106 G 6
Ballinluska .... 90 H 12
Ballinruan .... 99 F 9
Ballinskelligs Bay .... 88 B 12
Ballinspittle .... 90 G 12
Ballintober .... 106 G 6
Ballintogher .... 112 G 5
Ballintotty .... 100 H 9
Ballintoy .... 118 M 2
Ballintra *Donegal* .. 112 H 4
Ballintra *near Leabgarrow* .. 116 G 3
Ballintubber .... 105 E 6
Ballinunty .... 95 I 10
Ballinure .... 95 I 10
Ballinure (River) ..... 100 H 8
Ballinvarry .... 96 L 10
Ballitore .... 102 L 8
Ballivor .... 108 L 7
Ballon .... 96 L 9
Balloo Cross Roads .. 115 O 4
Balloor .... 112 G 4
Balloughter .... 97 M 10
Ballure .... 112 H 4
Ballyengland .... 94 F 10
Ballyallinan .... 94 F 10
Ballyalton .... 115 P 5
Ballyard .... 113 J 4
Ballybannon .... 102 L 9
Ballybay
  near Carrickmacross .. 108 L 5
Ballybay
  near Castleblayney .. 108 L 5
Ballybeg .... 95 I 11
Ballyboghil .... 109 N 7
Ballybogy .... 118 M 2
Ballyboy .... 101 I 8
Ballybrack *Dublin* .. 103 N 8
Ballybrack *Kerry* ... 88 B 12
Ballybrittas .... 101 K 8
Ballybrommel .... 96 L 9
Ballybrood .... 94 G 10
Ballybrophy .... 101 J 9
Ballybryan .... 101 K 7
Ballybunnion .... 93 D 10
Ballycahill .... 95 I 9
Ballycallan .... 95 J 10
Ballycanew .... 97 N 10
Ballycarney .... 97 M 10
Ballycarry .... 115 O 3
Ballycastle *Mayo* .. 111 D 5
Ballycastle *Moyle* .. 119 N 2
Ballycastle Bay ...... 119 N 2
Ballyclare *Newtonabbey* .. 115 N 3
Ballyclare *Roscommon* .. 107 I 6
Ballyclerahan .... 95 I 10
Ballyclery .... 99 F 8
Ballyclogh .... 94 F 11
Ballycolla .... 101 J 9
Ballycommon .... 100 H 9
Ballyconneely .... 104 B 7
Ballyconneely Bay .. 104 B 7
Ballyconnell *Cavan* .. 113 J 5
Ballyconnell *Sligo* .. 112 G 4
Ballycorick .... 99 E 9
Ballycotton .... 91 H 12
Ballycotton Bay ..... 91 H 12
Ballycrossaun .... 100 H 8
Ballycrovane Harbour .. 88 C 12
Ballycroy .... 110 C 5
Ballycuirke Lough ... 99 E 8
Ballycullane .... 96 L 11
Ballycullen .... 103 N 8
Ballycumber .... 101 I 8
Ballydangan .... 100 H 7
Ballydavid *Galway* .. 100 G 8
Ballydavid *Kilmalkedar* .. 92 A 11
Ballydavid Head .... 92 A 11
Ballydavis .... 101 K 8
Ballydehob .... 89 D 13
Ballydesmond ...... 93 E 11
Ballydonegan .... 88 B 13
Ballydonegan Bay .. 88 B 13
Ballyduff *Dingle* ... 92 B 11

Ballyduff *Kerry* ..... 93 D 10
Ballyduff *Waterford* .. 91 H 11
Ballyduff *Wexford* .. 97 M 10
Ballyeaston .... 115 O 3
Ballyeighter Loughs .. 99 F 9
Ballyfad .... 97 N 9
Ballyfair .... 102 L 8
Ballyfarnagh .... 105 F 6
Ballyfarnan .... 106 H 5
Ballyfasy .... 96 K 10
Ballyfeard .... 90 G 12
Ballyferis Point .... 115 P 4
Ballyfin .... 101 J 8
Ballyfinboy .... 100 H 8
Ballyforan .... 106 H 7
Ballyfoyle .... 96 K 9
Ballygalley .... 119 O 3
Ballygalley Head ... 119 O 3
Ballygar .... 106 H 7
Ballygarrett .... 97 N 10
Ballygarries .... 105 E 6
Ballygarvan .... 90 G 12
Ballygawley *Dungannon* .. 114 K 4
Ballygawley *Sligo* .. 112 G 5
Ballyglass
  near Cornanagh ... 105 E 6
Ballyglass *near
  Kilmovee* .... 106 G 6
Ballygorman .... 117 K 1
Ballygowan *Ards* ... 115 O 4
Ballygowan
  Newry-Mourne ... 109 N 5
Ballygriffin .... 95 I 10
Ballyhack .... 96 L 11
Ballyhacket .... 102 L 9
Ballyhaght .... 94 G 10
Ballyhahill .... 93 E 10
Ballyhaise .... 107 K 5
Ballyhalbert .... 115 P 4
Ballyhale *Galway* .. 105 E 7
Ballyhale *Kilkenny* .. 96 K 10
Ballyhar .... 93 D 11
Ballyhaunis /
  Béal Átha hAmhnais .. 106 F 6
Ballyhean .... 105 E 6
Ballyhean .... 105 E 6
Ballyheelan .... 107 J 6
Ballyheerin .... 117 I 2
Ballyheige .... 93 C 10
Ballyheige Bay .... 93 C 10
Ballyhillin .... 117 J 1
Ballyhoe Bridge ... 118 N 2
Ballyhoe Lough ... 108 L 6
Ballyhoge .... 96 M 10
Ballyhooly .... 94 G 11
Ballyhornan .... 115 P 5
Ballyhoura Mountains .. 94 G 11
Ballyhuppahane ... 101 J 8
Ballyjamesduff ... 107 K 6
Ballykean .... 101 K 8
Ballykeefe .... 95 J 10
Ballykeel .... 114 N 4
Ballykeeran .... 107 I 7
Ballykelly .... 118 K 2
Ballykilleen .... 102 K 8
Ballykinler .... 115 O 5
Ballyknockan ..... 103 M 8
Ballylacy .... 97 N 9
Ballylaghnan ..... 99 G 9
Ballylanders ..... 94 G 10
Ballyleague ...... 95 J 11
Ballylesson ...... 115 O 4
Ballylickey ...... 89 D 12
Ballyliffin .... 117 J 2
Ballyline .... 95 J 10
Ballylintagh .... 118 L 2
Ballylongford ... 93 D 10
Ballylongford Bay .. 93 D 10
Ballylooby ...... 95 I 11
Ballyloughbeg .. 118 M 2
Ballylynan ...... 102 K 9
Ballymacarbry ... 95 I 11
Ballymacaw ...... 96 K 11
Ballymachugh ... 107 K 6
Ballymack ...... 96 K 10
Ballymackey ... 100 H 9
Ballymackilroy .. 114 K 4
Ballymacoda .... 91 I 12
Ballymacrevan .. 115 N 4
Ballymacurly ... 106 H 6
Ballymacward ... 106 G 7
Ballymadog ..... 91 I 12
Ballymagan ..... 117 J 2
Ballymagaraghy .. 118 K 2
Ballymagorry .... 117 J 3
Ballymakeagh ... 91 I 12

A
B
C
D
E
F
G
H
I
J
K
L
M
N
O
P
Q
R
S
T
U
V
W
X
Y
Z

Ballymakeery /
  Baile Mhic Íre ....89 E 12
Ballymakenny .... 109 M 6
Ballymartin .... 109 O 5
Ballymartle ....90 G 12
Ballymena ....119 N 3
Ballymoe .... 106 G 6
Ballymoney *Ballymoney* ...118 M 2
Ballymoney *Limavady* ....118 K 3
Ballymore *Donegal* ....117 I 2
Ballymore *Westmeath* ....107 I 7
Ballymore Eustace .... 103 M 8
Ballymore Lough .... 111 E 5
Ballymurphy ....96 L 10
Ballymurragh ....93 E 10
Ballymurray .... 106 H 7
Ballynabola ....96 L 10
Ballynacallagh ....88 B 13
Ballynacally ....99 E 9
Ballynacarrick ....116 H 3
Ballynacarriga ....89 E 12
Ballynacarrigy .... 107 J 7
Ballynacarrow ....112 G 5
Ballynaclogh .... 100 H 9
Ballynacorra ....90 H 12
Ballynacourty ....91 J 11
Ballynadrumny .... 102 L 7
Ballynafid .... 107 J 7
Ballynagaul ....91 J 11
Ballynagoraher .... 105 D 6
Ballynagore .... 101 J 7
Ballynagree ....90 F 12
Ballynaguilkee ....95 I 11
Ballynahinch ....115 O 4
Ballynahinch Lake .... 104 C 7
Ballynahow ....88 A 12
Ballynahown *Kilcummin* ....98 D 8
Ballynahown *Westmeath* .. 101 I 7
Ballynakill *Carlow* ....96 L 9
Ballynakill *Offaly* .... 101 K 8
Ballynakill *Westmeath* ... 107 I 7
Ballynakill Harbour .... 104 B 7
Ballynakilla ....88 C 13
Ballynakilly Upper ......88 C 11
Ballynamallaght ....117 K 3
Ballynamona ....90 G 11
Ballynamult ....95 I 11
Ballynana ....92 A 11
Ballynare .... 103 M 7
Ballynashannagh ....117 J 2
Ballynaskeagh ....114 N 5
Ballynaskreena ....93 C 10
Ballynastangford ...... 105 E 6
Ballynastraw ....97 M 10
Ballynchatty ....113 K 4
Ballyneaner ....118 K 3
Ballyneety ....94 G 10
Ballyneill ....95 J 10
Ballynoe *Cork* ....90 H 11
Ballynoe *Down* ....115 O 5
Ballynure ....115 O 3
Ballyorgan ....94 G 11
Ballypatrick ....95 J 10
Ballypatrick Forest .....119 N 2
Ballyporeen ....95 H 11
Ballyquin ....92 B 11
Ballyquintin Point .....115 P 5
Ballyragget .... 101 J 9
Ballyrashane ....118 M 2
Ballyreagh *Dungannon* ...114 L 4
Ballyreagh *Fermanagh* ...113 J 4
Ballyroan .... 101 K 9
Ballyroddy .... 106 H 6
Ballyroebuck ....97 M 10
Ballyronan ....114 M 3
Ballyroney ....115 N 5
Ballyroon ....88 C 13
Ballysadare ....112 G 5
Ballysadare Bay ....112 G 5
Ballyshannon *Donegal* ...112 H 4
Ballyshannon *Kildare* ... 102 L 8
Ballysloe ....95 J 10
Ballysteen ....94 F 10
Ballyteige Bay ....96 L 11
Ballytoohy .... 104 C 6
Ballyvaughan ....99 E 8
Ballyvaughan Bay ....99 E 8
Ballyvester ....115 P 4
Ballyvoge /
  Baile Uí Bhuaigh .....89 E 12
Ballyvoneen .... 106 G 7
Ballyvourney /
  Baile Bhuirne ....89 E 12
Ballyvoy ....119 N 2
Ballyvoyle Head ....91 J 11
Ballywalter ....115 P 4
Ballyward ....115 N 5

Ballywilliam ....96 L 10
Balnamore ....118 M 2
Balrath .... 108 M 7
Balrothery .... 109 N 7
Balscaddan .... 109 N 7
Baltimore ....89 D 13
Baltray .... 109 N 6
Banada .... 106 F 5
Banagher .... 101 I 8
Banagher Forest ....118 L 3
Banbridge ....114 N 4
Bandon River ....89 F 12
Bangor *Mayo* ....111 C 5
Bangor *North-Down* .....115 O 4
Bangor Trail ....111 C 5
Bann (River)
  Lough Neagh ....115 N 5
Bann (River) *River Slaney* ...97 M 10
Banna ....93 C 10
Banna Strand ....93 C 10
Bannow ....96 L 11
Bannow Bay ....96 L 11
Bansha ....95 H 10
Banteer ....94 F 11
Bantry / *Beanntraí* ......89 D 12
Bantry Bay ....89 C 13
Barefield ....99 F 9
Barley Cove ....88 C 13
Barna *Limerick* ....94 H 10
Barna *Offaly* .... 101 I 9
Barnacahoge .... 105 F 6
Barnaderg .... 106 F 7
Barnesmore ....113 H 3
Barnesmore Gap ....113 I 3
Barnmeen ....115 N 5
Barnycarroll .... 105 F 6
Baronscourt Forest ....113 J 3
Barr na Trá / *Barnatra* ...110 C 5
Barra (Lough) ....117 H 3
Barrack Village .... 101 K 9
Barraduff ....89 D 11
Barrigone ....93 E 10
Barringtonsbridge ......94 G 10
Barrow (River) .... 102 K 8
Barrow Harbour ....93 C 11
Barry .... 107 I 7
Barry's Point ....90 F 13
Batterstown .... 108 M 7
Baunskeha ....96 K 10
Bauntlieve ....99 E 9
Baurtregaum ....93 C 11
Bawn Cross Roads .....94 F 11
Bawnboy ....113 I 5
Beagh *Galway* .... 105 F 7
Beagh *Roscommon* .....112 H 5
Beagh (Lough) ....117 I 2
Beagh (Slieve) ....113 K 4
Beal ....93 D 10
Béal an Átha / *Ballina* ...111 E 5
Béal an Átha Mhóir /
  Ballinamore .... 107 I 5
Béal an Mhuirthead /
  Belmullet ....110 C 5
Béal Átha an Ghaorthaidh /
  Ballingeary ....89 E 12
Béal Átha na Muice /
  Swinford .... 105 F 6
Béal Átha na Sluaighe /
  Ballinasloe .... 100 H 8
Béal Átha Seanaidh /
  Ballyshannon ....112 H 4
Béal Deirg / *Belderrig* ...111 D 5
Beal Point ....93 D 10
Béal Tairbirt / *Belturbet* ...107 J 5
Bealach Conglais /
  Baltinglass .... 102 L 9
Bealach Féich /
  Ballybofey ....117 I 3
Bealaclugga / *New Quay* ...99 E 8
Bealad Cross Roads ...89 F 13
Bealadangan .... 105 D 8
Bealaha ....98 D 9
Bealalaw Bridge ....88 C 12
Bealanabrack .... 104 C 7
Bealin .... 107 I 7
Bealnablath ....90 F 12
Beara ....89 C 12
Bearna / *Barna* ....99 E 8
Beaufort ....89 D 11
Bective .... 108 L 7
Beehive Huts ....92 A 11
Beenmore ....88 B 11
Beennaskehy ....90 G 11
Beenoskee ....92 B 11
Beg (Lough) *Antrim* ...114 N 4
Beg (Lough) *River Bann* ...114 M 3
Beginish Island ....88 B 12

Behy ....88 C 11
Bekan .... 105 F 6
Belcarra .... 105 E 6
Belclare .... 105 F 7
Belcoo ....113 I 5
Belderg Harbour ....111 D 5
Belfarsad .... 104 C 6
Belfast ....115 O 4
Belfast Lough ....115 O 3
Belgooly ....90 G 12
Belhavel Lough ....112 H 5
Bellacorick ....111 D 5
Belladrihid ....112 G 5
Bellagarvaun ....110 C 6
Bellaghy ....114 M 3
Bellahy .... 106 F 6
Bellameeny .... 106 H 7
Bellamont Forest ...... 108 K 5
Bellanaboy Bridge ......111 C 5
Bellanacargy .... 107 K 5
Bellanagare .... 106 G 6
Bellanagraugh Bridge ...112 F 5
Bellanaleck ....113 J 5
Bellanamore ....117 H 3
Bellanamullia .... 107 H 7
Bellananagh .... 107 J 6
Bellanode ....114 K 5
Bellarena ....118 L 2
Bellavary .... 105 E 6
Belleek ....114 M 5
Bellewstown .... 109 M 7
Belmont .... 101 I 8
Belmore Mountain .....113 I 5
Beltra *Croaghmoyle* .... 105 D 6
Beltra *Sligo* ....112 G 5
Beltra Lough .... 105 D 6
Belvelly ....90 H 12
Belview Port ....96 K 11
Belville ....111 D 5
Ben Gorm .... 104 C 7
Benbane Head ....118 M 2
Benbaun .... 104 C 7
Benbo ....112 H 5
Benbrack ....113 I 5
Benbreen .... 104 C 7
Benbulben ....112 G 4
Benburb ....114 L 4
Bencroy or
  Gubnaveagh ....113 I 5
Bendooragh ....118 M 2
Benettsbridge ....96 K 10
Benmore ....111 D 5
Benmore or Fair Head ...119 N 2
Bennacunneen .... 105 D 7
Benwee Head ....111 C 4
Beragh ....114 K 4
Bere Haven ....88 C 13
Bere Island ....88 C 13
Bernish Rock ....114 M 5
Berrings ....90 F 12
Bertraghboy Bay ...... 104 C 7
Bessbrook ....114 M 5
Bettystown .... 109 N 6
Big Dog Forest ....113 I 4
Big Island .... 100 H 8
Big Trosk ....119 N 2
Bilboa .... 102 K 9
Bilboa (River) ....95 H 10
Billis Bridge .... 108 K 6
Bills Rocks .... 104 B 6
Binevenagh ....118 L 2
Binn Éadair / *Howth* ...103 N 7
Biorra / *Birr* .... 101 I 8
Birdhill ....99 G 9
Birreencorragh .... 105 D 6
Bishops Court ....115 P 5
Black *Galway* .... 105 E 7
Black (River) *Longford* ...107 I 6
Black Ball Head ....88 B 13
Black Bull .... 103 M 7
Black Gap (The) ....113 I 4
Black Head *Clare* ......99 E 8
Black Head *Larne* ......115 O 3
Black Lion .... 101 J 8
Black Rock ....110 B 5
Blacklion ....113 I 5
Blackpool ....94 G 10
Blackrock *Cork* ....90 G 12
Blackrock *Louth* ...... 109 M 6
Blackrock *Rathdown* ... 103 N 8
Blackskull ....114 N 4
Blacksod Bay ....110 B 5
Blacksod Point ....110 B 5
Blackstairs Mountains ...96 L 10
Blackwater ....97 M 10
Blackwater (River) *Cork* ...89 F 11

Blackwater (River)
  Lough Neagh ....114 L 4
Blackwater (River)
  River Boyne .... 108 L 6
Blackwater Bridge
  Innfield .... 102 L 7
Blackwater Bridge *Tahilla* ....88 C 12
Blackwater Harbour ....97 N 10
Blackwatertown ....114 L 4
Blanchardstown .... 103 M 7
Blane Bridge ....93 E 10
Blaney ....113 I 4
Blarney ....90 G 12
Blasket Sound ....92 A 11
Bleach ....99 G 8
Bleach Lake ....94 F 10
Blennerville ....93 C 11
Blessington .... 103 M 8
Bloody Foreland ....116 H 2
Blue Ball .... 101 J 8
Blue Stack Mountains ...113 H 3
Blueford ....93 E 11
Boa Island ....113 I 4
Boardmills ....115 O 4
Boardwater ....93 E 11
Boderg (Lough) .... 107 I 6
Bodyke ....99 G 9
Bofeenaun .... 105 E 6
Bofin ....104 B 7
Bofin (Lough) *Galway* ...105 D 7
Bofin (Lough)
  Roscommon .... 107 I 6
Bogay .... 117 J 3
Boggan *Meath* .... 108 L 6
Boggan *Tipperary* ......95 J 9
Boggaun .... 101 I 9
Boggeragh Mountains ...89 F 11
Bohateh ....99 G 9
Bohaun .... 105 D 6
Boheeshil ....88 C 12
Boher ....94 G 10
Boheraphuca .... 101 I 8
Boherbue ....93 E 11
Bohereen ....94 G 10
Boherlahan ....95 I 10
Bohermeen .... 108 L 7
Boherquill .... 107 J 6
Boho ....113 I 4
Bohola .... 105 E 6
Bola (Lough) .... 104 C 7
Bolea ....118 L 2
Boleran ....118 L 2
Boley .... 102 L 8
Bolinglanna .... 104 C 6
Boliska Lough ....99 E 8
Bolton's Cross Roads ...93 D 10
Bolus Head ....88 A 12
Boola ....91 I 11
Boolakennedy ....95 H 10
Boolattin ....95 J 11
Boolteens ....93 C 11
Boolyduff ....99 E 9
Boolyglass ....96 K 10
Borris ....96 L 10
Borris in Ossory .... 101 J 9
Borrisoleigh .... 100 I 9
Boston ....99 F 8
Bottlehill ....90 G 11
Bouladuff ....95 I 9
Boviel ....118 L 3
Bow ....99 G 9
Boyerstown .... 108 L 7
Boyle (River) .... 106 H 6
Boyne (River) .... 102 K 7
Brackagh .... 101 K 8
Brackley Lough ....113 I 5
Bracklin .... 108 K 7
Brackloon *Mayo* ...... 106 F 6
Brackloon *Roscommon* ...106 G 6
Bracknagh *Offaly* .... 102 K 8
Bracknagh *Roscommon* ...107 H 7
Brackwanshagh ....111 E 5
Brandon Bay ....92 B 11
Brandon Head ....92 B 11
Brandon Hill ....96 L 10
Brannock Islands ....98 C 8
Brannockstown .... 102 L 8
Bray Head *Kerry* ....88 A 12
Bray Head *Wicklow* ... 103 N 8
Bré / *Bray* .... 103 N 8
Breaghva ....98 C 10
Breaghwy .... 105 E 6
Bree ....96 M 10
Breenagh ....117 I 3
Brickeens .... 105 F 6
Bricklieve Mountains ...106 G 5
Bride *Cork* ....89 F 12

Bride River Blackwater ...91 I 11
Bridebridge ....90 H 11
Brideswell *Ballyellis* ....97 M 9
Brideswell *Ballynamona* ...106 H 7
Bridge End ....117 J 2
Bridgeland .... 103 M 9
Bridget Lough ....99 G 9
Bridgetown
  Cannock Chase ......96 M 11
Bridgetown *Clare* .....99 G 9
Bridgetown *Donegal* ...112 H 4
Briensbridge ....99 G 9
Brittas *Limerick* ....94 G 10
Brittas *Saggart* ...... 103 M 8
Brittas Bay .... 103 N 9
Britway ....90 H 11
Broad Haven ....110 C 5
Broad Meadow .... 109 N 7
Broadford *Clare* ....99 G 9
Broadford *Limerick* ....94 F 10
Broadway ....97 M 11
Brookeborough ....113 J 5
Broomfield .... 108 L 5
Brosna ....93 E 11
Brosna (River) .... 101 I 8
Broughal .... 101 I 8
Broughane Cross Roads ...93 D 11
Brougher Mount ....113 J 4
Broughshane ....119 N 3
Brow Head ....88 C 13
Brown Flesk ....93 D 11
Brownstown ....96 K 11
Brownstown Head ......96 K 11
Bruckless ....112 G 4
Bruff ....94 G 10
Bruree ....94 G 10
Bryansford ....115 O 5
Buckna ....119 N 3
Buckode ....112 H 4
Buiríos Uí Chéin /
  Borrisokane .... 100 H 9
Bulgaden ....94 G 10
Bull (The) ....88 B 13
Bull Point ....119 N 2
Bullaba ....117 I 3
Bullaun ....99 G 8
Bull's Head ....92 B 11
Bun Cranncha / *Buncrana* ...117 J 2
Bun Dobhráin / *Bundoran* .112 H 4
Bun na hAbhna /
  Bunnahowen ....110 C 5
Bun na Leaca / *Brinlack* ...116 H 2
Bunaclugga Bay ....93 D 10
Bunacurry ....110 C 6
Bunatrahir Bay ....111 D 5
Bunaveela Lough ....111 D 5
Bunaw ....88 C 12
Bunbrosna .... 107 J 7
Bunclody ....96 M 10
Buncrana ....117 J 2
Bunlahy .... 107 J 6
Bunmahon ....91 J 11
Bunnafollistran .... 105 E 7
Bunnaglass ....99 F 8
Bunnahown .... 104 C 7
Bunnanaddan ....112 G 5
Bunny (Lough) ....99 F 8
Bunnyconnellan ....111 E 5
Bunowen .... 105 C 6
Bunratty ....99 F 9
Burnchurch ....96 K 10
Burncourt ....95 H 11
Burnfoot *Birdstown* ...117 J 2
Burnfoot *Limavady* ...118 L 3
Burnfort ....90 G 11
Burr Point ....115 P 4
Burren *Clare* ....99 E 8
Burren *Cork* ....90 F 12
Burren *Mayo* .... 106 F 6
Burren (The) ....99 E 8
Burren Centre Kifenora ...99 E 8
Burrenfadda ....99 E 8
Burrishoole Abbey .... 105 D 6
Burrow ....97 M 11
Burtown .... 102 L 9
Bush ....118 M 2
Bush (The) *Dungannon* ...114 L 4
Bush (The) *Rathcor* ... 109 N 6
Bushfield .... 100 G 8
Bushmills ....118 M 2
Butler's Bridge .... 107 J 5
Butlerstown ....90 F 13
Buttevant ....94 F 11
Butts (The) .... 101 K 9
Bweeng ....90 F 11

C

Cabragh ....114 L 4

Cadamstown *Kildare* ... 102 L 7
Cadamstown *Offaly* ... 101 J 8
Caddy ....114 N 3
Caggan .... 105 D 7
Caha Mountains ....89 C 12
Caha pass ....89 D 12
Caher *Clare* ....99 G 9
Caher *Mayo* .... 105 E 7
Caher Island .... 104 B 6
Caher Roe's Den ....96 L 10
Caheradrine ....99 F 8
Caheragh ....89 E 13
Caherbarnagh
  Corcaigh / Cork .....89 E 11
Caherbarnagh *Kerry* ...88 B 12
Caherconlish ....94 G 10
Caherconnel ....99 E 8
Caherconree ....92 C 11
Caherdaniel ....88 B 12
Caherea ....99 E 9
Caherlistrane .... 105 E 7
Cahermore *Cork* ....88 B 13
Cahermore *Galway* ....99 F 8
Cahermurphy ....98 D 9
Cahernahalla ....95 H 10
Cahore Point ....97 N 10
Caiseal / *Cashel* ....95 I 10
Caisleán an Bharraigh /
  Castlebar .... 105 E 6
Caisleán an Chomair /
  Castlecomer .... 101 K 9
Calafort Ros Láir /
  Rosslare Harbour ....97 M 11
Caledon ....114 L 4
Calf Islands ....89 D 13
Callaghansmills ....99 F 9
Callainn / *Callan* ....95 J 10
Callow *Galway* .... 104 B 7
Callow *Mayo* .... 105 E 6
Callow *Roscommon* ... 106 G 6
Caltra .... 106 G 7
Caltraghlea .... 100 H 7
Calverstown .... 102 L 8
Cam Forest ....118 L 2
Camlin (River) .... 107 I 6
Camlough ....114 M 5
Camoge ....94 G 10
Camolin ....97 M 10
Camowen ....113 K 4
Camp ....92 C 11
Campile ....96 L 11
Campsey ....118 K 2
Camross .... 101 J 8
Camus Bay .... 105 D 8
Canglass Point ....88 B 12
Canningstown .... 108 K 6
Canon Island ....99 E 9
Cappagh *Dungannon* ...114 L 4
Cappagh *Limerick* .....94 F 10
Cappagh River .... 100 G 8
Cappagh White ....95 H 10
Cappaghmore ....99 F 8
Cappalinnan .... 101 J 9
Cappamore ....94 G 10
Cappanacreha .... 105 D 7
Cappanrush .... 101 J 7
Cappataggle .... 100 G 8
Cappeen ....89 F 12
Car (Slieve) ....111 D 5
Caragh (Lough) ....88 C 11
Caragh (River) ....89 C 12
Caragh Bridge ....92 C 11
Caragh Lake ....92 C 11
Carbery's Hundred Isles ...89 D 13
Carbury .... 102 L 7
Cardy ....115 P 4
Cargan ....119 N 3
Carhan House ....88 B 12
Cark ....117 I 3
Cark Mountain ....117 I 3
Carland ....114 L 4
Carlanstown .... 108 L 6
Carlinge .... 109 N 5
Carlingford Lough ..... 109 N 5
Carn ....113 I 4
Carna .... 104 C 8
Carnageer ....119 O 3
Carnaghan ....117 J 2
Carnalbanagh Sheddings ...119 N 3
Carnanelly ....114 L 3
Carnanreagh ....118 K 3
Carnaross .... 108 L 6
Carnaween ....113 H 3
Carncastle ....119 O 3
Carndonagh /
  Carn Domhnach .....118 K 2
Carnduff ....119 N 2

Carne .....97 M 11
Carneatly .....119 N 2
Carnew .....97 M 9
Carney *Sligo* .....112 G 4
Carney *Tipperary* .....100 H 9
Carnlough .....119 O 3
Carnlough Bay .....119 O 3
Carnmore .....99 F 8
Carnoneen .....105 F 7
Carnowen .....117 J 3
Carnsore Point .....97 M 11
Carnteel .....114 L 4
Carntogher .....118 L 3
Carra (Lough) .....105 E 6
Carracastle .....106 F 6
Carragh .....102 L 8
Carraholly .....105 D 6
Carraig Airt / Carrigart .....117 I 2
Carraig Mhachaire Rois /
  Carrickmacross .....108 L 6
Carraig na Siúire /
  Carrick-on-Suir .....95 J 10
Carran .....99 E 8
Carrantuohill .....89 C 11
Carrick *Wexford* .....96 L 11
Carrick / An Charraig
  Donegal .....112 G 4
Carrick-a-Rede
  Rope Bridge .....118 M 2
Carrick-on-Shannon /
  Cora Droma Rúisc .....107 H 6
Carrickaboy .....107 K 6
Carrickashedoge .....108 L 6
Carrickboy .....107 I 7
Carrickfergus .....115 O 3
Carrickhugh .....118 K 2
Carrickmore .....114 K 4
Carrickroe .....114 K 4
Carrig .....94 G 11
Carrig Island .....93 D 10
Carrigadrohid .....90 F 12
Carrigafoyle Castle .....93 D 10
Carrigagulla .....90 F 11
Carrigaholt .....93 C 10
Carrigaholt Bay .....93 C 10
Carrigahorig .....100 H 8
Carrigaline .....90 G 12
Carrigallen .....107 J 6
Carrigan .....107 J 6
Carrigan Head .....112 F 4
Carriganimmy .....89 E 12
Carrigans .....117 J 3
Carrigatogher .....100 H 9
Carrigfadda .....89 E 13
Carrigglass Manor .....107 I 6
Carriggower .....103 N 8
Carrigkerry .....93 E 10
Carrignavar .....90 G 12
Carrigrohane .....90 G 12
Carrigtohill .....90 H 12
Carrowbehy .....106 G 6
Carrowdore .....115 P 4
Carrowkeel *Donegal* .....117 J 2
Carrowkeel *Galway* .....99 G 8
Carrowkennedy .....105 D 6
Carrowmore *Galway* .....99 F 8
Carrowmore *Kilmacowen* ..112 G 5
Carrowmore
  near Cloonacool .....112 F 5
Carrowmore
  near Crossboyne .....105 E 6
Carrowmore
  near Killasser .....105 F 6
Carrowmore
  near Killogeary .....111 E 5
Carrowmore Lake .....110 C 5
Carrowmore Point .....98 D 9
Carrowmoreknock .....105 E 7
Carrownacon .....105 E 6
Carrowneden .....112 F 5
Carrownisky .....104 C 6
Carrowntanlis .....105 F 7
Carrowreagh
  Roscommon .....100 H 7
Carrowreagh *Sligo* .....112 F 5
Carrowrory .....107 I 7
Carry Bridge .....113 J 5
Carrybeg .....95 J 10
Carryduff .....115 O 4
Casheen bay .....98 C 8
Cashel *Donegal* .....117 I 2
Cashel *Mayo* .....104 C 6
Cashel
  near Glennamaddy .....106 G 7
Cashel / An Caiseal
  Galway .....104 C 7
Cashel (Rock of) .....95 I 10

Cashelgarran .....112 G 4
Cashelmore .....117 I 2
Cashen River .....93 D 10
Cashla .....99 F 8
Cashla Bay .....98 D 8
Cashleen .....104 B 7
Casla / Costelloe .....98 D 8
Castlepollard .....107 K 6
Cassagh .....96 L 10
Castle Carry .....118 K 2
Castle Coole .....113 J 4
Castle Gardens .....90 F 13
Castle Haven .....89 E 13
Castle Island .....89 D 13
Castle Point .....98 C 10
Castlebaldwin .....112 G 5
Castlebar (River) .....105 E 6
Castlebellingham .....109 M 6
Castleblakeney .....106 G 7
Castlebridge .....97 M 10
Castlecaulfield .....114 L 4
Castleconnell .....99 G 9
Castleconor .....111 E 5
Castlecor .....94 F 11
Castlecove .....88 B 12
Castlecuffe .....101 J 8
Castledawson .....114 M 3
Castlederg .....113 J 3
Castledermot .....102 L 9
Castlefinn .....117 J 3
Castlefreke .....89 F 13
Castlegal .....112 G 4
Castlegar .....99 E 8
Castlegregory .....92 B 11
Castlehill *Ballycroy South* ..110 C 6
Castlehill
  near Rake Street .....111 D 5
Castlejordan .....102 K 7
Castleknock .....103 M 7
Castlelis .....97 M 10
Castlelyons .....90 H 11
Castlemaine .....93 C 11
Castlemaine Harbour .....92 C 11
Castlemartyr .....90 H 12
Castleplunket .....106 G 6
Castlequin .....88 B 12
Castlerahan .....108 K 6
Castlerock .....118 L 2
Castleroe .....118 M 2
Castleshane .....114 L 5
Castletown *Clare* .....99 E 8
Castletown *Cork* .....89 F 12
Castletown *Laois* .....101 J 9
Castletown *Limerick* .....94 F 10
Castletown *Meath* .....108 L 6
Castletown *near Finnea* ....107 K 6
Castletown *Westmeath* ....107 J 7
Castletown *Wexford* .....97 N 9
Castletown House .....103 M 7
Castletownbere .....88 C 13
Castletownroche .....94 G 11
Castletownshend .....89 E 13
Castleville .....105 E 7
Castleward House .....115 P 4
Castlewarren .....96 K 9
Castlewellan .....115 O 5
Castlewellan Forest Park ..115 O 5
Cathair na Mart /
  Westport .....105 D 6
Cathair Saidhbhín /
  Cahersiveen .....88 B 12
Cathedral Rocks .....104 B 6
Causeway .....93 C 10
Causeway Head .....118 M 2
Cavan / An Cabhán .....107 J 6
Cavanagarvan .....114 L 5
Ceanannas / Ceanannas Mór
  (Kells) .....108 L 6
Ceann Toirc / Kanturk .....94 F 11
Ceapach Choinn /
  Cappoquin .....91 I 11
Ceatharlach / Carlow .....102 L 9
Ceathrú Thaidhg /
  Carrowteige .....111 C 5
Cecilstown .....94 F 11
Celbridge .....103 M 7
Chanonrock .....108 M 6
Chapeltown *Down* .....115 P 5
Chapeltown
  near Portmagee .....88 A 12
Chapeltown *near Tralee* ....93 C 11
Charlemont .....114 L 4
Charlestown *Craigavon* ....114 M 4
Charlestown *Mayo* .....106 F 6
Cheekpoint .....96 K 11

Cherryville .....102 L 8
Chesney's Corner .....114 M 3
Church Ballee .....115 P 5
Church Cross .....89 D 13
Church Hill *Donegal* .....117 I 3
Church Hill *Fermanagh* ....113 I 4
Church Quarter .....119 N 2
Church Town .....117 J 3
Church Village .....105 E 6
Churchstreet .....106 G 6
Churchtown *Cookstown* ....114 L 3
Churchtown *Cork* .....90 H 12
Churchtown *Down* .....115 P 4
Churchtown *Wexford* .....96 L 11
Churchtown Point .....114 M 3
Cill Airne / Killarney .....89 D 11
Cill Chainnigh / Kilkenny ....96 K 10
Cill Chaoi / Kilkee .....98 D 9
Cill Dalua / Killaloe .....99 G 9
Cill Dara / Kildare .....102 L 8
Cill Mhantáin / Wicklow ....103 N 9
Cill Mocheallóg /
  Kilmallock .....94 G 10
Cill Orglan / Killorglin .....93 C 11
Cill Rois / Kilrush .....93 D 10
Cill Rónáin / Kilronan .....98 C 8
Cionn tSáile / Kinsale .....90 G 12
City Walls .....96 K 11
Clabby .....113 J 4
Cladagh .....113 I 5
Claddagh .....106 F 7
Claddaghduff .....104 B 7
Clady *Antrim* .....115 N 4
Clady *Magherafelt* .....118 M 3
Clady *Strabane* .....117 J 3
Clady (River) .....116 H 2
Clady Milltown .....114 M 5
Claggan *Donegal* .....117 J 2
Claggan *Mayo* .....104 C 6
Clamper Cross .....93 E 11
Clanabogan .....113 J 4
Clane .....102 L 8
Clár Chlainne Mhuiris /
  Claremorris .....105 F 6
Clara .....103 N 9
Clara (Valle of) .....103 N 9
Clarahill .....101 J 8
Clare *Armagh* .....114 M 5
Clare *Craigavon* .....114 N 4
Clare (River) .....105 F 7
Clare Island .....104 B 6
Clarecastle .....99 F 9
Clareen .....101 I 8
Clarina .....94 F 10
Clarinbridge .....99 F 8
Clark's Cross Roads .....107 J 7
Clash .....100 H 9
Clash North .....93 E 10
Clashmore .....91 I 11
Claudy .....118 K 3
Clear (Cape) .....89 D 13
Cleggan / An Cloigeann ....104 B 7
Cleggan Bay .....104 B 7
Cléire (Oileán) /
  Clear Island .....89 D 13
Cleristown .....96 M 11
Clew Bay .....104 B 7
Clifden Bay .....104 B 7
Cliff .....112 H 4
Clifferna .....108 K 6
Cliffony .....112 G 4
Clogga *Kilkenny* .....96 K 11
Clogga *Wicklow* .....97 N 9
Clogh *Antrim* .....119 N 3
Clough *Ballymena* .....119 N 3
Clogh *Kilkenny* .....101 K 9
Clogh *Laois* .....101 J 9
Clogh *Wexford* .....97 M 10
Cloghan *Offaly* .....101 I 8
Cloghan *Westmeath* .....107 K 7
Cloghane .....92 B 11
Cloghaneely .....117 H 2
Clogharinka .....102 K 7
Cloghaun .....105 F 7
Cloghboley .....112 G 4
Cloghbrack *Cloonbur* .....105 D 7
Cloghbrack *Meath* .....108 K 7
Clogheen .....95 I 11
Clogher *Dungannon* .....113 K 4
Clogher *Kerry* .....93 D 11
Clogher
  near Carrownacon .....105 E 6
Clogher *near Westport* ....105 D 6
Clogher *Roscommon* .....107 H 6
Clogher Head *Kerry* .....92 A 11
Clogher Head *Louth / Lú* ....109 N 6
Cloghera .....99 G 9
Clogherhead .....109 N 6

Cloghjordan .....100 H 9
Cloghmacoo .....108 L 6
Cloghoge .....109 M 5
Cloghroe *Cork* .....90 G 12
Cloghroe *Donegal* .....117 I 3
Cloghy .....115 P 4
Cloghy Bay .....115 P 4
Clohamon .....96 M 10
Clohernagh .....96 K 11
Cloich na Coillte /
  Clonakilty .....89 F 13
Clóirtheach / Clara .....101 J 7
Clomantagh .....95 J 9
Clonakenny .....101 I 9
Clonakilty Bay .....90 F 13
Colbinstown .....102 L 8
Coldwood .....99 F 8
Colebrooke .....113 J 5
Colehill .....107 I 7
Coleraine .....118 L 2
Colgagh .....112 G 5
Colgagh Lough .....112 G 5
Colligan (River) .....95 I 11
Collin Top .....119 N 3
Collinstown .....107 K 7
Collon .....109 M 6
Collooney .....112 G 5
Colly .....88 C 12
Colmanstown .....106 G 7
Comber .....115 O 4
Comeragh Mountains ....95 J 11
Commeen .....117 H 3
Commons .....95 J 10
Conay Island .....112 G 5
Cong / Conga .....105 E 7
Conlig .....115 O 4
Conn (Lough) .....111 E 5
Conna .....90 H 11
Connagh .....100 G 9
Connemara .....104 C 7
Connemara
  National Park .....104 C 7
Connkeevy .....112 G 5
Connly .....99 E 9
Connonagh .....89 E 13
Connor .....115 N 3
Connor Pass .....92 B 11
Convoy .....117 I 3
Coogue .....105 F 6
Cookstown .....114 L 4
Coola .....112 G 5
Coolagarry .....106 H 7
Coolaney .....112 G 5
Coolattin .....97 M 9
Coolbaun .....101 K 9
Coolbawn .....100 H 9
Coolboy .....97 M 9
Coolcull .....96 L 11
Coolderry .....101 I 8
Coole (Castle) .....113 J 4
Coole Abbey .....90 H 11
Cloon Lake .....88 C 12
Coolea / Cúil Aodha .....89 E 12
Coolearagh .....102 L 8
Cooley Point .....109 N 6
Coolgrange .....96 K 10
Coolgreany .....97 N 9
Coolkeeragh .....117 K 2
Coolkellure .....89 E 12
Coolmeen .....93 E 10
Coolmore .....112 H 4
Coolnareen .....101 J 9
Coolrain .....101 J 9
Coolroebeg .....96 K 10
Coolshaghtena .....107 H 6
Coolteige .....106 H 6
Coomacarrea .....88 B 12
Coomakesta Pass .....88 B 12
Coomasaharn Lake .....88 C 12
Coomhola .....89 D 12
Coomhola Bridge .....89 D 12
Coonagh .....94 F 10
Cooraclare .....98 D 9
Coorleagh .....96 K 9
Coornagillagh .....89 C 12
Cootehall .....106 H 6
Copany .....113 H 4
Copeland Island .....115 P 3
Cora Droma Rúisc /
  Carrick-on-Shannon .....107 H 6
Corbally
  Castleconor West .....111 E 5
Corbally *Clare* .....98 D 9
Corbally *Kildare* .....102 L 8
Corbay Upper .....107 I 6
Corbet Milltown .....115 N 4
Corcaigh / Cork .....90 G 12
Corclogh .....110 B 5
Corcomroe Abbey .....99 E 8

Cloyne .....90 H 12
Cluain Eois / Clones .....113 K 5
Cluain Meala / Clonmel ....95 I 10
Cluainín / Manorhamilton ..112 H 5
Clydagh .....105 E 6
Clynacantan .....88 A 12
Coachford .....90 F 12
Coagh .....114 M 4
Coalbrook .....95 J 10
Coalisland .....114 L 4
Coan .....101 K 9
Cod's Head .....88 B 13
Coill an Chollaigh /
  Bailieborough .....108 L 6
Colin Hill .....107 I 6
Cornafulla .....101 H 7
Cornagillagh .....117 I 3
Cornamona .....105 D 7
Cornanagh .....105 E 6
Corracloona .....113 H 4
Corrakyle .....99 G 9
Corraleehan .....113 I 5
Corran Cross Roads .....114 M 5
Corrandulla .....105 F 7
Corranny .....113 K 5
Corraree .....106 H 7
Corraun Hill .....104 C 6
Corraun Peninsula .....104 C 6
Corraun Point .....110 B 5
Corrawaleen .....107 I 5
Correllstown .....107 K 7
Corrib (Lough) .....105 E 7
Corries .....96 L 10
Corriga .....107 I 6
Corrigeenroe .....106 H 5
Corrofin .....99 E 9
Corronoher .....94 F 10
Corroy .....111 E 5
Corry .....112 H 5
Corstown .....95 J 10
Cortown .....108 L 6
Corvally .....108 L 6
Corvoley .....111 D 5
Cottoners .....89 C 11
Coulagh Bay .....88 B 12
Coumfea .....95 J 11
Courtmacsherry .....90 F 13
Courtmacsherry Bay ....90 G 13
Courtown .....97 N 10
Cousane Gap .....89 E 12
Craanford .....97 M 9
Craffield .....103 M 9
Crag Cave .....93 D 11
Craggaunowen
  Megalithic Centre .....99 F 9
Craig .....118 K 3
Craigantlet .....115 O 4
Craigavad .....115 O 4
Craigavon .....114 M 4
Craignamaddy .....114 K 3
Craigs .....118 M 3
Crana .....117 J 2
Cranagh .....114 K 3
Cranfield Point .....109 N 5
Cranford .....117 I 2
Crannogeboy .....116 G 3
Cranny .....99 E 9
Cratloe .....99 F 9
Craughwell .....99 F 8
Crawfordsburn .....115 O 4
Crazy Corner .....107 K 7
Creagh .....113 J 4
Creagh (The) .....114 M 3
Creaghanroe .....114 L 5
Crean's Cross Roads .....90 F 12
Crecora .....94 F 10
Creegh .....98 D 9
Creeslough .....117 I 2
Creevagh .....111 D 5
Creevagh Head .....111 E 5
Creeves .....93 E 10
Creevykeel .....112 G 4
Cregg *Clare* .....99 E 8
Cregg *Cork* .....89 E 13
Cregg *Galway* .....105 E 7
Cregg *Sligo* .....112 G 5
Creggan *Armagh* .....108 M 5
Creggan *Dungannon* ....114 K 4
Creganbaun .....104 C 6
Creggaun .....94 F 10
Creggs .....106 G 7
Crilly .....114 L 4
Crindle .....118 L 2
Crinkill .....101 I 8
Croagh *Donegal* .....112 G 3
Croagh *Limerick* .....94 F 10
Croagh Patrick .....105 C 6
Croaghaun .....110 B 6
Croaghmoyle .....105 D 6
Croaghnakeela Island ....104 C 8
Croaghrimbeg .....105 D 6

A
B
C
D
E
F
G
H
I
J
K
L
M
N
O
P
Q
R
S
T
U
V
W
X
Y
Z

A B C D E F G H I J K L M N O P Q R S T U V W X Y Z

Croan (Lough) 106 H7
Croangar (Lough) 116 H3
Crockaneel 119 N2
Crockets Town 111 E5
Crockmore 113 I4
Crocknasmug 118 L2
Croghan Offaly 101 K7
Croghan Roscommon 106 H6
Croghan Mountain 103 N9
Crohane 89 D12
Crohy Head 116 G3
Crois Mhaoilíona / Crossmolina 111 E5
Croithlí / Crolly 116 H2
Cromane 92 C11
Cromoge 101 J9
Croob (Slieve) 115 N4
Crookedwood 107 K7
Crookhaven 88 C13
Crookstown Kildare 102 L8
Crookstown Moviddy 90 F12
Croom 94 F10
Croos 106 H7
Cross Cong 105 E7
Cross Waterford 91 I11
Cross (River) 105 D7
Cross Barry 90 G12
Cross Keys Cavan 107 K6
Cross Keys Meath 108 K6
Cross Keys Meath 108 M7
Cross Roads 117 I3
Crossabeg 97 M10
Crossakeel 108 K6
Crossboyne 105 E6
Crossconnell 100 H8
Crossdoney 107 J6
Crossea 107 J7
Crosserlough 107 K6
Crossgar 115 O4
Crossgare 118 L2
Crosshaven 90 H12
Crossmaglen 108 M5
Crossna 106 H5
Crossooha 99 F8
Crosspatrick Kilkenny 101 J9
Crosspatrick Wicklow 97 M9
Crosswell 106 G7
Crove 112 G3
Crow Head 88 B13
Crownarad 112 G4
Cruit Island 116 G2
Crumlin Antrim 115 N4
Crumlin Cong 105 D7
Crusheen 99 F9
Crutt 101 K9
Cúil an tSúdaire / Portarlington 101 K8
Cuilcagh 113 I5
Cuilkillew 111 E5
Cuilmore 105 F6
Culdaff 118 K2
Culdaff Bay 118 K2
Culfadda 106 G5
Culfin 104 C7
Culky 113 J5
Cullahill 101 J9
Cullane 94 G10
Cullaun 94 H10
Cullaville 108 M5
Culleens 111 F5
Cullen Cork 94 H10
Cullen Tipperary 93 E11
Cullenagh (River) 99 E9
Cullenstown near Duncormick 96 L11
Cullenstown near Newbawn 96 L10
Cullin 105 E6
Cullin (Lough) 105 E6
Cullybackey 118 M3
Cullyhanna 108 M5
Culmore 117 K2
Culnady 118 M3
Cummeragh 88 B12
Cunningburn 115 P4
Curlew Mountains 106 G6
Curracloe 97 M10
Curragh 91 I12
Curragh (The) 102 L8
Curragh Camp 102 L8
Curragh West 106 G7
Curragha 109 M7
Curraghbonaun 106 F6
Curraghboy 106 H7
Curraghmore Gardens 95 J11
Curraghroe 107 H6
Curraglass 91 H11

Currahchase Forest Park ... 94 F10
Curran 114 M3
Currane (Lough) 88 B12
Currans 93 D11
Curraun 105 D7
Curreel (Lough) 104 C7
Curreeny 100 H9
Currow 93 D11
Curry 105 E6
Curryglass 88 C12
Curryskeskin 118 M2
Cushendall 119 N2
Cushendun 119 N2
Cusher 114 M5
Cushina 101 K8
Cut (The) 101 J8
Cutra (Lough) 99 F8

D

Dahybaun (Lough) 111 D5
Daingean 101 K8
Dalgar 105 F7
Dalkey 103 N8
Damastown 109 N7
Damerstown 101 K9
Damhead 118 M2
Dan (Lough) 103 N8
Danesfort Kilkenny 96 K10
Danesfort Longford 107 I6
Dangan Cork 91 H12
Dangan Waterford 96 K11
Darby's Gap 97 M10
Dargle 103 N8
Dark Hedges (The) 118 M2
Darkley 114 L5
Darragh 99 E9
Dartry Mountains 112 G4
Davagh Forest Park 114 L3
Davidstown 103 M9
Dawros 104 C7
Dawros Head 116 G3
Dead 94 H10
Dealagh 98 D9
Dee 108 L6
Deel Limerick 94 F10
Deel Mayo 111 D5
Deel Westmeath 108 K7
Deel Bridge 111 D5
Deele (River) 117 I3
Deelish 89 E12
Deenish Island 88 B12
Delamont 115 O4
Delgany 103 N8
Delphi 104 C7
Delvin 108 K7
Delvin (River) 109 N7
Dennet (Burn) 117 J3
Derg 113 J3
Derg (Lough) near Donegal 113 I4
Derg (Lough) near Nenagh 100 H9
Dergalt 117 J3
Dernagree 93 E11
Derravaragh (Lough) 107 J7
Derreen near Ballynagoraher 105 D6
Derreen near Cloghmore .. 104 C6
Derreen near Formoyle 99 E8
Derreen near Lahinch 98 D9
Derreen Gardens 89 C12
Derreendarragh 89 C12
Derreeny 88 C12
Derreeny Bridge 89 E13
Derriana Lough 88 C12
Derries 101 J8
Derry 112 G5
Derryadd 114 M4
Derryanvil 114 M4
Derrybeg 116 H2
Derryboye 115 O4
Derrybrien 99 G8
Derryclare Lough 104 C7
Derrycooly 101 I8
Derrycraff 105 D6
Derrydruel 116 G3
Derryerglinna 105 D7
Derryfadda 101 J9
Derrygolan 101 J8
Derrygonnelly 113 I4
Derrygoolin 100 G9
Derrygrogan 101 J8
Derrykeevan 114 M4
Derrykeighan 118 M2
Derrylea 104 C7
Derrylin 113 J5
Derrylough 116 G3

Derrymore 93 C11
Derrymore Island 93 C11
Derrynane 88 B12
Derrynane House 88 B12
Derrynasaggart Mountains .. 89 E11
Derrynawilt 113 K5
Derryneen 104 C7
Derrynoose 114 L5
Derryrush 104 C7
Derrytrasna 114 M4
Derryveagh Mountains 117 H3
Derryvohy 105 E6
Derrywode 106 G6
Dervock 118 M2
Desertmartin 114 L3
Devenish Island 113 J4
Devilsbit 101 I9
Devilsmother 105 D7
Diamond (The) Antrim 114 N4
Diamond (The) Cookstown 114 M4
Diamond (The) Omagh 113 J4
Dingle / Daingean Uí Chúis .. 92 B11
Dingle Bay 92 B11
Dingle Harbour 92 B11
Divis 115 N4
Doagh Newtownabbey 115 N3
Doagh Rosguill 117 I2
Doagh Beg / Dumhaigh Bhig 117 J2
Doagh Isle 117 J2
Dodder 103 M8
Doe Castle 117 I2
Dolla 100 H9
Dollingstown 114 N4
Domhnach Phádraig / Donaghpatrick 108 L6
Donabate 109 N7
Donacarney 109 N6
Donadea 102 L7
Donagh 113 J5
Donaghadee 115 P4
Donaghaguy 109 N5
Donaghcloney 114 N4
Donaghey 114 L4
Donaghmore 114 L4
Donaghmore Meath 109 M7
Donard Wexford 96 L10
Donard Wicklow 103 M8
Donard (Slieve) 115 O5
Donaskeagh 95 H10
Donegal / Dún na nGall 113 H4
Donegal Airport 116 G2
Donegal Bay 112 G5
Donegal Point 98 D9
Doneraile 94 G11
Donohill 95 H10
Donore 109 M6
Donoughmore 90 F12
Doo (Lough) 99 E9
Doo Lough 104 C7
Doo Lough Pass 104 C7
Dooagh 110 B6
Doobehy 111 D5
Doocastle 106 G5
Dooega Head 104 B6
Dooey Point 116 G3
Doogary 107 J5
Dooghbeg 104 C6
Doogort 110 B5
Doohooma 110 C5
Dooish Mount 117 J3
Doolough Point 110 C5
Doon Galway 100 G7
Doon Limerick 94 H10
Doon Lough 99 F9
Doona 110 C5
Doonaha 93 D10
Doonbeg 98 D9
Doonloughan 104 B7
Doonmanagh 92 B11
Doorin Point 112 H4
Dooyork 110 C5
Dore 116 H2
Dorrusawillin 107 H5
Dough 88 C13
Douglas 90 G12
Douglas Bridge 113 J3
Doulus Bay 88 A12
Doulus Head 88 A12
Dowdallshill 109 M5
Dowling 96 K10
Downhill 118 L2
Downpatrick 115 O5
Downpatrick Head 111 D5
Downs (The) 107 K7
Dowra 113 H5
Dowth 109 M6

Dowth 109 M6
Drains Bay 119 O3
Drangan 95 J10
Draperstown 114 L3
Dreen 118 K3
Dreenagh 92 C10
Drimoleague 89 E13
Drinagh Cork 89 E13
Drinagh Wexford 97 M11
Drinaghan 111 E5
Dring 107 J6
Dripsey 90 F12
Dripsey (River) 90 F11
Drishaghaun 105 D7
Drishane Bridge 89 D13
Drom 101 I9
Dromahair 112 H5
Dromara 115 N4
Dromcolliher 94 F10
Dromin Limerick 94 G10
Dromin Louth 109 M6
Dromina 94 F11
Dromineer 100 H9
Dromiskin 109 M6
Dromkeen 94 G10
Drommahane 90 F11
Dromod 107 I6
Dromoland Castle 99 F9
Dromore Banbridge 115 N4
Dromore Omagh 113 J4
Dromore Lake 94 F10
Dromore West 112 F5
Dromtrasna 93 E10
Drones (The) 118 M2
Drowes 112 H4
Drum Monaghan 108 K5
Drum Roscommon 101 H7
Drum Sligo 112 G5
Drum Hills 91 I11
Drum Manor Forest Park ... 114 L4
Drumahoe 117 K3
Drumandoora 99 F8
Drumaness 115 O4
Drumanoo Head 112 G4
Drumatober 100 G8
Drumbane 95 I10
Drumbeg Feddyglass 117 J3
Drumbeg Lisburn 115 O4
Drumbo 115 O4
Drumbologe 117 I3
Drumcar 109 M6
Drumcard 113 I5
Drumcliff 112 G5
Drumcliff Bay 112 G5
Drumcondra 108 M6
Drumcong 107 I5
Drumcree 108 K7
Drumcullen 114 M3
Drumduff 113 J4
Drumena Cashel 115 O5
Drumfea 96 L10
Drumfin 112 G5
Drumfree 117 J2
Drumgoft 103 M9
Drumintee 109 M5
Drumkeary 99 G8
Drumkeen 117 I3
Drumkeeran 112 H5
Drumlaheen Lough 107 I5
Drumlea 107 I5
Drumlegagh 113 J4
Drumlish 107 I6
Drumlosh 101 I7
Drummannon 114 M4
Drummin 96 L10
Drummullin 106 H6
Drumnakilly 114 K4
Drumone 108 K6
Drumquin 113 J4
Drumraney 107 I7
Drumreagh 110 B5
Drumsallan 107 H5
Drumshanbo 107 H5
Drumsna 107 I6
Drumsurn 118 L3
Duagh 93 D10
Dually 95 I10
Dublin Bay 103 N7
Duff 112 H4
Duffy 102 L7
Duleek 109 M7
Dumha Éige / Dooega 104 B6
Dún Aengus 98 C8

Dún A'Rí Forest Park 108 L6
Dún Chaoin / Dunquin 92 A11
Dún Dealgan / Dundalk 109 M5
Dún Garbhán /Dungarvan .. 91 J11
Dun Laoghaire 103 N8
Dún Mánmhaí / Dunmanway 89 E12
Dún Mór / Dunmore 106 F7
Dún na nGall / Donegal 113 H4
Dunabrattin Head 91 K11
Dunadry 115 N3
Dunaff 117 J2
Dunaff Head 117 J2
Dunaghy 118 M2
Dunagree Point 118 L2
Dunamase (Rock of) 101 K8
Dunamon 106 H7
Dunany 109 N6
Dunany Point 109 N6
Dunbel 96 K10
Dunboyne 103 M7
Dunbrody Abbey 96 L11
Dunbulcaun Bay 99 F8
Duncannon 96 L11
Duncormick 96 M11
Dundalk Bay 109 N6
Dunderrow 90 G12
Dunderry 108 L7
Dundonald 115 O4
Dundrod 115 N4
Dundrum Down 115 O5
Dundrum Dublin 103 N8
Dundrum Tipperary 95 H10
Dundrum Bay 115 O5
Dunfanaghy 117 I2
Dungannon 114 L4
Dunganstown 96 L10
Dungarvan Harbour 91 J11
Dungiven 118 L3
Dungloe / An Clochán Liath 116 G3
Dungonnell Dam 119 N3
Dungourney 90 H12
Dunguaire Castle 99 F8
Dunhill 91 K11
Duniry 100 G8
Dunkellin 99 F8
Dunkerrin 101 I9
Dunkineely 112 G4
Dunkitt 96 K11
Dunlavin 102 L8
Dunleer 109 M6
Dunlewy 117 H2
Dunloe (Gap of) 89 D11
Dunloy 118 M2
Dunluce Castle 118 M2
Dunmanus 89 D13
Dunmanus Bay 88 C13
Dunmore 109 O5
Dunmore Cave 96 K9
Dunmore East 96 L11
Dunmore Head Dunquin ... 92 A11
Dunmore Head near Culdaff 118 K2
Dunmore Head near Portnoo 116 G3
Dunmurry 115 N4
Dunnamaggan 96 K10
Dunnamanagh 117 K3
Dunnamore 114 L3
Dunnycove Bay 89 F13
Dunowen Head 89 F13
Dunree Head 117 J2
Dunsany 108 M7
Dunshaughlin 108 M7
Durlas / Thurles 95 I9
Durrow 101 J9
Durrus 89 D13
Dursey Head 88 B13
Dursey Island 88 B13
Duvillaun Beg 110 B5
Duvillaun More 110 B5
Dyan 114 L4
Dysart 107 J7
Dysert O'Dea 99 E9

E

Éadan Doire / Édenderry ... 102 K7
Eagle (Mount) 92 A11
Eagle Island 110 B5
Eagles Hill 88 B12
Eany 112 H4
Eanymore 112 H3
Easky 111 F5
Easky Lough 112 F5
East Ferry 90 H12

East Town 116 H2
Eddy Island 99 F8
Eden 115 O3
Ederny 113 J4
Edgeworthstown 107 J6
Edgeworthstown / Meathas Troim 107 J6
Egish (Lough) 108 L5
Eglinton 118 K2
Eglish 114 L4
Eighter 108 K6
Eleven Lane Ends 114 M5
Ellistrin 117 I3
Elly Bay 110 B5
Elphin 106 H6
Elton 94 G10
Elva (Slieve) 99 E8
Emmoo 106 H7
Emly 94 G10
Emmoo 106 H7
Emo 101 K8
Emo Court 101 K8
Emyvale 114 L4
Ennel (Lough) 107 J7
Ennis / Inis 99 F9
Enniscorthy / Inis Córthaidh 97 M10
Enniskean 89 F12
Enniskerry 103 N8
Enniskillen 113 J4
Ennistimon / Inis Díomáin .. 99 E9
Eochaill / Youghal 91 I12
Erne (Lower Lough) 113 I4
Erne (River) 107 J6
Erne (Upper Lough) 113 J5
Erra 107 I6
Errew Abbey 111 E5
Erriff (River) 105 D7
Errigal Mountain 117 H2
Erril 101 I9
Erris Head 110 B5
Errisbeg 104 C7
Errislannan 104 B7
Errit Lough 106 F6
Ervey Cross Roads 118 K3
Eshnadarragh 113 K5
Eshnadeelada 113 K5
Eske 113 H3
Eske (Lough) 113 H3
Esker 99 F8
Esker South 107 I6
Eskeragh 111 D5
Eskragh 113 K4
Eyeries 88 C12
Eyrecourt 100 H8

F

Faha 91 J11
Fahamore 92 B11
Fahan 117 J2
Fahy 100 H8
Fahy Lough 110 C5
Fair Green 99 F9
Fair Head 88 C13
Fairyhouse 108 M7
Fairymount 106 G6
Fallmore 110 B5
Fanad 117 I2
Fanad Head 117 J2
Fane River 108 M5
Fanore 99 E8
Farahy 94 G11
Fardrum 101 I7
Fardurris Point 98 D8
Farmer's Bridge 93 D11
Farnagh 101 I7
Farnagh 107 I6
Farnanes Cross Roads 90 F12
Farnoge 96 K10
Farran 90 F12
Farran Forest Park 90 F12
Farrancassidy Cross Roads 112 H4
Farranfore 93 D11
Fastnet Rock 89 D13
Faughan 118 K3
Fawney 117 K3
Fea (Lough) 114 L3
Feagarrid 95 I11
Feakle 99 G9
Feale (River) 93 D10
Fearn Hill 113 J3
Fedamore 94 G10
Fee (Lough) 104 C7
Feeagh (Lough) 105 D6
Feeard 93 C10
Feenagh 94 F10

Feeny ...118 K3
Feevagh ...106 H7
Fenagh ...107 I5
Fenit ...92 C11
Fennagh ...96 L9
Fennor ...91 K11
Feohanagh *Kerry* ...92 A11
Feohanagh *Limerick* ...94 F10
Feohanagh (River) ...92 B11
Ferbane ...101 I8
Fergus (River) ...99 E9
Fern (Lough) ...117 I2
Ferns ...97 M10
Ferry Bridge ...94 F10
Ferrybank ...97 N9
Ferrycarrig ...97 M10
Ferta ...88 B12
Fethard ...96 L11
Fews ...95 J11
Feystown ...119 O3
Fiddown ...96 K10
Fieries ...93 D11
Finavarra ...99 E8
Finglas ...103 N7
Finglass ...89 C11
Finn (Lough) ...117 H3
Finn (River) ...117 J3
Finnea ...107 J6
Finnisglin ...104 C7
Fintona ...113 K4
Fintragh Bay ...112 G4
Finuge ...93 D10
Finvoy ...118 M2
Fiodh Ard / Fethard ...95 I10
Fionnaithe / Finny ...105 D7
Firkeel ...88 B13
Fisherhill ...105 E6
Five Corners ...115 N3
Fivealley ...101 I8
Fivemilebridge ...90 G12
Fivemiletown ...113 K4
Flagmount *Corlea* ...99 G9
Flagmount *Kilkenny* ...96 K10
Flat Head ...90 G12
Flesk ...89 D11
Florence Court ...113 I5
Florence Court Forest Park ...113 I5
Foaty Island/Fota Island ...90 H12
Foilycleara ...95 H10
Folk Park ...99 F9
Fontstown ...102 L8
Forbes (Lough) ...107 I6
Fordstown ...108 L6
Fore ...107 K6
Forkill ...109 M5
Forlorn Point ...96 M11
Formoyle *Lonford* ...107 I7
Formoyle *Mayo* ...104 C6
Formoyle *near Ballivaghan* ...99 E8
Formoyle *near Inagh* ...99 E9
Formoyle (Lough) ...105 D7
Fort Stewart ...117 J2
Forthill ...107 I7
Fota Island ...90 H12
Foul Sound ...98 D8
Foulksmills ...96 L11
Fountain Cross ...99 E9
Four Mile House ...106 H6
Four Roads ...106 H7
Fourknocks ...109 N7
Foxford ...105 E6
Foxhall ...105 E7
Foyle (Lough) ...118 K2
Foynes ...93 E10
Foynes Island ...93 E10
Francis' Gap ...99 G8
Freemount ...94 F11
Frenchpark ...106 G6
Freshford ...95 J9
Freynestown ...102 L8
Frosses ...112 H3
Frower Point ...90 G12
Fuerty ...106 H7
Funshin More ...99 F8
Funshinagh (Lough) ...106 H7
Funshion ...94 G11
Furbogh ...99 E8
Furnace ...105 D7
Furnace Lough ...105 D6
Furness ...103 M8
Fyagh (Slieve) ...111 D5

G
Gabriel (Mount) ...89 D13
Gaddagh ...89 C11

Gaillimh / Galway ...99 E8
Gainestown ...107 K7
Galbally *Dungannon* ...114 L4
Galbally *Limerick* ...94 H10
Galbally *Wexford* ...96 M10
Galbolie ...108 K6
Galey ...93 D10
Galgorm ...118 N3
Gallarus Oratory ...92 A11
Galley Head ...89 F13
Gallion (Slieve) ...114 L3
Galmoy ...101 J9
Galty Mountains ...95 H10
Galtymore Mountain ...95 H10
Galway Bay ...98 D8
Galways Bridge ...89 D12
Gaoth Dobhair / Gweedore ...116 H2
Gaoth Sáile / Geesala ...110 C5
Gap (The) ...95 I11
Gara (Lough) ...106 G6
Garadice ...102 L7
Garadice Lough ...107 I5
Garbally ...100 H8
Garinish Island ...88 C12
Garnavilla ...95 I10
Garnish Point ...88 B13
Garrane ...89 E12
Garranlahan ...106 G6
Garraun *Clare* ...98 D9
Garraun *Galway* ...100 C9
Garraun (Mount) ...104 C7
Garries Bridge ...89 D12
Garrison ...112 H4
Garristown ...109 M7
Garron Point ...119 O2
Garrycloonagh ...111 E5
Garrycullen ...96 L11
Garryduff ...118 M2
Garryfine ...94 F10
Garrykennedy ...100 G9
Garryspillane ...94 G10
Garryvoe ...91 H12
Gartan Lough ...117 I3
Gartree Point ...114 N4
Garty Lough ...107 J6
Garvagh *Coleraine* ...118 L3
Garvagh *Rowan* ...107 I6
Garvaghy ...114 K4
Garvary ...113 J4
Gattabaun ...101 J9
Gearagh (The) ...90 F12
Gearha Bridge ...88 C12
Geashill ...101 K8
Geevagh ...112 H5
George (Lough) ...99 F9
Gerahies ...89 D13
Giant's Causeway ...118 M2
Giles Quay ...109 N6
Gilford ...114 M4
Gill (Lough) *near Sligo* ...112 G5
Gill (Lough) *nearTralee* ...92 B11
Glanaruddery Mountains ...93 D11
Glandore ...89 E13
Glandore Harbour ...89 E13
Glangevlin ...113 I5
Glanmire ...90 G12
Glanmore Lake ...89 C12
Glanoe ...93 D10
Glantane ...90 F11
Glanworth ...94 G11
Glarryford ...118 M3
Glasdrumman ...109 O5
Glaslough ...114 L5
Glasmullan ...117 J2
Glassan ...107 I7
Glasshouse Lake ...107 J5
Glassillaun ...104 C6
Glastry ...115 P4
Gleann Cholm Cille / Glencolumbkille ...112 F3
Gleann Domhain / Glendowan ...117 I3
Gleann na Muaidhe / Glenamoy ...111 C5
Glen ...117 I2
Glen (River) *Cork* ...90 F11
Glen (River) *Donegal* ...112 G3
Glen Bay ...112 F3
Glen Head ...112 F3
Glen Lough *Donegal* ...117 I2
Glen Lough *Westmeath* ...107 J7
Glenaan ...119 N2
Glenade ...112 H4
Glenade Lough ...112 H4
Glenamoy (River) ...111 D5
Glenariff ...119 N2

Glenariff Forest Park ...119 N2
Glenariff or Waterfoot ...119 N2
Glenarm ...119 O3
Glenavy ...115 N4
Glenballyemon ...119 N2
Glenbeg Lough ...88 C12
Glenbeigh ...92 C11
Glenboy ...112 H5
Glenbridge Lodge ...103 M8
Glenbrohane ...94 G10
Glenbrook ...90 G12
Glencar ...88 C12
Glencar Lough ...112 G4
Glencloy ...119 O3
Glencolmcille Folk Village ...112 F3
Glencree ...103 N8
Glencullen ...103 N8
Glendalough *Brockagh* ...103 M8
Glendalough *Waterford* ...95 J11
Glenderry ...92 C10
Glendorragha ...116 G3
Glendovan Mountains ...117 H3
Glendree ...99 F9
Glendum ...119 N2
Glenealy ...103 N9
Gleneely *near Ballybofey* ...113 I3
Gleneely *near Cardonagh* ...118 K2
Glenelly ...114 K3
Glenelly Valley ...114 K3
Glenfarne ...113 I5
Glenflesk ...89 D11
Glengad Head ...118 K1
Glengarriff (River) ...89 D12
Glengarriff Harbour ...89 D12
Glengesh Pass ...112 G3
Glengormley ...115 O3
Glenhead ...118 K2
Glenhull ...114 K3
Glenicmurrin Lough ...98 D8
Glenmacnass ...103 M8
Glenmalur ...103 M9
Glenmore *Clare* ...99 E9
Glenmore *Kilkenny* ...96 K10
Glennagevlagh ...105 D7
Glennamaddy ...106 G7
Glennascaul ...99 F8
Glenoe ...115 O3
Glenshane Pass ...118 L3
Glenshesk ...119 N2
Glentaisie ...119 N2
Glentane ...106 G7
Glenties ...116 H3
Glentogher ...118 K2
Glentrasna ...105 D7
Glenvale ...118 M3
Glenvar / Gleann Bhairr ...117 J2
Glenveagh National Park ...117 I2
Glenville ...90 G11
Glin ...93 E10
Glin Castle ...93 E10
Glinsce / Glinsk ...104 C7
Glinsk *Donegal* ...117 I2
Glinsk *Mayo* ...111 D5
Glounthaune ...90 G12
Glyde (River) ...108 M6
Glynn *Carlow* ...96 L10
Glynn *Larne* ...115 O3
Gneevgullia ...93 E11
Gob an Choire / Achill Sound ...104 C6
Gobbins (The) ...115 O3
Gokane Point ...89 E13
Gola Island / Gabhla ...116 G2
Golagh Lough ...113 H4
Golam Head ...98 C8
Golden ...95 I10
Golden Vale ...95 H10
Goleen ...88 C13
Goold's Cross ...95 I10
Goresbridge ...96 K10
Gorey / Guaire ...97 N9
Gormanston ...109 N7
Gort an Choirce / Gortahork ...117 H2
Gortaclare ...113 K4
Gortahill ...113 I5
Gortaleam ...106 F7
Gortarevan ...100 H8
Gortaroo ...91 I12
Gortaway ...117 J2
Gorteen ...106 G6
Gorteen Bridge ...101 J8
Gortgarriff ...88 C12
Gortgarrigan ...112 H5
Gortin ...113 K3
Gortin Glen Forest Park ...113 K3

Gortletteragh ...107 I6
Gortmore *near Ballycastle* ...111 D5
Gortmore *near Bangor* ...111 C5
Gortmullan ...113 J5
Gortnadeeve ...106 G7
Gortnahoo ...95 J9
Gortnasillagh ...106 G6
Gortree ...117 J3
Gortymadden ...100 G8
Gorumna Island ...98 C8
Gosford Forest Park ...114 M5
Gougane Barra Forest Park ...89 D12
Gougane Barra Lake ...89 E12
Gouladoo ...89 C13
Gowla ...104 C7
Gowlaun ...104 C7
Gowlin ...96 L10
Gowna (Lough) ...107 J6
Gowran ...96 K10
Gracehill ...118 N3
Graffy ...116 H3
Gráig na Manach / Graiguenamanagh ...96 L10
Graigue ...102 L9
Graigue Hill ...96 L9
Graigue More ...96 M10
Graigues ...88 B12
Granabeg ...103 M8
Gránard / Granard ...107 J6
Grand Canal ...101 I8
Graney ...102 L9
Graney (Lough) ...99 G9
Graney (River) ...99 G9
Grange *Kildare* ...102 K7
Grange *Kilkenny* ...96 K10
Grange *Louth* ...109 N5
Grange *Sligo* ...112 G4
Grange *Waterford* ...91 I12
Grange (River) ...106 F7
Grange Con ...102 L9
Grangebellew ...109 M6
Grangeford ...102 L9
Grangegeeth ...108 M6
Granias Gap ...117 K2
Grannagh ...99 F8
Gransha ...115 O3
Granville ...114 L4
Greagh ...107 I6
Great Blasket Island ...92 A11
Great Island ...90 H12
Great Newtown Head ...96 K11
Great Skellig ...88 A12
Great Sugar Loaf ...103 N8
Greatman's Bay ...98 D8
Greenan ...103 N9
Greenanstown ...109 N7
Greenasland ...115 O3
Greencastle *Donegal* ...118 L2
Greencastle *Newry-Mourne* ...109 N5
Greencastle *Omagh* ...114 K3
Greenfield ...105 E7
Greenisland ...115 O3
Greenore ...109 N5
Greenore Point ...97 N11
Gregans Castle ...99 E8
Gregory's Sound ...98 D8
Grey Abbey ...115 P4
Grey Point ...115 O3
Greysteel ...118 K2
Greystone ...114 L4
Grianan of Aileach ...117 J2
Grogan ...101 I8
Gubaveeny ...113 I5
Gubbaroe Point ...113 I4
Gulladuff ...118 M3
Gullaun Lough ...107 J6
Gullion (Slieve) ...109 M5
Gur (Lough) ...94 G10
Gurteen *Cappalusk* ...99 G7
Gurteen *Leitrim* ...112 H5
Gusserane ...96 L11
Gweebarra Bridge ...116 H3
Gweebarra ...116 H3
Gweebarra Bay ...116 G3
Gweestin ...93 D11
Gweedore ...116 G2
Gweestion ...105 E6
Gyleen ...90 H12

H
Hacketstown ...103 M9
Hags Head ...98 D9
Hamiltonsbawn ...114 M4
Hand Cross Roads (The) ...99 E9
Hannahstown ...115 N4

Hare Island ...89 D13
Harristown ...96 K10
Harrow (The) ...97 M10
Healy Pass ...89 C12
Helen's Bay ...115 O3
Helvick Head ...91 J11
Herbertstown ...94 G10
High Island ...104 B7
Highwood ...112 H5
Hill Street ...107 H6
Hillsborough ...115 N4
Hilltown *Harristown* ...96 L11
Hilltown *Newry and Mourne* ...115 N5
Hind ...106 H7
Hog's Head ...88 B12
Holeopen Bay West ...90 G13
Hollyford ...95 H10
Hollyfort ...97 N9
Hollymount ...105 E7
Hollywood ...103 M8
Holy Cross ...95 I10
Holy Island ...99 G9
Holycross ...94 G10
Holywell ...113 I5
Holywell Hill ...117 J2
Holywood ...115 O4
Hook Head ...96 L11
Hore Abbey ...95 I10
Horn Head ...117 I2
Horse and Jockey ...95 I10
Horse Island ...89 D13
Horseleap ...101 J7
Hospital ...94 G10
Hugginstown ...96 K10
Hungry Hill ...88 C12
Hurlers Cross ...99 F9
Hurley ...109 M7
Hyne (Lough) ...89 E13

I
Ilen ...89 E13
Illaunstookagh ...92 C11
Illauntannig ...92 B11
Illies ...117 J2
Illnacullin ...89 D12
Inagh ...99 E9
Inagh (Lough) ...104 C7
Inch ...92 C11
Inch *Donegal* ...117 J2
Inch *near Whitegate* ...90 H12
Inch *near Youghal* ...91 I12
Inch *Tipperary* ...95 H9
Inch *Wexford* ...97 N9
Inch Abbey ...115 O4
Inch Island ...117 J2
Inchagoill ...105 E7
Inchamore Bridge ...108 L7
Inchbeg ...96 J9
Inchcleraun ...107 H7
Inchee Bridge ...89 D12
Inchicronan Lough ...99 F9
Inchigeelagh ...89 E12
Inchiquin ...105 E7
Inchiquin Lough *Clare* ...99 E9
Inchiquin Lough *Kerry* ...89 D12
Inchmore ...107 I7
Inchnamuck ...95 H11
Inchydoney Island ...90 F13
Indreabhán / Inveran ...98 D8
Inis / Ennis ...99 F9
Inis Bó Finne / Inishbofin ...117 H2
Inis Meáin / Inishmaan ...98 D8
Inis Mór / Inishmore ...98 C8
Inis Oírr / Inisheer ...98 D8
Inishannon ...90 G12
Inishbarra ...98 C8
Inishbiggle ...110 C6
Inishbofin ...104 B7
Inishcarra ...90 G12
Inishcarra Reservoir ...90 F12
Inishcrone ...111 E5
Inishdoorus ...105 D7
Inishfarrard ...88 B12
Inishfree Bay ...116 G2
Inishfree Upper ...116 G3
Inishglora ...110 B5
Inishkea North ...110 B5
Inishkea South ...110 B5
Inishmaine Island ...105 E7
Inishmicatreer ...105 E7
Inishmurray ...112 G4
Inishnabro ...92 A11
Inishnee ...104 C7
Inishowen ...117 J2
Inishowen Head ...118 L2
Inishshark ...104 B7

Inishtooskert ...92 A11
Inishtrahull ...118 K1
Inishtrahull Sound ...118 K1
Inishturk ...104 B6
Inishvickillane ...92 A11
Inistioge ...96 K10
Innfield ...102 L7
Innisfree ...112 G5
Inniskeen ...108 M5
Inny (River) ...107 J6
Inver *Donegal* ...112 H4
Inver *Mayo* ...110 C5
Inver Bay ...112 H4
Ireland's Eye ...103 N7
Irish Agricultural Museum ...97 M11
Irishtown ...105 F7
Iron (Lough) ...107 J7
Iron Mountains ...113 I5
Irvinestown ...113 J4
Island Lake ...106 F6
Island Reavy (Lough) ...115 N5
Islandmagee ...115 O3
Islandmore ...115 P4
Iveragh ...88 B12

J
J. F. Kennedy Park ...96 L11
Jamestown *Cloonteem* ...107 H6
Jamestown *Laois* ...101 K8
Japanese Gardens ...102 L8
Jerpoint Abbey ...96 K10
Jerrettspass ...114 M5
Johnstown *Kildare* ...103 M8
Johnstown *Kilkenny* ...101 J9
Johnstown *Meath* ...108 M7
Johnstown *near Arklow* ...103 N9
Johnstown *near Coolgreany* ...97 N9
Johnstown Bridge ...107 I6
Johnstownbridge ...102 L7
Jonesborough ...109 M5
Joyce ...105 D7
Julianstown ...109 N6

K
Kanturk Castle ...94 F11
Katesbridge ...115 N5
Keadew ...107 H5
Keady ...114 L5
Keady Mountain ...118 L2
Kealduff ...89 C12
Kealkill ...89 D12
Kearney ...115 P4
Kearney Point ...115 P4
Keeagh ...99 E8
Keel ...110 B6
Keel (Lough) ...117 I2
Keel Lough ...110 B6
Keeloges ...106 G7
Keem Strand ...110 B6
Keenagh *Longford* ...107 I7
Keenagh *Mayo* ...111 D5
Keeraunnagark ...98 D8
Keereen ...91 I11
Keimaneigh (The pass of) ...89 E12
Kells *Ballymena* ...115 N3
Kells *Kerry* ...88 B12
Kells *Kilkenny* ...96 K10
Kells (Ceanannus Mor) / Ceanannas *Meath* ...108 L6
Kells Bay ...88 B12
Kells Priory ...96 K10
Kellysgrove ...100 H8
Kenmare River ...88 B12
Kentstown ...108 M7
Kerry (Ring of) ...88 B12
Kerry Head ...92 C10
Kesh *Fermanagh* ...113 I4
Kesh *Toomour* ...106 G5
Keshcarrigan ...107 I5
Key (Lough) ...106 H5
Kid Island ...110 C5
Kilbaha ...93 C10
Kilbaha Bay ...93 C10
Kilbane ...99 G9
Kilbarry ...89 E12
Kilbeacanty ...99 F8
Kilbeggan ...101 J7
Kilbeheny ...94 H11
Kilbennan ...105 F7
Kilberry *Bert* ...108 L6
Kilberry *Kildare* ...102 K8
Kilbreedy ...94 F10
Kilbrickan ...105 D7
Kilbricken ...101 J9
Kilbride *near Blessington* ...103 M8

A B C D E F G H I J K L M N O P Q R S T U V W X Y Z

Kilbride *near Ratoah* .... 103 M 7
Kilbride *near Trim* .... 108 L 7
Kilbride *near Wicklow* .... 103 N 9
Kilbrien .... 95 J 11
Kilbrin .... 94 F 11
Kilbrittain .... 90 F 12
Kilcaimin .... 99 F 8
Kilcar .... 112 G 4
Kilcarn .... 108 L 7
Kilcatherine Point .... 88 B 12
Kilcavan .... 101 J 8
Kilchreest .... 99 G 8
Kilclaran .... 99 G 9
Kilclief .... 115 P 5
Kilcloher .... 93 C 10
Kilclonfert .... 101 J 8
Kilclooney .... 116 G 3
Kilcock .... 102 L 7
Kilcogy .... 107 J 6
Kilcolgan .... 99 F 8
Kilcolman *Cashel* .... 90 F 12
Kilcolman
    Dunmoylan East .... 93 E 10
Kilcoltrim .... 96 L 10
Kilcomin .... 101 I 9
Kilcommon *near Caher* .... 95 I 10
Kilcommon *near Milestone* .... 95 H 9
Kilcon .... 111 E 5
Kilconly *Galway* .... 105 F 7
Kilconly *Kerry* .... 93 D 10
Kilcoo .... 115 N 5
Kilcoole .... 103 N 8
Kilcormac .... 101 I 8
Kilcornan .... 94 F 10
Kilcotty .... 97 M 10
Kilcredan .... 91 I 12
Kilcredaun Point .... 93 C 10
Kilcrohane .... 89 C 13
Kilcrow .... 100 H 8
Kilcullen .... 102 L 8
Kilcummin *Kerry* .... 92 B 11
Kilcummin *Mayo* .... 111 E 5
Kilcummin Farmhill .... 93 D 11
Kilcurly .... 109 M 5
Kilcurry .... 109 M 5
Kildalkey .... 108 L 7
Kildangan .... 102 K 8
Kildavin .... 96 L 9
Kilderry .... 96 K 9
Kildoney Point .... 112 H 4
Kildorrery .... 94 G 11
Kildress .... 114 L 4
Kildrum .... 115 N 3
Kilfeakle .... 95 H 10
Kilfearagh .... 98 D 10
Kilfenora .... 99 E 9
Kilfinnane .... 94 G 10
Kilfinny .... 94 F 10
Kilflyn .... 93 D 10
Kilgarvan .... 89 D 12
Kilglass *Galway* .... 106 G 7
Kilglass *Sligo* .... 111 E 6
Kilglass Lough .... 107 H 6
Kilgobnet *Kerry* .... 89 C 11
Kilgobnet *Waterford* .... 91 J 11
Kilgory Lough .... 99 F 9
Kilgowan .... 102 L 8
Kiljames .... 96 K 10
Kilkea .... 102 L 9
Kilkeary .... 100 H 9
Kilkeasy .... 96 K 10
Kilkeel .... 109 N 5
Kilkeeran High Crosses .... 95 J 10
Kilkenny West .... 107 I 7
Kilkerrin .... 106 G 7
Kilkieran / Cill Chiaráin .... 104 C 8
Kilkieran Bay .... 104 C 7
Kilkiernan .... 96 K 9
Kilkinamurry .... 115 N 5
Kilkinlea .... 93 E 10
Kilkishen .... 99 F 9
Kill *Cavan* .... 108 K 5
Kill *Waterford* .... 91 J 11
Killabunane .... 89 D 12
Killaclug .... 94 H 11
Killacolla .... 94 F 10
Killadangan .... 105 D 6
Killadeas .... 113 I 4
Killadoon .... 104 C 6
Killadysert .... 99 E 9
Killafeen .... 99 F 8
Killag .... 96 M 11
Killagan Bridge .... 118 M 2
Killaghteen .... 93 E 10
Killahy .... 95 J 9
Killakee .... 103 N 8
Killala .... 111 E 5

Killala Bay .... 111 E 5
Killallon .... 108 K 6
Killaloo .... 118 K 3
Killamery .... 95 J 10
Killane .... 102 K 8
Killanena .... 99 F 9
Killann .... 96 L 10
Killard .... 98 D 9
Killard Point .... 115 P 5
Killarga .... 112 H 5
Killarney National Park .... 89 D 11
Killarone .... 105 E 7
Killary Harbour .... 104 C 7
Killashandra .... 107 J 5
Killashee .... 107 I 6
Killasser .... 105 F 6
Killavally *Mayo* .... 105 D 6
Killavally *Westmeath* .... 101 J 7
Killavil .... 106 G 5
Killavullen .... 94 G 11
Killea *Donegal* .... 117 J 3
Killea *Tipperary* .... 101 I 9
Killeagh .... 91 H 12
Killealy .... 115 N 3
Killeany .... 98 D 8
Killedmond .... 96 L 10
Killeedy .... 93 E 10
Killeen *Ardamullivan* .... 99 F 9
Killeen *Armagh* .... 114 M 5
Killeen *Dungannon* .... 114 M 4
Killeenaran .... 99 F 8
Killeeneenmore .... 99 F 8
Killeenleagh Bridge .... 88 B 12
Killeevan .... 113 K 5
Killeglan .... 106 H 7
Killeigh .... 101 J 8
Killen .... 113 J 3
Killenagh .... 97 N 10
Killenaule .... 95 I 10
Killeshil .... 101 K 8
Killeshin .... 102 K 9
Killeter .... 113 I 3
Killeter Forest .... 113 I 3
Killevy .... 109 M 5
Killevy Churches .... 109 M 5
Killilan Bridge .... 99 G 8
Killimer .... 93 D 10
Killimor .... 100 H 8
Killinaboy .... 99 E 9
Killinaspick .... 96 K 10
Killinchy .... 115 O 4
Killincooly .... 97 N 10
Killiney *Dublin* .... 103 N 8
Killiney *Kerry* .... 92 B 11
Killiney Bay .... 103 N 8
Killinick .... 97 M 11
Killinierin .... 97 N 9
Killinkere .... 108 K 6
Killinny .... 99 F 8
Killinthomas .... 102 K 8
Killinure Lough .... 107 I 7
Killiskey .... 103 N 8
Killkelly .... 105 F 6
Killmuckbridge .... 97 N 10
Killogeary .... 111 E 5
Killogeenaghan .... 101 I 7
Killonecaha .... 88 B 12
Killoran .... 100 G 8
Killoscobe .... 106 G 7
Killough .... 115 P 5
Killough .... 103 N 8
Killowen .... 109 N 5
Killucan .... 108 K 7
Killukin .... 107 H 6
Killurin .... 96 M 10
Killurly .... 88 B 12
Killusty .... 95 J 10
Killwaughter .... 115 O 3
Killyclogher .... 113 J 4
Killyclug .... 117 I 3
Killyclogher .... 113 K 4
Killycolpy .... 114 M 4
Killygar .... 107 J 5
Killygordon .... 117 I 3
Killykeen Forest Park .... 107 J 5
Killylea .... 114 L 4
Killyleagh .... 115 P 4
Killyon .... 101 I 8
Kilmacanoge .... 103 N 8
Kilmacduagh Monastery .... 99 F 8
Kilmacoo .... 103 N 9
Kilmacow .... 96 K 11
Kilmacrenan .... 117 I 2
Kilmacteige .... 111 F 5
Kilmacthomas .... 95 J 11
Kilmactranny .... 106 H 5
Kilmacurragh .... 103 N 9
Kilmaganny .... 96 K 10

Kilmaine .... 105 E 7
Kilmainham Wood .... 108 L 6
Kilmakilloge Harbour .... 88 C 12
Kilmaley .... 99 E 9
Kilmalkedar .... 92 B 11
Kilmanagh .... 95 J 10
Kilmeadan .... 96 K 11
Kilmeage .... 102 L 8
Kilmeedy .... 94 F 10
Kilmeelickin .... 105 D 7
Kilmeena .... 105 D 6
Kilmessan .... 108 M 7
Kilmichael
    near Castletownbere .... 88 B 13
Kilmichael *near Macroom* .... 89 E 12
Kilmichael Point .... 97 N 9
Kilmihil .... 98 E 9
Kilmona .... 90 G 12
Kilmoon .... 89 D 13
Kilmore *Armagh* .... 114 M 4
Kilmore *Clare* .... 99 G 9
Kilmore *Down* .... 115 O 4
Kilmore *Mayo* .... 105 E 6
Kilmore *Roscommon* .... 107 H 6
Kilmore *Wexford* .... 96 M 11
Kilmore Quay .... 96 M 11
Kilmorna .... 93 D 10
Kilmorony .... 102 L 9
Kilmovee .... 106 F 6
Kilmurry *Cork* .... 90 F 12
Kilmurry *Limerick* .... 94 G 10
Kilmurry *near Kilkishen* .... 99 F 9
Kilmurry *near Milltown* .... 98 D 9
Kilmurry *Wicklow* .... 102 L 9
Kilmurry Mac Mahon .... 93 E 10
Kilmyshall .... 96 M 10
Kilnagross .... 107 I 6
Kilnalag .... 106 G 6
Kilnaleck .... 107 K 6
Kilnamanagh .... 97 M 10
Kilnamona .... 99 E 9
Kilntown .... 115 N 4
Kilpatrick .... 90 F 12
Kilpeacan Cross Roads .... 88 B 12
Kilpedder .... 103 N 8
Kilquigguin .... 97 M 9
Kilraghts .... 118 M 2
Kilrane .... 97 M 11
Kilrea .... 118 M 3
Kilrean .... 116 H 3
Kilreekill .... 100 G 8
Kilroghter .... 99 E 8
Kilross *Donegal* .... 117 I 3
Kilross *Tipperary* .... 94 H 10
Kilruddery .... 103 N 8
Kilsallagh *Galway* .... 106 G 7
Kilsallagh *Mayo* .... 104 C 6
Kilsallaghan .... 103 N 7
Kilsally .... 114 M 4
Kilsaran .... 109 M 6
Kilshanchoe .... 102 L 7
Kilshannig .... 92 B 11
Kilshanny .... 99 E 9
Kilsheelan .... 95 J 10
Kilskeer .... 108 L 6
Kilskeery .... 113 J 4
Kiltealy .... 96 L 10
Kilteel .... 103 M 8
Kilteely .... 94 G 10
Kiltegan .... 103 M 9
Kilternan .... 103 N 8
Kiltimagh .... 105 E 6
Kiltober .... 101 J 7
Kiltoom .... 107 H 7
Kiltormer .... 100 H 8
Kiltullagh .... 99 G 8
Kiltyclogher .... 113 H 4
Kilvine .... 105 F 7
Kilworth .... 94 H 11
Kilworth Mountains .... 94 H 11
Kinale (Lough) .... 107 J 6
Kinard .... 93 E 10
Kinawley .... 113 J 5
Kincasslagh .... 116 G 2
Kindrohid .... 117 J 2
Kindrum .... 117 I 2
Kingarrow .... 117 H 3
Kings River .... 95 J 10
Kingscourt .... 108 L 6
Kingsland .... 106 G 6
Kingsmill .... 114 M 4
Kingstown .... 104 B 7
Kinlough .... 112 H 4
Kinnadoohy .... 104 C 6
Kinnagoe Bay .... 118 K 2
Kinnegad .... 108 K 7

Kinnitty .... 101 I 8
Kinsale (Old Head of) .... 90 G 13
Kinsale Harbour .... 90 G 12
Kinsalebeg .... 91 I 12
Kinsaley .... 103 N 7
Kinvarra
    near Camus Bay .... 105 D 7
Kinvarra
    near Kinvarra Bay .... 99 F 8
Kinvarra Bay .... 99 F 8
Kippure .... 103 N 8
Kircubbin .... 115 P 4
Kirkhills .... 118 M 2
Kirkistown .... 115 P 4
Kitconnell .... 100 G 8
Knappagh .... 105 D 6
Knappogue Castle .... 99 F 9
Knight's Town .... 88 B 12
Knock *Clare* .... 93 E 10
Knock *Mayo* .... 105 F 6
Knock *Tipperary* .... 101 I 9
Knockaderry .... 94 F 10
Knockadoon Head .... 91 I 12
Knockainy .... 94 G 10
Knockalla Mount .... 117 J 2
Knockalongy .... 112 F 5
Knockalough .... 99 E 9
Knockanaffrin .... 95 J 11
Knockananna .... 103 M 9
Knockanefune .... 93 E 11
Knockanevin .... 94 G 11
Knockanillaun .... 111 E 5
Knockanimpaha .... 93 E 10
Knockanore .... 93 D 10
Knockaunalour .... 90 G 11
Knockaunavoher .... 94 G 10
Knockaunnaglashy .... 92 C 11
Knockboy *near Dungarvan* .... 95 I 11
Knockboy *near Waterford* .... 96 K 11
Knockboy (Mount) .... 89 D 12
Knockbrack .... 117 I 3
Knockbrandon .... 97 M 9
Knockbride .... 108 L 6
Knockbridge .... 109 M 6
Knockbrit .... 95 I 10
Knockcloghrim .... 114 M 3
Knockcroghery .... 106 H 7
Knockdrin .... 107 K 7
Knockerry
Knockferry .... 105 E 7
Knocklayd .... 119 N 2
Knocklofty .... 95 I 10
Knocklomena .... 89 C 12
Knocklong .... 94 G 10
Knockmealdown .... 95 I 11
Knockmealdown
    Mountains .... 95 H 11
Knockmore .... 104 B 6
Knockmore (Mount) .... 104 C 6
Knockmourne .... 90 H 11
Knockmoy Abbey .... 106 F 7
Knocknaboul Cross .... 93 E 11
Knocknacarry .... 119 N 2
Knocknacree .... 102 L 9
Knocknadobar .... 88 B 12
Knocknagantee .... 88 C 12
Knocknagashel .... 93 D 11
Knocknagree .... 93 E 11
Knocknahilan .... 90 F 12
Knocknalina .... 110 C 5
Knocknalower .... 110 C 5
Knockowen .... 89 C 12
Knockraha .... 90 G 12
Knocks *Cork* .... 89 F 12
Knocks *Fermanagh* .... 113 J 5
Knocks *Laois* .... 101 J 8
Knockshanahullion .... 95 H 11
Knockskagh .... 89 F 12
Knocktopher .... 96 K 10
Knocktown .... 96 M 11
Knockundervaul .... 93 D 10
Knockvicar .... 106 H 5
Knowth .... 108 M 6
Kylemore .... 100 H 8
Kylemore Abbey .... 104 C 7
Kylemore Lough .... 104 C 7

L

Laban .... 99 F 8
Labasheeda .... 93 E 10
Lack .... 113 J 4
Lackagh .... 102 K 8
Lackan *Carlow* .... 96 K 9
Lackan *Wicklow* .... 103 M 8
Lackan bay .... 111 E 5
Lackareagh .... 89 F 12

Laconnell .... 116 G 3
Ladies View .... 89 D 12
Lady's Island Lake .... 97 M 11
Ladysbridge .... 90 H 12
Ladywell .... 96 K 10
Laffansbridge .... 95 I 10
Lag .... 117 K 2
Lagan (River) .... 115 N 4
Lagan Valley .... 115 O 4
Lagavara .... 118 M 2
Lagganstown .... 95 I 10
Laghey Corner .... 114 L 4
Laghtnafrankee .... 95 J 11
Laghy .... 113 H 4
Lahardaun .... 111 E 5
Lakyle .... 93 E 10
Lambay Island .... 109 N 7
Lambeg .... 115 N 4
Lamb's Head .... 88 B 12
Lanesborough .... 107 I 6
Laney (River) .... 89 F 12
Laracor .... 108 L 7
Laragh *Kildare* .... 102 L 7
Laragh *Monaghan* .... 108 L 5
Laragh *Wicklow* .... 103 N 8
Largan *Mayo* .... 111 D 5
Largan *Sligo* .... 111 F 5
Largy .... 112 G 4
Largydonnell .... 112 H 4
Larne .... 115 O 3
Larne Lough .... 115 O 3
Lattin .... 94 H 10
Laune (River) .... 93 C 11
Lauragh .... 88 C 12
Laurelvale .... 114 M 4
Laurencetown .... 100 H 8
Lavagh .... 112 F 5
Lavagh More .... 117 H 3
Lawrencetown .... 114 N 4
Leabgarrow .... 116 G 3
League (Slieve) .... 112 F 4
League Point .... 89 D 13
Leamaneh Castle .... 99 E 9
Leamlara .... 90 H 12
Leamore Strand .... 103 N 8
Leane (Lough) .... 89 D 11
Leannan (River) .... 117 I 2
Leap .... 89 E 13
Leap (The)
    near Enniscorthy .... 96 M 10
Leap (The) *near New Ross* .... 96 L 10
Lecale Peninsula .... 115 O 5
Lecarrow *Leitrim* .... 112 H 5
Lecarrow *Roscommon* .... 107 H 7
Leckanarainey .... 112 H 4
Leckanvy .... 105 C 6
Leckaun .... 112 H 5
Leckavrea Mountain .... 105 D 7
Leckemy .... 118 K 2
Lee .... 93 C 11
Lee (River) .... 90 G 12
Lee Reservoir .... 90 F 12
Leek Point .... 93 C 10
Leenane .... 104 C 7
Legan or Lenamore .... 107 J 7
Legananny Dolmen .... 115 N 5
Leggah .... 107 J 6
Legoniel .... 115 O 4
Lehardan .... 117 J 2
Leighlinbridge .... 96 L 9
Leinster (Mount) .... 96 L 10
Leitir Mealláin /
    Lettermullan .... 98 C 8
Leitir Mhic an Bhaird /
    Lettermacaward .... 116 H 3
Leitrim *Banbridge* .... 115 O 5
Leitrim *Creegh* .... 98 D 9
Leitrim *Leitrim* .... 107 H 6
Leixlip .... 103 M 7
Lemanaghan .... 101 I 8
Lemybrien .... 91 J 11
Lenadoon Point .... 111 E 5
Lenan Head .... 117 J 2
Lene (Lough) .... 107 K 7
Lerrig .... 93 C 10
Leslie Hill .... 114 L 5
Letterbarra .... 112 H 3
Letterbreen .... 113 I 5
Lettercallow .... 98 C 8
Lettercraffroe Lough .... 105 D 7
Letterfinish .... 88 C 12
Letterfrack .... 104 C 7
Letterkelly .... 99 E 9
Letterkenny /
    Leitir Ceanainn .... 117 I 3
Letterleague .... 117 I 3
Lettermore .... 98 D 8

Lettermore Island .... 98 C 8
Levally .... 106 F 7
Levally Lough .... 105 E 6
Licketstown .... 96 K 11
Liffey (River) .... 102 M 8
Lifford .... 117 J 3
Light House Island .... 115 P 3
Limavady .... 118 L 2
Limerick / Luimneach .... 94 G 10
Limerick Junction .... 95 H 10
Lios Dúin Bhearna /
    Lisdoonvarna .... 99 E 8
Lios Mór / Lismore .... 91 I 11
Lios Póil / Lispole .... 92 B 11
Lios Tuathail / Listowel .... 93 D 10
Lisacul .... 106 G 6
Lisbane .... 115 O 4
Lisbellaw .... 113 J 5
Lisburn .... 115 N 4
Liscannor .... 98 D 9
Liscannor Bay .... 98 D 9
Liscarney .... 105 D 6
Liscarroll .... 94 F 11
Liscolman .... 118 M 2
Liscooly .... 117 J 3
Lisdoart .... 114 K 4
Lisdowney .... 101 J 9
Lisduff *Cavan* .... 108 K 6
Lisduff *Leitrim* .... 107 I 6
Lisduff *Offaly* .... 101 I 8
Lisgarode .... 100 H 9
Lisgoold .... 90 H 12
Lislea *Magherafelt* .... 118 M 3
Lislea *Newry-Mourne* .... 114 M 5
Lismacaffry .... 107 J 6
Lismoghry .... 117 J 3
Lismoyle .... 106 H 7
Lisnacree .... 109 N 5
Lisnageer .... 108 K 5
Lisnagleer .... 114 L 4
Lisnagry .... 94 G 9
Lisnagunogue .... 118 M 2
Lisnamuck .... 118 L 3
Lisnarrick .... 113 I 4
Lisnaskea .... 113 J 5
Lisnavagh .... 102 L 9
Lispatrick .... 90 G 13
Lisroe .... 99 E 9
Lisronagh .... 95 I 10
Lisryan .... 107 J 6
Lissadell House .... 112 G 4
Lissalway .... 106 G 6
Lissamona .... 89 D 13
Lissatinnig Bridge .... 88 C 12
Lissavaird .... 89 F 13
Lisselton .... 93 D 10
Lissinagroagh .... 112 H 5
Lissiniska .... 112 H 4
Lissycasey .... 99 E 9
Listellick .... 93 C 11
Listerlin .... 96 K 10
Listooder .... 115 O 4
Lisvarrinane .... 94 H 10
Little Bray .... 103 N 8
Little Island .... 90 G 12
Little Skellig .... 88 A 12
Littleton .... 95 I 10
Lixnaw .... 93 D 10
Loanends .... 115 N 4
Lobinstown .... 108 M 6
Loch Garman / Wexford .... 97 M 10
Loghill .... 93 E 10
Lombardstown .... 94 F 11
Londonderry .... 117 K 3
Lonehort Point .... 88 C 13
Long Island .... 89 D 13
Longford .... 101 I 8
Longhill .... 101 K 9
Longwood .... 108 L 7
Loo Bridge .... 89 D 12
Loobagh .... 94 G 10
Loop Head .... 92 C 10
Lorrha .... 100 H 8
Loskeran .... 91 J 11
Losset *Cavan* .... 107 J 6
Losset *Donegal* .... 117 I 2
Lough Bradan Forest .... 113 J 4
Lough Gowna .... 107 J 6
Lough Key Forest Park .... 106 H 6
Lough Navar Forest .... 113 I 4
Loughanavally .... 107 J 7
Loughanillaunmore .... 98 D 8
Loughanure .... 116 H 2
Loughbrickland .... 114 N 5
Lougher .... 92 C 11
Loughermore .... 118 K 3
Loughfad Hill .... 113 I 4

Loughgall ....114 M 4
Loughglinn ....106 G 6
Loughguile ....119 N 2
Loughinisland ....115 O 4
Loughlinstown ....103 N 8
Loughmoe ....101 I 9
Loughmorne ....108 L 5
Loughros More Bay ....116 G 3
Loughros Point ....116 G 3
Loughsalt Mount ....117 I 2
Loughshinny ....109 N 7
Louisburgh ....104 C 6
Loup (The) ....114 M 3
Louth ....108 M 6
Lower Ballinderry ....114 N 4
Lower Lake ....103 N 8
Lowertown ....89 D 13
Lowerymore ....113 I 3
Lowtown ....115 N 5
Lucan ....103 M 7
Luggacurren ....101 K 9
Lugnaquillia Mountain ....103 M 9
Luimneach / Limerick ....94 G 10
Lukeswell ....96 K 10
Lullymore ....102 L 8
Lurgan *Craigavon* ....114 N 4
Lurgan *Frenchpark* ....106 G 6
Lurganboy *Donegal* ....117 J 2
Lurganboy *Leitrim* ....112 H 5
Lusk ....109 N 7
Lyle ....115 N 3
Lyracrumpane ....93 D 10
Lyre ....90 F 11
Lyrenaglogh ....95 H 11

M

Maas ....116 G 3
Mac Gregor's Corner ....119 N 3
Mac Laughlins Corner ....118 M 3
Mac Mahon's Town ....114 K 4
Mac Swyne's Bay ....112 G 4
Mace ....105 D 6
Mace Head ....104 C 8
Macgillycuddy's Reeks ....89 C 12
Machugh (Lough) ....116 G 3
Mackan ....113 J 5
Macnean Lower (Lough) ....113 I 5
Macnean Upper (Lough) ....113 I 5
Macosquin ....118 L 2
Macroom /
   Maigh Chromtha ....89 F 12
Maddan ....114 L 5
Maddockstown ....96 K 10
Maganey ....102 L 9
Maghaberry ....115 N 4
Maghanlawaun ....89 C 12
Maghera *Clare* ....99 F 9
Maghera *Donegal* ....116 G 3
Maghera *Down* ....115 O 5
Maghera *Magherafelt* ....118 L 3
Magherabane ....117 J 2
Magherafelt ....114 M 4
Magheragall ....115 N 4
Magheralin ....114 N 4
Magheramason ....117 J 3
Magheramorne ....115 O 3
Magheraveely ....113 K 5
Maghery *near Dungannon* ....114 M 4
Maghery *near Dunglow* ....116 G 3
Magilligan ....118 L 2
Magilligan Point ....118 L 2
Magilligan Strand ....118 L 2
Maguiresbridge ....113 J 5
Mahee Island ....115 P 4
Mahon ....95 J 11
Mahon (Lough) ....90 G 12
Mahoonagh ....93 E 10
Maigh Chromtha /
   Macroom ....89 F 12
Maigh Cuilinn /
   Moycullen ....105 E 7
Maigh Nuad / Maynooth ....103 M 7
Maigue (River) ....94 F 10
Main ....118 N 3
Maine (River) ....93 C 11
Mainham ....102 L 8
Mainistir Fhear Maí /
   Fermoy ....90 H 11
Mainistir na Búille /
   Boyle ....106 H 6
Mainistir na Corann /
   Midleton ....90 H 12
Máistir Gaoithe /
   Mastergeehy ....88 B 12
Mal Bay ....98 D 9
Mala / Mallow ....94 G 11
Málainn Bhig / Malin Beg ....112 F 3

Malin ....118 K 2
Malin Bay ....112 F 3
Malin Head ....117 J 1
Malin More ....112 F 3
Mallusk ....115 N 3
Mamore (Gap of) ....117 J 2
Manger ....112 H 4
Mangerton Mountain ....89 D 12
Mannin Bay ....104 B 7
Mannin Lake ....105 F 6
Manorcunningham ....117 J 3
Manselstown ....95 I 9
Mansfieldstown ....109 M 6
Mantua ....106 H 6
Manulla ....105 E 6
Manulla (River) ....105 E 6
Maothail / Mohill ....107 I 6
Marble Arch Caves ....113 I 5
Marble Hill ....117 I 2
Mardyke ....95 J 10
Markethill ....114 M 5
Marshalstown ....96 M 10
Martin ....90 G 12
Martinstown *Emlygrennan* ....94 G 10
   Grennanstown ....108 L 7
Martinstown
   South Somerset ....119 N 3
Mask (Lough) ....105 D 7
Massford ....115 N 4
Masshill ....112 F 5
Masterstown ....95 I 10
Matehy ....90 G 12
Matrix (Castle) ....94 F 10
Mattock (River) ....108 M 6
Mauherslieve ....95 H 9
Maum ....105 D 7
Maumakeogh ....111 D 5
Maumeen Lough ....104 B 7
Maumtrasna ....105 D 7
Maumturk Mountains ....104 C 7
Mauricesmills ....99 E 9
Mayo ....105 E 6
Mayo (Plains of) ....105 E 6
Mayobridge ....114 N 5
Mazetown ....115 N 4
Mealagh ....89 D 12
Meanus ....94 G 10
Meathas Troim /
   Edgeworthstown ....107 J 6
Meela (Lough) ....116 G 3
Meelick ....100 H 8
Meelin ....93 E 11
Meenaclady ....116 H 2
Meenacross ....116 G 3
Meenanarwa ....117 H 3
Meenaneary /
   Mín na Aoire ....112 G 3
Meenatotan ....116 H 3
Meenavean ....112 F 3
Meencorwick ....116 H 3
Meenglass ....113 I 3
Meenlaragh ....117 H 2
Meenreagh ....113 I 3
Meentullynagarn ....112 G 3
Meenybraddan ....112 H 3
Meeting of the Waters ....103 N 9
Mellifont Abbey ....109 M 6
Melmore Head ....117 I 2
Melvin (Lough) ....112 H 4
Menlough ....106 G 7
Mew Island ....115 P 3
Michelstown Caves ....95 H 11
Middletown ....116 H 2
Middletown *Armagh* ....114 L 5
Midfield ....105 F 6
Mile ....117 J 2
Milebush ....115 O 3
Milehouse ....96 M 10
Milemill ....102 L 8
Milestone ....95 H 9
Milford *Armagh* ....114 L 5
Milford *Cork* ....94 F 10
Mill Town ....114 L 5
Millbay ....115 O 3
Millbrook *Derry* ....118 K 3
Millbrook *Larne* ....115 O 3
Millbrook *Oldcastle* ....108 K 6
Milleen ....93 E 11
Millford ....117 I 2
Millisle ....115 P 4
Millroad ....96 M 10
Millstreet *Cork* ....89 E 11
Millstreet *Waterford* ....91 I 11
Milltown *Armagh* ....114 L 5
Milltown *Ballymoney* ....118 M 2
Milltown *Banbridge* ....114 N 5

Milltown *Cavan* ....107 J 5
Milltown *Craigavon* ....114 M 4
Milltown *Dublin* ....103 M 8
Milltown *Kildare* ....102 L 8
Milltown *near Dingle* ....92 B 11
Milltown
   near Mount Bellew ....106 G 7
Milltown *near Tralee* ....93 C 11
Milltown *near Tuam* ....105 F 7
Milltown *Omagh* ....114 K 4
Milltown *Wexford* ....97 M 10
Miltownpass ....107 K 7
Minane Bridge ....90 G 12
Minard Head ....92 B 11
Mine Head ....91 J 12
Minerstown ....115 O 5
Minterburn ....114 L 4
Mizen Head ....88 C 13
Moanmore ....98 D 9
Modelligo ....91 I 11
Modreeny ....100 H 9
Mogeely ....90 H 12
Moglass ....95 I 10
Moher (Cliffs of) ....98 D 9
Moher Lough ....105 D 6
Mohil ....96 K 9
Móinteach Milic /
   Mountmellick ....101 K 8
Moira ....115 N 4
Moll's Gap ....89 D 12
Monard ....95 H 10
Monaseed ....97 M 9
Monaster ....94 G 10
Monasteraden ....106 G 6
Monasteranenagh Abbey ....94 G 10
Monasterboice ....109 M 6
Monasterevin ....102 K 8
Monavullagh Mountains ....95 J 11
Mondello Park ....102 L 8
Monea ....113 I 4
Moneen *Clare* ....93 C 10
Moneen *Galway* ....105 F 7
Money Point ....93 D 10
Moneydig ....118 M 3
Moneygall ....101 I 9
Moneyglass ....114 M 3
Moneygold ....112 G 4
Moneylahan ....112 G 4
Moneymore ....114 L 3
Moneyneany ....118 L 3
Moneyreagh ....115 O 4
Monilea ....107 K 7
Monivea ....106 F 7
Monkstown *Cork* ....90 G 12
Monkstown
   Newtownabbey ....115 O 3
Monroe ....107 J 7
Montpelier ....99 G 9
Mooncoin ....96 K 11
Moone ....102 L 9
Moord ....91 I 12
Moore Bay ....98 C 9
Moorfields ....115 N 3
More (Island) ....105 D 6
Morenane ....94 F 10
Morley's Bridge ....89 D 12
Morningstar ....94 G 10
Mornington ....109 N 6
Mosney ....109 N 7
Moss-Side ....118 M 2
Mossley ....115 O 3
Mothel ....95 J 11
Motte Stone ....103 N 9
Mount Falcon ....111 E 5
Mount Garret ....96 L 10
Mount Hamilton or Sperrin ....114 K 3
Mount Melleray Monastery ....95 I 11
Mount Norris ....114 M 5
Mount Nugent ....107 K 6
Mount Stewart Gardens ....115 P 4
Mount Talbot ....106 H 7
Mount Temple ....107 I 7
Mount Uniacke ....91 H 12
Mount Usher Gardens ....103 N 8
Mountbolus ....101 J 8
Mountcastle ....117 J 3
Mountcharles ....112 H 4
Mountcollins ....93 E 11
Mountfield ....114 K 4
Mounthenry ....105 E 7
Mountjoy *Dungannon* ....114 M 4
Mountjoy *Omagh* ....113 J 4
Mountrath ....101 J 8
Mountrivers Bridge ....98 D 9
Mountshannon ....100 G 9
Mourne (Lough)
   near Ballybofey ....113 I 3

Mourne (Lough)
   near Carrickfergus ....115 O 3
Mourne Beg ....113 I 3
Mourne Mountains ....109 N 5
Mourne River ....113 J 3
Moveen ....98 C 10
Moville / Bun an Phobail ....118 K 2
Mowhan ....114 M 5
Moy ....114 L 4
Moy (River) ....111 E 5
Moyagh ....117 J 3
Moyallan ....114 M 4
Moyard ....104 B 7
Moyarget ....118 N 2
Moyasta ....98 D 9
Moydow ....107 I 7
Moygashel ....114 L 4
Moyglass ....99 G 8
Moylough *Galway* ....106 G 7
Moylough *Sligo* ....106 F 5
Moynalty ....108 L 6
Moynalvy ....108 L 7
Moyne *Roscommon* ....106 G 6
Moyne *Tipperary* ....107 J 6
Moyne *Wicklow* ....103 M 9
Moyne Abbey ....111 E 5
Moyrus ....104 C 7
Moyteoge Head ....110 B 6
Moyvally ....102 L 7
Moyvore ....107 J 7
Moyvoughly ....107 I 7
Muck (Isle of) ....115 O 3
Muckamore ....115 N 3
Muckanagh Lough ....99 F 9
Muckish Mountain ....117 H 2
Mucklon ....102 L 7
Muckno Lake ....108 L 5
Muckros Head ....112 G 4
Muckross ....89 D 11
Muff ....117 K 2
Muggort's Bay ....91 J 11
Muine Bheag /
   Bagenalstown ....96 L 9
Muineachán / Monaghan ....114 L 5
Muing ....111 D 5
Muingnabo ....111 C 5
Mulhuddart ....103 M 7
Mulkear ....94 G 10
Mullach Íde / Malahide ....103 N 7
Mullagh *Cavan* ....108 L 6
Mullagh *Galway* ....100 G 8
Mullagh *Mayo* ....104 C 6
Mullagh *Meath* ....103 M 7
Mullaghanattin ....88 C 12
Mullaghanish ....89 E 12
Mullaghareirk Mountains ....93 E 10
Mullaghash ....118 K 3
Mullaghbane ....109 M 5
Mullaghboy ....115 O 3
Mullaghcarn ....113 K 3
Mullaghcleevaun ....103 M 8
Mullaghclogha ....114 K 3
Mullaghmore
   Cliffony North ....112 G 4
Mullaghmore *Magherafelt* ....118 L 3
Mullaghmore Head ....112 G 4
Mullan *Coleraine* ....118 L 2
Mullan *Figullar* ....114 L 4
Mullany'sCross ....111 F 5
Mullartown ....109 O 5
Mullen ....106 G 6
Mullenbeg ....96 K 10
Mullet Peninsula ....110 B 5
Mullinahone ....95 J 10
Mullinasole ....112 H 4
Mullinavat ....96 K 10
Mulroy Bay ....117 I 2
Multeen ....95 H 10
Multyfarnham ....107 J 7
Mungret ....94 F 10
Muntervary
   or Sheep's Head ....88 C 13
Murley ....113 K 4
Murlough Bay ....119 N 2
Murntown ....97 M 11
Murreagh ....92 A 11
Murrisk ....105 D 6
Murroe ....94 G 10
Murroogh ....99 E 8
Musheramore ....89 F 11
Mussenden Temple ....118 L 2
Mutton Island ....98 D 9
Mweelrea Mountains ....104 C 7
Mweenish Island ....104 C 8
Myshall ....96 L 9

N

Na Cealla Beaga /
   Killybegs ....112 G 4
Na Clocha Liatha /
   Greystones ....103 N 8
Na Dúnaibh / Downies ....117 I 2
Na Sceirí / Skerries ....109 N 7
Nacorra (Lough) ....105 D 6
Nacung (Lough) ....117 H 2
Nad ....90 F 11
Nafooey (Lough) ....105 D 7
Nagles Mountains ....90 G 11
Nalughraman (Lough) ....116 G 3
Namin (Lough) ....117 J 2
Namona (Lough) ....88 B 12
Nanny ....108 M 7
Narin ....116 G 3
Narraghmore ....102 L 8
Narrow Water Castle ....109 N 5
Naul ....109 N 7
Neagh (Lough) ....114 M 4
Neale ....105 E 7
Nealstown ....101 I 9
Neidín / Kenmare ....89 D 12
Nenagh ....100 H 9
Nephin ....111 D 5
Nephin (Glen) ....105 D 6
Nephin Beg ....111 D 5
Nephin Beg Range ....111 C 5
New Birmingham ....95 J 10
New Buildings ....117 J 3
New Inn *Cavan* ....108 K 6
New Inn *Galway* ....100 G 8
New Kildare ....94 F 10
New Quay / Bealaclugga ....99 E 8
New Twopothouse Village ....94 G 11
Newbawn ....96 L 10
Newbliss ....113 K 5
Newbridge *Fingal* ....109 N 7
Newbridge *Limerick* ....94 F 10
Newbridge
   near Tuomard ....106 G 7
Newbridge /
   An Droichead Nua ....102 L 8
Newcastle *Down* ....115 O 5
Newcastle *Dublin* ....103 M 8
Newcastle *Galway* ....99 F 7
Newcastle *Tipperary* ....95 I 11
Newcastle *Wicklow* ....103 N 8
Newcestown ....90 F 12
Newchapel ....95 I 10
Newferry ....114 M 3
Newgrange ....109 M 6
Newinn ....95 I 10
Newmarket *Cork* ....93 F 11
Newmarket *Kilkenny* ....96 K 10
Newmarket on Fergus ....99 F 9
Newmills *Donegal* ....117 I 3
Newmills *Dungannon* ....114 L 4
Newport *Tipperary* ....100 G 9
Newport Bay ....105 C 6
Newport Trench ....114 M 4
Newry ....114 M 5
Newtown *Cork* ....94 G 11
Newtown *Galway* ....99 F 8
Newtown *Kildare* ....102 L 7
Newtown *Laois* ....101 K 9
Newtown *Limerick* ....94 G 10
Newtown *near Knock* ....101 I 9
Newtown *near Nenagh* ....100 H 9
Newtown *Offaly* ....100 H 8
Newtown *Roscommon* ....100 H 7
Newtown *Tipperary* ....95 H 10
Newtown *Waterford* ....95 J 11
Newtown *Wexford* ....96 M 11
Newtown *Cashel* ....107 I 7
Newtown Cloghans ....111 E 5
Newtown-Crommelin ....119 N 3
Newtown Cunningham ....117 J 3
Newtown Forbes ....107 I 6
Newtown Gore ....107 I 5
Newtown
   Mount Kennedy ....103 N 8
Newtown Sandes ....93 D 10
Newtownabbey ....115 O 4
Newtownards ....115 O 4
Newtownbreda ....115 O 4
Newtownbutler ....113 J 5
Newtownhamilton ....114 M 5
Newtownlow ....101 J 7
Newtownlynch ....99 E 8
Newtownshandrum ....94 F 10
Newtownstewart ....113 J 4
Nier ....95 J 11
Ninemilehouse ....95 J 10
Nobber ....108 L 6

Nohaval ....90 G 12
Nore ....101 J 9
Nore (River) ....96 K 10
North Channel ....119 O 2
North Ring ....90 F 13
North Sound ....98 C 8
Nose of Howth ....103 N 7
Noughaval *Doora* ....99 F 9
Noughaval *Noughaval* ....99 E 8
Nowen Hill ....89 E 12
Nuns Quarter ....115 O 4
Nurney *Carlow* ....96 L 9
Nurney *Kildare* ....102 L 8
Nutt's Corner ....115 N 4

O

Oaghley ....93 D 10
Oatfield ....99 F 9
Oatquarter ....98 C 8
O'Brien's Tower ....98 D 9
O'Flynn (Lough) ....106 G 6
Oghil *Clare* ....100 H 8
Oghil *Galway* ....98 C 8
Ogonnelloe ....99 G 9
O'Grady (Lough) ....99 G 9
Oileán Ciarraí /
   Castleisland ....93 D 11
Oilgate ....97 M 10
Oily ....112 G 4
Old Court ....89 E 13
Old Head *Ballymackean* ....90 G 13
Old Head *Louisburgh* ....104 C 6
Old Kilcullen ....102 L 8
Old Kildimo ....94 F 10
Old Ross ....96 L 10
Old Town *Donegal* ....117 I 3
Old Town *Laois* ....101 J 9
Old Town *Roscommon* ....100 H 8
Old Town *Wexford* ....96 L 10
Old Twopothouse ....94 G 11
Oldleighlin ....96 K 9
Oldmill Bridge ....93 E 10
Oldtown *Dublin* ....109 N 7
Oldtown *Roscommon* ....101 I 7
Omagh ....113 K 4
Omeath ....109 N 5
Omey Island ....104 B 7
Onaght ....98 C 8
Oola ....94 H 10
Oorid Lough ....105 D 7
Oranmore ....99 F 8
Oriel (Mount) ....108 M 6
Oristown ....108 L 6
Oritor ....114 L 4
Ossian's Grave ....119 N 2
Ougther (Lough) ....107 J 6
Oulart ....97 M 10
Ovens ....90 G 12
Owel (Lough) ....107 J 7
Owenascaul ....92 B 11
Owenator ....116 H 3
Owenavorragh ....97 M 10
Owenbeagh ....117 H 3
Owenbeg ....111 F 5
Owenbeg (River) ....112 G 5
Owenboliska ....99 E 8
Owenboy ....90 G 12
Owenbristy ....99 F 8
Owencarrow ....117 I 2
Owendalulleegh ....99 G 8
Owenea ....116 G 3
Owengarve *Clew Bay* ....105 D 6
Owengarve *River Moy* ....106 F 5
Owenglin ....104 C 7
Oweniny ....111 D 5
Owenkillew *Glenelly* ....114 K 3
Owenkillew *Lough Swilly* ....117 J 2
Owenmore Bridge ....105 D 6
Owennacurra ....90 H 12
Owenreagh Hill ....117 J 3
Owenriff ....105 D 7
Owentaraglin ....93 E 11
Owentocker ....116 H 3
Owenur (River) ....106 H 6
Ower ....105 E 7
Owning ....95 J 10
Owroe Bridge ....88 B 12
Owvane ....89 D 12
Oysterhaven ....90 G 12

P

Palace ....96 L 10
Palatine ....102 L 9
Pallas ....101 J 8
Pallas Cross ....100 I 9
Pallas Green ....94 G 10
Pallaskenry ....94 F 10

A B C D E F G H I J K L M N O P Q R S T U V W X Y Z

Paps (The) ....89 E 11
Park *Bellavary* ....105 E 6
Park *Derry* ....118 K 3
Parke's Castle ....112 H 5
Parkgate ....115 N 3
Parkmore ....99 F 8
Parkmore Point ....92 A 11
Parknasilla ....88 C 12
Parteen ....99 G 9
Partry ....105 E 6
Partry Mountains ......105 D 7
Passage ....106 H 7
Passage East ....96 L 11
Passage West ....90 G 12
Patrickswell ....94 F 10
Patterson's Spade Mill ..115 N 3
Paulstown ....96 K 9
Peake ....90 F 12
Peatlands ....114 M 4
Peterswell ....99 F 8
Pettigoe ....113 I 4
Phoenix Park ....103 M 7
Piercetown ....97 M 11
Pigeons (The) ....107 I 7
Pike ....100 H 8
Pike (The) *near Boola* ..91 I 11
Pike (The) *near Lamybrien* ..91 J 11
Pike (The) *Tipperary* ..100 H 8
Pike Corner ....108 L 7
Pike of Rush Hall ......101 J 9
Piltown ....95 K 10
Pluck ....117 J 3
Plumbridge ....113 K 3
Pollagh ....101 I 8
Pollan Bay ....117 J 2
Pollatomish ....111 C 5
Pollnalaght ....113 J 4
Pollshask ....106 G 7
Pomeroy ....114 L 4
Pontoon ....105 E 6
Port ....116 F 3
Port Ballintrae ....118 M 2
Port Durlainne / Porturlin ..111 C 5
Port Láirge / Waterford ..96 K 11
Port Laoise / Portlaoise ..101 K 8
Port Omna / Portumna ..100 H 8
Portacloy ....111 C 5
Portadown ....114 M 4
Portaferry ....115 P 4
Portaleen ....118 K 2
Portavogie ....115 P 4
Portbradden ....118 M 2
Portglenone ....118 M 3
Portland ....100 H 8
Portlaw ....96 K 11
Portmagee ....88 A 12
Portmagee Channel ....88 A 12
Portmarnock ....103 N 7
Portmuck ....115 O 3
Portnablagh ....117 I 2
Portnoo ....116 G 3
Portrane ....109 N 7
Portroe ....100 G 9
Portrush ....118 M 2
Portsalon ....117 J 2
Portstewart ....118 L 2
Poulaphouca Reservoir ..103 M 8
Poulnamucky ....95 I 10
Poulnasherry Bay ......98 D 10
Power Head ....90 H 12
Power's Cross ....100 H 8
Powerscourt Demesne ..103 N 8
Powerstown ....96 K 10
Poyntz Pass ....114 M 5
Priesthaggard ....96 L 11
Prosperous ....102 L 8
Puckaun ....100 H 9
Puffin Island ....88 A 12
Punchestown ....103 M 8

Q

Quarrytown ....119 N 3
Querrin ....93 D 10
Quigley's Point ......118 K 2
Quilty ....98 D 9
Quin ....99 F 9
Quoile ....115 O 4

R

Rabbit Islands ....89 E 13
Race End ....117 I 2
Raffrey ....115 O 4
Raghly ....112 G 5
Raghtin More ....117 J 2
Rahan ....101 J 8
Rahanagh ....93 E 10
Rahara ....106 H 7

Raharney ....108 K 7
Raheen ....96 L 10
Raigh ....105 D 7
Railyard ....101 K 9
Rake Street ....111 D 5
Ram Head ....91 I 12
Ramor (Lough) ....108 K 6
Ramore Head ....118 M 2
Rams Island ....114 N 4
Ramsgrange ....96 L 11
Randalstown ....114 N 3
Rapemills ....101 I 8
Raphoe ....117 J 3
Rasharkin ....118 M 3
Rashedoge ....117 I 3
Rath ....101 I 8
Ráth Caola / Rathkeale ..94 F 10
Ráth Droma / Rathdrum ..103 N 9
Rathangan ....102 L 8
Rathaspick ....107 J 7
Rathbrit ....95 I 10
Rathcabban ....100 H 8
Rathconrath ....107 J 7
Rathcool ....89 F 11
Rathcoole ....103 M 8
Rathcor ....109 N 6
Rathcore ....102 L 7
Rathcormack *near Fermoy* ..90 H 11
Rathcormack *near Sligo* ..112 G 5
Rathcroghan ....106 H 6
Rathdangan ....103 M 9
Rathdowney ....101 J 9
Rathduff ....90 G 11
Rathedan ....96 L 9
Rathfeigh ....108 M 7
Rathfriland ....115 N 5
Rathfylane ....96 L 10
Rathgarogue ....96 L 10
Rathgormuck ....95 J 11
Rathkeevin ....95 I 10
Rathkenny ....108 M 6
Rathlackan ....111 E 5
Rathlee ....111 E 5
Rathlin Island ....119 N 2
Rathlin O'Birne Island ..112 F 4
Rathlin Sound ....119 N 2
Rathmelton ....117 J 2
Rathmines ....103 N 8
Rathmolyon ....108 L 7
Rathmore ....89 E 11
Rathmullan ....117 J 2
Rathnew ....103 N 9
Rathnure ....96 L 10
Rathoma ....111 E 5
Rathowen ....107 J 7
Rathvilla ....101 K 8
Rathvilly ....102 L 9
Ratoath ....108 M 7
Raven Point (The) ....97 M 10
Ravensdale ....109 M 5
Ray *near Dunfanaghy* ..117 H 2
Ray *near Rathmillan* ..117 J 2
Ray (River) ....117 H 2
Rea (Lough) ....99 G 8
Reaghstown ....108 M 6
Reanagowan Cross Roads ..93 D 11
Reananeree /
  Rae na nDoirí ......89 E 12
Reanascreena ....89 E 13
Rear Cross ....95 H 9
Red Bay ....119 N 2
Redcastle ....118 K 2
Redcross ....103 N 9
Redgate ....97 M 10
Redhills ....107 K 5
Ree (Lough) ....107 I 7
Reelan ....117 H 3
Reen ....89 D 12
Reens ....94 F 10
Reevanagh ....96 K 9
Relaghbeg ....108 L 6
Rerrin ....88 C 13
Rhode ....101 K 7
Richhill ....114 M 4
Ridge ....96 K 9
Ridge Point ....110 C 5
Rine (River) ....99 F 9
Rineanna Point ......99 F 9
Ringabella Bay ......90 H 12
Ringarogy Island ....89 D 13
Ringaskiddy ....90 H 12
Ringboy ....115 P 4
Ringfad Point ....115 P 5
Ringsend ....118 L 2
Ringstown ....101 J 8
Ringville / An Rinn ....91 J 11
Rinmore Point ....117 I 2

Rinn (River) ....107 I 6
Rinn Lough ....107 I 6
Rinneen *Clare* ......98 D 9
Rinneen *Cork* ......89 E 13
Rinroe Point ....110 C 5
Rinville ....99 F 8
Rinvyle ....104 C 7
Rinvyle Castle ......104 B 7
Rinvyle Point ....104 B 7
River ....110 B 6
Riverchapel ....97 N 10
Riverstick ....90 G 12
Riverstown *Cork* ....90 G 12
Riverstown *Sligo* ..112 G 5
Riverstown *Tipperary* ..101 I 8
Riverville ....93 D 11
Roadford ....98 D 8
Roaninish ....116 G 3
Roaringwater Bay ....89 D 13
Robe ....105 E 6
Robert's Head ......90 H 12
Robertstown ....102 L 8
Robinstown ....108 L 7
Roche's Point ....90 H 12
Rochestown ....96 K 11
Rochfortbridge ......101 K 7
Rock (The) ....114 L 4
Rock Island ....98 C 8
Rockabill ....109 N 7
Rockchapel ....93 E 11
Rockcorry ....108 K 5
Rockhill ....94 F 10
Rockmills ....94 G 11
Rodeen ....107 H 6
Roe ....118 L 3
Roe Valley ....118 L 2
Roney Point ....97 N 10
Rooaun ....100 H 8
Roonagh Quay ......104 C 6
Roonah Lough ......104 C 6
Roosky *Leitrim* ....112 H 4
Roosky *Mayo* ......106 F 6
Roosky *Roscommon* ..107 I 6
Ropefield ....112 G 5
Ros an Mhil / Rossaveel ..98 D 8
Ros Comáin /
  Roscommon ......106 H 7
Ros Cré / Roscrea ....101 I 9
Ros Láir / Rosslare ..97 M 11
Ros Mhic Thriúin /
  New Ross ....96 L 10
Rosapenna ....117 I 2
Rosbercon ....96 L 10
Rosegreen ....95 I 10
Rosenallis ....101 J 8
Rosguill ....117 I 2
Roskeeragh Point ....112 F 4
Rosmuck ....105 D 7
Rosmult ....95 I 9
Rosnakill ....117 I 2
Ross *Lough Leane* ..89 D 11
Ross *Lough Sheelin* ..107 K 6
Ross Abbey ....105 E 7
Ross Lake ....105 E 7
Ross Port ....111 C 5
Ross West ....105 E 6
Rossan Point ....112 F 3
Rossbeg ....116 G 3
Rossbeigh Creek ....92 C 11
Rossbrin ....89 D 13
Rosscahill ....105 E 7
Rosscarbery ....89 E 13
Rosscarbery Bay ....89 E 13
Rosscor ....113 H 4
Rossdohan Island ....88 C 12
Rosserk Abbey ......111 E 5
Rosses (The) ....116 G 2
Rosses Bay ....116 G 2
Rosses Point ....112 G 5
Rossgeir ....117 J 3
Rossglass ....115 O 5
Rossinver ....112 H 4
Rosslare Bay ....97 M 11
Rosslare Point ......97 M 11
Rosslea ....113 K 5
Rossmore *Cork* ....89 F 12
Rossmore *Laois* ..102 K 9
Rossmore Forest Park ..114 L 5
Rossmore *Meath* ..88 C 12
Rossnowlagh ....112 H 4
Rostellan ....90 H 12
Rostrevor ....109 N 5
Rosturk ....105 C 6
Rough Point ....92 B 11
Roughty ....89 D 12
Roundfort ....105 E 7
Roundstone ....104 C 7

Roundwood ....103 N 8
Roury ....89 E 13
Rousky ....114 K 3
Rowallane Gardens ..115 O 4
Rower (The) ....96 L 10
Royal Canal ....107 I 7
Royaloak ....96 L 9
Ruan ....99 F 9
Rubane ....115 P 4
Rue Point ....119 N 2
Runabay Head ......119 N 2
Runnabackan ....106 H 6
Rushen (Slieve) ......113 J 5
Russborough House ..103 M 8
Rutland Island ......116 G 3
Ryefield ....108 K 6
Ryehill ....106 F 7
Rylane Cross ....90 F 12

S

Saddle Head ....110 B 5
Saggart ....103 M 8
St. Finan's Bay ......88 A 12
St. John's Lough ....107 I 5
St. John's Point ......115 P 5
St. John's Point ......112 G 4
St. Johnstown ......117 J 3
St. Macdara's Island ..104 C 8
St. Margaret's ......103 N 7
St. Mochta's House ..108 M 6
St. Mullin's ....96 L 10
Saintfield ....115 O 4
Saleen *Cork* ......90 H 12
Saleen *Kerry* ......93 D 10
Salia ....104 C 6
Sallahig ....88 B 12
Sallins ....102 M 8
Sally Gap ....103 N 8
Sallybrook ....90 G 12
Sallypark ....100 H 9
Salrock ....104 C 7
Saltee Islands ......96 M 11
Salthill ....99 E 8
Sandholes ....114 L 4
Sandyford ....103 N 8
Santry ....103 N 7
Saul ....115 O 4
Sawel Mountain ....118 K 3
Scalp Mountain ....117 J 2
Scardaun *Mayo* ..105 E 7
Scardaun *Roscommon* ..106 H 7
Scarnagh ....97 N 9
Scarriff / An Scairbh ..99 G 9
Scarriff Island ......88 B 12
Scartaglin ....93 D 11
Scarva ....114 M 5
Scattery Island ....93 D 10
Schull / Skull ......89 D 13
Scolban (Lough) ....113 H 4
Scotch Town ....114 K 3
Scotshouse ....113 K 5
Scotstown ....114 K 5
Scrabo Hill ....115 O 4
Scramoge ....107 H 6
Screeb Cross ......105 D 7
Screen ....97 M 10
Screggan ....101 J 8
Scribbagh ....113 H 4
Scullogue Gap ......96 L 10
Scur (Lough) ....107 I 5
Seaforde ....115 O 5
Seapatrick ....114 N 4
Seefin ....95 J 11
Seskinore ....114 K 4
Seskinryan ....96 L 9
Seven Heads ....90 F 13
Seven Hogs or
  Magharee Islands (The) ..92 B 11
Shalwy ....112 G 4
Shanacashel ....88 C 11
Shanagarry ....90 H 12
Shanaglish ....99 F 8
Shanagolden ......93 E 10
Shanahoe ....101 J 9
Shanballard ....99 G 7
Shanbally *Cork* ....90 G 12
Shanbally *Galway* ..106 G 7
Shanballymore ......94 G 11
Shanco ....114 L 4
Shanes Castle ......114 N 3
Shankill ....103 N 8
Shanlaragh ....89 E 12
Shanlis ....108 M 6
Shannagh (Lough) ..115 N 5
Shannakea ....93 E 10
Shannawona ....105 D 7
Shannon ....99 F 9

Shannon (River) ....100 H 8
Shannon Airport ....99 F 9
Shannon Harbour ..101 I 8
Shannonbridge ......100 H 8
Shanragh ....101 K 9
Shantonagh ....108 L 5
Sharavogue ....101 I 8
Sheddings (The) ....119 N 3
Sheeanamore ......103 M 9
Sheeaun ....99 G 9
Sheeffry Hills ......105 C 6
Sheehan's Point ....88 B 12
Sheelin (Lough) ....107 K 6
Sheep Haven ......117 I 2
Sheever (Lough) ....107 K 7
Shehy Mountains ..89 D 12
Shercock ....108 L 6
Sherkin Island ......89 D 13
Sherky Island ......88 C 12
Sheskin ....111 D 5
Sheskinapoll ....117 J 3
Shillelagh ....97 M 9
Shinrone ....101 I 9
Shiven ....106 G 7
Shoptown ....115 N 3
Shot Head ....89 C 13
Shranamanragh Bridge ..110 C 5
Shrule ....105 E 7
Silent Valley ....109 O 5
Sillan (Lough) ......108 L 5
Silver Bridge ......108 M 5
Silver Strand ......104 C 6
Silvermine Mountains ..100 H 9
Silvermines ....100 H 9
Sinking ....106 F 7
Sion Mills ....113 J 3
Six Crosses ....93 D 10
Six Road Ends ......115 P 4
Six Towns (The) ....114 L 3
Sixmilebridge ......99 F 9
Sixmilecross ....114 K 4
Skannive (Lough) ..104 C 8
Skeagh ....107 J 7
Skehana ....101 K 9
Skehanagh ....106 G 7
Skerries (The) ......118 M 2
Skreen *Meath* ....108 M 7
Skreen *Sligo* ......112 F 5
Sky Road ....104 B 7
Slade ....96 L 11
Slane ....108 M 6
Slane (Hill of) ......108 M 6
Slaney (River) ......97 M 10
Slat (Lough) ....92 B 11
Slate (River) ....102 L 8
Slea Head ....92 A 11
Slemish Mountain ..119 N 3
Sliabh na Caillighe ..108 K 6
Slieve Anierin ......113 I 5
Slieve Aught Mountains ..99 G 8
Slieve Bernagh ......99 G 9
Slieve Bloom Mountains ..101 J 8
Slieve Gamph
  or the Ox Mountains ..111 F 5
Slieve Mish Mountains ..93 C 11
Slieve Miskish Mountains ..88 C 13
Slieveanorra ....119 N 2
Slievecallan ....99 E 9
Slievefelim Mountains ..94 H 9
Slievekimalta ......100 H 9
Slievekirk ....117 K 3
Slievemore *Dungannon* ..114 K 4
Slievemore *Mayo* ..110 B 5
Slievemurry ....106 G 7
Slievenamon ......95 J 10
Slieveroe ....96 K 11
Slievetooey ....116 G 3
Sligeach / Sligo ....112 G 5
Sligo Bay ....112 F 5
Slyne Head ....104 B 7
Smerwick ....92 A 11
Smerwick Harbour ..92 A 11
Smithborough ......114 K 5
Smithstown ....101 K 9
Snagh (Slieve)
  Derryveagh Mts. ..117 H 3
Snaght (Slieve) *Inishowen* ..117 J 2
Snave ....89 D 12
Sneem ....88 C 12
Soldierstown ......115 N 4
Sord / Swords ....103 N 7
South Sound ......98 D 8
Spa ....93 C 11
Spa (The) ....115 O 4
Spanish Point *Locality* ..98 D 9
Spanish Point *Mal Bay* ..98 D 9

Speenoge ....117 J 2
Spelga Dam ....115 N 5
Sperrin Mountains ..118 K 3
Spink ....101 K 9
Spittaltown ....101 J 7
Springfield ....113 I 4
Springhill ....114 M 3
Springwell Forest ..118 L 2
Squires Hill ....115 O 4
Sraghmore ....103 N 8
Srah / An tSraith ..105 E 6
Srahduggaun ......111 C 6
Srahmore *near Bangor* ..111 C 5
Srahmore *near Newport* ..105 D 6
Srahmore River ....105 D 6
Sráid na Cathrach /
  Milltown Malbay ..98 D 9
Stabannan ....109 M 6
Stackallan ....108 M 6
Stack's Mountains ..93 D 11
Staffordstown ......114 M 3
Stags (The) ....89 E 13
Stags of Broad Haven ..111 C 4
Staigue Stone Fort ..88 B 12
Stamullin ....109 N 7
Staplestown ....102 L 8
Stepaside ....103 N 8
Stewartstown ......114 L 4
Stickstown ....90 F 12
Stillorgan ....103 N 8
Stone Bridge ......113 K 5
Stonyford *Kilkenny* ..96 K 10
Stonyford *Lisburn* ..115 N 4
Stormont ....115 O 4
Strabane ....117 J 3
Stracashel ....117 H 3
Stradbally *Kerry* ..92 B 11
Stradbally *Laois* ..101 K 8
Stradbally *Waterford* ..91 J 11
Strade ....105 E 6
Stradone ....107 K 6
Stradreagh ....118 L 2
Straffan ....103 M 8
Stragar ....112 G 3
Strahart ....96 M 10
Straid *Donegal* ..117 J 2
Straid *Larne* ......115 O 3
Straid *Moyle* ....118 M 2
Straith Salach / Recess ..104 C 7
Strand ....93 E 10
Strandhill ....112 G 5
Strangford ....115 P 4
Strangford Lough ..115 P 4
Stranocum ....118 M 2
Stranorlar ....117 I 3
Stratford ....102 L 9
Stravally ....112 G 3
Streamstown ......104 B 7
Streedagh Point ....112 G 4
Streek Head ....89 C 13
Street ....107 J 6
Strokestown ......106 H 6
Stroove ....118 L 2
Struell Wells ......115 O 5
Strule ....113 J 3
Sturrakeen ....95 H 10
Suck (River) ....106 G 6
Suir (River) ....101 I 9
Summercove ......90 G 12
Summerhill ....108 L 7
Suncroft ....102 L 8
Sunderlin (Lough) ..107 I 7
Swan ....101 K 9
Swanlinbar ....113 I 5
Swan's Cross Roads ..114 K 5
Swatragh ....118 L 3
Sweep (The) ......95 J 10
Swilly (Lough) ....117 J 2
Swilly (River) ......117 J 2
Sybil Head ....92 A 11

T

Table Mountain ....103 M 8
Tacumshane ......97 M 11
Tacumshin Lake ..97 M 11
Taghmon ....96 M 11
Taghshinny ....107 I 7
Tagoat ....97 M 11
Tahilla ....88 C 12
Talbot Island ......104 B 7
Talbotstown ......102 M 9
Tallaght ....103 M 8
Tallanstown ......108 M 6
Tallow ....91 H 11
Tallowbridge ......91 H 11
Talt (Lough) ....111 F 5
Tamlaght *Fermanagh* ..113 J 5

Tamlaght *Magherafelt* ....118 M 3
Tamnamore ....114 M 4
Tandragee ....114 M 4
Tang ....107 I 7
Tangaveane ....116 H 3
Tappaghan Mount ....113 J 4
Tara (Hill of) ....108 M 7
Tarbert ....93 D 10
Tardree Forest ....115 N 3
Tarker (Lough) ....108 L 5
Tarmon ....112 H 5
Tarsaghaunmore ....111 C 5
Tassagh ....114 L 5
Taughblane ....115 N 4
Taur ....93 E 11
Tawin ....99 E 8
Tawin Island ....99 E 8
Tawny ....117 I 2
Tawnyinah ....106 F 6
Tawnylea ....112 H 5
Tay ....95 J 11
Tay (Lough) ....103 N 8
Taylor's Cross ....101 I 8
Tearaght Island ....92 A 11
Tedavnet ....114 K 5
Teelin ....112 G 4
Teemore ....113 J 5
Teeranea ....98 D 8
Teeranearagh ....88 B 12
Teerelton ....89 F 12
Teermaclane ....99 E 9
Teernakill ....105 D 7
Teeromoyle ....88 B 12
Teevurcher ....108 L 6
Temple (The) ....115 O 4
Temple of the Winds ....115 P 4
Templeboy ....112 F 5
Templederry ....100 H 9
Templeglentan ....93 E 10
Templehouse Lake ....112 G 5
Templemartin ....90 F 12
Templenoe ....89 C 12
Templeoran ....101 J 7
Templepatrick ....115 N 3
Templeshanbo ....96 L 10
Templetouhy ....101 I 9
Templetown ....96 L 11
Tempo ....113 J 4
Terenure ....103 N 8
Termon ....98 D 10
Termonbarry ....107 I 6
Termonfeckin ....109 N 6

Terryglass ....100 H 8
Tevrin ....107 K 7
Thomas Street ....106 H 7
Thomastown *Meath* ....108 L 6
Thomastown *Tipperrary* ......95 H 10
Thoor Ballylee ....99 F 8
Three Castle Head ....88 C 13
Three Castles ....96 J 9
Three Rock ....103 N 8
Tiduff ....92 B 11
Tievealehid ....116 H 2
Tievemore ....113 I 4
Tillyvoos ....112 H 4
Tiltinbane ....113 I 5
Timahoe ....102 L 8
Timoleague ....90 F 13
Timolin ....102 L 9
Tinahely ....103 M 9
Tinnahinch ....96 L 10
Tinriland ....102 L 9
Tiobraid Árann /
    Tipperary ....95 H 10
Tirnaneill ....114 L 5
Tirneevin ....99 F 8
Toames ....89 F 12
Tobar an Choire /
    Tubbercurry ....112 F 5
Tober ....101 J 7
Toberbeg ....102 M 8
Toberdoney ....118 M 2
Tobermore ....114 L 3
Tobernadarry ....105 E 7
Toberscanavan ....112 G 5
Toe Head ....89 E 13
Toem ....95 H 10
Togher *Cork* ....89 E 12
Togher *Louth* ....109 N 6
Togher *Offaly* ....101 K 8
Tolka ....103 M 7
Tollymore Forest Park ......115 O 5
Tombrack ....97 M 10
Tomdarragh ....103 N 8
Tomhaggard ....97 M 11
Tonabrocky ....99 E 8
Tonakeera Point ....104 C 7
Tonyduff ....108 K 6
Toomaghera ....99 E 8
Toomard ....106 G 7
Toombeola ....104 C 7
Toome ....114 M 3
Toomyvara ....100 H 9
Toor ....100 H 9

Tooraree ....93 E 10
Tooreencahill ....93 E 11
Toorlestraun ....112 F 5
Toormore ....89 D 13
Toormore Bay ....89 D 13
Toornafulla ....93 E 10
Toraigh /
    Tory Island ....116 H 2
Torc Waterfall ....89 D 11
Torneady Point ....116 G 2
Torr Head ....119 N 2
Tory Sound ....117 H 2
Tourig (River) ....91 I 11
Tower ....90 G 12
Trá Lí / Tralee ....93 C 11
Trá Mhór /
    Tramore ....96 K 11
Trabane Strand ....112 F 4
Tracton ....90 G 12
Tragumna ....89 E 13
Tralee Bay ....92 C 11
Tramore Bay ....96 K 11
Tranarossan Bay ....117 I 2
Travara Bridge ....88 C 12
Trawbreaga Bay ....117 K 2
Trawenagh Bay ....116 G 3
Trawmore Bay ....110 C 5
Trean ....105 D 7
Treantagh ....117 I 2
Treehoo ....107 K 5
Trien ....106 G 6
Trillick ....113 J 4
Tristia ....110 C 5
Trory ....113 J 4
Trostan ....119 N 2
Truskmore ....112 G 4
Trust ....100 G 7
Tuaim / Tuam ....105 F 7
Tuamgraney ....99 G 9
Tuar Mhic Éadaigh /
    Tourmakeady ....105 D 7
Tubber ....99 F 8
Tubbrid *Kilkenny* ....95 J 9
Tubbrid *Tipperary* ....95 I 11
Tulach Mhór /
    Tullamore ....101 J 8
Tulla *near Ennis* ....99 F 9
Tulla *near Gort* ....99 F 8
Tullagh Point ....117 J 2
Tullaghan ....112 G 4
Tullaghan Bay ....110 C 5

Tullaghanstown ....108 L 7
Tullagher ....96 K 10
Tullaghobegly ....117 H 2
Tullaherin ....96 K 10
Tullahought ....95 J 10
Tullakeel ....88 C 12
Tullamore ....93 D 10
Tullaroan ....95 J 10
Tullig ....92 C 11
Tullig Point ....93 C 10
Tullokyne ....105 E 7
Tully
    Lower Lough Erne ......113 I 4
Tully *near Ballyshannon* ....113 H 4
Tully *Upper Lough Erne* ....113 J 5
Tully Cross ....104 C 7
Tully National Stud ....102 L 8
Tullyallen ....109 M 6
Tullyamalra ....108 L 5
Tullycanna ....96 L 11
Tullydush ....117 J 2
Tullyhogue ....114 L 4
Tullylease ....94 F 11
Tullymacreeve ....109 M 5
Tullynaha ....112 H 3
Tullynally Castle ....107 J 6
Tullyroan ....114 M 4
Tullyvin ....108 K 5
Tulrohaun ....105 F 6
Tulsk ....106 H 6
Turlough ....105 E 6
Turloughmore ....105 F 7
Turner's Rock Tunnel ......89 D 12
Turreen ....107 I 7
Tuskar Rock ....97 N 11
Twelve Pins (The) ....104 C 7
Twomileborris ....95 I 9
Tylas ....108 M 7
Tynagh ....100 G 8
Tynan ....114 L 5
Tyrella ....115 O 5
Tyrellspass ....101 J 7

Uachtar Ard /
    Oughterard ....105 E 7
Uaigh / Owey Island ....116 G 2
Ugga Beg (Lough) ....98 D 8
Ulster American
    Folk Park ....113 J 4
Ulster Folk
    Museum (The) ....115 O 4

Union Hall ....89 E 13
Unshin ....112 G 5
Upper Ballinderry ....115 N 4
Upper Lake ....103 M 8
Upperchurch ....95 H 9
Upperlands ....118 M 3
Urbalreagh ....117 K 1
Urglin Glebe ....102 L 9
Urlaur ....106 F 6
Urlingford ....95 J 9

V

Valencia Island ....88 A 12
Valley ....110 C 5
Valleymount ....103 M 8
Vartry Reservoir ....103 N 8
Ventry ....92 A 11
Ventry Harbour ....92 A 11
Vicarstown ....102 K 8
Victoria Bridge ....113 J 3
Villierstown ....91 I 11
Virginia ....108 K 6
Virginia Road ....108 K 6
Vow ....118 M 3

W

Waddingtown ....96 M 11
Walshestown ....97 M 11
Walshtown ....90 H 12
Ward ....103 N 7
Ward (River) ....103 N 7
Waringsford ....115 N 4
Waringstown ....114 N 4
Warrenpoint ....109 N 5
Warrenpoint ....114 M 4
Washing Bay ....114 M 4
Watch Ho.-Village ....96 M 9
Waterfall ....90 G 12
Waterfoot or Glenariff ......119 N 2
Waterford Harbour ....96 L 11
Watergrasshill ....90 G 11
Waterworks ....114 L 3
Wattle Bridge ....113 J 5
Welchtown ....117 I 3
Wellington Bridge ....96 L 11
Wells Cross ....114 M 4
Wesport Bay ....105 C 6
West Town ....116 H 2
Westcove ....88 B 12
Westport House ....105 D 6
Westport Quay ....105 D 6
Wexford Bay ....97 N 10

Wexford Harbour ....97 M 10
Whale Head ....117 J 2
Wheathill ....113 I 5
Whiddy Island ....89 D 12
White *Limerick* ....93 E 10
White *Louth* ....109 M 6
White Castle ....118 K 2
White Hall ....89 D 13
White Island ....113 I 4
White Park Bay ....118 M 2
White Strand ....98 D 9
Whiteabbey ....115 O 3
Whitechurch *Cork* ....90 G 12
Whitechurch *Waterford* ....91 I 11
Whitecross ....114 M 5
Whitegate ....90 H 12
Whitehall *Roscommon* ....107 I 6
Whitehall *Westmeath* ......107 K 7
Whitehead ....115 O 3
Whites Town ....109 N 6
White'sCross ....90 G 12
Whitesides Corner ....114 M 3
Wicklow Gap ....103 M 8
Wicklow Mountains ....103 N 8
Wicklow Way ....103 N 8
Wildfowl
    and Wetlands Trust ....115 O 4
Wilkinstown ....108 L 6
Willbrook ....99 E 9
Williamstown *Galway* ......106 G 6
Williamstown
    Westmeath ....107 I 7
Windgap ....95 J 10
Windmill ....102 L 7
Windy Gap *Kerry* ....89 D 12
Windy Gap *Louth* ....109 N 5
Windy Gap *Mayo* ....105 E 6
Wolfhill ....101 K 9
Womanagh ....91 I 12
Woodburn ....115 O 3
Woodcock Hill ....99 F 9
Woodenbridge ....103 N 9
Woodford (River) ....99 G 8
Woodstown ....96 L 11

Y

Yellow Furze ....108 M 6
Yganavan (Lough) ....92 C 11
Youghal ....100 H 9
Youghal Bay ....91 I 12

A B C D E F G H I J K L M N O P Q R S T U V W X Y Z

Town plans

Sights
Place of interest
Interesting place of worship:
Church - Protestant church

Roads
Motorway - Dual carriageway
Numbered junctions: complete, limited
Major thoroughfare
Unsuitable for traffic or street subject to restrictions
Pedestrian street - Tramway
Car park - Park and Ride
Tunnel
Station and railway
Funicular
Cable-car

Various signs
Tourist Information Centre
Mosque - Synagogue
Tower - Ruins
Windmill
Garden, park, wood
Cemetery

Stadium - Golf course - Racecourse
Outdoor or indoor swimming pool
View - Panorama
Monument - Fountain
Pleasure boat harbour
Lighthouse
Airport - Underground station
Coach station
Ferry services:
passengers and cars - passengers only

Main post office with poste restante - Hospital
Covered market
Gendarmerie - Police
Town Hall
University, College
Public buildings located by letter:
Museum
Theatre

Plans

Curiosités
Bâtiment intéressant
Édifice religieux intéressant : catholique - protestant

Voirie
Autoroute - Double chaussée de type autoroutier
Échangeurs numérotés : complet - partiels
Grande voie de circulation
Rue réglementée ou impraticable
Rue piétonne - Tramway
Parking - Parking Relais
Tunnel
Gare et voie ferrée
Funiculaire, voie à crémaillère
Téléphérique, télécabine

Signes divers
Information touristique
Mosquée - Synagogue
Tour - Ruines
Moulin à vent
Jardin, parc, bois
Cimetière

Stade - Golf - Hippodrome
Piscine de plein air, couverte
Vue - Panorama
Monument - Fontaine
Port de plaisance
Phare
Aéroport - Station de métro
Gare routière
Transport par bateau :
passagers et voitures, passagers seulement

Bureau principal de poste restante - Hôpital
Marché couvert
Gendarmerie - Police
Hôtel de ville
Université, grande école
Bâtiment public repéré par une lettre :
Musée
Théâtre

Stadtpläne

Sehenswürdigkeiten
Sehenswertes Gebäude
Sehenswerter Sakralbau:Katholische - Evangelische Kirche

Straßen
Autobahn - Schnellstraße
Nummerierte Voll - bzw. Teilanschlussstellen
Hauptverkehrsstraße
Gesperrte Straße oder mit Verkehrsbeschränkungen
Fußgängerzone - Straßenbahn
Parkplatz - Park-and-Ride-Plätze
Tunnel
Bahnhof und Bahnlinie
Standseilbahn
Seilschwebebahn

Sonstige Zeichen
Informationsstelle
Moschee - Synagoge
Turm - Ruine
Windmühle
Garten, Park, Wäldchen
Friedhof

Stadion - Golfplatz - Pferderennbahn
Freibad - Hallenbad
Aussicht - Rundblick
Denkmal - Brunnen
Yachthafen
Leuchtturm
Flughafen - U-Bahnstation
Autobusbahnhof
Schiffsverbindungen:
Autofähre, Personenfähre
Hauptpostamt (postlagernde Sendungen) - Krankenhaus
Markthalle
Gendarmerie - Polizei
Rathaus
Universität, Hochschule
Öffentliches Gebäude, durch einen Buchstaben
gekennzeichnet:
Museum
Theater

Plattegronden

Bezienswaardigheden
Interessant gebouw
Interessant kerkelijk gebouw: Kerk - Protestantse kerk

Wegen
Autosnelweg - Weg met gescheiden rijbanen
Knooppunt / aansluiting: volledig, gedeeltelijk
Hoofdverkeersweg
Onbegaanbare straat, beperkt toegankelijk
Voetgangersgebied - Tramlijn
Parkeerplaats - P & R
Tunnel
Station, spoorweg
Kabelspoor
Tandradbaan

Overige tekens
Informatie voor toeristen
Moskee - Synagoge
Toren - Ruïne
Windmolen
Tuin, park, bos
Begraafplaats

Stadion - Golfterrein - Renbaan
Zwembad: openlucht, overdekt
Uitzicht - Panorama
Gedenkteken, standbeeld - Fontein
Jachthaven
Vuurtoren
Luchthaven - Metrostation
Busstation
Vervoer per boot:
Passagiers en auto's - uitsluitend passagiers

Hoofdkantoor voor poste-restante - Ziekenhuis
Overdekte markt
Marechaussee / rijkswacht - Politie
Stadhuis
Universiteit, hogeschool
Openbaar gebouw, aangegeven met een letter::
Museum
Schouwburg

Piante

Curiosità
Edificio interessante
Costruzione religiosa interessante: Chiesa - Tempio

Viabilità
Autostrada - Doppia carreggiata tipo autostrada
Svincoli numerati: completo, parziale
Grande via di circolazione
Via regolamentata o impraticabile
Via pedonale - Tranvia
Parcheggio - Parcheggio Ristoro
Galleria
Stazione e ferrovia
Funicolare
Funivia, cabinovia

Simboli vari
Ufficio informazioni turistiche
Moschea - Sinagoga
Torre - Ruderi
Mulino a vento
Giardino, parco, bosco
Cimitero

Stadio - Golf - Ippodromo
Piscina: all'aperto, coperta
Vista - Panorama
Monumento - Fontana
Porto turistico
Faro
Aeroporto - Stazione della metropolitana
Autostazione
Trasporto con traghetto:
passeggeri ed autovetture - solo passeggeri

Ufficio centrale di fermo posta - Ospedale
Mercato coperto
Carabinieri - Polizia
Municipio
Università, scuola superiore
Edificio pubblico indicato con lettera:
Museo
Teatro

Planos

Curiosidades
Edificio interessante
Edificio religioso interessante: católica - protestante

Vías de circulación
Autopista - Autovía
Enlaces numerados: completo, parciales
Vía importante de circulacion
Calle reglamentada o impracticable
Calle peatonal - Tranvía
Aparcamiento - Aparcamientos «P+R»
Túnel
Estación y línea férrea
Funicular, línea de cremallera
Teleférico, telecabina

Signos diversos
Oficina de Información de Turismo
Mezquita - Sinagoga
Torre - Ruinas
Molino de viento
Jardín, parque, madera
Cementerio

Estadio - Golf - Hipódromo
Piscina al aire libre, cubierta
Vista parcial - Vista panorámica
Monumento - Fuente
Puerto deportivo
Faro
Aeropuerto - Estación de metro
Estación de autobuses
Transporte por barco:
pasajeros y vehículos, pasajeros solamente

Oficina de correos - Hospital
Mercado cubierto
Policía National - Policía
Ayuntamiento
Universidad, escuela superior
Edificio público localizado con letra :
Museo
Teatro

Plans de ville
Town plans / Stadtpläne / Stadsplattegronden
Piante di città / Planos de ciudades

GREAT BRITAIN

- Aberdeen 150
- Bath 150
- Birmingham............. 151
- Bournemouth 152
- Brighton and Hove 153
- Bristol 154
- Cambridge............. 155
- Canterbury............. 156
- Cardiff 157
- Chester 158
- Coventry............... 159
- Dundee................. 159
- Durham................. 160
- Edinburgh 161
- Exeter.................. 162
- Glasgow 163
- Leeds 164
- Leicester 165
- Lincoln................. 165
- Liverpool 166-167
- Greater London 168-169
- London 170-171
- Manchester 172
- Newcastle-upon-Tyne ... 173
- Norwich 174
- Nottingham............. 174
- Oxford 175
- Perth 176
- Plymouth 177
- Portsmouth
  and Southsea 178
- Southampton 179
- Stirling................. 180
- Stratford-upon-Avon 181
- Winchester............. 182
- Windsor................. 183
- York 184

IRELAND

- Belfast 185
- Cork 186
- Galway................. 187
- Dublin 188-189
- Killarney 190
- Limerick 191

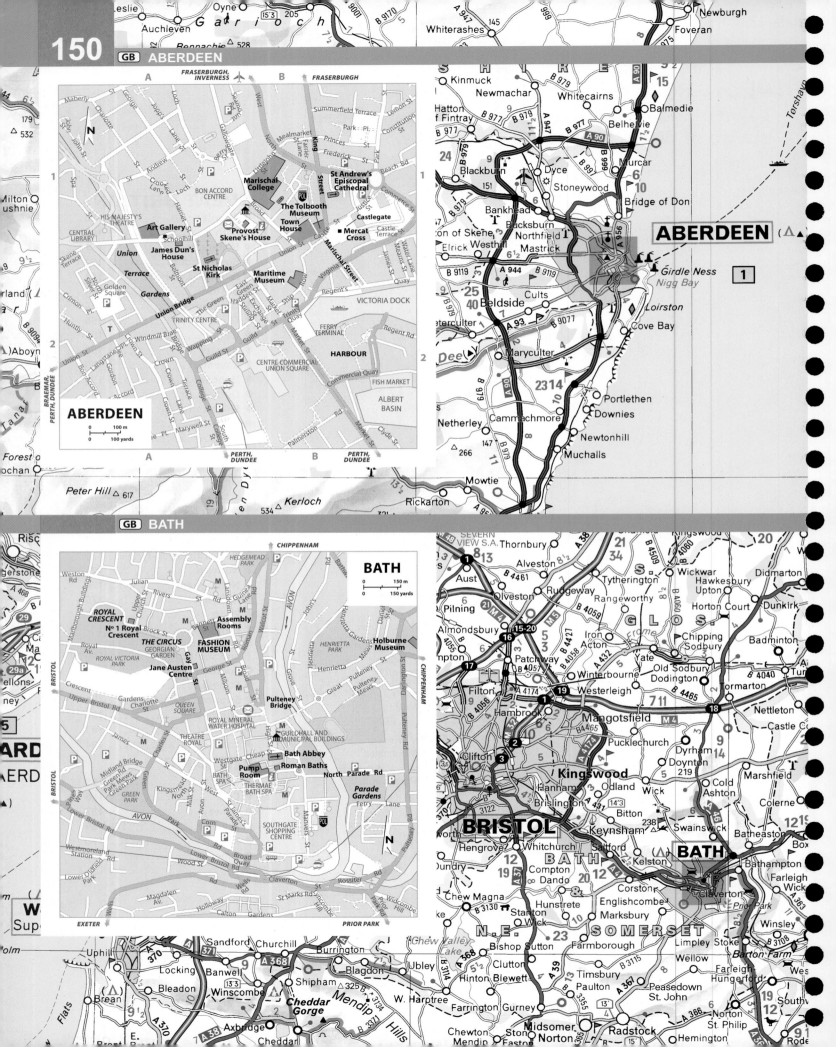

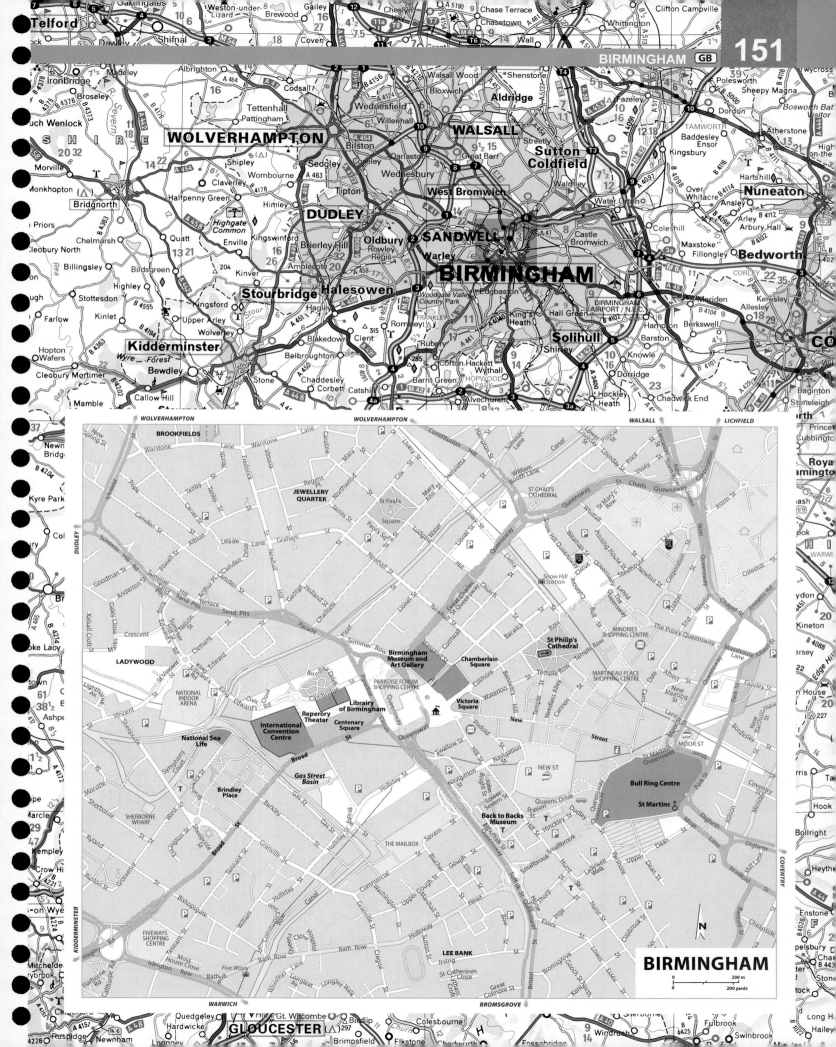

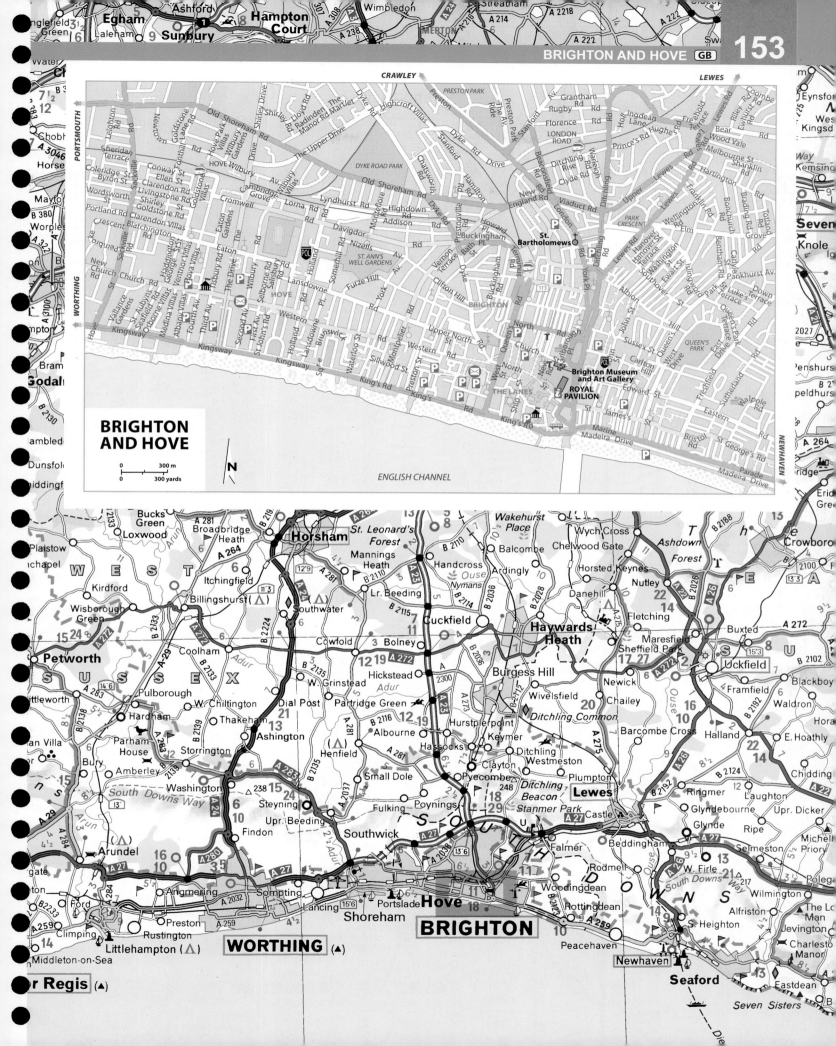

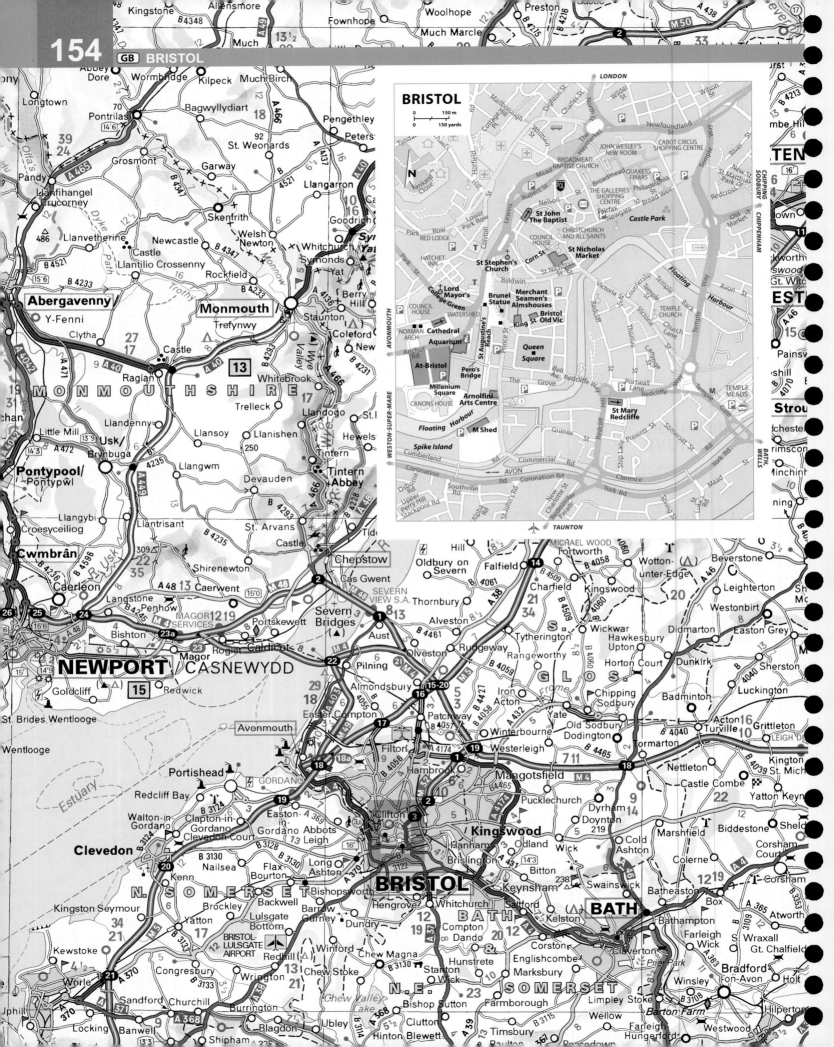

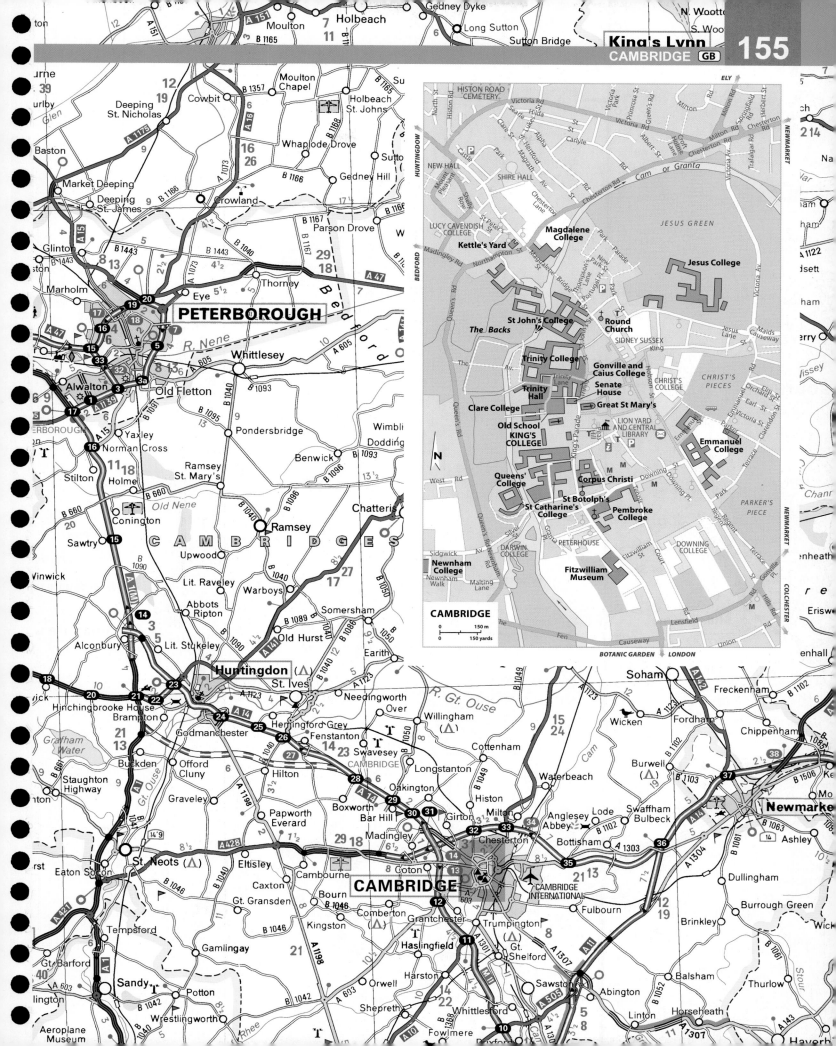

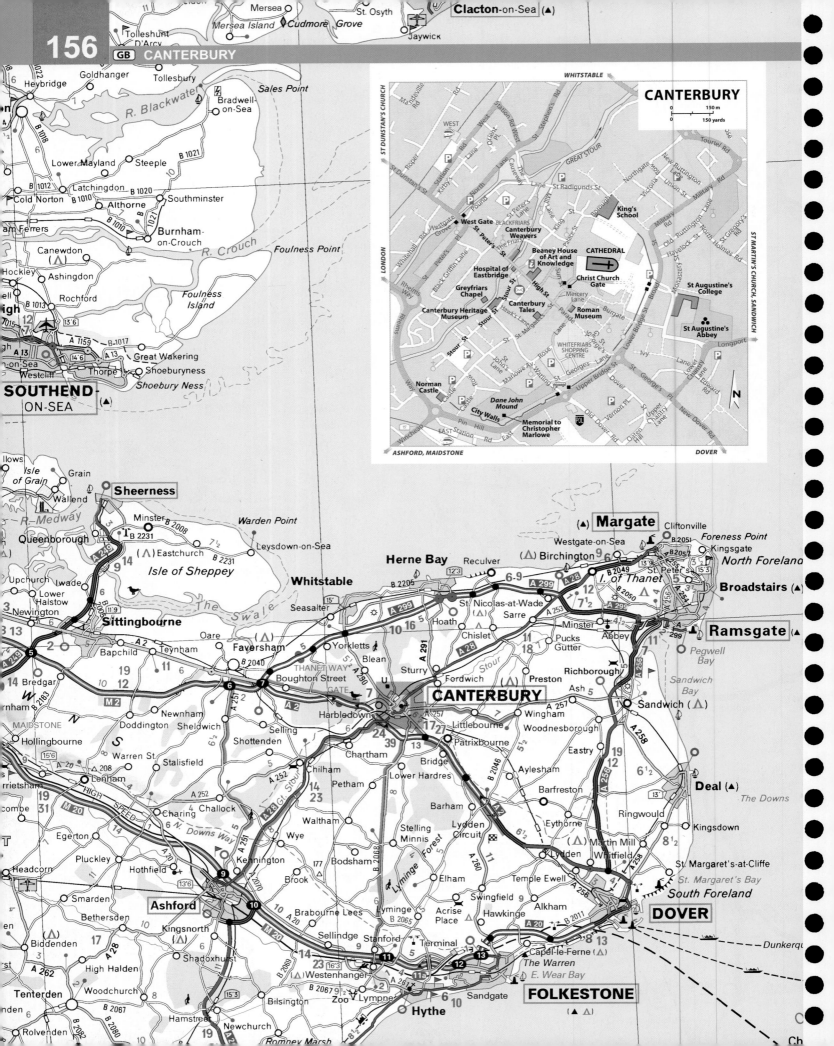

CARDIFF

SWANSEA • MERTHYR TYDFIL • CAERPHILLY • BRISTOL

WELSH OFFICE • UNIVERSITY COLLEGE • CATHAYS
TEMPLE OF PEACE • National Museum Cardiff
ALEXANDRA GARDENS • City Hall • Gorsedd Gardens
OLD COUNTY HALL • Bute Park • Law Courts
CARDIFF NEW SYNAGOGUE
Cardiff Castle • Military Museums • St John's Church
CAPITOL CENTRE • ST DAVID'S SHOPPING CENTRE
Cardiff Arms Park • Central Market • The Old Library • Queen St
Millennium Stadium • CARDIFF CENTRAL
SWAMINARAYANA TEMPLE
Pendyris St • CALLAGHAN SQUARE
SEVENOAKS PARK • Bute East Dock
GRANGETOWN MUSLIM CULTURAL CENTRE
THE SALVATION ARMY
BUTETOWN • THE RED DRAGON CENTRE
Coal Exchange • CARDIFF BAY
ST CUTHBERT'S • Wales Millennium Centre
Techniquest • Pierhead Building • Y Senedd
MERMAID QUAY • Norwegian Church
HAMADRYAD PARK • CARDIFF BAY
CARDIFF YACHT CLUB • CARDIFF BAY WETLANDS RESERVE
QUEEN ALEXANDRA DOCK
LECKWITH WOODS • N
0 200 m
0 200 yards

PENARTH • BRIGEND

CAERPHILLY • Risca • Caerleon • Caerwent • SEVERN VIEW S.A.
Cymmer • Senghenydd • Llanbradach • Machen • Langstone • Penhow • SEVERN BRIDGES • Aust
Tonyrefail • Bedwas • Rogerstone • MAGOR SERVICES • Portskewett • Severn Bridges
Pontypridd • Caerphilly / Caerffili • Bishton • Roglet • Caldicot • Pilning
Beddau • Thornhill • Parc Cefn Onn • Castleton • NEWPORT / CASNEWYDD • Magor • Almondsbury
Talbot Green • Llantrisant • Pentyrch • Tongwynlais • Goldcliff • Redwick • Easter Compton
Miskin • Pontyclun • Lisvane • Marshfield • St. Brides Wentlooge • Avonmouth • Filton
Llanharry • Radyr • Llanishen • St. Mellons • Peterstone Wentlooge • Portishead • GORDANO
CARDIFF WEST • Whitchurch • Rumney • Redcliff Bay • Clapton-in-Gordano
Hensol • St. Brides-Super-Ely • St. Fagans • CARDIFF / CAERDYDD • Walton-in-Gordano • Gordano Court
Pendoylan • Ely • Clevedon • Clevedon Court • Abbots Leigh
Bonvilston • St. Nicholas • Dinas Powys • Bishopsworth
Beaupre Castle • Wenvoe • Penarth • Kenn • Nailsea • Long Ashton • Clifton
GLAMORGAN • Penmark • N. SOMERSET • BRIST
Eglwys Brewis • St. Athan • Sully • Kingston Seymour • Brockley • Backwell • Barrow Gurney • Dundry
East-Aberthaw • Rhoose • Porthkerry • Swanbridge • Flat Holm • Yatton • Lulsgate Bottom
Barry / Barri • CARDIFF AIRPORT • BRISTOL-LULSGATE AIRPORT • Redhill • Winford • Chew Magna
Weston-Super-Mare • Congresbury • Wrington • Chew Stoke

CHESTER (city inset map)

HOYLAKE · ELLESMERE PORT · MANCHESTER, LIVERPOOL

Northgate Arena
Northgate
The Walls
King Charles' Tower
Kaleyard's Gate
Chester Cathedral
Town Hall
Eastgate
FORUM SHOPPING CENTRE
THE ROWS
Grosvenor Shopping Centre
Dewa Roman Experience
Newgate
Three Old Arches
Stanley Palace
Grosvenor Park
St John's
ROMAN AMPHITHEATRE
Grosvenor Museum
Bridgegate
Roodee
QUEEN'S PARK
CASTLE
Old Dee Bridge

CHESTER
0 — 150 m
0 — 150 yards

WREXHAM · CONWY

MANCHESTER, NANTWICH, WHITCHURCH

Road map

SOUTHPORT
Birkdale
Mere Brow
Croston
Rufford Old Hall
Rufford
Scarisbrick
Ainsdale
Halsall
Burscough Bridge
Parbold
Burscough
Formby
Ormskirk
Newburgh
Skelmersdale
Gt. Altcar
Aughton
Lydiate
Ince Blundell
Up Holland
Hightown
Maghull
Rainford
Blundellsands
Litherland
Crosby
Kirkby
ST. HELENS
Bootle
Knowsley
New Brighton
LIVERPOOL
Roby
Huyton
Prescot
Wallasey
BIRKENHEAD
West Kirby
Irby
Port Sunlight
Woolton
Farnworth
Thurstaston
Pensby
Bebington
Hough Green
Ditton
Heswall
Bromborough
Widnes
Speke
Parkgate
Thornton Hough
LIVERPOOL JOHN LENNON AIRPORT
Hale
Runcorn
Neston
Eastham
River Mersey
Frodsham
Willaston
Ellesmere Port
Rhyl
Prestatyn
Talacre
Point of Ayr
Welsh Channel
River Dee / Afon Dyfrdwy
Elton
Helsby
Kinmel Bay
Llanasa
Flint / Fflint
Whitby
Backford Cross
CHESTER
Pensarn
Rhuddlan
Trelawnyd
Dyserth
Mostyn
Holywell / Treffynnon
Greenfield
Puddington
Stoak
Bridge Trafford
Abergele
Bodelwyddan
St. Asaph
Rhuallt
Babell
Bagillt
Little Barrow
Llannefydd
Caerwys
Halkyn
Connah's Quay
Saughall
Sealand
Great Barrow
Trefnant
Afon-wen
Queensferry
Upton
Henllan
Bodfari
Northop
Ewloe
Hawarden
Lache
Christleton
Llansannan
Nannerch
FLINTS
Northop Hall
Waverton
Bylchau
Denbigh / Dinbych
Mold / Yr Wyddgrug
Buckley / Bwcle
Saltney
Llanrhaeadr
Cilcain
Handbridge
Huxley
DENBIGHSHIRE
Moel Fammau
Loggerheads
Broughton
CHESHIRE WEST
Ruthin / Rhuthun
Nercwys
Penyffordd
Pulford
Aldford
Tattenhall
Cyffylliog
Llanferres
Leeswood
Hope
Burton
Handley
Higher Burwardsley
AND CHESTER
Clocaenog
Treuddyn
Waun y Llyn
Caergwrle
Rossett
Pentre Celyn
Llanfynydd
Farndon
Broxton
Llandegla
Gresford
Holt
Clawdd-newydd
Bwlchgwyn
Brymbo
Llanarmon-yn-Ial
Bettws Gwerfil Goch
Bryneglwys
Coedpoeth
Wrexham / Wrecsam
Rhostyllen
Erddig
Tilston
Malpas
Llanfihangel Glyn Myfyr
Llanelidan
Rhoslannerchrugog
Marchwiel
Worthenbury

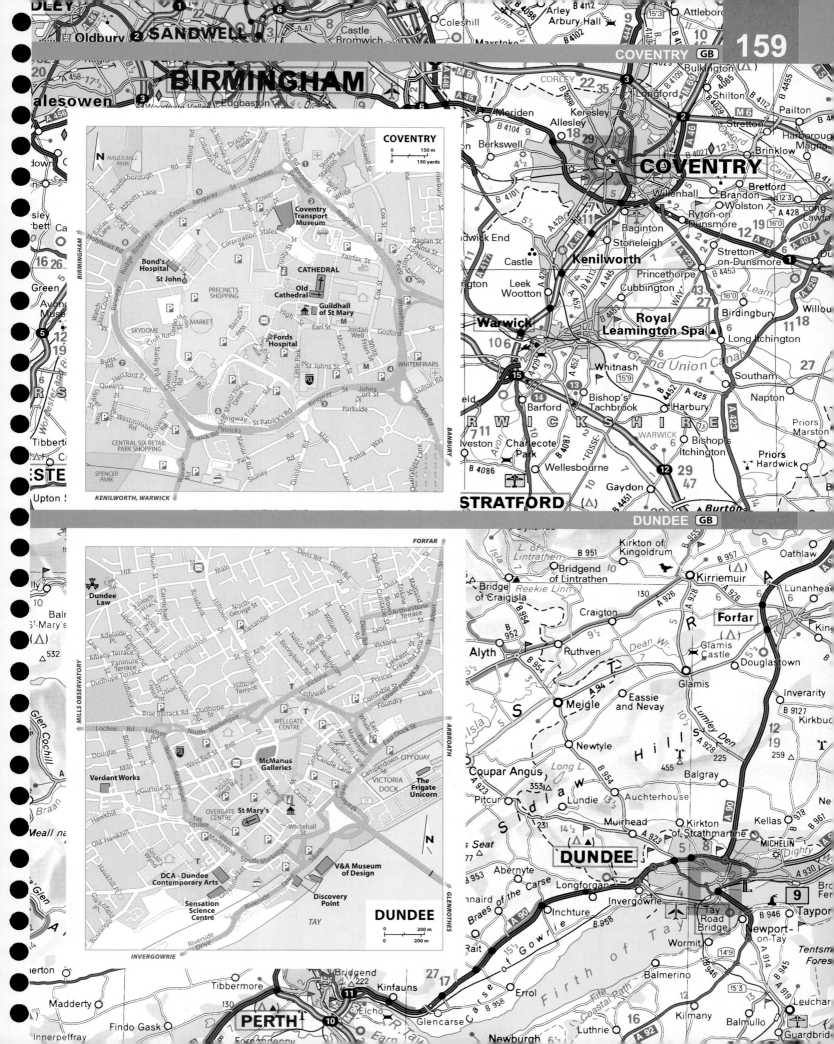

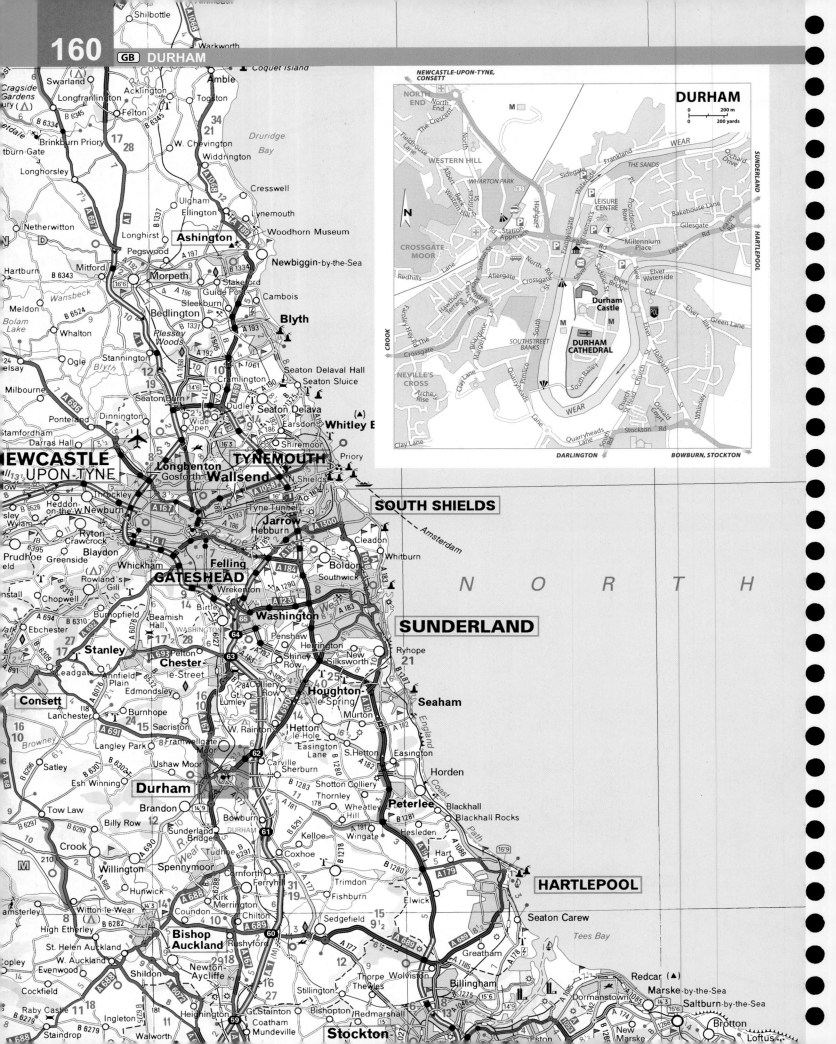

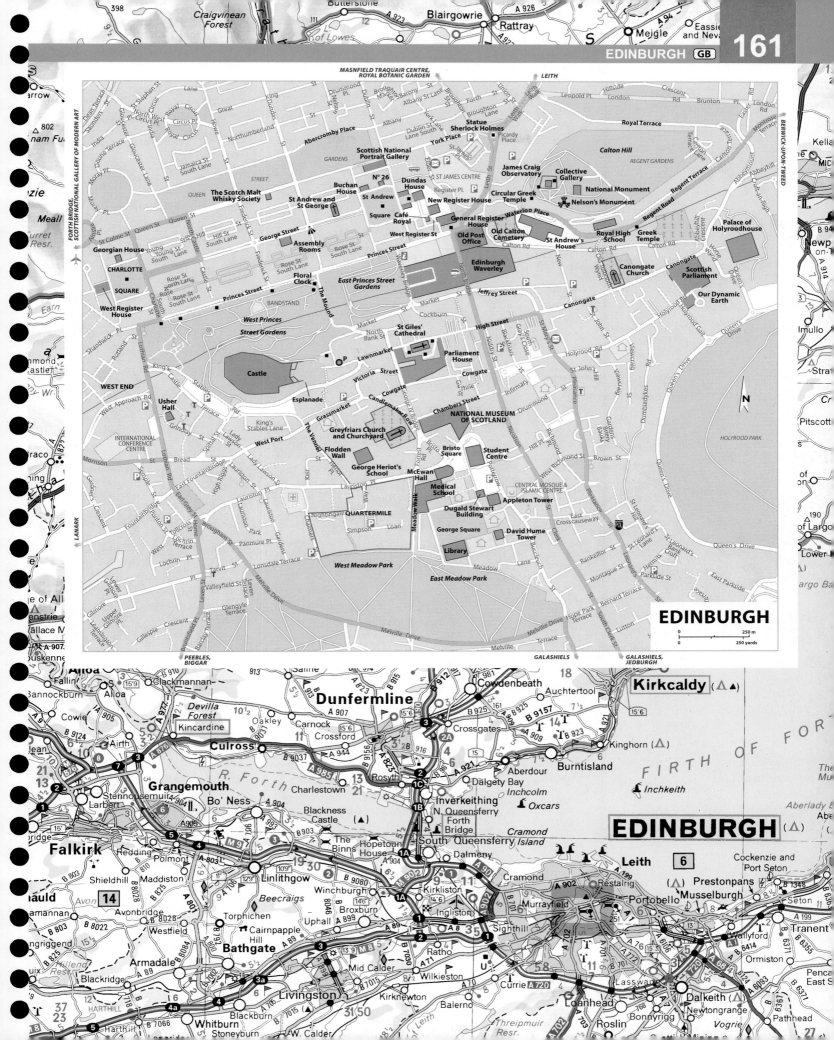

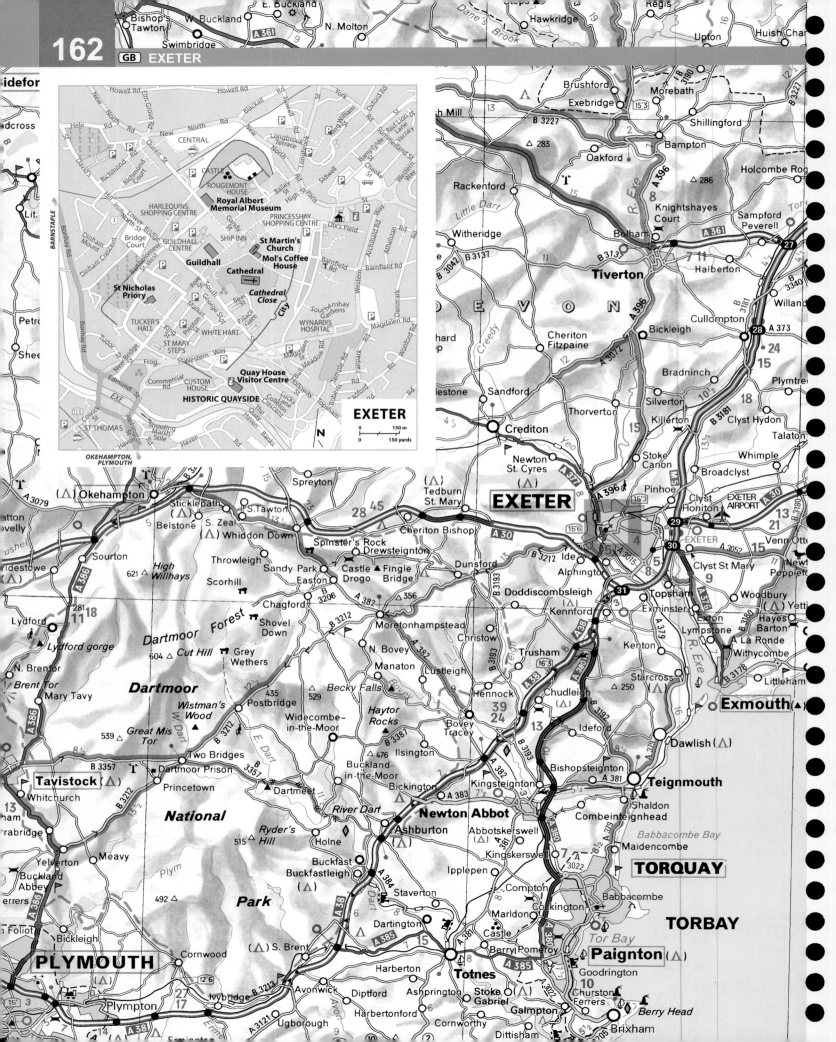

EXETER

0   150 m
0   150 yards

N

OKEHAMPTON, PLYMOUTH

Historic Quayside map labels:
Howell Rd, Howell Rd, Hele Rd, New North Rd, Elm Grove Rd, Blackall Rd, York Rd, Oxford Rd, King William St, Summerland St, Verney St, CENTRAL, Longbrook Terrace, Cheeke St, Western Way, CASTLE, ROUGEMONT HOUSE, Royal Albert Memorial Museum, HARLEQUINS SHOPPING CENTRE, PRINCESSHAY SHOPPING CENTRE, Bailey St, High St, Sidwell St, Dix's Field, Paris St, Gandy St, SHIP INN, St Martin's Church, Mol's Coffee House, Guildhall, GUILDHALL CENTRE, Cathedral, St Nicholas Priory, Cathedral Close, Fore St, George St, Market, Preston, WHITE HART, TUCKER'S HALL, WYNARD'S HOSPITAL, Southernhay Gardens, King St, St Mary Steps, Frog St, Magdalen St, W Western Way, Quay House Visitor Centre, CUSTOM HOUSE, Commercial Rd, Edmund St, ST THOMAS, Cowick St, Okehampton Rd, Shooting Marsh Stile, HISTORIC QUAYSIDE

Main map place names:

E. Buckland, W. Buckland, Bishop's Tawton, Swimbridge, N. Molton, Hawkridge, Dane's Brook, Upton, Huish Cham, Brushford, Morebath, Exebridge, Shillingford, h Mill, Rackenford, Oakford, Bampton, Holcombe Rog, Knightshayes Court, Sampford Peverell, Bolham, Halberton, Willand, Tiverton, Cullompton, Witheridge, Bickleigh, Cheriton Fitzpaine, Bradninch, Plymtre, Silverton, Clyst Hydon, Sandford, Thorverton, Killerton, Talaton, Crediton, Newton St. Cyres, Stoke Canon, Whimple, Broadclyst, Pinhoe, Clyst Honiton, EXETER AIRPORT, Venn Otte, Okehampton, Spreyton, Tedburn St. Mary, EXETER, Ide, Clyst St Mary, Newt Popplefo, Stickepath, S. Tawton, Cheriton Bishop, Alphington, Woodbury, Belstone, Whiddon Down, Spinster's Rock, Drewsteignton, Dunsford, Doddiscombsleigh, Topsham, Exminster, Exton, Sourton, S. Zeal, Throwleigh, Sandy Park, Castle Drogo, Fingle Bridge, Kennford, Lympstone, A La Ronde, High Willhays, Scorhill, Easton, Chagford, Moretonhampstead, Christow, Trusham, Kenton, Withycombe, Littleham, Lydford, Lydford gorge, Cut Hill, Grey Wethers, Shovel Down, N. Bovey, Manaton, Lustleigh, Hennock, Chudleigh, Starcross, Exmouth, N. Brentor, Brent Tor, Mary Tavy, Dartmoor, Wistman's Wood, Postbridge, Becky Falls, Haytor Rocks, Bovey Tracey, Ideford, Dawlish, Great Mis Tor, Widecombe-in-the-Moor, Ilsington, Bishopsteignton, Tavistock, Dartmoor Prison, Buckland-in-the-Moor, Bickington, Kingsteignton, Teignmouth, Whitchurch, Princetown, Dartmeet, Newton Abbot, Ashburton, Abbotskerswell, Shaldon, Combeinteignhead, National, River Dart, Holne, Kingskerswell, Maidencombe, Babbacombe Bay, Buckland Abbey, Yelverton, Meavy, Buckfast, Ipplepen, TORQUAY, Babbacombe, Park, Buckfastleigh, Compton, Marldon, Cockington, TORBAY, PLYMOUTH, Cornwood, Dartington, Staverton, Castle, Berry Pomeroy, Paignton, Tor Bay, Plympton, Ivybridge, Avonwick, Diptford, Ashprington, Stoke Gabriel, Goodrington, Churston Ferrers, Berry Head, Brixham, Totnes, Harberton, Harbertonford, Cornworthy, Dittisham, Ugborough, Errmington

DEVON

Dartmoor Forest

Dartmoor Forest

National Park

GLASGOW

450 m
450 yards

N

DUMBARTON | STIRLING | KIRKINTILLOCH

Botanic Gardens
Queen's Cross Church
Hunterian Art Gallery
MACKINTOSH HOUSE
MAIN BUILDING
Hunterian Museum
University Gilmorehill Building
WESTERN INFIRMARY
Kelvingrove Park
Park Circus
KELVINGROVE ART GALLERY AND MUSEUM
KELVIN HALL
Old Dumbarton Rd
The National Piping Centre
Tenement House
Beresford
Glasgow School of Art
The Mitchell Library
CCA
Willow Tearoom
Sauchiehall Street
BUCHANAN STREET BUS STATION
Martyr's School
Royal Infirmary
CATHEDRAL
Necropolis
St Mungo Museum of Religious Life and Art
Provand's Lordship
Scottish Exhibition and Conference Center
EXHIBITION CENTRE STATION
Merchants' House
Willow Tea Rooms
The Lighthouse
Gallery of Modern Art
City Chambers
George Street
High Street
Clyde Auditorium - The "Armadillo"
Glasgow Tower
Science Centre
Imax
BBC Building
La grue Finnieston
Clyde Arc
Princes Square
Trades Hall
CENTRAL STATION
ST ENOCH SHOPPING CENTRE
Glasgow Cross
Tolbooth Steeple
The Barras
Clyde River
Bridgegate Steeple
Saltmarket
Glasgow Green
People's Palace
Doulton Fountain
Templeton Business Centre
Scotland Street School Museum

KILMARNOCK | MOTHERWELL HAMILTON KILMARNOCK | EAST KILBRIDE

Greenock
Port Glasgow
Dumbarton
Erskine Bridge
Duntocher
Milngavie
Kirkintilloch
Cumbernauld
Kilpatrick Hills
R. Clyde
Loch Thom
Langbank
Old Kilpatrick
Bearsden
Lenzie
Condorrat
Slamannan
Garvock
Bishopton
Clydebank
Stepps
Longriggend
Creuch Hill
Kilmacolm
Renfrew
Muithead
Riggend
Caldercruix
Houston
Bridge of Weir
Linwood
Coatbridge
Airdrie
Chapelhall
Johnstone
Ranfurly
Kilbarchan
Heathfield
Muirshiel
Stake
GLASGOW
Rutherglen
Mossend
Holytown
Salsburgh
PAISLEY
Uddingston
BOTHWELL
Bellshill
Garfin
Lochwinnoch
Barrhead
Howwood
Cambuslang
Bothwell
Blantyre
Cleland
Kilbirnie
Neilston
Busby
HAMILTON
Motherwell
Beith
Newton Mearns
East Kilbride
Hamilton
Wishaw
Barrmill
Lugton
Eaglesham
Larkhall
Overtown
Dunlop
Auldhouse
Dalry
Newmains
Law
Dalserf

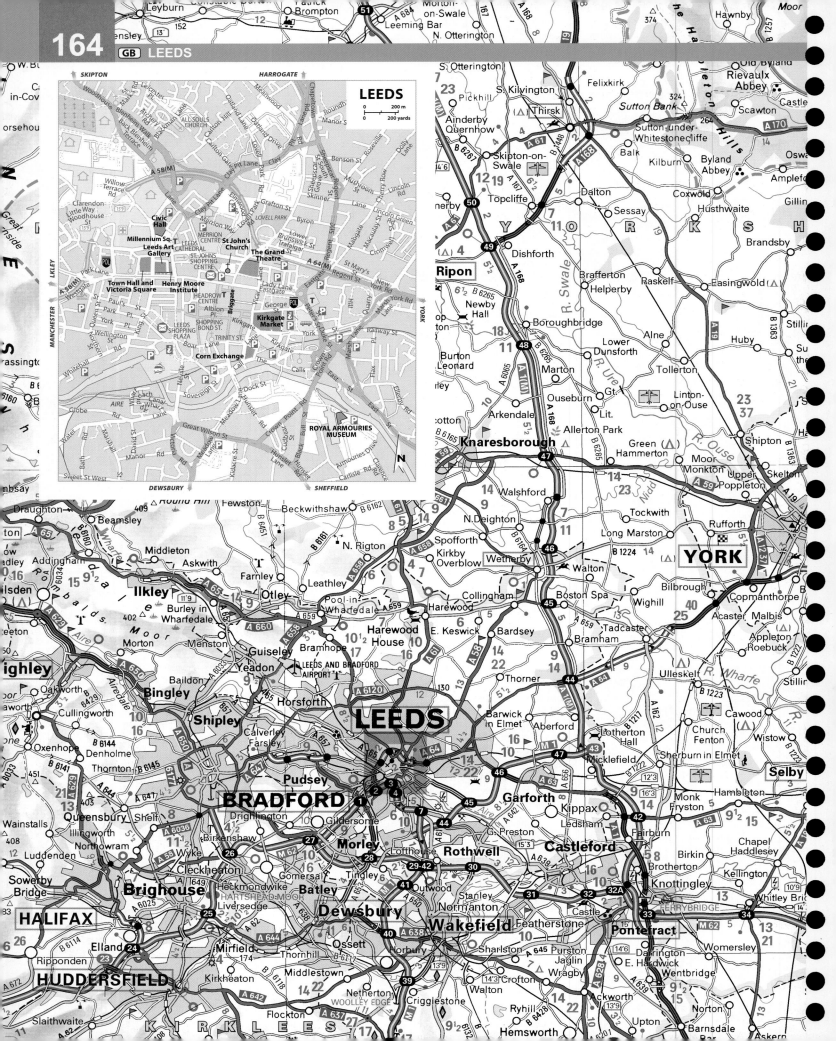

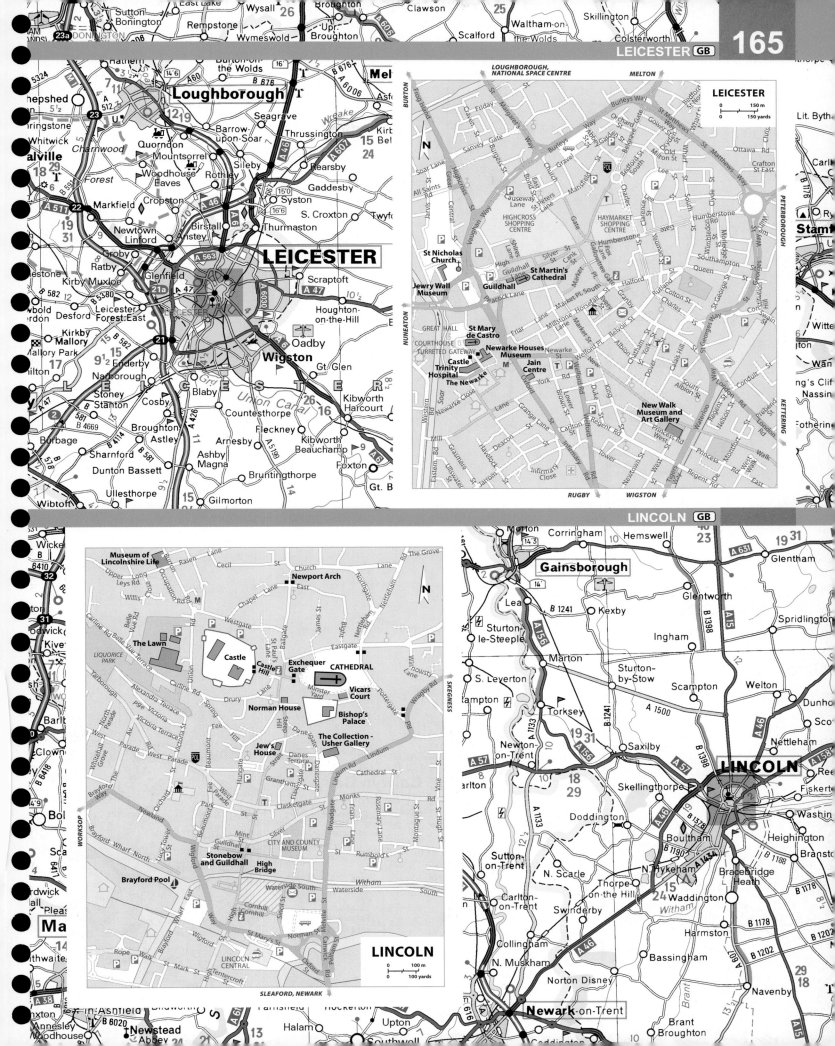

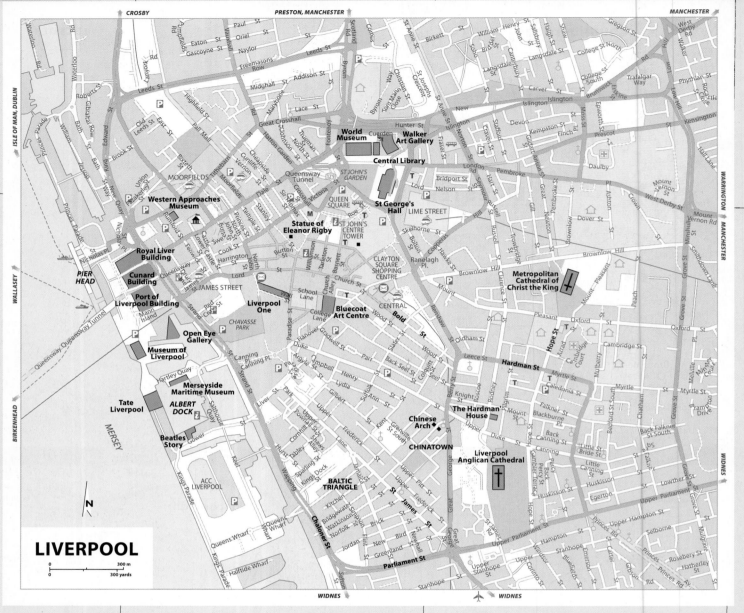

LIVERPOOL

0 | 300 m
0 | 300 yards

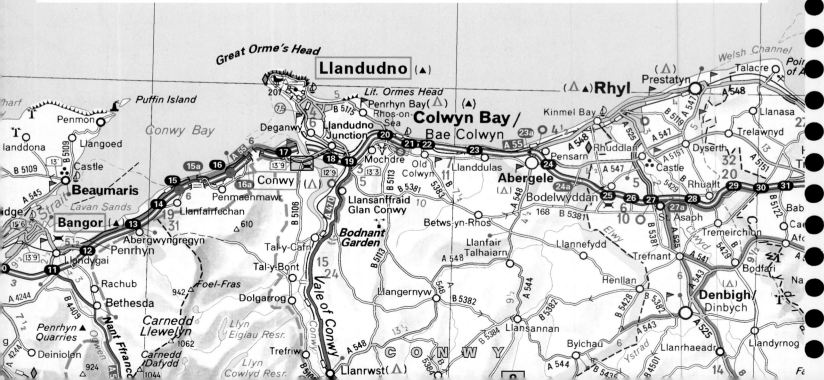

Chesham · Amersham · Beaconsfield · Slough · Windsor · Eton · Ascot · Guildford · Woking · Staines · Egham · Sunbury · Chertsey · Weybridge · Walton-on-Thames · Esher · Leatherhead · Dorking · Reigate · Redhill · Epsom · Ewell · Banstead · Kingston upon Thames · Hampton Court · Richmond · Twickenham · Wimbledon · Hounslow · Heathrow Airport · Uxbridge · Harrow · Wembley · Ealing · Watford · Bushey · Rickmansworth · Chorleywood · Borehamwood · Edgware · Mill Hill · Finchley · Barnet · Potters Bar · St. Albans · South Mimms

Woking · Guildford

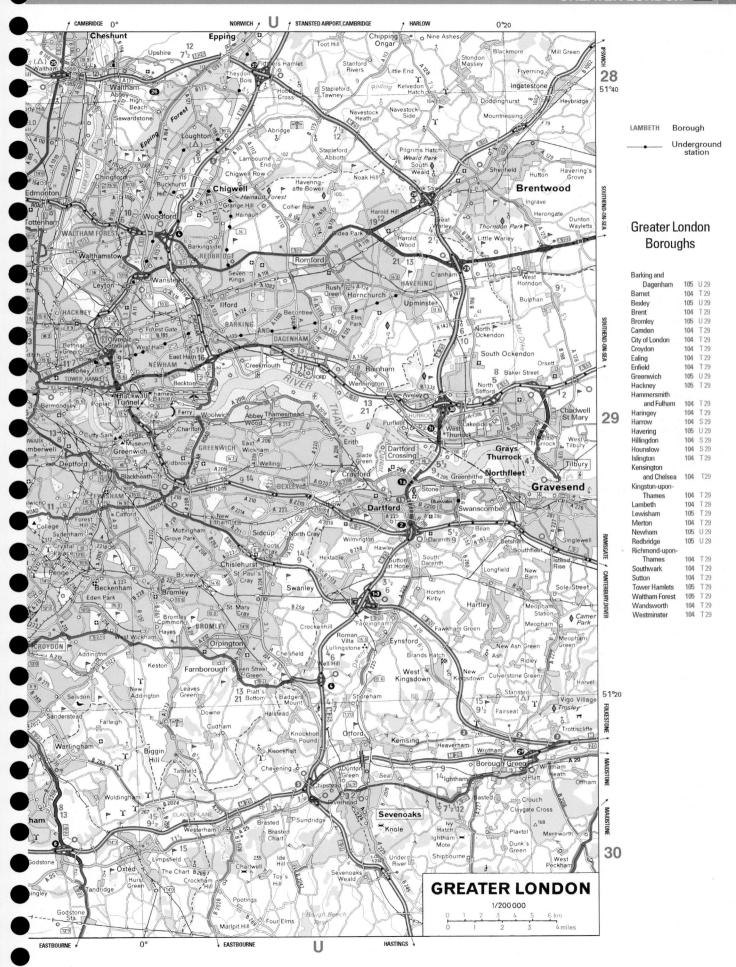

LAMBETH Borough
•——•—— Underground station

Greater London Boroughs

Borough		
Barking and Dagenham	105	U 29
Barnet	104	T 29
Bexley	105	U 29
Brent	104	T 29
Bromley	105	U 29
Camden	104	T 29
City of London	104	T 29
Croydon	104	T 29
Ealing	104	T 29
Enfield	104	T 29
Greenwich	105	U 29
Hackney	105	U 29
Hammersmith and Fulham	104	T 29
Haringey	104	T 29
Harrow	104	T 29
Havering	105	U 29
Hillingdon	104	S 29
Hounslow	104	S 29
Islington	104	T 29
Kensington and Chelsea	104	T 29
Kingston-upon-Thames	104	T 29
Lambeth	104	T 29
Lewisham	105	T 29
Merton	104	T 29
Newham	105	U 29
Redbridge	105	U 29
Richmond-upon-Thames	104	T 29
Southwark	104	T 29
Sutton	104	T 29
Tower Hamlets	105	T 29
Waltham Forest	105	U 29
Wandsworth	104	T 29
Westminster	104	T 29

GREATER LONDON

1/200 000

0 1 2 3 4 5 6 km
0   1   2   3   4 miles

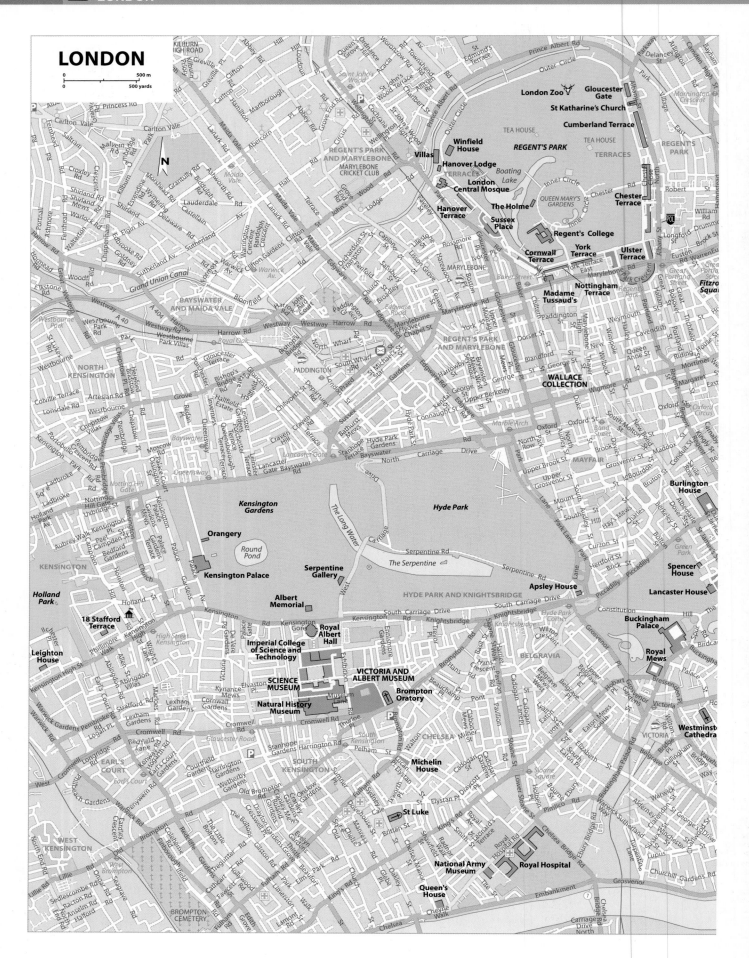

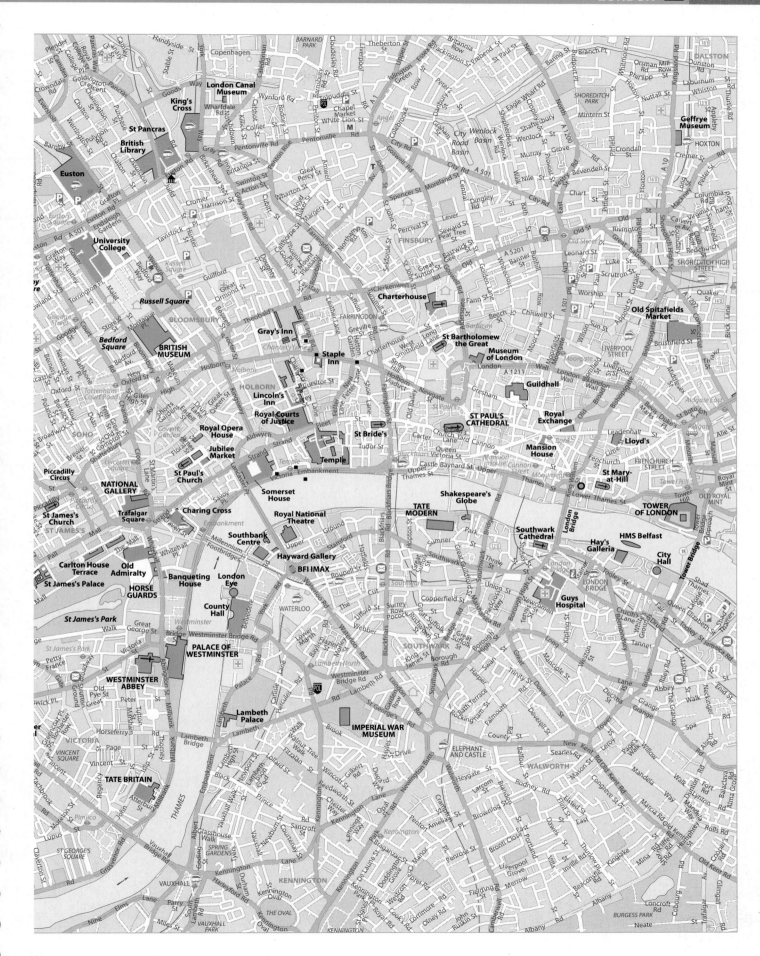

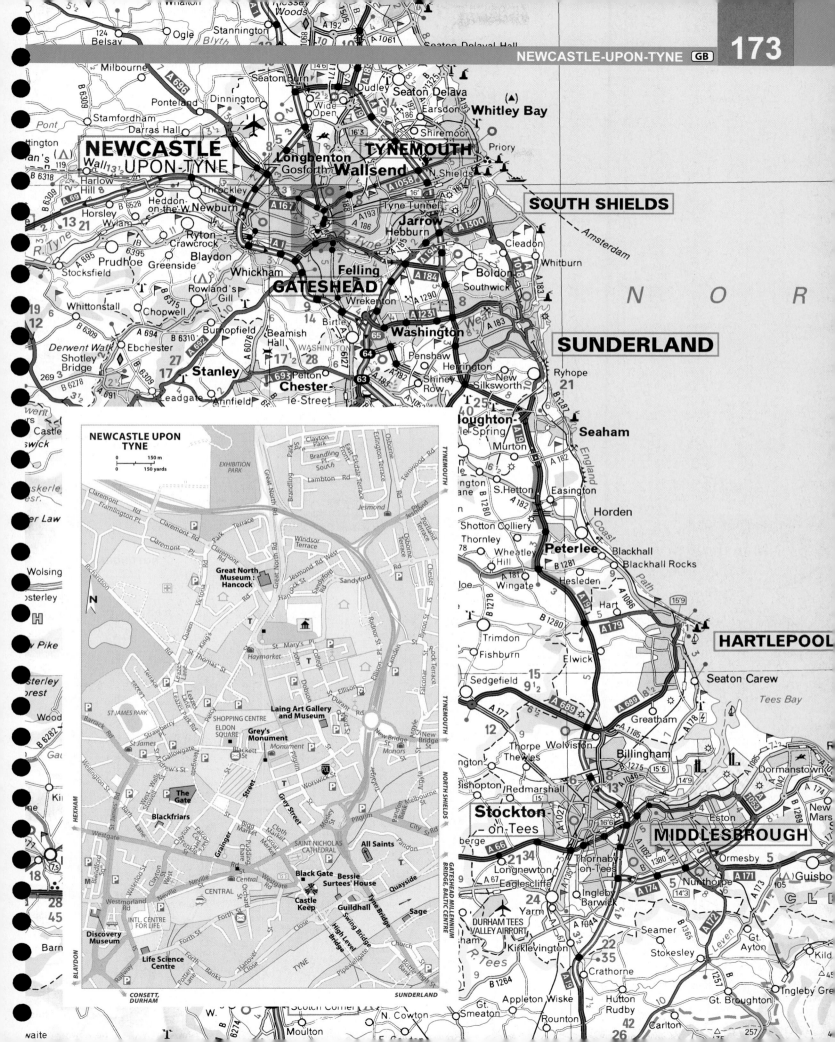

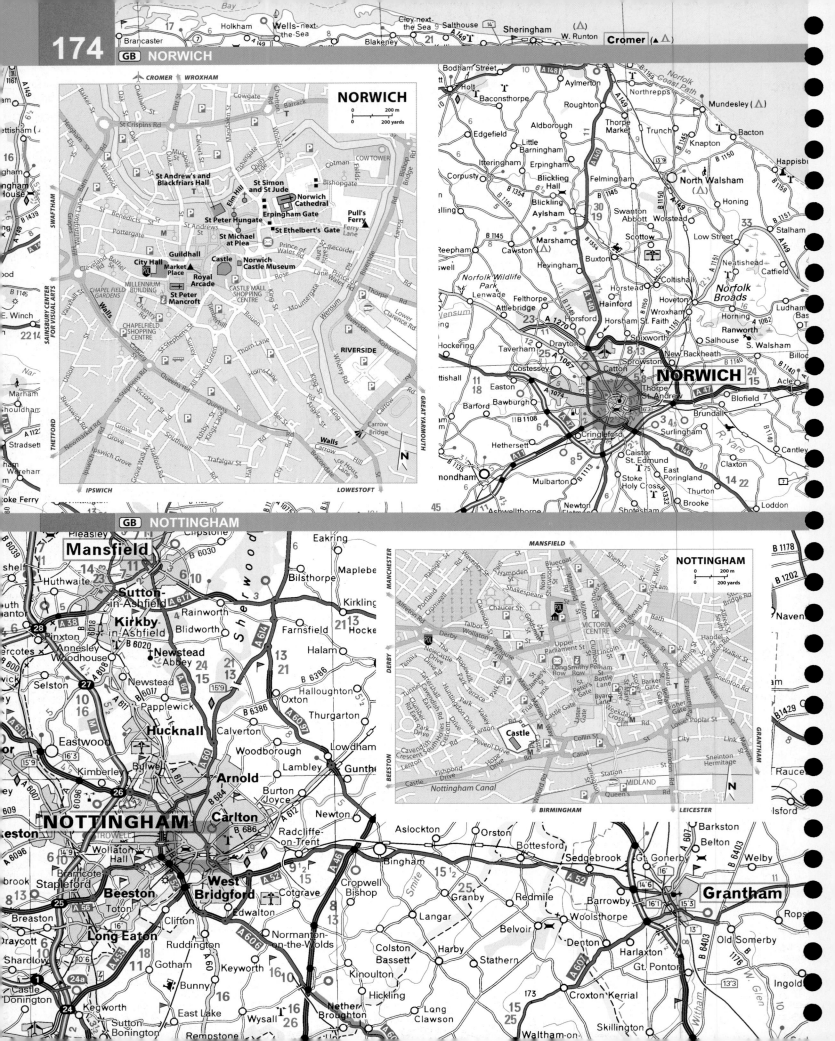

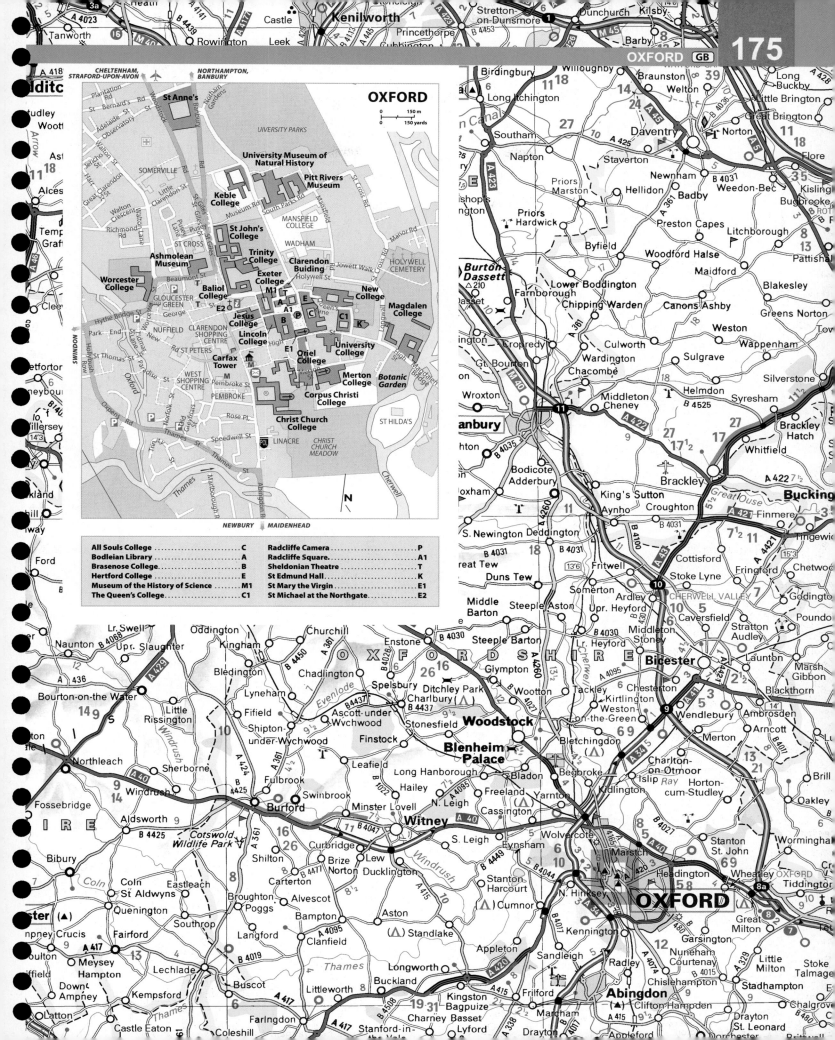

Perth (inset map)

PERTH

0 — 100 m
0 — 100 yards

BRAEMAR, SCONE PALACE — COUPAR ANGUS

- Black Watch Regimental Museum
- North
- Bell's Sports Centre
- Inch
- Barossa Place
- N°10
- Rose Terrace
- Georgian Terraces
- Old Perth Academy
- Atholl Crescent
- Riverside Park
- Perth Bridge
- St Ninian's Cathedral
- Union Lane
- Charlotte St
- Fair Maids House
- Foundry Lane
- Charlotte Square
- Lower City Mills
- Murray St
- Perth Museum and Art Gallery
- Perth Concert Hall
- St John's Centre
- St John's
- City Hall
- Maison des Évêques de Dunkeld
- King James VI Hospital
- Salutation Hotel
- Sheriff Court
- Alexandra St
- Exchange Lane
- Andrew St
- Canal St
- Victoria St
- South William St
- Nelson St
- Water Works et Fergusson Gallery
- St Leonard's in the Fields
- South Inch
- King James Pl
- King's Pl
- Moncreiffe Island
- Branklyn Garden, Friarton Bridge
- Kinnoull Hill
- Riverside
- Dundee Rd
- Gowrie Commercial St
- Queen's Bridge
- Tay
- N
- INVERNESS, CAITHNESS GLASS
- CRIANLARICH, CRIEFF
- STIRLING
- CHERRYBANK
- FORTH ROAD BRIDGE

Main map

Loch Muick · Glas-allt · 998 · 920
Inchgrundle · Loch Lee · Glen
Braedownie · Glen Clova · Ben Tirran · 896 · 778 · White Hill · 741 · 691 · West Knock
Clova · B 955 · Waterhead · 726
Runtaleave · Glen Prosen · Glenprosen Village · 246
Isla Forest · Cat Law 678 · Dykehead · Ogil · Fern · 173
Backwater Resr. · Balintore · Pearsie · 481 · White
Dykends · Kirkton of Kingoldrum · B 957 · Oathlaw · Tannadice
L. of Lintrathen · Bridgend of Lintrathen · B 951 · Kirriemuir · Lunanhead
Reekie Linn · Craigisla · B 954 · 130 · Craigton · A 926 · A 978 · A 926 · Forfar · Kingsmuir
B 952 · Ruthven · Dean Wr. · Glamis Castle · A 94 · B 9128
B 954 · Glamis · Douglastown · Inverarity · B 9127
Meigle · Eassie and Nevay · A 94 · Kirkbuddo · 12 19 · 259
Dunkeld · Inver · Birnam · Clunie · A 984 · Meikleour · A 984 · Newtyle · Hill · A 928 · 225 · Mor
Trochry · Strathbraan · Tay · Caputh · Kinclaven · Coupar Angus · A 923 · Pitcur · Balgray · Newbiggi
A 822 · 28 45 · B 867 · 101 · Cargill · Burrelton · A 94 · Long L. · Lundie · Auchterhouse · Kellas · B 961 · A 92
Little Glenshee · Bankfoot · B 9099 · 16 · 31 · King's Seat · 377 · Muirhead · Kirkton of Strathmartine · MICHELIN · Dighty
nan Caorach 623 · Stanley · A 9 · 132 · Guildtown · Kinrossie · B 953 · Abernyte · DUNDEE · 5 8 · A 930
Logiealmond · Harrietfield · B 8063 · Moneydie · A 93 · Balbeggie · Kinnaird of the Carse · Longforgan · Broughty Ferry
Buchanty · Almond · Luncarty · Scone Palace · Braes of Gowrie · Inchture · Invergowrie · 4 · Tay Road Bridge · 9 · Tayport
Fowlis Wester · 18 · Huntingtower Castle · A 85 · New Scone · Rait · A 90 · Newport-on-Tay · Tentsmuir Forest
Methven · Tibbermore · Bridgend · Kinfauns · 27 17 · Errol · Wormit · Balmerino · 14.9
Madderty · 130 · 11 · Elcho · Glencarse · Carse of Gowrie · Firth of Tay · Fife Coastal Path · 16 · Kilmany · Balmullo · Leuchars
Findo Gask · PERTH · 10 · R. Tay · R. Earn · Newburgh · Luthrie · A 92 · Guardbridge
pffray · Forgandenny · 934 · Bridge of Earn · 9 · Lindores · A 913 · Dairsie · Strathkinness
Kinkell Bridge · Aberuthven · B 9141 · Forteviot · 935 · A 912 · Abernethy · Letham · Cupar · A 91
Auchterarder · Dunning · B 8062 · Pitmedden Forest · B 936 · Springfield · Hill of Tarvit · Pitscottie · Ceres · A 915
31 50 · Common of Dunning · Path of Condie · Glenfarg · Gateside · Strathmiglo · Auchtermuchty · A 91 · Ladybank · Scotstarvit Tower · Craigrothie · Peat Inn
Steele's Knowe · Water of May · 365 · 522 · Lomond Hills · Falkland · A 914 · Kingskettle · Backmuir of New Gilston
Glen Eagl · 485 · 497 · 11 · Freuchie · 15 · Largoward

Dartmoor

Lydford gorge
604 △ Cut Hill
N. Brentor
Brent Tor
Mary Tavy
Wistman's
Wood
Great Mis
Tor
Two Bridge
Dartmoor Prison
Princetown

National

Tavistock (△)
Whitchurch

Werrington Broadwoodwidger
Ottery
Yeolmbridge
Davidstow 26
tagel 308 △
Camelford
(△)
Laneast
Launceston
Linton
Chillaton
Milton Abbot
Lamerton
Delabole
Altarnun
A 30
S. Petherwin
Lewannick
Lezant
B 3362
Gulworthy
Horrabridge
Michaelstow
420 △
Brown
Willy
Bolventor
North Hill
Kilmar
Tor
The Cheesewring
Bray
Shop
Stoke
Climsland
Morwellham
Gunnislake 13
Yelverton
Meavy
St. Teath
St. Breward
34
21
301
Kelly Bray
A 390
Cotehele House
Calstock
Buckland
Abbey
492 △
Bodmin Moor
The Hurlers
Caradon
Hill
369
Callington
St. Dominick
Bere
Alston
Bere Ferrers
Helland
(△)
Cardinham
Pensilva
(△)
St. Mellion
Landulph
Tamerton Foliot
Bickleigh
Cornwood
Bodmin
A 38
12 19
St. Cleer
St. Ive
18
162
Pillaton
(△)
PLYMOUTH
(△)
Lanhydrock
A 390
St. Neot
Dobwalls
A 390
Liskeard
Menheniot
27
17
Landrake
A 38
Saltash
Plympton
27
17
Restormel
Castle
18
29
Taphouse
Widegates
St. Germans
Antony House
Torpoint
Ivybr
Lanlivery
(△)
Lostwithiel
Duloe
Morval
Hessenford
A 374
Antony
Devonport
Plymstock
Ermington
Eden
Project
St. Blazey
Tywardreath
Lanreath
Pelynt (△)
Downderry
Crafthole
Cremyll
Mt. Edgcumbe
The
Sound
Plymstock
Brixton
Golant
Fowey
W. Looe (△)
Cornwall Coast Path
Millbrook
Polkerris
Carlyon Bay
Polruan
Lansallos
Talland-by-Looe
Polperro (△)
Cawsand
Wembury
Newton
Ferrers
Holbeton
Charlestown
Gribbin Head
Black Head
Rame Head
Whitsand
Bay
Wembury
Bay
Noss Mayo
S. Devon
Stoke
Point
Dunstone
Yealmpton
Kingst
Bigbury-on-S
Burgh-
Island
Thu
Bigbury Bay
Santander
Roscoff
Bolt T

PLYMOUTH

0   200 m
0   200 yards

VICTORIA
PARK
TAVISTOCK
ARMADA
SHOPPING
CENTRE
City Museum
and Art Gallery
DRAKE
CIRCUS
CENTRE
STONEHOUSE
Devonport Stonehouse Bridge
PLYMOUTH
PAVILIONS
GUILDHALL
COUNCIL
HOUSE
St Andrew's
Prysten
House
SUTTON
HARBOUR
STONEHOUSE
POOL
Elizabethan
House
National Marine
Aquarium
Mayflower
Museum
FERRY
TERMINAL
MILLBAY
DOCKS
The Promenade
THE HOE
Royal
Citadel
Smeaton's
Tower

THE SOUND

N

EXETER
DARTMOUTH

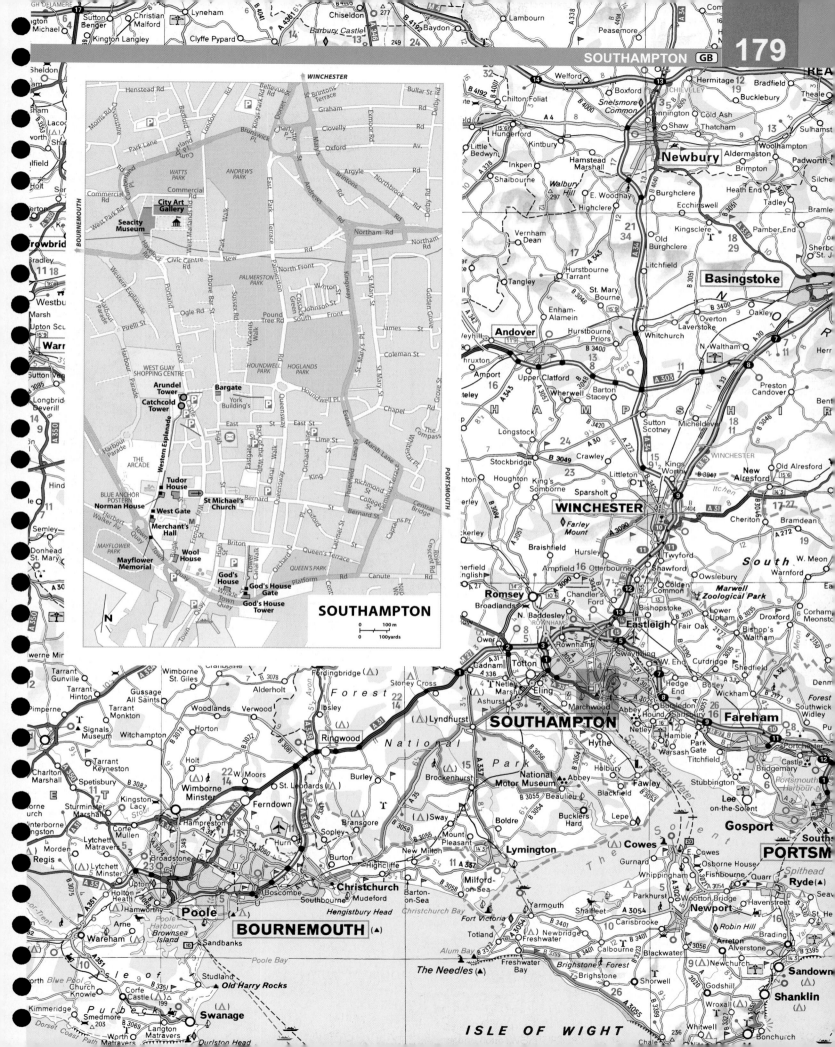

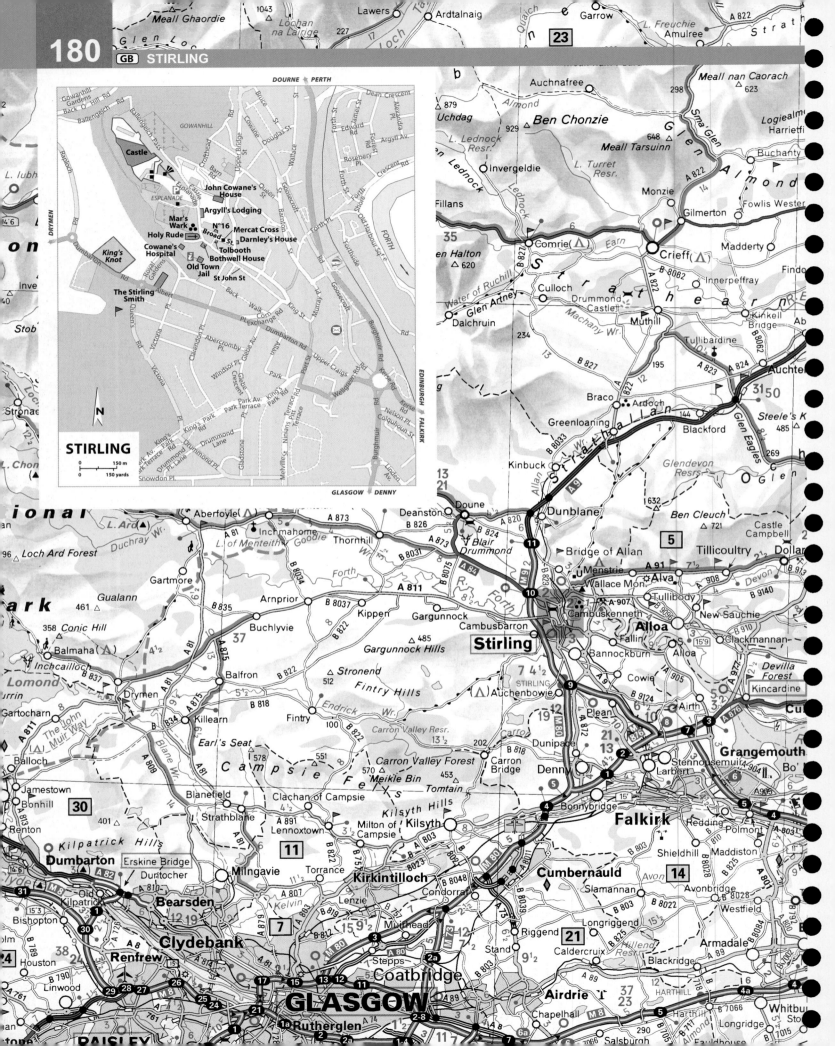

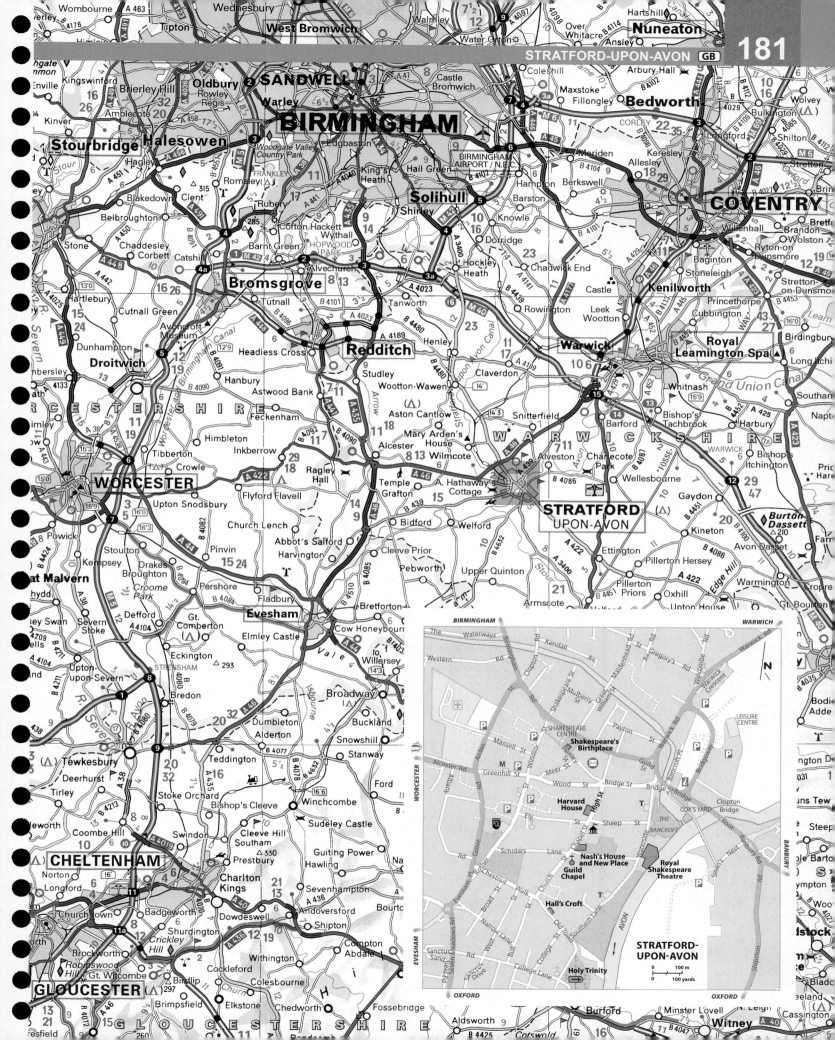

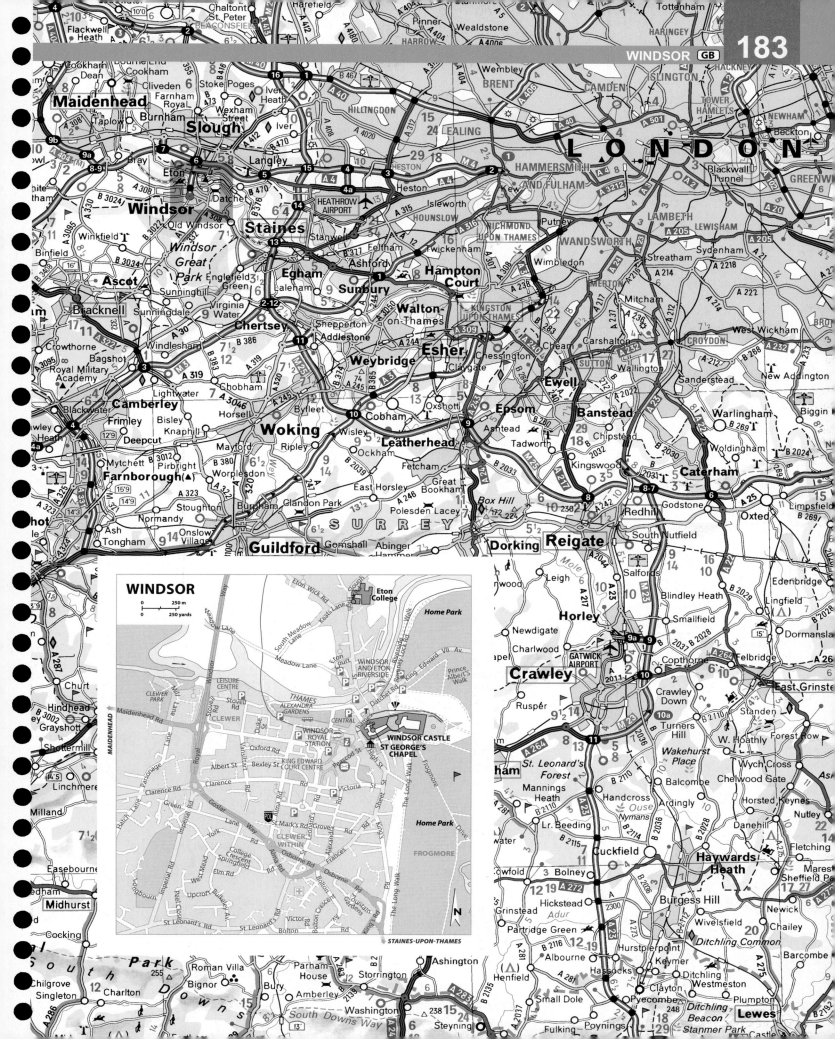

WINDSOR

Scale: 0 — 250 m / 0 — 250 yards

STAINES-UPON-THAMES

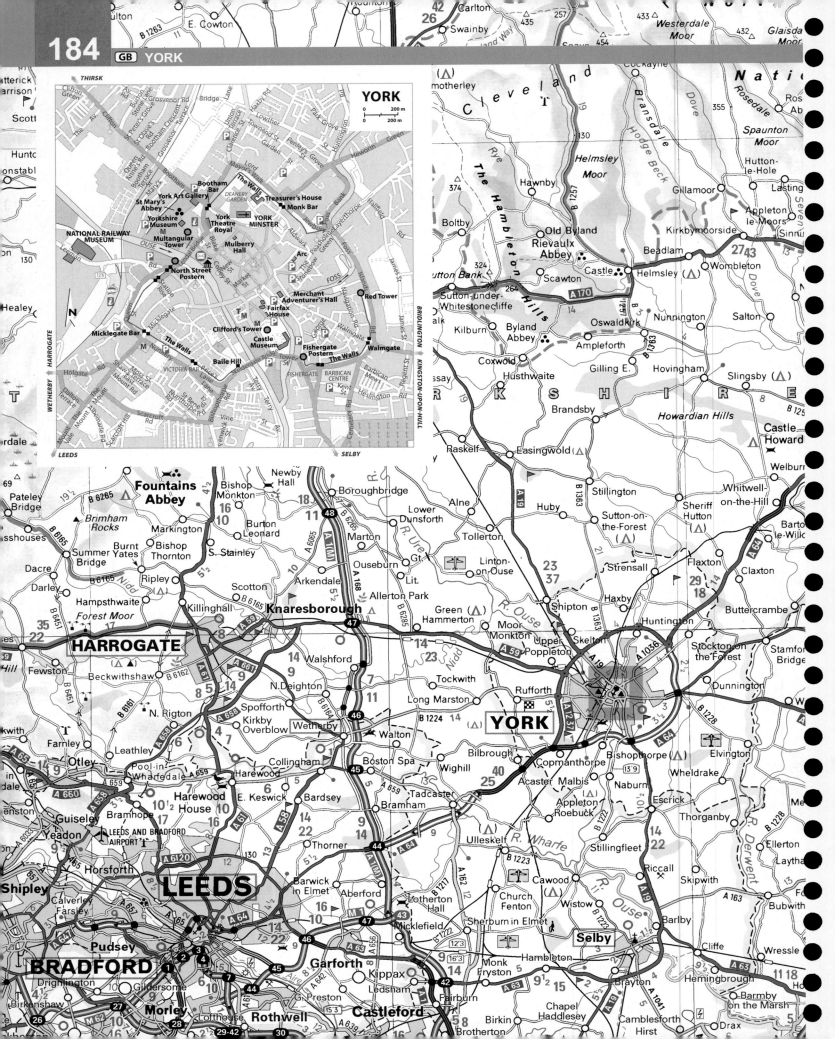

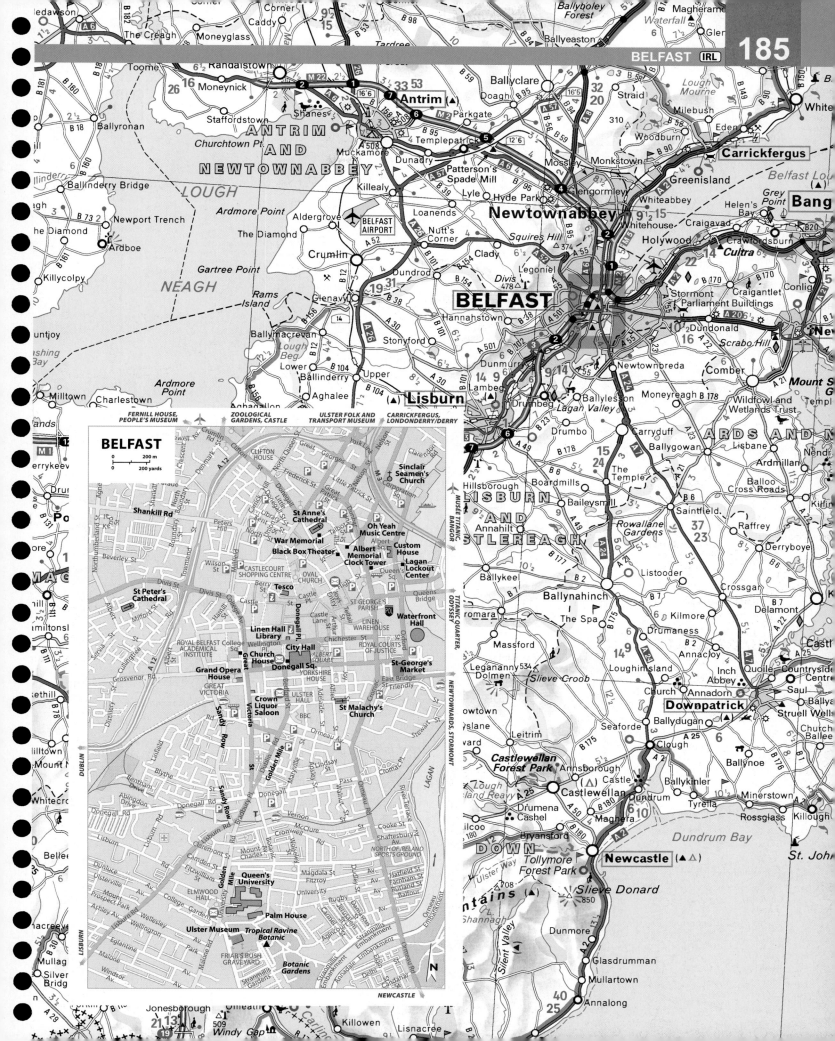

BELFAST

0   200 m
0   200 yards

FERNILL HOUSE, PEOPLE'S MUSEUM
ZOOLOGICAL GARDENS, CASTLE
ULSTER FOLK AND TRANSPORT MUSEUM
CARRICKFERGUS, LONDONDERRY/DERRY

CLIFTON HOUSE
Shankill Rd
War Memorial
St Anne's Cathedral
Black Box Theater
St Peter's Cathedral
Oh Yeah Music Centre
Sinclair Seamen's Church
Custom House
Albert Memorial Clock Tower
Lagan Lookout Center
CASTLECOURT SHOPPING CENTRE
OVAL CHURCH
Tesco
ST GEORGE'S PARISH
LINEN WAREHOUSE
Waterfront Hall
Linen Hall Library
Church House
City Hall
Donegall Sq
ROYAL COURTS OF JUSTICE
Grand Opera House
YORKSHIRE HOUSE
St-George's Market
Crown Liquor Saloon
ULSTER HALL
BBC
St Malachy's Church
GREAT VICTORIA
Golden Mile
Sandy Row
NORTH OF IRELAND SPORTS GROUND
DUBLIN
LISBURN
Queen's University
ELMWOOD HALL
Palm House
Ulster Museum
Tropical Ravine Botanic
FRIAR'S BUSH GRAVEYARD
Botanic Gardens

MUSEE TITANIC, BANGOR
NEWTOWNARDS, STORMONT
MUSEE TITANIC, ODYSSEY

N

NEWCASTLE

Antrim
Randalstown
Moneynick
Moneyglass
The Creagh
Toome
Staffordstown
Shanes
Muckamore
Dunadry
Templepatrick
Parkgate
Doagh
Ballyclare
Straid
Milebush
Woodburn
Eden
White
Carrickfergus
Greenisland
Belfast Lou
Grey Point
Bang
Helen's Bay
Craigavad
Crawfordsburn
Cultra
Conlig
ANTRIM AND NEWTOWNABBEY
Churchtown Pt.
Ardmore Point
The Diamond
Aldergrove
BELFAST AIRPORT
Nutt's Corner
Patterson's Spade Mill
Mossley
Monkstown
Glengormley
Whitehouse
Whiteabbey
Newtownabbey
Holywood
Stormont Parliament Buildings
Craigantlet
Scrabo Hill
Dundonald
New
LOUGH
NEAGH
Ballinderry Bridge
Newport Trench
The Diamond
Ardboe
Killycolpy
Gartree Point
Rams Island
Milltown
Charlestown
Ardmore Point
Crumlin
Glenavy
Dundrod
Divis 478
Legoniel
Squires Hill
Divis 374
Hannahstown
BELFAST
Dunmurry
Lambeg
LISBURN
Lisburn
Stonyford
Ballymacrevan
Lough Beg Lower
Ballinderry Upper
Aghalee
Aghagallon
Hillsborough
Annahilt
Baileysmill
Boardmills
Saintfield
LISBURN AND CASTLEREAGH
Drumbeg
Lagan Valley
Ballylesson
Drumbo
Carryduff
Ballygowan
Lisbane
Ardmillan
Balloo Cross Roads
Newtownbreda
Moneyreagh
Comber
Mount S
G
Wildfowl and Wetlands Trust
Templ
ARDS AND N
Nendr
The Temple
Rowallane Gardens
Raffrey
Derryboye
Ballykee
Listooder
Crossgar
Delamont
Ballynahinch
Kilmore
Drumaness
The Spa
Massford
Annacloy
Quoile
Castl
Legananny 534 Dolmen
Slieve Croob
Loughinisland
Inch Abbey
Annadorn
Saul
Church
Downpatrick
Struell Wells
Seaforde
Ballydugan
Leitrim
Clough
Castlewellan Forest Park
Annsborough
Castlewellan
Dundrum
Ballykinler
Minerstown
Drumena Cashel
Maghera
Tyrella
Rossglass
Killough
Bryansford
Dundrum Bay
DOWN
Tollymore Forest Park
Newcastle
St. John
Slieve Donard 850
Glasdrumman
Mullartown
Annalong

M 22
M 2
A 6
A 26
A 57
A 2
A 52
A 23
A 55
A 24
A 7
A 25
A 50
A 20
A 21
A 49
A 1

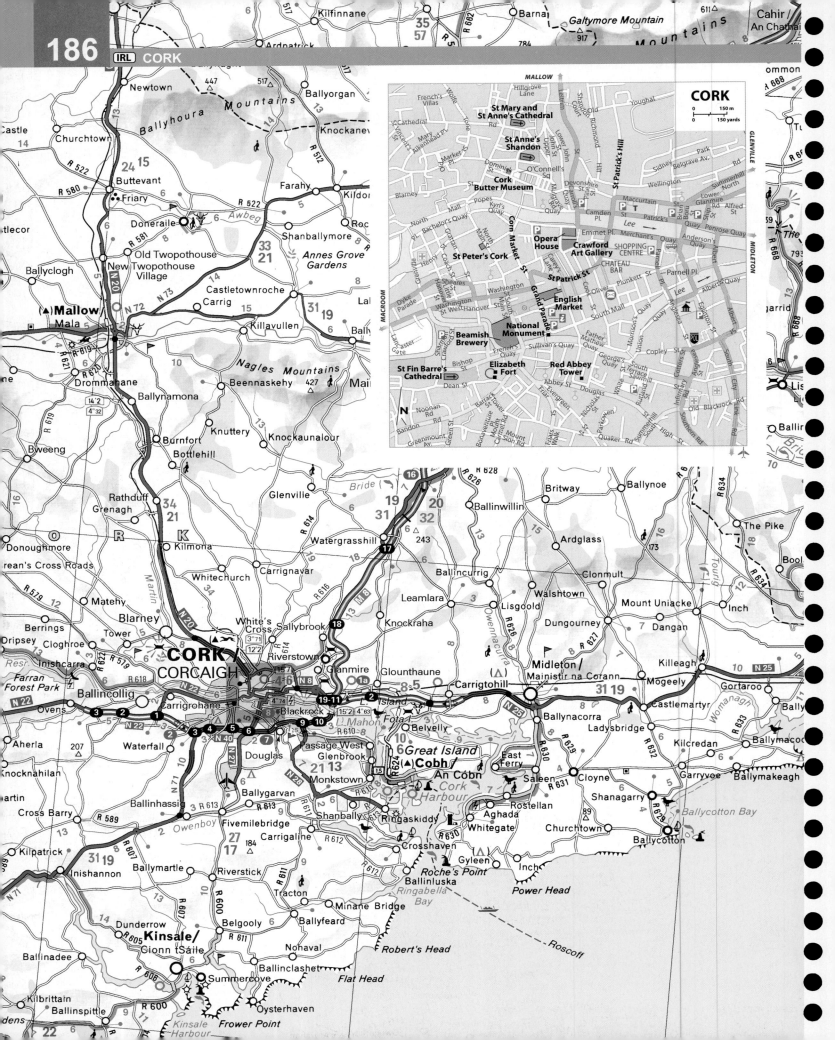

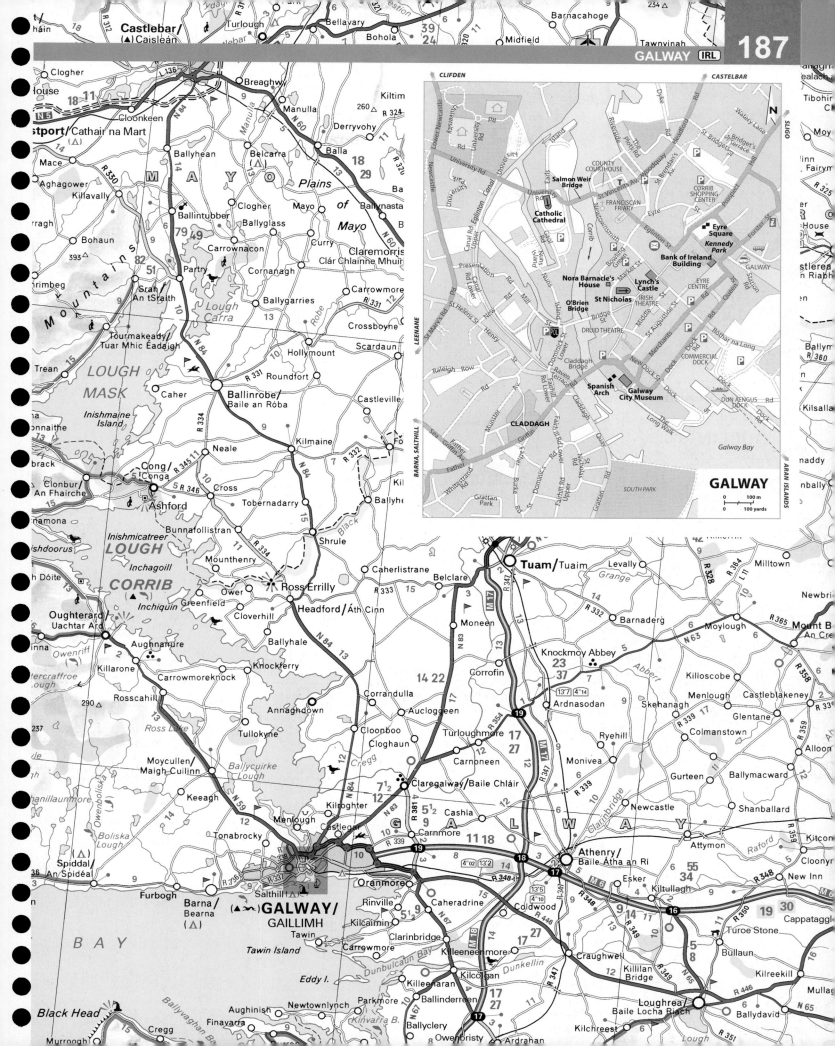

Map labels

Castlebar/ ▲Caisleán
Clogher
House
N 5 18 11
stport/ Cathair na Mart
▲
14
Mace
Aghagower
Killavally
rragh
Bohaun
393
rimbeg
Trean
15
Breaghwy
Turlough
Bellavary
Bohola
Manulla
Derryvohy
Kiltim
R 324
260
260
Ballyhean
Belcarra
(▲)
Balla
Clogher
Mayo
Curry
Ballynasta
Ballintubber
Ballyglass
Carrownacon
Party
Cornanagh
Claremorris
Clár Chlainne Mhuir
Srah/
An tSraith
Carrowmore
R 331
Ballygarries
Robe
Crossboyne
Tourmakeady/
Tuar Mhic Éadaigh
Roundfort
Hollymount
Scardaun
Caher
Ballinrobe/
Baile an Róba
Castleville
Neale
Kilmaine
Fo
Cong/
Conga
Cross
Ballyhe
Clonbur/
An Fhairche
Ashford
Tobernadarry
Ballyhe
namona
Bunnafollistran
Shrule
shdoorus
Mounthenry
Caherlistrane
Tuam/ Tuaim
Levally
Milltown
Ross Errilly
Belclare
Oughterard/
Uachtar Ard
Greenfield
Headford/ Áth Cinn
Moneen
Barnaderg
Moylough
Mount B
Aughnanure
Ballyhale
Corrofin
Knockmoy Abbey
Killoscobe
Killarone
Knockferry
Ardnasodan
Skehanagh
Menlough
Castleblakeney
Rosscahill
Carrowmoreknock
Corrandulla
Aucloggeen
Turloughmore
Ryehill
Glentane
Annaghdown
Colmanstown
Moycullen/
Maigh Cuilinn
Tullokyne
Cloonboo
Cloghaun
Carnoneen
Monivea
Alloon
Keeagh
Claregalway/ Baile Chláir
Cashla
Gurteen
Ballymacward
Kilroghter
Newcastle
Shanballard
Menlough
Castlegar
Carnmore
Spiddal/
An Spidéal
Tonabrocky
Oranmore
Athenry/
Baile Átha an Rí
Attymon
Furbogh
Salthill
Barna/
Bearna
▲
GALWAY/
GAILLIMH
(▲)
Tawin
Rinville
Caheradrine
Coldwood
Esker
Kiltullagh
New Inn
Cappatagg
Clarinbridge
Killeeneenmore
Craughwell
Killilan
Bridge
Killeenaran
Kilcolgan
Túroe Stone
Bullaun
Kilreekill
Mullag
Black Head
Aughinish
Newtownlynch
Parkmore
Ballinderreen
Loughrea/
Baile Locha Riach
Ballydavid
Cregg
Finavarra
Ballyclery
Kilchreest
N 65

BAY

LOUGH MASK
LOUGH CORRIB
Lough Carra
Plains of Mayo
MAYO
Mountains
GALWAY

Galway city inset

SLIGO
N

Salmon Weir Bridge
Catholic Cathedral
Franciscan Friary
Corrib Shopping Center
County Courthouse
Eyre Square
Kennedy Park
Bank of Ireland Building
Nora Barnacle's House
Lynch's Castle
St Nicholas
Irish Theatre
Eyre Centre
O'Brien Bridge
Druid Theatre
Claddagh Bridge
Spanish Arch
Galway City Museum
Commercial Dock
Dun Aengus Dock
CLADDAGH
South Park
Galway Bay
The Long Walk
Grattan Park

GALWAY

ARAN ISLANDS

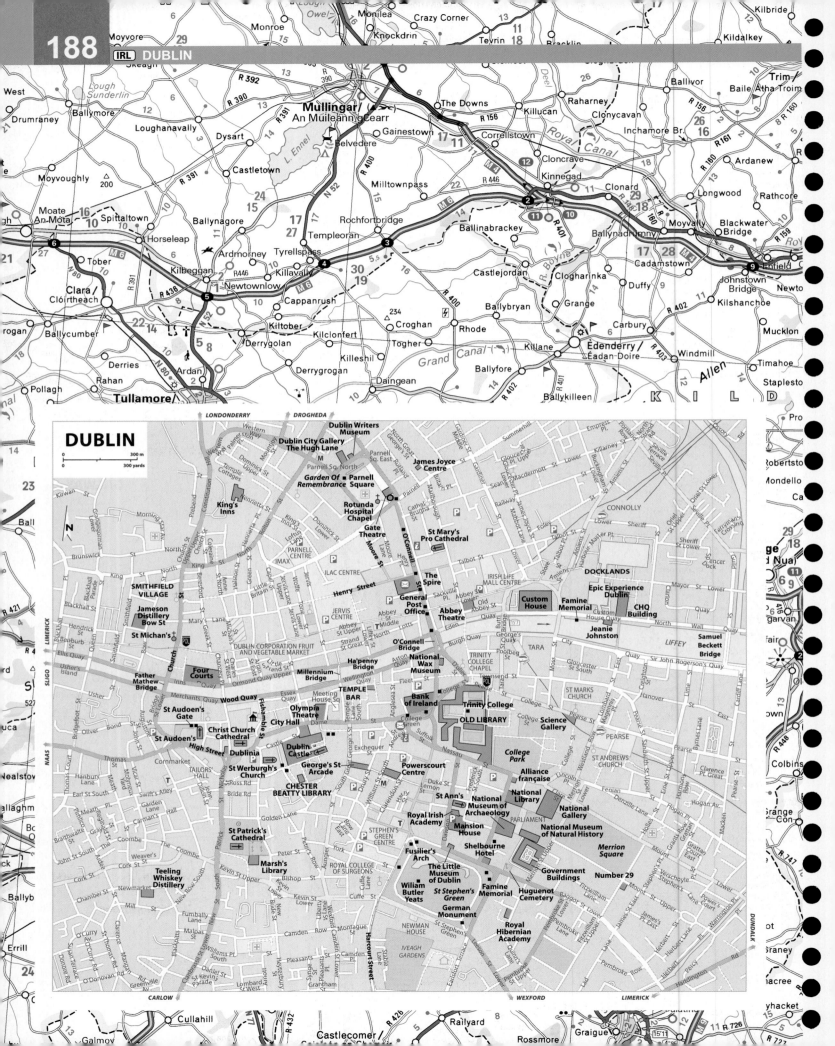

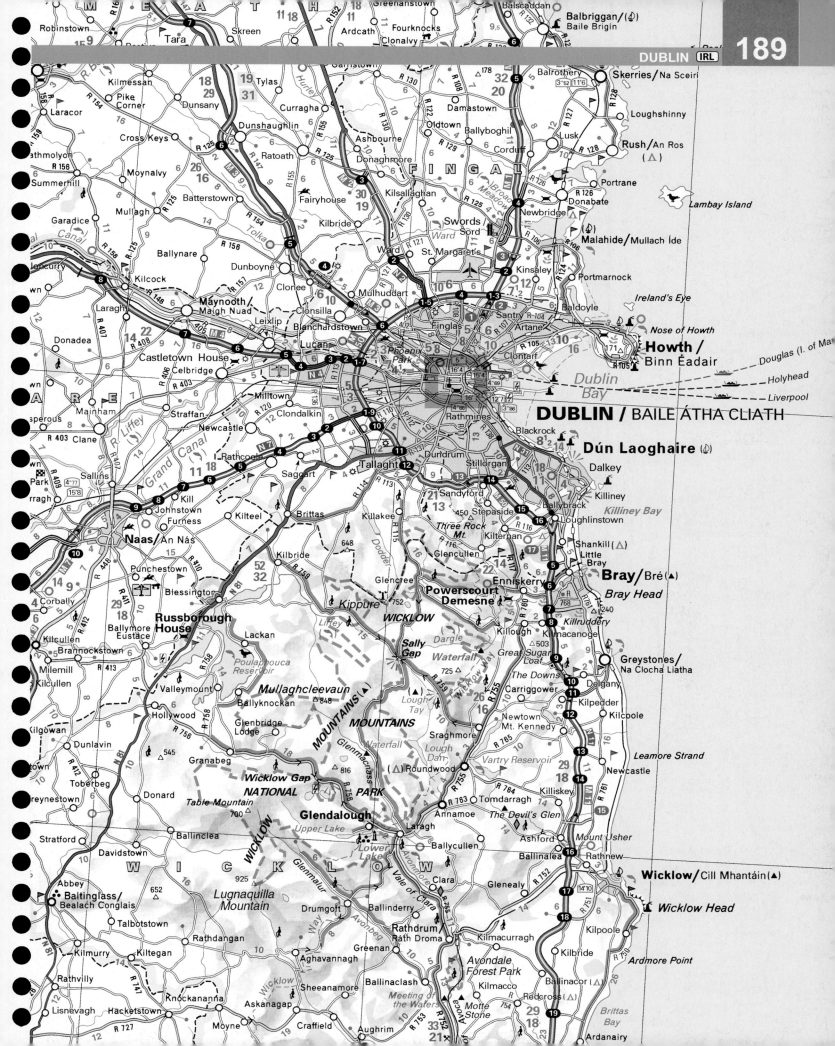

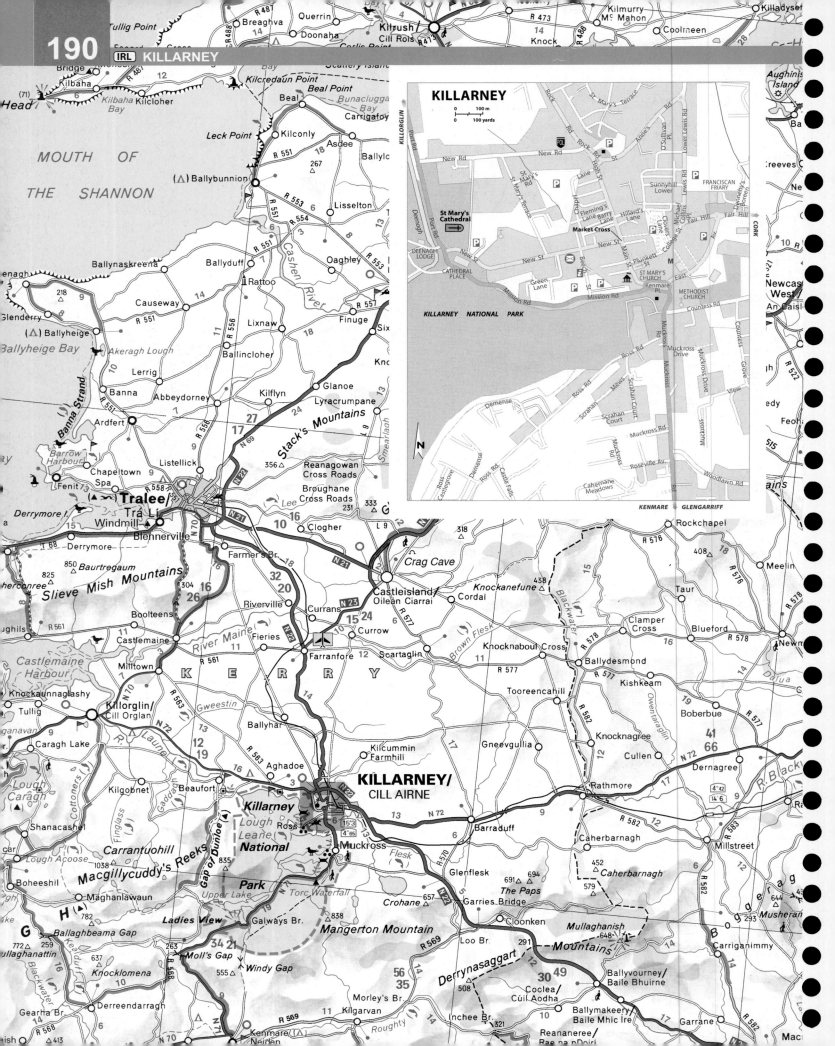

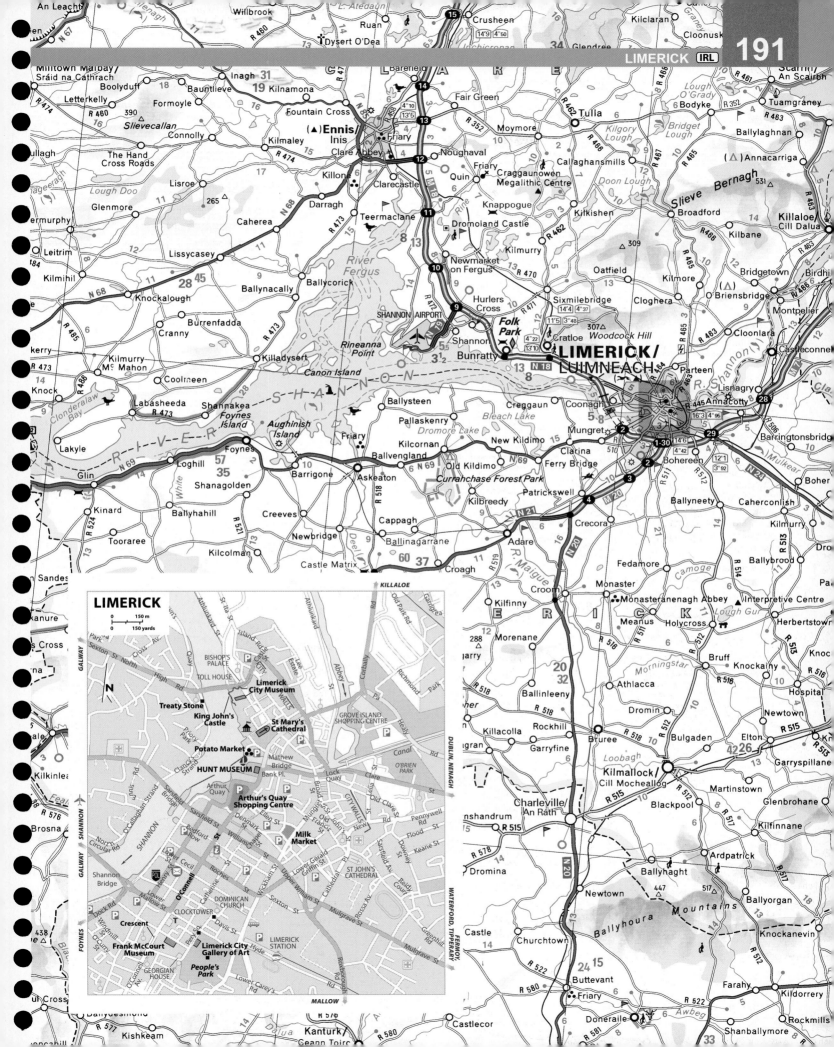

Eochair

Bóithre

Mótarbhealach - Limistéar seirbhíse
Carrbhealach dúbailte le saintréithe mótarbhealaigh
Acomhal mótarbhealaigh: iomlán - teoranta
Vimhreacha ceangail
Líonra idirnáisiúnta agus náisiúnta bóithre
Bóthar idir-réigiúnach nach bhfuil chomh plódaithe
Bóthar nuadheisithe - gan réitiú
Cosán - Conair mharcáilte / Cosán marcaíochta
Mótarbhealach, bóthar á dhéanamh
(an dáta oscailte sceidealta, mas eol)

Leithead bóithre

Carrshlí dhéach
4 lána - 2 leathanlána
2 lána - 2 chunglána

Fad bóthar (iomlán agus meánfhad)

Bhóithre dola ar an mótarbhealach
Saor ó dhola ar an mótarbhealach
i mílte - i gcilíméadair
ar an mbóthar

Aicmiú oifigiúil bóithre

Mótarshl - GB : Priomhbhealach
IRL: Bóithre eile ,

Priomhbóithre agus fobhóithre náisiúnta
Ceann scríbe ar ghréasán bóithre priomha

Constaicí

Timpeall - Bearnas agus a airde os cionn leibhéal na mara (i méadair)
Fána ghéar (suas treo an gha)
IRL: Bealach deacair nó baolach
Bóthar cúng le hionaid phasála (in Albain)
Crosaire comhréidh: iarnród ag dul, faoi bhóthar, os cionn bóthair
Bóthar toirmeasctha - Bóthar faoi theorannú
Bacainn dola - Bóthar aonslí
(Ar phríomhbhóithre agus a bhóithre réigiúnacha)
Teorainneacha airde (faoi 15'6" IRL, faoi 16'6" GB)
Teorann Mheáchain (faoi 16t)

Iompar

Leithead caighdeánach - Stáisiún paisinéirí
Aerfort - Aerpháirc
Longsheirbhísí : (Seirbhísí séasúracha: dearg)
Bád
Fartha (uas - ulach : tonnaí méadracha)
Coisithe agus lucht rothar

Lóistín - Riarachán

Teorainneacha riaracháin
Teorainn na hAlban agus teorainn na Breataine Bige

Teorainn idirnáisiúnta - Custam

Áiseanna Spóirt agus Súgartha

Machaire Gailf - Ráschúrsa
Timpeall rásaíochta - Cuan bád aeraíochta
Láthair champa , láthair charbhán
Conair mharcáilte - Páirc thuaithe
Zú - Tearmannéan mara
IRL: Lascaireacht - Ráschúrsa con Lamród thraein ghaile
Traein cábla
Carr cábla , cathaoir cábla

Amhairc

Príomhradharcanna:
féach AN EOLAÍ UAINE
Bailte nó áiteanna inspéise, baill lóistín
Foirgneamh Eaglasta - Caisleán
Fothrach - Leacht meigilíteach - Pluais
Páirc, Gáirdíní - Ionaid eile spéisiúla
IRL: Dunfort - Cros Cheilteach - Cloigtheach
Lánléargas - Cothrom Radhairc - Bealach Aoibhinn

Comharthaí Eile

Cáblashlí thionsclaíoch
Crann teileachumarsáide - Teach solais
Stáisiún Giniúna - Cairéal
Mianach - Tionsclaíocht
Scaglann - Aill
Páirc Fhoraoise Naisiúnta - Páirc Naisiúnta

Allwedd

Ffyrdd

Trafford - Mannau gwasanaeth
Ffordd ddeuol â nodweddion traffordd
Cyfnewidfeyd: wedi'i chwblhau - cyfyngedig
Rhifau'r cyffyrdd
Ffordd ar rwydwaith rhyngwladol a chenedlaethol
Ffordd rhyngranbarthol a llai prysur
Ffordd ac wyneb iddi - heb wyneb
Llwybr troed - Llwybr troed ag arwyddion / Llwybr ceffyl
Trafford - ffordd yn cael ei hadeiladu
(Os cyfydi yr achos: dyddiad agor disgwyliedig)

Ffyrdd

ffordd ddeuol
4 lôn - 2 lôn lydan
2 lôn - 2 lôn gul

Pellter (cyfanswm a'r rhyng-bellter)

Tollffyrdd ar y drafford
Rhan di-doll ar y drafford
mewn miltiroedd - mewn kilometrau
ar y ffordd

Dosbarthiad ffyrdd swyddogol

Trafford - GB : Prif ffordd

IRL: Prif ffordd genedlaethol a ffordd eilradd

Ffyrdd eraill
Cylchfan ar rwydwaith y prif ffrydd

Rhwystrau

Cylchfan - Bwlch a'i uchder uwchlaw lefel y môr (mewn metrau)
Rhiw serth (esgyn gyda'r saeth)
IRL: Darn anodd neu beryglus o ffordd
Yn yr Alban : ffordd gul â mannau pasio
Croesfan rheilffordd: croesfan rheilffordd, o dan y ffordd, dros y ffordd
Ffordd waharddedig - Ffordd a chyfyngiadau arni
Rhwystr Toll - Unffordd
(Ar brif ffyrdd a ffyrdd rhanbarthol)
Terfyn uchder (llai na 15'6" IRL, 16'6" GB)
Terfyn pwysau (llai na 16t)

Cludiant

Lled safonol - Gorsaf deithwyr
Maes awyr - Maes glanio
Llongau ceir: (Gwasanaethau tymhorol: mewn coch)
llong
Fferi (llwyth uchaf: mewn tunelli metrig)
Teithwyr ar droed neu feic yn unig

Llety - Gweinyddiaeth

Ffiniau gweinyddol
Ffin Cymru, ffin yr Alban

Ffin ryngwladol - Tollau

Cyfleusterau Chwaraeon a Hamdden

Cwrs golf - Rasio Ceffylau
Rasio Cerbydau - Harbwr cychod pleser
Leoedd i wersylla
Llwybr troed ag arwyddion - Parc gwlad
Parc saffari, sw - Gwarchodfa natur
IRL: Pysgota - Maes rasio milgwn
Trên twristiaid
Rhaffordd, car cêbl, cadair esgyn

Golygfeydd

Gweler Llyfr Michelin

Trefi new fannau o ddiddordeb, mannau i aros
Adeilag eglwysig - Castell
Adfeilion - Heneb fegalithig - Ogof
Gerddi, parc - Mannau eraill o ddiddordeb
IRL: Caer - Croes Geltaidd - twr crwn
Panorama - Golygfan - Ffordd dygyfeydd

Symbolau eraill

Lein gêbl ddiwydiannol
Mast telathrebu - Goleudy
Gorsaf bwer - Chwarel
Mwyngloddio - Gweithgarwch diwydiannol
Purfa - Clogwyn
Parc Coedwig Cenedlaethol - Parc Cenedlaethol

Comnarthaí ar phleanna bailte

Ionaid inspéise

Ionad inspéise agus

Ionad inspéise adhartha

Bóithre

Mótarbhealach, carrbhealach dúbailte le saintréithe mótarbhea

Acomhail mótarbhealaigh : iomlán - teoranta

Priomh-thrébhealach

Sráid: neamhoiriúnach do thrácht, ach í stáit speisialta

Sráid: coisithe

Carrchlós

Comhartha Éagsúla

Aerfort

Leithead caighdeánach - Staisiún paisinéirí

Ionad eolais turasóireachta - Ospidéal

Gairdín, páirc, coill - Reilig

Staidiam

Galfchúrsa

Stáisiún traenach faoi thalamh

Príomhoifi g phoist le poste restante

Foirgneamh poiblí curtha in iúl le litir thagartha:

Músaem

Amharclann

Póitíní (ceanncheathrú)

Symbolau ar gynlluniau'r trefi

Golygfeydd

Man diddorol

Lle diddorol o addoliad

Ffyrdd

Trafford, ffordd ddeuol

Cyfnewidfeyd: wedi'i chwblhau - cyfyngedig

Prif ffordd drwodd

Stryd : Anaddas i draffi g, cyfyngedig

Stryd: Cerddwr

Parc ceir

Arwyddion amrywiol

Maes awyr

Lled safonol - Gorsaf deithwyr

Canolfan croeso - Ysbyty

Gardd, parc, coedwig - Mynwent

Stadiwm

Cwrs golff

Gorsaf danddaearol

Prif swyddfa bost gyda poste restante

Adeilad cyhoeddus a ddynodir gan lythyren:

Amgueddfa

Theatr

Yr Heddlu (pencadlys)

Que pensez-vous de nos produits ?
Tell us what you think about our products.

Déposez votre avis
Give us your opinion: satisfaction.michelin.com